Sociology for AS AQA
4th edition

For Eirene

4th Edition

Sociology
for AS AQA

Ken Browne

Fully covers the complete specification

First edition published in 2002 by Polity Press
This edition published in 2013 by Polity Press

Polity Press
65 Bridge Street
Cambridge CB2 1UR, UK

Polity Press
350 Main Street
Malden, MA 02148, USA

ISBN-13: 978-0-7456-5550-5
ISBN-13: 978-0-7456-5551-2 (pb)

A catalogue record for this book is available from the British Library.

Typeset in 9.5 on 13 pt Utopia
by Servis Filmsetting Ltd., Stockport, Cheshire
Printed and bound in China by 1010 printing

The publisher has used its best endeavours to ensure that the URLs for external websites referred to in this book are correct and active at the time of going to press. However, the publisher has no responsibility for the websites and can make no guarantee that a site will remain live or that the content is or will remain appropriate.

Every effort has been made to trace all copyright holders, but if any have been inadvertently overlooked the publisher will be pleased to include any necessary credits in any subsequent reprint or edition.

For further information on Polity, visit our website: www.politybooks.com

Contents

Acknowledgements

I'd like to thank the anonymous readers approached by Polity, who provided me with some very constructively critical and supportive comments, many of which I have incorporated into the finished text, and Eirene Mitsos for some useful help and ideas, and for painstakingly – and painfully – reading and re-reading various drafts of the entire book. Martin Rathfelder of the Socialist Health Association, Becky Francis, Bonny Hartley, Kath Checkland, James Plaskitt and Mike Luck also provided some help and support on various aspects. I'd like to thank the staff at the Office for National Statistics (ONS). They constantly amaze me with the extent of their helpfulness in pointing the way to hard-to-access data, and the speed with which they respond and provide updates. This was particularly helpful after the difficulties that followed the launch of the new ONS website in 2011, when broken or missing links and unmigrated material constantly undermined my searches for data.

Ken Pyne has drawn some new cartoons to illustrate ideas in the text, and he has once again shown himself to be excellent at interpreting my vague suggestions, and I thank him for being so responsive.

I would like to thank all the staff at Polity, particularly Jonathan Skerrett, who has been a brilliant and supportive editor, and also Clare Ansell and Breffni O'Connor. Thanks too to Leigh Mueller for her excellent copy-editing.

I am grateful to Penguin Books, Tom Shakespeare, the Socialist Health Association, the Joseph Rowntree Foundation, the Mayor's Office (Greater London Authority) and Warwickshire County Council for permission to reproduce copyright material. The source of copyright material is acknowledged in the text. Should any copyright-holder have been inadvertently overlooked, the author and publishers will be glad to make suitable arrangements at the first possible opportunity.

Introduction to the 4th edition

This fourth edition has been completely restructured and rewritten, and is divided into chapters that provide complete coverage of each area in the AQA specification. Each of these chapters is sub-divided into topics, which correspond directly to the bullet points in the AQA specification. Each of these topics has been rewritten to include all the content suggested in the detailed schemes of work recommended and published by the AQA. This is backed up by a thorough analysis of the AQA mark schemes used by examiners and examiners' reports. There have been substantial changes to the Methods-in-Context area, with more extensive coverage, activities and examples at the end of the Education and Health chapters.

The book is based on the AQA specification, but much of the material can also be used for the OCR specification, particularly the chapters on the Family, Culture and Identity, Sociological Methods and Health.

The AS specification

The AQA AS specification involves the following units:

UNIT 1

Any *one* from these:

- Culture and Identity
- Families and Households
- Wealth, Poverty and Welfare

Answer all parts of one stimulus response/ structured question, chosen from *one* of the three topics. Each question in five parts – three short questions together worth 12 marks + two short essays each worth 24 marks. Total marks = 60. 40 per cent of AS-level marks and 20 per cent of the total A-level marks. Exam is 1 hour.

UNIT 2

Either

- Education
or
- Health
and
- Sociological Methods

Answer *three* questions chosen from one of the two sections provided on Education and Health

- One stimulus response/structured question on the chosen topic, each consisting of four parts – two short questions together worth up to 8 marks + two short essays, one worth 12 marks and the other worth 20 marks. And
- One stimulus response question on socio- logical research methods in the context of the chosen topic. Question has one part essay answer, with an either/or option, worth 20 marks. And
- One four-part question on free-standing sociological research methods. Three short questions together worth up to 10 marks + one essay, worth 20 marks.

Total marks = 90. 60 per cent of the total AS-level marks and 30 per cent of the total A-level marks. Exam is 2 hours.

ASSESSMENT

At AS Sociology, students are assessed on two main objectives:

1 Knowledge and understanding

This involves sociological theories, concepts and research, and an understanding of how sociologists use a range of methods and sources of information, and the practical, ethical and theoretical issues arising in sociological research.

Knowledge and understanding is likely to be tested in *questions* by the use of words like:

Outline	Explain
Examine	Describe
Discuss/Assess	Give reasons for

2 The skills of application, interpretation, analysis and evaluation

This involves things like being able to recognize and criticize sociologically significant information, to make sense of data, to recognize the strengths and weaknesses of sociological theories and evidence, and to reach conclusions based on the evidence and arguments presented.

The skills of application and interpretation are likely to be tested in *questions* by the use of words like:

Identify	Illustrate
Give an example	Suggest
How might . . . ?	In what ways . . . ?
With reference to item A	

To show the examiner that you are using the skills of *application and interpretation* you might consider using the following words and phrases:

as shown by item A/recent events in. . .	for example. . .
this shows. . .	as shown by Brainache's theory of/study of . . .
such evidence may be misleading because. . .	Brainache's study challenges/supports this view. . .
this is a value-judgement because. . .	Such statistics/other evidence show/s that. . .

The skills of *analysis* and *evaluation* are likely to be tested in *questions* by the use of words like:

Assess	Evaluate
To what extent . . . ?	How useful . . . ?
Critically discuss	Compare and contrast
. . . for and against the view . . .	

To show the examiner that you are using the skill of *analysis* you might consider using the following words and phrases:

the relevance of this is	this indicates
this is similar to/different from	so
therefore	this means/does not mean
hence	a consequence of
the implication of	the contrast between
put simply	

For *evaluation skills*, you might use the following words and phrases:

a strength/weakness of this	an argument for/against
an advantage/disadvantage of	the importance of
this is important because	this does not take account of
however	alternatively
a criticism of this is	others argue that
a different interpretation is provided by. . .	on the other hand
the problem with this is. . .	this does not explain why . . .
this argument/evidence suggests	to conclude

TWO THEMES

There are two themes or threads that run through the whole AS (and A2) course:

- socialization, culture and identity
- social differentiation, power and stratification

These are not expected to be taught as specific subjects, but rather as themes that should be referred to throughout the course. For example, in the family unit you might consider the socialization of children, or inequalities of power and status between men and women. In the poverty unit you might consider issues such as the way children are socialized into the culture of poverty or a dependency culture, or the way that the poor lack the power and resources to challenge and change their position. In education, you might consider the role of the hidden curriculum or the labelling process in forming student identities, or how the education system contributes to reproducing an unequal society. If you study the culture and identity topic in chapter 2, you will obviously cover socialization, culture and identity very thoroughly.

How to use this book

Each chapter of this book is designed to be more or less self-contained, and to cover the knowledge and skills required to achieve success at AS-level Sociology.

All students should read chapter 1, as it lays out some important introductory ideas which are developed and referred to in later chapters.

Important terms are highlighted in colour when they first appear in the text, and in **bold type** in the page margins. These are normally explained in the text, and listed at the end of the chapter. They are also included in a comprehensive glossary at the end of the book. Unfamiliar terms should be checked in the glossary or index for further explanation or clarification. The contents pages or the index should be used to find particular themes or references. The bibliography consists of all research referred to in the book, in case you should wish to explore further any of the topics. There are activity-based sections on research in chapter 5, as well as in the Methods-in-Context sections at the end of chapters 6 and 7. These should help to prepare you for that part of the examination question in Unit 2 which asks you to apply your knowledge of research methods to particular issues in education or health, as well as to the more general question on research methods.

Chapter summaries and revision checklists outline the key points that should have been learnt after reading each chapter. These should be used as checklists for revision – if you cannot do what is asked, then refer back to the chapter to refresh your memory. There is a list of the key terms that you should know after studying each chapter. These are defined in the margins or the text when they first occur, and are also included in the glossary at the end of the book. You should use this key terms list and the glossary as reference sources and as a revision aid, as you can check the meaning of terms. At the end of each topic, some typical examination-style questions are included to revise the topic, and at the end of every chapter, except for chapters 1 and 5, there is a typical examination question for that unit. Students should attempt these under timed conditions, both as practice and to gauge how ready they are for the examination.

Where 'Britain' is used in the text, it should be taken to mean mainland Britain and Northern Ireland.

Websites

The internet is a valuable source of information for sociologists and for exploring the topics in this book. However, there is a lot of rubbish on some internet sites, and information should be treated with caution. One of the best search engines to search for topics generally is www.google.com. Try this for any research topic – putting 'UK' at the end usually helps, e.g. 'poverty uk'. There are some useful websites referred to throughout this book, but you can find more, and other resources, at www.politybooks.com/browne.

CHAPTER **1** Introducing Sociology

Contents

1

Introducing Sociology

KEY ISSUES

- What is sociology?
- Sociology and common-sense and naturalistic explanations
- Key introductory ideas
- Sociological perspectives
- Sociological problems, social problems and social policy

This is an important chapter that introduces sociology and some of the key terms, ideas and sociological approaches that are referred to throughout this book. It is therefore worth spending some time on learning the main points covered.

Newcomers to sociology often have only quite a vague idea of what the subject is about, though they often have an interest in people. This interest is a good start, because the focus of sociology is on the influences from society which shape the behaviour of people, their experiences and their interpretations of the world around them. To learn sociology is to learn about how human societies are constructed and where our beliefs and daily routines come from; it is to re-examine in a new light many of the taken-for-granted assumptions which we all hold, and which influence the way we think about ourselves and others. Sociology is above all about developing a critical understanding of society. In developing this understanding, sociology can itself contribute to changes in society, for example by highlighting and explaining social problems like divorce, ill-health and poverty. The study of sociology can provide the essential tools for a better understanding of the world we live in, and therefore the means for improving it.

What is sociology?

Sociology is the systematic (or planned and organized) study of human groups and social life in modern societies. It is concerned with the study of **social institutions**.

These are the various organized social arrangements which are found in all societies. For example, the family is an institution which is concerned with arrangements for marriage, such as at what age people can marry, whom they can marry and how many partners they can have, and the upbringing of children. The education system establishes ways of passing on attitudes, knowledge and skills from one generation to the next. Work and the economic system organize the way the production of goods will be carried out, religious institutions are concerned with people's relations with the supernatural, and the law is concerned with controlling and regulating the behaviour of people in society. These social institutions make up a society's **social structure** – the building blocks of society.

Social institutions are the various organized social arrangements which are found in all societies.

Social structure refers to the social institutions and social relationships that form the 'building blocks' of society.

Sociology tries to understand how these various social institutions operate, and how they relate to one another, for example the way in which the family might influence how well children perform in the education system. Sociology is also concerned with describing and explaining the patterns of inequality, deprivation and conflict which are a feature of nearly all societies.

Sociology and common sense

Sociology is concerned with studying many things which most people already know something about. Everyone will have some knowledge and understanding of family life, the education system, work, the mass media and religion simply by living as a member of society. This leads many people to assume that the topics studied by sociologists and the explanations sociologists produce are really just common sense: what 'everyone knows'.

This is a very mistaken assumption. Sociological research has shown many widely held 'common-sense' ideas and explanations to be false. Ideas such as that there is no real poverty left in modern Britain, that the poor and unemployed are inadequate and lazy, that everyone has equal chances in life, that the rich are rich because they work harder, that men are 'naturally' superior to women, and that sickness and disease strike people at random havc all been questioned by sociological research. The re-examination of such common-sense views is very much the concern of sociology.

A further problem with common-sense explanations is that they are very much bound up with the beliefs of a particular society at particular periods of time. Different societies have differing common-sense ideas. The Hopi Indians' common-sense view of why it rains is very different from our own – they do a rain dance to encourage the rain gods. Common-sense ideas also change over time in any society. In Britain, we no longer burn witches when the crops fail, or see mental illness as evidence of satanic possession, but seek scientific, medical or psychiatric explanations for such events.

Not all the findings of sociologists undermine common scnse, and the work of sociologists has made important contributions to the common-sense understandings of members of society. For example, the knowledge most people have about the changing family in Britain, with rising rates of divorce and growing numbers of lone parents, is largely due to the work of sociologists. However, sociology differs from common sense in three important ways:

- Sociologists use a sociological imagination. This means that, while they study the familiar routines of daily life, sociologists look at them in unfamiliar ways or from a different angle. They ask if things really are as common sense says they are. Sociologists re-examine existing assumptions, by studying how things were in the past, how they've changed, how they differ between societies and how they might change in the future.
- Sociologists look at evidence on issues before making up their minds. The explanations and conclusions of sociologists are based on precise evidence which has been collected through painstaking research using established research procedures.
- Sociologists strive to maintain **objectivity** and **value freedom** in their work. These involve keeping an open mind, considering all the evidence, allowing others to scrutinize research findings, and keeping personal beliefs out of the research process.

Objectivity
means sociologists should approach their research with an open mind – a willingness to consider all the evidence, and to have their work available for scrutiny and criticism by other researchers.

Value freedom
means sociologists should try not to let their prejudices and beliefs influence the way they carry out their research and interpret evidence.

Sociology and naturalistic explanations

Naturalistic explanations are those which assume that various kinds of human behaviour are natural or based on innate (inborn) biological characteristics. If this were the case, then one would expect human behaviour to be the same in all societies. In fact, by comparing different societies, sociologists have discovered that there are very wide differences between them in terms of customs, values, beliefs and social behaviour. For example, there are wide differences between societies in the roles of men and women and what is considered appropriate 'masculine' and 'feminine' behaviour. This can only be because people learn to behave in different ways in different societies. Sociological explanations recognize that most human behaviour is learnt by individuals as members of society, rather than something with which they are born. Individuals learn how to behave from a wide range of social institutions right through their lives. Sociologists call this process of learning 'socialization'.

Some key introductory ideas

SOCIALIZATION, CULTURE AND IDENTITY

Socialization is
the lifelong process of
learning the culture of
any society

The term **culture**
refers to the language,
beliefs, values and
norms, customs, dress,
diet, roles, knowledge
and skills which make
up the 'way of life' of
any society.

Identity is
concerned with how
individuals see and
define themselves and
how other people see
and define them.

Socialization is the lifelong process by which people learn the **culture** of the society in which they live. Socialization is carried out by agencies of socialization, such as the family, the education system, religious institutions or the mass media. Culture is socially transmitted (passed on through socialization) from one generation to the next.

Socialization plays a crucial part in forming our identities. **Identity** is about how we see and define ourselves and how other people see and define us.

For example, we might define ourselves as gay, black, a Muslim, Welsh, English, a woman, a student or a mother. Many aspects of our individual identities will be formed through the socialization process, with the family, friends, school, the mass media, the workplace and other agencies of socialization helping to form our individual identities. Many chapters in this book refer to aspects of this socialization process and the formation of our identities.

However, while lifelong socialization plays a very important part in forming our identities, individuals also have the free will to enable them to 'carve out' their own personal identities and influence how others see them, rather than simply being influenced by them. Individuals are not simply the passive victims of the socialization process. While individual identities are formed by various forces of socialization, the choices individuals and groups make and how they react to these forces can also have an influence. For example, while the mass media might influence our lifestyles, attitudes and values, and how we see ourselves and how others see us, individuals may also react to what they read, see or hear in the media in different ways.

A woman from a minority ethnic background may define herself as black or Asian, but she may also see herself mainly as a woman, a mother, a teacher or a Muslim. Similarly, we have some choices in the consumption goods we buy, the clothes we wear, and the leisure activities we choose to pursue. Through these choices, we can influence how others see us, and the image of ourselves we project to them. Individuals may also have multiple identities, presenting different aspects of themselves in different ways to different groups of people. People may therefore not adopt the same identity all the time, and different people will see them in different ways.

Activity

1. Suggest three ways, with examples, in which individuals learn the culture of society in contemporary Britain.
2. Describe three factors, apart from the examples given, that others might use to define your identity, such as your dress or taste in music. Explain your answer with examples.
3. Suggest three ways that individuals' choices in consumer goods may influence how other people define them.
4. Suggest reasons why people may have difficulty in getting other people to accept whatever identity they wish to project to others.

ROLES, ROLE MODELS AND ROLE CONFLICT

Roles are very like the roles actors play in a theatre or television series. People in society play many different roles in their lifetimes, such as those of a man or a woman, a child and an adult, a student, a parent, a friend, and work roles like factory worker, police officer or teacher. People in these roles are expected by society to behave in particular ways. For example, police officers who steal or take bribes, the teacher who is drunk in the classroom and the parent who neglects his or her children are clearly not conforming to the ways society expects them to behave, and these examples show how important such expectations of others are.

Roles are often learnt by copying or imitating the behaviour and attitudes of others. Children, for example, will often learn how to behave by copying the behaviour of their parents, teachers or friends. Those whose behaviour we consciously or unconsciously copy are known as **role models**.

One person plays many roles at the same time. For example, a woman may play the roles of woman, mother, student, worker, sister and wife at the same time. This may lead to **role conflict**, where the successful performance of two or more roles at the same time may come into conflict with one another.

A woman who tries to balance, and is often torn apart by, the competing demands of being a night-class student, having a full-time job, looking after children and taking care of dependent elderly parents illustrates this idea of role conflict.

VALUES AND NORMS

Values provide general guidelines for behaviour. In Britain, values include beliefs about respect for human life, privacy and private property, about the importance of marriage and the importance of money and success. While not everyone will always share the same values, there are often strong pressures on people to conform to some of the most important values in any society, which are often written down as **laws**. These are official legal rules which often deal with matters that many people think are very important. Laws against murder and theft, for example, enforce the values attached to human life and private property in our society. Laws are formally enforced by the police, courts and prisons, and involve legal punishment if they are broken.

Norms are social rules which define the correct and acceptable behaviour in a society or social group to which people are expected to conform. Norms are much more precise than values: they put values (general guidelines) into practice in particular situations. The norm that someone should not generally enter rooms without knocking reflects the value of privacy, and rules about not drinking and driving reflect the values of respect

Roles are the patterns of behaviour which are expected from individuals in society.

Role models are people's patterns of behaviour which others copy and model their own behaviour on.

Role conflict is the conflict between the successful performance of two or more roles at the same time, such as those of worker, mother and student.

Values are general beliefs about what is right or wrong, and about the important standards which are worth maintaining and achieving in any society or social group.

Laws are official legal rules, formally enforced by the police, courts and prison, involving legal punishment if the rules are broken.

Norms are social rules which define the correct and acceptable behaviour in a society or social group to which people are expected to conform.

Role conflict for working women

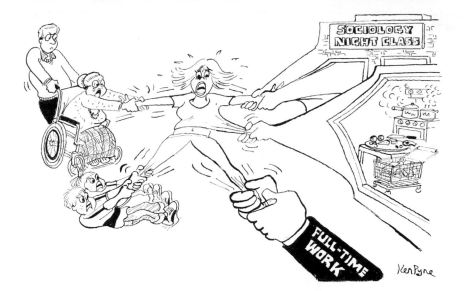

Norms control behaviour in nearly all aspects of our lives, with positive and negative sanctions to enforce them. Try jumping queues to see the sanctions that follow

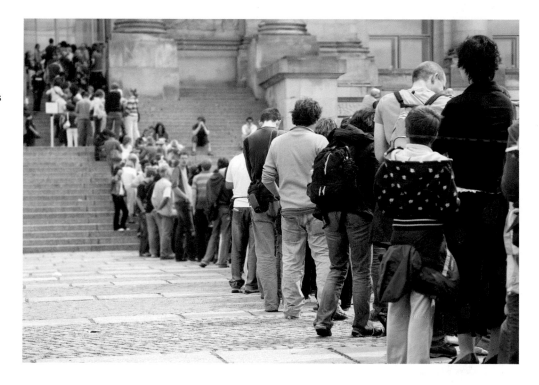

for human life and consideration for the safety of others. Norms exist in all areas of social life. In Britain, those who are late for work, jump queues in supermarkets, laugh during funerals, walk through the streets naked or never say 'hello' to friends when they are greeted by them are likely to be seen as unreliable, annoying, rude or odd because they are not following the norms of expected behaviour. Norms are mainly informally enforced – by the disapproval of other people, embarrassment or a telling off from parents or others.

Customs are norms which have lasted for a long time and have become a part of society's traditions – kissing under the mistletoe at Christmas, buying and giving Easter eggs or lighting candles at Divali are typical customs found in Britain.

Customs are norms which have lasted for a long time and have become a part of society's traditions.

Values and norms, and related customs and traditions, are embedded deeply within a society's culture. They include a large number of unwritten rules, some of which are tiny, and even trivial, but they are nonetheless important aspects making up the familiar and taken-for-granted characteristics of a society's culture. These are learnt by most people through socialization, but behaviour which passes for normal in one's own culture may be considered unacceptable in others.

1 Go to the following links to four videos on YouTube which illustrate some cultural differences, or do a search in YouTube for 'HSBC ads', or 'cultural differences'. You may come across similar videos in the same location, which you may also wish to view.
   http://youtu.be/WcEfzHB08QE
   http://youtu.be/JK_NinOmFWw
   http://youtu.be/8jrbu0lCWjk
   http://youtu.be/v1vvLQd53Ps

After viewing these videos:

2 Identify four differences in social norms, customs and traditions either between the different countries of the UK (England, Scotland, Northern Ireland and Wales) or between the UK and other cultures.

3 Suggest four social norms that you think people raised in another culture might find odd if they visited or came to live in the UK.

4 Explain how the videos you have watched show the importance of socialization in helping people to live together in society.

Values and norms are part of the culture of a society, and are learnt and passed on through socialization. They differ between societies – the values and norms of an African tribe are very different from those of people in modern Britain. They may also change over time and vary between social groups even in the same society. In Britain, living together without being married – a cohabiting relationship – is much more accepted today than it was in the past, and wearing turbans – which is seen as normal dress among Sikh men – would be seen as a bit odd among white teenagers.

SOCIAL CONTROL

Social control is the term given to the various methods used to persuade or force individuals to conform to the dominant social norms and values of a society, and to prevent **deviance** – a failure to conform to social norms.

Processes of social control may be formal, through institutions like the law or school rules, or they may be informal, through peer-group pressure, personal embarrassment at doing something wrong, or the pressure of public opinion.

Sanctions are the rewards and punishments by which social control is achieved and conformity to norms and values enforced. These may be either **positive sanctions**, rewards of various kinds, or **negative sanctions**, various types of punishment. The type of sanction will depend on the seriousness of the norm: positive sanctions may range from gifts of sweets or money from parents to children, to merits and prizes at school, to knighthoods and medals; negative sanctions may range from a feeling of embarrassment, to being ridiculed or gossiped about or regarded as a bit eccentric or 'a bit odd', to being fined or imprisoned.

Social control is the term given to the various methods used to persuade or force individuals to conform to the dominant social norms and values of a society.

Deviance is the failure to conform to social norms.

Sanctions are the rewards and punishments by which social control is achieved and conformity to norms and values enforced.

Positive sanctions are rewards of various kinds.

Negative sanctions are various types of punishment.

A **social class** is a group of people who share a similar economic situation, such as a similar occupational level, income and ownership of wealth.

Income is a flow of money which people obtain from work, from their investments, or from the state.

Wealth is property in the form of assets which can, in general, be sold and turned into cash for the benefit of the owner.

Life chances are the chances of obtaining those things defined as desirable and of avoiding those things defined as undesirable in any society.

Social mobility refers to the movement of groups or individuals up or down the social hierarchy, from one social class to another.

The **upper class** consists of those who are the main owners of society's wealth. It includes wealthy industrialists, landowners and the traditional aristocracy.

The **middle class** consists of those in non-manual work – jobs that don't require heavy physical work and are usually performed in offices and involve paperwork or computer work.

The **working class** consists of those working in manual jobs, involving physical work and, literally, work with their hands, such as factory or labouring work.

Activity

1. Identify three important values in Britain today and three norms relating to these values. Suggest ways in which these norms and values are enforced.
2. Identify at least four roles that you play, and describe the norms of behaviour to which you are expected to conform in each case.
3. Describe the sanctions you might face if you failed to conform to the norms you have identified.
4. Identify how the successful performance of one role might conflict with the successful performance of another.

SOCIAL CLASS, SOCIAL MOBILITY AND STATUS

Social class is a term you will read a lot about in sociology, including in this book. Social class is generally associated with inequality in industrial societies. It is often used in a very broad and imprecise way, but generally refers to a group of people sharing a similar economic situation, such as occupation, **income** and ownership of **wealth**.

Often, occupation, income and ownership of wealth are closely related to each other and to other aspects of individuals' lives, such as how much power and influence they have in society, their level of education, their social status (or position in society – see below), their type of housing, car ownership, leisure activities and other aspects of their lifestyle.

An individual's social class has a major influence on his or her **life chances**. Life chances include the chances of obtaining things like good-quality housing, a long and healthy life, holidays, job security and educational success, and avoiding things like unemployment, ill-health and premature death. **Social mobility** refers to the movement of groups or individuals up or down the social hierarchy, from one social class to another.

To help you to understand the different social classes in modern Britain, the following simplified classification will suffice for the purposes of this book:

- The **upper class** is a small class, and refers to those who are the main owners of society's wealth, including wealthy industrialists, landowners and the traditional aristocracy. Often these people do not work for others, as their assets are so large that work is not necessary for them to survive.
- The **middle class** is a large class, and refers to those in non-manual work – jobs which don't involve heavy physical effort, and which are usually performed in offices and involve paperwork or ICT (information and communication technology) of various kinds. Some argue that those in the lowest levels of non-manual work, such as supermarket check-out operators and those in routine office work, should really be included in the working class, as their pay and working conditions are more like those of manual workers than like those of many sections of the middle class.
- The **working class** is one of the largest social classes, referring to those working in manual jobs – jobs involving physical work and, literally, work with their hands, like factory or labouring work.
- The **underclass** is a small class, and refers to a group of people who are right at the bottom of the class structure, and whose poverty often excludes them from full participation in society. The term 'underclass' is used in different ways, and is a controversial concept. It is discussed more fully in chapter 4 on wealth, poverty and welfare.

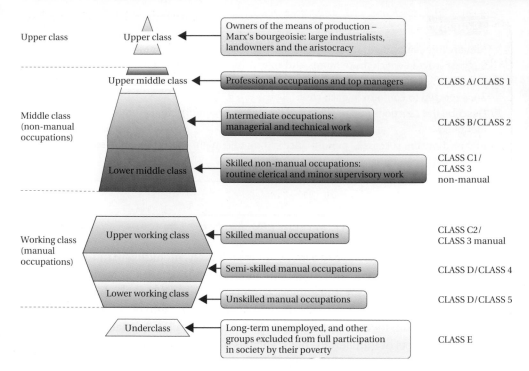

Figure 1.1 The class structure

The **underclass** is the social group right at the bottom of the social class hierarchy, consisting of those who are in some ways cut off, or excluded, from the rest of society.

Figure 1.1 illustrates the class structure of modern Britain, and is a guide to the use of the concept of social class in this book.

Status

The term **status** is used in sociology in two main ways. It is often used to refer to the role someone occupies in society, like a father, worker or consumer. It is also sometimes used to refer to the ranking of individuals in society according to the differing amounts of prestige or respect given to different positions by other members of that group or society – people's social standing in the eyes of others. **Ascribed status** is status given by birth or family background, which, in general, cannot be changed by individuals. Examples of such status include a person's age, ethnic group, sex, or place or family of birth. **Achieved status** refers to any social position or position of prestige that has been achieved by an individual's own efforts, such as through education, skill and talent, promotion at work and career success.

Status sometimes refers to the role position someone occupies in society, but more commonly refers to the amount of prestige or social importance a person has in the eyes of other members of a group or society. **Ascribed status** is status given by birth or family background, which, in general, cannot be changed by individuals. **Achieved status** is status that is achieved by an individual's own efforts or talents.

ETHNICITY AND GENDER

Three other concepts you will come across in sociology, and which are also referred to widely in this book, are those of **ethnicity**, **minority ethnic group**, and **gender**. Ethnicity refers to the shared culture of a social group which gives its members a common identity in some ways different from that of other social groups. A minority ethnic group is a social group which shares a cultural identity which is different from that of the majority population of a society, such as African-Caribbean, Indian Asian and Chinese ethnic groups in Britain. Gender refers to the culturally created differences between men and women which are learnt through socialization, rather than simply **sex** differences, which refer only to the biological differences between the sexes.

Ethnicity refers to the shared culture of a social group which gives its members a common identity in some ways different from that of other social groups. A **minority ethnic group** is a social group which shares a cultural identity which is different from that of the majority population of a society. **Gender** refers to the culturally created differences between men and women which are learnt through socialization. **Sex** refers to the biological differences between men and women, as opposed to culturally-created gender differences.

Activity

Using the word list below, fill in the blanks in the following passage. Each dash represents one word.

identity	social structure	values
social control	norms	social mobility
status	working class	role conflict
value freedom	ascribed status	status
social class	positive	upper class
achieved status	socialization	objectivity
ethnicity	roles	underclass
minority ethnic group	social institutions	negative sanctions
social classes	deviance	life chances
gender	social classes	

Sociology involves studying the social world, but as sociologists are themselves part of this social world, they need to take care that they look at things in a detached and impartial way. They should approach research in an open-minded way, considering all the evidence before making up their minds. This is known as _____. They should also try not to let their own beliefs and prejudices influence their research. This_____ _____ is important if sociology is to be seen as something more than newspaper journalism.

Society is constructed of a range of _____ _____, like the family, religion, the education system and the law. These make up the _____ _____ – the 'building blocks' of society. Sociologists generally believe that people learn the culture of their society, and this learning process is known as _____. For example, males and females often learn to behave in different ways. This difference is known as _____. The learning process influences the formation of the individual's _____ – how they see and define themselves and how others see and define them. _____ refers to the shared culture of a social group which gives its members a common identity in some ways different from that of other social groups. If a group has a cultural identity different from the majority population of a society, such as black and Asian groups in Britain, it is known as a _____ _____ _____.

Everyone in society is expected to behave in particular ways in particular situations, and these patterns of expected behaviour are known as _____, but sometimes these come into conflict with each other, causing _____ _____.

Every society has sets of guidelines for behaviour. _____ establish the important standards about what is important in a society and what is right or wrong. _____ provide rules about how to behave in particular situations.

People are encouraged to conform to these rules by _____ _____, which is carried out by a range of rewards and punishments known as _____ and _____ _____. Non-conformity to social rules is known as _____.

A _____ _____ is a group of people who share a similar economic situation, and this can have an important influence on their chances of obtaining the desirable, and avoiding the undesirable, things in life – their _____ _____. The two largest _____ _____ are the _____ _____ and the middle class. The main owners of society's wealth are known as the _____ _____, while the very poorest group, which is excluded from full participation in society by poverty, is known as the _____. Sometimes people can move up or down between _____ _____, and this is known as _____ _____. Some people and some positions in society are ranked by others in terms of different amounts of prestige or respect, and this is known as _____. If this is given by birth or family background, it is known as _____ _____. However, some people can achieve their _____ through their own individual efforts and talents. This is known as _____ _____

The solution to this activity can be found on the teachers' pages of www.politybooks.com/browne.

Sociological perspectives

A **perspective** is simply a way of looking at something. A **sociological perspective** is a way of looking at society. Newcomers to sociology often find the different perspectives in sociology difficult, as there appears to be no 'right answer'.

A useful insight might be gained from the following situation. Imagine there are five people looking at the same busy shopping street – a pickpocket, a police officer, a roadsweeper, a shopper and a shopkeeper (see cartoon below). The pickpocket sees wallets sticking out of pockets or bags, and an opportunity to steal. The police officer sees potential crime and disorder. The roadsweeper sees litter and garbage left by everyone else. The shopper might see windows full of desirable consumer goods to buy, and the shopkeeper sees only potential customers, and possibly shoplifters. All are viewing the same street, but are looking at different aspects of that street. What they see will depend on their 'perspective' – what they're looking for. They might all be seeing different things, but you can't really say any of their views is more correct than another – though you might think some views provide a more truthful, more rounded and fuller description of the street than others do.

Sociological perspectives are basically similar, in that they are the different viewpoints from which sociologists examine society. Different sociological perspectives simply emphasize and explain different aspects of society. Often, debates between and criticisms of these different perspectives help us to understand social issues much more clearly.

What follows is an introduction to some of these sociological perspectives. These perspectives are often best understood by looking at particular areas, and this book will explore them further in various chapters, building on and illustrating what is said below.

Sociological perspectives centre on the themes of how much freedom or control the individual has to influence society. To what extent is the individual's identity moulded by social forces outside her or his control? How much control does the

> A **perspective** is a way of looking at something.
> A **sociological perspective** involves a set of theories which influences what is looked at when studying society.

People may view the same scene from different perspectives

individual have over these social forces, and how free are individuals to form their own identities?

There are two main approaches here:

- the sociology of system, often referred to as **structuralism**.
- the sociology of action – social action or interpretivist theories.

STRUCTURALISM

Structuralism is concerned with the overall structure of society, and the way social institutions, like the family, the education system, the mass media and work, act as a constraint on, or limit and control, individual behaviour. Structuralist approaches have the following features:

- The behaviour of individual human beings, the way they act (their social action) and the formation of their identities are seen as being a result of social forces which are external to the individual – the individual is moulded, shaped and constrained by society through socialization, positive and negative sanctions, and material resources like income and jobs. For example, institutions like the family, the education system, the mass media, the law and the workplace mould us into our identities. According to the structuralist approach, the individual is like a puppet, whose strings are pulled by society. We might see people almost like jelly, poured into a 'social mould' to set.
- The main purpose of sociology is to study the overall structure of society, the social institutions which make up this structure, and the relationships between these social institutions (or the various parts of society) such as the links between the workplace and the economy, the economy and the political system, the family and the education system, and so on. The focus of sociology is on the study of social institutions and the social structure as a whole, not on the individual. This is sometimes referred to as a **macro approach**.

Structuralism is illustrated in the cartoon on the left.

> **Structuralism**
> is a perspective which is concerned with the overall structure of society, and sees individual behaviour moulded by social institutions like the family, the education system, the mass media and work.

> A **macro approach** focuses on the large-scale structure of society as a whole, rather than on individuals.

Structural approaches see individuals formed by the wider social forces making up the social structure of society

> ### Activity
>
> 1. How much is our behaviour moulded by social forces beyond our control? Try to think of all the factors which have contributed to the way you are now, and which prevent you from behaving in any way you like. You might consider factors like the influences of your parents and family background, the mass media, experiences at school, your friendship groups, income and so on.
> 2. Imagine you were creating an ideal society from scratch. Plan how you would organize it, with particular reference to the following issues:
>   - the care and socialization of children.
>   - the passing on of society's knowledge and skills from one generation to the next.
>   - the production of food and other goods necessary for survival.
>   - how you would allocate food and other goods to members of society.
>   - the establishment and enforcement of rules of behaviour.
>   - how you would deal with people who didn't conform to social rules.
>   - how you would coordinate things and resolve disputes between members of society.
> 3. Consider how your ideal society is similar to, or different from, the organization of contemporary Britain. How would you explain these differences?

There are two main varieties of structuralism: functionalism (consensus structuralism) and Marxism (conflict structuralism).

Functionalism (consensus structuralism)

Functionalism is most closely associated with the work of the French sociologist Émile Durkheim (1858–1917) and the American Talcott Parsons (1902–79), who are referred to in various parts of this book. Functionalism sees society built up and working like the human body, made up of interrelated parts which function for, or contribute to, the maintenance of society as a whole. For example, in order to understand the importance of the heart, lungs and brain in the human body, we need to understand what function or purpose each carries out and how they work together in providing and maintaining the basic needs of human life. Similarly, functionalists argue that any society has certain **functional prerequisites** (certain basic needs or requirements) that must be met if society is to survive. These include the production of food, the care of the young and the socialization of new generations into the culture of society. Social institutions like the family or education exist to meet these basic needs, in the same way as we have to have a heart and lungs to refresh our blood and pump it around our bodies.

Just as the various parts of the human body function in relation to one another and contribute to the maintenance of the body as a whole, so, according to functionalist sociology, social institutions meet functional prerequisites, maintaining the social system and order and stability in society. In this view, social institutions like the family, education and work are connected and function in relation to one another for the benefit of society as a whole. Stability in society is based on socialization into norms and values on which most people agree. These shared norms and values are known as a **value consensus**. It is this value consensus which functionalists believe maintains what they see as a peaceful, harmonious society without much conflict between people and groups.

> **Functionalism** is a sociological perspective which sees society as made up of parts which work together to maintain society as an integrated whole. Society is seen as fundamentally harmonious and stable, because of the agreement on basic values (value consensus) established through socialization.

> **Functional prerequisites** are the basic needs that must be met if society is to survive.

> **Value consensus** is a general agreement around the main values and norms of any society.

Activity

Try to think of all the connections or links you can between the following institutions – for example, how what happens in the family may influence what happens at school and educational achievement:
- the family and the education system
- the family and the workplace
- education and the workplace

Marxism (conflict structuralism)

The term **Marxism** comes from the work of Karl Marx, who lived from 1818 to 1883.

Base and superstructure   Marx believed that the economy was the driving force in society, and it was this that determined (or influenced) the nature of social institutions, and people's values and beliefs. Marxism sees the structure of society divided into two main parts, illustrated in figure 1.2.

1   The economic base, or *infrastructure*, which underpins and determines everything else in society; this consists of:

> **Marxism** is a structural theory of society which sees society divided by conflict between two main opposing social classes, due to private ownership of the means of production: the key resources necessary for producing society's goods, such as land, factories and machinery.

Figure 1.2 The base and superstructure in Marxist theory

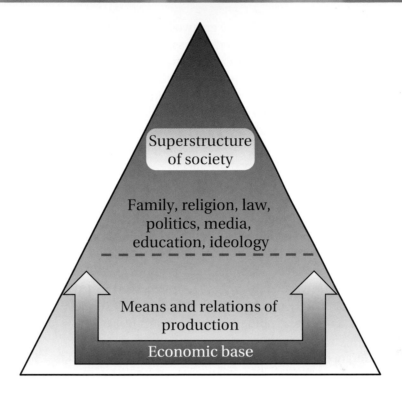

Superstructure of society

Family, religion, law, politics, media, education, ideology

Means and relations of production

Economic base

The **means of production** are the key resources necessary for producing society's goods, such as land, factories and machinery.

The **relations of production** are the forms of relationship between those people involved in production, such as cooperation or private ownership and control.

Ideology is a set of ideas, values and beliefs that represents the outlook, and justifies the interests, of a social group.

- the **means of production**, like the land, factories, raw materials, technology and labour necessary to produce society's goods.
- the **relations of production**: the relations, such as shared ownership or private ownership, between those involved in production; who controls production; and the relationship between owners and non-owners, e.g. whether people are forced to work, like slaves, or paid for their work.

2 *The superstructure*, which includes society's social institutions, such as the family, education, the mass media, religion and the political system, and beliefs and values (**ideology**), which Marx saw as primarily determined (or influenced) by the economic system.

Surplus value and exploitation   In a capitalist society, the means of production are privately owned, and most people depend on the owners for employment. Marx argued that workers produce more than is needed for employers to pay them their wages – this 'extra' produced by workers is what Marx called **surplus value**, and provides profit for the employer. For example, in a burger chain, it is the workers who make, cook, package and serve the burgers, but only half the burgers they sell are necessary to cover production costs and pay their wages. The rest of the sales provide profit for the owners of the burger chain. This means that the workers who produce the burgers do not get the full value of their work, and they are therefore being exploited.

Surplus value is the extra value added by workers to the products they produce, after allowing for the payment of their wages, and which goes to the employer in the form of profit.

> **Activity**
>
> Do you think those who produce the wealth should get the full share of what they produce? Do you think most goods today are produced because people need them, or because they can be persuaded to buy them by advertising? See what other people think about this.

Capitalists and workers   Marx argued that there were two basic social classes in capitalist industrial society: a small wealthy and powerful class of owners of the means of production (which he called the **bourgeoisie** or **capitalists** – the owning class) and a much larger, poorer class of non-owners (which he called the **proletariat** or working class). The proletariat, because they owned no means of production of their own, had no means of living other than to sell their labour, or **labour power** as Marx called it, to the bourgeoisie in exchange for a wage or salary. The capitalists exploited the working class by making profits out of them by keeping wages as low as possible instead of giving the workers the full payment for the goods they'd produced.

Class conflict   Marx asserted that this exploitation created major differences in interest between the two classes, and this created conflict. For example, the workers' interests lay in higher wages to achieve a better lifestyle, but these would be at the expense of the bosses' profits. The bosses wanted higher profits to expand their businesses and wealth, but this could only be achieved by keeping wages as low as possible and/or by making the workers produce more by working harder. The interests of these two classes are therefore totally opposed, and this generates conflict between the two social classes (**class conflict**). Marx believed this class conflict would affect all areas of life.

The ruling class   Marx argued that the owning class was also a **ruling class**. For example, because they owned the means of production, the bourgeoisie could decide where factories should be located, and whether they should be opened or closed down, and they could control the workforce through hiring or firing. Democratically elected governments could not afford to ignore this power of the bourgeoisie, otherwise they might face rising unemployment or other social problems if the bourgeoisie decided not to invest its money.

Dominant ideology   Marx believed the ruling or dominant ideas in any society, what he called the **dominant ideology**, were those of the owning class (hence it is sometimes also called **ruling class ideology**) and the major institutions in society reflected those ideas.

For example, the law protected the interests of the owning class more than it did those of the workers; religion acted as the 'opium of the people', persuading the working class to accept their position as just and natural (rather than rebelling against it), by

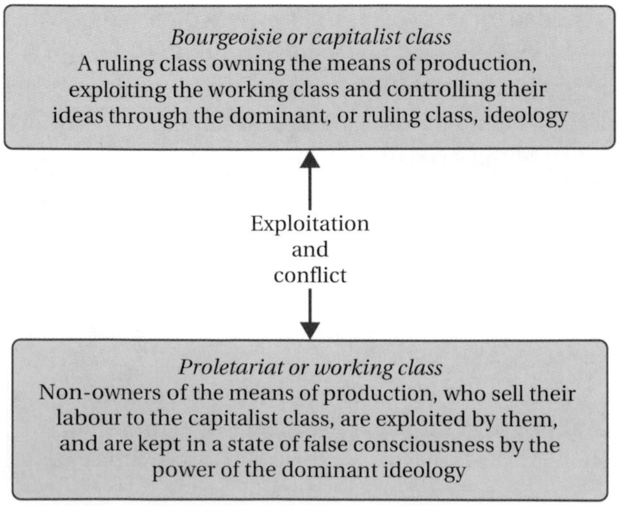

The **bourgeoisie** (or capitalists) is the class of owners of the means of production in industrial societies, whose primary purpose is to make profits.

The **proletariat** is the social class of workers who have to work for wages as they do not own the means of production.

Labour power refers to people's capacity to work. People sell their labour power to the employer in return for a wage, and the employer buys only their labour power, and not the whole person.

Class conflict is the conflict that arises between different social classes. It is generally used to describe the conflict between the bourgeoisie and proletariat in Marxist views of society.

The **ruling class** is the social class of owners of the means of production, whose control over the economy gives them power over all aspects of society, enabling them to rule over society.

The **dominant ideology** is the set of ideas and beliefs of the most powerful groups in society, which influences the ideas of the rest of society.

Bourgeoisie or capitalist class
A ruling class owning the means of production, exploiting the working class and controlling their ideas through the dominant, or ruling class, ideology

↑
Exploitation and conflict
↓

Proletariat or working class
Non-owners of the means of production, who sell their labour to the capitalist class, are exploited by them, and are kept in a state of false consciousness by the power of the dominant ideology

Figure 1.3 A summary of the Marxist view of society

Ruling class ideology is the set of ideas of the ruling class.
False consciousness is a failure by members of a social class to recognize their real interests.

'drugging' them and inducing hallucinations of future rewards in heaven for putting up with their present suffering; the bourgeoisie's ownership of the mass media meant only their ideas were put forward. In this way, the workers were almost brainwashed into accepting their position. They failed to recognize they were being exploited and therefore did not rebel against the bourgeoisie. Marx called this lack of awareness by the working class of their own interests **false consciousness**.

Revolution and communism   However, Marx thought that one day the circumstances would arise in which the workers did become aware of their exploitation. They would develop **class consciousness** (an awareness of their real interests and their exploitation) and would join together to act against the bourgeoisie through strikes, demonstrations and other forms of protest. This would eventually lead to a revolution against and overthrow of the bourgeoisie. The means of production would then be put in the hands of the state and run in the interests of everyone, not just of the bourgeoisie. Marx foresaw this leading to a new form of society which he called **communism**. This new communist society would be an equal society, in which the means of production would be the common property of all, and would be without exploitation, without classes and without class conflict.

Class consciousness is an awareness in members of a social class of their real interests.
Communism refers to an equal society, without social classes or class conflict, in which the means of production are the common property of all.

Marx therefore saw society based on the exploitation of one large class by a small group of owners, creating social classes with opposing interests, and inequalities of wealth and power in society. Rather than seeing society functioning harmoniously as the functionalists do, Marxists see society based on conflict between rival social classes (class conflict) with social institutions serving to maintain the interests of a ruling class. However, like functionalists, Marxists see the behaviour of individuals as still largely determined or moulded by social institutions.

Social action theories or **interpretivist** approaches are perspectives which emphasize the creative action which people can take, rather than seeing them as simply passive victims of social forces outside them. Social action theory suggests it is important to understand the motives and meanings people give to their behaviour, and how this is influenced by the behaviour and interpretations of others. The focus of research is therefore on individuals or small groups rather than on society as a whole.

Activity

Comparing the views of functionalists and Marxists, which view of society do you think provides the most accurate and useful insights into the way British society is currently organized? Is it mainly based on consensus or conflict? Give reasons for your answer, with examples to illustrate the points you make.

SOCIAL ACTION OR INTERPRETIVIST THEORIES

Individual behaviour in everyday social situations is the main focus of **social action** or **interpretivist** approaches. These theories are concerned with discovering and thereby understanding the processes by which interactions between individuals or small groups take place, how people come to interpret and see things as they do, how they define their identities, and how the reactions of others can affect their view of things and their sense of their own identity.

Social action or interpretivist theories include the following features:

Determinism is the idea that people's behaviour is moulded by their social surroundings, and that they have little free will, control or choice over how they behave.

- Society and social structures/institutions are seen as the creation of individuals. An emphasis is placed on the free will of people to do things, in how they act and form their identities, rather than on the **determinism** of structuralism. Determinism means that the activities and identities of individuals are moulded by forces beyond their control, and they have little control or choice in how they behave. It almost suggests people are programmed to behave the way they do by society.

- An emphasis is placed on the individual and everyday behaviour rather than the overall structure of society. The focus of sociology is on the individual or small groups of individuals, not on the social structure as a whole. Rather than studying general trends and the wider causes of crime, for example, interpretivists are more likely to study a juvenile gang, to see how they came to be seen and labelled as deviant, and how they themselves see the world. This is sometimes referred to as a **micro approach**.

- People's behaviour is viewed as being driven by the meanings they give to situations: their definitions of a situation, or the way they see things and therefore behave, become very important. For example, a parent might interpret a baby crying as a sign of tiredness, hunger, fear or illness. The action the parent takes – putting the baby to bed, feeding her, comforting her or taking her to the doctor – will depend on how the parent defines the situation, and to understand the parent's behaviour we have to understand the meaning he or she gives to the baby's crying. In turn, how the parent acts in response to the meaning given to the baby's behaviour is likely to affect the baby's behaviour – whether it stops crying because it is no longer tired, hungry, afraid or ill.

- The main purpose of sociology is to study, uncover and interpret the meanings and definitions individuals give to their behaviour.

Social action approaches are illustrated in the cartoon on the right.

> ### Activity
> 1 How do the attitudes and interpretations of other people affect your view of yourself? Give examples to illustrate the points you make.
> 2 Imagine you wanted to study the family and the education system. Suggest three things for each institution you might be interested in if you adopted a structuralist approach, and three things for each institution if you adopted an interpretivist approach.

> A **micro approach** focuses on small groups or individuals, rather than on the structure of society as a whole.

Social action or interpretivist theories emphasize the free will and choice of individuals, and their role in creating the social structure

Symbolic interactionism

Symbolic interactionism is a social action perspective particularly concerned with understanding human behaviour in face-to-face situations, and how individuals and situations come to be defined or classified in particular ways. This is known as **labelling**. It is also concerned with the consequences for individual behaviour of such definitions, since people will behave according to the way they see situations. For example, the sociologist's task is to understand the point of view and experience of, say, the disillusioned and hostile student who hates school, as well as of the teachers and others who label him or her as 'deviant'. Sociologists should try to understand how and why teachers classify some students as deviant, and what happens to the behaviour of those students once they have been classified in that way.

> **Symbolic interactionism** is a sociological perspective which is concerned with understanding human behaviour in face-to-face situations, and how individuals and situations come to be defined in particular ways through their encounters with other people.

STRUCTURATION: A MIDDLE WAY BETWEEN STRUCTURE AND ACTION

In real life, society is probably best understood using a mixture of both structural and action approaches. In other words, constraints from social institutions, like the family, work (and the income it does or doesn't produce), the law and education, limit and control the behaviour of individuals or groups, and have important influences on the formation of individual and group identities. However, individuals can, within limits,

> **Labelling** refers to defining a person or group in a certain way – as a particular 'type' of person or group.

What consequences might follow for someone who has been labelled a deviant?

make choices within those structures and act accordingly. For example, the school is part of the education system – a social structure. Young people are constrained (forced) by law to go to school, and that school continues to exist even after generations of young people have come and gone. It therefore has an existence separate from the individuals who attend that school at any one time. That structure continues only so long as people support the law and agree to attend school – if everyone stopped sending their children to school, the system would either have to be changed or it would collapse. This shows human beings create and reinforce, or can change or destroy, these structures.

If we take a particular school or group of schools, while they are constrained by the demands of the National Curriculum, the laws on education and the income they have, what happens within each individual school is controlled to some degree by the people closely connected to it – governors, students, teachers and parents. If attendance is poor, behaviour dreadful, teaching quality inadequate, exam results a catastrophe, and the school has a weak or incompetent headteacher, we may see this as a failing school. It might be inspected by Ofsted (the Office for Standards in Education, Children's Services and Skills), and officially classified as a school requiring 'special measures' to put it right. If parents opt to send their children to another school, it may face declining income, making things worse. As a result, it might face closure.

However, the school might be dramatically improved by teachers and others in the school community working harder to try and turn the school around. We might then eventually see it as a 'good' school. The school might be held up as a showpiece of improvement by the government, and used as a model or 'beacon school' for all other schools to follow. This change shows that, within social structures like education, human action – human activity – can make differences by changing those structures.

This means that, while people operate within the constraints of the social structure, they can also act, make choices, and sometimes change that social structure. It has to be supported by people, and constantly recreated: parents have to send their children to school because it is against the law not to do so, and most parents don't question this. But they do have to agree to this, and there are lots of cases where parents refuse

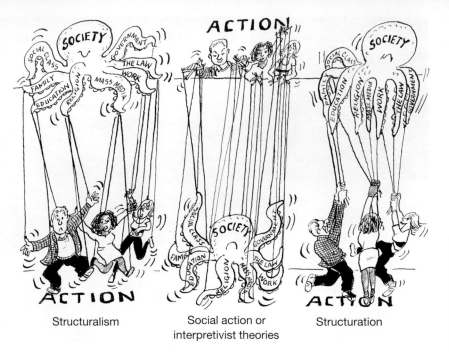

| Structuralism | Social action or interpretivist theories | Structuration |

to send their children to school because they believe there is something wrong with the school. If they refuse, especially a lot of them, then there would undoubtedly be a change in the schooling system.

This third or middle way, between structuralism and action theories, recognizes the importance both of the constraints of social structure and of choice: the actions people can take to accept or change those structures. This is Anthony Giddens's highly influential theory of **structuration**.

The three approaches, of structuralism, social action theory and structuration, are illustrated in the cartoon.

Activity

Some argue that living in society is like living in a goldfish bowl – you are constrained by the bowl, even though you can't see the glass walls. In the light of what you have read in this chapter, discuss in a group to what extent you think this is an accurate view of society. Give reasons for your answers.

FEMINIST PERSPECTIVES

Feminism examines society particularly from the point of view and interests of women. Feminists argue that a lot of mainstream sociology has been focused on the concerns of men – 'malestream sociology' – and has failed to deal with the concerns and interests of women and the unequal position they have traditionally occupied in society. There are a number of strands within feminist approaches, but three of the main ones are **Marxist feminism**, **radical feminism** and **liberal feminism**. Marxist feminism takes a Marxist approach to the study of women and women's interests, and emphasizes the way in which women are doubly exploited – both as workers and as women. Radical feminism tends to focus more on the problem of **patriarchy** – the system whereby males dominate in every area of society, such as the family, the workplace and politics. For radical feminists, the main focus is on the problem of men and male-dominated

Structuration is an approach between structuralism and social action theory. It suggests that, while people are constrained by social institutions, they also have choice and can at the same time take action to support or change those institutions.

Feminism is a view that examines the world from the point of view of women, who are seen as disadvantaged, with their interests ignored or devalued in society.
Marxist feminism takes a Marxist approach to the study of women and women's interests, and emphasizes the way in which women are doubly exploited – both as workers and as women.
Radical feminism focuses on the problem of men and male domination under **patriarchy** – the system whereby males dominate in every area of society.
Liberal feminism focuses on measures to ensure that women have equal opportunities with men within the present system.

society. Liberal feminism emphasizes the rights of women as individuals, and believes in removing all forms of discrimination to establish equality of opportunity for women with men. They want to ensure that women have equal opportunities with men within the present system, through steps such as changes to the law to stop sex discrimination, establishing equal pay, removing obstacles to women's full participation in society, and better childcare measures so that women can play their full part in paid employment. Marxist feminism and radical feminism fundamentally challenge the way society is presently organized and seek major social change, while liberal feminism basically accepts the system as it is but seeks to ensure women have equal opportunities with men within that system.

NEW RIGHT PERSPECTIVES

The **New Right** approach stresses individual freedom and self-help and self-reliance, reduction of the power and spending of the state, the free market and free competition between private companies, schools and other institutions, and the importance of traditional institutions and values.

The **New Right** is more a political philosophy than a sociological perspective, and is associated mainly with the years of the Conservative government in Britain between 1979 and 1997. This approach is, however, found in the work of some sociologists, and is referred to in various parts of this book. This approach has four main features:

- *An emphasis on individual freedom and self-interest*, and the need to reduce the power of the state to the minimum, reducing control of the individual by unnecessary state interference. Self-interest is given priority over the needs and welfare of others.
- *Reduced spending by the state*, by making individuals more self-reliant. An example is cutting welfare benefits and encouraging people into work to make them 'stand on their own two feet', and not expecting them to be dependent on the state for support if they are physically and mentally capable of supporting themselves. Lower taxes were seen as a means of increasing incentives for individuals and businesses to succeed.
- *A defence of the free market*. This means that free competition between individuals, companies, schools and other institutions is encouraged, to give individuals maximum choice between competing products, for instance in healthcare and education. An example might be giving parents a free choice of schools as consumers of education, and the right to reject some schools in favour of others, just as people choose between competing products in a supermarket. Support for private healthcare and the selling-off to private companies of state-owned industries like gas, electricity, water, British Airways and British Telecom were seen as ways of introducing competition in these areas, on the assumption that private companies with more competition would lead to lower prices and better-quality services or products.
- *A stress on the importance of traditional institutions and values*, such as traditional family life and traditional education, and a condemnation of anything that challenges these values. For example, lone parent families have been viciously attacked by the New Right, and blamed for a whole range of social problems, such as poor discipline and underachievement at school, immorality, crime, a culture of laziness, welfare dependency and the lack of a work ethic, and the existence of poverty.

POSTMODERNISM

Postmodernism is an approach that stresses that society is changing so rapidly and constantly that it is marked by chaos, uncertainty and risk, and is fragmented into many different groups, interests and lifestyles. Social structures are being replaced by a mass of individuals making individual choices about their lifestyles. Societies can no longer be understood through the application of general theories or grand stories (metanarratives), like Marxism or functionalism, which seek to explain society as a whole.

Postmodernism is an approach in sociology, as well as in other subjects, which stresses that society is changing so rapidly and constantly that it is marked by chaos, uncertainty and risk. Social structures like the family or social class are breaking down, and are being replaced by a whole range of different and constantly changing social relationships. Postmodernists argue that it is nonsense to talk of an institution called the family, for example, as people now live in such a wide range of ever-changing personal relationships. Gay and lesbian couples, cohabiting heterosexual couples who do not marry, multiple partners, divorce and remarriage, lone parents, stepparents and stepchildren, dual-income families with both partners working, people living alone, people living in shared households with friends, couples who have differing arrangements for organizing household tasks: all mean that any notion of the 'typical family' or 'the family as an institution' is absurd.

Postmodernists suggest society and social structures have ceased to exist, and have been replaced by a mass of individuals making individual choices about their lifestyles and identities, free from traditional constraints like social class, gender or ethnicity. Society is fragmenting into a mass of individuals and groups with such a wide diversity of interests and lifestyles, and is so constantly and rapidly changing, that it is essentially chaotic. This means that societies can no longer be understood through the application of 'big' theories or grand stories (called **metanarratives** – master narratives) like Marxism or functionalism, which seek to explain society as a whole. In any case, for postmodernists there is no single 'true' theory – no explanation is any better than any other, and different theories are just a variety of different points of view of equal value.

Postmodernists believe there are few of the social constraints on people that structuralist approaches identify. In postmodern societies, the emphasis is on individuals as consumers, making their own choices in education, health, their personal relationships and lifestyle. People can now form their own identities – how they see and define themselves and how others see and define them – and they can be whatever they want to be. People are free to make choices about their lifestyles, and the image they want to project to other people. Postmodern society involves a media-saturated consumer culture in which individuals are free to pick 'n' mix identities and lifestyles, chosen from a limitless range of constantly changing consumer goods and leisure activities, which are available from across the globe.

> A **metanarrative** is a broad all-embracing 'big theory' (literally, a 'big story') or explanation for how societies operate.

Activity

Go through the following statements, and classify them as one of the following:

- Functionalist
- Marxist feminist
- liberal feminist
- postmodernist
- New Right
- Marxist
- radical feminist
- interpretivist

(a) We will challenge all aspects of society not relevant to women, bring about a complete female takeover, eliminate the male sex and begin to create a female world.

(b) The family is one of the main building blocks in creating the shared values which are such an important part of a stable society.

(c) There are conflicts between the rich and the poor in our society. This is hardly surprising, given that the richest 10 per cent of the population own over half the country's wealth.

(d) To make sure women have equal opportunities with men, there must be more free childcare provided.

(e) Women are exploited both as women and as workers – they get exploited in paid employment, and they get exploited at home, where they do most of the housework and childcare and get nothing for it.

(f) The ruling ideas in society are those of the ruling class.

(g) Truth is whatever you choose to believe.

(h) Some people may see an amber traffic light as a warning to speed up before it turns red. Others may see it as a sign to slow down before stopping. In order to understand such behaviour, you need to understand the meaning people give to events.

(i) The education system is of major importance in preparing a well-trained and qualified labour force so the economy can develop and grow.

(j) The education system prepares an obedient workforce which won't rock the boat and complain about being exploited at work.

(k) A person's identity is purely a matter of her or his personal choice, regardless of social factors like their class, gender or ethnicity.

(l) If you think people are out to get you, even if they're not, then this is likely to affect the way you behave. To understand behaviour, we have to understand people's point of view.

(m) Women will never achieve equality as long as men hold all the positions of power in society.

(n) It is in everyone's interests to pull together at work for the benefit of society as a whole.

(o) Although girls now do better than boys in education, they could do better still. We must make sure that any obstacles to girls' progress in school are removed.

(p) We must make sure women get equal pay for equal work.

(q) Some students are almost bound to fail, because teachers give them the impression that they're thick, and this undermines the self-confidence of the students, who then think it isn't worth bothering.

(r) The welfare state has produced an underclass of people who are idle and don't want to work, and are content to scrounge off overgenerous welfare state benefits rather than get a job to support themselves.

The solution to this activity can be found on the teachers' pages of www.politybooks.com/browne.

Sociological problems, social problems and social policy

> A **social problem** is something that is seen as being harmful to society in some way, and needs something doing to sort it out.

> A **sociological problem** is any social issue that needs explaining.

Social problems are matters that are seen as being harmful to society in some way, and as needing some action to sort them out. A social problem is nearly always a **sociological problem** – a social issue that needs explaining – but not all sociological problems are social problems.

Very often sociologists have been able to show by research that many social problems are not simply a result of the behaviour of individuals, but are created by wider social factors. A useful example is that of accidents.

ACCIDENTS AS A SOCIAL AND A SOCIOLOGICAL PROBLEM

Accidents are a social problem, and the accident statistics show a clear social pattern in terms of age, class and gender. For example, young people and old people, the poor and males are more likely to die or be seriously injured because of an accident. Accidents may happen to us individually, and sometimes randomly, but the causes are often socially influenced, by factors such as poor-quality housing, inadequate home care for the elderly, low income, dangerous working conditions and a dangerous environment, with busy roads and no safe play areas for children. Accidents provide an often dramatic and tragic, but nevertheless excellent, example of how seemingly random or individual experiences and events are in fact socially patterned and socially influenced.

The study of accidents shows how clear-sighted C. Wright Mills (1970) was when he wrote about the distinction between 'the personal troubles of milieu' (immediate social surroundings) and 'the public issues of social structure'. Every single accident is a personal experience but the social pattern of these experiences in Britain every year is for all of us a social problem – not least because of the harm they cause and the billions of pounds spent treating them by the National Health Service. This social problem is also a sociological problem – something which needs explaining by sociologists. The pattern of accident statistics illustrates well Mills's distinction between 'personal troubles' and 'public issues' to which we referred above. To paraphrase Mills, when, in a nation of 60 million, only 1 person has an accident, then that is his or her personal trouble, and for its solution we look at the circumstances of that person. But when, in a nation of 60 million, 8 million have accidents, with a clear social pattern, that is a public issue and a social problem, and we cannot hope to find a solution within the personal situations and characteristics of individuals.

Sociological research has often made major contributions to the **social policy** solutions needed to tackle social problems like accidents, ill-health, crime, poverty or educational failure. Social policy refers to the packages of plans and actions taken to solve social problems or achieve other goals that are seen as important. These are usually adopted by national and local government or various voluntary agencies. Examples are measures taken to solve social problems like obesity and alcohol abuse and to achieve the goal of a healthier nation, such as the Change4Life campaign (www.nhs. uk/Change4Life), or to improve the educational performance of boys compared to girls. However, sociologists also try to explain social issues that aren't social problems, like the improved performance of females in the educational system, or why the birth rate is declining and why people are having smaller families.

It is this ability of sociology to explain social events and to contribute to the understanding and solution of social problems, and to the social policy solutions adopted, which makes it such a worthwhile, useful and exciting subject.

> **Social policy**
> refers to the packages of plans and actions adopted by national and local government or various voluntary agencies to solve social problems or achieve other goals that are seen as important.

The Change4Life campaign is one example of a social policy which seeks to address social problems (in this case, obesity and unhealthy lifestyles)

CHAPTER SUMMARY AND REVISION CHECKLIST

After studying this chapter, you should be able to:

- explain what is meant by a 'social institution' and 'social structure'.

- explain how sociology is different from common-sense and naturalistic explanations.

- define the meaning of socialization, culture, identity, roles, role models, role conflict, values, laws, norms, social control, deviance, and positive and negative sanctions, and explain their importance in understanding human behaviour in human society.

- explain what is meant by 'social class' and identify the main social classes in the contemporary United Kingdom.

- explain what is meant by a sociological perspective, and identify the main features of the structuralist approaches of functionalism and Marxism, and the social action or interpretivist approaches, including symbolic interactionism.

- explain what is meant by structuration, and how it provides a middle way between structural and action perspectives.

- explain the variety of feminist perspectives, and the features of the New Right approach in sociology.

- outline some of the features of postmodernism.

- explain what is meant by, and the differences between, a sociological problem and a social problem, and the contribution of sociology to social policy.

KEY TERMS

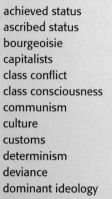

(these are already defined in the text, and may also be found in the glossary at the end of the book)

achieved status	ideology	objectivity	social mobility
ascribed status	income	patriarchy	social policy
bourgeoisie	interpretivism	perspective	social problem
capitalists	labelling	positive sanctions	social structure
class conflict	labour power	postmodernism	socialization
class consciousness	laws	proletariat	sociological perspective
communism	liberal feminism	radical feminism	sociological problem
culture	life chances	relations of production	status
customs	macro approach	role conflict	structuralism
determinism	Marxism	role models	structuration
deviance	Marxist feminism	roles	surplus value
dominant ideology	means of production	ruling class	symbolic interactionism
ethnicity	metanarrative	ruling class ideology	underclass
false consciousness	micro approach	sanctions	upper class
feminism	middle class	sex	value consensus
functional prerequisites	minority ethnic group	social action theory	value freedom
functionalism	negative sanctions	social class	values
gender	New Right	social control	wealth
identity	norms	social institution	working class

There are a variety of free tests and other activities that can be used to assess your learning at

www.politybooks.com/browne

UNIT 1

Culture and Identity

Families and Households

Wealth, Poverty and Welfare

Culture and Identity

Contents

CHAPTER 2

Culture and Identity

SPECIFICATION TOPICS

- **Topic 1** Different conceptions of culture, including subculture, mass culture, high and low culture, popular culture, global culture
- **Topic 2** Sources and different conceptions of the self, identity and difference
- **Topic 3** The socialization process and the role of the agencies of socialization
- **Topic 4** The relationship of identity to age, disability, ethnicity, gender, nationality, sexuality and social class in contemporary society
- **Topic 5** Leisure, consumption and identity

Topic 1

SPECIFICATION AREA

Different conceptions of culture, including subculture, mass culture, high and low culture, popular culture, global culture.

The meaning and importance of culture

As discussed in the first chapter, the term 'culture' is used by sociologists to refer to the language, beliefs, values and norms, customs, dress, diet, roles, knowledge and skills, and all the other things that people learn that make up the 'way of life' of any society. Culture is passed on from one generation to the next through the process of socialization. Although there are many aspects of everyday life which are shared by most members of society, there are a range of different aspects of culture within this general concept of culture, such as subculture and dominant, folk, high, low, popular, mass and global cultures. These different aspects of culture are discussed below.

DOMINANT CULTURE

> The **dominant culture** of a society refers to the main culture in a society, which is shared, or at least accepted without opposition, by the majority of people.

The **dominant culture** of a society refers to the main culture in a society, which is shared, or at least accepted without opposition, by the majority of people. For example, it might be argued that the main features of British culture include it being

29

white, patriarchal and unequal, with those who are white and male having things they regard as worthwhile rated as more important than those who are female or from a minority ethnic group. Similarly, those who are rich and powerful (who are mainly also white and male) are in a position to have their views of what is valuable and worthwhile in a culture regarded as more important, and given higher status, than those of others.

SUBCULTURE

When societies are very small, such as small villages in traditional societies, then all people may share a common culture or way of life. However, as societies become larger and more complicated, a number of smaller groups may emerge within the larger society, with some differences in their beliefs, values and way of life. Each group having these differences is referred to as a **subculture**. Figure 2.1 illustrates this.

A few subcultures, like some of those found in schools, among young people or in minority ethnic groups, may be not simply different from the dominant culture in some ways, but also in active opposition to it. In these cases we might refer to them as **subcultures of resistance**. For example, Willis (1977) found an anti-school subculture in his study of a group of working-class lads, in which resistance to schooling and the culture of the school was highly valued. Among younger South Asians and African Caribbeans, ethnic subcultures may form as a way of resisting racism and disadvantage. Hall and Jefferson (1976) saw particular youth subcultural styles (such as among Teddy Boys, Mods, Skinheads and Punks) as forms of resistance to dominant culture.

Further discussion of various subcultures can be found on pages 55–60 (class subcultures), pages 77–82 (minority ethnic group subcultures), pages 95–8 (youth subcultures), pages 247–8 (subculture of poverty) and pages 360–3 (anti- and pro-school subcultures).

A **subculture** is a smaller culture held by a group of people within the main culture of a society, in some ways different from the main culture but with many aspects in common. Examples of subcultures include those of some young people, Travellers (including New Age Travellers, Irish Travellers and Romani (commonly called 'Gypsies')), gay people, different social classes and minority ethnic groups.

A **subculture of resistance** is one that not only has some differences from the dominant culture, but also is in active opposition to it.

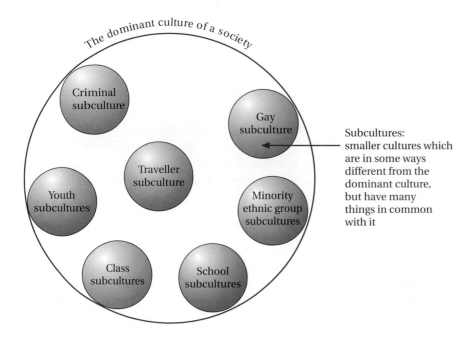

Figure 2.1 Culture and subcultures

Subcultures: smaller cultures which are in some ways different from the dominant culture, but have many things in common with it

Morris dancing is an example of traditional folk culture

FOLK CULTURE

Folk culture is
the culture created
by local communities
and is rooted in the
experiences, customs
and beliefs of the
everyday life of ordinary
people.

Folk culture is the culture created by local communities and is rooted in the experiences, customs and beliefs of the everyday life of ordinary people. It is 'authentic' rather than manufactured, as it is actively created by ordinary people themselves. Examples include traditional folk music, folk songs, storytelling and folk dances which are passed on from one generation to the next by socialization and often by direct experience. Folk culture is generally associated with pre-industrial or early industrial societies, though it still lingers on today among enthusiasts in the form of folk music and folk clubs, and the Morris dancing which features in many rural events.

HIGH CULTURE

High culture
refers to cultural
products seen to be
of lasting artistic or
literary value, which are
particularly admired and
approved of by elites
and the upper middle
class.
An **elite** is a small group
holding great power and
privilege in society.

High culture is generally seen as being superior to other forms of culture, and refers to aspects of culture that are seen as of lasting artistic or literary value, aimed at small, intellectual **elites**, predominantly upper-class and middle-class groups, interested in new ideas, critical discussion and analysis, and who have what some might regard as 'good taste'.

High culture is seen as something set apart from everyday life, something special, to be treated with respect and reverence, involving things of lasting value and part of a heritage which is worth preserving. High culture products are often found in special places, like art galleries, museums, concert halls and theatres. Examples of high culture products include serious news programmes and documentaries, classical music like that of Mozart or Beethoven, the theatre, opera, ballet, jazz, foreign language or specialist 'art' films, and what has become established literature, such as the work of Charles Dickens, Jane Austen or Shakespeare, and visual art like that of Monet, Gauguin, Picasso or Van Gogh.

MASS, POPULAR AND LOW CULTURE

Mass culture, sometimes referred to as **popular culture** or **low culture**, is generally contrasted with high culture. The term 'low culture' is a derogatory term (critical and insulting) to describe popular culture. Its usage suggests popular or mass culture is of inferior quality to the 'high' culture of the elite discussed above. The term 'popular culture' is often used as an alternative, suggesting it is culture liked and enjoyed by ordinary people, worthy of study, and avoiding and rejecting the suggestion that it is somehow of an inferior quality or of lower value than high culture.

Mass or popular culture is a product of industrial societies. It is commercially produced culture, spread on a wide scale throughout society, and aimed at the mass of ordinary people, but it lacks roots in their daily experiences as in folk culture, and is commercially manufactured by businesses for profit rather than created by the community itself and reflecting its own experiences of daily life. Strinati (1995) sees mass culture as popular culture involving cultural products produced for profit by mass-production industrial techniques, for sale to and consumption by the mass of ordinary people. These mass-produced, standardized products are generally short-lived, and regarded by many as inferior to high culture. Rather than something 'set apart' and 'special', mass culture is seen as consisting of trivial products, dumbed down to appeal to as many people as possible, which demand little critical thought, analysis or discussion, and are of no lasting artistic value. Mass culture is everyday popular culture – simple, undemanding, easy-to-understand entertainment. It is often produced on a global scale, appealing to millions of people across local communities and national divisions, with the mass media spreading a common mass culture across the globe. It is largely concerned with making money for large corporations, especially the mass media.

Popular culture might include mass-circulation magazines, with extensive coverage of celebrities and lifestyles, 'red top' tabloid newspapers like the *Sun* or the *Mirror*, television soaps and reality TV shows, dramas and thrillers, rock and pop music, video

> **Mass culture**, sometimes called popular culture or low culture, refers to commercially produced culture, involving cultural products produced for sale to the mass of ordinary people. These involve mass-produced, standardized, short-lived products, which many see as of little lasting value, and which demand little critical thought, analysis or discussion.

> **Low culture** is a derogatory (critical and insulting) term used to describe mass culture or popular culture, suggesting these are of inferior quality to the **high culture** of the elite.

> **Popular culture** refers to the cultural products liked and enjoyed by the mass of ordinary people. It is sometimes referred to as mass culture or low culture.

Video games are an example of popular culture

games, blockbuster feature films for the mass market, romances and thrillers bought for reading on the beach, and websites like Facebook. Such culture is largely seen as passive and unchallenging, often fairly mindless entertainment, aimed at the largest number of people possible.

Evaluation of mass culture

Bourdieu (1971) was a French Marxist, who argued that the alleged superiority of high culture compared to mass or popular culture was because the dominant class had the power to impose on the rest of society its own cultural ideas about what counts as good and bad taste, worthwhile knowledge, good books, music, art, films and so on. The rest of society are socialized into accepting the continuing superiority of high culture, although they themselves are more likely to participate in mass or popular culture, which is regarded by the dominant class as an inferior and worthless low culture.

Strinati (1995) suggests that mass or popular culture is often attacked for diverting people away from more useful activities, for driving down cultural standards (like those established in high culture art and literature) and for having harmful effects on audiences.

Frank and Queenie Leavis, writing between the 1930s and 1960s, had nothing but contempt for mass culture, which they saw as processed, packaged, trivial and mindless escapist fantasy, and inferior to the lasting artistic and literary value found in high culture. They saw it as ruining the proper use of language, exploiting people's emotional needs and fears, and encouraging greed and mindless social conformity.

MacDonald (1965) was another critic of mass culture. Unlike folk culture, which he saw as authentic and generated by ordinary people, and high culture which expressed serious and long-established authentic cultural values, he saw mass culture as trivial and inauthentic. He saw mass culture as simply mass-produced manufactured products imposed on the masses by businesses for financial profit. This view is also shared by some Marxists, who argue that the culture industries produce mass cultural products of little artistic merit to make a profit, and manipulate people into wanting and consuming them through advertising and the mass media.

Some Marxists and other critical theorists argue that mass culture is a form of social control, which maintains the ideological **hegemony** (or the dominance of a set of ideas) and the power of the dominant social class in society. This is because the consumers of mass culture are lulled into an uncritical, undemanding passivity, making them less likely to challenge the dominant ideas, groups and interests in society. Marcuse (2002 [1964]), for example, suggested consumption of mass culture, particularly the mass media, undermined people's ability to think critically about the world, or to oppose and change it. Marcuse saw this as a form of social repression – a means of locking people into the present system, and undermining the potential for revolution.

Strinati rejects these views. He sees mass culture as popular culture, having value and as worthy of study. He doesn't accept the suggestion that there is a single mass audience and mass culture, which people passively and uncritically consume, and points to a wide diversity and choice within popular culture, which people select from and critically respond to.

Livingstone (1988) found that the writers and producers of TV soap operas, a form of popular culture watched by millions, saw them as having positive benefits for society. They saw them as educating and informing the public by raising and commenting

Hegemony refers to the acceptance of the dominant ideology by the working class, as a result of the power of the ruling class to persuade others to accept and consent to its ideas.

on important or controversial social issues, presenting a range of political opinions, generating public controversies and discussion, and giving insights into the sometimes tough and grim lives of others. Rather than killing off public debate and lulling mass audiences into uncritical passivity, soap operas like *Eastenders* and *Coronation Street* have generated huge debate and critical discussion about issues that might otherwise rarely get aired in public, or only in crude media stereotypes. In recent years the public has been encouraged to discuss social issues through soap stories about, for example, child rape, incest, false imprisonment, lesbianism, child cot death, child abuse, religious cults, paedophilia, drug addiction and relationship breakdown. The controversies surrounding these soap stories have frequently dominated the headlines of the red-top tabloid press, promoting public discussions that might never otherwise have happened.

Many of those who consume and enjoy popular culture suggest its critics are basically elitist snobs, who rank cultural preferences on a 'snob-to-slob' scale based on their own cultural preferences. These snobs simply prefer high culture and have contempt for what they regard as the slob culture of the masses.

The changing distinction between high culture and mass culture

Some now argue that the distinction between high culture and mass culture is weakening. Postmodernist writers, in particular, argue that mass markets and consumption now make the distinction between high and popular culture meaningless. There has been a huge expansion of the creative and cultural industries, such as advertising, television, film, music, and book and magazine publishing. This means there is now a huge range of media and cultural products available to all.

Technology in industrial societies makes cultural products of all kinds almost infinitely reproducible. Mass-communication technology like the internet; music downloads; cable, satellite and digital television; film and radio; printing for both mass production and personal use in the home; the global reach of modern mass-media technology; the mass production of goods on a world scale and easier international transportation – these make all forms of culture freely available to everyone. Such technology enables original music and art and other cultural products to be consumed by the mass of people in their own homes without visiting specialized institutions like theatres or art galleries. High culture is no longer simply the preserve of cultural elites.

People now have a wider diversity of cultural choices and products available to them than ever before in history, and can pick 'n' mix from either popular or high culture. High culture art galleries, like Tate Modern in London, are now attracting huge numbers of visitors, from very diverse backgrounds. Live opera is now available to the masses, through popular figures like the OperaBabes, or concerts in the park.

Strinati (1995) argues that elements of high culture have now become a part of popular culture, and elements of popular culture have been incorporated into high culture, and that there is therefore no longer any real distinction between high and popular culture, and it is ever more difficult for any one set of ideas of what is worthwhile culture to dominate in society.

Storey (2003) points out that what is also changing is that members of the dominant class are no longer only consuming high culture, but now consume much of what they had previously dismissed as mass culture, and the masses themselves are now consuming high culture through mass production. For example, artist Andy Warhol painted thirty pictures of Leonardo da Vinci's *Mona Lisa* in different colours, arguing that 'thirty was better than one', turning high culture art into popular culture. Although Warhol's work has been marketed to millions through postcards and posters, at the same time it is widely admired by the supporters of high culture, and original Warhol paintings and creations now sell for millions of pounds. In 2007 there was some controversy in Britain when the Victoria and Albert Museum in London, generally seen as an institution of high culture, held 'Kylie: The Exhibition' – an exhibition of costumes, album covers, accessories, photos and videos from the career of the then 38-year-old pop singer Kylie Minogue. This drew widespread accusations from critics that high culture was being 'dumbed down'.

High culture art forms are themselves increasingly being turned into products for sale in the mass market for consumption by the mass of ordinary people, and there is no longer anything special about art, as it is incorporated into daily life. Giddings (2010) points out that forms of high culture are now often used to produce mass culture products; he gives the example of modern video games – which are considered to be part of mass culture – which often bring together art, architecture, classical music, actors and writers which alone would be classified as 'high culture'.

Technology now means mass audiences can see and study high culture products, such as paintings by artists like Van Gogh, on the internet or TV, and have their own framed print hanging on their sitting-room wall. Internet websites, like those of museums and galleries and Google (see www.googleartproject.com), mean people can build their own private high culture virtual museums and art galleries. The originals may still only be on show in art galleries and museums, but copies are available to everyone. High culture art like the *Mona Lisa* or Van Gogh's *Sunflowers* are now reproduced on everything from socks and T-shirts to chocolate boxes and can lids, mugs, mouse mats, tablemats, jigsaws and posters. (Visit www.studiolo. org/Mona or www.megamonalisa.com for some bizarre images and uses of the *Mona Lisa*.) Classical music is used as a marketing tune by advertisers, and literature is turned into TV series and major mass movies, such as Jane Austen's *Pride and Prejudice*.

Giddings, from a postmodernist approach, suggests the lines between high culture and mass culture are like the borders between countries: 'they are only there because we are told they are there, and people will always disagree on where those borders lie, whether they should be acknowledged at all, or who has the right to move them'. He suggests it is impossible to draw distinctions for anyone other than oneself, and this effect is amplified as mass culture becomes more globalized and cultures intertwine.

> **Global culture** refers to the way cultures in different countries of the world have become more alike, sharing increasingly similar consumer products and ways of life. This has arisen as **globalization** has undermined national and local cultures.

> **Globalization** is the growing interdependence of societies across the world, with the spread of the same culture, consumer goods and economic interests across the globe.

GLOBAL CULTURE

Global culture refers to the way **globalization** has undermined national and local cultures, with cultural products and ways of life in different countries of the world becoming more alike. The same cultural and consumer products are now sold across the world, inspired by media advertising and a shared mass culture spread through a media-generated culture industry, and they have become part of the ways of life of many different societies. The globalization of culture has meant that people now have access to a wide diversity of global media, and to religions, music, food and clothing from across the world. For example, television companies sell their programmes and programme formats like *Big Brother*, *The X Factor*, *The Weakest Link* and *Who Wants to be a Millionaire?* globally. Companies like McDonald's, Coca Cola, Vodaphone, Starbucks, Nescafé, Sony and Nike are now symbols that are recognized

The *Mona Lisa*. . .

. . .now has a spliff to relax and a mobile to keep in touch

Fine art is now available on cubes to play with

Who's that in the window? The *Mona Lisa* is transformed into a window blind

In what ways do these pictures illustrate the erosion of the distinction between high culture and popular culture? Try to think of other examples of this.

Globalization means that many of the same product brands are now found in many countries of the world

across the world, along with the consumer lifestyles and culture associated with them. As Ritzer (2004) shows, using the example of the American food industry, companies and brands now operate on a global scale. For example, McDonald's is a worldwide business, with more than 33,000 restaurants in 119 countries (in 2012), Pizza Hut, Kentucky Fried Chicken and Subway operate in 100 countries, with Starbucks in 59 countries and growing at a colossal speed. It is now possible to buy an identical food product practically anywhere in the world, promoting a global culture and also weakening local cultures, as local food outlets close in the face of competition and local diets change. Combined with global marketing of films, music, computer games, food, clothes, football and other consumer products, these have made cultures across the world increasingly similar, with people watching the same TV programmes and films, listening to the same music, eating the same foods, wearing the same designer clothes and labels, and sharing many aspects of their lifestyles and identities.

Activity

1 Refer to the pictures on this page, and explain in what ways they illustrate global culture. Try to think of other consumer products that are also global.
2 In what ways do you think consuming these products also involves lifestyle choices? For example, what's the difference between having a coffee in Starbucks and in the local café (apart from the coffee itself)? Explain what lifestyle you think is identified with your selected products.

Exam-style questions

1 Explain what is meant by a 'subculture of resistance'. *(2 marks)*

2 Suggest two ways that folk culture differs from mass culture. *(4 marks)*

3 Explain the difference between 'high culture' and 'popular culture'. *(4 marks)*

4 Explain the difference between a dominant culture and a subculture. *(4 marks)*

5 Suggest three ways in which globalization is affecting contemporary culture in the United Kingdom. *(6 marks)*

6 Suggest three reasons why the distinction between high culture and popular culture might be weakening. *(6 marks)*

7 Examine sociological contributions to our understanding of mass culture. *(24 marks)*

8 Examine the ways that technology and/or industrialization have influenced culture in contemporary societies. *(24 marks)*

9 Assess the view that the difference between high culture and mass culture has largely disappeared in society today. *(24 marks)*

Topic 2

SPECIFICATION AREA

Sources and different conceptions of the self, identity and difference

The concept of identity

Identity is not the same as personality. Personality is about the psychological aspects of a person's character, such as whether she or he is introverted (shy and withdrawn) or extroverted (outgoing and confident), tense or laid-back, selfish or generous, and so on. Personality tends to be a more fixed aspect of a person's character, while identity is more fluid and changeable. Identity is about how individuals or groups see and define themselves, and how other individuals or groups see and define them. Identity is formed through the socialization process and the influence of social institutions like the family, the education system and the mass media.

The concept of identity is an important one, as it is only through establishing our own identities and learning about the identities of other individuals and groups that we come to know what makes us similar to some people and different from others, and therefore to form social connections with people. How you see yourself will influence the friends you have, who you will marry or live with, and the communities and groups to which you relate and belong. If people did not have an identity, they would lack the means of identifying with or relating to their peer group, to their neighbours, to the communities in which they lived or to the people they came across in their everyday lives. Identity therefore 'fits' individuals into the society in which they live.

The identity of individuals and groups involves both elements of personal choice and the responses and attitudes of others. Individuals are not free to adopt any identity

'Look, don't identify me by the size and shape of my body, my social class, my job, my gender, my ethnicity, my sexuality, my nationality, my age, my religion, my education, my friends, my lifestyle, how much money I earn, the clothes I wear, the books I read, where I go shopping, the way I decorate my house, the television programmes and movies I watch, my leisure and sports activities, the car I drive, the music I listen to, the drinks I like, the food I eat, the clubs I go to, where I go on holiday, the way I speak or my accent, the things I say, the things I do, or what I believe in. I'm just me. OK?'

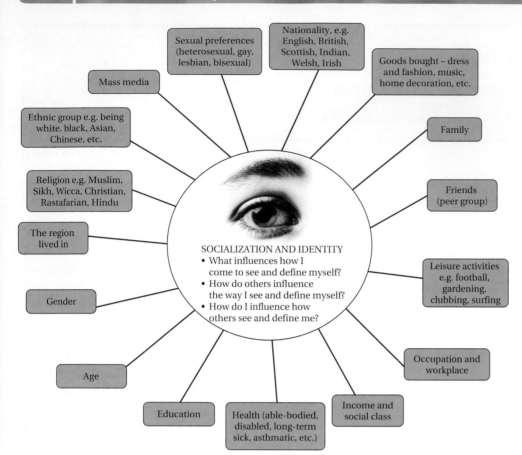

Figure 2.2 Some social influences on the formation of identities

they like, and factors like their social class, their ethnic group and their sex are likely to influence how others see them. The identity that an individual wants to assert and which they may wish others to see them having may not be the one that others accept or recognize. An Asian woman, for example, may not wish to be identified primarily as an Asian or a woman, but as a senior manager or entertainer. However, if others still continue to see her primarily in terms of her ethnic and gender characteristics, she may find it difficult to assert her chosen identity. Similarly, the pensioner who sees him or herself as 'young at heart' may still be regarded as an old person by others.

Individuals have multiple identities, asserting different identities in different circumstances. An individual may, for example, define herself primarily as a Muslim in her family or community, as a manager at her work, as a lesbian in her sexual life, or as a designer-drug-user in her peer group. While the example of the Muslim, lesbian, drug-taking manager might seem a somewhat unlikely mix of identities, it does suggest that it is possible for people to assert different identities or impressions of themselves in different social situations.

Identities may also change over time. For example, as people grow older they may begin to see themselves as different from when they were younger, and may well be viewed differently by others, particularly as their status changes as they move into retirement, and are detached from the identities arising from their job in paid employment.

Figure 2.2 shows a wide range of factors which may influence individuals' identity, but some of the main sources of identity include their social class, their gender, their ethnicity, their nationality, their disabilities, their age, their sexuality, their leisure activities and their consumption patterns. These sources of identity will be examined in Topics 4 and 5.

Different types of identity

INDIVIDUAL OR PERSONAL IDENTITY

Woodward (2000) suggests that individual identity is concerned with the question 'Who am I?' – how individuals define themselves, what is important and matters to them, how they see themselves as individuals different from other people, and the things that give them their own unique personal or individual characteristics. Their name, their passport, their National Insurance number, their fingerprints, their DNA, their birth certificate and their signature are some obvious examples of these, as well as people's personal histories, friends and relationships and their own understanding of who they really are as individuals: their own self-concept of the 'inner me', or 'I', as Mead referred to it.

SOCIAL IDENTITY

Social identity offers little choice and defines individuals in relation to the social groups with which they are identified and to which they belong, and how they differ from other social groups and individuals. Such groups might include men and women, ethnic groups, or national groups like the English, Scots or Welsh. The formation of social identities may also arise from the characteristics associated with the social roles that people play – for example, the identities and the related behaviour that might be expected of them when playing their social roles as mothers and fathers, sons and daughters, students or workers, or as members of social groups like males or females, Muslims or Sikhs, gays, lesbians or heterosexuals, or Welsh or Scottish.

COLLECTIVE IDENTITY

A collective identity is an identity shared by a social group, and involves elements of both personal and social identities, but differs from both as it involves considerable elements of choice by individuals in that they actively choose to identify with a group and adopt the identity associated with it. For example, while social identities like gender, ethnicity or nationality are largely defined by others and individuals have only limited choice in whether or not to adopt them, being identified as a football or rock music fan, a Goth, a gang member, a Hell's Angel, a feminist, an eco-warrior protecting the environment, an anti-war, animal rights or Labour Party activist is almost completely a matter of personal choice.

To what extent do you think going to festivals like Glastonbury is an important aspect of the identity of young people? What other groups or activities do young people engage with to form their collective identities?

MULTIPLE IDENTITIES

The idea of multiple identities simply means that people have several identities, rather than just one. Individuals may draw on more than one source of identity, such as identities formed around their social class, and/or their ethnicity, their sexuality, their gender, their nationality and/or their age, etc., or a combination of all of them. Individuals may assert different 'selves' in different circumstances. For example, at home they may assert the identity of a good son or daughter or a good Muslim; at school or college they may assert their identity as a good student; in their personal relations, as gay; in their peer group, as a Goth; in their leisure activities, as a sporty type or drinker; in their workplace, as a good worker; or as primarily having an Asian Muslim identity in the UK, but a British identity while travelling abroad.

STIGMATIZED OR 'SPOILED' IDENTITIES

A **stigma** might be:

- a physical impairment, like being blind, losing the use of lower limbs, or having an illness like AIDS or a sexually-transmitted disease
- a social characteristic, like being mentally ill, a sex offender, a criminal or a child abuser.

Goffman (1990a) said a **stigmatized identity** is an identity that is in some way undesirable or demeaning, excluding people from full acceptance in society. The disabled, for example, are often said to have a stigmatized identity in a society which places a high premium on bodily perfection. Those with stigmatized identities can face serious social consequences, with others treating them with contempt, poking fun at them, denying them proper medical treatment (as happens with some older people and the disabled),

> A **stigma** is any undesirable physical or social characteristic that is seen as abnormal or unusual in some way, that is seen as demeaning, and stops an individual being fully accepted by society.
> A **stigmatized identity** is an identity that is in some way undesirable or demeaning, and excludes people from full acceptance in society.

or refusing them employment (as with former prisoners, the mentally ill or the elderly). Having a stigmatized identity nearly always means that any attempts made by individuals to present an alternative 'normal' impression of themselves will fail. This alternative 'failed' identity is sometimes called a spoiled identity. As Goffman put it, 'stigma is a process by which the reaction of others spoils normal identity'.

Exam-style questions

1   Explain what is meant by a stigmatized identity.   *(2 marks)*
2   Explain the difference between personality and identity.   *(4 marks)*
3   Suggest two ways in which individuals might adopt different identities in different social situations.   *(4 marks)*
4   Suggest three sources from which individuals may construct their identity.   *(6 marks)*
5   Suggest three ways in which individuals might have multiple identities.   *(6 marks)*
6   Suggest three factors influencing an individual's identity other than social class, gender or ethnicity.   *(6 marks)*
7   Assess the view that there is no single source of identity, and that identities are increasingly varied in today's society.   *(24 marks)*

Socialization and resocialization

The newborn child is not born with an understanding of culture, and human societies are not based on instinctive behaviour, like that of animals. Children born in the UK will most likely develop into members of society much like any other British child, but if those same children were born in France, India, China or Peru, they would be likely to develop many different ways of behaving because they would learn different cultures.

Learning culture through the socialization process, and the values, norms and roles that are part of this culture, enables individuals to operate in the societies into which they are born and helps to ensure some stability in society. Socialization is a life-long process that changes and develops as we grow older and encounter new experiences and cultures. For example, a common language enables people to communicate with each other, to learn and share meanings and to develop ideas. People need to know what is expected of them in the societies in which they live, and in the social situations they encounter, and the learning of social roles generally means we know how we are expected to behave when we are, for example, teachers or students, or sons or daughters, and how to behave towards and what to expect from the people we meet. Socialization therefore makes possible some predictability in social life, and avoids the chaos and confusion in everyday life that would arise if we had to reinvent or guess at social rules every time we met someone or entered a new situation, or if people made up their own rules and meanings as they went along.

RESOCIALIZATION

The concept of **resocialization** helps to reinforce and emphasize the importance of the socialization process. This occurs when people are removed from their usual everyday situations, and encounter new social environments. It involves learning, or relearning, appropriate new norms and values to operate in this new environment. Resocialization may involve only mild changes, such as adapting to a new school or workplace, or quite extensive changes when moving to a new society, or entering (or leaving) institutions like the military, prison or a psychiatric hospital.

When people move to other societies, they will often have to learn new norms and values that are very different from those they were used to in the society in which they were raised, as found by many first-generation immigrants to Britain, or British people who choose to live in foreign countries.

A prison provides a dramatic example of resocialization, as here the staff of the institution remove the identity of the individual and replace it by one imposed by the prison, by enforcing new rules, cutting hair, removing personal possessions, requiring a uniform and so on. Prisoners who don't rapidly learn the new norms and values are likely to find themselves in a lot of trouble, with both prison staff and other prisoners.

> **Resocialization** is the learning of appropriate new norms and values to enable people to operate in a changed social environment when they enter a new and different society or social situation, or when their life circumstances otherwise change.

Goffman (1991 [1961]) found a similar process of resocialization in psychiatric hospitals, with the hospital seeking to impose new values and norms that met the needs of the hospital rather than necessarily those of the patient. You can read more on Goffman and this process of resocialization on pages 516–17.

Nature versus nurture

Socialization gives people enough in common with others to relate to them and know what is expected of them as they share a broadly similar way of life. The importance of nurture (socialization and upbringing) rather than nature (biology) in making people fully social members of society, was discussed briefly in the first chapter (see pages 5–8). The significance of socialization in binding humans into society is also shown by cases of feral children. These children have in some way missed out on the normal processes of human socialization and so fail to develop what we might regard as normal human behaviour. As the following activity shows, such children therefore fail to adopt many of the cultural features, like values, norms, beliefs and language, which bind others into society.

Activity

Feral children

Evidence of the importance of culture and socialization in binding the individual into society is found in the study of feral ('feral' means 'wild' or undomesticated) children. Feral children are children who, for one reason or another, miss out on some important stages of human learning as they have been removed from human contact and the normal processes of human socialization. They remain unaware of human social behaviour and language from a very early age and therefore fail to develop many aspects of behaviour we would regard as 'human'. Feral children are extremely rare, and many studies of so-called feral children need to be treated with care. Some of the cases may appear to be feral, but, rather than lacking human socialization, they actually had severe learning or physical disabilities before they were abandoned and were abandoned because of these disabilities. There are many possible examples of feral children at www.feralchildren.com. One example is Tissa, the 'Monkey Boy of Sri Lanka', who was found in Sri Lanka in 1973, and who showed more animal than human characteristics. For example, he walked on all fours with a group of monkeys, yelped and snarled at humans, ate his food off the ground and did not smile.

Go to www.feralchildren.com

1 Identify two case studies in which children are raised differently from normal human children.
2 Identify in each case study the characteristics these children display that children raised in human societies usually don't.
3 Explain carefully the ways these examples might show that human behaviour is learnt rather than based on instinct.

A **social construction** means that the important characteristics of something – such as statistics, health, childhood, old age or what is regarded as deviance – are created and influenced by the attitudes, actions and interpretations of members of society. They only exist because people define them as such.

Socialization and the social construction of self and identity

Identity is something that is socially constructed – a **social construction**. That is, it is something created by the socialization process, and the individual and social interpretations and actions of people. It is not something that is given by biology or nature. For example, being black or white, or male or female, only have significance in society because people attach some importance to these characteristics, and define people in terms of these categories.

There is a close link between culture, identity and socialization. It is the socialization process that transmits both culture and identities from one generation to the next, though the precise forms of this socialization process will vary between, for example, ethnic groups, sexes, age groups and nationalities. Jenkins (1996) argues that identities are formed in the socialization process. Through learning their culture, and through their involvement with other individuals, social groups and subcultures, people come to develop ideas about what makes them similar to, or different from, others, and their identities are formed. Learning the culture of a society involves learning the roles, or patterns of behaviour, that are expected from individuals in different positions in society. These roles entail individual and social identities, such as the identities adopted in the roles of mother or father, son or daughter, worker or student, or masculine or feminine gender roles. During the socialization process, and through meeting other people, individuals learn to know what they can expect from others, and to have a particular view of themselves, and also learn about how others see and define them. These all contribute to the formation of identities.

Primary and secondary socialization

Socialization is carried out by a number of agencies of primary and secondary socialization.

PRIMARY SOCIALIZATION

Primary socialization refers to socialization during the early years of childhood in the family, by pre-school carers and others in the close community. It is through primary socialization that children first begin to learn about the basic values and norms of society, and begin to acquire their sense of who they are as individuals – their individual identities – and significant elements of their social identities such as their gender, ethnicity and sexuality. In most cases, these identities formed during childhood will remain throughout people's lives and are much more difficult to change in adulthood than other identities.

SECONDARY SOCIALIZATION

Secondary socialization is that which takes place beyond the family and close community. It is carried out through agencies of secondary socialization, like those outlined below:

- *The education system.* It is at school that most children learn a great deal of knowledge about the society in which they live, as well as the values and norms to which they will be expected to conform as adults.
- *The peer group.* The desire for approval and acceptance by peers is a powerful socializing influence, and **peer group** pressure to conform, and the fear of rejection and ridicule by peers, may exert an enormous influence on an individual's self-identity and behaviour. Such pressure may promote conformity to the wider norms of society, such as acceptance of traditional gender roles.
- *The workplace.* The very fact of finding and keeping a job, and getting along with workmates, involves learning about and conforming to the social rules governing

Primary socialization is socialization during the early years of childhood, and is carried out by the family or close community.

Secondary socialization is socialization which takes place beyond the family and close community, such as through the education system, the peer group, the workplace, the mass media and religious institutions.

The **peer group** is a group of people of similar age and status, with whom a person often mixes socially.

In what ways does the peer group influence the individual's socialization and sense of identity?

work, like getting there on time, regular attendance and obeying the instructions of managers. The workplace has traditionally been seen as an important source of the individual and social identities of adults, as what people do for a living affects people's view of themselves, how others define them, and the kind of lives they are able to lead outside work.

- *The mass media* are major sources of information, ideas, norms and values, as well as spreading images of, for example, fashion, music, role models and lifestyles that can influence people's values and behaviour.

- *Religious institutions* spread beliefs which influence people's ideas about right and wrong behaviour, important values and norms, and morality, and these may in turn affect the behaviour of individuals. In some cases, religious beliefs and institutions are important aspects of both the culture of communities and the identities of individuals, as for example in the case of Islam and Sikhism among the minority ethnic communities in Britain.

Activity

Suggest two ways in each case that (a) the mass media, (b) peer groups and (c) religion might be a source of identity and meaning for individuals.

Theoretical approaches to the role of socialization in the formation of culture and identity

There are different theoretical approaches to the understanding of the socialization process and the formation of culture and identity. These are the structural and action approaches which were outlined in the first chapter. If you haven't yet read the relevant section of chapter 1, you should read it now.

STRUCTURAL APPROACHES

Structuralists, like functionalists and most Marxists, adopt a macro approach, seeing culture and individual identities created by the wider social forces making up the social structure of society. Individuals are seen like puppets or programmed robots, who are socialized and manipulated by social institutions like the agencies of socialization mentioned above. Wider social forces, with culturally defined norms and values, form and limit the identities that are adopted, and individuals have little choice or control over their identity formation. Their identities are handed down to them by the socialization process, based on sources like social class, ethnicity, gender and age, and they are compelled to conform to them by various positive and negative sanctions. It is therefore wider social forces – rather than individual choice – that shape the identities of individuals.

Functionalist writers like Durkheim and Parsons see learning culture through socialization as a benevolent process – the means by which individuals are integrated or 'stitched' into the societies to which they belong. Socialization acts as a kind of social glue, with shared values and norms – a value consensus – bonding people together and enabling them to live in relative harmony. Marxists, on the other hand, would argue that there is not a value consensus, but, rather, that people are socialized into the beliefs and values of the dominant social class in society – what is known as the dominant ideology. The socialization process is seen as a form of social control, which, in a divided conflict-ridden society, is used to limit conflict and dissent. Feminists would also emphasize how socialization can often reinforce and reproduce patriarchy – the dominance of men over women. However, all recognize that it is culture and socialization that form the integrating link between the individual and society.

Criticisms of structural approaches

Criticisms of these approaches are that individuals are seen simply as puppets, what Garfinkel (1984) called 'cultural dopes', passively consuming and accepting norms and values handed down through socialization, with little input from the individual. Structural approaches don't recognize that individuals have free will, and can take initiatives, make choices, challenge and disobey social rules, and have a role in carving out their own identities in interaction with others. The social action approaches discussed below see individuals having control over the formation of their identities, rather than identities simply being formed by the social structure.

SOCIAL ACTION APPROACHES

Social action or interpretivist and interactionist theories adopt a micro approach, focusing much more on the individual and everyday behaviour rather than the overall structure of society. This micro approach places much more emphasis on the role of individuals in creating culture and defining their identities, and is concerned with the meanings and interpretations individuals give to situations as they interact with other individuals and groups in the socialization process. Such theories suggest that identity is something individuals can create rather than simply have imposed on them. Norms, values and roles are not orders but guidelines that individuals can interpret, and they provide flexibility for individuals to manoeuvre within – they may alter some rules, ignore others, or can, of course, reject them altogether.

The looking-glass self

These approaches suggest individual and social identities are produced by the interaction between individuals and the culture and society to which they belong. The way that interaction between individuals can form and change identities is illustrated in works by Goffman, Mead and Cooley.

The 'looking-glass self'   Mead (1863–1931) argued that, as children grow up, they learn to develop a sense of themselves – their self-concept – and the qualities they have that make them different from others. As they relate to (or interact with) other people, they begin to develop ideas about how others see them and, by seeing how people respond to them, they may modify their self-concept and sense of identity and begin to see themselves as others see them. This means the self-concepts and identities of individuals are changing and developing all the time as they go through daily life in society. Cooley (1998), writing in 1902, developed the concept of the 'looking-glass self' to explain this. The 'looking-glass self' is the idea that our image of ourselves is reflected back to us (like a mirror) in the views of others. As we consider the image of ourselves reflected in the reactions of other people to us, we may modify and change our view of ourselves and our behaviour. An individual, for example, might see her- or himself as outgoing, friendly and sociable, but if others see them as introverted, unfriendly and stand-offish, then they might adopt a new self-identity in accordance with how others see them, or modify their behaviour and try to change people's views of them. Our self-concept or our individual identity is therefore a social construction, and not a purely individual one.

Goffman: the presentation of self and impression management   Goffman (1990b) sees society like a stage, with people acting out performances like actors do in a play or TV drama. Good actors are able to persuade audiences or viewers that they really are the characters they are playing. Similarly, in society people try to project particular impressions of themselves – what Goffman calls 'the presentation of self' – by putting on dramatic performances or a 'show' to try to influence or manipulate how others see them. By managing the impressions they give to other people – Goffman calls this **impression management** – individuals try to convince others of the identities they wish to assert. This is often achieved by the use of symbols of various kinds to demonstrate the kind of person they want to be seen as.

Impression management is the way individuals try to convince others of the identity they wish to assert by giving particular impressions of themselves to other people.

Symbols of identity reveal how we see ourselves, and act as signs or signals to others of the type of person we'd like them to see us as. Such symbols and signs include things like:

- the way people speak and the words they use (like using a lot of swear or 'cool' words).
- styles of clothing and jewellery, such as designer labels or minority ethnic dress.
- body adornment, such as body piercing, tattoos and hairstyles.
- the choice of leisure activities, such as types and destinations of holiday, choices of clubs and music.
- choice in consumer goods.
- choices in media and technology, such as magazines, newspapers, TV programmes, websites and mobile devices.

As Bourdieu (2010 [1979]) points out, these are symbols of taste, lifestyle and identity through which we try to present a particular impression to others, and which become the basis for the social judgements of others.

Goffman says everyone is engaged in this process of manipulating others and being manipulated by them to give the best possible impression of themselves. Through adopting social roles – like those of actors in a theatrical performance who put on costumes and speak from scripts to convince audiences that they really are who they seem to be – and by responding to the reactions of others, individuals therefore develop their individual and social identities. Goffman also compares the performance of individuals in daily life to the front and back regions of a theatre. In the front or public area (the stage), people (actors) aim to give particular impressions to audiences. However, there is also a private back region (back-stage in the dressing room) where actors can shed their stage identity, stop performing, and be themselves. In other words, when individuals finally get home into the privacy of their bedrooms, they can stop performing, abandon impression management of their identities, and be themselves.

While the individual may try to present a certain impression to others, there is no certainty that their impression management will always succeed. This is particularly the case for those with stigmatized identities. For example, someone with a physical impairment – like being confined to a wheelchair, for example – may not wish to give the impression that they are primarily a disabled person, but rather a black person, a Muslim, a woman, a news reporter or a doctor, but other people may continue to define them in terms of their impairment. People's failure to establish their chosen identity through such impression management then spoils their preferred identity.

Criticisms of social action approaches

Critics of the social action approach suggest that individuals are seen as having too much control over their identity formation, and not enough emphasis is given to the importance of power inequalities in society and the role of social institutions in limiting and controlling the identities that individuals can adopt. While individuals might be able to choose some aspects of their identity, they are limited in their choices by factors such as the social disapproval that may arise if values and norms are not complied with, and by the need to work and earn money to feed themselves or their families, or to purchase the consumer goods necessary to assert an alternative identity. A road sweeper for a local council cannot simply choose to adopt the identity of a council manager, or a horse-riding, fox-hunting, shooting member of the upper class, because he or she probably lacks the financial means, social background, educational qualifications or skills to do so.

A THIRD WAY: STRUCTURATION

Giddens (2006) argues that there is a middle way between these structure and action approaches, which he calls 'structuration'. He accepts that social structures limit how people may act and the identities they may adopt, but also sees that they make it possible for people to act and form identities in the first place. The culture and structure of society provide people with the means of establishing their identities and the tools necessary to make sense of society, and provide some degree of predictability in social life through an understanding of and agreement on basic social norms and values and a common language. Without these, it would be very difficult for individuals to establish their identities. While people can make choices and have opportunities to form and change their identities, they can only make choices within the cultural framework of the society in which they live. Social structure and social action are therefore interdependent.

The reflexive self

The **reflexive self** refers to the idea that an individual's identity is formed and develops through a process of reflecting on, or thinking about, her or his identity in interaction with other individuals and the agencies of socialization.

As suggested above, individuals are not simply passive receivers of identities handed down by agencies of socialization like the family and education, or factors like social class, gender, ethnicity or community. The **reflexive self** refers to the idea that the identity of individuals is formed and develops as they reflect on, or think about, their identity, as they interact with other individuals and the agencies of socialization. Individuals have the capacity to alter their identities through this interaction as they reflect on (look at) themselves. Giddens (1991) sees identity like an evolving narrative or biographical story that individuals are continuously reflecting on, working on and re-working as they go through life. This 'identity story' is about reflecting on our interactions with others and the agencies of socialization, on who we are now, our past – where we've come from – and where we're going next. If the identity of individuals and relations with others are to be maintained, this identity story needs to make sense to them, but also to be easily explained to others and maintained through devices like impression management. It is through this reflexive process that identities are formed, developed and changed.

Activity

1 Explain what Garfinkel meant by a 'cultural dope' and Goffman by 'impression management'.
2 Suggest ways in which you try to manage the impressions of yourself that you give to other people, drawing on things like behaviour, speech, dress, consumer goods, personal appearance and so on. Do you always succeed in giving the impression you want? Explain why you might or might not succeed.
3 With reference to Cooley's idea of the 'looking-glass self', explain, with examples, how the reactions of others might encourage people to change how they view themselves.

Exam-style questions

1   Explain what is meant by an agency of socialization.   *(2 marks)*

2   Suggest two ways that the socialization process helps to integrate people into society.   *(4 marks)*

3   Explain the difference between primary and secondary socialization.   *(4 marks)*

4   Explain the difference between 'culture' and 'identity'.   *(4 marks)*

5   Suggest three ways in which individuals might present their preferred identities to others.   *(6 marks)*

6   Suggest three reasons why individuals may not always succeed in adopting their preferred identity.   *(6 marks)*

7   Assess sociological contributions to our understanding of the process of socialization.   *(24 marks)*

8   Examine different sociological approaches to the formation of identities through socialization.   *(24 marks)*

Topic 4

SPECIFICATION AREA

The relationship of identity to age, disability, ethnicity, gender, nationality, sexuality and social class in contemporary society

Social class and identity

SOCIAL CLASS

The identities that people adopt are formed within the cultures and subcultures to which they belong. One of the factors that has traditionally had a major effect on people's identity is their social class, and the class subcultures into which they are socialized.

Social class is a term that refers to a group of people who share a similar economic situation, such as a similar occupational level, income and ownership of wealth. Often occupation, income and ownership of wealth are closely related to each other and influence the lives of individuals, for example:

- how much power and influence they have in society
- their level of education
- their social status
- their type of housing
- their car ownership
- their leisure activities
- the consumer goods bought and lifestyle adopted

Occupation – work – is often a central part of how people see themselves – their individual identity – as well as how other people define them – their social identity. It is usually one of the first things we find out about people when we meet them for the first time. The time and money available to participate in social life, enjoy leisure activities and buy the consumer goods and services to support the lifestyles we aspire to, which are also important aspects of our identity, are all linked to some degree to the work we do.

> **Activity**
>
> List all the ways you can think of how a person's occupation might affect their self-identity and how others see them. Think about aspects of his or her life, such as family life, status in society, housing, health, leisure activities, beliefs and values, future planning and so on. Make sure you explain precisely how the effects on identity you mention are linked to a person's job.

LIFE CHANCES

Social class is an important influence on people's lives, and pretending that it is not significant will not make it go away, any more than not being able to see a plate-glass door will stop you from hurting yourself when you walk into it. An individual's social class has a major influence on his or her life chances – that is, the chances of obtaining those things defined as desirable and of avoiding those things defined as undesirable in any society. There are wide, measurable differences in life chances between social classes:

- higher social classes have better housing, cars, food, holidays, incomes and job security.
- just 10 per cent of the population owned around 44 per cent of the UK's wealth (in 2008–10), and 20 per cent of the population owned around 62 per cent. The poorest 50 per cent of the population owned only about 10 per cent.
- the top 20 per cent of income earners get over five times the share of the bottom 20 per cent, and Britain has one of the widest gaps between the high-paid and the low-paid in Europe.
- around one-fifth of the population of Britain lives in relative poverty.
- a man from the top social class on average lives seven years longer than a man from the lowest social class.
- nearly twice as many babies die at birth or in the first year of life in the bottom social class as in the highest social class.
- sickness increases as one moves down the social class hierarchy. Lower-working-class people suffer more from almost all diseases than those in the upper middle class.
- smoking, drug and alcohol abuse and obesity are all more commonly found in the lower social classes.

Given all these class inequalities, it is perhaps not surprising that social class has been an important influence on people's identities.

OBJECTIVE AND SUBJECTIVE DIMENSIONS OF CLASS

There are two dimensions of social class: the objective and the subjective dimensions. The objective dimension refers to those aspects of social class which exist independently of people's thoughts and ideas – these are the material differences in people's life chances, such as those discussed above. Belonging to a social class is not, however, simply an objective fact.

The subjective dimension of class refers to people's personal perception of the social class they think they belong to – their class identity. While people's income means they don't always have a free choice in adopting the activities of any class they wish, the class they identify with will influence their attitudes, beliefs and values, and cultural choices, such as the music they listen to, the films and TV programmes they watch, the books, magazines and newspapers they read and their tastes in food, fashion and leisure, which are all part of the subculture of the class with which people identify. These subjective dimensions are part of what Bourdieu has called a '**habitus**'.

> A **habitus** is the cultural framework and set of ideas possessed by a social class, into which people are socialized, initially by their families, and which influences their cultural tastes and choices.

Bourdieu and class 'habitus'

Bourdieu (1971) was a French Marxist, who argued that each social class possesses its own cultural framework or set of ideas, which he called a habitus. Individuals will operate according to the social class habitus they have learnt during socialization, and this will influence:

- the knowledge they have.
- the way they use language and their accent.
- manners and forms of behaviour.
- attitudes and values.
- cultural tastes, including choices in cultural preference (high/popular culture), diet and leisure activities, consumer goods, clothing and fashion, and general lifestyles.

This cultural framework contains ideas about what counts as 'good' and 'bad' taste, 'good' books, music, food, newspapers, TV programmes and so on. The dominant class has the power to impose its own views on what counts as good taste on the rest of society. The high culture which was discussed earlier reflects the good taste of the habitus of the dominant class, while the working class is more associated with the inferior tastes of popular or mass culture. Those who have access to the habitus of the dominant class possess what Bourdieu called **cultural capital'**.

> **Cultural capital** is the knowledge, education, language, attitudes and values, and network of social contacts and lifestyle possessed by the upper and upper middle class.

SOCIAL CLASS SUBCULTURES

Social class influences how people orientate themselves in society, as they are socialized into class identities from quite an early age, through living with and encountering in their communities people in the same social class as themselves, who are like them, who share similar lifestyles, attitudes and values, and with whom they feel comfortable in their everyday lives. The following sections give a brief outline of some of the traditional cultural features of the various social classes in British society, which provide sources of identity for those subjectively identifying with them.

Upper-class subculture and identity

The upper class is a small class, and refers to those who are the main owners of society's wealth. The upper class includes three main groups.

1   The traditional upper class. This consists of Royalty and the 'old rich' traditional landowning aristocracy, as well as the titled ranks of dukes, duchesses, lords, ladies, earls and so on.
2   The owners of industry and commerce – the 'corporate rich' of the business world, such as Sir Richard Branson of Virgin.
3   Stars of entertainment, media and sport make up the third group, including people such as Sir Paul McCartney, Sir Mick Jagger, Sir Elton John and Sir Sean Connery, J. K. Rowling (author of the Harry Potter books) and David and Victoria Beckham.

Traditional upper-class culture and identity are largely associated with the first group (the 'old rich'), which has a strong sense of identity created by the socialization process and close family networks established through intermarriage, inherited wealth, a shared educational experience and a shared subculture. Scott (1991) suggested features of upper-class subculture include:

- socialization through a family life providing an exclusive upbringing and lifestyle, and close kinship relations through intermarriage with similar families; secondary socialization through an education based around private boarding schools, particularly the public schools, like Eton and Harrow, followed by Oxford and Cambridge Universities. These provide cultural capital, and develop an appreciation of high culture, and a sense of leadership and superiority; contacts are established among their peers, forming the 'old boys' network', which provides a self-help network in later life, and the links around which marriages are formed.

Traditional upper-class culture includes a taste for opera and ballet, military service as commissioned officers, and the employment of domestic servants

- military service (in regiments like the Guards or Cavalry).
- the employment of domestic staff, like nannies, butlers, cooks and gardeners.
- a taste for high culture, like opera, ballet and classical music.
- particular codes of etiquette and manners.
- leisure activities like hunting and shooting, tennis at Wimbledon, horse racing at 'Royal' Ascot, and weekends at country houses; these all provide a network for meeting others like themselves and reinforcing helpful social contacts.
- a sense of leadership, self-confidence and superiority over others.

The other two groups both make up the 'nouveau riche' (new rich), who have acquired their wealth in their own lifetimes rather than through inheritance, and sometimes come from humble origins. These groups may attempt to achieve acceptance by the traditional upper class by attempting to copy their lifestyles, but they often find acceptance difficult, as the 'old rich' tend to regard the nouveau riche as culturally inferior, lacking cultural capital, with poor taste, prone to splashing out with their wealth in conspicuous 'flashy', 'in-your-face' ways, like buying expensive sports cars, houses and clothes. They are thought to lack the sophisticated taste, 'breeding' and high culture of the traditional upper class. The nouveau riche more commonly establish their identities independently through their lifestyles and extravagant consumption patterns, which are discussed later in this chapter.

Middle-class subculture and identity

The middle class is a large class, and refers to those in non-manual work – jobs which don't involve heavy physical effort, and which are usually performed in offices and involve paperwork or ICT (Information and Communication Technology) work of various kinds.

The middle class has expanded rapidly in recent years, and it consists of such a wide range of different groups, with different occupations, educational qualifications, incomes and lifestyles, that, as writers such as Savage (1995) and Roberts (2001) argue, it is difficult to generalize with any accuracy about a shared middle-class culture and identity. Despite this, some general features that might distinguish the middle class from the working class, and that are found in aspects of the identity of most sections of the middle class and into which children are socialized, include:

- a commitment to education, including private education, and recognition of its importance for career success.
- a recognition of the importance of individual effort, personal ambition and self-help for success in life.
- a sense of individual and family self-interest.
- a concern with future orientation (planning for the future) and deferred gratification (putting off today's pleasures for future gains).
- a commitment to, or a leaning towards, greater respect for high culture than for popular culture.
- a concern with their own fitness, health and well-being.

Lawler (2005) draws on Bourdieu's (2010 [1979]) use of the concept of 'taste' (mentioned earlier on page 50) and how this becomes a symbol of identity, and a basis for judging others and establishing differences from them. Lawler suggests that taste is one way the middle class helps to secure and maintain its identity, through a sense of its own superiority over and opposition to white working-class culture. She suggests that working-class people are viewed by the middle class as variously worthless, disgusting, contemptible, frightening and threatening, with bad clothes, bad food, bad behaviour and bad taste. Jones (2011) echoes this view, with the middle class seen as sneering at and ridiculing the white working class, treating them as the 'scum of the earth', and demonizing and stereotyping them as 'chavs'.

Groups in the middle class Several major groups make up the middle class, and each of them may display variations from the features identified above. The following five groups give some idea of the characteristics of the major groups in the middle class.

1   *The professionals*, such as lawyers, doctors, teachers and social workers, who value education, their independence, high culture products, and possess high levels of what Bourdieu called cultural capital.
2   *Managers in the private sector of business, and government officials* (senior civil servants). These will have upper-range salaries, and their identity is likely to be formed in terms of their consumer spending and the lifestyles and leisure activities their incomes will support. They are likely to adopt identities associated with more traditional middle-class respectability, valuing politeness, respect for the law and refined behaviour, including an appreciation of high culture, moderation in behaviour – such as not overindulging in alcohol or drugs – and visiting museums, National Trust properties and so on.
3   *The self-employed small business owners*. These are likely to have a very individualistic identity, as they are forced to stand on their own two feet, and they are likely to be very work-centred.
4   *The financial and creative middle class*. This consists of those involved in finance (stockbrokers, investment managers, etc.) and the media and advertising. These groups tend to be young and very well-off, with high levels of consumer spending. Features include elements of both high and popular culture, clubbing, expensive restaurants, use of designer drugs, with lots of specialized leisure activities and holidays to reveal the affluent identity they wish to project. This group tends to be very individualistic, concerned primarily with its own self-interest, earning a lot of money and consuming things to mould and show off their identities.
5   *The lower-middle-class 'white-collar' workers*. These are employed in routine, non-manual work, like routine clerical and sales staff, with limited promotion prospects, and with lifestyles very similar to those of the new working class (see pages

In what ways do business people try to present identities associated with middle-class respectability?

59–60). People in this group are more likely to have a shared collective identity than other middle-class groups, expressed through membership of trade unions to protect against declining status and pay.

Working-class subculture and identity

The working class is one of the largest social classes, and refers to those working in manual jobs – jobs involving physical work and, mainly, work with their hands, like factory or labouring work. There are two broad groups within the working class: the traditional working class and the 'new' working class.

The traditional working class The traditional working class declined rapidly in the last quarter of the twentieth century, as the industries in which it was found closed down, and it has practically disappeared in Britain today. It was associated mainly with the north of England and Scotland, and was found in traditional (long-established) basic industries, such as mining, docking, iron and steel, fishing and shipbuilding.

Cultural features included:

- a close-knit community and community life: as people knew each other and were in the same boat, they 'looked out' for and protected one another.
- men were the main breadwinners, and women primarily housewives, looking after their men and their children.
- as Willis (1977) found, hard manual work was central to men's sense of masculinity as 'real men', and was their main source of identity.
- obtaining a skill and getting a job and money were seen as more important than educational qualifications.
- a strong sense of working-class identity and loyalty to their social class, with class solidarity expressed through a strong commitment to trade unions and the joining together ('collectivism') this involved.
- a strong commitment to the old Labour Party, as it was then seen as the party of the working class.

In what ways might traditional working-class jobs like coal mining create a sense of solidarity and be a source of masculine identity?

- a view of society based on a struggle between the social classes, identifying the workers – 'us' – as engaged in a conflict with 'them' – the bosses.
- enjoyment of and participation in popular culture, and some elements of traditional folk culture (like brass bands in mining communities).
- as Charlesworth (2000) found in his study of a traditional working-class community in Rotherham, language may involve a lot of swearing, and the use of insults (like 'shit fo' brains' or 'daft fucka') as forms of endearment to display friendship.

According to writers such as Hoggart (1969), there were very strong moral values, with clear conceptions of right and wrong, and maintaining respectability in the community was closely linked to 'doing the right thing'. The insecurity of life in the traditional working class, with few chances of promotion at work, and ever-present risks of unemployment, industrial injury, ill-health, premature death and poverty, led to three particular attitudes:

- *immediate gratification*: enjoying pleasures today while the going's good rather than putting them off for later.
- *a present orientation*: a focus on the here and now rather than the future and long-term goals
- *a sense of fatalism*: an acceptance of the situation they found themselves in, as they didn't see much hope of improving or changing their lives. In traditional working-class jobs, educational qualifications were often not very important for work, and parents tended not to encourage ambition and educational success.

The 'new' working class   By far the largest section of the working class today is what is commonly called the 'new' working class, though it is actually quite old now as it first emerged in the 1960s. The new working class originally emerged in the south of England, but it has now spread to become by far the largest section of the working class.

Consumption and lifestyle are likely to be more important than work in forming the identity of the new working class

Cultural features include:

- a privatized, home-centred family lifestyle, with little involvement with neighbours or the wider community.
- an instrumental approach to life and work. Work is more likely to be seen as a means simply of making money, rather than as a means of making friends or as a major source of identity.
- there is little sense of loyalty to others in the same class. Those identifying with this class don't regard social class and power differences between classes as very important – the only real difference between people is that some have more money and possessions than others.
- women are more likely to be in paid employment, though still retaining prime responsibility for the home.
- there are high levels of home-ownership, with home-centred lifestyles and consumption of popular culture.
- there is more emphasis on consumer goods, leisure activities and lifestyle in forming identity, than on work.

Is social class of declining importance in forming identities?

Some writers, like Clarke and Saunders (1991), suggest that social class is of declining importance today as a source of identity, as classes become fragmented into a range of different groups, and are being replaced by a whole range of other influences on identity, including gender, religion, ethnicity and consumer lifestyles. Pakulski and Waters (1996) suggest that class is dead as an important factor in a person's identity, being replaced with the lifestyle and consumption patterns of different status groups. Lash and Urry (1987) argue that class subcultures have weakened, and people's cultural choices, tastes and lifestyles have become more individualistic and less influenced by their close communities and work situations. Postmodernist writers suggest that identities have become much more fluid and changeable, and people can now choose, pick 'n' mix, chop and change any identities they want from a range of different life-styles presented to them through the mass media, and by the choices they make in their leisure activities and the lifestyles they express through their consumer spending. For postmodernists, consumer culture has replaced class culture as the major influence on people's identity. This is discussed in the last section of this chapter.

Activity

1 Refer to the section above and mark the following statements as more likely to be true or false:
   (a) Traditional working-class people are less likely to value education than the middle class.
   (b) Members of the new working class are less likely to be involved in community activities than the traditional working class.
   (c) The traditional working class is likely to have a lifestyle more like that of the lower middle class.
   (d) People in the new working class are more likely to live in a tight-knit community than the traditional working class.
   (e) Traditional working-class people are likely to identify with others in their class.
   (f) The middle class is likely to be concerned with planning for the future.
   (g) Members of the middle class are more likely to be interested in high culture than the traditional working class.
   (h) Members of the traditional working class are likely to see society divided by conflict between opposing social classes.
   (i) The traditional upper class is likely to have a sense of its own superiority to others.
   (j) The traditional upper class sees itself as having a similar identity to the corporate rich and the stars of sport, entertainment and the media.
2 Identify and briefly explain two characteristics of: (i) upper-class subculture, (ii) middle-class subculture, (iii) traditional working-class subculture and (iv) the subculture of the new working class.
3 Suggest two ways in which the experience of education may reinforce class identity.
4 What social class do you think you belong to? Give reasons for your answer.
5 Do you subjectively identify yourself as a member of a particular social class? Which one, and explain why.
6 Explain what is meant by the subjective dimension of class, and why this might be important when considering whether class is still a source of identity.
7 Conduct a short survey among people you know to see how they identify social class and what social class they would put themselves in, and why.

The continuing importance of social class

The views discussed above tend to underestimate the importance that social class still has today. Class remains a common social identity, and in surveys many people continue to identify themselves with a social class. For example, the British Social Attitudes Survey published in 2007 found:

● 95 per cent of people identified themselves with a social class, with only 5 per cent saying they did not identify with any class.

- 38 per cent of people identified themselves as middle class.
- 57 per cent identified themselves as working class.

In addition, those who suggest that identity is now formed around people's choices in leisure activities and consumer goods don't take adequate account of the fact that these are not free choices, but are influenced by people's income. Sky-diving, swimming with dolphins, up-to-the-minute worn-once fashion clothing, lots of latte coffees, designer kitchens and exotic foreign holidays are not lifestyle options that are available to everyone. Social class is a major limitation on people choosing any identity they may desire.

Social class is still the major influence on people's standard of living and lifestyle, their chances of educational success, their health and life expectancy, their home ownership, their risks of unemployment and poverty, and other life chances. We may no longer be able to assume that social class is the key influence on people's identity. However, whether or not people express their identities in traditional terms of social class is one thing; escaping the influence of social class on identity formation is another thing altogether.

Gender and identity

One of the first questions we ask when someone has a baby is: 'Is it a boy or a girl?', and the sex of a person is one of the first things we notice about someone when we meet them for the first time.

Stratification by sex is a feature found in most societies, with men generally being in a more dominant position in society than women. Our sex has major influences on how we think about ourselves, how others think about us, and the opportunities and life chances open to us. This section will examine how the different gender identities of men and women are constructed by socialization in modern Britain, and how they might be changing.

SEX AND GENDER

The term **sex** (whether someone is male or female) refers to the natural or biological differences between men and women, such as differences in genitals, internal reproductive organs and body hair, while **gender** (whether someone is masculine or feminine) refers to the socially constructed cultural, social and psychological differences between the two sexes. It refers to the way a society encourages and teaches the two sexes to behave in different ways through socialization. These different ways of behaving, which society expects from individuals of either sex – how a boy/man or girl/woman should behave in society – are known as **gender roles. Gender identity** refers to how people see themselves, and others see them, in terms of their gender roles and biological sex – the meaning that being a man or a woman has to people.

GENDER AND BIOLOGY

Our sexual or biological characteristics do not determine or decide gender roles and identities. We know this because, although the biological differences between men and women are the same everywhere, the behaviour and identities adopted by men and women differ both within the same society, and between societies. Mead (2001)

Sex refers to the biological differences between men and women, while **gender** refers to the culturally created differences between men and women which are learnt through socialization.

A **gender role** is the pattern of behaviour which is expected from individuals of either sex.

Gender identity refers to how people see themselves, and how others see them, in terms of their gender roles and biological sex.

Male and female babies have the same biological differences across the world, but socialization means there are wide variations in the ways boys and girls behave in different societies

carried out research on three distinctly different tribes from New Guinea, which led her to believe that many so-called 'masculine' and 'feminine' characteristics are not based on fundamental sex differences, but reflect the cultural conditioning of different societies. She uncovered examples where male and female behaviour was quite different from that most commonly found in today's UK. For example, in the Tchambuli tribe in New Guinea, the traditional gender roles found in modern Britain were reversed – it was the men who displayed what we might regard as traditional 'feminine' characteristics, such as doing the shopping and putting on make-up and jewellery to make themselves attractive. Women were the more aggressive, practical ones, who made the sexual advances to men and did all the trading.

Even in Britain today, there is a diversity of masculine and feminine behaviour, with both males and females adopting a range of identities. There are, for example, women who present themselves as very traditional feminine figures, while others are tomboyish, or tough as nails in girl gangs, or adopt the masculine styles of hard drinking, yobbish 'ladettes'. Similarly, men may be sharing, caring, emotional 'New Men', 'macho' men and so on.

It is evidence like this that has led sociologists to conclude that masculine and feminine gender identities are primarily constructed through socialization, rather than simply a result of the biological differences between men and women.

THE SIGNIFICANCE OF GENDER AS A SOURCE OF IDENTITY

Throughout our lives, our gender is an important source of identity. Whether we see ourselves as masculine or feminine, and which aspects of masculinity and femininity we identify ourselves with, influence how we think about ourselves, how we behave towards others, how others see us, the expectations they have of us and the way they treat us.

Having a feminine or masculine identity enables individuals to share things with others (like playing sport or going shopping) and gives people guidelines for identifying with and relating to others like themselves, for example through the way they dress, the language they use, the way they sit, their body language, the way they style their hair and the activities they share. The particular gender identity people adopt marks them out as similar to some people and different from others, and they will generally adopt forms of behaviour which 'fit' the identities they construct.

While we may be able to some extent to influence the exact details of our own gender identities – after all, men and women do not display the same masculine and feminine characteristics in a uniform, unchanging way – the options available to us are not unlimited. We are influenced by agencies of socialization such as the family, the school, the peer group and the mass media, which frequently promote socially approved forms of masculine and feminine behaviour.

Activity

1 List some of the socially approved ways that men and women are expected to behave, and how they should not behave, in contemporary Britain.
2 Suggest ways in which these expectations might be beginning to change.

GENDER STEREOTYPES AND HEGEMONIC GENDER IDENTITIES IN BRITAIN

Gender differences are socially constructed by the agencies of socialization, which steer people towards gender stereotypes and encourage them to identify themselves with these stereotypes. A gender **stereotype** is a generalized view of the 'typical' or 'ideal' characteristics of men and women. The gender stereotype of men involves a **hegemonic identity** that Connell (1995) called a 'hegemonic masculinity', but we could also consider there to be a 'hegemonic femininity'.

Some possible features of these are summarized in table 2.1.

Girls and women who fail to identify themselves with and conform to the feminine stereotype are liable to be seen as 'tomboys', while men and boys who fail to conform to the masculine stereotype are likely to be seen as 'wimps' or 'sissies'. It is still the case that one of the worst taunts a male child can face, which is a challenge to his emerging masculine identity, is to be called 'girl' by his peer group.

Feminist sociologists particularly emphasize the ways the processes of socialization into these hegemonic masculine and feminine identities reproduce and reinforce male dominance (patriarchy), and make it difficult for either men or women to construct gender identities different from the hegemonic stereotypes.

Activity

1 Discuss the suggested features of the hegemonic stereotypes of masculinity and femininity shown in table 2.1. To what extent do you think they give an accurate impression of gender characteristics in Britain? Back up your view with evidence of both child and adult behaviour.
2 Suggest ways that these stereotypes might be changing in modern Britain, with evidence drawn from areas such as work, education and the mass media to back up your view.

A **stereotype** is a generalized, over-simplified view of the features of a social group, allowing for few individual differences among members of the group. The assumption is made that all members of the group share the same features. Examples of stereotypes include views such as 'all women are lousy drivers', 'all young people are vandals and layabouts' or 'those on welfare benefits are all on the fiddle'.

A **hegemonic identity** is one that is so dominant that it makes it difficult for individuals to assert alternative identities.

Heterosexuality involves a sexual orientation towards people of the opposite sex.
Sexual orientation refers to the type of people to whom individuals are either physically or romantically attracted, of the same or the opposite sex.

Table 2.1

Hegemonic masculine characteristics	Hegemonic feminine characteristics

Heterosexuality	**Heterosexuality**
Sexual dominance	Sexually passive (or a 'slapper' if sexually active)
Repression of emotions/emotional distance (except in sport, when males tend to get very emotional indeed)	Expression of emotions/emotional warmth, caring and sensitive
Physical strength/muscular/tall	Weak, fragile/small
Aggression	Gentleness and non-aggressive
Independence and self-reliance	Dependence (on men)
Competitiveness and ambition	Non-competitive
Lack of domesticity (housework and childcare) – only occasional practical DIY around the home	Concerned with and responsible for housework and practical and emotional aspects of childcare
Rational and practical	Emotional and unpredictable
Risk-taking	Avoids risk
Task-oriented – focus on 'doing things' like work success, playing sports, making things, DIY in the home or activities to escape from work	People-oriented – focus on forming and maintaining friendships, family, children, and 'customer care' (keeping customers happy)
Lack of concern with or interest in personal appearance, taste in dress or personal health and diet	Major concern with physical appearance (being slim and pretty), health, diet, dress sense, and attractiveness to men

THE SOCIAL CONSTRUCTION OF HEGEMONIC GENDER IDENTITIES THROUGH SOCIALIZATION

There is a wide range of primary and secondary agencies of socialization which establish traditional gender roles and mould males and females into the hegemonic gender identities. Examples of this are considered below, and summarized later in figure 2.3 on page 69.

The role of the family

Parents and relatives tend to hold stereotyped views of the typical or ideal characteristics of boys and girls, and they often try to bring up their children in accordance with what they regard as normal masculine or feminine behaviour. Oakley (1985) identifies four processes during primary socialization:

1 *Manipulation*: boys and girls are handled differently – e.g. boys are more likely to be bounced in physical play, with girls treated more gently and more likely to be cuddled.

2 *Canalization*: boys and girls are directed towards different toys and games – e.g. construction kits, cricket bats, footballs, chemistry sets, electronic toys, guns, cars and trucks, aeroplanes, and computer games for boys, developing the technological interest and technical and sporting skills regarded as part of a 'normal' masculine environment; sewing machines, dolls, prams, cookers, teasets, drawing books and playing with domestic technology like microwaves and vacuum cleaners for girls, developing the skills and interests reflected in their mothers' traditional roles in the kitchen and as nurturers. When girls play the role of nurse to their brother's doctor, or play with dolls and make-up and different types of clothing, and wear clothes bought by parents that are generally more colourful and pretty, while the boys get more practical clothing, they are learning adult gender stereotypes by mimicking them.

3 *Verbal appellations*: boys and girls are exposed to different language and praised or rebuked for different things – e.g. parental praise, such as 'you're such a brave boy' or 'you're such a sweet girl', rewarding behaviour which is seen as appropriate for their gender.

4 *Differential activity exposure*: boys and girls are exposed to and encouraged to do different activities, for example by watching and imitating the role models provided by the usually different activities carried out by their fathers and mothers. Other examples include boys and girls being given different rules to follow, or jobs around the home – e.g. girls are more likely to do indoor housework, generally helping their mothers with domestic jobs, while boys are more likely to do outdoor jobs with their fathers, like cleaning the car, sweeping the paths and being shown how to do repairs and make things.

Activity

While Oakley was mainly concerned with these processes during primary socialization, they can probably also be identified as being at work during secondary socialization. Try to think of examples of the ways these processes are also carried out at school, at work, by the peer group and by the mass media.

In what ways are gender identities formed through socialization and play in the early years?

The role of the school

Much of this gender socialization goes on through the school's **hidden curriculum**. This consists of the hidden teaching of attitudes and behaviour, which are taught at school through the school's organization and teachers' attitudes but which are not part of the formal timetable. Examples of this include:

> The **hidden curriculum** refers to the attitudes and behaviour which are taught through the school's organization and teachers' attitudes, but which are not part of the formal timetable.

- *Teachers' attitudes*, with teachers traditionally encouraging boys more in sciences and computing, placing more emphasis on their progress than that of girls; giving different career advice to boys and girls; and treating disruptive, unruly behaviour by boys and girls differently.
- *Subject choice*: girls and boys have traditionally been counselled by parents and teachers into taking different subjects. Within the National Curriculum, girls are more likely to study home economics, textiles and food technology, while boys are more likely to choose electronics, woodwork or graphics technology. After the age of 16, other subject divisions still remain, with girls more likely to take arts subjects (like English literature, history and foreign languages) and boys more likely to choose the sciences. This gender division is also found in sport, with rugby and cricket for the boys and hockey and netball for the girls.

There is a further discussion of how the school creates and reinforces gender stereotypes in the chapter on education, and it would be useful to refer to pages 389–94 now.

The importance of the peer group

Generally, people try to gain acceptance among their peers by conforming to the norms of their peer group, and this frequently involves conformity to stereotyped masculine or feminine identities. A boy, for example, who saw himself as a collector of soft toys would be quite likely to face ridicule from his peer group; a girl who identified herself as a rugby player or a boxer might be seen as a bit of a tomboy. There are also double standards in terms of the sexual aspects of masculine and feminine identities. Among teenage boys (and often adult men too), sexual promiscuity and sexual 'conquest' are encouraged and admired as approved masculine behaviour, and are seen as a means of achieving status in the male peer group. However, males – and other women – will condemn this same promiscuity among women – promiscuous girls and women are most likely to be seen as 'up for it', and have a spoiled identity of slappers, slags or sluts or some other insulting term assigned to them.

Willis confirmed this in his study of a group of working-class 'lads'. The 'lads' constantly chased girls for sex, but then often dropped them, labelling them as 'loose' once they had had sex with the boys who had been after it. Girls and women who have sex outside some steady relationship are likely to find themselves condemned by men and women alike. In short, promiscuous men are seen as 'stags' or 'studs'; promiscuous women are seen as 'slags' or 'sluts'.

This double standard helps to encourage conformity to separate gender identities for men and women, with the stereotyped man as sexual athlete and stereotyped woman as the passive and faithful lover, wife or girlfriend.

The role of the mass media

The mass media create and reinforce gender stereotypes in a number of ways. Comics, for example, present different images of men and women. Girls are usually presented as pretty, romantic, helpless, easily upset and emotional, and dependent on boys for support and guidance. Boys are presented as strong, independent, unemotional and

assertive. Boys and girls are often presented in traditional stereotyped gender roles such as soldiers (boys) or nurses (girls). A similar pattern is shown on children's television, and much TV and other advertising shows gender stereotypes. Around 80 per cent of TV advertising voice-overs are male voices – suggesting authority. The media, particularly advertising, often promote the 'beauty myth' – the idea that women should be assessed primarily in terms of their appearance.

There are often very different types of story and magazine aimed at males and females. Romantic fiction is almost exclusively aimed at a female readership. A glance at the magazine shelves of any large newsagent's will reveal different sections for 'women's interests' and 'men's interests', reflecting the different hegemonic masculine and feminine identities which men and women are encouraged to adopt. Women have been traditionally presented in the mass media in a limited number of stereotyped roles, for example:

- as a 'sex object': the image of the slim, sexually seductive, scantily clad figure typically found on page 3 of the *Sun* newspaper is used by the advertising industry to sell everything from peanuts to motorbikes and newspapers. 'Celebrity culture' provides strong role models for the ways girls should dress and behave, and 'super-models' are the beauty queens of today, at a time when Miss World beauty contests are seen by many as redundant and unacceptable. Such imagery encourages women to believe the key to their happiness lies in how much they appeal to men sexually.
- in their relationships with men, such as bosses, husbands, and lovers.
- as emotional and unpredictable.
- in the housewife/mother role: as the content, capable and caring housewife and mother, whose constant concern is with the whiteness of clothes, the cleanliness of floors, and the evening meal; and as the person who keeps the family together and manages its emotions.

Men are presented in a wider range of roles, and men's magazines reflect interests that are seen as part of the hegemonic masculine identity. These include photography, music systems and gadgets, computers, DIY and all manner of transport: cars, motorbikes, aircraft, trains and boats. The 'top shelf' soft-porn magazines are aimed exclusively at men.

Figure 2.3 The social construction of hegemonic gender identities through socialization

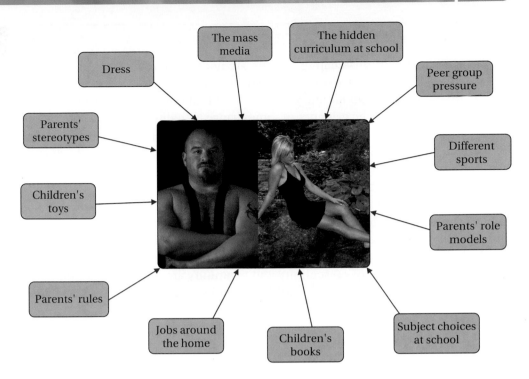

Dress

The mass media

The hidden curriculum at school

Peer group pressure

Parents' stereotypes

Different sports

Children's toys

Parents' role models

Parents' rules

Jobs around the home

Children's books

Subject choices at school

Activity

1 Refer to figure 2.3, which shows a range of ways in which hegemonic gender identities are constructed in modern Britain. Working in groups, take some of the ways and identify examples showing how gender stereotypes are constructed, and how these influence how people come to see themselves, and how others see them.

2 Look at the following list of words, and divide them into three groups: those you might use to describe women, those you might use to describe men, and those you might use to describe both men and women.

clever	passive	sulky	thoughtful	bastard
powerful	assertive	gentle	caring	attractive
bimbo	emotional	gossip	elegant	soft
aggressive	pretty	tart	kind	tender
cold	sweet	logical	quiet	competitive
sly	ruthless	delicate	brave	active
muscular	bitchy	weak	clinging	slag
domineering	slim	submissive	frigid	gracious
hideous	hunk	handsome	raving	plain
hysterical	blonde	beautiful	player	stud
cute	babe	fit	mover	dickhead
loose	dog	trophy bird	easy	slut

3 Now compare the two lists of words used to describe men and women. Do they present gender stereotypes? You will probably have found there are some words in both lists that have a similar meaning. Why are some words generally restricted to one gender? Discuss why these words are not used to describe both sexes, and how they show stereotyped assumptions about women and men. Consider generally the way language is used to create gender identities.

CHANGING GENDER IDENTITIES

As suggested earlier in this chapter, people are not simply robots or puppets. Both males and females play active roles in the construction of their gender identities and people are beginning to adopt and experiment with alternative gender identities. In recent years, there has been evidence of some change in traditional ideas about masculine and feminine gender identities, and related sexuality. Soap operas give us insights into lesbian and gay relationships, and other images of sexual identities with which we may not be very familiar. People are becoming more tolerant of gays and lesbians, and more accepting of cohabitation.

More males and females are adopting gender identities which combine elements of both genders, and these are constantly changing. We see more unisex hairstyles and clothing, more men wearing what were once seen as women's jewellery or women's clothes, and using a range of cosmetics. Some writers suggest that the old hegemonic conceptions of masculinity and femininity are outdated, and that more people are choosing to ignore the traditional gender stereotypes, and to adopt new identities.

Changing female identities

Females are now doing better than males in education, and more positive role models are replacing traditional stereotypes in daily life and in the media.

Women are becoming more successful than men in many areas of the labour market, such as in the music industry and in business and the professions, like law and medicine. Girls and women often have better 'people' and communication skills than men, and these are the skills that are required for success in the new service economy – dealing with customers, orders, clients and complaints. The traditional stereotype of women as mothers and carers, with prime responsibility for running the home and family, is being replaced by role models of strong, independent and successful women in all spheres of life. With women's growing labour market success, the traditional idea of a single main male family breadwinner is being undermined, and as women's independent income increases, their financial need for marriage reduces. A woman no longer needs a man, through marriage and the family, to achieve status in society. There is now a new and wider range of roles for women, and as traditional stereotypes are eroded, so women can choose from a range of feminine identities: 'being feminine' can increasingly mean a lot of different things.

Some argue that traditional feminine identities are being eroded, and that there is some convergence, or growing similarity, between masculine and feminine identities. There has been the emergence of 'ladettes' – females taking on aspects of lads' masculinity associated with loutishness and loudness, heavy drinking and aggressive sexuality in both dress and behaviour. There has been the emergence of increasingly violent girl gangs, and a 2006 World Health Organization survey found girls in the UK were among the most violent in the world, with nearly one in three Scottish and English adolescent girls admitting to having been involved in a fight in the past year, and it seemed likely these high levels of violence among adolescent girls were linked to binge drinking and 'ladette' culture. Jackson's (2006) research among 13- to 14-year-old boys and girls found this 'ladette' behaviour in schools too, with more girls adopting the same assertive, boisterous and crude 'laddish' culture and confrontational anti-school activity more traditionally found among boys.

Changing male identities

The traditional power of men in the family and the labour market, and in society generally, is, some suggest, being challenged by women's growing success and equality. Men used to establish their identities through the public world of work and as family breadwinners, and women through the private realm of family and home. However, women are becoming increasingly assertive and successful in a wide range of areas, and they can now do everything men can do, and they are often doing it more successfully. At the same time, the prospects for young men are diminishing:

- males are underachieving in education.
- traditional employment in 'macho' manual work is disappearing, with the closure of long-established heavy industries, such as mining, shipbuilding and steel.
- women are increasingly doing better than men in the labour market, particularly in the new service industries.
- men's dominant position in the family, as main breadwinner and decision-maker, is increasingly under threat with the rise of women's equality and their independent incomes: 70 per cent of divorces are initiated by women, and more women are choosing to remain single and childless; marriage and parenthood are in decline; advances in technology are reducing men's role in reproduction, and women can now have children without the necessity of a male partner.
- equal opportunities laws and policies, and independent taxation and equality in pensions have all undermined male power.

'New Men' and other male identities Since the 1980s there has been speculation about the emergence of a so-called 'New Man', who was allegedly more caring, sharing, gentle, emotional, sensitive in his attitudes to women, children and his own emotional needs, and willing to do his fair share of housework. Love, family, personal relations and getting in touch with his own emotions were meant to be more important than achieving career success and power in the family and society. Male bodies are now emerging in advertising as sex objects to sell things, in much the same way women's bodies have always been used. New emerging masculine identities are becoming more concerned with appearance (a traditional feminine concern): 10 per cent of cosmetic surgery is now carried out on men, and the proportion is rising, with the growing use by men of face lifts, 'boob jobs', 'nose jobs' and 'tummy tucking', and beauty treatments such as facials and waxing to remove body hair. An *Observer* and Nivea for Men survey in 2004 found that 83 per cent of men were fairly or extremely interested in their own physical appearance, and 21 per cent of men had been in the past, or were currently, on a diet. The male grooming market has grown by 800 per cent since 1998. Recent research shows that males of all ages are now worrying about their appearance. A survey of teenage boys by a teen magazine in 2005 said that they agonized about their physique as much as teenage girls did. The growth of eating disorders, like anorexia, among men, and Men's Health weeks, suggest a new concern with men's health and attractiveness.

New and ever-changing male identities are often created by the mass media, and by marketing campaigns by big business to sell new products, and these open up the range of identity choices for men. Apart from the New Man, other identities that have made appearances in the mass media include:

- *New Lad* – a reaction against the New Man, and associated with the 'yob culture' of aggressive and promiscuous sex, lager, football and loutishness.
- *New Bloke* – a New Lad who has become a recent father, but who, as well as hanging around the pub, is also to be found changing nappies.

- *New Dad* – a New Man who discovers the joys of fatherhood.
- *Emo Boy* – a version of the New Man, who reads books, appreciates the arts, watches his diet, isn't afraid to show his emotions, and dresses with more care and style than most girls, usually in tight sweaters and pants.
- *Metrosexuals* – heterosexual men who embrace their feminine side, are in touch with their feelings, use moisturiser and designer cosmetic products, who have refined tastes in clothing, and incorporate elements of the gay lifestyle.

Activity

1 Suggest two ways in each case that (a) men and (b) women might use gender representations in the mass media as a source of personal identity and meaning.
2 Try to identify three examples of how men are being represented more as sex objects in the contemporary mass media, including advertising.
3 Drawing on your own experiences of the mass media, discuss examples of the ways new masculine and feminine identities might be emerging in contemporary society.

Are more men now 'New Dads' and involved in the care of their children? How does this challenge traditional concepts of hegemonic masculinity?

The rise of the gay movement and the growth of anti-sexist ideas have further contributed to the undermining of men's traditional role, and opened up the possibility for aspects of masculine identity to merge with aspects of traditional femininity.

IS THERE A CRISIS OF MASCULINITY?

Though the New Man has turned out to be a very rare specimen, with the New Lad emerging in the 2000s as a reaction against the New Man, men are said to be facing anxiety, uncertainty and confusion about what their role and identity are in today's society. A growing sense of insecurity accompanies the loss of men's sense of purpose in relation to the traditional hegemonic masculine identity of what Gilmore (1991) described as 'the provider, the protector and the impregnator'. Mac an Ghaill (1994) argues that the changes discussed above, summarized in figure 2.4, are creating a 'crisis

Figure 2.4 A crisis of masculinity?

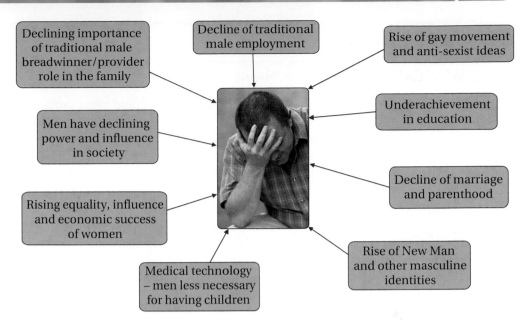

Declining importance of traditional male breadwinner/provider role in the family

Decline of traditional male employment

Rise of gay movement and anti-sexist ideas

Men have declining power and influence in society

Underachievement in education

Rising equality, influence and economic success of women

Decline of marriage and parenthood

Medical technology – men less necessary for having children

Rise of New Man and other masculine identities

of masculinity', with men feeling lost and searching for a gender identity that fits in the modern world.

IS GENDER STILL AN IMPORTANT SOURCE OF IDENTITY?

The material above suggests that gender identities may be changing and becoming much more fluid, with both men and women having a wider choice in the gender identities available to them. Postmodernists, as will be seen later, suggest that people are now free to choose any identity they like, without the constraints of gender identities.

However, it is easy to exaggerate the extent of the changes. The narrow, stereotyped gender roles of thirty years ago are still held by many of today's children, and many still grow up forming their identities around these stereotypes. People may have more choice today over the elements of masculinity and femininity they adopt, but traditional gender roles have not changed as much as we might like to think. Women still earn less than men, and still do most of the housework, childcare and emotional work in the family. The majority of women still strive to conform to the hegemonic femininity discussed earlier in this chapter, and often have feelings of guilt and inadequacy when their physical appearance and sense of self fail to 'measure up' to this stereotype. Similarly, most men still conform to the fairly typical, 'unreconstructed' hegemonic masculinity. There is still some way to go before people are so freed from the constraints of gender role socialization and social pressures to conform that they can pick 'n' mix their gender identity in any way they wish, or reject it altogether as a source of identity.

Activity

1 Explain what is meant by a 'crisis of masculinity'. To what extent do you think there is such a crisis? Give reasons for your answer.
2 Suggest evidence for the view that there is a new femininity emerging, which is more assertive and less dependent on men.
3 Suggest three arguments for, and three against, the view that there is a 'New Man' emerging.

Sexuality and identity

GENDER, SEXUALITY AND 'NORMAL SEX'

Like gender identity, sexual behaviour is socially constructed, and what counts as normal sexual behaviour, or 'normal sex', is part of the culture of any society and established through the socialization process, and can vary by time, place and culture. For example, in ancient Greece, **homosexuality** among men was seen as part of normal everyday sex. In contemporary Britain, the dominant view of normal **sexuality** is that of heterosexuality, which is a central aspect of the hegemonic masculine and feminine identities discussed in the previous section. In the case of women, this has traditionally been linked to romance and/or steady and meaningful personal relationships.

Sexuality has always been a central part of the hegemonic feminine identity, as women have been defined, in Britain and other Western countries, by their physical attractiveness and sexual appeal to men. Women have traditionally been regarded as sex objects, subjected to what Mulvey (1975/2009) called the '**male gaze**', particularly in the mass media, like the top-shelf soft-porn magazines and page 3 of the *Sun* newspaper, in advertising, and through media pictures and stories of the exploits of female celebrities. In terms of normal sex, it is worth recalling the point that was made earlier – that there is still a double standard of sexual morality for men and women, with sexually promiscuous females likely to be condemned by both sexes.

> **Homosexuality** involves a sexual orientation towards people of the same sex, with lesbian women attracted to other women, and gay men attracted to other men.
> **Sexuality** refers to people's sexual characteristics and their sexual behaviour.

> The **male gaze** is where men look (gaze) at women as sexual objects.

CHANGING SEXUAL IDENTITIES

In recent years, the physical-appearance and 'sex-appeal' aspects of sexuality long associated with femininity have become a more important part of masculinity as well. New alternative masculine identities appear to be emerging, with the rise of the gay movement and the growing crisis of masculinity opening up new choices for men. This is reflected in much of the material in the earlier discussion on gender. Men's increasing concerns with things like their appearance and attractiveness, their body size and shape, their diet, their health and their dress sense; their growing use of cosmetics and cosmetic surgery; and the increase in eating disorders among men – all point to men's rising concern with sexual attractiveness.

Men's bodies have also become much more sexualized, with more naked men's bodies appearing in the media and advertising, on a greater scale than ever before, with a growing importance attached to men's physical body image, rather than just women's.

An example of this, almost paralleling the traditional obsession with women's breasts, was the media obsession with 'moobies' (men's boobs) in the 2000s. This began with the *Sun* newspaper publishing in 2005 a 'Hall of Shame' series of pictures showing the different shapes and sizes of famous men's breasts, and making disparaging comments about them. Other tabloid newspapers soon followed with criticisms of flabby stomachs – 'holiday podges' – and love handles.

The release of *Casino Royale* in 2006, with actor Daniel Craig appearing as the new James Bond, was met with endless comments about Craig's body, and how he appeared mostly naked more than anyone else in the film, where even 'the hotsy-totsy women kept their kits on', as one reviewer put it, with 'Craig's ripped pecs being the most public symbol of British masculinity'.

The point is that men are beginning to face almost the same physical scrutiny, by both women and other men, as women always have. As McRobbie (1994) put it: 'The beauty stakes have gone up for men, and women have taken up the position of active viewers.'

STIGMATIZED OR SPOILED SEXUAL IDENTITIES

Individuals whose view of themselves – their conception of self – is that reflected in the hegemonic gender identities discussed earlier are likely to regard sexuality outside 'normal sex', such as homosexuality, as deviant activities, and those practising them as having stigmatized or spoiled identities. The consequences of this for gay men and lesbians include hostility in pubs and clubs and in the street, bullying at school, mockery in the mass media (anti-gay jokes, for example) and discrimination in employment. Some forms of sexuality, such as paedophilia, sado-masochism, transvestism, necrophilia and some forms of exhibitionism, can be even more stigmatized. It is for this reason that many forms of sexuality which do not conform with normal sex are concealed, with practitioners using what Goffman called 'impression management' to conceal these aspects of their sexuality from others, to prevent them from becoming part of their public identity and the stigmatization that would accompany this.

GAY AND LESBIAN IDENTITIES

In Britain, stigmatization of homosexual identities, particularly of gay men, is reducing, and is much diminished compared to what it once was. There is more fluidity about sexual identity, and new identities are emerging, with more TV soaps and dramas featuring gay and lesbian relationships. However, the changes are fairly recent, particularly in relation to the law. While lesbianism has never been specifically against the law in the UK, it was only in 1968 that it became legal for there to be sexual relations between men over the age of 21 in England and Wales, with Scottish men having to wait until 1980. The age of consent for gay men only became the same as for heterosexual adults (age 16) in 2000, and it was as recently as 2005 that gay and lesbian couples were allowed to achieve the same legal status as heterosexual married couples by forming civil partnerships.

The rise of the gay movement, the importance of gay spending (the 'pink pound') and newly emerging forms of masculinity have overcome much of the stigma attached to male homosexuality, as well as weakening the sense of difference and opposition between gay and straight masculine identities. In this sense, masculine sexual identity has become more fluid and changeable, and homosexuality much more widely accepted.

As a result of the gay movement, gay people who 'come out' (openly declare themselves to be gay) and participate in the gay subculture now have a wide range of sexual identities open to them beyond the effeminate 'gay' or 'butch' stereotypes found in the media, such as 'camp' queens, macho men, cross-dressers, gay cowboys, leather boys, etc.

Many people are now more tolerant of gay and lesbian relationships, and there is a wider range of sexual identities available today, particularly for men

A NOTE OF CAUTION

There is some evidence that attitudes to sexuality have become more relaxed, with wider acceptance of homosexuality and **bisexuality**, and people having more freedom to choose from a range of sexual identities. However, it is important not to exaggerate the extent of these changes. The norms of sexual behaviour, and the sexual identities arising from them, are still constructed by the agencies of socialization, and homosexuality, let alone other sexual practices, is still regarded as deviant by many people. **Homophobia**, an irrational fear of or aversion to homosexuals, is still very common.

Queer Bashing, a national survey by Stonewall of hate crimes against lesbians and gay men, found that one in three gay men and one in four lesbians had experienced at least one violent attack in the period between 1990 and 1996, and, because of fear of becoming the victim of homophobic violence, 65 per cent of respondents always or sometimes avoided telling people they were gay. Of those aged under 18, 90 per cent had experienced verbal abuse, and 48 per cent violence, because of their sexuality. A 2007 survey by Stonewall found that, while nine out of ten people supported laws to protect gay people, almost one in six adults in Britain had seen gay or lesbian colleagues being physically or verbally bullied at work as a direct result of their sexuality.

Women are still very much more likely to be seen as sex objects than men, particularly in pornography, with even young boys and girls widely exposed to sexualized images of females. Porn now seems quite deeply embedded, through the internet and mobile phone technology, in the culture of young men. In 2007, the Sex Education Forum found that half of children using the internet were exposed to porn and that almost a third of children receive unwanted sexual comments via email, instant messaging or text. It does then still appear that men have more choice in choosing their sexual identities than women, who remain constrained by traditional stereotypes.

Bisexuality involves a sexual orientation towards people of both sexes.

Homophobia is an irrational fear of or aversion to homosexuals.

Activity

1 With examples, suggest ways that advertising, the mass media and shop displays show a sexual image of men today.
2 Do you think that men are as concerned with their physical appearance as women?
3 To what extent do you think that young people today have more freedom to express their sexuality?
4 To what extent have you been aware of gay and lesbian relationships in contemporary soap and reality TV shows?
5 Do you think there is now less stigma attached to 'non-normal' sexuality?

Ethnicity and identity

Ethnicity is not the same as race or skin colour, as there are many groups that may appear physically similar, but come from different ethnic backgrounds – for example, the English and the Scots, or Indian Sikhs and Pakistani Muslims. Everyone has an ethnicity, with the largest ethnic group in Britain being white British, though the concept of ethnicity is generally used in everyday life in connection with **minority ethnic groups**, such as African-Caribbean, Indian Asian, Chinese and Polish ethnic groups in Britain.

Ethnicity refers to the shared culture of a social group which gives its members a common identity in some ways different from that of other social groups. A **minority ethnic group** is a social group that shares a cultural identity which is different from that of the majority population of a society.

WHAT IS MEANT BY AN ETHNIC IDENTITY?

An ethnic identity is one in which individuals assert their identity primarily in terms of the ethnic group and culture to which they belong. Ethnic identity is formed and transmitted from one generation to the next by agencies of socialization, such as the family, peer group, religious institutions, education and the mass media. Anwar (1998) and Ghuman (1999), for example, found that South Asian families emphasized the values of family obligation and loyalty, and a commitment to their religion, which they sought to instil in their children during the socialization process. The education system may reinforce ethnic identities either through the establishment of ethnic-based religious schooling, such as Muslim or Sikh schools, or through the effects of racism in mainstream schools. Sewell (1998) found that black identities were reinforced as young black students coped with racist teacher stereotypes of 'black machismo' by forming peer group-related black school subcultures – an example of how both the experience of education and the peer group can reinforce ethnic identities.

Sewell (1996) found many aspects of the macho black identity of young African Caribbeans were derived from the mass media. The global media, through satellite TV, DVDs and the internet, also enable minority ethnic communities to draw on the cultures in their countries of origin. Bhangra music and Bollywood films (Bollywood is the name given to the Mumbai-based Hindi-language film industry in India) in South Asian communities might be an example.

Religion is often an important socializing agent in minority ethnic communities, and, as Jacobson (1998) found, Islam, particularly, has become of growing significance as a source of identity among some young British Pakistani Asians, partly as a response to the social exclusion, racism and lack of opportunity they encounter in British society.

Sources of ethnic identity drawn on during the socialization process might include values, beliefs, traditions, geographical and cultural origins, a shared history, language, music, diet, dress, religious ideas, and experiences of racism and discrimination. These shape ethnic identities, give them meaning and provide a sense of self-identity, of cultural distinctiveness and of belonging with others like themselves.

Ethnicity is just one identity, and individuals can adopt more than one identity depending on the social context in which they find themselves. For example, British Asians may have multiple identities, adopting an Asian identity at home, what Fanon (2008 [1952]) (see also Johal (1998) considered below) called a '**white mask**' identity (see margin box and box below) at school or in other situations, and another identity as very fashionable, with designer gear and awesome musical tastes and so on, in their leisure and consumption patterns. These multiple identities, sometimes merging into 'hybrid' identities (discussed below) help them to fit into the different communities and social groups in which they find themselves.

> The **white mask** refers to the idea of non-white minority ethnic groups seeking to overcome prejudice and racism and gain acceptance in white society by playing down their own ethnicity and culture, and adopting the features (the 'white mask') of majority white culture.

White Masks

Black Skin, White Masks is a 1952 anti-racist book written by Frantz Fanon, attacking the racist oppression of black people. The book examines the feelings of inadequacy and injustice that black people experience living in a dominant racist white culture. The 'White Masks' refers to the self-identity of black people who as a survival strategy deny their own ethnic origins and culture. Putting on 'white masks' – adopting the culture of the dominant white society in which they live – is an attempt to achieve social acceptance in predominantly white groups and communities. Although originally written about black people, it can apply to any minority ethnic group attempting to survive in the face of discrimination and prejudice.

Activity

1 Suggest and explain, with examples, three ways in each case that (a) the family, (b) religious institutions, (c) the mass media and (d) peer groups might form ethnic identities and pass them on from one generation to the next.
2 Explain what you understand by a 'white mask' identity, and suggest ways that people from minority ethnic groups might adopt such an identity. Why might they do this?

DIASPORA AND GLOBALIZATION

Diaspora is the dispersal of an ethnic population from its original homeland, and its spreading out across the world, while retaining cultural and emotional ties to its area or nation of origin. Diaspora suggests that a dispersed ethnic population adopts two (or more) ethnic identities: it will retain some links to its original culture and heritage, while also adopting elements of the culture of the host societies in which individuals now live, and will manoeuvre between them. An example might be the Sikh community in Britain maintaining close links with family and culture in the Punjab region of India, speaking Punjabi and observing Sikh customs at home, and speaking English and adopting what may be radically different peer-group values and norms at school or college.

Globalization, including the impact of the global mass media and popular culture, also means that cultures may be beginning to lose their separate identities. With diasporas and globalization, different cultures interact, and new cultural and ethnic **hybrid identities** emerge, formed from a mix of other identities. For example, the diaspora created by the centuries of slavery, and the mass emigration in the 1950s and 1960s from the Caribbean and the Indian subcontinent, means that black and Asian populations are now dispersed around the globe, and in Britain new ethnic identities like British Asian, Brasian, black British and Muslim British have emerged.

As discussed above, some minority ethnic people may adopt a 'white mask' as part of their hybrid identity, as a means of 'fitting in' in social situations and gaining acceptance in groups and communities which they might otherwise find difficult to achieve.

> **Diaspora** is the dispersal of an ethnic population from its original homeland, and its spreading out across the world, while retaining cultural and emotional ties to its area or nation of origin.

> A **hybrid identity** is a new identity formed from a mix of two or more other identities.

In what ways does this picture suggest a hybrid identity? What other hybrid identities are you aware of?

CHANGING ETHNIC IDENTITIES: NEW ETHNICITIES AND HYBRID ETHNIC IDENTITIES

Hall (1992) suggests that ethnic identities are becoming harder to identify, with globalization and diasporas merging cultures and creating 'new ethnicities'. For example, African Caribbean music and dress are now popular among Punjabi and Bengali males, minority ethnic cultures are becoming integrated into mainstream culture, such as in reggae, hip hop and rap music, as well as in dress and diets. Burdsey (2004) found evidence of the consumption of designer clothes, recreational drugs and other leisure activities among young British Asians that was previously associated with young white and black males.

People of all ethnic groups are drawing on a range of cultures to create either new hybrid ethnic identities (this is called 'hybridization'), or multiple identities. Ethnic identity is also becoming more confused by new, predominantly British-born, ethnic minorities, with more children born to parents of inter-ethnic partnerships, involving a fusion of two ethnic groups. Bradford (2006) showed that the Mixed ethnic group in the United Kingdom included children of white and black Caribbean parents, white and Asian parents, and white and black African parents, as well as a number of other mixed identities. The majority of people who had a Mixed ethnic identity had a white parent and were born in Britain. For such groups, it is difficult to establish whether they identify themselves as having a white ethnic identity drawn from one parent, an identity arising from the ethnic minority group of the other parent, or a new hybrid identity drawing on both parental ethnic groups.

ETHNICITY AS RESISTANCE

Ethnicity as an identity has often been asserted as a way of resisting racism and disadvantage, especially among African-Caribbean youth, as Sewell (1996) found in anti-school male black subcultures as a response to racism at school, and among younger South Asians. By asserting an ethnic identity and drawing on the strengths of their cultures, they can resist their denial of status and the devaluing of their own culture by racism. They may seek to reclaim their identity through, for example, embracing Rastafarianism (among black youth), or Islam (as Jacobson found among young British Pakistanis) or other aspects derived from their cultures of origin.

ETHNIC IDENTITIES IN BRITAIN

What follows below are brief profiles of some of the main ethnic identities in Britain today. Britain is a multicultural society, with a wide diversity of ethnic groups, and, as Trevor Phillips (2007), Chair of the Equality and Human Rights Commission (EHRC), pointed out: 'There are more and more different kinds of people rubbing up against each other than at any time in human history.'

Some minority ethnic groups have fairly distinctive cultures, with relatively clear customs and values to draw on in constructing their ethnic identities, like the Indian Asian community. Others have more hybrid identities drawing on a range of cultures, as discussed above. Minority ethnic groups in Britain are, however, limited in their attempts to establish the identity they might want, as they may face racist stereotypes fuelled by labelling by teachers, an **ethnocentric** school curriculum, negative reporting by the media, unfair treatment by the police and the refusal of some white British people to regard them as British at all, or to see them only in terms of their ethnicity (whether they want to be seen that way or not).

Ethnocentrism is a view of the world in which other cultures are seen through the eyes of one's own culture, with a devaluing of the others.

White identities

The identities of white British people in Britain are largely taken for granted, as much of British society and the main agencies of socialization promote and favour white people and their culture. White British people do not generally need to assert their identities as they have the power in society that minority ethnic groups lack, and do not face the racism, discrimination and devaluing of their culture that minority ethnic groups experience. The assertion of a White British identity is also associated with racism, and the sense that white people are superior to other ethnic groups. This is promoted by right-wing groups like the British National Party, which seek aggressively to promote a British and white identity based on a 'pure white Britishness' that has probably never really existed, but which excludes other ethnic identities. It is also worth pointing out that 'white' is not an ethnic group with a shared culture, history and national identity. There are different cultural traditions and different identities amongst the English, Scottish, Irish, Welsh and Polish communities in Britain, for example. Some white minority ethnic groups may also face discrimination and disadvantage. In the past, the Irish in Britain suffered a lot of racism, and today recent immigrants from the European Union countries of Eastern Europe, like Romania and Bulgaria, often encounter racism from White British people.

African-Caribbean identities

Gilroy (1993, 2002) believes there is no single black identity or black culture, but that the historical experience of slavery affects the perceptions of black people, and black identity and culture have roots in the 'Black Atlantic' – a cultural network and source of support to black people, spanning Africa, the Americas, the Caribbean and Britain, reflecting the diaspora of slavery and its legacy. For second-generation younger African Caribbeans, who were born in Britain, certain styles of dress and tastes in music, like hip hop and reggae, the use of the patois dialect, dreadlocks and a sense of pride in their black skin as a form of resistance to racism all help to establish a distinctive black identity. This may be reinforced by distinctive black subcultures, like Rastafarianism, or the anti-school subculture discussed in research by Fuller (1980) among African-Caribbean girls in a London comprehensive school. Fuller saw this black anti-school subculture as a means for the girls to resist and overcome negative stereotyping by teachers.

Asian identities

It is simplistic to talk of an 'Asian identity', as there is a diversity of different Asian groups, with important differences between them. Modood et al. (1994) carried out a study using interviews and group discussions to explore what ethnic identity meant to people of Caribbean or South Asian origin. The authors suggest that the identity of the various Asian groups is defined in terms of their different cultures, languages and religions. In Britain, the largest Asian groups include Indian Asians, Bangladeshis and Pakistanis. Extended families and **arranged marriages** are common to all these groups, as well as enjoyment of Bollywood films and Bhangra music and dance.

However, there are differences between these groups. They speak different languages (Punjabi, Hindi, Gujarati, Urdu), often have different forms of dress (such as turbans for men and veils for women), have different diets (Hindus and Sikhs eat no beef, Muslims eat halal food – food that is permissible according to Islamic law, with no pork or alcohol), have different religions (Hinduism, Sikhism, Islam, Buddhism and, occasionally, Christianity) and religious institutions (mosques and temples), and celebrate different festivals (such as Ramadan (a month of fasting) and Eid to celebrate the end of

An **arranged marriage** is one which is arranged by the parents of the marriage partners, with a view to compatibility of background and status. More a union between two families than between two people, and romantic love between the marriage partners is not necessarily present.

Bhangra music and Bollywood films are important aspects of Asian ethnic identity. RSVP (left) is a popular Bhangra band (www.rsvpmusic.co.uk) and *3 Idiots* (the film still on the right) is one of the highest-grossing Bollywood films of all time

Ramadam for Muslims, Divali for Hindus and Sikhs, and Versaiki (celebrating the birth of Gurus, or 'teachers') for Sikhs).

Religion is particularly important in the different Asian groups, and religious institutions frequently provide a focus for community life as well as religious belief. Of particular significance here is the worldwide growth of Islam, and their religion is an important part of the identity of British Muslims. As Jacobson found, for many young Pakistani Muslims, Islam and its symbols and values have become central features in building a positive identity which they see as otherwise denied to them by a white, racist, **Islamophobic** British culture. This is discussed below.

Those wishing to assert their ethnicity as their main source of identity are likely to emphasize aspects of their minority ethnic cultures in their 'impression management' to others. This was illustrated by Mirza et al. (2007), when they suggested the growing popularity for wearing of the hijab (headscarf) by Muslim girls was not due to family or religious pressure or about preserving a cultural tradition, but mostly influenced by 'peer behaviour or pressure and a sense that the headscarf marks out one's identity as a Muslim. This is a statement of difference, perhaps more than a desire to be religious.' The hijab is essentially a statement of identity: 'This is who I am, these are my values, and this is the group I identify with.' On the other hand, Giddens (2005) shows how such symbols of ethnic identity as the hijab can have a diversity of meanings, with some feminists seeing it as liberating women from the traditional male sexual gaze, while others see it as a symbol of the oppression of women; some women wear it as a fashion statement along with Western-style dress, while others do see it, as Mirza et al. suggest, as a marker of their ethnic and religious identity.

Islamophobia is an irrational fear and/or hatred of or aversion to Islam, Muslims or Islamic culture.

Mirza et al suggest that the growing popularity for wearing the hijab (headscarf) by Muslim girls is not driven by religious pressure, but by peer pressure, and is essentially a means of marking out the group they identify with

Changing Asian identities   Among the younger Asian generations, Johal (1998) suggests there is evidence of the emergence of two new ethnic identities – British Asians and 'Brasians'. British Asians have two identities – the Asian one they inherit through socialization from their family and ethnic group, and the British one they learn through the agencies of secondary socialization and living daily life in British society. Johal argues British Asians adopt whichever identity is appropriate for the context in which they find themselves, switching between the Asian identity at home and in their ethnic community they have inherited through family and community socialization, and adopting a 'white mask' – the white British culture they have learnt through the agencies of secondary socialization – when encountering and interacting with white culture, such as at school, college or work.

Johal uses the term 'Brasians' (derived from both 'British' and 'Asian') to describe a single new hybrid identity drawing on and fusing or blending both British and Asian cultures. This entails elements of both cultures, but with a strong dimension of personal choice, and picking 'n' mixing between them to forge a new identity. For example, the religious beliefs of Brasians might be important to them, but they might expect to marry whomsoever they wish, rather than have an arranged marriage or a partner from the same ethnic or religious group, and they may not necessarily follow traditional customs, such as constraints over diet, drinking alcohol or dress. Butler's (1995) interviews with 18- to 30-year-old Muslim women in Bradford and Coventry showed that while the family and religion remained important in shaping the identities of young Muslim women, these women were also attempting to mould a new identity with more independence. They were seeking the same opportunities in terms of education and careers and the same legal equality as white British women, and challenging some of the restrictions that traditional Asian Muslim culture imposed on them, while still having some attachment to the values of their culture.

Activity

1 Those wishing to assert their ethnicity as their main source of identity are likely to emphasize aspects of their ethnic cultures in their 'impression management' to others. With reference to the pictures opposite, identify five 'symbols' that people might use to project their ethnic identity to others, and explain briefly how they do this.
2 Identify three cultural features associated with the identities of three different minority ethnic groups in Britain, and three with the ethnic majority group (White British).
3 To what extent do you think there are new hybrid ethnic identities emerging in modern Britain? Give examples.

'Muslim' – a stigmatized identity?   Since the later years of the twentieth century, there has been a huge international surge in Islam, particularly Islamic **fundamentalism**. Islamic fundamentalism has become associated with the removal of Western, particularly American, 'decadent' cultural influences, changes in the position of women (such as the wearing of veils, being confined mainly to the home, being banned from driving and going out in public unaccompanied, and being refused access to some education and occupations) and the establishment of Islamic law involving legal punishments which to most Western eyes are barbaric, such as public flogging, the amputation of the hands of persistent thieves, and death by stoning or beheading. The atrocities of the Taliban regime in Afghanistan in the 1990s, the worldwide terrorist network of Al-Qaeda, which was responsible for the bombing of the Twin Towers in New York in 2001

Fundamentalism is a return to the literal meaning of religious texts and associated behaviour.

and behind the London bombings in July 2005, and the media reporting of the activities of a tiny minority of Muslims in Britain have all formed the basis for the stereotyping of all Muslims in the popular imagination. As a result, the identity 'Muslim' has practically become a stigmatized identity, which brings with it harassment and fear for many Muslims who have little sympathy with Islamic fundamentalism, much less terrorism of any kind. Baroness Warsi in 2011, then Co-Chair of the Conservative Party and Cabinet Minister, complained of 'fashionable Islamophobia', and suggested prejudice against Muslims was now seen as normal. She said anti-Muslim hatred in Britain did not attract the social stigma attached to prejudice against other religious and ethnic groups, and had passed what she called 'the dinner-table test' – where it had become acceptable to talk about Muslims in a prejudiced, bigoted way. As Phillips pointed out, the balance of media reporting of Muslims in the 2000s was such 'that the very word "Muslim" is conjuring up images of terrorism and extremist preachers, rather than Mrs Ahmed down the road, who might be the mother of your son's best friend'.

Research among Muslims living in Britain suggests that 'Mrs Ahmed down the road' is in fact far more typical than the media might suggest: according to a 2005 Mori poll conducted for the *Sun* newspaper, 86 per cent felt strongly that they belonged to Britain, and felt part of British society. Mirza et al. (2007) found:

- 59 per cent of Muslims preferred to live under British law, compared to 28 per cent who would prefer to live under sharia (Muslim) law.
- 59 per cent felt they had as much, if not more, in common with non-Muslims in Britain as with Muslims abroad.
- 84 per cent believed they had been treated fairly in British society.

- the majority of British Muslims were moderates who accepted the norms of Western democracy.

This research suggests that the stigmatizing stereotyping of Muslims by non-Muslims may be wholly unjustified, and may actually generate resentment among them because of the way in which they and their beliefs are treated.

Activity

1 Explain what is meant by diaspora, and why this might lead to the emergence of hybrid ethnic identities.
2 What tensions do you think there might be for young people from minority ethnic or mixed ethnic backgrounds seeking to establish their identities in a predominantly white culture?
3 Suggest reasons why asserting an ethnic identity might help people from minority ethnic backgrounds resist the effects of racism.
4 Explain what is meant by a 'stigmatized identity'.
5 To what extent do you agree with the suggestion that a Muslim identity may have become a stigmatized identity in contemporary Britain? Give reasons for your answer.

Nationality and identity

WHAT IS NATIONALITY?

A **nation** may or may not be a **nation-state**. Most of those living within a nation-state will have citizenship, which gives people their legal **nationality**. Nationality usually involves the rights and responsibilities attached to being a citizen, with rights such as being able to access government services like healthcare and education, having a passport and the right of residence, and responsibilities such as obeying the law and paying taxes. Nationality is most commonly based on place of birth or marriage, but can also be achieved by naturalization, whereby people choose their nationality after meeting legal requirements.

Hall (1992) suggests that every nation has a collection of stories, images and symbols about its shared experiences, which people draw on to construct and express their national identity. Examples might include a flag, a national anthem, festivals, national heroes and stories, national sports teams, national drinks or foods (in Britain, perhaps tea and fish and chips?), national dress or music.

A national identity is formed by the agencies of socialization, through which it is passed on from one generation to the next. For example, the education system tends to promote national identity, through teaching citizenship, language, literature and history, and understanding and respect for national values. It is through the agencies of socialization that people learn a common language, which is an important aspect of a national identity, and the mass media generally promote a national identity by giving higher priority to national over foreign news, and celebrating national sporting events, like national football matches. National identity is reinforced through rituals and ceremonies, such as the State Opening of Parliament, Royal events like weddings and funerals, and Bonfire Night on 5 November (in Britain), Burns Night (in Scotland) and 'National days' like the Fourth of July celebrations (United States), Bastille Day (France) and St Patrick's Day (Ireland)

A **nation** is a particular geographical area with which a group of people identify, to which they share among themselves a sense of belonging based on a common sense of culture, history and usually language.
A **nation-state** is a nation which has its own independent government controlling a geographical area.
Nationality is having citizenship of a nation-state, including things like voting rights, a passport, and the right of residence.

A national identity is often promoted and maintained by attracting tourists to historic sites, like those shown here: the Eiffel Tower in Paris, the Colosseum in Rome, the Acropolis in Athens, the guards at Buckingham Palace in London, and the Statue of Liberty in New York. Try to think yourself of some tourist sites which are also symbols of national identity, in both Britain and across the world

Palmer (1999) discusses how a national identity is promoted and maintained by heritage tourism, using the historic symbols of the nation as a means of attracting tourists. For example, she suggests symbols like Edinburgh Castle, Buckingham Palace and the Tower of London, and the Eiffel Tower in Paris, are presented as symbols to encourage tourists to celebrate and share Scottish, British and French identities. In Britain, all manner of castles, palaces, stately homes, museums, heritage centres and picturesque villages are used to promote a distinctive sense of national identity to tourists, and also build this identity for residents.

NATIONALITY AS A SOURCE OF IDENTITY

Generally, having a particular nationality involves a national identity. National identity usually involves a sense of belonging to a nation-state and sharing things in common with others of the same nationality, and a consciousness of differences from those of other nationalities.

National identity and **nationalism** are usually linked to nationality and membership of a nation-state, but this is not necessarily the case. For example, the British nation-state includes the nations of England, Scotland, Wales and Northern Ireland, together forming the United Kingdom. Citizens of the United Kingdom all have British nationality, but they do not all have this nationality as their main source of national identity. There is a growing sense of nationalism and national identity within the countries making up the British state, and a declining number of people are identifying themselves as 'British', adopting instead distinct English, Scottish or Welsh identities, or regional identity in Northern Ireland. For example, a 2011 survey by Populus on behalf

Nationalism involves a sense of pride in, and commitment to, a nation, and a very strong sense of national identity.

of the Searchlight Educational Trust identified a resurgence of English identity, with 39 per cent of people in England preferring to call themselves 'English' rather than 'British', with strong support for policies to make it a legal obligation for all public buildings to fly the (English) flag of St George. This growth of national identities *within* the UK has resulted in elected Assemblies for Wales and Northern Ireland, and a Parliament for Scotland. These have further accelerated the growth of nationalism and national identities in these countries. This was shown when the Scottish National Party formed the government with an overall majority in the Scottish Parliament in 2011, fuelling speculation about growing independence for Scotland.

WHAT IS MEANT BY A BRITISH IDENTITY?

Britain is made up of a wide variety of ethnic groups, including the Welsh, Irish, Scottish, English, Poles, Indian-, Bangladeshi- and Pakistani-Asians and African Caribbeans, so it can sometimes be difficult to identify a specific British identity and a British culture, and a national identity shared by all citizens. What is sometimes suggested as making up 'British culture' or a 'British identity' may just be a reflection of the ability of those with power to impose their view of 'Britishness' on the rest of society.

It is relatively easy to describe some British national symbols, like the Queen, the Union Jack flag and the British passport, and some common cultural bonds like the English language (though British minority ethnic groups, including the Welsh, have their own languages too). However, identifying features of 'Britishness' beyond these becomes quite difficult. The 2004 British Social Attitudes survey found that most people now define Britishness as speaking English, holding citizenship and respecting the country's laws and institutions. The 2011 Populus/Searchlight survey (see above) asked what it was that most defined someone as British, and the most popular answer was essentially self-definition – 34 per cent of people thought it meant putting 'being British or English ahead of belonging to a particular ethnic or religious group', while 24 per cent thought it meant being born here.

Surveys have found that many children from all cultural and class backgrounds have no strong sense of a British identity. Former Labour Prime Minister Gordon Brown (in 2007) and Conservative Prime Minister David Cameron (in 2011) both expressed concern about the weakening of a clear collective British identity and sense of national belonging. Brown stressed that the idea of 'Britishness' and 'British values' was not based on ethnicity and race, but on shared values held in common. These included a commitment to liberty for all, a commitment to social responsibility shown by all, and a commitment to fairness to all. Cameron saw commitment to the values of freedom of speech, freedom of worship, democracy, the rule of law, equal rights, regardless of race, sex or sexuality, as defining characteristics of British identity.

However, it is difficult to see these values as being a defining feature of British identity,

Activity

1   Suggest two examples, with explanation, of how each of the following helps to form and promote a British identity that is different from other national identities: (a) the family, (b) the education system, (c) the mass media, (d) religious institutions, (e) sport.
2   The photos opposite show the flags of England, Scotland, Wales, the United Kingdom and the European Union. Carry out a small survey and ask people which flag they most closely identify themselves with, and try to draw up some conclusions about people's national identity.

as they are found in most Western democratic countries. It is equally difficult to identify a history that is shared by all Britons. For example, British history is littered with battles between the English and the Scots and Irish, and the history of the British Empire is not something that black and minority ethnic Britons are likely to want to relate to, with its associations with violent repression, slavery and exploitation of non-white peoples.

The British Home Office has devised a 'Life in the UK Test' for those wishing to apply for British citizenship, which is meant to identify features of 'Britishness' that immigrants should be familiar with. However, it is doubtful whether even most people who were born and bred in Britain would pass the test. The activity below includes some of the sample questions available on the Home Office website.

Activity

1 Suggest *three* ceremonies and *three* symbols which you think show a *British* national identity.

2 The following questions are samples from the UK government's 'Life in the UK Test'. You can read more about this at www.lifeintheuktest.gov.uk. Try to answer the questions, and discuss whether you think they are a fair test of 'Britishness'.

   (a) Where have migrants come from in the past and why?
   (b) Do women have equal rights and has this always been the case?
   (c) Do many children live in single-parent families or stepfamilies? When do children leave home?
   (d) When do children take tests at school? How many go on to higher education?
   (e) What are the minimum ages for buying alcohol and tobacco? What drugs are illegal?
   (f) What is the census and how are census data collected and used?
   (g) How many people belong to an ethnic minority and which are the largest minority groups? Where are there large ethnic communities?
   (h) How many people say they have a religion and how many attend religious services? What are the largest religious groups?
   (i) What is the Church of England and who is its head? What are the main Christian groups?
   (j) Where are Geordie, Cockney and Scouse dialects spoken?
   (k) What and when are the main Christian festivals? What other traditional days are celebrated?
   (l) What are MPs? How often are elections held and who forms the government?
   (m) What is the Queen's official role and what ceremonial duties does she have?
   (n) How are local services managed, governed and paid for?
   (o) What rights do citizens of European Union states have to travel and work?
   (p) What rights and duties do UK citizens have?
   (q) Who has the right to vote and at what age? How and when do you register to vote?

3 Some believe that some members of minority ethnic groups living in the UK and who are British citizens do not mainly identify themselves as British, but identify with the country from which they or their families originally came. The most famous 'test' of this was made by Conservative politician Norman Tebbit in 1990, in what became known as the 'Tebbit test'. Tebbit said: 'A large proportion of Britain's Asian population fail to pass the cricket test. Which side do they cheer for? It's an interesting test. Are you still harking back to where you came from or where you are?' Do you think the Tebbit test is a fair test of British identity?

4 Woodlands Junior School in Kent has a website called 'Project Britain: Your Guide to British Life, Culture and Customs'. You can see this at http://projectbritain.com/. Have a look at this website, and, using this and also using the material in questions 1 and 2 above if you wish, draw up a questionnaire containing ten questions about Britain which you think might find out whether there is such a thing as a British identity. Explain why you think the questions you have drawn up show a British identity.

GLOBALIZATION AND DECLINING NATIONAL IDENTITIES

As discussed earlier, globalization is changing national cultures, and blurring national identities. Hall suggests that one possible consequence of globalization is that national cultures may decline, leading to new **cultures of hybridity** and new hybrid identities. There does seem to be some evidence for this. Decisions and events in one part of the world can now have significant consequences for people across the globe. The mass media now report events across the world almost instantaneously, as well as exposing people to other cultures, including attitudes, values, religious beliefs, fashions and diets. It is no longer easy, for example, to identify a 'British diet', with lattes, curries, samosas, chicken tikka, pasta and pizza, and Chinese, Thai, Italian and Indian foods all now widely eaten in Britain. People travel abroad much more than they used to, and more British people are buying homes in foreign countries. Britain's membership of the European Union means that some decisions affecting British life are now taken in collaboration with other European countries, and the same currency (the euro) is now used across much of Europe. Widespread immigration means there are substantial minority ethnic groups in Britain as well as in many other countries. Individual countries appear to be of declining importance, with national identities becoming diluted. Postmodernists see such changes opening up more opportunities for people to choose from a far wider range of cultures and identities than they had in the past. Consequently, nationality and national cultures may be less significant as a source of identity, and people might see a European or global identity, for example, as more significant than a British or English identity.

On the other hand, while globalization may be undermining traditional conceptions of national identity, Hall recognizes that this, as well as the growth of wider political units like the European Union, can also give rise to nationalism and a reassertion of national identity as a means of opposing the trend. This idea of asserting national identity as a means of opposing changes like globalization and the European Union has been described by Orr (2011) as part of a more general trend towards constructing what she calls *negative identities*, as people rage at anyone seen to be different. This is where people construct and define their identities by who they are *not* – for example, *not* Muslim, *not* a global citizen, *not* European or East European, *not* Scottish or *not* Welsh. In Britain, the appearance in recent years of groups like the British National Party, the UK Independence Party and the English Democrats might all be seen as attempts to reassert national identity, often mixed with racism and hostility to immigration, which is seen as diluting British or English identity. Certainly, in national sporting events, national identities are strongly asserted, with millions of flags of St George sold to English football supporters, and the Welsh and Scottish similarly asserting their national identities.

A **culture of hybridity** is a culture that is a 'mix' of two or more other cultures, creating a new culture (a 'hybrid').

A BRITISH IDENTITY CRISIS?

There does appear to be a growing identity crisis in the UK, and particularly over what is meant by a 'British identity'. This identity is becoming less important to the majority of people, and the survey evidence below suggests that the 'British' identity is fraying, with English, Scottish and Welsh identities replacing it.

- 67 per cent of adults in Wales considered their national identity as wholly or partly Welsh (2001 Labour Force Survey).
- 77 per cent of people in Scotland thought 'Scottish' best described their national identity; 86 per cent thought of themselves as Scottish compared to just 50 per cent who thought of themselves as British (2001 Scottish Social Attitudes survey).

The British Social Attitudes Survey of 2006–7 found:

- 44 per cent of the British public thought 'British' was the best or only way to describe their national identity, and less than half of even those living in England (48 per cent).
- 40 per cent of people living in England identified themselves as primarily or solely English. The only exception to this is among the minority ethnic groups, the majority of whom were more likely to identify themselves as 'British' than as any other national identity, according to the Office for National Statistics.

> **Activity**
>
> 1 Suggest reasons why minority ethnic groups living in Britain might be more likely than any other groups to identity themselves as British rather than English, Scottish or Welsh.
> 2 Identify and explain three reasons why British national identity appears to be in decline.

Disability and identity

THE SOCIAL CONSTRUCTION OF DISABILITY

An **impairment** is some abnormal functioning of the body or mind, either that one is born with or which arises from injury or disease.

Disability is a physical or mental impairment which has a substantial and long-term adverse effect on a person's ability to carry out normal day-to-day activities.

Impairment is some abnormal functioning of the body, which only becomes a **disability** when it prevents people from carrying out normal day-to-day activities. Impairment is therefore not the same as disability. Shakespeare (1998) suggests that disability should be seen as a social construction – a problem created by the attitudes of society and not by the state of our bodies.

Shakespeare argues that disability is created by societies that don't take into account the needs of those who do not meet with that society's ideas of what is 'normal'. The stereotype in any society of a 'normal' or acceptable body may generate a disabled identity among those with bodies that do not conform to this stereotype, particularly those with a physical impairment, even when the impairment does not cause mobility or other physical difficulties for that person. An example of this might be people of very small stature (dwarfs), or with facial disfigurements that cause an adverse reaction among others.

Whether someone is disabled or not is then a social product – it is social attitudes which turn an impairment into a disability, as society discriminates against people with impairments. For example, people parking their cars on pavements make it difficult for those in wheelchairs or the blind to get by; the design of buildings may make access difficult or impossible for those who have lost the use of their lower limbs and need wheelchairs to aid their mobility. People who are short-sighted only become disabled if they have no access to glasses to correct their sight, or if documents are printed in small type or colours which people with visual impairments find hard to read. Workplaces can be disabling if adjustments to the working environment are not made to enable people with impairments to perform their jobs successfully. People with facial disfigurement only become disabled because of the reactions of other people to this deviation from a 'normal' appearance.

As Shakespeare argues, 'people become disabled, not because they have physical or mental impairments, but because they have physical or mental differences from the majority, which challenge traditional ideas of what counts as "normal". Disability is about the relationship between people with an impairment and a society which discriminates against them.'

DISABILITY, SOCIALIZATION AND STEREOTYPING

Most of us learn about disability as part of the socialization process, rather than as a result of personal experience. Popular views of disability, for those without direct experience, are often formed through the mass media. Media images of disability are often linked with socially unacceptable behaviours, or suggest that we have good reasons to fear people with impairments, especially those with mental or behavioural difficulties, or who display violent or inexplicable behaviour.

Stereotypes of disability

Barnes (1992) suggested stereotypes of disability, particularly those generated by the mass media, include ideas that disabled people are:

- dependent on others
- unable to contribute to society
- non-sexual and have no sex life
- unable to express and speak up for themselves
- less than human
- monsters or wicked people, with maladjusted personalities and 'aren't like other people'
- to be made fun of, pitied, or praised for their courage in coping with their disability

Only rarely do the media treat disability as a perfectly normal part of everyday life. Disability therefore becomes an identity marking people out as different from others.

DISABILITY AS A 'MASTER IDENTITY'

A person has multiple identities, and disabled people may not see their impairment as the defining characteristic of their identity – they may regard themselves, and wish others to see them, for example, mainly as black, and/or working class and/or gay, rather than as disabled.

However, many people with impairments may experience difficulty in asserting their own choice of identity in the face of the 'disabled' identity, based on stereotypes, that others seek to impose on them. They may find it hard to make others see the 'real me'

Disability is often seen by the non-disabled as a stigmatized identity – as something to be hidden or ashamed of. This sculpture, formerly on display in Trafalgar Square in London, by Marc Quinn, *Alison Lapper Pregnant*, is of disabled artist Alison Lapper, who was born in 1965 without arms and with shortened legs. As Alison Lapper herself said, 'It is so rare to see disability in everyday life – let alone naked, pregnant and proud. This sculpture makes the ultimate statement about disability – that it can be as beautiful and valid a form of being as any other.'

inside the disabled person. The other dimensions of their identity, in terms of ethnicity, social class, gender, sexuality or lifestyle, for example, may be ignored once the label of 'disabled person' is applied by others. To borrow and adapt the term 'master status' from the sociology of deviance, disability might be regarded as a 'master identity' – an identity that overrides all other aspects of that person's identity, whether they want it to or not.

DISABILITY – A STIGMATIZED OR SPOILED IDENTITY: AN IDENTITY OF EXCLUSION

The label 'disabled' frequently carries with it a stigma arising from stereotyping, which prevents people with impairments from achieving full social acceptance. An impairment may be seen by others as involving total disablement, rather than as just one aspect, and remaining abilities may not be recognized. A person with no legs, for example, can function and think perfectly normally, and it may only be in activities requiring the use of their lower limbs that they experience difficulties. The stigma attached to disability, leading to what Goffman called a stigmatized or spoiled social identity, means it can also become an identity of exclusion, excluding disabled people from full participation in society, as they face, for instance, unnecessary physical barriers in buildings and streets, discrimination in employment, inadequate medical care, negative portrayals in the media, and mocking, patronizing or dismissive attitudes from others. For example, wheelchair users often find that people will look at and talk to the person pushing a wheelchair (if one is present), rather than the disabled person, or patronize the disabled person or speak in a loud voice, giving the impression the disabled person is either deaf or stupid, and that the disability is total. Disabled people may fail at what Goffman called 'impression management', because stereotypes of disability spoil their presentation of self, and the identity they wish to project to others through managing the impressions others have of them.

Activity

1 Suggest three ways that disability may be a stigmatized social identity.
2 Suggest two ways that people with impairments may face difficulties in managing the impressions other people have of them.
3 Explain what is meant by the idea that disability is an 'identity of exclusion'.
4 The six pictures below show people with various impairments. Although you can't know how they identify themselves, try to put them in rank order, 1–6, of those you think most likely to those you think least likely to identify themselves mainly in terms of their disability. Give reasons for your answer, and compare your answers with other people in your class. What does this suggest, if anything, about different views on disability and identity?

  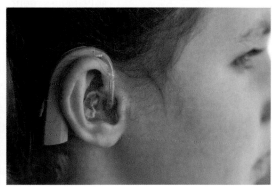

Age and identity

THE SOCIAL CONSTRUCTION OF AGE

How old you are is not simply, or even most importantly, a matter of biological development. There is also a social dimension to ageing, and there are often different norms, values and expectations of behaviour associated with different ages. Age is a social construction, in the sense that the identity and status allocated to people of different biological ages is created by society and social attitudes, and not simply moulded by biology.

There can be wide biological differences between people of the same age, which may impact on how others see and define them, and attitudes to age vary between cultures. In some societies old people have high status as the 'elders' of a community, while in modern Britain older people generally tend to lack status and authority, though this can vary between ethnic groups. In the Asian community, for example, elderly people are still often held in high esteem.

Social attitudes to people of different ages can change over time. Philippe Ariès (1973) showed that in medieval times childhood did not exist as a separate status. Children often moved straight from infancy, when they required constant care, to working roles in the community. Children were seen as 'little adults'. They did not lead separate lives, and dressed like, and mixed with, adults. 'Childhood' was certainly not the specially protected and privileged time of life we associate with children today, with their legal protection, extended education and freedom from work. There is more about childhood on pages 187–98 and you might wish to take a look at this now.

AGE GROUPS AND IDENTITY

The social construction of age means that we tend to think of people in terms of age groups in contemporary British culture, such as 'infancy', 'childhood', 'teenager', 'youth', 'young' and 'mature' adulthood, 'middle age' or 'old age'. The age group to which we belong can have important consequences for identity and status, particularly for the young and the old. For example, our age influences whether we can get employment, or keep employment, go into pubs, clubs and films, and whether it is legally possible to marry or socially acceptable to have sex.

There are often broad cultural stereotypes and assumptions about the lifestyles of some of these age groups, and different norms and expectations of behaviour associated with them, which can help to mould the identities of those in these groups. For example, behaviour considered appropriate for a child might be regarded as very odd in a middle-aged man. These age groups are therefore a form of social identity and may be a source of individual identity as well. In other words, how old you are can have a direct impact on your own sense of identity, how you behave and how others see you. For example, being a 'teenager' involves a frequently difficult period of transition between childhood and adulthood, and the teenage identity may be seen as confusing, troublesome and angst-ridden for the individual, and 'trouble' for others.

Bradley (1995) sees age as an important aspect of identity for individuals. She recognizes that it tends to be a short-lived and changing identity as people spend only a short period in a particular age group (though this may be changing for the retired elderly, with growing life expectancy). The 2010–11 British Social Attitudes report found that age

In what ways might teenagers be regarded as having a stigmatized identity?

was the strongest 'bonding factor' when it came to identity (above factors like social class, gender and ethnicity) with all age groups having a sense of common interest with their own age group, though this was stronger among the young than older age groups. Of those describing themselves as 'young', 66 per cent felt they had more in common with those in the same age group, compared to 53 per cent of those describing themselves as 'older'.

Bradley suggests that age becomes a particularly significant aspect of identity in two main age groups – the young (teenagers and 20-somethings) and older people who are retired from work.

OLDER PEOPLE AND IDENTITY

With greater life expectancy, retired people may be in the 'older' age group for perhaps longer than in any other age group. Retirement brings with it a loss of identity that arises from work, as well as the associated income. Older people today are healthier and more affluent than they have ever been, but there is still widespread poverty among the old, particularly among working-class widowed women and/or those without occupational pension schemes. Even relatively well-off pensioners will face a substantial drop in income compared to those who are working, and this makes it harder for some older people, especially the poor, to establish alternative identities through their leisure and consumption patterns (see Topic 5).

In 2010 nearly one in four people in the UK were aged 60 or over. The 'grey pound' (older people's spending) is very important to businesses and, increasingly, new businesses are opening up that market to older people and are dedicated to their needs, such as SAGA.

Despite being a significant proportion of the population and a major market for business, older people often suffer prejudice and discrimination, with negative stereotyped assumptions that they are less intelligent, forgetful, 'grumpy' and 'moaning', in poor health, incapable and dependent on others and so on – simply because they are old. Older people, particularly, are likely to encounter **ageism**.

Ageism can have detrimental effects on older people, and they may face being called derogatory names and having negative media images ('dirty old man', 'boring old fart', 'grumpy old woman'), being infantilized (treated like infants/children), being denied a sexual identity, facing barriers to proper medical treatment (such as not being referred to a consultant, for being too old) and losing jobs or facing obstacles to getting jobs on the grounds of being too old. Old age might be regarded as an example of a stigmatized identity, which prevents older people from establishing identities other than that of simply being the 'old person' found in negative stereotypes.

> **Ageism** is stereotyping, prejudice and discrimination against individuals or groups on the grounds of their age.

Why is old age in Britain often a stigmatized social identity?

YOUTH AND IDENTITY: YOUTH CULTURE

The identity of young people has often found expression through youth subcultures.

The term 'youth subculture' refers to groups of young people who share some cultural features which are in some ways different (often visibly) from that of the dominant, mainstream culture of society.

The last sixty years or so have seen the appearance of a wide range of youth subcultures in the UK. Teddy Boys, Mods and Rockers, Hippies, Skinheads, Punks, Ravers, Goths and Rastas have all emerged as very distinctive youth identities, with related styles of dress, appearance, language, behaviour and music. These styles act as symbols which distinguish them from the dominant culture and also from other youth subcultures. Hebdige (1979) pointed out youth subcultures often involve **bricolage**, whereby otherwise ordinary, everyday readily available objects are combined to create new styles and identities. For example, punk subculture involved the bricolage of bondage gear, household glue, bin liners, toilet chains, safety pins, body piercing, home-made tattoos, spitting, as well as extraordinary Mohican hairstyles. Other style symbols include the Dr Martens boots, braces and shaved heads of skinheads, and the death-attachment skulls and vampire-inspired black dress, make-up and hair of the Goth subculture.

These symbols draw attention to those wearing them, and may turn youth subcultures into spectacles to be looked at, as well as sometimes expressing active hostility and contempt for the values, dress and fashion codes of the dominant culture.

Sociological approaches to youth subculture

Functionalist approaches Functionalists like Eisenstadt (1956) and Parsons and Bales (1956) suggest youth subcultures emerge as a way of dealing with the **status frustration** that arises during the extended period of transition from childhood to independent adulthood in contemporary Western societies. Economic dependency on parents, often living with them well into their 20s, and extended periods in education mean that many young people find difficulty in establishing a clear independent adult status, and this leads to status frustration. Youth culture enables young people to assert and practise their growing independence and carve out an identity for themselves separate from that established by family, school or work.

Functionalists see the formation of youth subcultures as a fairly normal transitional stage as young people move towards the establishment of an independent adult

> **Bricolage** refers to the use of readily available ordinary objects to create something new. For example, in the study of youth culture, it refers to the use of everyday items like bin liners, safety pins as ear and nose rings, toilet chains, and habits like spitting to create a new distinctive punk identity.

> **Status frustration** is a sense of frustration arising in individuals or groups because they are denied status in society.

Young people commonly establish their identities through youth subcultures. What youth subcultures are around today, and why do you think people identify with them?

identity. Youth culture is seen as a short-lived passing phase, expressed mainly through pleasure-seeking in leisure activities in the company of the peer group. Once the period of status frustration is over and a clear adult identity established, interest in youth culture withers.

The functionalist view outlined above has been criticized for not explaining the wide variety of youth subcultures and youth styles, the class, gender and ethnic differences between them and their occasional dysfunctional aspects, such as their links to racism, sexism, crime, delinquency and anti-social behaviour.

Marxist approaches   While functionalists tended to look at youth culture as a whole, Marxists try to explain the diversity of subcultures and their differences in style in terms of their social class positions. Hall and Jefferson (1976) saw particular youth styles, such as Skinheads, Punks, Teddy Boys and Mods, as subcultures of resistance to the dominant social class and dominant culture and ideology of society. Hebdige (1976), for example, saw the Mod style as a reaction by lower middle-class youth to the tedium of their life and work.

Cohen (1972) saw working-class youth subcultures arising as a means of re-establishing a sense of community and **social cohesion** lost in their parents' culture due to the break-up of traditional working-class communities, through rehousing and high unemployment. This is shown by Clarke et al. (1976) and Hebdige (1979), who saw skinhead style, like Dr Martens workboots, braces and ultra-short shaved skinhead hair styles, as an attempt to re-create the lost traditional working-class community, through an exaggerated emphasis on masculinity, toughness, independence, resistance to authority, and other features of traditional working-class identity. Brake (1985) saw working-class youth subcultures as expressions of hostility and resistance to the dominant culture and social class of a society which had destroyed the traditional working-class life.

Hebdige saw the bricolage of the punk subculture of the late 1970s as a form of resistance to dominant cultural values and norms, which they saw as offensive and ugly. This was achieved by turning existing values on their head. Through deliberately attempting to be shocking, ugly and offensive, by, for example, spitting, swearing, and adopting offensive names, as well as the style bricolage discussed above, punks were expressing their view that the society they lived in was also ugly and offensive.

Marxist theories of youth subcultures have been criticized:

> **Social cohesion** refers to the bonds or 'glue' that bring people together and integrate them into a united society.

- For studying only the 'spectacular' or high-profile white male working-class youth subcultures. They didn't pay much attention to middle-class youth subcultures, minority ethnic youth, girls and the majority of ordinary youth who may not have been involved in subcultures or in non-resisting subcultures.
- By postmodernists (see below) for assuming youth subcultures reflect the influences of social class, and other wider social conditions, and that they are subcultures of resistance against the dominant culture. Bennett (2001) points out that youth subcultures may not have the same meaning to those taking part as Marxist sociologists assume, and it is possible, for example, that young people involved in youth subcultures don't see themselves as resisting anything, and may well be doing it just for fun.
- By Cohen (2002[1972]), from an interactionist perspective, and by Thornton (1995), from a postmodernist perspective. They suggest youth subcultures are not created by factors like social class, gender, ethnicity or neighbourhood, but are largely manufactured by the mass media. Cohen suggests the media, in their search for

exciting headlines, link up unconnected events, styles of dress and behaviour, and label them as 'groups', such as Mods, Rockers, Punks, Skinheads, Goths and Ravers. The people involved then start to see themselves as part of a group with things in common, and a youth subculture that previously didn't exist begins to form. Thornton sees young people developing a sense of identity and of their position in society, and choosing their styles through what they see and hear in the media in a media-saturated society.

Feminist approaches   Feminists have emphasized that many youth culture studies were 'malestream': written by men about male subcultures. Females were either invisible, ignored or only considered as girlfriends tagging along with male members of the subculture. McRobbie (2000), a Marxist feminist, saw many youth subcultures of the 1970s and 1980s, such as the Skinhead and Punk subcultures, as male-dominated patriarchal groups.

Feminists suggested girls were less involved in male-dominated subcultures for three main reasons:

- gender role socialization (discussed earlier)
- stricter control by parents of girls' leisure time
- concerns about their personal safety

Traditionally, girls were consequently more confined to the private space of the home rather than the public space of pubs, clubs and the streets, which are more dominated by males and where the more visible forms of youth culture were expressed.

McRobbie and Garber (1976) found girls' subculture took the form of what they called 'bedroom culture'. This focused on activities like listening to and discussing music, make-up, beauty, fashion, magazines and celebrities, and talking about boys, romance, dance routines, personal issues and so on. Lincoln (2004) found this 'bedroom culture' is still significant in the lives of contemporary teenage girls, though the private space of the bedroom has taken on greater significance for boys too, with internet access and networking sites like Facebook. That these activities take place in the private space of the home does, of course, make it difficult for sociologists to study, and particularly for male sociologists.

Contemporary young women seem to be much more involved in youth subcultures outside the home, which have become less patriarchal, with growing female equality and success in education and employment. Hollands (1995) found girls' roles in youth culture were becoming more similar to those of men, with females going out more frequently, spending a higher percentage of their income on nights out than their male counterparts, and more involved in dance and drug subcultures.

Postmodernist approaches   Postmodernists reject the concept of subculture, and they regard theories of youth culture (like those discussed above) as just **metanarratives** – 'big stories' trying to fit people into the social structural boxes of class, gender or ethnicity. In postmodern society, structural factors such as social class, gender and ethnicity have become less significant as sources of identity and the formation of groups. Culture itself is now so fragmented that it is no longer possible to talk about things like dominant culture, mainstream culture, subcultures or subcultures of resistance, because all culture is now just so many different tastes within a wide range of freely chosen consumer choices.

Young people are now more likely to respond to the uncertainties and insecurities involved in the transition to adulthood in a more individual way, reflecting a consumer

A **metanarrative** (literally, a 'big story') is a broad, all-embracing 'big theory' or explanation for how societies operate.

culture based on individual choice. They will identify with many cultural groups, but these groups will be fluid and changing, temporary and short-lived. Young people will mix 'n' match cultural choices, changing styles and shifting loyalties, picking, choosing and changing identities from the endless range of possibilities open to them in a consumer society presented to them by globalized mass media.

Thornton sees youth subcultures as replaced by media-generated taste-based club and music cultures. Young people, reared on global media, the internet and mobile technology adopt and adapt images and ideas from media-generated globalized culture as sources of multiple identities. They relate less to class, gender or ethnicity as sources of their identity, and more to websites like Facebook, YouTube, and raves, clubs and dance music.

Instead of youth subcultures, Bennett (1999) prefers to describe the cultural activities of the young as **neo-tribalism**. This refers to the idea that youth are no longer forming cohesive and fixed youth subcultures, formed around features like class, gender and ethnicity. They now make consumer choices to identify themselves for short periods with a range of groups (tribes) which they move between. These tribes have very loose and fluid boundaries, an ever-changing floating membership, and they only appear when they come together for particular lifestyle rituals (like clubbing and dancing).

In the individualized, media-saturated, consumer-driven, 'mix and match' postmodern world, where people can, allegedly, be whatever they want to be, nobody knows quite what's happening next in the fluid lives of young people.

Postmodernist approaches to youth, as in most other areas, have been the subject of much discussion. The cultural activities of youth take place in leisure time, and the next topic (Topic 5), examines whether leisure activities are now as free from the influences of factors like social class, gender and ethnicity as postmodernists believe.

> **Neo-tribalism**
> refers to groups with very loose fluid boundaries and an ever-changing floating membership, that only exist when they come together for particular lifestyle rituals (like clubbing and dancing). They are not the cohesive and fixed social groups, with clear identities, styles and lines of division between them, associated with the concept of a subculture.

Activity

1 Suggest **three** ways that the law enforces age-related identities.
2 Explain what is meant by 'ageism', and suggest **three** ways that both older people and younger people experience ageism.
3 Suggest **three** reasons why the peer group might be particularly important in establishing the identities of young people.
4 Suggest reasons why both 'old age' and 'teenager' might be regarded as stigmatized identities.

Exam-style questions

1   Suggest **two** ways that ethnic identities are formed through socialization.
    (4 marks)

2   Suggest **two** differences between working-class and upper-class culture.   *(4 marks)*

3   Explain **two** ways that social class may be of declining significance as a source of
    identity.   *(4 marks)*

4   Suggest **two** reasons why disability may be a stigmatized social identity.   *(4 marks)*

5   Suggest **three** ways in which national identities are formed.   *(6 marks)*

6   Examine sociological contributions to our understanding of youth subcultures.
    (24 marks)

7   Examine the extent to which traditional gender identities are changing in
    contemporary Britain.   *(24 marks)*

8   Examine sociological contributions to our understanding of how identity is formed
    by any two of the following: sexuality, age, ethnicity, social class, nationality.
    (24 marks)

9   Assess the view that social class is no longer a significant factor in shaping social
    identity.   *(24 marks)*

Topic 5

SPECIFICATION AREA

Leisure, consumption and identity

Postmodernism and identity

Much of this chapter has suggested that identities are strongly influenced by social position, with factors such as social class and occupation, gender, ethnicity and age providing the basic sources of identity formation and difference from others.

However, postmodernist writers argue that these social factors are no longer significant in forming identities. Lyotard (1984) argues these all-embracing explanations or 'big theories' (like class, gender or ethnicity) for identity – what he calls metanarratives – no longer explain the identities people adopt and the differences between them, and people no longer relate to these metanarratives in forming their identities.

Postmodernists argue that identities are now much more fluid and subject to constant change. Rojek (1995) and Roberts (1978, 1986) believe that what we choose to do in our leisure time, the products we consume and the lifestyles we follow are far more significant in forming our identities today. They suggest that most people now have an almost unlimited free choice of leisure activities and lifestyle, and they can adopt any identity or image they wish.

Bocock (2004) believes that people's consumer choices – their tastes and the type, image and style of the goods they buy – are important aspects in defining their identities and the image and status they wish to project to others. Through their leisure and consumption choices, people are shopping for lifestyles, and in effect buying and creating identities.

Their identities are established through their consumption of the huge diversity of consumer leisure goods and services now on offer, such as music, household decor, holiday destinations or clubs, the type of shops they buy from, the 'labels' they purchase, the type of food and drinks they buy to display in their homes, and the leisure activities they follow.

Holidays, for example, are no longer simply about sun, sea and sand, but about lifestyle identity – showing people how well-off, interesting, successful or imaginative you are. Going llama trekking in the Andes, wine-tasting in Australia, staying in a villa in Tuscany or having winters in Barbados gives a quite different indication to others of who you are than going clubbing in Ibiza or having a week in Blackpool; shopping from the Oxfam shop projects a different image from that of buying your clothes from Gap; bungee-jumping, surfing, white-water rafting or 'extreme' sports suggest a different identity from knitting or being a 'couch potato' television viewer.

Leisure activities are now an important aspect of people's identities

Leisure in postmodernity

In contemporary British society, much leisure has become more privatized and home-centred. Entertainment that was once available primarily outside the home, like football, music and films, is now available inside the home, through technology like television, computers and music systems. Postmodernists point to the way the leisure industries have now been transformed to provide a vast range of lifestyle activities that people can buy into to promote their identities. A useful example of this is tourism in contemporary societies, through which individuals seek out means of expressing and developing their taste and identities.

TOURISM IN POSTMODERN SOCIETY

Tourism is now not simply about having a break away from home and work, but offers a variety of opportunities to consume cultural experiences and objects to enhance and explore lifestyles and identity. Heritage centres, theme parks, self-improvement activities (like spas, meditation and crafts), museums and galleries and other tourist attractions and destinations try to attract people by marketing themselves as both popular entertainment and lifestyle choices. Museums and art galleries, once seen as bastions of high culture with exhibitions to be looked at, are increasingly presented as places of fun and entertainment, with activities and interactive things to do. As Urry (1995) suggests, much tourism is now sold on the basis of identity packaging. For example, the countryside is now sold to tourists as enabling them to consume the same locations as literary figures, as in Shakespeare or Brontë country, as well as to buy a whole range of symbols linked to them, like the vast range of Shakespeare paraphernalia on sale in 'Shakespeare country'.

The 'tourist gaze'

Urry (2002) talks of the **tourist gaze**, whereby tourists gaze upon or view and consume different objects, scenes, experiences, landscapes or townscapes. These are organized by paid tourism experts to provide pleasurable experiences and spectacles which are out of the ordinary, different from everyday life, and designed to be looked at or gazed upon with interest and curiosity.

The tourist gaze illustrates many aspects of leisure in postmodern societies. For

The **tourist gaze** refers to the viewing and experiencing of objects and locations with curiosity and interest, organized by professional experts to provide pleasurable experiences for tourists that are different from everyday life.

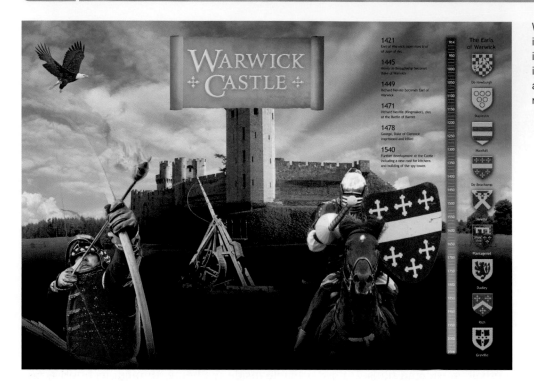

Warwick Castle's attractions illustrate Baudrillard's idea of simulations, where imaginary reconstructions are presented as if they are real

example, heritage tourism, to locations like castles, stately homes, and Shakespeare and Brontë country, appeals to the nostalgia of past times, and encourages tourists to gaze on a once-secure world under threat in the uncertainty of postmodern society.

Postmodern societies are dominated by images, and tourism is no exception. Tourists are not gazing at real things, but imaginary reconstructions and images manufactured to appeal to their imaginations. Baudrillard (2001) refers to such reconstructions as 'simulations', where imaginary things are presented as real. Examples might be the Jorvik Viking Centre in York, where people can travel around and *smell* life in an imaginary reconstructed Viking Britain, or Warwick Castle, where tourists can consume reconstructed history, through a range of themed events and re-enactments, such as the dungeon attraction, where 'gore seekers will be greeted by decaying bodies, chanting monks, torture implements, execution and "the labyrinth of lost souls" – a fantastic scary mirror maze' (from the Warwick Castle website).

Postmodernists see this blend of tourism, entertainment and simulations as providing one way for individuals to consume the cultural symbols that enable them to carve out their identities through leisure in postmodern societies.

THE CREATION OF IDENTITY IN A MEDIA-SATURATED SOCIETY

Strinati (1995) emphasizes the importance and power of the mass media and popular culture in shaping consumer choices. Popular culture, like the culture of celebrity, and media images and messages bombard us daily, through books, magazines, newspapers, TV, radio, advertising and computers, and form our sense of reality and increasingly dominate the way we define ourselves. We live in what Baudrillard called a media-saturated society. In this media-saturated society, the mass media create desires and pressures to consume, and individual identity is no longer formed predominantly by factors such as class, ethnicity or gender, but by information and images gained from the media. In a globalized popular culture, the mass media present to us a massive choice of lifestyles, images and identities drawn from across the world. Bradley (1995) argues that new identities are created by globalization, bringing different cultural groups into contact. People now adopt different identities to meet the diversity in their lives – they no longer identify with class alone, but with ethnicity, gender, disability, race, religion, nationality, music, fashion designer labels, dress, sport and other leisure activities – they can pick 'n' mix to create whatever identities they wish.

Shopping for identities – who do you want to be today?

In today's consumer society, as Miller et al. (1998) point out, shopping has become a major leisure activity in its own right, particularly for women. Featherstone (2007) suggests shopping is not just about buying products, but about buying into lifestyles, giving meaning to people's lives and establishing identities. Even something as basic as the human body can now be 'bought' to establish an identity, with diet products, fitness clubs and equipment, cosmetic surgery, breast implants, body piercing, tattoos, hair extensions and so on encouraging people to shape their bodies in accordance with the image they wish to project of themselves. This idea of people 'buying' an identity, and working on what Giddens called 'projects of the self' is very much in keeping with Giddens's idea of the reflexive self discussed earlier (see page 51).

Bauman and May (2004) suggest that advertising for consumer products like perfumes, alcoholic drinks, cars and clothing is not simply about selling the products, as these goods have symbolic significance – the label, the make of trainer, is more important than the product, the trainer, itself. These products come packaged with an associated lifestyle, as shown in the dress, language, pastimes, home decor and physical appearance of people in advertisements. These provide lifestyle models which people are encouraged to buy into, and from which they can choose to shape their personal identities, and establish their individuality and difference from others. Advertising and shopping provide what Bauman and May call 'do-it-yourself identity kits'. The founder of Revlon, Charles Revson, summed it up neatly when he said: 'In the factory we make cosmetics; in the store we sell hope.'

Shopping for identity

Bauman (1996) argues that life has become a shopping mall, to stroll around consuming whatever you want, trying out and constructing whatever identities you choose, and changing them whenever you want. As Taylor (1999) put it, society is transformed into 'something resembling an endless shopping mall where people now have much greater choice about how they look, what they consume, and what they believe in'. In the postmodern pick 'n' mix consumer society, the influences of class, gender and ethnicity are no longer relevant, and people can become whatever they want to be, adopting lifestyles and identities built around the almost unlimited choice of leisure activities and consumer goods available.

HOW MUCH FREE CHOICE IS THERE IN CHOOSING IDENTITIES AND LIFESTYLE?

The postmodernist view that we now have unrestrained choice in our leisure activities, and that we are completely free to adopt any lifestyle and identity we like through our leisure choices and consumer spending, ignores a range of factors which still have important influences, or constraints, on the consumption patterns, leisure activities and lifestyles we can choose, and the identities we can adopt and project onto others. These are considered below.

Occupation and work experience

Work remains an important element in occupying, directing and structuring the individual's time – the demands of working life involve a high degree of discipline if paid jobs are to be kept. It is, for most people, the single biggest commitment of time in

The work we do has important effects on our status in society, and our leisure activities and consumption patterns

any week, and it is perhaps one of the most important experiences affecting people's entire lives. How money is earned, how much, in what working conditions, the length of working hours and the amount of pension all decide in many ways a person's status and the kind of life they will lead. Work has major effects on the time and money people have to enjoy and spend on the leisure and consumer goods which are an increasingly important source of identity.

Parker (1971, 1976) believes that people's occupations and the way they experience their work, such as the amount of independence and satisfaction they have there, have important influences on their leisure. He suggests that there are three patterns in the link between work and leisure, which he calls the opposition, neutrality and extension patterns. These are shown in table 2.2.

Table 2.2 Patterns of relationship between work and leisure

Work–leisure pattern	Nature of work	Typical occupations	Nature of leisure
Opposition	Physically hard and dangerous male-dominated occupations, hostility to work	Mining, deep-sea fishermen, steelworkers.	Opposition to work. Leisure is a central life interest – a sharp contrast in opposition to work, and an opportunity to escape from the hardships of work.
Neutrality	Boring and routine work, with little job satisfaction, leading to apathy and indifference to work.	Routine clerical workers, assembly-line workers, supermarket staff.	Nothing much to do with work (neutral); leisure for relaxation with home and family, like DIY and going out with the family.
Extension	Work involving high levels of personal commitment, involvement and job satisfaction.	Professionals and managers – doctors, teachers, social workers, business executives.	Because work is so interesting and demanding, leisure is work-related, and there is a blurring of the distinction between work and leisure. Work extends into leisure time, which may be used to improve work performance. For example, business executives playing golf or eating out with clients, teachers using their own time to run school trips/holidays with students, or preparing lessons or developing computer skills at home.

Criticisms of Parker   Parker's emphasis on the way the experience of work influences leisure patterns has been heavily criticized, particularly for putting too much importance on work experience, and not paying enough attention to factors other than work that might shape leisure patterns.

- *Parker over-emphasizes the importance of work in shaping leisure activities.* In the UK in 2012, only about 58 per cent of the population over the age of 16 were in employment, and more than one in four of these (about 27 per cent) was working part-time. Experiences at work therefore cannot explain the leisure activities of substantial sections of the population, including those who are retired, those in full-time education, full-time housewives, others who are economically inactive and the unemployed.
- *Parker over-simplifies the influence of work on leisure,* even for those in full-time paid employment. Roberts (1978, 1986) and Clarke and Critcher (1995) say he doesn't take into account the choices that people can make in leisure activities, and such activities vary among those even in the same occupation.
- *Parker's research is focused primarily on men in full-time paid employment.* Feminist writers like McIntosh (1988) and Deem (1990) say that Parker does not take into account the way gender influences leisure, particularly as many women work only part-time and their leisure is far more influenced by the demands of domestic labour (housework and childcare) and control by men, than by paid employment.

Social class

Scraton and Bramham (1995) argue that the postmodernist view that people have a free choice of leisure and create their own identities through participating in leisure-based consumer activities, like shopping, ignores the fact that such activities are only available to the most well-off members of society. Bauman and May point out that choice takes place within a society in which resources are unequally distributed. This means that for some the opportunity to choose is more real than for others, and most people simply don't have enough money to make free choices. People's choices will also be influenced by the amount of cultural capital they possess (Bourdieu's concept, as discussed earlier in this chapter). Their taste will influence what they choose to buy and the identity they project to others, regardless of how much money they have.

Many leisure activities have become highly commercialized, moneymaking businesses, and some leisure activities are denied to the working class simply because of the high costs involved. For example, the high membership fees of private golf clubs and the expense of activities such as flying and motor-racing effectively prevent the working class, and much of the middle class, from undertaking such activities. For many people, shopping is not about buying identities, but about seeking out the cheapest bargains to stretch limited incomes to feed and clothe themselves and their children. Those in the poorest social classes, who are unemployed or in low-paid work, have few opportunities to establish their personal identities through buying into consumer products and the associated lifestyles. Freedom of consumer choice is limited by social class and the unequal distribution of wealth and income.

Age

Age continues to influence the choice of leisure activities, and identities established through them. The leisure of young single people tends to be spent outside the home in the company of their peer group. They may gain some economic independence from either a wage packet or benefits obtained on training schemes, but lack the financial commitments and responsibilities of household bills, children and the burden of paying rent or a mortgage. This means that young people are more leisure-centred than perhaps any other age group except the retired. They are therefore more likely to have the opportunity of forming their identities through participation in leisure-based consumer lifestyles, expressed through the purchase of clothes and music, and the clubs, pubs and concerts they go to.

The family life cycle

The family life cycle will also influence leisure activities and opportunities. Young couples who set up households together and have children will face more restrictions on their leisure activities, with household costs, mortgages and the costs of children. As children become less dependent on their parents, and as mortgages get paid off, people will have more disposable income to spend on leisure activities and consumer goods. Ill-health as people get older, with reduced income in retirement, may once again limit leisure opportunities.

Gender

Gender has an important influence on the choice of leisure activity. As a result of gender role socialization, men and women show different leisure interests, and some leisure activities are more associated with one sex than the other. Shopping is a good example of this – men tend to view shopping as a chore, a necessary way of obtaining things they need; for women it is more likely to be seen as an enjoyable leisure activity in its own right, concerned with improving their personal appearance and making themselves feel good.

Feminist researchers have shown that women generally have less time and opportunity for leisure activities than men, as they often have responsibility for housework and childcare, and sometimes for dependent elderly relatives or the sick and disabled, on top of paid employment. Women also earn less than men, which further restricts their opportunity to participate in commercial leisure activities.

Research by Deem (1986) in Milton Keynes found that women's leisure activities were often combined with aspects of childcare, such as driving the children to leisure centres and going swimming with them. This does raise questions of how far such activities are really freely chosen and enjoyable leisure activities, rather than aspects of unpaid domestic labour.

Deem's research in Milton Keynes, and Green, Hebron and Woodward's (1990) research in Sheffield, found that patriarchy and patriarchal control (dominance

A night out with the girls – but patriarchal control and the demands of family life often mean that women have more restricted leisure opportunities than their male partners, particularly for those independent leisure activities that might bring them into contact with other men

and control by men) restricted women's leisure opportunities to 'approved' activities. Male partners often felt threatened by women's independent participation in leisure activities that might bring them into social contact with other men. Activities like clubbing and pubs in a 'night out with the girls' are often not approved of by men.

Patriarchy also restricts women's independence and choice in leisure activities, through the harassment that women may face in public places, such as getting 'chatted up' if they go into pubs, clubs or leisure centres on their own, or the risks they face in walking home alone at night. It seems then that gender still remains a very important aspect in leisure choices and identity formation.

Activity

1 Identify and explain two ways that the leisure activities of males and females differ.
2 The evidence suggests women have less leisure time and opportunities than men. What effects do you think this might have on women forming individual identities and lifestyles?

Ethnicity

Ethnicity has important influences on leisure activities, and people will often make cultural choices of leisure activity in accordance with the ethnic group to which they belong, such as their tastes in food, music and films. Some minority ethnic groups may find their activities restricted by racism.

Asian women are more likely to be restricted to home- and family-based activities because of culturally defined roles. Roberts (1983) found many Asian workers will put in long working hours so they can afford, and have time, to visit kinfolk in their countries of origin.

However, as seen earlier, younger British-born people from minority ethnic groups may be adopting less culturally defined leisure choices and lifestyles, and forming

Apple's iPhone and other Apple products like the iPod Nano and the iPad were 'must have' symbols of identity in the 2000s, which were still selling in their millions at the time of writing (2012), and reaping huge profits for the Apple Corporation, making it one of the richest corporations in the world

identities that are less constrained by the cultural inheritance of their parents' culture. Whether this reflects everyday life for most people is questionable, and may not be true of everyday life for ethnic minorities who value traditional culture.

The pursuit of profit

Marxist writers like Clarke and Critcher (1995) point out that leisure has become a highly organized and commercialized multinational industry, employing millions of people worldwide, and concerned with making profits. Sport, for example, is a huge international and highly profitable business, with merchandising of goods, and global TV and satellite deals worth millions of pounds. Tourism, together with the associated airline and hotel chains, is a major global industry. Clarke and Critcher argue that large corporations shape and manipulate people's choices of leisure activities, consumer goods and shopping habits. Global marketing of consumer goods through advertising in a media-saturated society creates endless demand for new 'must have' products and services. Rather than having free choices of leisure activities and consumer goods, advertising aims to convince people that their sense of self – their very identity – depends on buying into the very latest and ever-changing lifestyle trends, to the benefit of the large businesses making the products required to establish those identities.

CONCLUSION ON LEISURE, CONSUMPTION AND IDENTITY

The preceding section outlines a range of factors which suggest that the postmodernist idea that people can now pick 'n' mix any identities they wish, through free choices of leisure activities and consumer goods, is somewhat exaggerated. Jenkins (1996) believes that identity remains rooted in social experience and membership of social groups, and is not something that can be changed at will. Bradley (1995) argues that social inequalities remain important, though these no longer shape identities as strongly as they once did. She accepts there is more fluidity and choice now, and that people are less likely to have a single identity, like social class, gender or ethnicity, that overarches all others. She suggests that, while there is some choice over identity, and people have become more aware of the multiple sources of identity open to them, there are still constraints on this choice.

Activity

Working in a group, discuss answers to the following questions:
1 What are the 'must have' products which you would like to own, and why?
2 To what extent do you think owning these products is important in the way others see you?
3 Explain briefly what is meant by 'leisure has become a commercialized activity'.

4 Do you think you are manipulated by advertising into buying leisure goods and services, and taking part in some leisure activities rather than others?

5 Identify and explain three factors that may limit an individual's ability to have a free choice of leisure activity.

Exam-style questions

1 Explain what is meant by a 'media-saturated' society. *(2 marks)*

2 Suggest **two** ways that leisure is changing in contemporary societies. *(4 marks)*

3 Suggest **two** differences between the leisure patterns of men and women. *(4 marks)*

4 Explain what is meant by pick 'n' mix identities. *(4 marks)*

5 Suggest **three** ways in which a person's identity may be formed by their consumer spending and lifestyle choices. *(6 marks)*

6 Suggest **three** ways in which social class and occupation may influence people's choice of leisure activities. *(6 marks)*

7 Assess the postmodernist view that identity is now almost exclusively established through consumption and lifestyle choices. *(24 marks)*

8 Examine the view that a person's social position (such as their social class, gender, ethnicity or age) is still the main influence on their leisure patterns and identity. *(24 marks)*

CHAPTER SUMMARY AND REVISION CHECKLIST

After studying this chapter, you should be able to:

- explain, with examples, the meaning of culture; dominant culture; subculture; subculture of resistance; folk culture; high culture; mass, popular and low culture; global culture; and the differences between them, and suggest ways the distinction between high culture and mass culture might be disappearing.

- explain, with examples, what is meant by identity, individual identity, social identity, collective identity, multiple identities, hybrid identities and stigmatized or spoiled identities, and how identity is established by the agencies of socialization.

- explain the importance of the process of socialization in the formation and transmission between generations of culture and identity, and the structural and social action theoretical approaches to the role of socialization in the formation of culture and identity.

- explain what is meant by the 'looking-glass self', the 'reflexive self' and 'impression management'.

- explain what is meant by the social construction of identities.

- explain the meaning and importance of social class, gender, sexuality, ethnicity, nationality, disability and age as sources of identity.

- examine postmodernist approaches to identity, including how identities are formed through consumer, leisure and lifestyle choices, and the extent to which people now have a free choice in the identities they adopt and are less constrained by traditional sources of identity.

- explain what is meant by a 'media-saturated society' and how this might affect people's choice of identity.

- examine the factors that influence and restrict people's choice of leisure activities, including occupation and work experience, social class, age, family life cycle, gender, ethnicity, and businesses' search for profits.

- examine the extent to which people's identities today are formed by their social position, drawing on all the material in this chapter.

KEY TERMS

(these are already defined in the text, and may also be found in the glossary at the end of the book)

ageism	gender identity	low culture	secondary socialization
arranged marriage	gender role	male gaze	sex
bisexuality	global culture	mass culture	sexual orientation
bricolage	globalization	metanarrative	sexuality
cultural capital	habitus	minority ethnic group	social cohesion
culture of hybridity	hegemonic identity	nation	social construction
diaspora	heterosexuality	nationalism	status frustration
disability	hidden curriculum	nationality	stereotype
dominant culture	high culture	nation-state	stigma
elite	homophobia	neo-tribalism	stigmatized identity
ethnicity	homosexuality	peer group	subculture
ethnocentrism	hybrid identity	popular culture	subculture of resistance
folk culture	impairment	primary socialization	tourist gaze
fundamentalism	impression management	reflexive self	white mask
gender	Islamophobia	resocialization	

There are a variety of free tests and other activities that can be used to assess your learning at

www.politybooks.com/browne

EXAM QUESTION

SECTION A: CULTURE AND IDENTITY

Time allowed: 1 hour   **Total for this section: 60 marks**

Read Items **1A** and **1B** below and answer parts $\boxed{0}\,\boxed{1}$ to $\boxed{0}\,\boxed{5}$ that follow.

Item 1A

Postmodernists suggest that mass markets and consumption now make the distinction between high and popular culture meaningless. There is now a huge range of media and cultural products available to all. Mass communication technology like the internet, music downloads, cable, satellite and digital television, film and radio, printing for both mass production and personal use in the home, the global reach of modern mass media technology, the mass production of goods on 5 a world scale, and easier international transportation, make all forms of culture freely available to everyone.

Item 1B

Identity is socially constructed. This means it is something created by the socialization process, and the individual and social interpretations and actions of people. It is not something that is given by biology or nature. For example, being black or white, or male or female, only have significance in society because people attach some importance to these characteristics, and define people in terms of these categories. Through learning their culture, and through their involvement 5 with other individuals, social groups and subcultures, people come to develop ideas about what makes them similar to, or different from, others, and their identities are formed. The socialization process transmits both culture and identities from one generation to the next. 10

$\boxed{0}\,\boxed{1}$ Explain **two** ways in which high culture differs from popular culture (**Item 1A**, line 2).
                                            (4 marks)

$\boxed{0}\,\boxed{2}$ Suggest **two** ways in which 'mass markets and consumption now make the distinction between high and popular culture meaningless' (**Item 1A**, lines 1–2).   *(4 marks)*

$\boxed{0}\,\boxed{3}$ Suggest **two** ways in which there may be a 'crisis of masculinity' in contemporary Britain.
                                            (4 marks)

$\boxed{0}\,\boxed{4}$ Examine sociological explanations for the formation of identities.   *(24 marks)*

$\boxed{0}\,\boxed{5}$ Using material from **Item 1B** and elsewhere, assess the view that **either** ethnicity **or** gender are no longer significant sources of identity in contemporary Britain.   *(24 marks)*

Families and Households

Contents

CHAPTER 3

Families and Households

SPECIFICATION TOPICS

- **Foundation** Introducing the family: What is the family and a household? Different forms of the family and marriage
- **Topic 1** The relationship of the family to the social structure and social change, with particular reference to the economy and to state policies
- **Topic 2** Changing patterns of marriage, cohabitation, separation, divorce, child-bearing and the life-course, and the diversity of contemporary family and household structures
- **Topic 3** The nature and extent of changes within the family, with reference to gender roles, domestic labour and power relationships
- **Topic 4** The nature of childhood, and changes in the status of children in the family and society
- **Topic 5** Demographic trends in the UK since 1900; reasons for changes in birth rates, death rates and family size

---

A **family** is a social institution consisting of a group of people who are related by kinship ties: relations of blood, marriage/civil partnership or adoption. Cohabiting couples not formally linked by kinship are also often regarded as a family unit.

Kinship refers to relations of blood, marriage / civil partnership or adoption.

Foundation
Introducing the family

What is the family?

A **family** is a group of people who are related by **kinship** ties: relations of blood, marriage / civil partnership or adoption. Cohabitation (living together without the legal bonds of a marriage or civil partnership) is becoming a very common alternative to marriage or a civil partnership, so for couple families, cohabitation ought also to be included as a family relationship. The family unit is one of the most important social institutions, found in some form in nearly all known societies. It is a basic unit of social organization, and plays a key role in socializing children into the culture of their society.

What is a household?

A **household** is either one person living alone or a group of people who live at the same address and share living arrangements. Most families will live in a household, but not all households are families. For example, students sharing a house together make up a household, though they are not a family. Similarly, in pre-industrial Britain, average household sizes were often larger than they are today, but this was generally because they contained domestic servants or other non-family members. Increasingly today, more households are containing people living alone rather than families. In 2011, around one in three households consisted of people living alone.

> A **household** simply means one person living alone or a group of people who live at the same address and share living arrangements.

Different forms of the family and marriage

Even though the family is found in nearly every society, it can take many different forms. Marriage and family life in earlier times in Britain, and today in many other societies, can be organized in quite different ways from family life in modern Britain. Sociologists use a number of different terms to describe the wide varieties of marriage and household type. Table 3.1 below summarizes these varieties.

Table 3.1 Forms of the family, marriage and household

Forms of:	Description
Marriage	
Monogamy	One husband and one wife
	Found in Europe, the USA and most Christian cultures
Serial monogamy	A series of monogamous marriages
	Found in Europe and the USA, where there are high rates of divorce and remarriage
Arranged marriage	Marriages arranged by parents to match their children with partners of a similar background and status
	Found in the Indian sub-continent and Muslim, Sikh and Hindu minority ethnic groups in Britain
Civil partnership	A legal form of marriage for gay and lesbian couples. Civil partnership gives legal recognition to the relationships of same-sex couples, giving civil partners equal treatment to married couples in a wide range of legal matters
Polygamy	Marriage to more than one partner at the same time
	Includes polygyny and polyandry
Polygyny	One husband and two or more wives
	Found in Islamic countries like Egypt and Saudi Arabia
Polyandry	One wife and two or more husbands
	Found in Tibet, among the Todas of southern India, and among the Marquesan Islanders
Family and household structure	
Nuclear family	Two generations: parents and children living in the same household
Extended family	All kin including and beyond the nuclear family

Table 3.1 (continued)

Forms of:	Description
Family and household structure	
Classic extended family	An extended family sharing the same household or living near each other
Modified extended family	An extended family living far apart, but keeping in touch by phone, letters, email, networking websites like Facebook and frequent visits
Beanpole family	A multi-generation extended family, which is long and thin, with few aunts, uncles and cousins, reflecting fewer children being born in each generation, but people living longer
Patriarchal family	Authority held by males
Matriarchal family	Authority held by females
Symmetrical family	Authority and household tasks shared between male and female partners
Reconstituted family or stepfamily or blended family	One or both partners previously married, with children of previous relationships
Lone parent family	Lone parent with dependent children, most commonly after divorce or separation (though may also arise from death of a partner or unwillingness to marry or cohabit)
Gay or lesbian family	Same-sex couple living together with children
Single person household	An individual living alone

Activity

Refer to table 3.1 and:

1　Interview a few people and try to find out what types of family they live in today. Is there any 'typical' family or is there a variety of family types? Write a report or do a presentation on your findings.

2　Fill in the blanks in the following passage. Each dash represents one word.

The ___ ___ means just the parents and children, living together in one household. This is sometimes called the two-generation family, because it contains only the two generations of parents and children. The ___ ___ is a grouping consisting of all kin. The ___ ___ ___ consists of several related nuclear families or family members who live in the same household, street or area and who see one another regularly. The ___ ___ ___ is one where related nuclear families, although they may be living far apart, maintain close relations made possible by modern communications, such as car travel, phone, letters or email. This is probably the most common type of family arrangement in Britain today. The ___ ___ is a form of the extended family in a pattern which is long and thin, reflecting the fact that people are living longer but are having fewer children. The ___ ___ ___ is today largely a result of the rise in the divorce rate, although it may also arise from the death of a partner, the breakdown of cohabiting relationships, or a simple lack of desire to get married. Nine out of ten of these families are headed by women. The ___ ___ is one where one or both partners have been married previously, and they bring with them children of a previous marriage. It remains a popular impression that the most usual kind of family in contemporary Britain is the ___ ___ where both husbands and wives or cohabiting partners are likely to be wage earners, and to share the housework and childcare. However, some argue that men still dominate in the family and make most of the decisions, and it therefore remains ___ . ___ is the only legal form of marriage allowed in Britain. In modern Britain, most of Western Europe and the United States there are high rates of divorce and remarriage, and some people keep marrying and divorcing a series of different partners. The term ___ ___ is sometimes used to describe these marriage patterns. This type of marriage pattern has been described as 'one at a time, one after the other and they don't last long!'. ___ ___ are those where parents organize the marriages of their children to try and ensure a good match with partners of a similar background and status. They are typically found among Muslim, Sikh and Hindu minority ethnic groups. However, this custom is coming under pressure in Britain as younger people demand greater freedom to choose their own marriage partner in the same way as in wider society. While marrying a second partner without divorcing the first is a crime in Britain, in many societies it is perfectly acceptable to have more than one marriage partner at the same time. ___ is a general term used to describe this form of marriage.

The solution to this activity can be found on the teachers' pages of www.politybooks.com/browne.

Is the nuclear family a universal institution?

Functionalist writers like Murdock (1949) suggest that the **nuclear family** is such an important social institution, playing such vital functions in maintaining society, that it is found in some form in every society. In other words, it is a universal institution. However, although most societies in the world have some established arrangements for the production, rearing and socialization of children, this does not mean that these arrangements always or necessarily involve prime responsibility resting on the family or biological parents. The examples below help to illustrate some alternative arrangements which suggest the nuclear family is not always or necessarily the only way of bringing up children.

> The **nuclear family** is a family with two generations, of parents and children, living together in one household.

THE NAYAR

Among the Nayar of south-west India, before the nineteenth century, there was no nuclear family. A woman could have sexual relations with any man she wished (up to a maximum of twelve) and the biological father of children was therefore uncertain. The mother's brother, rather than the biological father, was responsible for looking after the mother and her children. Unlike our society, where in most cases the biological parents marry and/or live together and are responsible for rearing their children, among the Nayar there was no direct link between having sexual relations, child-bearing, child-rearing and cohabitation.

COMMUNES

Communes developed in Western Europe, Britain and the United States in the 1960s, among groups of people wanting to develop alternative lifestyles to those of conventional society because of the political or religious beliefs they held. Communes often try to develop an alternative style of living and a kind of alternative household, with an emphasis on collective living rather than individual family units.

A number of adults and children all aim to live and work together, with children being seen as the responsibility of the group as a whole rather than of natural parents. Many communes tended to be very short-lived, and only a few remain in Britain today.

> **Communes** are self-contained and self-supporting communities.

THE KIBBUTZ

In the early **kibbutzim**, childrearing was separated as much as possible from the marriage relationship, with children kept apart from their natural parents for much of the

> The Israeli **kibbutz** (plural – 'kibbutzim') is a form of commune, and is one of the most famous and successful attempts to establish an alternative to the family. Here, the emphasis is on collective childrearing, with the community as a whole taking over the tasks of the family.

time and brought up in the children's house by metapelets. These were a kind of professional parent, combining the roles of nurse, housemother and educator. The role of the natural parents was extremely limited, and they were only allowed to see their children for short periods each day. The children were seen as the children of the kibbutz – they were the responsibility of the community as a whole, which met all of their needs. Children would move through a series of children's houses with others of the same age group until they reached adulthood.

In recent years, the more traditional family unit has re-emerged in the kibbutzim, with natural parents and children sharing the same accommodation, but the kibbutz remains one of the most important attempts to find an alternative to conventional family structures.

LONE PARENT FAMILIES

The lone parent family is becoming increasingly common in Western societies, and is usually headed by a woman. Lone parents represent a clear alternative to the conventional nuclear family. This is discussed later in this chapter.

GAY AND LESBIAN FAMILIES

Same-sex couples with children are becoming more common, though they are still relatively rare. Most same-sex couples with children tend to be lesbian couples – that is, two women. However, there are more cases emerging of gay (male) couples adopting children or having children through surrogate mothers. A high-profile celebrity example of this was Sir Elton John and his partner David Furnish, who in 2010 become parents to a son born to a surrogate mother in California.

Lesbian wedding party

The Civil Partnership Act of 2004 gave legal recognition to the relationships of same-sex couples who enter a civil partnership, involving similar arrangements to a legal marriage. Entering a civil partnership gives gay and lesbian couples equal treatment to married couples in a wide range of legal matters. Couples who form a civil partnership now have a new legal status of 'civil partner'. You might argue that gay and lesbian couples are families like any other, but they do offer an alternative to more conventional views of the nuclear family.

FOSTER CARE AND CHILDREN'S HOMES

It is worth remembering that a considerable number of children are 'looked after' by local authorities, and brought up by foster parents or in children's homes. This does demonstrate that the link between natural parents and the rearing of children can be, and sometimes is, separated.

Even though the nuclear family is probably one of the main means of bringing up children in the world today, the examples above mean it would be incorrect to assume that the conventional nuclear family is a universal institution. This is particularly the case today, when new forms of relationship are developing, and when the idea of a life-time relationship is increasingly diminishing as more people have a series of partners during their lifetimes, and abandon traditional styles of family living.

Exam-style questions

1   Explain what is meant by the term 'serial monogamy'.   *(2 marks)*

2   Explain what is meant by a 'civil partnership'.   *(2 marks)*

3   Explain the difference between a family and a household.   *(4 marks)*

4   Suggest **three** ways that children may be brought up, other than in families.
    (6 marks)

Topic 1

SPECIFICATION AREA

The relationship of the family to the social structure and social change, with particular reference to the economy and to state policies

Sociological perspectives on the family

What is the role of the family in society? The consensus approach of functionalist writers sees the family as a beneficial institution, contributing to social stability and the creation of a harmonious society, and providing a source of practical and emotional support for individuals. On the other hand, conflict theorists, like Marxist and many feminist writers, tend to see the family as an agency of social control, and emphasize the way the family reproduces social inequality from one generation to the next, such as the inequalities between social classes and between men and women. Marxists see the family as a means of teaching its members to submit to the ideology – values and beliefs – of the wealthy upper class, and not to be critical of the society around them. The family is seen as working to dampen down the inevitable social conflict that is bound to appear in unequal societies.

Feminist writers see the family as a unit based on **patriarchy**, reproducing and supporting a society in which men have most of the power, status and authority.

These competing approaches to the role of the family in society are considered below.

THE FUNCTIONALIST PERSPECTIVE

As we saw in the first chapter, functionalism is a consensus theory that emphasizes integration and harmony between the different parts of society, and the way these parts work together to maintain society. With regard to the family, functionalists see the family as a vital 'organ' in maintaining the 'body' of society, just as the heart is an important organ in maintaining the human body. Functionalists suggest that the family has a number of responsibilities placed upon it – these are the *functions* it performs in society. These functions are primarily concerned with the family's role in the preparation of children to fit into adult society, and with contributing to satisfying the functional prerequisites, or basic needs, which enable society to survive. Functionalists are also interested in how the family fits with other social institutions (like education or work) so that society functions efficiently and harmoniously.

Murdock (1949) argued there are four main functions of the family:

- *sexual* – expressing sexuality in a socially approved context (note the social disapproval attached to, for example, incest, adultery and homosexuality in many societies).
- *reproduction* – the family providing some stability for the reproduction and rearing of children.
- *socialization* – the family is an important unit of **primary socialization**, of children, whereby children learn socially acceptable behaviour and the culture of their

Patriarchy refers to male dominance with men having power and authority.

Primary socialization refers to socialization during the early years of childhood (contrasted with secondary socialization, when other social institutions exert an ever increasing influence on individuals, such as the school, the peer group and the mass media).

society. This helps to build the shared ideas and beliefs (value consensus) which functionalists regard as important to maintaining a stable society.

- *economic* – the family provides food and shelter for family members.

Murdock regards these functions as necessary in any society, and he suggests that the nuclear family is found in every society to carry them out. However, as seen in the previous Foundation section, the nuclear family is not the only form of arrangement possible for carrying out these functions, and other institutions and arrangements can and do take them over.

Parsons was an American functionalist writer who examined family life in the 1950s. He argued that there are two basic functions of the family that are found in every society. These are the primary socialization of children and the stabilization of human personalities.

The primary socialization of children

Parsons (1951) sees primary socialization as involving the learning and internalization of society's culture, such as the language, history and values of a society. He argues that society would cease to exist if the new generation were not socialized into accepting society's basic norms and values. In his view, this socialization in the family is so powerful that society's culture actually becomes part of the individual's personality – people are moulded in terms of the central values of the culture and act in certain ways almost without thinking about it. Parsons therefore argues that families are factories producing human personalities, and only the family can provide the emotional warmth and security to achieve this.

The stabilization of human personalities

In industrial societies, the need for work and money, the lack of power and independence combined with boredom at work, the pressure to achieve success and support the family all threaten to destabilize personalities. Parsons suggests the family helps to stabilize personalities by the **sexual division of labour**, in the family.

In Parsons's view, women have an **expressive role**, in the family, providing warmth, security and emotional support to their children and male partner. The male partner carries out an **instrumental role** as family breadwinner, which leads to stress and anxiety and threatens to destabilize his personality. However, the wife's expressive role relieves this tension by providing love and understanding: the sexual division of labour into expressive and instrumental roles therefore contributes to the stabilization of human personalities.

The fit between the nuclear family and contemporary society

Writers like Parsons, Young and Willmott (1973) and Fletcher (1966) have suggested that the **classic extended family**, has largely disappeared in modern society, and the structurally isolated, **privatized nuclear family**, or some form of **modified extended family**, has emerged as the main family form in contemporary British society.

The privatized nuclear family is a self-contained, self-reliant and home-centred unit, with free time spent doing jobs around the house, and leisure time mainly spent with the family. In this isolated privatized family, family members will often know more, and care more, about the lives of media soap stars, celebrities and computer game heroes than they do about the real people who live in their street. This privatized nuclear family has been called by Parsons the 'structurally isolated' family, since it has also lost many of its functions and links to other social institutions. According to Parsons, this family

The **sexual division of labour** refers to the way jobs are divided into 'men's jobs' and 'women's jobs'.

The **expressive role** is the nurturing, caring and emotional role. The **instrumental role** is the provider/breadwinner role in the family.

In the **classic extended family**, several related nuclear families or family members live in the same house, street or area. It may be horizontally extended, where it contains aunts, uncles, cousins, etc., or vertically extended, where it contains more than two generations. The **privatized nuclear family** is a self-contained, self-reliant and home-centred family unit that is separated and isolated from its extended kin, neighbours and local community life. The **modified extended family** is a family type in which related nuclear families, although living apart geographically, nevertheless maintain regular contact and mutual support through visiting, the phone, email, social networking websites and letters.

Is the nuclear family the typical shape of the contemporary family?

form has emerged because it is well adapted to meet both the needs of modern society and the needs of individuals.

There are six main reasons why there is thought to have been a decline in extended family life, with the isolated nuclear family fitting contemporary society. These are explained below and summarized in figure 3.1.

The need for geographical mobility Contemporary society has a specialized **division of labour**, with a wide range of different occupations with different incomes and lifestyles. This means that the labour force needs to be geographically mobile – to be able to move around the country to areas where their skills are required, to improve their education or gain promotion. This often involves leaving relatives behind, thus weakening and breaking up traditional extended family life. The isolated nuclear family is ideally suited to this requirement because it is small in size and it is not tied down by responsibilities for extended kin who, in earlier times, might have been living with them.

The higher rate of social mobility in contemporary societies Social mobility means that people can move up or down the social scale compared to the family they were born into. Higher levels of social mobility mean that different members of the extended family may find themselves in different jobs, with differences in education, income, lifestyle, opportunities, and attitudes and values between kin. These differences weaken relations between kin, as they have less in common.

The growth in people's wealth and income as society has got richer and the welfare state has developed People are much better-off today, and the welfare state has taken over a number of functions previously performed by the family, such as in education, healthcare and welfare. This has reduced dependence on kin for support in times of distress. This further weakens the extended family.

> The **division of labour** is the division of work or occupations into a large number of specialized jobs or tasks, each of which is carried out by one worker or group of workers.

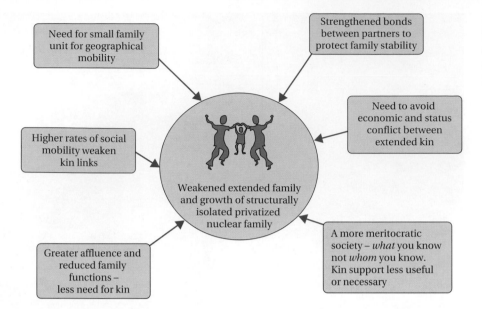

The growth in meritocracy in contemporary societies Contemporary societies require more skills and education for jobs, and are more **meritocratic**, than in the past – it is *what you know*, rather than *who you know*, that is the most important factor in getting jobs. Extended kin therefore have less to offer family members, such as job opportunities, therefore reducing reliance on kin. However, while this is true for most people, kin links remain very important in the upper class, for the inheritance of wealth and for access to the top elite jobs.

The need to avoid the possibility of economic and status differences in an extended family unit causing conflict and family instability The different occupations, incomes, lifestyles and statuses of extended family members who live together might be a source of family conflict and instability, with disputes over where to live when different job opportunities arise, and over different incomes and lifestyles in the same family unit. The fact that adult children generally move away from the family home to establish their own independent lives avoids such potential problems.

The need to protect family stability by strengthening the bonds between married or cohabiting partners There is a lack of support from kin in the isolated nuclear family, and Parsons argues that this helps to cement family relationships by increasing the mutual dependency of partners in a married or cohabiting relationship. This increases the stabilization of adult personalities, which are under particular stress in the face of the impersonal competitive relations of contemporary society as people fight for higher status, more money and promotion at work to support the consumer-led lifestyles of contemporary society. Young and Willmott suggest that rising living standards have made the home a more attractive place to spend time, and family life has become more home-centred. Free time is spent by both partners doing jobs around the home, watching TV and so on, and the family becomes a self-contained and more intimate unit.

The changing functions of the family

Functionalist writers suggest that, in contemporary society, many of the functions once performed by the family in pre-industrial society have been removed from the family. These have been transferred to other more specialized institutions, such as the National

A **meritocracy** (or a meritocratic society) is a society where occupational status is mainly achieved on the basis of talent, skill and educational qualifications, rather than who you know or the family you were born into.

Health Service and the education and welfare systems (see table 3.2 on page 126 for more detail on this). Parsons calls this process **structural differentiation**, He claims this process of structural differentiation has meant the modern, more specialized family has only two basic functions left: the primary socialization of children and the stabilization of adult personalities outlined on page 122.

CRITICISMS AND EVALUATION OF THE FUNCTIONALIST PERSPECTIVE

The criticisms made of the functionalist perspective see it as:

- *Downplaying conflict* Both Murdock and Parsons paint very rosy pictures of family life, presenting it as a harmonious and integrated institution. However, they downplay conflict in the family, particularly the 'darker side' of family life, such as violence against women and child abuse. Children may become emotionally disturbed by conflict between parents, and children may often be used as **scapegoats** by parents.

- *Being out of date.* Parsons's view of the 'instrumental' and 'expressive' roles of men and women is very old-fashioned. It may have held some truth in the 1950s when many married women were full-time housewives, and men the breadwinners in most households. However, this is clearly not the case today, when most married and cohabiting women are wage-earning breadwinners. Nowadays, both partners are likely to be playing expressive and instrumental roles at various times, especially if men are taking on greater responsibilities for childcare, as we are sometimes led to believe.

- *Ignoring the exploitation of women.* Functionalists tend to ignore the way women suffer from the sexual division of labour in the family, with their responsibility for housework and childcare undermining their position in paid employment, for example through restricted working hours because of the need to prepare children's meals, take them to and from school, and look after them when they are ill. Housework also causes stress, leading to mental illness. These concerns are typically raised by feminist writers, discussed below.

- *Ignoring the harmful effects of the family.* Leach (1967) asserts that, in modern society, the nuclear family has become so isolated from kin and the wider community (this is called **privatization**,) that it has become an inward-looking institution that leads to emotional stress. Family members expect and demand too much from one another, and this stress generates conflict within the family. He argues that, 'Far from being the basis of the good society, the family, with its narrow privacy and tawdry secrets, is the source of all our discontents.' Marxists like Laing and Esterson (1970) and Cooper (1972) also argue the family can be a destructive and exploitative institution. They see life in families smothering the development of individuality, leading to unquestioning obedience to authority in later life, and contributing to the mental illness of schizophrenia. Feminist writers are particularly critical of the functionalist view for playing down the 'darker side' of family life, including the domestic violence and child abuse that goes on there. This is discussed in more detail in Topics 3 and 4 (see pages 183–6 and 194–6).

Other criticisms of the functionalist view are considered below.

The case against the functionalist view that the family has lost its functions

Fletcher (1966) denied that the family has lost many of its functions in contemporary society. He suggested that in pre-industrial and early industrial society poverty meant

---

Structural differentiation refers to the way new, more specialized social institutions emerge to take over a range of functions that were once performed by a single institution.

Scapegoats are individuals or groups who get blamed for things that aren't their fault.

Privatization is the process whereby households and families become isolated and separated from the community and from wider kin, with people spending more time together in home-centred activities.

functions such as welfare, education or recreation were often not carried out. Children were frequently neglected, and male peasants often cared more about their animals than about their wives. Fletcher argues that the family now has more, not fewer, responsibilities (functions) placed on it. For example, the health and welfare functions of the family have been strengthened by the welfare state, and parents today are more preoccupied with their children's health, and retain responsibility for diagnosis of minor illness and referral to doctors and other welfare state agencies. Social services departments, with their powers to intervene in families if children are neglected or abused, have increased the responsibilities on parents, not reduced them.

Fletcher says that the family plays an important economic role as a unit of consumption. The modern family is particularly concerned with raising its living standards and keeping up with the neighbours through buying a whole host of goods targeted at family consumers, such as washing machines, home media and broadband packages, music systems, computers and computer games and package holidays. Marxists see this pressure to purchase consumer goods as a means of motivating workers in boring, unfulfilling jobs.

Feminist writers see the modern family as a unit of production, since women's unpaid **domestic labour**, (housework and childcare) produces a wide range of goods and services in the family which would prove very expensive if they were provided and paid for outside the family.

The discussion of what the traditional functions of the family were, how these have changed and the extent to which the family has lost its functions is outlined in table 3.2.

> **Domestic labour**
> is unpaid housework, including cooking, cleaning, childcare and looking after the sick and elderly.

Table 3.2 Traditional functions of the family and how they have changed

Traditional functions of the family	How they have changed
• *Reproduction of the population* – the reproduction and nurturing of children. Having children was often seen as the main reason for marriage, as a means of passing on family property and providing a future workforce.	• In Britain since the 1970s, there has been a steady increase in the reproduction of children and sexual relations before, alongside and outside marriage.
• Before industrialization and the growth of factory production in Britain, the family was a unit of production. This means that the family home was also the workplace, and the family produced most of the goods necessary for its own survival. Children would learn the skills needed for working life from their parents, and the family ascribed the occupational roles and status of adults. In other words, children generally followed in their parents' footsteps.	• Since the early nineteenth century in Britain, work has moved outside the home to factories and offices (with the exception of housework / domestic labour). Families no longer generally produce the goods they need – they go out to work for wages so they can buy them. The skills required for adult working life are no longer learnt in the family but at the place of work, at colleges and universities or on government-supported job training schemes. Occupational roles and status in society are less likely to be ascribed by the kinship network, and more likely to be achieved by individual merit.
• The family and kinship network traditionally played a major role in *maintaining and caring for dependent children* – that is, those who were still unable to look after themselves.	• The modern nuclear family is less dependent on relatives for help and assistance with maintaining and caring for children. State welfare services, like the National Health Service, social services departments, including social workers working with families, and a range of welfare benefits, plus various pre- and after-school clubs, playgroups and nurseries all help parents to maintain their children.
• The family provided most of the *help and care for the young, the old, the sick, and the poor* during periods of illness, unemployment and other crises. Poverty often meant poor health and poor healthcare.	• This has become shared with the welfare state through the NHS and the social services. Homes for the elderly, hospitals, welfare clinics, GPs, old age pensions, unemployment benefit and income support reduce the dependence on kin for money and support.

Table 3.2 (continued)

Traditional functions of the family	How they have changed
• The *primary socialization and social control of children*. The family is where society's new recruits first learn the basic values and norms of the culture of the society they will grow up in. For example, it is in the family that children first learn the difference between what is seen as right and wrong, good and bad behaviour, and the acceptance of parental and other adult authority.	• The family still retains the major responsibility for the socialization and social control of young children, but the increase in the number of children's centres, childminders, pre-schools and playgroups, and free nursery education for 15 hours a week for 3- and 4-year-olds has meant this is no longer restricted to the family. The state educational system now helps the family with the socialization of school-age children, and the mass media also play an important socializing role.
• The family used to be one of the only sources of *education* for young people in Britain. Before compulsory schooling was provided by the state in Britain from 1880, many children from working-class families were very poorly educated by today's standards, and illiteracy rates were extremely high.	• The education of children has been mainly taken over by the state, and is now primarily the responsibility of professional teachers rather than parents. All young people between the ages of 5 and 16 (age 17 from 2013, age 18 from 2015) now have to attend school or college by law. However, the family continues to play an important socializing and supporting role in preparing a child for school, and encouraging and supporting her or him while at school. The family still has a major effect on a child's level of educational achievement.

Activity

1 To what extent do you consider the family has lost its functions? Examine the arguments in table 3.2 and on pages 125–6, weigh up the strengths and weaknesses of each argument and reach a conclusion. (This is evaluation.)

2 Do you think the welfare state has placed more or fewer demands on the family? Give reasons for your answer.

3 Look at TV, newspaper or magazine advertising. Can you find any evidence that the image of family life presented in advertising is used as a way of persuading people to buy consumer goods – for example, by making it appear that buying goods will lead to happier lives, or will make children feel more cared for? If you're in a group, collect or record some adverts and discuss them in your group.

4 Do you have any evidence, from your own experience, of families buying goods to keep up with the neighbours? If so, why do you think they do this?

Has the extended family disappeared?

While the functionalists are broadly correct in their view that the nuclear family fits contemporary society, and it is true that many families with dependent children in Britain today are nuclear families, we must not assume that just because family members may live apart geographically, all links with kin are severed and destroyed. Kin beyond the nuclear family still play an important part in the lives of many families, and it is more realistic to talk of a modified extended family rather than the structurally isolated nuclear family as the most common family form. This modified extended family is one in which related nuclear families, although they may be living far apart geographically, nevertheless maintain regular contact and mutual support made possible by modern communications and easy transportation.

It would also be wrong to suggest that classic extended family life has completely disappeared. It is still to be found in Asian and traditional working-class communities.

Families are changing rapidly, and there is no longer a 'typical' family type. There is a wide diversity (or range) of family structures alongside the isolated nuclear family. The issue of family diversity is discussed later in Topic 2 following this.

Don't forget you can also criticize the functionalist approach by referring to arguments drawn from other perspectives – like the Marxist and feminist approaches discussed below.

THE NEW RIGHT

The New Right supports traditional values and institutions, and its views of the role, importance and functions in society of the traditional family unit are very similar to the functionalist approach discussed above.

New Right theorists see the nuclear family and the kinship network as performing important and beneficial functions in securing social stability, through providing emotional security for children, socializing them into the culture of society, and establishing respect for and conformity to social and moral values and norms. Like the functionalists, they see the traditional heterosexual nuclear family, with two natural parents and a traditional division of gender roles in the family, with men playing the instrumental roles as authority figures and providers, and women playing the expressive roles of providing affection and nurture, as the best means of bringing up children to become conformist, responsible adults. They therefore see it as crucial that the nuclear family should remain the dominant form of the family.

The New Right sees traditional family life as under threat from social changes like the rising divorce rate, more stepfamilies, more lone parents, cohabitation as an alternative to the commitment of marriage, births outside marriage, and gay marriage (civil partnership), and welfare state policies that support relationships outside the conventional nuclear family. They argue these changes undermine social stability, and point to rising lack of respect and anti-social behaviour among the young, lack of discipline in school and educational underachievement, alcohol and drug abuse, crime and dependency on welfare benefits as symptoms of the decline of traditional family life. For example, they argue that working mothers put their own careers above the needs of their children, and they point to the lack of successful male role models for young people in fatherless families, with uncontrollable children the fault of lone mothers who are unable to discipline youngsters (particularly young males) as effectively as if families had fathers.

Murray (1989, 1990) and Marsland (1989) argue that the welfare state has undermined personal responsibility and self-help, and the importance of support from families. They are particularly scathing about welfare support for lone parents, as they argue this encourages single women to have children they could not otherwise afford, knowing they can get help from state benefits. They see the decline of the traditional family, and particularly growing numbers of lone parent families, as contributing to the emergence of a **dependency culture** and a work-shy **underclass** which wants to avoid work by living off welfare benefits. This underclass is marked out by high levels of illegitimacy, lone parenthood and family instability, which the New Right sees as contributing to wider social problems, such as alcohol abuse and 'yob culture', crime, fiddling of the benefit system and drug abuse, exclusion from school and educational failure.

The New Right argues for a return to traditional family values, with government policies to reverse the decline of the traditional family unit. These might include measures to reduce divorce and births outside marriage, and the reduction of welfare state benefits to non-conventional family units. Such policies seek to make alternative means of living or bringing up children less attractive options, while at the same time policies

A **dependency culture** is a set of values and beliefs, and a way of life, centred on dependence on others, particularly benefits from the welfare state.

The **underclass** is a social group right at the bottom of the social class hierarchy, whose members are in some ways different from, and cut off or excluded from, the rest of society.

are adopted to support conventional nuclear family units, with traditional gender roles in parenting and support to strengthen legal marriage over cohabitation, through measures like tax relief for married couples.

Criticisms of the New Right approach to the family are similar to those of the functionalist perspective discussed above, and the criticisms derived from Marxist and feminist writers discussed below. Perhaps the most significant criticisms are that it has a particularly rosy view of what family life is like, ignoring much of its darker side (see pages 183–6), and harks back to the reestablishment of a romanticized era of happy families that probably never existed.

THE MARXIST PERSPECTIVE: THE FAMILY AS AN AGENCY OF SOCIAL CONTROL

Like functionalists, Marxists adopt a structural perspective on the family, looking at how the family contributes to the maintenance of society's structure. However, unlike functionalists, Marxists do not regard the nuclear family as a functionally necessary (and therefore universal) institution. Marxists see the family within the framework of a capitalist society, which is based on private property, driven by profit, and riddled with conflict between social classes with opposing interests. Marxists argue that the nuclear family is concerned with social control by teaching its members to submit to the capitalist class, and they emphasize the ways the family reproduces unequal relationships and works to damp down inevitable social conflict.

> **Monogamy** is a form of marriage in which a person can only be legally married to one partner at a time.

Early traditional Marxists like Engels (1820–95) believed that the monogamous nuclear family developed as a means of passing on private property to heirs. The family, coupled with **monogamy**, was an ideal mechanism as it provided proof of paternity (who the father was) and so property could be passed on to the right people. Women's position in this family was not much different from that of prostitutes in that a financial deal was struck – she provided sex and heirs in return for the economic security her husband offered.

> **Ideological state apparatuses** are agencies which serve to spread the ideology, and justify the power, of the dominant social class.

Althusser, a Marxist writing in 1971, argued that, in order for capitalism to survive, the working class must submit to the ruling class or bourgeoisie. He suggested that the family is one of the **ideological state apparatuses**, along with others such as the education system and the mass media, which are concerned with social control and passing on the ideology (the ideas and beliefs) of the ruling class. Through socialization into this ideology in the family, the ruling class tries to maintain false class consciousness by winning the hearts and minds of the working class.

Zaretsky (1976) also emphasizes this ideological role of the family in propping up capitalism. He sees the family as an escape route from oppression and exploitation at work – a private place where people, particularly male workers, can enjoy a personal life and be valued as individuals, and have some measure of control over their lives. This release in the family helps them to live with their daily oppression in the world of work, and thereby helps to undermine opposition to capitalism. However, this seems a very romanticized view of the family, without family conflicts and rows, and, as Marxist feminists have pointed out (see below) this is very much a male Marxist perspective on the family, as much of the work that might make the family a haven and refuge is done by, and at the expense of, women.

Criticisms of the Marxist perspective

The traditional Marxist perspective tends to be a bit old-fashioned. The idea that men marry and have children to pass on property ignores other reasons for getting married or forming families. Many women now work and have independent incomes, and in many cases they are more successful than men in some areas of the labour market. Women are therefore far less likely to marry for economic security. Marriage is now less of a social necessity. The idea that families exist basically to pass on ruling-class ideology ignores the many other things that go on in families. A 2003 report by the Institute of Education, *Changing Britain, Changing Lives,* found that people are now more likely to marry for love and affection rather than as a social obligation, with a growing emphasis on the emotional aspects of relationships and personal fulfilment both for men and, especially, for women. Marxist analysis of the family is now mainly explored by Marxist feminists, as considered below.

THE FAMILY, SOCIAL CONTROL AND SURVEILLANCE

Another way the family exercises ideological control is derived from Foucault's idea of surveillance. Foucault (1991) developed the concept of surveillance – the state keeping an eye on you – to describe how the state can exercise social control over people. Surveillance is traditionally associated with external pressure, through social institutions like the criminal justice system, the mass media and the education system which watch over people to encourage them, through force and persuasion, to conform to social norms, such as what proper family life and good parenting should be like. However, in postmodern societies, Foucault sees this surveillance as internalized – people come to accept the norms of behaviour as their own, and follow them because they think it is in their interests to do so. They then exercise self-surveillance, and police their own behaviour. Social institutions no longer need to enforce social control over how people behave because they do it themselves as they constantly monitor and keep an eye on their own behaviour.

Henderson et al. (2010) applied Foucault's concept of surveillance to the family and motherhood. They suggest that conformity to social norms relating to family life, such as those presented in the media, or by social workers, is established as mothers exercise surveillance over themselves and one another informally, as they observe, talk to, criticize, judge and reproach themselves and one another about parenting styles, about what products to buy for their children, child discipline, access to computer games, the internet and television, diet and so on. Henderson et al. found that this self-surveillance was often accomplished and accompanied by guilt if mothers were not living up to their own self-imposed parenting expectations.

This process of self-surveillance was confirmed in a Netmums survey of 5,000 mothers in 2011. This found mothers were under so much pressure – from both themselves and other mothers – to appear like perfect parents and to give a good impression of themselves that they covered up or lied about things like how much television their children watched, what they cooked for their families and how much 'quality time' they spent playing with and talking to their children.

This process of self-surveillance establishes a self-imposed pattern of conformity to the accepted norms of family life, and is another means by which the family can operate as an agency of social control. For functionalists, this is seen as part of a desirable process of ensuring social stability and conformity, but for Marxists and feminists it is seen as repressive, promoting submission and conformity in an unequal society, and exploitative, especially for women whose guilt underpins it.

FEMINIST PERSPECTIVES ON THE FAMILY

In recent years, feminist approaches have probably had more influence on the study of the family than any other perspective, and they have been extremely valuable in introducing new areas into the study of the family, such as housework and its contribution to the economy; domestic violence; the negative effects of family life on women's careers in paid employment; and the continuing inequality between men and women in the family. These themes are explored further elsewhere in this chapter.

Feminist perspectives emphasize the harmful effects of family life upon women, and the role of the family in the continuing oppression of women. They provide a healthy antidote to functionalist and New Right accounts, which tend to emphasize the 'functional' aspects of the family and downplay the negative side of family life. For feminists, the family and marriage are major sources of female oppression and gender inequalities in society – whether we examine housework, childcare, power and authority or women's employment outside the home.

Themes in feminist analysis of the family

- *The family as a place of work.* Feminist writers were among the first to state that housework is work – as real as waged work outside the home. Housework and childcare in the family, which are mainly performed by women, are unpaid, and not really recognized as work at all. Men are often the ones who gain from this, as it is they who have their meals cooked, their children looked after and their homes kept clean by women's work. Oakley (1974) has emphasized that housework is hard, routine and unrewarding (both personally and in a financial sense), and housework remains the primary responsibility of women, though men might sometimes help. This will be examined later in this chapter.
- *The myth of the* **'symmetrical family'**. Feminists attack the notion (put forward originally by Young and Willmott in *The Symmetrical Family* (1973)) that there is growing equality between partners in the family. These issues are discussed later in this chapter, but feminists emphasize it is still mainly women who:

> A **symmetrical family** is one in which the roles of husband and wife or cohabiting partners have become more alike (symmetrical) and equal.

Feminists emphasize that housework is unpaid labour. If women ironed clothes, cooked and cleaned for others outside the family they would be paid for it, but in the family they are not

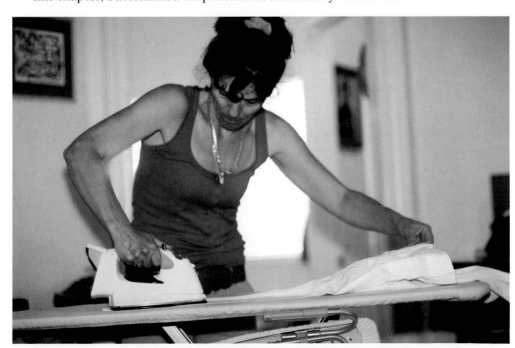

○ perform most housework and childcare tasks.
○ make sacrifices to buy the children clothes, and to make sure other family members are properly fed.
○ are less likely to make the most important decisions in the family.
○ are more likely to give up paid work, or suffer from lost or restricted job opportunities, as they are expected to look after children, the old, the sick, and male partners. Many women now work both outside the home in paid employment and inside the home doing domestic labour. In effect, they have two jobs to their male partner's one.

● *The greater dependency of women on men's earnings,* as the average pay of women is only about 83 per cent of that of men, largely linked to women's traditional roles as housewife and mother in the family.
● *Domestic violence* – women are far more likely than men to be the victims of serious domestic violence.

Liberal feminism   Liberal feminism recognizes that women's position in the family, with women taking on the major responsibility for housework and childcare, can have adverse effects on their power, careers and health. They believe the best way to improve the position of women in the family and society is through reform measures within the present system that remove all forms of discrimination to establish equality of opportunity for women with men, and allow them to make free choices between motherhood, a career or a combination of both. These measures include:

● *changing socialization and parenting practices,* to avoid the gender stereotyping which steers women into the housewife–mother role.
● *establishing and asserting the legal rights of women as individuals,* with laws to establish equal pay and stop sex discrimination, such as the Equal Pay Act (1970), the Sex Discrimination Act (1975) and the Equality Act (2010).
● *the establishment of equality in maternity and paternity leave,* so both fathers and mothers have the same legal rights to time off work when children are born, and parenting is seen as the responsibility of both parents, rather than mainly the mother's.
● *better and cheaper childcare* to enable women and men to combine childcare with successful careers in paid employment.
● *more sharing of housework and childcare tasks with men.*
● *stronger action against domestic violence* – the most serious of which is by men against women.

The major criticism of liberal feminist approaches is that, while they make proposals that might improve the position of women within existing society, they do not tackle the fundamental inequalities that women face as a result of patriarchy and capitalism – points that are made by radical and Marxist feminists.

Radical feminism   Radical feminists focus on the problem of patriarchy in society and in the family as the main obstacle to women's equality. Greer (2007) argues that many relationships between men and women in all spheres of life in contemporary society remain highly patriarchal and exploitative. Radical feminists see the family as a patriarchal institution, which benefits men at the expense of women, and through which men exercise their patriarchal power and control over women, sometimes backed up with physical and sexual violence (domestic violence). They believe women are better-off if they steer clear of patriarchal families. Their solution is basically to reject the family and family life, and in many cases to reject relationships with men altogether.

Marxist feminism   Marxist feminism emphasizes the way in which women are doubly exploited – both as workers in an unequal, exploitative capitalist society, and as women. They see the family, and particularly women's work in the family, as contributing to the maintenance of capitalism in the following ways.

The social reproduction of labour power

The social reproduction of labour power simply means the family providing a place where children can be born and raised with a sense of security, and the ruling class is supplied with a readily available and passive labour force for its factories and offices. The family achieves this in three ways:

- by providing a place for eating, drinking and relaxing, helping to ensure that members of the workforce are able to go to work each day with their ability to work (their labour power) renewed.
- by producing and maintaining labour which is free of cost to the capitalists through the unpaid housework of women (what is called *domestic labour*), as women are not paid for their labour in rearing children and looking after male partners.
- by socializing children into the dominant ideas in society (the dominant ideology), and preparing them for the necessity and routines of work, such as the need to work for a living, and to be punctual and obedient at work. Through day-to-day relationships in the family, with parents having power and control over their children, and men over women, family members come to accept, often without questioning them, the power inequalities they will face as adults in capitalist society. The family therefore lays the groundwork for submission to 'the boss' in later life, and is one of the mechanisms by which capitalism produces and recruits a moulded and obedient workforce.

Social control of the working class

Social control refers to the means of keeping people conforming to the dominant norms and values of society. The expectation that what are defined as 'good parents' must work to provide material comforts and good life chances for their children helps to keep people in unsatisfying, boring and unrewarding jobs. It is harder for workers to go on strike for higher pay if there is a family to support, because it might mean cuts in the living standards of themselves and their children. This weakens workers' bargaining power at work, and discourages them from taking action that might disrupt the system.

The family can also act as a 'safety valve', providing a release from the tedium, frustration and lack of power and control at work that many workers experience. As Zaretsky said above, the family can be a place to escape from the world and relax – a 'sanctuary' into which adults withdraw to recover, and enjoy the feel-good emotional factors of friendship, love and support. Delphy and Leonard (1992) argue this safety valve is provided by women, whose emotional work is an important aspect of women's domestic labour. This safety valve helps to prevent frustration at work from spilling over into action against the system, and contributes to the stabilization of the capitalist system, to the benefit of the dominant class.

Criticisms of the Marxist feminist and radical feminist perspectives

Criticisms of the Marxist feminist and radical feminist perspectives include the following points:

- Women's roles are not the same in all families. Many families now consist of dual-worker couples, with both partners in paid employment.

- These perspectives assume that women are passive victims in the family, and do not have any choices. Hakim (2011) suggests that women's inequality in the family, and what is treated as self-evident proof of widespread sex discrimination and sex-role stereotyping, may be the result of women's personal choices and preferences, and that most men and women have different career aspirations, life goals and priorities. Some women may choose to become full-time housewives and mothers because they enjoy it and find it fulfilling and rewarding, and they are not forced to do this. Many choose to take paid employment, even though they still have to combine this with the major responsibilities for housework and childcare (see later in this chapter).

- More women are working and have independent incomes, and this means they may have more power in the family than some feminist writers imply.

- That around 70 per cent of divorces are initiated by women shows that women can, and do, escape from relationships which are unsatisfactory or oppressive.

- Day-to-day relationships in the family are less likely today to create an unquestioning and obedient workforce. Children have much more status and power in the family than they used to, with families becoming more child-centred (see pages 190–2), and children are empowered by knowledge and experience gained through exposure to a much wider range of socializing experiences outside the family, such as education and the mass media, including the internet. Women too are much more likely to assert themselves in family life.

Table 3.3 summarizes functionalist, Marxist feminist and radical feminist perspectives on the family.

Table 3.3 Sociological perspectives on the family

Functionalism	Marxist feminism	Radical feminism
The family meets the needs of society by socializing children into shared norms and values, leading to social harmony and stability	The family meets the needs of capitalism by socializing children into ruling class norms and values (the ruling class ideology), leading to a submissive and obedient workforce, with false consciousness, and stability for capitalism	The family meets the needs of patriarchy by socializing children into traditional gender roles, with men as 'breadwinners' and women having responsibility for housework and childcare
The family is a social institution providing security for the conception, birth and nurture of new members of society	The family is a social institution responsible for the reproduction of labour power for capitalism	The family is a social institution responsible for the reproduction of unequal roles for women and men
The sexual division of labour in the family, with men performing instrumental roles and women performing expressive roles, stabilizes adult personalities and thereby helps to maintain a stable society	The male's instrumental role as wage earner maintains the family, pays for the reproduction of labour power and acts as a strong control on workers' behaviour in the workplace thereby helping to maintain the stability of an unequal, exploitative capitalist society	The sexual division of labour in the family exploits women, since their responsibilities for domestic labour and childcare are unpaid, undermine their position in paid employment and increase dependency on men. It thereby maintains an unequal patriarchal society
The family is a supportive and generally harmonious and happy social institution	The family is an oppressive institution that stunts the development of human personalities and individuality. There is a 'dark side' to family life that functionalist accounts play down	The family is an oppressive institution that benefits men and oppresses and exploits women. There is a 'dark side' to family life that includes violence and abuse against women and children

Activity

Refer to pages 121–34 and table 3.3 and to the following statements, and classify each one as nearly as possible as functionalist, New Right, traditional Marxist, Marxist feminist, liberal feminist or radical feminist. Give a brief justification of your reasons in each case.

1 The family is a socially useful and happy institution providing the best context for bringing up children.

2 The family is an important institution because of its contribution to maintaining social stability.

3 The family is a patriarchal and unequal institution controlled by and for men.

4 Children are socialized by the family and other institutions to conform to the dominant ideology.

5 Only the family provides the warmth, security and emotional support necessary to keep society stable.

6 Patterns of obedience laid down in the family form the basis for acceptance of the hierarchy of power and control in capitalist society.

7 Women's role in the family is to do housework, to care for children, the sick and the elderly, and to flatter, excuse, sympathize with and pay attention to men. This often disadvantages women in many aspects of their lives.

8 The family always benefits either men or capitalism.

9 It is important to make further progress in the sharing of housework and childcare by men and women to remove the disadvantages that many women face in the home and paid employment.

10 The image of the caring and loving family ignores the violence against women and the sexual crimes, like rape within marriage, which go on there.

11 The family exists primarily to pass on private property from one generation to the next, and to prepare a submissive and obedient workforce.

12 The family is an important institution in maintaining male power.

13 Marriage is perhaps the best antidote to the celebrity, self-obsessed culture we live in, for it is about understanding that our true value is lastingly expressed through the lives of others we commit to.

14 When wives play their traditional role as 'takers of shit', they often absorb their husbands' anger and frustration at their own powerlessness and oppression in the world of work, and stop rebellion in the workplace.

15 Families are factories producing stable human personalities.

16 It is highly unlikely that any society will find an adequate substitute to take over the functions of the nuclear family.

17 Policies like equal pay and anti-discrimination laws, improved educational opportunities and paid maternity leave have improved women's prospects in paid employment, giving them the confidence and encouraging them to assert their demands for equal treatment with men in all their personal, family and workplace relationships. This has led to much improved and more equal relationships between men and women in all spheres of life.

18 Women's unpaid domestic labour reproduces the workforce at no cost to the capitalist.

19 Family breakdown is not only damaging for individuals, it also imposes incredibly high financial and social costs on society as a whole. The government should encourage couples to make a commitment through marriage by offering financial support to those who choose to do so.

20 Social policy should aim to remove laws and traditions that discriminate against women who take time out of paid employment to raise children; women should be placed on an equal footing with men, through measures such as cheaper and greater availability of childcare.

POSTMODERNISM AND THE FAMILY

Postmodernists believe that contemporary society is rapidly changing and full of uncertainties, with people questioning a whole range of traditionally accepted values, morals and norms. No longer are individuals constrained by social structures, like the family, social class or religion, and they are rejecting ideas about the traditional family as a mainstay of social order. Society has become fragmented into a mass of individuals who are making their own choices about what they choose to believe in, and how they live their daily lives.

Diversity and consumer choice are two key features of postmodern society, and this consumer choice is reflected, postmodernists argue, in the disintegration of the traditional family. This is being replaced by a wide diversity of relationships in which people are choosing to live. They no longer feel bound by traditional ideas and expectations about marriage, lifelong monogamy, parenthood and family life, or traditional sexual identities. Rising divorce rates, cohabitation, multiple partners, serial monogamy and births outside marriage all reflect the way people are adopting new lifestyles and ways of relating to one another suited to their needs, rather than being constrained by traditional norms.

Many of the changes in family life discussed in this chapter – such as the decline in family size and marriage rates, the rising divorce rate, growing lone parenthood and individuals living alone, more shared households and 'families of choice', changing roles in the family and civil partnerships (gay marriage) – are widely regarded by politicians and social policymakers as a threat to the family and something to worry about, as support networks are weakened, and individuals face growing insecurity, uncertainty and anxiety in their lives.

Postmodernists see these changes as simply reflecting individuals making their consumer choices. Individuals pick and choose and 'mix and match' relationships as it suits them, and change these over a period of time – just like buying goods in a supermarket and going to another one if the quality and price aren't right. The rise of alternative family units, cohabitation, multiple partners and more diversity in sexual relationships, with greater tolerance of homosexuality, make the notion of the traditional family as a social institution redundant, as it has been replaced by a huge range of ever-changing personal relationships and household arrangements in which people are choosing to live.

Politics, social policy and the family

Debates over family life have become a major feature of politics in Britain. Politicians of all the major parties have expressed similar views on the importance of the family, seeing it as one of society's central and most important institutions, as the bedrock of a strong society, social stability and security for children, and encouraging support for and strengthening of family units. The political parties often blame family breakdown for wider social problems, such as teenage pregnancies, sexual promiscuity, educational failure, welfare dependency, poverty, drug abuse, and crime and delinquency. Despite a changing world where a majority of the population no longer lives in families, or families with dependent children, family life still seems to be central to the thinking of the major political parties.

SOCIOLOGICAL APPROACHES AND FAMILY POLICIES: FAMILY IDEOLOGY

Family ideology is that dominant set of beliefs, values and images about how families are and how they ought to be.

A **stereotype** is a generalized, oversimplified view of an institution or social group.

The **cereal packet family** refers to the stereotype of the ideal family found in the mass media and advertising. It is generally seen as involving first-time married parents and their own natural children, living together, with the father as the primary breadwinner and the mother as primarily concerned with the home and children.

Feminist and Marxist writers suggest that many state policies are formed around a dominant **family ideology**. This refers to a dominant set of ideas, beliefs and images about family life, family structure and family relationships which suggests what the perfect and best form of family is and how family life ought to be lived. This ideology reflects in many ways the functionalist view of the family, and the policy ideas of the New Right. At the heart of this ideology is a **stereotype** which has been called the patriarchal **'cereal packet' family**. This is a nuclear family unit consisting of two married parents who are the biological parents of their children. The husband plays the instrumental role as the main breadwinner and decision-maker, and takes primary responsibility for family discipline; the wife is primarily concerned with carrying out the expressive, nurturing role, through caring for the home (housework) and expressing maternal love through childcare, and perhaps doing some part-time paid employment to supplement the family income. This ideology also often includes ideas that this family is based on romantic love, as well as love of children (particularly maternal love), and that it is a nurturing, caring and loving institution – a safe and harmonious refuge from an uncaring outside world. This family is seen as the best and most desirable form of family, particularly by the New Right, and is presented as a symbol of natural, wholesome goodness, and supporting such a traditional family and parental responsibilities is often seen as crucial to maintaining moral values in society. This family ideology represents a powerful view of how people *should* lead their lives, even if this ideology does not reflect the reality of how most people do actually live their lives.

Feminist writers such as Barrett and McIntosh (1982) have argued that this stereotype found in family ideology is patriarchal, harmful and anti-social:

- *It is patriarchal* because it involves the exploitation of women through the triple burden of domestic and emotional labour in the family, on top of paid employment. This benefits men to the disadvantage of women. Women remain disadvantaged in paid work compared to men because of their assumed or actual responsibilities for housework, childcare and looking after other dependants, like

The 'cereal packet' family, with a working father in a first marriage to a home-based mother, caring for their own two natural children, makes up only about 5 per cent of all households

disabled or elderly relatives. This increases women's dependency on men in relationships. State policies, such as giving more generous maternity leave than paternity leave, encourage a traditional gendered division of labour in the family, and perpetuate patriarchal gender inequality there.

- *It is harmful* because it suggests that those living in other relationships, or living alone, are somehow deviant, are a threat to normal family life and lack any meaningful relationships in their lives. Every time politicians or policy-makers make appeals to 'strengthen the family' (meaning something resembling the cereal packet image in family ideology), they are at the same time condemning those who live outside such a family, such as lone parents, lesbian and gay couples, and those living alone. Lone parents, particularly, have been subject to attack by conservative politicians of the New Right and the mass media because they are seen as inadequate units for bringing up children, and the source of a range of social problems. Attacks on gays are often justified by the threat they are perceived to present to heterosexual relationships found in family ideology. Yet those living outside conventional families now make up a substantial proportion of the population. The stereotype is also harmful because it pretends there is no darker side of family life, with domestic violence and child abuse, and prevents such issues being treated as seriously as they should be, at great cost to the women and children who are mainly the ones victimized in the family. The stereotyped image of family ideology overlooks the way women become isolated at home with children, or struggle to combine paid work with childcare, situations which may be very stressful and lead many women towards tranquillizer use and mental illness. Lone parent and other non-conformist household units may face discrimination by social workers, teachers, the police and magistrates, and therefore face higher risks of labelling or stereotyping, with children being branded failures at school, or being taken into care, or arrested and prosecuted, because their parents are seen as inadequate and deviant.
- *It is anti-social* because it devalues life outside the family. Much of social life today centres around family activities, and it is often difficult for those outside such conventional arrangements to participate. For example, schools are organized in such a way that it is difficult for lone parent families and dual-worker families to combine paid work with childcare. Package holidays are overwhelmingly geared to families, and those who are lone parents or who live alone may often find it difficult to get the same financial deals as family groups. Fox Harding (1995) points out that housing policy favours married couples, with single parents receiving the worst social housing, and houses themselves are often designed for nuclear families, not larger household groups or for people living alone. Family ideology separates people from one another – from 'us' in the family and 'them' outside the family – and therefore sets up barriers between people. It devalues life outside the family, and discourages alternative forms of household organization and relationships between people from developing, such as living alone, same-sex relationships, lone parenthood, communal living or serial monogamy.

LAWS AND SOCIAL POLICIES AFFECTING THE FAMILY AND HOUSEHOLDS

Given the political importance attached to the family, and the dominance of the family ideology considered above, it is perhaps not surprising that there are a huge number of laws and social policies influencing families and households. Practically all government policies affect families in some way. These include: those on tax, welfare and housing; compulsory education and the welfare state, which have affected family size and divorce, and have enabled both partners in a couple-relationship with children to undertake paid employment; laws protecting children and promoting women's rights; and laws defining rules and procedures for marriage / civil partnership and divorce, and establishing monogamy as the only legal form of marriage.

There are a huge range of changes going on in contemporary families, such as rising divorce, cohabitation, lone parenthood, births outside marriage and people choosing to live alone. Governments face the dilemma of whether they accept these trends, and adopt policies to support all those raising children, in whatever family shape, size or other form that might take, and therefore adapt social policies to a changing world. Alternatively, they may adopt policies which try to stop these changes and even reverse them. So, although there may be a whole range of policies affecting families, there is often no agreement on what the best family policies are, and whether the policies adopted should encourage people to live in some family structures and discourage others.

There are two main types of social policies specifically aimed at families:

- *Those aimed at providing direct material support for families,* such as cash benefits like tax credits and child benefit to increase family prosperity and reduce adult and child poverty, and the Child Support Agency to ensure absent fathers contribute to the costs of bringing up their children.
- *Those to help parents balance the demands of paid employment and family life, and support children.* Such policies include things like maternity and paternity leave, early years childcare and support through nursery education and schemes like Sure Start Children's Centres, advice services to improve parenting skills, child protection policies, and supporting lone parents into paid employment.

As seen earlier, functionalist sociologists have suggested that state policies have assisted the family in carrying out its functions more effectively (see pages 125–7), and the New Right (see pages 128–9) has tended to promote policies that support traditional family units. They see the family as being under threat from increasing divorce rates, rising numbers of lone parents and births outside marriage, with the growing diversity of alternative lifestyles undermining the stability of society and generating serious moral decline. The blame generally falls on the inadequate socialization and supervision of children by parents, and in some cases the lack of a male role model for boys. Social policy is seen as a means of strengthening traditional families, and promoting self-reliance rather than reliance on the state.

1980s and 1990s: Conservative Party policy

The New Right approach was very influential through the years of Conservative Party government in the 1980s and 1990s. Social policy aimed to strengthen nuclear families, by emphasizing self-help through increasing reliance on the family, as it tried to save money by reducing welfare benefits. For example, the Child Support Agency was established in 1993 to ensure absent fathers took financial responsibility for their children, and this was accompanied by cuts in the value of benefits paid to single mothers.

1997–2010: Labour Party policy

Between 1997 and 2010, the Labour Party formed the government. Some of the New Right ideas were continued in this period, with continual concerns expressed over 'dysfunctional' families and the lack of male role models in female-headed lone parent families being linked to a range of social problems. At the same time, social policy showed a recognition of the growing diversity of family forms, with more emphasis placed on the care, protection and development of children than on the social institution in which they were raised. These policies reflected more the concerns of feminist critics of the family. There were policies – 'New Deals' – to support lone parents in moving from dependence on welfare back into employment, the introduction of Britain's first National Minimum Wage to help the most poorly paid, and child tax credits and measures to reduce child poverty and to help the poorest families, regardless of the form these families took. An increase in free childcare and nursery education, with all 3- and 4-year-olds guaranteed five half-days of nursery education each week, supported parents with dependent children, where a lone parent or both partners in a couple family were in, or wanted to be in, paid employment, without the crippling costs of childcare. The Civil Partnership Act in 2005 enabled gay and lesbian couples to, in effect, get legally married through forming civil partnerships. This recognized gay and lesbian couples as an acceptable form of family for the first time.

2010 onwards: ConDem policy

In 2010, a new ConDem (Conservative – Liberal Democrat) coalition government took power. Family policies took on some of the New Right characteristics of those of the Conservative years of the 1980s and 1990s. There was a renewed emphasis on the importance of marriage, and the promotion of marriage, as opposed to cohabitation, to cement relationships and ward off family breakdown. Once again, family breakdown was seen as damaging for individuals and as imposing what the Work and Pensions Secretary Duncan Smith called 'incredibly high financial and social costs on society as a whole'. The Conservative Party manifesto in 2010 made a commitment to offer tax benefits for married couples as a means of encouraging people to get married. Cuts in major areas of public spending (spending by central and local government) on welfare services, such as children's services and care of the elderly, reflected the traditional New Right concerns of self-help and reliance on the family, not the state.

The activity below is designed to encourage you to examine and think about how social policies and laws affect families and households, and what the political parties currently have to say about families.

Activity

1 The column on the left in the table below lists a range of issues, social policies and laws that might be considered to have an effect on families and households. The column on the right is left blank, for you to explain what social policies or laws there are on the issues, to describe how these social policies work, and how they might affect families and households, and roles and relationships within them. Take two of them (or if you're in a class, several could be shared out) or suggest ones of your own choosing in the light of the latest developments. You can probably find a lot of references to these issues by searching on the internet, but the following sites might be useful:

   - www.dwp.gov.uk (Department for Work and Pensions)
   - www.familyandparenting.org (the Family and Parenting Institute)
   - www.gingerbread.org.uk (issues around lone parenthood)
   - www.crae.org.uk (Children's Rights Alliance for England)
   - www.homeoffice.gov.uk (the Home Office – useful for investigating family or child-related crimes, including forced marriage)
   - www.cmoptions.org (information about child maintenance options, including the Child Support Agency)

- www.ondivorce.co.uk (providing advice and support for those getting divorced)
- www.childrenscommissioner.gov.uk/ (the Children's Commissioner)
- www.dfe.gov.uk (Department for Education)
- www.direct.gov.uk (access to information about all aspects of government services – search for parents, children or families)

Issue, law or social policy	Description of issue, law or policy, and effects on families and households, and roles and relationships within them
Abortion law	
Child benefit	
Child protection policies	
Child Support Agency	
Children Act (2004)	
Civil Partnership Act 2005	
Compulsory education	
Divorce laws (including custody of and access to children)	
Domestic violence laws/policies	
Equality laws to improve the rights and position of women	
Eradicating child poverty	
Early years education for all 3- and 4-year-olds	
Free NHS healthcare	
Laws and policies on adoption and fostering of children	
Maternity and paternity leave	
National Minimum Wage	
Support for lone parents	
Sure Start programmes	

2 Take any one trend in families in Britain today, such as rising births outside marriage, rising levels of cohabitation, divorce or lone parenthood, and suggest: (a) two social policies feminists might adopt to support people through these changes; (b) two social policies the New Right or functionalists might adopt to try to stop or reverse these changes.

3 What are the main political parties currently saying about family roles and relationships? Go to the websites of the political parties below, and briefly outline two policies on the family and family roles and relationships. Identify any differences you can between them. Look for a 'policy' heading or button, but be prepared to search (try 'policy', 'manifesto' or 'family' first).
- www.labour.org.uk (the Labour Party)
- www.libdems.org.uk (the Liberal Democrats)
- www.conservatives.com (the Conservative Party)

Exam-style questions

1 Explain what is meant by the 'modified extended family'. *(2 marks)*

2 Explain what is meant by the 'expressive role'. *(2 marks)*

3 Explain what is meant by 'family ideology'. *(2 marks)*

4 Explain **two** characteristics of the 'cereal packet family'. *(4 marks)*

5 Explain **two** characteristics of the privatized nuclear family. *(4 marks)*

6 Identify **three** features of the New Right view of the family. *(6 marks)*

7 Suggest **three** reasons for the decline of the classic extended family. *(6 marks)*

8 Assess the view that the main role of the family is to carry out social control. *(24 marks)*

9 Assess feminist contributions to our understanding of the family. *(24 marks)*

10 Examine the view that the nuclear family is ideally suited to the needs of contemporary society. *(24 marks)*

11 Assess the view that social policies on the family favour the traditional nuclear family. *(24 marks)*

Topic 2

SPECIFICATION AREA

Changing patterns of marriage, cohabitation, separation, divorce, child-bearing and the life-course, and the diversity of contemporary family and household structures

Changing families and households

Sex and childbirth were once, for most people, linked to – and only acceptable within – marriage, and most people followed a fairly standard family life cycle. They were born to and raised by their two natural parents, who were married to each other, and then themselves moved on to marriage. They then started their own family, until their children left home and the couple settled down in their empty nest to work, enjoy more leisure, enjoy grandchildren, and await retirement and death. Contemporary families and households bear little resemblance to this traditional family life cycle.

Families and households in Britain are constantly changing over time, but since about the 1970s there have been a series of major changes. There has been a huge increase in the number of divorces, and a decline in the idea that marriage – itself a declining arrangement – is a lifelong – 'till death us do part' – commitment; there is a decline in marriage and growing cohabitation; women are having fewer children, at older ages, and increasingly none at all, as they begin to free themselves from traditional housewife–mother roles; there is more serial monogamy as people cohabit with or marry a series of partners; there are many more stepfamilies; there are growing numbers of lone parents – who are now responsible for raising about a quarter of all dependent children; gays and lesbians can now openly form families, legally cemented through civil partnerships; ever-growing numbers of people are living alone; there are more births outside marriage, to both single and cohabiting women; more people are experimenting with living in non-family households; and there is growing ethnic diversity between and within families. These changes mean that families and households today bear little resemblance to those of forty or fifty years ago, and there is no longer such a thing as the 'typical family'. As Lewis (2001) suggests, marriage, sex and parenthood are no longer linked, and individuals today have much greater freedom of choice in their personal behaviour and the arrangements in which they choose to live their lives, rather than these being regulated by an externally imposed public moral code. These changes are apparent in many European countries.

This topic discusses a number of these changes. However, the other topic areas also consider various other changes in the family. It is important that you remember all these changes, and for revision purposes, figure 3.2 provides a summary of the main changes that are discussed in this topic and other parts of this chapter.

DIVORCE

One of the most startling changes in the family in the United Kingdom in the last century has been the general and dramatic increase in the number of marriages

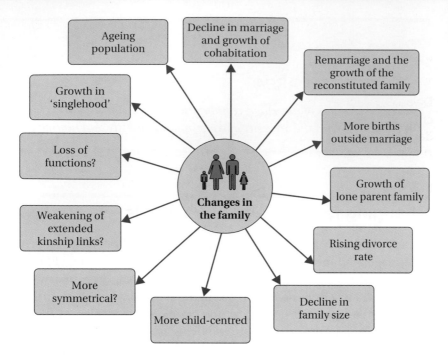

Figure 3.2 Changes in the family

Ageing population

Decline in marriage and growth of cohabitation

Remarriage and the growth of the reconstituted family

Growth in 'singlehood'

More births outside marriage

Loss of functions?

Changes in the family

Growth of lone parent family

Weakening of extended kinship links?

Rising divorce rate

More symmetrical?

Decline in family size

More child-centred

Activity

With reference to figure 3.2, discuss with different generations, such as friends, parents and grandparents or great-grandparents, how the family has changed during the course of the last fifty years. If you are in a group, pool all your findings and discuss the changes you have discovered.

---

ending in divorce, with a similar trend found in many developed Western countries. The number of divorces rose from 27,000 in 1961 to a peak of 180,000 in 1993, and then fell back to around 126,000 by 2009, which was the lowest since 1974; during the 1960s the number doubled, and then doubled again in the 1970s. Although the number of divorces and the **divorce rate** have been dropping in the last few years, this partly reflects the fact that fewer people are getting married in the first place, and there is a lower number of married people in the population. Measuring the number of divorces against the number of marriages each year shows that divorce is still much higher than in the past: in 1974, for example, there was about one divorce for every four marriages, but by 2009 this had more than doubled to just over two divorces for every four marriages. These trends are shown in figure 3.3. Britain still has one of the highest divorce rates in the European Union. About one-half of new marriages today are likely to end in divorce, and, if present rates continue, more than one in four children will experience a parental divorce by the time they are 16.

The **divorce rate** is the number of divorces per 1,000 married people per year.

Divorce statistics

Divorce statistics are presented in three main ways:

- *the total number of divorce petitions per year* (the number of people applying for a divorce but not necessarily actually getting divorced).

- *the total number of decrees absolute granted per year* (the number of divorces actually granted).
- *the divorce rate* (the number of divorces each year per thousand married people in the population).

Divorce statistics must be treated with considerable caution, and assessed against changing legal, financial and social circumstances, if misleading conclusions about the declining importance of marriage and the family are to be avoided. The increase may simply reflect easier and cheaper divorce procedures enabling the legal termination of already unhappy 'empty shell' marriages, rather than a real increase in marriage breakdowns. It could be that people who in previous years could only separate are now divorcing as legal and financial obstacles are removed.

Divorce statistics only show the legal termination of marriages. They do not show:

- the number of people who are separated but not divorced.
- the number of people who live in empty shell marriages – many couples may want to split up but are deterred from doing so by their roles as parents.

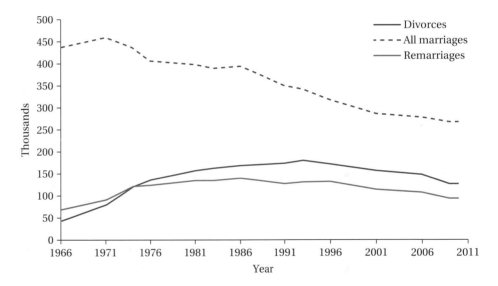

Figure 3.3 Marriages, remarriages* and divorces, UK 1966–2010

* Remarriage for one or both partners

Source: Office for National Statistics

Activity

Look at figure 3.3
1. Approximately how many divorces were there in 1971?
2. About how many divorces were there in 2006?
3. Describe the trend in the number of remarriages compared to all marriages between 1966 and 2010.
4. Write a short paragraph on what the trends in marriage, remarriage and divorce in Figure 3.3 might suggest about changing attitudes to marriage and divorce in the UK.
5. Suggest two reasons why remarriages might be growing as a proportion of all marriages.

- how many unstable or unhappy marriages existed before divorce was made easier by changes in the law and changing social attitudes to divorce.

These points could mean either that divorce figures underestimate the extent of family and marriage breakdowns or that rising divorce rates only reflect legal changes and do not represent a real increase in marital instability.

Divorce and 'broken homes'

Divorce is the legal termination of a marriage, but this is not the only way that marriages and homes can be 'broken'. Homes and marriages may be broken in 'empty shell marriages', in which the marital relationship has broken down, and the couple continue to live together, but no divorce has taken place. Separation – through either choice or necessity (like working abroad or imprisonment) – may also cause a broken home, as may the death of a partner. So homes may be broken for reasons other than divorce, and divorce itself is often only the end result of a marriage which broke down long before.

Reasons for the increase in the divorce rate

There are two broad groups of reasons for the increase in the divorce rate:

- *changes in the law* which have gradually made divorce easier and cheaper to get.
- *changes in society* which have made divorce a more practical and socially acceptable way of terminating a broken marriage. These are discussed in the next sections, and figure 3.4 summarizes these changes.

Changes in the law as a reason for the rising divorce rate

Changes in the law over the last century have made divorce easier and cheaper to get, and have given men and women equal rights in divorce. This partly accounts for the

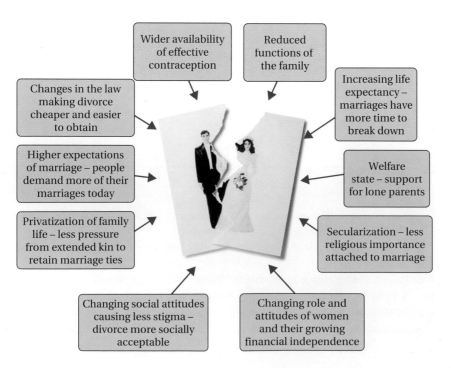

Figure 3.4 Causes of the rising divorce rate

steep rise in the divorce rate over the last fifty years, particularly in the 1970s and 1980s. These changes in the law are listed in the box below. However, changes in the law reflect changing social attitudes and norms, and there are a number of wider social explanations that must also be considered.

A brief history of the divorce laws

In the nineteenth century, divorce could only be obtained by the rich. As a result, there were very few divorces, and in 1911, there were only about 600 divorces a year. Men also had more rights in divorce than women until 1923, when equal rights in divorce were established. Since 1971, changes in the law have made it easier to get a divorce.

- *The Divorce Law Reform Act of 1969*, which came into effect in 1971, was a major change. Before the 1969 Act, a person wanting a divorce had to prove before a court that his or her spouse had committed a 'matrimonial offence', such as adultery, cruelty, desertion or unreasonable behaviour. This frequently led to major public scandals, as all the details of unhappy marriages were aired in a public lawcourt. This may have deterred many people whose marriage had broken down from seeking a divorce. Also, marriages may have broken down – become empty shell marriages – without any matrimonial offence being committed. The 1969 Act changed all this, and made 'irretrievable breakdown' of a marriage the only grounds for divorce. It is now no longer necessary to prove one partner guilty of a matrimonial offence or at fault in some way: it simply has to be demonstrated that a marriage has broken down beyond repair. After 1971, one new way of demonstrating irretrievable breakdown of a marriage was by two years of separation (with both partners consenting) or five years without both partners consenting, in addition to existing grounds of adultery, unreasonable behaviour or desertion. This change in the law led to a massive increase in the number of divorces after 1971.
- *The Matrimonial and Family Proceedings Act of 1984* allowed couples to petition for divorce after only one year of marriage, whereas previously couples could normally divorce only after three years of marriage. This led to a record increase in the number of divorces in 1984 and 1985.
- *The Family Law Act of 1996* came into effect in 1999. This increased the amount of time a couple had to be married before a divorce could be granted from twelve to eighteen months, introduced compulsory marriage counselling for a 'period of reflection and consideration', and required children's wishes and financial arrangements for children to be agreed before a divorce was granted. This was an attempt to stem the rising number of divorces by increasing the time for 'cooling off'. These compulsory counselling sessions were later abandoned because it was found they were more likely to encourage people to go through with a divorce, even when they were initially uncertain.
- In 2011, the government decided that, as a quicker and cheaper alternative to resorting to the over-worked family courts, disputes between divorcing couples (over things like money and custody of children) should be referred to mediation to be sorted out before couples are allowed to resort to the courts.

Changes in society as a reason for the rising divorce rate

The changing role of women

This is a very important explanation for the rising divorce rate. Around three-quarters of divorce petitions (requests to a court for a divorce) are initiated by women, and around seven out of ten of all divorces are granted to women. This suggests that more women than men are unhappy with the state of their marriages, and are therefore more likely to take the first steps in ending them. This may well be because, as feminists argue, women's expectations of life and the quality of their relationships have risen during the course of the last century, and they are less willing to accept the patriarchal nature of marriage and the family, and the traditional housewife–mother role, with the sacrifices of their own leisure activities, careers and independence this involves. The employment of married women has increased dramatically over the last century, and it is now the norm for married women to be in employment, even when they have small children. This has increased their financial independence, and reduced the extent of dependence on their husbands. There is also a range of welfare state benefits to help divorced women, particularly those with children. Marriage has therefore become less of a financial necessity for women, and this makes it easier for them to escape from unhappy marriages.

Rising expectations of marriage

Functionalist writers like Parsons and Fletcher argue that the divorce rate has risen because couples (especially women) expect and demand more in their relationships today than their parents or grandparents might have settled for. Love, companionship, understanding, sexual compatibility and personal fulfilment are more likely to be the main ingredients of a successful marriage today. The growing privatization and isolation of the nuclear family from extended kin and the community have also meant that couples are likely to spend more time together. The higher expectations mean couples are likely to end a relationship which earlier generations might have tolerated.

Have rising expectations of marriage made relationships more 'fragile' and therefore more likely to break up?

This functionalist approach suggests that higher divorce rates therefore reflect better quality in surviving marriages and remarriages. This view of the higher expectations of marriage is reflected in the fairly high rate of remarriage among divorced people. In other words, families split up to re-form happier families – a bit like old banger cars failing their MOT test, being taken to the scrapyard and being replaced with a better-quality car, thereby improving the general quality of cars on the road.

Growing secularization

Secularization refers to the declining influence of religious beliefs and institutions. Writers such as Goode (1971) and Gibson (1994) argue that this has resulted in marriage becoming less of a sacred, spiritual union and more a personal and practical commitment which can be abandoned if it fails. Evidence for this lies in the fact that less than a third of marriages today involve a religious ceremony. The church now takes a much less rigid view of divorce, and many people today probably do not attach much religious significance to their marriages.

Changing social attitudes

From a postmodernist perspective, Beck and Beck-Gernstein (1995) see rising divorce rates as a product of the growing individualization and uncertainty of postmodern societies. All aspects of our lives are now subject to more choice, negotiation and decision-making. In family relationships, for example, individuals now choose and negotiate more about things like who does which household chores, where to live, and how to organize household finances, rather than these being taken on by men or women because that is the way things have always been before. Postmodernists argue people now have much greater individual freedom of choice, and are less constrained by traditional controls of morality, social expectations and norms, and family ties. Giddens (1993) suggests the idea of romantic love and personal fulfilment in relationships has gained in significance, and intimate relationships are no longer based on ideas of permanence, and people are less willing to stay with unsatisfactory partners. Rising divorce rates reflect the pursuit of individual choice as people continually keep swapping partners in their search for personally fulfilling relationships in a rapidly changing society where the future seems less certain and secure than it appeared in the past. These factors weaken commitment, particularly long-term commitment, to institutions like the family.

These changes are reflected in changing social attitudes to divorce, which has become more socially acceptable. There is less social disapproval and condemnation (stigmatizing) of divorcees. Divorce no longer hinders careers through a public sense of scandal and outrage. As a result, people are less afraid of the consequences of divorce, and are more likely to seek a legal end to an unhappy marriage rather than simply separating or carrying on in an empty shell marriage.

The greater availability of, and more effective, contraception

The greater availability of, and more effective, contraception has made it safer to have sex outside the marital relationship, and with more than one person during marriage. This weakens traditional constraints on fidelity to a marriage partner, and potentially exposes relationships to greater instability.

The growth of the privatized nuclear family

Functionalists contend that the growing privatization and isolation of the nuclear family from extended kin and the community in contemporary society have meant it is no longer so easy for marriage partners to seek advice from, or temporary refuge, with relatives. This isolation can increase the demands on and expectations of each partner in a marriage. There is also less social control from extended kin pressuring couples to retain marriage ties. In this sense, there is both more pressure on marriage relationships arising from the points above, and fewer constraints preventing people abandoning marriage, and increasingly the decision whether to divorce or not lies with the married couple alone.

The reduced functions of the family

As we saw earlier in this chapter, some functionalist writers like Parsons argue that in contemporary society a number of traditional family functions have transferred to other social institutions. This has perhaps meant that marriage has become less of a

" I'VE GOT ANOTHER FORTY YEARS TO LIVE ! "

practical necessity, and there are fewer bonds linking marriage partners. Love and companionship and personal compatibility are the important dimensions of contemporary marriages, and if some or all of these disappear, there may be nothing much left to hold marriages together.

Increasing life expectancy

People live to a greater age today than they did in the early years of the twentieth century, and this means the potential number of years a couple may be together, before one of them dies, has increased, and is continuing to increase as life expectancy lengthens. This gives more time for marriages to go wrong (as the cartoon suggests) and for divorces to occur. Some suggest that the divorce courts have taken on the role in finishing unhappy marriages once performed by the undertaker.

Variations in divorce rates between social groups

While divorce affects all groups in the population, there are some groups in which divorce rates are higher than the average. The highest rate of divorce is among men and women in their late 20s. Teenage marriages are twice as likely to end in divorce as those of couples overall, and there is a high incidence of divorce in the first five to seven years of marriage and after about ten to fourteen years (when the children are older or have left home). The working class, particularly semi-skilled and unskilled, has a higher rate of divorce than the middle class. Childless couples and partners from different social class or religious backgrounds also face a higher risk of divorce, as do couples whose work separates them for long periods. The rising divorce rate therefore does not affect all groups of married people equally, and some face higher risks of divorce than others.

Figure 3.5 Facts proven at divorce and to whom divorce granted: England and Wales, 2010

Source: Office for National Statistics

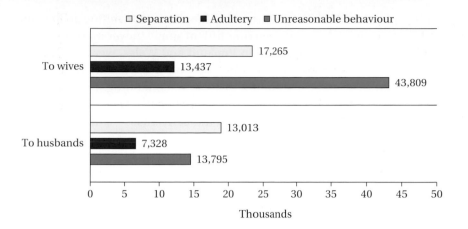

| | □ Separation | ■ Adultery | ■ Unreasonable behaviour |

To wives
- 17,265
- 13,437
- 43,809

To husbands
- 13,013
- 7,328
- 13,795

Thousands

Activity

1 Suggest reasons why the following groups might be more at risk of divorce than other groups in the population:
   - teenage marriages
   - childless couples
   - couples where each partner is from a different social class or ethnic background
2 Suggest reasons why women are more likely to apply for divorce than men.
3 Refer to figure 3.5, which shows the different numbers and reasons for divorce by husbands and wives:
   (a) Which reason for divorce shows the largest difference between husbands and wives?
   (b) Approximately how many more divorces were granted to wives than husbands?
   (c) Outline the main differences in the reasons for divorce by husbands and wives, and suggest explanations for them. What conclusions might you draw about the different behaviour of men and women in marriage?

CHANGING PATTERNS OF MARRIAGE: THE DECLINE IN MARRIAGE AND THE GROWING INCIDENCE AND ACCEPTANCE OF COHABITATION

The decline of marriage and the growth of living together before or outside marriage were two of the major social changes at the turn of the twenty-first century. **Marriage rates** are declining in Britain. In the last fifty years, the marriage rate has declined by around two-thirds – from around 68 (men) and 51 (women) marrying per 1,000 unmarried men/women, to 21.3 (men) and 19.2 (women) in 2009. In 2009, about 65 per cent of marriages were first marriages for both partners, compared to 80 per cent in 1971, so a growing proportion – around 1 in 3 – of the declining number of marriages that do take place are remarriages for one or both partners, suggesting a growing trend towards serial monogamy, as people divorce and remarry a series of partners. In 2009, there were around 267,000 marriages in the UK – the lowest number of marriages since 1895, and about 42 per cent fewer than in 1971. The number of first-time marriages for both partners has halved since 1971. Those who do marry are putting off marriage until they are older. Between 1981 and 2010, the average age at first marriage increased by about 7 years for both men and women, to age 32 for men and age 30 for women.

As marriage rates decline, more couples are cohabiting rather than seeking official recognition of their relationships through marriage. In the early 1960s in Britain,

> The **marriage rate** is the number of men or women marrying per 1,000 unmarried men or women aged 16 or over each year.

fewer than 1 in 100 adults under 50 are estimated to have been cohabiting at any one time, compared with 1 in 6 in 2010. Between one-fifth of single (never married) men, and a quarter of single women, over age 16 in England and Wales, were cohabiting in 2008, more than twice the proportion recorded around twenty years previously. Of all men and women over age 16, around 1 in 10 were cohabiting. By the 2000s, about four-fifths (80 per cent) of people in first marriages had lived with their partner beforehand – compared to less than 2 per cent in the early 1950s – and even more prior to a second marriage. Of all couples married in 2006, 8 in 10 gave identical addresses for both partners – and this, what was once seen as 'living in sin', included 65 per cent of those getting married in a religious ceremony. It is estimated that 22 per cent of couples who live together will be in a cohabiting, rather than married, relationship by 2021 – twice the proportion in 1996. In 2011, nearly 15 per cent of all families with dependent children consisted of cohabiting couples, who were neither married nor in a civil partnership.

The meaning of cohabitation

Although cohabitation is rapidly becoming the norm rather than the exception, it can have different meanings for the couples involved:

- *As a fairly temporary, informal arrangement,* spending a lot of time together and sharing accommodation, but within what is seen as a fairly temporary and casual relationship.
- *As an alternative or substitute to marriage* – as a long-term stable and committed partnership, but without the legal commitments, or the patriarchal dimensions feminists identify, associated with marriage. For some devout Catholics, who regard divorce as a sin, such an arrangement enables them to form a new relationship without divorcing.
- *As a preparation for or trial marriage* – what a young woman in the *Daily Mirror* described as 'a bit like membership of a club or gym. You try it out for a bit and, if it's a hit, you become a life member.' For most couples, cohabitation is such a trial run, and about 80 per cent of first-time marriages have been preceded by a period of cohabitation.

Younger people are more likely to cohabit, and have children outside marriage, and the trend is rising

The reasons for the decline of marriage and growing cohabitation

The reasons for the decline of marriage and growing cohabitation are similar to some of those for the rising divorce rate considered earlier, including:

- *The changing role of women*, whose growing economic independence has given them more freedom to choose their relationships. This is a very important explanation for the decline of marriage. Women now are more successful than men in education, and this is gradually being reflected in the labour market, as women seek to pursue their own careers. Women's expectations of life and marriage have risen during the course of the last century, and they are less willing to take on the demands associated with the housewife–mother role which, as feminists point out, still seems to dominate women's roles in marriage (this is discussed in the next topic). Evidence suggests that women in cohabiting relationships carry out less housework than those in married relationships. Women who do choose to marry often postpone this until they are older, when their careers are more established. Women's growing financial independence means they have less need for the security of marriage and support by men. Marriage has therefore become less of a financial necessity for women, and cohabitation provides an alternative relationship for personal fulfilment without the legal, financial and housework commitments involved in marriage. Cohabitation also avoids the potential complexity and bitterness of legally unravelling finance, housing and other possessions, and disputes over the custody of children, involved in marriage breakdown.
- *The reduced functions of the family.* As seen earlier in Topic 1, some functionalist writers argue that, in contemporary society, a number of family functions have either been transferred to or shared with other social institutions. This has perhaps meant that marriage has become less of a practical necessity.
- *Changing social attitudes and reduced social stigma.* Young people are more likely to cohabit than older people. This may in part reflect the evidence that older people, compared to younger people, are more likely to think that 'living together outside marriage is always wrong'; this reveals more easygoing attitudes to cohabitation among the young, showing the reduced social stigma attached to it. This may partly be a result of growing secularization.
- *Growing secularization*, discussed under divorce earlier, has meant that the influence of religiously based morality regarding the importance of marriage, and the condemnation of cohabitation, have declined. Marriage and cohabitation are now more about individual and practical choices than sacred, spiritual unions. Evidence for this lies in the fact that less than a third of marriages today involves a religious ceremony (though this is partly because many are second marriages arising from divorce, and many churches won't marry divorced people).
- *The rising divorce rate* may well deter couples from what they see as the risk involved in marriages not lasting. On the other hand, the high number of second marriages (remarriages) for one or both partners is itself due to the increased number of first marriages ending in divorce, as people give marriage another go.
- *Reducing risk.* Beck (1992) suggests we are living in what he calls a 'risk society'. Individuals are less controlled by traditional structures and institutions like the family, and there is less loyalty and commitment demanded by the social norms of marriage and family life. For example, a whole range of socially acceptable alternatives to the traditional nuclear family are now available. In this situation, individuals face increased risks, as they are constantly forced to reflect on their lives, weigh up choices, and make decisions, such as whether to get married or cohabit or live

alone, or what sort of family or other relationship they wish to live in, rather than relying on what was once seen as traditional and socially acceptable. In this situation, more people may simply be choosing to avoid the risk involved in long-term legal commitments like marriage.

CHANGES IN CHILD-BEARING AND MORE BIRTHS OUTSIDE MARRIAGE

The pattern of child-bearing has changed in Britain over the last hundred years or so. Families have been getting smaller, as the number of births has been dropping, with women having fewer children – and delaying having them until they are older – and more women choosing to remain childless. These trends are discussed further in Topic 5 on demography. However, one of the major changes in regard to child-bearing is the growing proportion of births outside of marriage. Nearly half of all births (47 per cent in 2011) in the UK are now outside marriage / civil partnership – about five times more than the proportion in 1971 – and this is a trend found in most European countries. In the European Union, around 37 per cent of children were born outside marriage in 2009, more than double the proportion twenty years earlier, and in Estonia, Sweden, Bulgaria, France and Slovenia the majority of live births were outside of marriage. This changing pattern clearly illustrates Lewis's point, mentioned earlier, that marriage, sex and parenthood are no longer linked.

Despite the record numbers of children being born outside marriage/civil partnership, nearly nine out of ten of those births in 2011 were registered jointly by the parents. Both parents in three out of four of these cases gave the same address. This suggests the parents were cohabiting, and that children are still being born into a stable couple relationship, even if the partners are not legally married or in a civil partnership.

The explanations for the increase of births outside marriage are very similar to those for the increase in the divorce rate, the decline in the marriage rate and the increase in cohabitation, which were discussed above. These include, particularly, a reduction in the social stigma attached to births outside marriage, and the changing position of women.

> **Activity**
>
> Refer back to the reasons for the increase in divorce, the decline of marriage and the increase in cohabitation, and identify and explain four reasons why there are now more births outside of marriage or civil partnership. Make sure you link your explanations to having children, rather than just making general points.

LONE PARENTHOOD: THE GROWTH OF THE LONE PARENT FAMILY

One of the biggest changes in the family has been the growth of the lone parent family (also known as the single parent or one parent family). The percentage of lone parent families has tripled since 1971, and Britain has one of the highest proportions of lone parent families in Europe. Around one in four of all families with dependent children were lone parent families in 2011 – nine out of ten of them headed by women. Nearly one in four (24 per cent) of dependent children now live in such families, compared to just 7 per cent in 1972. Most lone parents are women. This is because women are more likely to be awarded custody of children by the courts when divorces occur, reflecting the cultural norm that women are expected to bring up children. A further explanation is that fathers may have abandoned the mother before the birth of the child.

Why are there more lone parent families?

The rapid growth in the number of lone parent families can be explained by a number of factors, some of which have already been discussed earlier in explaining the rising divorce rate. These include:

- *The greater economic independence of women.* Women have greater economic independence today, both through more job opportunities and through support from the welfare state. This means marriage, and support by a husband, is less of an economic necessity today, compared to the past.
- *Improved contraception, changing male attitudes, and fewer 'shotgun weddings'.* With the wider availability and approval of safe and effective contraception, and easier access to safe and legal abortion, men may feel less responsibility to marry or cohabit with women and support them should they become unintentionally pregnant, and women may feel under less pressure to marry or cohabit with the future father. There are therefore fewer 'shotgun weddings' (where reluctant couples are forced into marriage by the father of the pregnant woman wielding an imaginary shotgun to ensure that the man marries his daughter).
- *Reproductive technology is available to women,* enabling them to bear children without a male partner, through surrogate motherhood and fertility treatments like IVF (in vitro fertilization).
- *Changing social attitudes.* There is less social stigma (or social disapproval and condemnation) attached to lone parenthood today. Women are therefore less afraid of the social consequences of becoming lone parents.

Those with New Right views particularly blame the generosity of the welfare state for the growth in lone parenthood. Writers such as Charles Murray (1990) argue that generous welfare benefits encourage women to have children they could not otherwise afford to support. This is often linked to his idea of the underclass, which is discussed in chapter 4 (see page 248).

The growth in lone parenthood has been seen by the New Right as one of the major signs of the decline of conventional family life and marriage. Lone parent families – and particularly lone never-married mothers – have been portrayed by some of the media and conservative politicians of the New Right as promiscuous parasites, blamed for everything from a decline in the importance of family life, and juvenile crime, through to housing shortages, rising drug abuse, educational failure of children and the general breakdown of society. The problems created by lone parenthood, particularly for boys, are usually explained by the lack of a male role model in the home, and consequently inadequate socialization.

Lone parenthood has therefore been presented as a major social problem, and there have been periodic **moral panics** about lone parenthood in the mass media.

In an effort to cut the welfare costs to the state of lone parents, the Child Support Agency was established in 1993. This was designed to encourage absent fathers to take financial responsibility for their children, thereby reducing benefit costs to the state. There have been a number of attempts to encourage lone parents to support themselves through paid employment. For example, in 1997, a new Childcare Tax Credit was introduced to help with the costs of childcare, along with a national childcare strategy to ensure good-quality affordable childcare, the expansion of nursery places

A **moral panic** is a wave of public concern about some exaggerated or imaginary threat to society, stirred up by overblown and sensationalized reporting in the mass media.

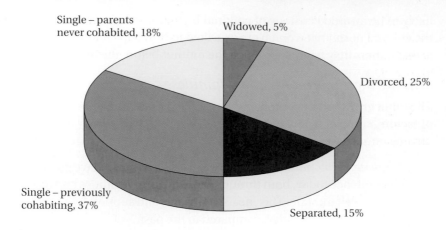

Single – parents never cohabited, 18%

Widowed, 5%

Divorced, 25%

Single – previously cohabiting, 37%

Separated, 15%

Figure 3.6 Lone mother families with dependent children, by marital status: Great Britain, 2010

Source: data from General Lifestyle Survey, Office for National Statistics

for children aged 3 and 4, and more pre- and after-school clubs. These policies arose from the fact that it is the lack of affordable childcare that is the major deterrent to lone parents working. The National Minimum Wage helps to prevent the exploitation of lone parents, who are mainly women, by unscrupulous employers, and the New Deal for Lone Parents helped many lone parents to find paid employment. In 2010, about 57 per cent of lone parents were in employment.

Nailing the myths

Never-married lone mothers only account for just over half of all lone parents with dependent children, with the other half mostly arising from divorce and separation, and occasionally widowhood, as figure 3.6 shows. Even among never-married lone mothers, the vast majority previously cohabited with the father and have registered his name on the child's birth certificate.

Only around 16 per cent of births are to parents who are neither married nor cohabiting.

The problems allegedly created by absent fathers have been questioned on the grounds that it is not the presence or absence of a father that is important, but whether fathers actually involve themselves in the children's upbringing. There are probably many fathers in two-parent families as well who fail to involve themselves in the care and discipline of their children, and problems like juvenile delinquency are likely to arise in any household where children are inadequately supervised and disciplined. This problem, often blamed on lone parenthood, is therefore just as likely to occur among two-parent families. A Home Office report has found no difference in crime rates between youngsters from lone parent and from two-parent families, and the Social Justice Policy Group in 2007 found youth crime was linked to a range of factors, all of which are as likely to be found in two-parent families, such as inadequate parenting, child abuse/maltreatment, family disruption, poor parental supervision, parental or sibling criminality, having teenage parents, unstable living conditions and economic disadvantage. Even if there were a link between lone parenthood and crime, it is more likely to be caused by poverty rather than lone parenthood – because lack of childcare facilities means many lone parents have to depend on inadequate state benefits to live, and lone parents are more likely to live in overcrowded or poor-quality housing. This probably explains other factors linked in the popular imagination to lone parenthood, such as lower educational achievement.

A misleading myth is that of lone teenage mothers getting pregnant to jump the queue for social (council and housing association) housing. There is very little evidence for this. Gingerbread (www.gingerbread.org.uk) pointed out that the average age of a lone parent in 2011 was 38, and that, at any one time, less than 2 per cent of all lone parents are teenagers. Only about 18 per cent of lone mothers have never married or lived with their child's father. Research in 1996 commissioned by the Economic and Social Research Council found that only 10 per cent of the small minority of women who were not in a regular relationship with the father when they became mothers were living alone with their child in social (council) housing six months after the birth. Many live with their parents, and many single, never-married parents have been in cohabiting relationships which broke down. In effect, this is no different from marriages that break down.

Feminist sociologists have been highly critical of New Right and other attacks on lone parents – particularly lone mothers. Silva (1996) argues that media-fuelled public concerns over lone mothers and the welfare of children are little more than an attempt to force women back into the traditional roles of housewife and homemaker, thereby undermining steps towards gender equality and women's independence. She suggests such attacks are patriarchal, as they challenge women's right to careers, to live independently from men and to raise children on their own.

Activity

1. Suggest reasons why, in the event of divorce, women are more likely than men to be given custody of the children.
2. Suggest explanations why most lone parent families are headed by women.
3. To what extent do you agree with the following statements, and why?
   - 'A lone mother can bring up her child as well as a married or cohabiting couple.'
   - 'People who want children ought to get married.'
   - 'To grow up happily, children need a home with both their mother and father.'
4. What are the advantages and disadvantages of lone parenthood compared to two-parent families?
5. Suggest reasons why the stereotypes held by professionals (like teachers, police officers and social workers) might mean children from lone parent families are more likely (a) to underachieve in education, and (b) to be overrepresented in the official crime statistics.
6. Visit the following websites, and identify five issues that seem to be of particular concern to lone parents. Describe each issue briefly, and outline any solutions that are suggested.
   www.gingerbread.org.uk
   www.lone-parents.org.uk

REMARRIAGE AND THE GROWTH OF THE RECONSTITUTED, STEP- OR BLENDED FAMILY

Around a third of marriages now involve a remarriage for one or both partners, mainly reflecting the increase in the divorce rate. A lot more divorced men remarry than divorced women, reflecting women's greater dissatisfaction or disillusionment with marriage. This is perhaps not surprising, given the way women often have to balance the triple and competing demands of paid employment, domestic labour and childcare, and emotional management of the family (see Topic 3).

The same factors that have increased divorce and separation, and that have generated more lone parenthood, have also meant there is an increasing trend towards serial monogamy, as individuals divorce and then form new married or cohabiting monogamous relationships with a series of different partners.

When these individuals getting involved in a series of married or cohabiting relationships are also parents, this creates more reconstituted families (sometimes called *stepfamilies* or *blended families* – as two or more different families are blended together) with stepparents, stepchildren, and stepbrothers and stepsisters arising from a previous relationship or relationships of one or both partners. Stepfamilies are the fastest-growing family type. Stepfathers are more common than stepmothers, since most children remain with the mother after a break-up, and around eight out of ten stepfamilies consist of a couple with at least one child from a previous relationship of the woman. This reflects the fact that it is nearly always women who gain custody of children in the event of a relationship breakdown. One in six men in their thirties are now stepfathers, raising other men's children – nearly double the proportion in the mid-1990s. Official estimates suggest there are around three-quarters of a million stepfamilies with dependent children in the UK – 10 per cent of all families with dependent children.

Life in stepfamilies

Allan et al. (2011) have pointed out life in stepfamilies can be complex. The sense of unity which may be present in families with the two natural parents (what Allan calls *natural families*), such as shared family history, commitments and interests, is not necessarily so evident in stepfamilies. For example, children may feel greater loyalty and closer to their natural parents, both the one who is present in the stepfamily and the one who is absent, than to their stepparent. There may also be divisions between children when there are two sets of children from previous families, each identifying with their own natural parent in the new blended family. As Allan points out, within natural families, disputes over things like how the household is organized, who does what, parenting and child discipline inevitably arise, with the two parents sometimes taking different positions. Within natural families, the right of both parents to be involved in these things is taken for granted and rarely questioned, but the family role of the stepparent in such matters is much less clear, and may depend on his or her relationship with the natural parent, rather than being asserted and taken-for-granted as in a natural family. For example, as Allan points out, depending on their age, children may be less willing to accept control and discipline, whatever its form, from stepparents than from natural parents, and some of the natural parents in these households may also have reservations about the degree to which a stepparent should be involved in child discipline and in other aspects of day-to-day childcare.

FAMILY AND HOUSEHOLD DIVERSITY

Many of the changes described in this topic, and in other parts of this chapter, have meant there is a wide range – or diversity – of households and family types in contemporary Britain.

The myth of 'cereal packet' families

There is no typical family or household in contemporary Britain, but there is a persistent myth of the 'cereal packet' family as the best, most desirable and most common form of family and household arrangement, as found in family ideology (see pages 137–8). The cereal packet family is the stereotype often promoted in advertising and other parts of the mass media, with family-size breakfast cereals, toothpaste and a wide range of other consumer goods. New Right theorists and functionalist sociologists often continue to see this as the most desirable type of family in Britain. This cereal packet happy family stereotype often gives the impression that the best form of family that people could live in, and for children to be raised in, is what Allan et al. have referred to as the 'natural family', in which a married or cohabiting couple are the biological parents of their children. The stereotype also portrays the ideal number of children as about two, with their natural parents as ideally tied together in first-time marriages for both of them. In this family, the instrumental husband is the main breadwinner and responsible for family discipline, and the wife plays the expressive nurturing role, through looking after the family home (housework) and taking primary responsibility for childcare, and maybe doing some part-time paid employment to supplement the family income. This family is seen as a nurturing, caring and loving institution – a safe and harmonious refuge from an uncaring outside world.

Why is the cereal packet stereotype misleading?

This image of the cereal packet stereotyped conventional or typical family is very misleading because there have been and continue to be important changes in family patterns, and there is a wide range of family types and household arrangements in contemporary Britain. This growing diversity of relationships that people live in shows that traditional family life is being eroded as people constantly develop new forms of relationship and choose to live in different ways. The meaning of 'family' and 'family life' is therefore changing for a substantial number of parents and children.

Households and families

Figure 3.7 shows the different types of household in the United Kingdom in 2011, and what percentages of people were living in them. In 2011, only 21 per cent of households contained a married / civil partnership or cohabiting couple with dependent children, and only 36 per cent of people lived in such a household. Meanwhile, 29 per cent of households consisted of one person living alone, and at least 70 per cent of households had no dependent children in them; 12 per cent of people lived in lone parent families, and 11 per cent of households were lone parent families. This alone shows that the cereal packet image of the nuclear family does not represent the arrangement in which most people in Britain live.

Families with dependent children

Figure 3.8 examines families with dependent children. This shows that, in 2011, about 26 per cent of such families were lone parent families, with more than nine out of ten of them (92 per cent) headed by women. Although a married/civil-partner or cohabiting couple headed 74 per cent of families with dependent children, this doesn't mean that most of these families conformed to the cereal packet image.

- A number of these families involved a cohabiting rather than a married/civil-partner relationship. In 2011, around one in four families consisting of a couple with dependent children involved a cohabiting rather than a married/civil-partner relationship. Such arrangements do not conform to the cereal packet stereotype.
- A number were reconstituted families, in which one or both of the partners were previously married. More than two in five marriages currently taking place will end in divorce, and around 40 per cent of all marriages now involve remarriage for one or both of the partners. About 10 per cent of all couple families with dependent

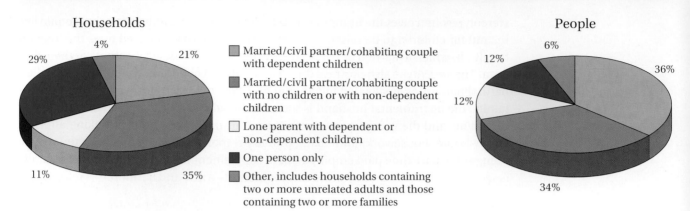

Households

4%
29%
21%
11%
35%

☐ Married/civil partner/cohabiting couple with dependent children

☐ Married/civil partner/cohabiting couple with no children or with non-dependent children

☐ Lone parent with dependent or non-dependent children

■ One person only

☐ Other, includes households containing two or more unrelated adults and those containing two or more families

People

6%
12%
12%
36%
34%

Figure 3.7 Households and people, by type of household: United Kingdom, 2011

Source: Labour Force Survey, Office for National Statistics

All families with dependent children

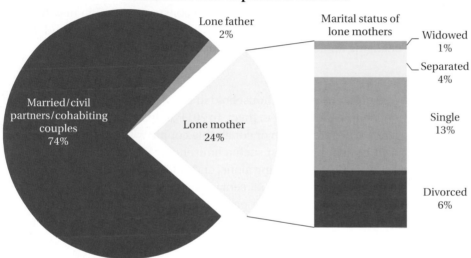

Lone father
2%

Married/civil partners/cohabiting couples
74%

Lone mother
24%

Marital status of lone mothers

Widowed
1%

Separated
4%

Single
13%

Divorced
6%

Figure 3.8 Families with dependent children, by family type and, for lone mothers, by marital status: United Kingdom, 2011*

* Data on marital status of lone mothers is from 2010

Source: Labour Force Survey, Office for National Statistics and General Lifestyle Survey 2010

Activity

Refer to figures 3.7 and 3.8

1 What percentage of households in 2011 consisted of one person only?
2 What percentage of people in 2011 were living in households consisting of a married / civil partner or cohabiting couple with no children or with non-dependent children?
3 In 2011, what percentage of all families with dependent children were headed by a lone mother who was widowed?
4 What is the main cause of lone motherhood?
5 Suggest reasons why so many people seem to believe that the 'cereal packet' family is the best and the most common type of family.

children were stepfamilies in 2010, and the stepfamily is today the most rapidly growing family type, along with cohabitation.

- Most of these families were dual-worker families, in which both parents were working. In 2011, about 90 per cent of couples with dependent children were both either in or looking for paid employment. Large numbers of mothers with dependent children work in paid employment, with the numbers increasing as children get older. In 2011, nearly three-quarters (71 per cent) of women in couples with dependent children were in paid employment. This often involves complex and costly alternative arrangements for childcare while both parents are working.

The cereal packet happy family stereotype of family ideology, of a working father married to a home-based mother caring for two small children now makes up only about 5 per cent of all households.

The classic extended family

As seen in Topic 1, functionalist writers have suggested that the classic extended family has largely disappeared in contemporary Britain, as the isolated privatized nuclear family emerges as the form most suited to life in contemporary societies.

While the isolated nuclear family may be more common than the classic extended family today, the classic extended family still survives in modern Britain in two types of community:

Traditional working-class communities These are long-established communities dominated by one industry, like fishing and mining, in the traditional working-class industrial centres of the north of England, and also occur in inner-city working-class areas. In such communities, there is little geographical or social mobility, and children usually remain in the same area when they get married. People stay in the same community for several generations, and this creates close-knit community life – it is the type of community shown in TV soaps such as *Coronation Street* and *EastEnders*.

Members of the extended family live close together and meet frequently, and there is a constant exchange of services between extended family members, such as washing, shopping and childcare between female kin, and shared work and leisure activities between male relatives. Such extended family life declined in the second half of the twentieth century, particularly in the 1990s, as traditional industries closed down and people were forced to move away in search of new employment.

The Asian community There is evidence that the extended family is still very common among those who came to Britain in the 1960s and 1970s from India, Pakistan and Bangladesh. The extended family usually centres on the male side of the family, with grandfathers, sons, grandsons and their wives, and unmarried daughters. Such family life continues to be an important source of strength and support in these communities.

The modified extended family

While it is true that many families with dependent children in Britain today are nuclear families, we must not assume that just because family members may live apart geographically, all links with kin are severed and destroyed. Kin beyond the nuclear family still play an important part in the lives of many families, particularly in the early years of relationships when homes are purchased or rented and children arrive. Often, in the age of modern communications and easy transportation, the closeness and mutual support between kin typical of classic extended family life are retained through email

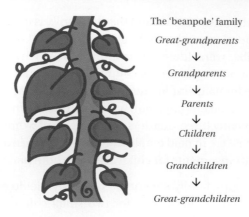

The 'beanpole' family

Great-grandparents

↓

Grandparents

↓

Parents

↓

Children

↓

Grandchildren

↓

Great-grandchildren

Figure 3.9 The 'beanpole' Family. Declining numbers of children in each generation and greater life expectancy mean the family tree has become thinner and less bushy – more beanpole-like – with fewer brothers and sisters, cousins, aunts and uncles, but more grandparents and great-grandparents

communication, social networking websites like Facebook, letter writing, telephone and visiting, despite geographical separation. We might therefore conclude that the most common family unit in contemporary society is a modified form of the extended family. This modified extended family is one in which related nuclear families, although they may be living far apart geographically, nevertheless maintain regular contact and mutual support made possible by modern communications and easy transportation. This, rather than the isolated nuclear family, is probably the most common type of family arrangement in Britain today.

The 'beanpole' family: the return of the extended family?

As discussed later in this chapter (see Topic 5), Britain's ageing population means that a growing number of people are reaching old age, and often living well into their 80s and many into their 90s. At the same time, couples are having fewer children and nuclear families are getting smaller. This means that there is an increase in the number of extended three-, four- and five-generation families. There are declining numbers of children in families, but more of them are growing up in extended families alongside several of their grandparents and even great-grandparents. Brannen (2003) calls this new shape of the extended family the '**beanpole family**'. This is because the family tree is 'thinner' and less 'bushy': fewer brothers and sisters in one generation leads to fewer cousins, aunts and uncles in the next. It is also longer, with several generations of older relatives, as people live longer. This trend towards a new emerging 'beanpole' form of the extended family can only be expected to increase with the growing numbers of the elderly, and fewer children being born.

A **beanpole family** is a multi-generation extended family, which is long and thin, with few aunts, uncles and cousins, reflecting fewer children being born in each generation, but people living longer.

Cultural diversity

Cultural diversity refers to differences in family structure and lifestyles between ethnic and religious groups.

Caribbean families   Berthoud (2001) sees family life in the Caribbean community as based on 'modern individualism'. This emphasizes individual choice, independence and commitment based on the quality of relationships rather than custom, duty or a marriage certificate. Marriage is just one lifestyle option among many, which people may or may not choose, according to their individual circumstances and preferences, and whether or not they fancy taking on family commitments. Modern individualism finds expression in Caribbean communities through low rates of marriage – with marriage relatively unimportant to the Caribbean self-image – and high levels of lone parenthood. Berthoud points out that Caribbeans are less likely to live with a partner than either white people or South Asians, and those who do have a partner are less likely to have married them, and those who have married are more likely to separate or divorce – the proportion who separate or divorce is around twice as high as for white people. Mixed partnerships are common, with half of black men who have partners living with a white woman, and a third of black women with partners living with a white man. Berthoud suggests mixed marriages are widely accepted among Caribbeans – more than among whites, and much more than among Asians. He points out that this pattern of high numbers of mixed partnerships among Caribbeans, combined with the low rate of partnership and marriage in the first place, means that very few Caribbean men and women are married to each other.

Lone parenthood is higher among Caribbean women than any other ethnic group – over half of Caribbean mothers are never-married lone parents, compared to one in ten white mothers. This partly reflects a cultural tradition, but also high rates of black male unemployment and men's inability and reluctance to support families. As Berthoud points out, the combination of low rates of partnership, and high rates of single parenthood and of mixed marriage means that only a quarter of black children live with two black parents.

South Asian families Ballard (1982) found extended family relationships are more common in minority ethnic groups originating in South Asia – from Pakistan, Bangladesh and India. Such families are still commonly patriarchal in structure, with seniority going to the eldest male, and males in general.

Berthoud sees family life in South Asian communities as based on 'old-fashioned values', in the sense that many of their present family characteristics were once found in the past among white families, but have now been rejected. These include a commitment to marriage, tight-knit families with a strong sense of family loyalty, births within marriage, respect for parents, **arranged marriages** (a custom derived from their countries of origin), husbands' authority over wives, women's roles as housewives and mothers, and having large numbers of children.

Today, the highest rates of marriage are in South Asian communities. Around three-quarters of Pakistani and Bangladeshi women are married by age 25, compared with about two-thirds of Indian women and half of white women. Virtually all South Asians with a partner are in a formal marriage. A majority of Bangladeshi and Pakistani women look after their home and family full-time, rather than taking paid employment. Family sizes tend to be larger than other ethnic groups, particularly among Pakistanis and Bangladeshis, with families of four or more children quite common. In many ways, the traditional British 'cereal packet' family of a working male married to a home-based female is more likely to be found among Pakistanis and Bangladeshis than any other ethnic group. Divorce rates are low in such communities because of strong social disapproval and a wide support network of kin for families under stress. Berthoud points out that, for South Asians, the key question is not whether they are married but how they choose their marriage partner. Arranged marriages are still common in such communities, with Pakistanis and Bangladeshis particularly continuing to have their marriage partners chosen for them by their parents or other family elders. This custom is a source of some conflict between young South Asians and their parents, with rising expectations of young people having some choice in their marriage partner.

An **arranged marriage** is one which is arranged by the parents of the marriage partners, with a view to compatibility of background and status. More a union between two families than between two people, and romantic love between the marriage partners is not necessarily present.

Social class diversity

Social class diversity refers to differences between upper-class, middle-class and working-class families. Classic extended families – where they still exist – are more likely to be found in what remains of traditional working-class communities, although such families are disappearing everywhere. For example, in a study of Swansea, Charles (2008) found that classic extended families were practically extinct, even in the working class, and the only group in which such families remained was the ethnic minority population. Classic extended families in the working class have been largely replaced by modified extended or privatized nuclear families. Modified extended families tend to be more common in the working class, and privatized nuclear families more common in the middle class. Differences in income and wealth will also lead to differences in lifestyle, and possibly in parenting practices and the household division of labour, between families from different social classes.

Life cycle and life-course diversity

Life cycle diversity refers to the way families may change through life, for example as partners have children, as the children grow older and eventually leave the home, as partners separate and form new relationships, as people retire, grow older and have grandchildren. All these factors mean the family will be constantly changing. For instance, levels of family income will change as children move from dependence to independence, levels of domestic labour and childcare will change, and levels of participation in paid employment will alter, particularly for women, depending on the absence or presence of children and the children's age. This means there will always be a diversity of family types at different stages of the family life cycle. Figure 3.10 shows an example of a family life cycle, and reflects some of the different forms the family may take at different stages of the **life course** of individuals. The life course refers to the various significant events, such as marriage or cohabitation, parenthood, divorce and retirement, that individuals experience as they make their way through life, and the choices they make and the meanings they give to these events.

> The **life course** refers to the various significant events individuals experience as they make their way through life, and the choices they make and the meanings they give to events such as marriage or cohabitation, parenthood, divorce, and retirement.

Allan and Crow (2001) point out that in contemporary societies the traditional family life cycle and life course have changed dramatically. In the past, the typical family life cycle took the form of a series of set stages, with a fairly standard life course for individuals: young people would grow up in two-parent natural families, finish their education, leave home, get married and then start their own family, and then the family life cycle would be reborn as their own children left home.

In contemporary Britain, there have been huge changes in family formation, and young people face growing uncertainty about *what* they should do, and *when* they should do it. They are confronted with a range of choices as they make their way through life, which contributes to ever more diverse family forms. For example, they face choices about whether or not to leave home and get their own place; whether to marry, cohabit or live alone; whether to have children; whether or not to leave their current partner, to get divorced or to remarry. They face choices over which partner does the cooking or housework or whether it should be shared, whether or not to work part-time to look after the children, or whether or not to retire early. The life course for individuals is now characterized more than ever by uncertainty, risk, choice, diversity and change; there are multiple paths through the life course, and events no longer occur in any set pattern. In the face of declining marriage, remarriage, more stepfamilies, serial monogamy and fewer long-term relationships, rising cohabitation, lone parenthood, more births outside marriage, rising divorce and so on, individuals will have a wide variety of experiences of personal relationships and family life, and no longer will these necessarily be age-related. The boundaries between family and friendship are also becoming blurred, and the formation of friendships may become more significant than traditional family-related life events (see, for example, 'Adult-kids, kippers, shared households and "families of choice"' below).

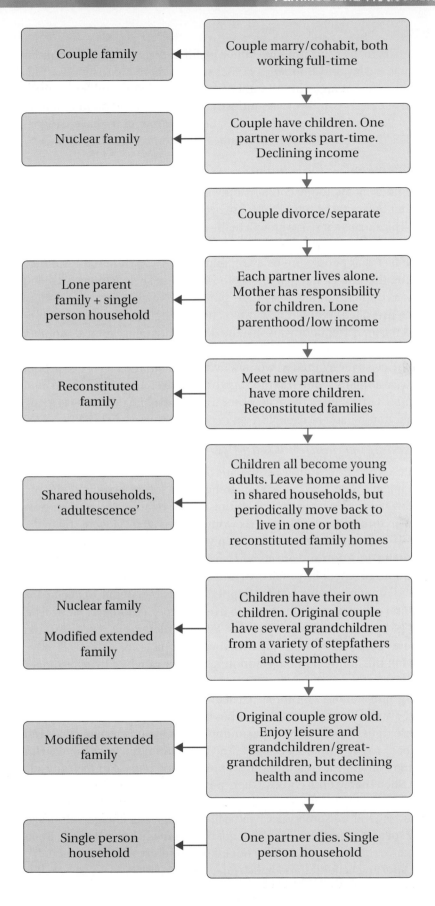

Figure 3.10 A family life cycle

Regional diversity

Regional diversity refers to the way family life differs in different geographical locations around the country. Eversley and Bonnerjea (1982) suggest there are distinctive patterns of family life in different areas of Britain. For example, on the south coast there is a high proportion of elderly couples; older industrial areas and very traditional rural communities tend to have more extended families; and the inner cities have a higher proportion of families in poverty, lone parent families and ethnic minority families.

The growth in 'singlehood' – living alone

About one in three households today contains only one person, compared to one in twenty in 1901. Under half of these households are over pensionable age, compared to two-thirds in 1971. This means there is a growth in the number of younger people living alone. This trend can be explained by the decline in marriage, the rise in divorce and separation, and the fact that people are delaying marriage or cohabitation until they are older, or rejecting this choice altogether. There is also less social stigma attached to living alone now, as opposed to the idea of the 'left-on-the-shelf' unwanted solitary individual that once prevailed. Women now often choose singlehood as they wish to pursue careers, and this may frequently involve the demand for geographical mobility (moving to other areas) and this is easier if not bogged down by a partner's job.

There are nearly twice as many men as women living alone in the 25–44 age group, but there are over twice as many women as men aged 65 and over, because women tend to live longer than men. Longer lives, particularly for women, explain the increase in the number of pensioner one-person households.

Adult-kids, kippers, shared households and 'families of choice'

Heath (2004) has described how young people are now less likely to follow the traditional route of living at home, leaving school, going into a job or higher education, and then 'settling down' into a married or cohabiting couple relationship in their own homes. In 2011, one in three men, and one in six women, aged 20 to 34 were still living with their parents – a 20 per cent increase in fifteen years. Some of these 'adult-kids', who have finished their education and are in their working years, live with their parents because they can't afford to rent or buy their own homes. But others are staying through choice. This group is sometimes referred to as 'kippers' – 'kids in parents' pockets' – as it's cheaper, easier and often more comfortable to live at home, although it may mean eroding their parents' planned retirement savings. Even by their early 30s, one in ten men and one in twenty women are still living with their parents.

Those who have left the family home are adopting a wider range of living arrangements before forming couple relationships (or living alone) later in life. Shared households are becoming much more common, particularly among young people. This transitional period between youth and adult roles has been described as 'kidulthood' or 'adultescence'. These transitional living arrangements might include moving between living alone, going back to live with their parents, and living in shared households with their peers. There may often be a greater loyalty among young people to their friends than to their family. Such shared households, where people choose to live and form relationships with a group of people with whom they have closer relations than with their families of birth, have therefore sometimes been called 'families of choice' (although they are not strictly speaking families as they are not based on kinship relations). Such households may involve shared domestic life (cooking, eating and socializing together), and shared leisure, sporting activities and holidays.

Figure 3.11 Family and household diversity

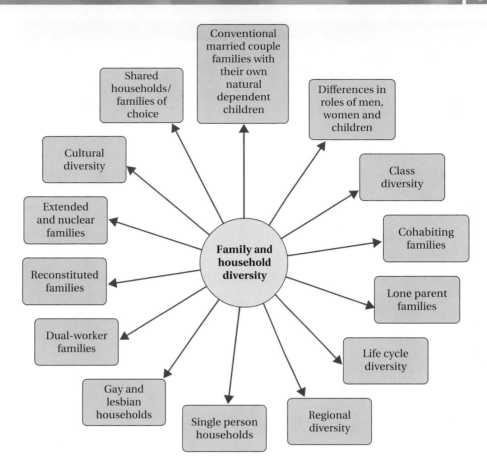

These households are on the increase because of the high costs of buying or renting houses, the growing numbers of young people entering higher education, and the desire of young people to explore alternative living arrangements rather than simply settling down into a conventional couple household.

Figure 3.11 summarizes the range of family diversity in contemporary Britain.

Activity

1 Identify all the ways that family life might change during its life cycle.
2 Discuss with others in your group, and outline three different life courses of individuals in relation to their family and personal lives.
3 Suggest two ways in each case in which (a) the increase in the divorce rate, (b) immigration, (c) more births outside marriage and (d) more civil partnerships (gay marriages), contribute to family diversity in contemporary Britain.
4 Suggest three differences you might expect to find between working-class and middle-class families.

Exam-style questions

1   Explain what is meant by the term 'divorce rate'.   *(2 marks)*

2   Explain what is meant by the term 'family diversity'.   *(2 marks)*

3   Suggest **two** reasons why there has been an increase in births outside marriage/civil partnership. *(4 marks)*

4   Suggest **two** reasons why couples may choose to cohabit rather than get married or form a civil partnership.   *(4 marks)*

5   Suggest **three** ways in which families may differ between ethnic groups.   *(6 marks)*

6   Suggest **three** reasons why the conventional nuclear family no longer remains the norm in contemporary Britain.   *(6 marks)*

7   Examine the view that there is no general or 'typical' family or household in Britain today.   *(24 marks)*

8   Examine the reasons for changes in the patterns of marriage, divorce and cohabitation since the 1970s.   *(24 marks)*

Topic 3

SPECIFICATION AREA

The nature and extent of changes within the family, with reference to gender roles, domestic labour and power relationships

Gender roles, domestic labour and power in the family

A SYMMETRICAL FAMILY?

The **domestic division of labour** refers to the division of roles, responsibilities and work tasks within a household.
Segregated conjugal roles show a clear division and separation between the male and female roles.
Integrated (or joint) **conjugal roles** show few divisions between male and female partners' roles.
Conjugal roles simply means the roles played by a male and female partner in marriage or in a cohabiting relationship.

Young and Willmott (1973) argued that the modern family is what they called a 'symmetrical family'. This is a family that has strong bonds between married or cohabiting partners, with the relationship becoming more symmetrical (the same on both sides) – less patriarchal, or male-dominated, and much more an equally balanced partnership of equals. Both partners share household chores, childcare and decision-making, and both partners are more likely to be involved in paid employment. The assumption has been that there has been a change in the **domestic division of labour** from **segregated conjugal roles** to more equally balanced **integrated** (or joint) **conjugal roles**. Whether there really is more equality between partners in relationships today, or whether the family remains a patriarchal, male-dominated unit, is the issue in this topic.

Some of the differences between segregated and integrated conjugal roles are identified in table 3.4.

This greater equality in marriage or cohabiting relationships is often thought to be shown by women taking on more of traditional 'men's work' (especially working outside the home) and men doing 'women's work' (housework, shopping and childcare), with shared leisure and decision-making. This has often been combined with discussion, mainly in the mass media, about the emergence of a so-called 'New Man', who was more caring, sharing, gentle, emotional and sensitive in his attitudes to women, children and his own emotional needs, and committed to doing his fair share of housework and childcare.

Table 3.4 Differences between segregated and integrated conjugal roles

Segregated conjugal roles	Integrated conjugal roles
Partners in a married or cohabiting relationship have clearly separated roles.	Partners in a married or cohabiting relationship have interchangeable and flexible roles.
Men take responsibility for bringing in money, major decisions and doing the heavier and more technical jobs around the home, such as repairing household equipment and doing DIY. Women are mainly housewives, with responsibility for housework, shopping, cooking, childcare, etc.; they are unlikely to have full-time paid employment.	Both partners are likely to be either in paid employment or looking for a job. Household chores and childcare are shared, with males taking on traditional female jobs like housework, cooking, shopping, etc., and female partners taking on traditional male jobs, such as household repairs, looking after the car, etc.
Partners are likely to have separate friends and different leisure activities.	Partners share common friends, leisure activities and decision-making.

WHAT CAUSES THESE APPARENT CHANGES?

The growing equality in family relationships which is thought to be occurring is often explained by the following factors.

Improved living standards in the home

Improved living standards such as central heating, TV, DVDs, computers and the internet, and all the other modern consumer goods, have encouraged husbands and wives, or cohabiting couples, to become more home-centred, building the relationship and the home.

The decline of the close-knit extended family and greater geographical and social mobility

In contemporary society more geographical and social mobility has weakened the close-knit ties of the extended family. This has meant there is less pressure from kin on newly married or cohabiting couples to retain traditional roles and it is therefore easier to adopt new roles in a relationship. There are often no longer the separate male and female networks (of friends and especially kin) for male and female partners to mix with. This increases their dependence upon each other, and may mean men and women who adopt new roles avoid being teased by friends who knew them before they got married or started cohabiting (see Bott's research in the box below).

Elizabeth Bott, 'Conjugal roles and social networks' (1957)

Bott tried to explain the apparent changes in conjugal roles. Although her research is old, the theoretical aspects of her work still have some use today.

Bott found that the most important factor influencing whether couples had segregated or integrated conjugal roles was the social network of friends, kin and acquaintances built up by each partner before marriage. Where couples had a tight-knit network, where the members of the network knew each other well and were in regular contact, this helped to reinforce the separation between men's and women's roles. Both husband and wife, or cohabiting partners, had people of their own sex for companionship or help with household tasks. The closeness of the network acted as a form of social control on the couple, and things such as teasing prevented the couple drifting from traditional segregated roles. By contrast, a loose-knit network would make movement towards more role integration easier, because those constraints would be removed.

Using Bott's framework, one would expect that the geographical and social mobility of contemporary societies would lead to looser social networks, more reliance on the partners in the relationship, and therefore more role integration.

The improved status and rights of women

The general improvements in women's status in society, with most women now in paid employment, may encourage men to accept women more as equals and not simply as housewives and mothers, while at the same time women have become more assertive in demanding that household tasks are shared.

The increase in the number of women working in paid employment

That most women are now in paid employment has increased their independence and authority in the family, and reduced the time they spend on housework.

Gershuny (1994) and Laurie and Gershuny (2000) found that as wives moved into paid employment or from part-time to full-time work, they did less housework, and men did a bit more. Laurie and Gershuny saw this as leading to *some* progress in reducing gender inequalities in the home, but they stressed this was a very slow process and was leading to only small reductions. Kan et al. (2011) found that, while men have increased their contribution to domestic work, this is in what has been traditionally seen as the masculine-defined tasks, such as DIY, outside work like gardening, and general 'fixing'. These tasks are non-routine, and do not need doing every day, day in, day out, and Kan points out that women still do the bulk of caring activities and routine chores such as cooking, cleaning and clothes care – traditionally defined as 'feminine' tasks.

Nonetheless, where the female partner has her own income, she is less dependent on her male partner, and she therefore has more power and authority. Decision-making is thus more likely to be shared. The importance of the female partner's earnings in maintaining the family's standard of living may also have encouraged men to help a bit more with housework – a recognition that the women cannot be expected to do two jobs at once.

The commercialization of housework

The commercialization of housework refers to the way there are a whole host of consumer goods and services to help with reducing the burden of housework compared to previous generations. This includes things like freezers, fridges, automatic washing machines and dryers, vacuum cleaners, electric irons, takeaway foods, supermarket ready-meals and other convenience foods, online shopping, including online ordering and home delivery of groceries (like those provided by Tesco, Ocado and Sainsbury's), and a whole host of other companies providing a wide range of domestic services to the home, like pet care and cleaning services. Silver (1987) and Schor (1992) suggested that this commercialization has taken away some of the drudgery and time-consuming aspects of housework (though Schor suggested there was actually more time spent on it as standards are now higher). This means that housework is now easier and less skilled, so, perhaps, enabling women to do a bit less and encouraging men to do a bit more, and if women are in paid employment this boosts the family income to pay for these things. However, all these things still need to be organized and the fact that there may be less to do doesn't in itself reduce gender inequality if women have to do all the related organizing and running around. This reducing burden of housework through commercialization is also most available only to the well-off. This is perhaps why women, but particularly men, do less housework as they earn more, as they can afford to pay others to do it for them.

Weaker gender identities

Postmodernists would argue that men and women now have much more choice in how they see themselves and their roles. Couples are free to 'pick 'n' mix' roles and identities based on personal choice, and are therefore less constrained by traditional masculine and feminine gender roles and identities. Postmodernists suggest this may weaken traditional gender divisions in housework and childcare, and encourage men to do more, though Kan's research above suggests this might perhaps be a hope rather than reflecting actual experience.

CRITICISMS OF THE VIEW THAT MODERN MARRIAGES AND COHABITING RELATIONSHIPS ARE REALLY MORE EQUAL

The view that there is more equality in modern family relationships has been subject to very strong criticism, particularly by feminist writers, and there is not really much evidence that the family is now typically 'symmetrical'. While there does seem to be some evidence of more role integration in leisure activities and some decision-making, housework and childcare remain predominantly women's work. While men are perhaps more involved in childcare than they used to be, this would appear to be in the more enjoyable activities like playing with the children and taking them out. The more routine jobs such as bathing and feeding and taking children to the doctor are still done predominantly by women, and it is still mostly women who get the blame if the house is untidy or children are dirty or badly dressed.

Evidence from a number of surveys shows that, in most cases, women still perform the majority of domestic tasks around the home, even when they have paid jobs themselves. This is true even among full-time working women, where one would expect to find the greatest degree of equality. Knudsen and Wærness (2008), in a comparative study of women's and men's housework in thirty-four countries, found there were no modern countries in the world where men do housework more than, or as much as, women, and women perform two-thirds of all domestic work in the world. In many cases, traditional segregated roles still remain. Review the evidence yourself by studying the data on pages 173–4, and doing the related activity, and reading about the additional evidence on inequalities in the domestic division of labour in the section below.

Activity

Refer to items A–E. These show the results of surveys which were conducted between 1992 and 2008. Then answer the following questions:

1 Which three household tasks were the most likely to be performed mainly by women? (see Item A)
2 Which two household tasks were the most likely to be performed mainly by men? (Item A)
3 Who is most likely to look after sick family members? (Item A)
4 Which household task is the least likely to be performed mainly by men? (Item A)
5 Which three household tasks are most likely to be shared equally? (Item A)
6 Who is most likely to prepare the evening meal, and either to be solely responsible for washing evening dishes or to share it with their partners? (Item A)
7 What percentage of men never iron clothes? (Item B)
8 What percentage of women never do DIY repair work? (Item B)
9 According to Item C, which two groups spend the most time each day on food-related housework?
10 According to Item C, which activity do married men and women seem to spend roughly equal amounts of time on each day?
11 Refer to Items D and E. (a) Identify two differences between the housework done by men and that done by women, and (b) suggest how these differences might make paid work more difficult for women.
12 Reviewing the evidence in Items A–E, suggest three pieces of evidence that might be used to show family relationships are becoming more equal, and three pieces indicating that they are not.

13 Drawing on all the work you have done on the issue, to what extent do you agree with the view that it is largely a myth that the contemporary family is a partnership of equals? How would you explain any differences between what women and men do in the home?

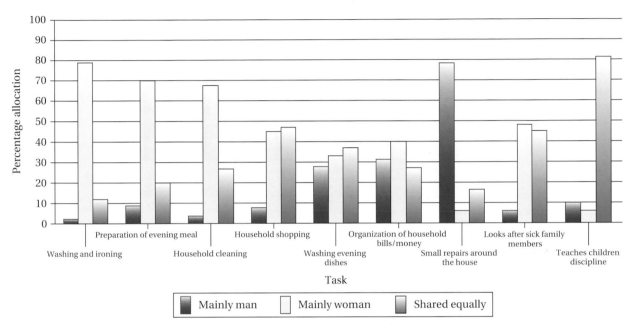

Item A Household division of labour among married and cohabiting couples: Great Britain, 1990s

Source: Data from *British Social Attitudes Survey* (1992, 1994); *Social Trends* (1997); *British and European Social Attitudes Report* (1998)

Item B Percentage who never do selected household tasks: United Kingdom, 2001

Activity	Does not do activity	
	Men	Women
Cooking a meal	15	3
DIY repair work	16	46
Gardening	20	22
Non-food shopping	7	3
Food shopping	12	5
Cooking a meal (special occasion)	33	10
Decorating	8	27
Tidying the house	13	4
Helping children with homework	66	60
Washing clothes	39	5
Ironing clothes	42	8

Source: Adapted from UK Time Use Survey, Office for National Statistics

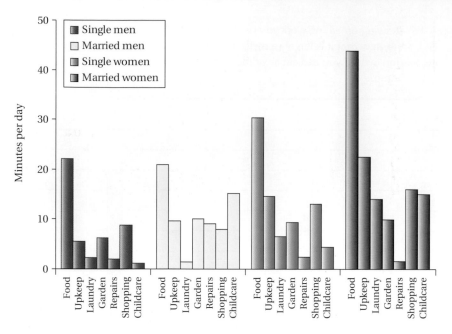

Item C Time spent on housework each day: full-time workers

Source: Adapted from Bryan and Sevilla Sanz (2008)

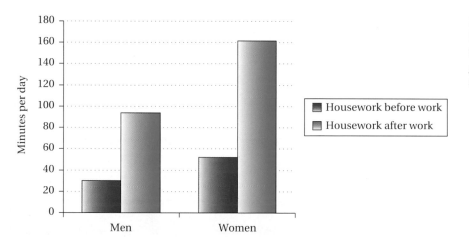

Item D Time spent on housework before and after work: full-time workers

Source: Adapted from Bryan and Sevilla Sanz (2008)

Item E

Housework may affect wages because it reduces the amount of energy and flexibility that can be brought to the labour market. Individuals who go to work tired after doing the housework are likely to perform less well than others with no housework commitments; similarly, having the responsibility of organising domestic activities may make it more difficult to concentrate at work. Furthermore, those who need to do housework at certain times (for example cooking meals) cannot be as flexible in their working hours as those with no commitments and so may be more restricted in the types of jobs they can do. As well as doing more total hours of housework than men (or single women), married women specialise in routine tasks (like cooking and laundry) which are done at times that may interfere with paid employment. In particular there is evidence that the married women's housework may limit their paid employment activities towards the end of the working day. Married men, by contrast, tend to specialise in housework tasks, like gardening and household repairs, that can be put off to the weekend.

Source: Adapted from Bryan and Sevilla Sanz (2008)

Inequalities in the domestic division of labour

Women still perform the majority of domestic and childcare tasks around the home, even when they have paid jobs themselves. They spend on average nearly twice as long as men each day on household and childcare tasks, such as household shopping, cooking the evening meal, cleaning, washing and ironing, looking after the children and caring for sick family members. The 2008 British Social Attitudes Survey reported that 80 per cent of women with partners said that they 'always or usually did the laundry'. A 2008 mumsnet.com survey found 75 per cent of mothers do most of the cooking for their children, compared to just 7 per cent of fathers. The 2007 European Social Reality Report found 85 per cent of women in the European Union did the ironing (79 per cent in the UK). A 2009 survey by cleaning firm Vileda found that four out of ten British men still thought that housework was a woman's job, with one in five men admitting that they did absolutely no cleaning around the home (and 78 per cent of those doing no cleaning were married and/or fathers). One in three men said they had never tackled the bathroom with a mop, bucket or cloth. The Food Standards Agency's 'Consumer Attitudes to Food Standards' survey (2007) found that 77 per cent of women took all or most of the responsibility for household food shopping. Data published in 1997 by the Office for National Statistics showed that women spent on average nearly twice as long as men each day (five hours) cooking, cleaning, shopping, washing and looking after the children. Housework is the second-largest cause of domestic rows, after money. It is women who are most likely to have to make sacrifices, if money is tight, to buy the children clothes, and to make sure other family members are properly fed.

Research on families where both partners are working in full-time career jobs, such as Elston's (1980) research on doctors and Rapoport and Rapoport's (1976) study of professional and business couples, suggests that these professional wives are still expected to take major responsibility for dealing with childcare arrangements, sick children and housework. Harkness (2005) found this was still true a quarter of a century later. Three-quarters of households now have dual incomes, with both partners working, but she found that women still take responsibility for most of the housework, and that it is still mainly women who take time off to look after sick children, including more than half of women who earn the same as or more than their partners. Harkness found working mothers with children put twice as many hours into housework as their partners, and mothers working full-time in dual-earner couples faced long working hours, with

Have conjugal roles really become more equal?

the burden of unpaid housework and childcare responsibilities increasing the time pressures for many women. A 2011 survey by the Social Issues Research Centre, *The Changing Face of Motherhood*, found even though most mothers work full- or part-time today, they are twice as likely to be involved in childcare as fathers.

These pressures of housework and childcare on top of full-time careers have led to the suggestion by the *Guardian* newspaper that many full-time married career women effectively have the status of 'married lone parents'.

So women who are in full-time demanding career jobs are still treated primarily as housewives–mothers at home, and this is the group Young and Willmott argued would be most likely to display symmetry in marriage.

Activity

Do a small survey in your own home or in any household where there are children, and find out who performs the various jobs around the home – mainly the man, mainly the woman, or shared equally. You might like to investigate whether children do any work.

(a) Make a note about whether or not one or both partners are working in paid employment, and whether they do this full-time or part-time. Why might this be important information?

(b) Use the various tasks included in items A–E on pages 173–4 to draw up a checklist of jobs. You might also consider some of the following tasks: cleaning floors; cleaning the loo; drawing up the shopping list or working out what's needed when going to the supermarket; changing nappies; bathing the baby; buying children's clothes.
You might also consider decision-making in the family, by asking about who finally decides whether to spend a large amount of money (say, over £1,000), buy new furniture, whether and where to go on holiday, whether to buy a new car, colour schemes when redecorating, what plants to put in the garden, and so on. A further aspect to explore might be who takes responsibility for children, such as making sure they have the right gear for school every day, buying them new shoes, arranging parties and so on.

(c) Examine your results to see if there is any evidence to suggest family roles are becoming more equal. If you are in a group, bring all the results together and discuss what the evidence shows.

Women still do most of the housework and childcare, even when they have full-time jobs in paid employment

Figure 3.12 How domestic labour differs from paid employment

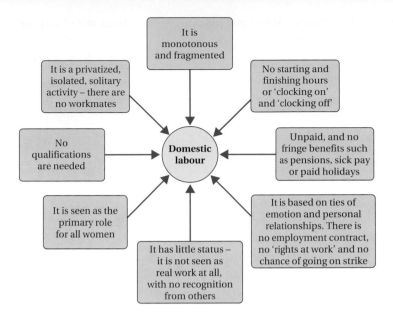

The nature and value of domestic labour   Domestic labour refers to unpaid house-work and childcare, and, as seen above, most of this still falls to women. This is a clear inequality between men and women, and this problem is made worse by some of the features of domestic labour that make it different from a paid job. These include no pay, no pensions, no holidays, and unlimited working hours. These features of domestic labour are illustrated in figure 3.12 above.

The Office for National Statistics in 1997 calculated that, if the time spent on unpaid work in the home (childcare, washing, ironing, cleaning, shopping and cooking) was valued at the same average pay rates as equivalent jobs in paid employment (for example, if cooking were paid as it is for chefs, or childcare as for nannies and child-minders), it would be worth (in 2002) £700 billion a year. Legal & General's 2011 'Value of a Parent' survey found that women with children spend an average 71 hours a week on household chores and childcare, valued at £30,032 a year. This is £578 per week, or a modest £8.14 an hour. This is a much higher amount than most households could afford to pay to purchase these services outside the home if mothers stopped providing them for free. The survey found mothers put in 42 per cent more time than fathers on housework and childcare, who spent 50 hours a week on such tasks.

Activity

Refer to figure 3.12
1 Suggest reasons why domestic labour is often not seen as 'real work'.
2 What might make it difficult for those doing domestic labour to go on strike?
3 Explain what is meant by domestic labour being 'seen as the primary role for all women'.
4 In what ways do you think domestic labour might be (a) more satisfying and (b) less satisfying than work in paid employment?
5 Women who are full-time housewives suffer higher rates of stress, anxiety and depression, and suffer from poorer mental health, than women and men working in paid employment. With reference to figure 3.12, suggest reasons why this might be the case.
6 To what extent do you agree with the view that it is mainly men who benefit from domestic labour?
7 What kind of evidence would you use to judge whether there is 'symmetry' in your own family or relationship, or that of others? Identify the main issues you would want to look at.

Who benefits from domestic labour?   There are differing views about who benefits from domestic labour:

- For *radical feminists*, men are seen as the main people who benefit from domestic labour, since it is overwhelmingly women who do it. From this point of view, the inequalities in domestic labour are part of the problem of patriarchy, with the family seen as a patriarchal unit, institutionalizing, reinforcing and reproducing male power.
- *Marxist feminists* see domestic labour as benefiting capitalism by contributing to the reproduction of labour power. Unpaid domestic labour reproduces the labour force at no cost to the capitalist, through the free production and rearing of children, and support for male workers. From this point of view, the family is a 'social factory' producing human labour power. Domestic labour also contributes to the daily reproduction of the labour force by providing for the physical and mental well-being of family members so they are capable of performing labour each day for the capitalist. However, Marxist feminists recognize it is also a problem of patriarchy, as it is women who do most of this unpaid work and it is predominantly men who benefit from it.

Measuring the domestic division of labour   Crude indicators are often used to measure whether or not there are integrated roles. For example, shared friends are often seen as evidence of 'jointness', but shared friends may mean the male partner's friends, and involve the woman being cut off from her friends, resulting in more dependence on her male partner and greater inequality.

Oakley (1974) is a feminist sociologist who did much of the pioneering work on housework and roles in the family. Oakley argues that Young and Willmott's evidence for 'jointness' in *The Symmetrical Family* is totally unconvincing. Of married men, 72 per cent claimed to 'help their partners in the home in some way other than washing up at least once a week'. As Oakley points out, this could mean anything – a quick run over with the vacuum cleaner, tucking children into bed, making breakfast occasionally, going out with the children on Saturday mornings, or even a man ironing his own trousers. This is hardly convincing evidence for symmetry or equality in marriage, and fewer than three-quarters of husbands in Young and Willmott's research did even this much.

While there is some evidence of more sharing of childcare than household tasks, Boulton (1983) argued that many surveys exaggerate how much childcare men really do. As she sees it, while men may help with childcare, it is their female partners who take the main responsibility for children, often at the expense of other aspects of their lives, like paid employment. This seems still to be the case thirty years later.

The extent to which some of the research on conjugal roles can be applied to the whole population is seriously questionable. For example, Bott's research was based on a small sample of twenty families, the research by Oakley on forty couples, and by Boulton on fifty couples. Much of this research was based in London. These samples are too small and too specific to London to be applied to the whole country. The only surveys which can really claim to be representative of everyone are large-scale surveys, like the British Social Attitudes Survey, which uses much larger samples (around 3,000 people) and very careful sampling techniques. These issues are discussed in chapter 5 on sociological methods.

The emotional side of family life and women's 'triple shift'

There is evidence that women take the major responsibility for emotional labour and 'managing' the emotional side of family life. Delphy and Leonard (1992) described emotional work as concerned with maintaining the bonds of affection, moral support, friendship and love which give family members a sense of belonging and which underpin family solidarity and cohesion. In short, it is concerned with the things that make people feel good in their family lives. This emotional work requires active effort, as it involves talking to partners and children about things that interest them, smiling at their jokes, taking pleasure in their successes, doing things that give them pleasure and so on. Delphy and Leonard see this emotional work as an important dimension of women's work in the home.

Duncombe and Marsden (1995) found that many long-term relationships were held together by women, rather than men, putting in the emotional work necessary to keep their relationships alive. As well as with their partners, women also seem to be more involved in the emotional aspects of childcare, such as talking to, listening to, understanding and supporting children, including older children. This emotional work also involves liaising between family members when there are rows, and acting as the family mediator. This additional work of women is very much in keeping with the functionalist view that Parsons was talking about in the 1950s when he wrote about the 'expressive role' of women. However, this expressive role of women in the emotional side of family life now often comes on top of their 'instrumental' responsibilities in paid employment and domestic labour. This means many female partners often have major responsibility for three jobs (paid work, domestic labour and childcare, and emotional work) to their male partner's one. That women mainly undertake this aspect of family life is perhaps illustrated by the fact that, after separation or divorce, 40 per cent of fathers lose contact with their children within two years.

Women's triple shift

The points discussed in this section mean many female partners now often have three jobs – paid work, domestic labour and childcare, and emotional work – to their male partner's one. This has sometimes been referred to as women's 'triple shift'.

Activity

Do you agree with the view that women are the main managers of family emotions? What evidence from your own or other families can you think of which shows this is or is not the case?

The sections above suggest that, in terms of 'who does what' around the home, there is little evidence of integrated roles or symmetry in modern relationships, and public attitudes do not seem to have shifted as much as some might think. Taylor-Gooby (2005) found that, while public attitudes increasingly assume a high degree of gender equality in paid work, this does not apply to home and family life. This research found there was still a widely held belief among the public that women should be responsible for the care of the home and young children. Asked about whether mothers should work, nearly half (48 per cent) thought they should stay at home while children are under school age, with just a third (34 per cent) supporting part-time working, and even less full-time working.

It seems that patriarchal ideology still sees housework and childcare as women's work, and research over the past forty years has repeatedly shown that nothing much has changed since Oakley wrote, in *The Sociology of Housework* in 1974:

> As long as the blame is laid on the woman's head for an empty larder or a dirty house it is not meaningful to talk about marriage as a 'joint' or 'equal' partnership. The same holds of parenthood. So long as mothers and not fathers are judged by their children's appearance and behaviour . . . symmetry remains a myth.

Inequalities in power and authority in contemporary families

An important issue to consider when assessing whether there is more equality or not in contemporary families is to examine the distribution of power and authority. This is concerned with how much control over decision-making each partner has, and who is most able to get their own way, and make decisions about important matters affecting family life. These might include decisions about how to spend and manage money, where to go on holiday, where to live, parenting styles – how children should be raised – and where they should go to school, and so on. The bulk of evidence suggests that power and authority are not equally distributed in marriage and cohabiting relationships.

Decision-making   While some decisions in the family are taken jointly, very few are taken by women alone, as opposed to men alone. Edgell (1980) found women had sole responsibility for decisions only in relatively unimportant areas like home decoration and furnishing, children's clothes, food and other domestic spending. Women were less likely than men to have the final say on the most important decisions in the family, and decisions which couples thought of as 'very important', such as moving house or taking out loans, were finally taken by men alone. Things appear to have improved over the period since Edgell's research, with more joint or independent decision-making, particularly in money matters. However, as seen earlier, women's major areas of power and authority still lie predominantly in housework and childcare, but these responsibilities carry major penalties for women in terms of their own careers and income, which undermines their power in other areas of family life (see below). This is a crucial issue, as in many families the partner who earns the most money will often have the greatest power to make and implement decisions.

Financial decision-making and money management   A Bright Grey / Opinium Research survey in 2011, *Women and Protection*, found that although three in five (59 per cent) of married couples say they consult each other on all financial issues, less than half (44 per cent) of working women were mainly responsible for making financial decisions for the family, compared to just over half (53 per cent) of working men who stated they would make them.

Pahl (2005, 2008) found that there is growing individualization in couple's finances, whereby each partner has some independence in financial matters (like their own bank account and credit card). This was more likely among younger couples, those without children, and those where the woman was in full-time work. In these cases nearly half of men and women maintained some financial independence. But this dropped to a third where the woman worked part-time, and very few couples maintained financial independence where women were not in paid work or were retired. Given that, in contemporary Britain, more men than women are in paid employment, and of those women who are in employment, over four in ten (43 per cent in 2012) work part-time, compared to just 13 per cent of men, this does not point to much sharing or financial independence in many families.

Pahl points out that, though a couple's decision to keep their money separate may appear to lead to more equality and independence in decision-making, it may actually increase financial inequality between the partners. This is because, overall, men earn around 15 per cent more than women, so, for every £100 that men take home, women are typically earning about £85. This means that men are not only better-off, but will probably have better credit ratings enabling them to borrow more money if they so wish. This inequality can widen further if the woman's income drops, for example when children are born. Pahl suggests that, as long as women's earnings are lower than men's and women are responsible for paying for the costs of children and childcare, then individualization in money management can be a route to inequality in married and cohabiting couples. Even if household and childcare costs are shared equally, if men have more money to start with, such costs are more affordable and less of a burden for him than for his female partner.

In many households today, men are still often the major earners, and this puts men in a stronger bargaining position than women, and often puts their female partners in a position of economic dependence. Men still hold the purse strings of financial power in many families.

THE CONSEQUENCES OF INEQUALITY IN THE FAMILY

The effects of housework and childcare on women's careers

Women's continuing responsibility for housework and childcare often means women's careers suffer, holding back the earning power of all women, and particularly mothers. Surveys suggest many working women are limited in the jobs they can do and the hours they can work because they are still expected to take the main responsibility for housework and childcare, and to be at home when the children leave for and return from school. These family commitments allow little opportunity for working mothers to concentrate on the actions necessary for progressing their careers, and women consequently have lower pay, less security of employment and poorer promotion prospects than men, and this reinforces men's economic superiority and greater authority in the family.

About three-quarters of part-time workers are women, and about 43 per cent of women in paid employment work only part-time, compared with about 13 per cent of men. The presence of dependent children (under the age of 18) and the age of the youngest child are the most important factors bearing on whether or not women are in paid employment, and whether they work full-time or part-time. The age of their children has no similar impact on the working patterns of fathers. Indeed, the age of their children has *no* impact on their likelihood of being in employment, and around 90 per cent of men with dependent children are in employment regardless of the age of

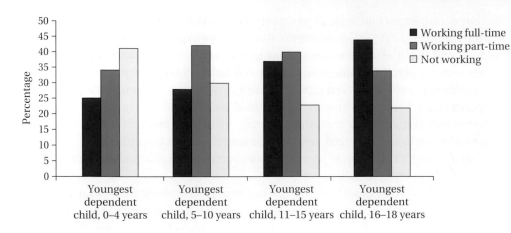

Figure 3.13 Working patterns of women with dependent children, United Kingdom, 2011

Source: ONS Labour Force Survey

their youngest child. Figure 3.13 illustrates the importance of this link between dependent children and work status, and provides clear evidence that it is women who retain primary responsibility for childcare.

Activity

Refer to figure 3.13

1 What percentage of mothers whose youngest child was aged 0–4 years was not working in 2011?
2 Identify two trends which occur as the youngest dependent child gets older.
3 What does figure 3.13 suggest might be the main restriction on mothers with dependent children going out to work? Suggest ways this restriction might be overcome.
4 How do you think having dependent children might affect the working lives of fathers in couple relationships? Give reasons for your answer.

Inequalities in employment There is still a lot of male prejudice about women in career jobs and senior positions, and women face a number of disadvantages:

- Women who have children are seen as unreliable by some employers, because of the assumption they will get pregnant again, or be absent to look after sick children or when schools unexpectedly close for some reason.
- Employers are sometimes reluctant to invest in expensive training programmes for women, as they may assume women will leave work eventually to produce and raise children.
- Women with promising careers may have temporarily to leave jobs to have children, and therefore miss out greatly on pay and promotion opportunities. Top jobs require a continuous career pattern in the 20–30 age period, yet these are the usual child-bearing years for women, so while men continue to work and get promoted, women miss their opportunities. Women with young children may also find difficulty in attending extra meetings and other gatherings after work, and this may affect their chances of promotion. This is why a growing number of women are choosing to delay motherhood until they are older and their careers have been established.
- Highly qualified women who leave jobs to have children, or who take career breaks to spend time with young children, often face hidden discrimination when they return to their jobs. Gatrell (2004) found many of these returning women, labelled

'jelly heads' by hostile employers, had no other option but to accept a downgraded position if they wished even to stay in their chosen professions, particularly if they asked for more flexible working arrangements to cope with their children. Although downgrading like this is illegal, many women don't fight their cases for fear of being labelled as 'awkward' and consequently facing even further career disadvantages.

- It is mainly women who give up paid work (or suffer from lost/restricted job opportunities) to look after children, the elderly or the sick.
- Married or cohabiting women are still more likely to move house and area for their male partner's job promotion rather than the other way round. This means women interrupt their careers and have to start again in a new job, often at a lower level, while the men are getting promoted at the expense of lost opportunities for their partners.

Gatrell et al. (2011) suggested that employers' views about mothers being the main or only carer were increasingly becoming out-of-date. She suggested a growing number of fathers want to be more involved with their children than fathers in the past, and in some cases fathers are the main or only carers, and mothers who go out to work might require fathers to work flexibly so childcare can be shared. However, until such time as changes occur, with housework and childcare fully shared and no longer regarded as the primary responsibility of women, it seems that the inequality of women inside the home will continue to lead to disadvantages and inequality for them in the labour market. This will in turn reflect back and further reinforce existing inequalities in power and decision-making inside the home.

The 'darker side' of family life

Feminists of all kinds are very critical of functionalist and New Right views that the cereal packet family, with a division of labour into men's instrumental roles and women's expressive roles, is the most desirable type of family. They suggest that the various dimensions of family inequality discussed in this topic area are particularly disadvantageous for women. The cumulative effects of inequality in the family manifest themselves in what has been called the 'darker side' of family life, which challenges the functionalist and New Right view of the warm and supportive happy cereal packet family stereotype.

While the family may often be a warm and supportive unit for its members, it can also be a hostile and dangerous place. The growing privatization of family life can lead to emotional stress in the family. Family members are thrown together, isolated from and lacking the support of extended kin, neighbours and the wider community. Tempers become easily frayed, emotional temperatures and stress levels rise, and – as in an overloaded electrical circuit – fuses blow, and family conflict is the result. This may lead to violence, divorce, and psychological damage to children, perhaps even mental illness and crime.

The breakdown of marriages which leads to divorce is often the end result of long-running and bitter disputes between partners. The intense emotions involved in family life, and the inequalities within families, often mean that incidents that would appear trivial in other situations take on the proportion of major confrontations inside the family. The extent of violence in the family is coming increasingly to public attention, with rising reports of sexual and physical abuse of children, emotional neglect of children, the rape of women by their husbands or partners, and women and baby battering. One in four murders takes place in the family. This is the darker side of family life.

Because of the private nature of the family, accurate evidence on the extent of violence and abuse inside the family is difficult to obtain, and fear or shame means that it is almost certain that many such incidents are covered up. However, the evidence suggests that it is primarily women and children who are on the receiving end of much of the most serious violence and abuse in the family, and that men are the main perpetrators. Feminists see this as an extension of the other dimensions of family inequality discussed above. The abuse of children is discussed in Topic 4 (see pages 194–6), but you should be aware that violence against children is also an important dimension of family inequality.

Domestic violence   There is widespread evidence of violence by men and women against their partners. It is estimated that one in four women, and one in six men, will suffer some form of domestic violence at some point in their relationships. Most of the assaults and physically most violent incidents – 89 per cent – are committed by men against their female partners. Each year about 150 people are killed by a current or former partner, and 80 per cent of them are women.

Domestic violence accounted for around 18 per cent of all violent crime in 2010–11, and the British Crime Survey estimates there were nearly 400,000 incidents of domestic violence in that year. Around four out of five of the victims are women. Around 45 per cent of all violent crime experienced by women is domestic, and estimates suggest there may be as many as 6.5 million violent incidents each year, including repeat victimization.

It is women who are most likely to experience domestic violence, to experience repeated violence, and to sustain injuries requiring medical treatment. Female victims of domestic violence will suffer an average of 35–7 assaults for an average period of seven years before informing any agency. Every year, in England and Wales, approximately 63,000 women and children spend at least one night in a refuge for battered women. For many women, home is neither a secure nor a safe place to be.

Statistics such as those discussed above reflect the extent and seriousness of the problem of violence in the home, particularly against women, much of which goes

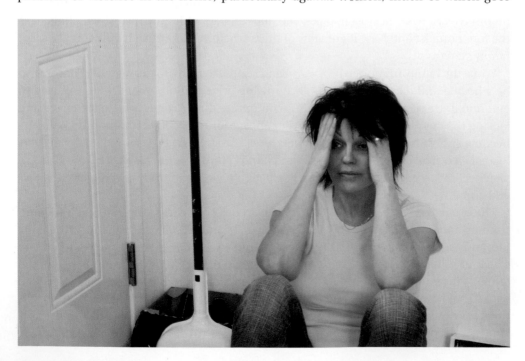

Domestic violence is overwhelmingly committed by men against their female partners. Why do you think this is?

unreported and undiscovered. The type of physical violence carried out in the family, mainly by male partners, would quite probably result in prosecution and imprisonment if it was carried out against a stranger outside the family. Nonetheless, an estimated two-thirds of victims of domestic violence do not seek help because they are afraid the violence will get worse, are ashamed, or see it as a private matter, and only about a quarter of all serious domestic violence incidents are reported to the police, but they still receive one domestic violence call every minute in the UK. However, only around one in twenty of those that are reported result in a conviction.

In the past, domestic violence was often not taken very seriously by the police or courts: it was often dismissed as a 'domestic' which they did not see as their responsibility but, rather, as a private family or personal matter. However, in recent years the police and courts have been beginning to treat domestic violence more seriously, with domestic violence units, rape suites and specially trained officers in many police stations.

Despite the high level of violence against women in married and cohabiting relationships, many women do not leave their violent partners. This is often because of fear, shame and embarrassment, financial insecurity, lack of alternative housing and concerns about disruption to their children's lives.

Disturbingly, many young women today still seem to believe that violence and aggression are acceptable parts of relationships. A 2005 survey conducted by *Sugar* magazine found that 16 per cent of teenage girls had been hit by a boyfriend – a quarter of them regularly. Yet over two-thirds of the girls who had been hit then stayed with their boyfriends. Of all the teenage girls who replied to the survey, 43 per cent thought it acceptable for a boyfriend to get aggressive, and 6 per cent thought it was OK for a boy to hit his girlfriend, for reasons such as cheating on him, flirting with someone else or if she was 'dressing outrageously'. Over 40 per cent of all the girls said they would 'consider giving a boy a second chance if he hit them'. A 2009 survey by the NSPCC and the University of Bristol found a third of teenage girls suffered sexual abuse by their boyfriends, with a quarter suffering physical violence, including being slapped, punched or beaten. Such evidence suggests that patriarchal relations exist even before entry into married or cohabiting relationships.

Rape in marriage   Rape is when someone is forced to have sex against her or his will, often accompanied by the actual or threatened use of violence. Estimates suggest more than one in four women has been raped, with most rapes being committed by men on their female partners, yet government estimates suggest that as many as 95 per cent of rapes are never reported to the police at all. About three-quarters of rapes, according to the British Crime Survey, take place in the home of the victim or offender. Nearly half of rapes within marriage are accompanied by the actual or threatened use of violence, and one in five women suffer physical injury.

Such sexual violence in the family, then, would appear to be disturbingly common, but it was only as recently as 1991 that rape within marriage was confirmed as a criminal offence by the Court of Appeal. Nonetheless, only about 6 per cent of all reported rapes lead to a rapist being convicted, and the most difficult cases in which to prove in court that there was no consent are those of rape in marriage or cohabiting relationships.

Feminist explanations for domestic violence

Radical feminists (and many other feminists) explain domestic violence as a means for men to exercise patriarchal power, to control and intimidate women, and to keep them in a state of submission. Marxist feminists emphasize structural factors as well. These include social deprivation (with factors like overcrowded homes and low incomes generating stress and disputes about money), a culture of violence – particularly in some parts of the working class – and the generally lower status of women in society. Dobash and Dobash (1992) argue male violence against women in the family is the means by which women's subordinate role and unequal power are enforced and maintained, and that this is tolerated and reinforced by political and cultural institutions. Ganley and Schechter (1995) suggest male violence, including sexual violence, against women is a result of women's inequality in society, with violence used by men to enforce and maintain this inequality, and exert power over women by gaining control over their partner's actions, thoughts and feelings. It is essentially about men showing women who is in charge.

Feminists of all kinds would agree that domestic violence has its roots in structural inequalities in society, and it is only by increasing the power and independence of women through improving their position in society generally – for example by making housing, childcare and employment policies, and the criminal justice system, more responsive to their needs – that domestic violence can be tackled at its roots.

Activity

1. Suggest three reasons why domestic violence statistics are likely to understate the extent of this social problem.
2. Do you think domestic violence by women against men is more or less likely to be reported than domestic violence by men against women? Give reasons for your answer.
3. Suggest three problems or difficulties sociologists might face in trying to research into domestic violence.
4. Go to www.womensaid.org.uk (the Women's Aid site), or www.crimereduction.gov.uk (search 'domestic violence') and find out the extent of domestic violence and the policy measures being taken to combat it.

Exam-style questions

1. Explain what is meant by the term 'symmetrical family'. *(2 marks)*
2. Explain what is meant by women's 'triple shift'. *(2 marks)*
3. Explain what is meant by the 'commercialization of housework'. *(2 marks)*
4. Suggest **two** ways in which family life may disadvantage women. *(4 marks)*
5. Explain the difference between segregated and integrated roles in the family. *(4 marks)*
6. Suggest **three** inequalities between men and women that may be found in contemporary families. *(6 marks)*
7. Assess the view that modern families have become a partnership of equals. *(24 marks)*
8. Examine sociological contributions to our understanding of the effects of inequality in the family. *(24 marks)*

Topic 4

SPECIFICATION AREA

The nature of childhood, and changes in the status of children in the family and society

Popular views of childhood

In contemporary Britain, and in most Western societies, many people take it for granted that children are fundamentally different from adults. Children are seen as innocent and vulnerable, and as needing protection from the dangers lurking in the adult world. We tend to think of childhood as a clear and separate period of life, with the child's world being a special time of life that is different and separate from the world of adults, with a long period of support and socialization by adults, usually in the family, necessary before they are themselves able to take on the responsibilities of adults.

In many ways, childhood today in Britain has become quite a privileged time of life compared to that of adults. For example, children are protected by laws to discourage them from smoking, drinking alcohol, accessing pornography, viewing unsuitable films, being exploited at work, or being neglected or abused by parents and other adults, and they get cheaper travel, and have special foods, clothes, toys and leisure activities designed for them. They even have special arrangements made for them by the state, such as schools to educate them, child benefits to help their parents support them and a range of child protection agencies designed to protect their interests. It is often thought that this is a perfectly natural result of children's biological immaturity, which makes them vulnerable and in need of the care and protection of adults. However, sociologists would argue that the identity and status of children, and childhood as a separate phase of life, have been created by society and social attitudes, and are not simply moulded by biological immaturity. In short, they argue that childhood is a **social construction**.

> **Social construction** means that the important characteristics of something – such as statistics, health, childhood, old age or what is regarded as deviance – are created and influenced by the attitudes, actions and interpretations of members of society. They only exist because people define them as such.

To what extent do you think childhood in contemporary Britain might be regarded as a privileged time of life?

The social construction of childhood

Evidence supporting the idea that childhood is a social construction rather than simply a natural product of biological immaturity is found in three main areas:

- the differing status, responsibilities and treatment of children in different contemporary cultures.
- the way the view of the nature of children and of childhood, and the status, responsibilities and treatment of children have changed through history, and continue to change today.
- the differences between children's status and responsibilities even in the same society.

CROSS-CULTURAL DIFFERENCES IN CHILDHOOD

Looking at childhood from a cross-cultural perspective shows there is a wide variety or diversity of childhoods that exist across the world. The freedom from adult responsibilities experienced by many Western children is not found in all societies, especially those of developing countries. In many simpler societies the prolonged period of childhood and adolescence before the transition to adulthood found in contemporary Britain does not exist, and children take on adult roles as soon as they are physically able. In many societies children perform essential work necessary for the economic survival of the family. The International Labour Organization suggests that one in seven children in the world work, with 215 million children aged 5–17 involved in child labour. Around 115 million children work in hazardous conditions, with the highest proportion of child labourers in Sub-Saharan Africa, where 28 per cent of children (58 million) are involved in work. A more dramatic and disturbing example of the swift transition to adulthood is found in the case of child soldiers. A 2008 report by the Coalition to Stop the Use of Child Soldiers (www.child-soldiers.org) suggested that between 2004 and 2007 child soldiers were involved in active conflict in twenty-one countries around the world, with children both being brutalized and killed, and brutalizing and killing others, as part of adult conflicts. Girls as well as boys are involved, with girl soldiers frequently subjected to rape and other forms of sexual violence as well as being involved in combat and other roles.

Anthropologist Napoleon Chagnon (1996) found how different childhood among the Yanomamo of the Amazonian rainforest is from what we might expect in contemporary Britain. For example, a Yanomamo girl is expected to help her mother from a young age, and by the age of 10 will be running a house, and will probably be married and having children by the age of 12 or 13.

The experience of childhood can differ widely between societies, as suggested by these photos of a child labourer in a brickyard in Kabul, Afghanistan, and a child soldier in Sierra Leone

These examples suggest that the nature of childhood is not the same in every society, and in many countries of the world today, small children are expected to take on at an early age what in contemporary Britain might be regarded as adult responsibilities, with many of them being against the law for children.

HISTORICAL CHANGES IN CHILDHOOD

The notion of childhood as a distinctive phase of life between infancy and adulthood is a relatively modern development, and didn't develop in Western societies until the sixteenth and seventeenth centuries. Philippe Ariès (1973) showed that, in medieval times, childhood did not exist as a separate status. Children often moved straight from infancy, when they required constant care, to working roles in the community. Children were seen as miniature versions of adults – 'little adults' – and were expected to take on adult roles and responsibilities as soon as they were physically able to do so, and to participate in all aspects of social life alongside their parents. Family portraits of the fifteenth and sixteenth centuries, like the one shown here, often depicted children as these little adults – shrunken versions of their parents, wearing adult clothes.

This painting from the seventeenth century (1608) of what appears to be a small adult is in fact of a 2-year-old boy – he can be identified as a boy by the dagger in his belt: 400 years ago boys wore dresses until they were 8 years old. The picture shows how both ideas about childhood and gender identity have changed dramatically over time.

Children did not lead separate lives, and mixed with adults. None of the things we associate with childhood today, such as toys, games, books, music, special clothes, schooling and so on existed. Until the mid nineteenth century (the 1850s), child labour was commonly practised and accepted. Most children worked, starting around the age of 7. In the early part of the nineteenth century, many factory workers were children under the age of 11. Children worked as long and as hard as adults, and adolescent children often left home for years to work, with boys being taken on as apprentices and girls as servants in richer households. In poor families, parents sometimes forced their children to engage in scavenging and street selling, and occasionally they were used as thieves and prostitutes. Children frequently faced the same legal punishments as adults for criminal activity. The notion that children deserved special protection and treatment did not exist at this time.

In the nineteenth century, the father and husband was the head of the family – it was a patriarchal unit – and fathers often had a great deal of authority over other family members. They would often have little involvement in the care of their children.

Children might see relatively little of their parents and, generally, children had low status in the family and were expected to be 'seen and not heard'.

Ariès showed that the social construction of childhood was linked to industrialization. With industrialization, work moved outside the family home. Restrictions on child labour in mines and factories during the nineteenth century, designed to protect children from exploitation and hardship, isolated most children from the world of adult work and responsibilities. Children began to be seen as innocent and in need of protection, though they were also seen as weak and vulnerable to temptation. Strong discipline was applied to teach children appropriate behaviour, and they often experienced severe beatings in the name of discipline which we would regard as child abuse today.

The growing speed of technological change in the nineteenth century meant parents were frequently unable to pass on the knowledge and skills required for working life, and the requirements for a literate and numerate labour force in part led to the development of compulsory education from 1880. These changes made children dependent on parents or other adults. There then emerged a new conception of a phase of 'childhood', with children lacking in power and dependent on, and supported by, adults. This period of dependency is getting ever longer today, as more young people spend time in education and training.

DIFFERENCES BETWEEN CHILDREN IN THE SAME SOCIETY

It is important to recognize that the conception and experience of childhood are not the same for everyone, even in the same society. In contemporary Britain, inequalities based on social class, ethnicity and gender mean that not all children have the same experiences of growing up. For example, around 27 per cent of children in the UK in 2010–11 were living in officially defined poverty, and girls will often have a different and more restricted childhood than boys. This is particularly the case for Asian girls, with Brannen (1996; Brannen et al. 1994) and Bhatti (1999) finding them more strictly controlled by parents than their brothers. Margo et al. (2006) have pointed out that richer parents, unlike poorer groups, can afford to purchase activities, like dance and music lessons, and are more likely to attend constructive, organized or educational activities that can enhance their children's personal and social development. By contrast, poorer children are more likely to spend time hanging out with friends or watching TV, with less beneficial effects on their personal and social development. Some children are forced to take jobs as soon as possible, such as paper rounds or working in shops, in order to supplement any pocket money they may or may not get from their parents, and poorer children are likely to suffer more ill-health and disability, and to have fewer educational qualifications than those who are better-off.

Children in contemporary Britain

During the course of the twentieth century and in the early twenty-first, families have become more child-centred, with family activities and outings often focused on the interests of the children. The amount of time parents spend with their children has more than doubled since the 1960s, and parents are more likely to take an interest in their children's activities, discussing decisions with them, and treating them more as equals. Often, the children's welfare is seen as the major family priority, frequently involving the parents in considerable financial cost and sacrifice.

THE CAUSES OF CHILD-CENTREDNESS

- Families have got smaller since the end of the nineteenth century, and this means that more individual care and attention can be devoted to each child.
- In the nineteenth century, the typical working week was between 70 and 80 hours for many working-class people. Today it is more like 43 hours (including overtime), and is tending to get shorter. This means parents have more time to spend with their children.
- Increasing affluence, with higher wages and a higher standard of living, has benefited children, as more money can be spent on them and their activities.
- The welfare state provides a wide range of benefits designed to help parents care for their children, and has increased demands on parents to look after their children properly. Social workers, for example, have an extensive range of powers to intervene in families on behalf of children, and have the ultimate power to remove children from families if parents fail to look after them properly. The United Nations Convention on the Rights of the Child (1989) sets the international standard for protecting and promoting the rights of children, and the Children Acts of 1989 and 2004 established children's legal rights in the UK, and there is now a Minister for Children and a Children's Commissioner to champion the views of children and protect and promote their interests.
- Paediatrics, or the medical science of childhood, developed rapidly during the twentieth century, along with a wide range of research and popular books suggesting how parents should bring up their children to encourage their full development. The nurturing, protection and education of children are now seen as a vital and central part of family life, with parenting skills and early years education now recognized as an important aspect of children's educational and social development. There have been a number of TV programmes, like *Supernanny*, suggesting ways parents can avoid having, or learn to cope with, 'problem children'.
- Compulsory education and more time spent in further education and training have meant that young people are dependent on their parents for longer periods of time. Tuition fees for higher education and the abolition of student grants have

Figure 3.14 Reasons for a more child-centred society

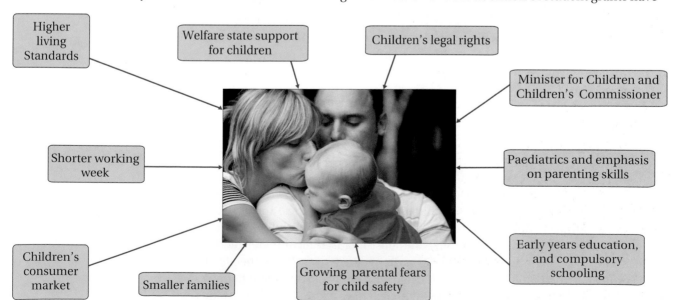

Family life has become more child-centred over the past fifty years

recently extended this period of dependency of young people on their parents. In this respect, 'childhood', including the dependency on adults it involves, has itself become extended.

- Compulsory education from age 5 has meant that children are better educated today, and mix with and learn more from other children. This means they are probably both more knowledgeable and more assertive in their dealings with parents.
- Children's lives have become more complex, with more educational, medical and leisure services for them. This frequently involves parents in ferrying children to schools, cinemas, friends and so on.
- Parental fears (largely unjustified) of 'stranger danger' – the perception that their children are at risk of assault or abduction by unknown adults – and growing traffic dangers and have meant that children now travel more with parents rather than being left to roam about on their own as much as they used to.
- Large businesses have encouraged a specific childhood consumer market. Businesses like Mothercare, ToysЯus, Nike, publishers and the music industry focus on the childhood consumer market, encouraging children to consume and parents to spend to satisfy their children's demands. Margot suggests children are taking greater control over family spending decisions, and 7- to 11-year-olds have become an increasingly lucrative target audience for advertisers eager to harness their 'pester power' – where advertisers target children to pester their parents into buying them CDs, clothes, toys, sweets and so on.

HAS THE POSITION OF CHILDREN IMPROVED OR WORSENED?

Most people would see the lives of children in contemporary Britain as a major improvement compared to the lives of children in earlier centuries, and as better than the lives of children in many other parts of the world. The status of children in the family and society has improved substantially, and most children have better diets, better medical care, more rights, more facilities in society geared towards their needs, and are better protected and cared for, better educated, and enjoy healthier and happier lives than ever before in history. Nonetheless, children do face a number of inequalities and other problems.

Inequalities and problems of children

Child-centredness does not mean children are equal to parents, nor are they always well cared for. Children are often told by parents what they can do, when they can do it, where they can go, and what's appropriate for them at their age, including things like hairstyles, dress, wearing of jewellery and so on.

Legal controls over children   Many laws restricting what children can do primarily arise from a desire to protect their overall health and safety, security and well-being, to protect them from exploitation – for example, by minimum wage regulations – and harm from child abuse and paedophilia. There are also many laws preventing children and young people from engaging in activities which they are thought not yet to be sufficiently mature or responsible to participate in. These include things such as:

- getting married (age 16 with parent/guardian consent, otherwise age 18).
- driving a car (age 17).
- voting and becoming a Member of Parliament or a local councillor (age 18).
- taking paid work: those under 14 (13 in some areas) aren't allowed to undertake paid work, except for odd jobs for a parent, relative or neighbour, babysitting, light work like a paper round, and some specially licensed sport, advertising, modelling or appearing in plays, films, television shows or other entertainment. Those under school-leaving age are not allowed to work during school hours or for more than two hours on any school day or 12 hours in any week, or before 7 a.m. or after 7 p.m.
- having sex: those under the age of 16 (the age of consent) cannot legally engage in sexual acts.
- buying some goods: shopkeepers cannot legally sell lottery tickets, aerosol paints and petrol to under-16s, or cigarettes, tobacco, solvents, lighter fuel, knives and alcohol to under-18s.
- watching or buying some films or computer games: films, DVDs, video and computer games have '12', '15' and '18' age restrictions.

Laws like these mean children have fewer legal rights than those of other ages. While they might be designed to protect children, they are at the same time a form of control over them, undermining their independence and enforcing dependence on adults.

Unhappy children   Womack (2011) reports that Britain's children are said to be the unhappiest in the West. Family breakdown is a cause of considerable childhood angst, with one-third of British 16-year-olds now living apart from their biological fathers. According to an international league table compiled by UNICEF, the United Nations Children's Fund, children growing up in the United Kingdom are more prone to bad physical and mental health, failure at school, and have the poorest relationships with their parents and friends, suffer greater deprivation, and are exposed to more risks from alcohol, drugs and unsafe sex than those in any other wealthy country in the world. Teenage pregnancy is among the highest in Europe. At some point, 10 per cent of British children develop a mental health problem and research suggests about half of adults with lifetime mental health problems first experienced difficulties in childhood.

Child poverty remains a problem in the UK, with 3.6 million children officially classified as living in poverty in 2010–11.

Margo indicates that British children spend more time in the company of peers, and less time with adults and parents, than young people in culturally similar countries, and she cites research showing many children are concerned that their parents are not there when they need them, and do not make them feel loved and cared for.

An estimated 11 per cent of young people ran away overnight on at least one occasion before their sixteenth birthday, according to a 2005 report from the Children's Society, and the NSPCC suggests around 77,000 children under 16 run away from home every year, for a range of reasons, such as being bullied, having trouble with their parents, or fear of being thrown out of home, or being abused.

Such evidence suggests that the experience of family life for many children in contemporary Britain may not be a happy one, and their dependency on adults and their inability to obtain legal paid employment means they have few opportunities to escape unhappy family lives.

Neither should we assume that children themselves are the innocents they are sometimes made out to be. Figures collected from police forces in England and Wales suggest that around 3,000 crimes, including criminal damage, arson and sex offences, in which the suspects are under the age of 10 – below the age of criminal responsibility, and therefore too young to be prosecuted – are reported every year. Every year an estimated 70,000 school-age children enter the youth justice system for various offences. Under-age drinking, drug abuse, anti-social behaviour and criminal activity are common complaints by older people about children and young people today, with parents often blamed for not socializing and supervising their children properly. Some may interpret this behaviour of children as a way for them to assert some independence from the suffocation of child-centredness which maintains their dependency on and regulation by adults, but it does nonetheless suggest that family life is not necessarily as child-centred or happy as some may believe it to be.

Internationally, the position of many children is a cause of grave concern, with reports of the sale and trafficking of children, child prostitution, child pornography, children involved in armed conflicts as soldiers and the illegal trafficking of children's organs and tissues.

Child abuse   As suggested above, child-centredness doesn't mean that all children are happy, or well looked after, and they remain unequal to adults in many respects.

Figure 3.15 Children and young people who were the subject of a Child Protection Plan (CPP), by category of abuse: England, year ending 31 March 2011

Source: Department for Education (DfE), *Children in Need Census* (2010-11)

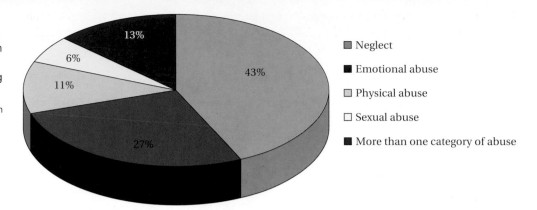

- Neglect
- Emotional abuse
- Physical abuse
- Sexual abuse
- More than one category of abuse

Further evidence of this, and a consequence of their dependence on adults and lack of control over their lives, comes in the form of child abuse, which is an all-too-common experience for some children.

There are several different types of abuse of children, as figure 3.15 shows. *Sexual abuse* refers to adults using their power to perform sex acts with children below the age of consent (age 16). *Physical abuse* refers to non-sexual violence. *Emotional abuse* refers to persistent or severe emotional ill-treatment or rejection of children, which has severe effects on their emotional development and behaviour. *Neglect* refers to the failure to protect children from exposure to danger, including cold and starvation, and failing to care for them properly so that their health or development is affected.

A report in 2011 from the NSPCC (the National Society for the Prevention of Cruelty to Children), *Child Abuse and Neglect in the UK Today*, found that around one in five children had been severely maltreated during childhood, with most of the ill-treatment committed by a parent or guardian. In 2005, the most comprehensive survey ever of teenagers and domestic abuse, conducted by the teen magazine *Sugar* in association with the NSPCC, found one-fifth of teenage girls were hit by parents – a quarter of them regularly. In 2011, statistics from the Department for Education (DfE) showed there were 42,690 children and young people under the age of 18 who were the subject of a Child Protection Plan (CPP) in England because of various forms of abuse (see figure 3.15). There were over a third of a million children registered as 'in need' who were at risk of not achieving or maintaining a reasonable standard of health or development without the provision of local authority services, and there were nearly three-quarters of a million episodes of need referred to and assessed by local authority social care services.

These figures were just for England (Scotland, Wales and Northern Ireland typically add around a further 20 per cent to this number) and only for cases that came to the attention of children's services departments. It is very likely that many children in need or experiencing abuse remain undiscovered. Some indication of this is given by statistics from ChildLine, the free confidential counselling service for children, established in 1986. ChildLine has counselled well over a million children and young people, and almost one in five of the calls received has been about sexual and physical abuse.

Sibling abuse   While most people think of child abuse as being committed by adults, it can also occur between brothers and sisters, and may take similar forms to that between adults, or of adults who abuse children. Sibling abuse may involve emotional, physical and sexually aggressive behaviour, like bullying, name calling, ridiculing, put-downs, hitting, slapping and punching, and unwelcome sexual touching (or worse). Womack, reporting results from the 2010 *Understanding Society* UK household longitudinal

Sibling abuse can have serious short-term and possibly long-term psychological effects on children

study, showed that 31 per cent of young people said they were hit, kicked or pushed by a brother or sister 'a lot' or 'quite a lot'; nearly 30 per cent of teenagers complained of being called 'nasty names' by brothers or sisters, while others reported having their belongings stolen by siblings. Nearly a third of children (30 per cent) with siblings were frequently bullied by their brother or sister, with 8 per cent scared of being hurt badly by him or her. Around 40 per cent of children admitted to bullying their brothers or sisters. In many families, such aggression between siblings is frequent and a source of great concern to parents. While most of us will probably have experienced such things as part of normal sibling rivalry, if it gets out of hand it can have very damaging consequences for the development of young people, and may even establish a pattern of abuse which resurfaces in their own adult relationships.

> **Activity**
>
> 1 Why do you think child abuse statistics are likely to understate the extent of these social problems?
> 2 How would you define child abuse? Do you think ideas about what child abuse is have changed over time? Give reasons for your answer.
> 3 What difficulties do you think sociologists might face in trying to research the area of child abuse?
> 4 What explanations might there be for child abuse?

Is childhood disappearing?

Postman (1994), first writing in 1982, was concerned with the disappearance of child-hood. He argues that the distinction between adults and children is disappearing, and that there is a merging of the taste and style of children and adults, with behaviour, language and attitudes becoming indistinguishable. Children in contemporary society are rapidly becoming exposed to a range of experiences that they share with adults, such as the globalized mass media, especially the internet and TV. This may be eroding the cultural divisions between childhood and adult status. In the contemporary world, children are increasingly exposed to the same issues, themes and experiences as adults, and are no longer sheltered from adult experiences and knowledge, including sex, pornography, crime, alcohol and drug abuse, and violence. Evidence for this was found in a 2007 report from the Cambridge University-based 'Primary Review' inquiry. This found children of primary school age expressing concern about adult-related themes like climate change, global warming and pollution, the gulf between rich and poor, terrorism, crime and street violence. A BBC News School Report survey of 11- to 16-year-olds in 2011 found they were most concerned about terrorism and climate change as threats to the world.

Cunningham (2005) argues that parental authority has been undermined by children having money from either parents (pocket money) or, for those who are older, from part-time work. A survey in 2008 found the average teenager received an allowance heading towards £1,000 a year, with some pocketing half as much again. On average, 13-year-olds were getting £45 a month, rising to £80 at 16. Average spending by children themselves (aged 7–15) in the UK in 2007–8 was £12.50 per week – a total of over £4 billion each year. Children are in most cases able to make their own decisions as to how to spend this money, reducing their dependency on parents. Margo also emphasizes that children's access to advertising is unprecedented, and transforms them into consumers, who demand access to the adult world earlier.

Adults and children, particularly older children, lead increasingly separate lives. Silva (1996) suggests that perhaps the roles of parents may be diminishing in face of the growing importance of peers, teachers, and other influences that children are exposed to through media such as film, television, DVDs, computer games, mobiles and the internet, including chat rooms and porn sites.

Many children now have their own rooms with their own televisions, computers with internet access, and mobile phones. This means parents are no longer able to control or manage the range of information, images and values that their children are exposed to, and this reduces the opportunities for parents to socialize their children, and regulate their behaviour. The Primary Review report mentioned above confirmed this, with parents saying they had little control over such things as mobile phones and the internet, through which children had access to unsuitable or harmful material, and both teaching assistants and parents were concerned about a 'loss of childhood'. Palmer (2007) has suggested that parents increasingly use modern technology like television, computer games, the internet and mobile phones, together with junk food, to keep children occupied. She argues that, combined with the increasingly busy and stressed life of parents, this is depriving children of a 'proper' childhood, with quality family time, like family meals with conversation and 'proper' food. She sees the contemporary world creating what she calls 'toxic childhood syndrome', developing a toxic new generation which potentially faces a whole range of social and behavioural problems.

The rapid pace of technological and social change often means that children are more up to date than their parents. Computer technology and use of the internet are good examples of this, as children are often far more adept at using these than their parents. The BBC News School Report online survey in 2011 (www.bbc.uk/schoolreport) found nearly 90 per cent of 11- to 16-year-olds had helped an adult in their family go online, and over half had helped with finding websites and emailing. The internet particularly gives young people access to a range of knowledge and imagery of which their parents in many cases have little awareness. This creates the possibility that young people will increasingly develop a culture that parents find goes beyond their comprehension or experience, and is far more in tune with the future than the culture of their parents. This may make parental involvement with their children's activities more difficult, and create a barrier between parents and children.

Margo suggests another indicator of a loss of childhood: that, over the past 50 years, the average age of first sexual intercourse fell from 20 for men and 21 for women in the 1950s to 16 for both by the mid-1990s. There is concern over the sexualization of childhood, with advertising and retailers encouraging children to dress and act in a sexually precocious way, and Margo points to the proliferation of sex tips for teenagers in youth magazines and health and beauty spas for young girls as evidence that children are exposed to, and expected to navigate, adult concerns at ever younger ages.

Exam-style questions

1   Explain what is meant by 'childhood is a social construction'.   *(2 marks)*

2   Explain what is meant by the 'loss of childhood'.   *(2 marks)*

3   Suggest **two** reasons why childhood is a relatively modern invention.   *(4 marks)*

4   Suggest **two** ways in which the position of children could be said to have improved over the last fifty years.   *(4 marks)*

5   Identify **three** ways in which the experience of childhood may differ between children in contemporary British society.   *(6 marks)*

6   Suggest **three** ways in which children have less power in society than adults. *(6 marks)*

7   Examine the view that the modern family has become more child-centred. *(24 marks)*

8   Examine the view that in contemporary society the distinction between 'childhood' and 'adulthood' is disappearing.   *(24 marks)*

Topic 5

SPECIFICATION AREA

Demographic trends in the UK since 1900; reasons for changes in birth rates, death rates and family size

Demographic change and the family

In order for a government to plan its policies with regard to social policy, the allocation of scarce resources, land, housing, education and finance, it is necessary to have accurate information and estimates of future trends in population size and distribution. It is important to know whether the population is increasing or decreasing, what typical family size might be in the future, whether more people are living alone, and what proportion of the population will be at school, working (or possibly unemployed) and retired in fifteen or twenty years' time. Such information will influence, for example, the number of schools and hospitals, and the number and sizes of houses that will need to be built, the number of teachers, doctors and nurses to be trained, the number of jobs that will be required, and the number of welfare benefits to be paid out. These changes cannot be made overnight, and so governments need this information to plan for the future.

DEMOGRAPHY

> **Demography** –
> the term used for
> the study of the
> characteristics of human
> populations, such as
> their size and structure
> and how these change
> over time.

Demography is the term used for the study of population. Information on population is obtained from a wide variety of sources, such as the compulsory registration of births, marriages and deaths, and national surveys like the Office for National Statistics Labour Force Survey and the General Lifestyle Survey. A main source is the census, which has been carried out every ten years since 1801, with the exception of 1941, when the Second World War made it impractical to hold one. The last census was in March 2011.

There are four main factors that influence the size of a country's population:

- births
- deaths
- **immigration**: the number of people *entering* the UK for a period of at least a year, so that the UK effectively becomes their country of usual residence
- **emigration**: the number *leaving* the UK for a period of at least a year, so that their country of destination effectively becomes their country of usual residence

---

SOME KEY TERMS IN DEMOGRAPHY

You should learn these definitions.

Birth rate – the number of live births per 1,000 of the population each year.

The **fertility rate** – a general term which is used to describe either the general fertility rate or the total fertility rate.

General fertility rate – the number of live births per 1,000 women of child-bearing age (15–44) per year.

The **total fertility rate (TFR)** is the average number of children women will have during their child-bearing years. The number of births in any society depends on both the fertility rates of women (how many children they have) and the numbers of women of child-bearing age.

Infant mortality rate – the number of deaths of babies in their first year of life per 1,000 live births per year.

Death rate (or mortality rate) – the number of deaths per 1,000 of the population per year.

Life expectancy – an estimate of how long the average person can be expected to live. Estimates of life expectancy can be based on any age, but the most common are life expectancy at birth and at one year.

Dependent population – that section of the population which is not in work and is supported by those who are, such as the under-18s (who are still at school or in training); pensioners; the unemployed and others living on welfare benefits.

The **dependent age groups** are those under age 17 (age 18 from 2015) in compulsory education, and those over retirement age.

Migration – changing the country of usual residence for a period of at least a year, so that the country of destination effectively becomes the country of usual residence.

Immigration – entering another country for a period of at least a year, so that country becomes the one of usual residence.

Emigration – leaving the usual country of residence for another country for a period of at least a year, so that the country of destination becomes the one of usual residence.

Net migration – the *difference* between immigration and emigration, and therefore whether the population of a country or area has gone up or gone down when both emigration and immigration are taken into account. Net migration is usually expressed in terms of a net gain or increase (+) or a net loss or decrease (–) of population.

Natural population change – changes in the size of a population due to changes in the number of births and deaths, excluding migration. Expressed as a *natural increase* (+) or *decrease* (–) in population.

Population projections – predictions of future changes in population size and composition based on past and present population trends.

MIGRATION: IMMIGRATION AND EMIGRATION

One influence on the population size and composition of the UK has been migration. Migration occurs because of 'push' and 'pull' factors. *Push factors* are those that may encourage someone to leave their home country, and *pull factors* are those that may attract them to a new country. Both of these can either encourage people to leave the UK to live abroad, or encourage those in other countries to move to the UK.

- *Push factors* include things like escaping poverty, unemployment or persecution.
- *Pull factors* include things like better opportunities for jobs, study, a higher standard of living, more political and religious freedom, and joining relatives.

In 2011, the two main pull reasons for immigration to the UK were for formal study (by far the largest group) and work-related reasons, followed by family reasons, with people from abroad joining their families in the UK. There is not much research on the push reasons for emigration from the UK, but these are likely to include better career and job opportunities, and higher earnings, the attraction of a better lifestyle, or simply wanting a fresh start. In 2011, a number of emigrants were former immigrants from the European Union who decided to return to their own countries.

The pattern of migration

Up to about 1930, and during the 1960s and 1970s, net migration showed a net loss of population, with more people leaving the UK each year than entering it. In the period between about 1930 and 1960, and in most years since the 1980s, immigration has exceeded emigration, that is, more people have entered the UK as migrants than left the UK – there was a net gain in population through migration.

In the twentieth century, there were two peak periods of immigration. During the 1930s and up until about 1945, several hundred thousand refugees fled to Britain from Europe to escape the effects of Nazi occupation and persecution. Most of these immigrants were white. During the 1950s and 1960s, widespread immigration from the black Commonwealth began, with immigrants arriving from the Caribbean in the 1950s, and from India, Bangladesh (then East Pakistan), Pakistan, Uganda and Kenya in the 1960s and 1970s. Much of this immigration was actively encouraged by the British government, which sent out recruiting teams to these countries to solve labour shortages in unskilled and poorly paid occupations in Britain, though Ugandan and Kenya Asians were fleeing persecution. This influx of people began to transform Britain into a more ethnically diverse country, and in 2011 around 10 per cent of the UK population were from a non-white ethnic group, and this in turn contributed to family diversity, with differences between, for example, white British families, South Asian families and Caribbean families (see pages 162–3)

Since 2001, the main pattern of migration suggests there has been an annual net increase of around an average of 183,000 people per year. In 2011, this reached 252,000, the highest calendar year figure on record, but this increase was mainly due to less emigration from the UK rather than any significant increase in immigration. In 2011, around 80 per cent of immigrants came from the following groups, a useful indicator of current trends in migration:

- around 15 per cent were British citizens returning home.
- around a third were citizens of the European Union.
- around a third were citizens of the New Commonwealth (countries like Bangladesh, Pakistan, India, Nigeria and Sierra Leone).
- around 6 per cent were citizens of the Old Commonwealth, which comprises Australia, Canada, New Zealand and South Africa.

Figure 3.16 shows the pattern of net migration from 1901, with projections until 2021.

Figure 3.16 Net migration to the UK 1901–2021*

*2011–21 based on 2010 projections

Source: Office for National Statistics

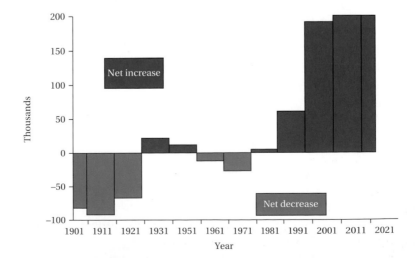

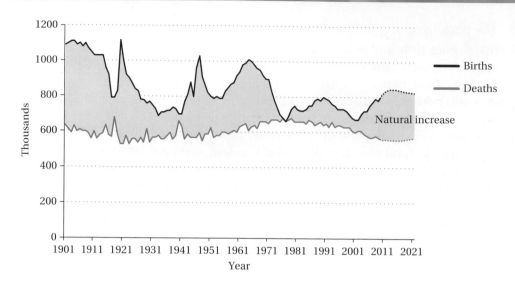

Figure 3.17 Natural population changes, UK 1901–2021*

*2010–2021 based on 2010 projections

Source: Office for National Statistics

NATURAL POPULATION CHANGE IN THE UNITED KINGDOM

Since 1900, most of the growth in the UK population has been due to natural increases, with more births than deaths, and greater **life expectancy**. The population of the United Kingdom rose from about 38.3 million in 1901 to around an estimated 64 million by the end of 2013. Since 1900, a continuing fall in the **death rate** combined with a falling **birth rate** has slowed down population growth compared to the nineteenth century, and there has been greatly improved life expectancy. The birth rate has been generally declining since 1900, but there have been some periodic increases in births – 'baby booms' – after the two world wars (1914–18 and 1939–45) as couples started families delayed by separation during the war years, with another baby boom in the 1960s as living standards rose, and another smaller baby boom in the 2000s, largely fuelled by mothers delaying children until they were older, and immigration of women of child-bearing age from Eastern and Central Europe, where women tend to have more children.

Figure 3.17 illustrates the main natural changes in population size since 1900, with projections until 2021.

THE DECLINE IN THE DEATH RATE AND INFANT MORTALITY RATE, AND INCREASING LIFE EXPECTANCY

In 1902 the death rate was 18 per 1,000, and this had declined to around 9 per 1,000 in 2010. The **infant mortality rate** has also fallen, from around 142 per 1,000 live births in 1902 to around 4.3 per 1,000 in 2010. Average life expectancy has consequently risen. In 2012–13, estimates suggest men can expect to live, on average, to around the age of 79, and women to around 83, though of course many will live beyond these average ages.

> **Life expectancy** is an estimate of how long the average person can be expected to live. Estimates of life expectancy can be based on any age, but the most common are life expectancy at birth and at one year.
> The **birth rate** is the number of live births per 1,000 of the population each year.
> The **death rate** (or mortality rate) is the number of deaths per 1,000 of the population per year.

> The **infant mortality rate** is the number of deaths of babies in their first year of life per 1,000 live births per year.

HOW DO WE COMPARE?

LIFE EXPECTANCY

Life expectancy from birth is higher than in the UK, for both males and females, in Japan, Iceland, Italy, Australia, Finland, Canada, Norway, New Zealand and the Netherlands.

Source: Matheson (2010)

Explanations for changes in the death rate, infant mortality rate and increased life expectancy

Improved hygiene, sanitation and medicine Public hygiene and sanitation have improved enormously since the early nineteenth century, with the construction of public sewer systems and the provision of clean running water. These changes, together with improved public awareness of hygiene and the causes of infection, have contributed to the elimination in Britain of the great epidemic killer diseases of the past, such as cholera, diphtheria and typhoid, which were spread through infected water and food. McKeown (1976) suggested these improvements in environmental conditions, coupled with a steady rise in living standards and better diet and nutrition, were more important than medical advances in wiping out these epidemic diseases. Advances in medicine and science, such as vaccines and the development of penicillin, antibiotics and other life-saving drugs, and advances in surgery and medical technology, such as transplant surgery, have further contributed to the decline in the death rate, and increased life expectancy. More sophisticated medical care means that people now survive illnesses that would have killed them even in the recent past. Before the twentieth century, the highest mortality rates were among babies and young children, but today death rates rise the older you get. The major causes of death today in Britain are from the non-infectious degenerative diseases, such as cancer and heart disease.

Higher living standards As McKeown suggested, rising standards of living have further assisted in reducing death rates. Higher wages, better food, more amenities and appliances in the home, and greatly improved housing conditions, with less damp, inside toilets and running hot water, have all assisted in improving the health and life expectancy of the population. Because of improved transportation and food technology, a wider range of more nutritious food is available, with improved storage techniques (such as freezing) making possible the import of a range of foodstuffs, including more affordable fresh fruit and vegetables all the year round.

Public health and welfare There has been a steep rise in state intervention in public health and welfare, particularly since the establishment of the welfare state in 1948. The NHS has provided free and comprehensive healthcare, and there is much better

Figure 3.18 Reasons for the decline in the death rate

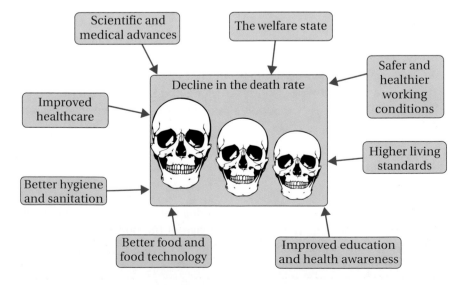

Websites like NHS Direct and Netdoctor provide useful sources of health education and advice

antenatal and postnatal care for mothers and babies. More women have children in hospitals today, and childbirth has become much safer for women (in the past, deaths of women in childbirth in the UK were not uncommon, and today around 500,000 women globally still die in childbirth each year). There are health visitors to check on young babies, which helps to explain the decrease in the infant mortality rate. The wide range of welfare benefits available helps to maintain standards of health in times of hardship, and older people in particular are better cared for today, with pensions and a range of services like home helps, social workers and residential care homes.

Health education   Coupled with these changes has been a growing awareness of nutrition and its importance to health. Improved educational standards generally, and particularly in health education, have led to a much better-informed public, who demand better hygiene and public health, and welfare legislation and social reforms to improve health. Websites like NHS Direct (www.nhsdirect.nhs.uk), Netdoctor (www.netdoctor. co.uk) and Patient.co.uk (www.patient.co.uk) provide guidance on the prevention and treatment of ill-health, and promote good health by advising and educating the public on issues such as the benefits of exercise, giving up smoking and eating a balanced diet.

Improved working conditions   Working conditions improved dramatically in the twentieth century. Technology has taken over some of the more arduous, health-damaging tasks, and factory machinery is often safer than it was 100 years ago. Higher standards of health and safety at work, shorter working hours and more leisure time have all made work physically less demanding and therefore have reduced risks to health.

THE AGEING POPULATION

The decline in the death rate and increased life expectancy have meant that more people are living longer. Britain, like most Western industrialized countries, today has an **ageing population**. This means that the average age of the population is getting higher, with a greater proportion of the population over retirement age, and a smaller proportion of young people.

An **ageing population** is one in which the average age is getting higher, with a greater proportion of the population over retirement age, and a smaller proportion of young people.

Britain has an ageing population, with one in six people now over the age of 65, and the proportion is growing

However, the decline in the birth rate has meant that fewer children are being born as well, and this has changed the overall age structure of the population. For example, in 1901, about 33 per cent of the population were under age 15, 63 per cent between the ages of 15 and 65, and only about 4 per cent were over age 65. By 2012, the proportion over age 65 had risen to about 17 per cent. Figure 3.19 shows this ageing population between 1901 and what it is projected to be in 2033. The changing shape shows that in 1901 there was quite a rapid decline in the proportion of people over the age of 50 in the population as a whole, as they began to die. By 2001 there is more of a bulge in the middle age groups, and by 2033 the older age groups make up a much larger proportion of the population, with most age groups taking up similar proportions. A quick glance at the proportion of over-70s in 1901 compared to 2033 shows this clearly.

The consequences of an ageing population

There is in many cases a long gap between people retiring from work and their becoming dependent on others. Men currently retire at age 65, and women at between 60 and 65, though all women will retire at 65 by 2020, and the retirement ages for both men and women look set to rise in the future, possibly to age 68. Many people in their 60s and 70s remain very healthy, active, self-supporting and involved in the lives of their families and communities.

Nonetheless, the growing proportion of elderly people in the population creates a growing burden of dependence, or an increasing **dependency ratio**. This simply means that an increasing number of older people have to be supported by a decreasing proportion of the working population. This could mean higher taxes on those working, to pay for higher levels of government spending on welfare benefits, health and social services, such as the costs of care for the elderly in residential and nursing homes. Around 42 per cent of all welfare spending goes to elderly people, and, without welfare reforms, this is expected to keep on rising. An alternative approach involves cutting pensions and services to the elderly, or charging for services that were formerly free.

Dependency ratio – the relationship between the proportion of the population who are working and those who are dependent or not working.

Figure 3.19 The ageing population: United Kingdom, 1901–2033

Source: Office for National Statistics

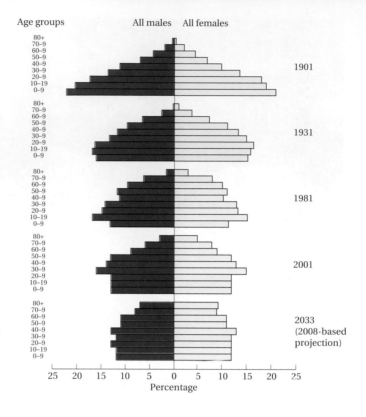

Activity

1 Refer to figure 3.19, and identify three pieces of data that show an ageing population between 1901 and 2033. Explain why they show this.
2 What evidence is there in figure 3.19 that women, in general, live longer than men? Identify data from the figure to back up your view.
3 Identity the largest age group in each of 1931, 2001 and 2033, and suggest two reasons for any differences you identify.

HOW DO WE COMPARE?

THE AGEING POPULATION

By 2009, the proportion of the UK population aged 65 and over (16 per cent) meant the UK had a mid-ranking status compared to other European countries. Germany and Italy, both with consistently low fertility, had the highest proportions of their populations aged 65 and over in 2009. Japan is the world's most aged country: in 2008, 22 per cent of the Japanese population were aged 65 or above. By 2035 one-third of Japan's population will be aged 65 or over and 14 per cent will be aged 80 or over. The number of centenarians (people aged 100 or over) in the UK is projected to reach 97,000 by 2035, more than an eight-fold increase from the 2009 figure of 11,600. Japan is projected to have around 420,000 centenarians by 2035, and Europe in total around 529,000. By contrast, by 2035 Africa is projected to have around 10,000.

Source: Matheson (2010)

Britain has an ageing population. What advantages or disadvantages might there be for families with older, retired relatives?

The growing proportion of elderly people and a relatively smaller proportion of young people have a number of potential effects on the family and individuals:

- There are more pensioner one-person households as partners die, particularly among women who live longer than men.
- Elderly relatives can help with childcare and babysitting, and maybe financially (especially in the middle class). With many families in contemporary Britain having both parents in paid employment, grandparents now often play an important role in providing unpaid childcare, such as babysitting services and taking small children to school and collecting them afterwards.
- If elderly relatives are poor due to inadequate pensions and savings, their family may have to support them. This may lead to financial hardship, as people face having to support not just themselves and their children, but also their parents and possibly grandparents too. This can be made worse if there is a loss of income if one partner has to give up work to care for elderly dependants.
- The growing isolation and loneliness of older people, as friends and partners die and health deteriorates, may lead to growing dependence on their children to visit and support them. This can create problems for planning family holidays and moving for work or promotion.
- There may be emotional strain and overcrowding if an elderly, and possibly infirm, relative moves in with his or her child's family. This might cause conflict between couples, or between children and grandparents, as well as increasing costs to the family.
- There could be more family and household diversity, with a return of the classic extended family, more one-person households and, combined with a declining birth rate, more beanpole families, as considered earlier in this chapter.
- There may be extra work for fully adult children, and particularly women. The practical burdens of caring for the elderly tend to fall mainly on their fully adult children. Increasingly, with longer life expectancy, many of these adult children are themselves elderly and facing more infirmity – for example, 65-year-olds caring for their 90-year-old parents. This responsibility falls particularly to women in the family, even though they already carry most of the burden of housework and childcare in their own homes, as discussed earlier in this chapter.

- There may well be increased stress and ill-health for relatives who have to devote large amounts of time to caring for infirm or disabled elderly relatives.
- Young people may have difficulty in finding affordable homes of their own, as older people occupy their homes for longer. They may find they have to live with their parents longer than they would otherwise choose.

Activity

1 If you have, or were to have, an elderly parent, grandparent or greatgrandparent living with you, what advantages and problems are or might be created for family life? Discuss these with others if you are in a group.
2 Go to www.ageuk.org.uk (Age UK) and identify five issues of concern to older-person households, and what Age UK suggests should be done to resolve them.
3 Suggest three possible consequences for families of a growing proportion of older people in society.

THE DECLINE IN THE BIRTH RATE, FERTILITY RATE AND AVERAGE FAMILY SIZE

Since 1900, the birth rate has been declining in the UK, from 29 per 1,000 in 1901 to about 13 per 1,000 in 2010. During the 2000s, the birth rate began to rise again each year, from 11.3 in 2002 to 13 in 2010. The **general fertility rate** (the number of live births per 1,000 women of child-bearing age (15–44) per year) and the TFR (the total fertility rate: the average number of children women will have during their child-bearing years) have also been declining. There was an average number of about 2.8 children per woman of child-bearing age in 1961, but this had reduced to about 2 by 2010. Like the birth rate, the general and the **total fertility rate** rose in the 2000s, with the TFR in 2010 the highest for thirty-seven years, creating a 'baby boom' in the 2000s.

> The **general fertility rate** is the number of live births per 1,000 women of child-bearing age (15–44) per year.
> The **total fertility rate (TFR)** is the average number of children women will have during their child-bearing years. The number of births in any society depends on both the fertility rates of women (how many children they have) and the numbers of women of child-bearing age.

HOW DO WE COMPARE?

FERTILITY

The UK's total fertility rate (1.98) in 2010 was:
- similar to the quite high level of much of northern Europe (France, Ireland, Belgium, the Netherlands and the Scandinavian countries) and Australia and New Zealand.
- higher than that of China and Brazil.
- lower than those of the USA, South Africa, India, Egypt, Kenya and Nigeria

Source: Matheson (2010)

These changes have meant that, since 1900, average family and household size have been dropping, from around 6 children per family to an average of around 1.7 children per family in 2009. The average household size in Britain has also almost halved in the last 100 years, from around 4.6 people to around 2.4 people per household in 2011. The trend towards smaller families, more lone parent families and, in particular, more people living alone explains this reduction in average household size.

A new baby boom?

In the 2000s there was a new 'baby boom' – a surge in births. While the total fertility rate of 1.6 children per woman in the UK was the lowest ever in 2001, between 2001 and 2008 it increased every year. By 2011, it had reached the highest (1.98) it had been since 1973, and there were more babies born than in any year since 1991. While younger British-born women are still choosing to have fewer or no babies, this is being made up for by higher numbers of births among older women. Women are now delaying having children until they are older, as they establish their careers, but also, with high rates of divorce and separation, may be starting new families after forming new partnerships later in life. Younger migrant women who were born outside the UK, many from the Eastern European countries of the European Union, and who tend to have larger families, also explain the rise in fertility. It remains to be seen whether these trends will continue, but they seem highly unlikely ever to return to anywhere near the levels of the last baby boom in the 1960s.

Reasons for the decline in the birth rate and fertility rate, and for smaller families

Contraception More effective, safer and cheaper methods of birth control have been developed over the last century, and society's attitudes to the use of contraception have changed from disapproval to acceptance. This is partly because of growing **secularization**, and the declining influence of the church and religion on people's behaviour and morality. The availability of safe and legal abortion since 1967 has also helped in terminating unwanted pregnancies. Family planning is therefore easier.

> **Secularization** is the process whereby religious thinking, practice and institutions decline and lose influence in society.

Compulsory education Since children were barred from employment in the nineteenth century, and education became compulsory in 1880, they have ceased to be an economic asset that can contribute to family income through working at an early age. Children have therefore become an economic liability and a drain on the resources of parents, because they have to be supported for a long period in compulsory education, and often in post-17/18 education and training, including university and college years. Parents today often have to support their children well into their 20s.

Figure 3.20 Reasons for the decline in the birth rate, fertility rate and smaller family size

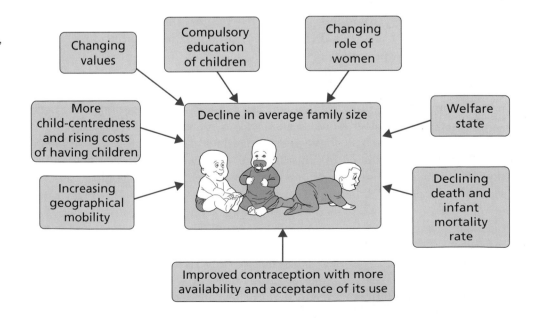

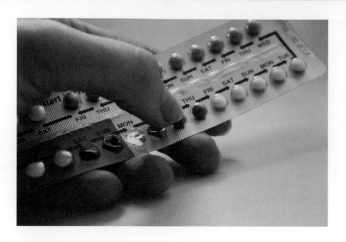

More effective methods of birth control, combined with changing attitudes to the use of contraception, have contributed to the decline in the birth rate

The rising costs of having children   Research carried out by Opinion Matters for insurance company Aviva in 2011 suggested that the average size of the British family is declining because of the costs of bringing up children. The number of married or cohabiting couples who have one child has risen from 16 per cent in 1972 to 20 per cent today. When asked why they were not going to have a second child, 58 per cent of parents with one child cited 'money' as the overwhelming reason. The average cost of raising a child from birth until the age of 21 is around £271,000, including costs for education, such as school trips and university costs, 'household services' such as internet connection, and train and bus fares, clothing and food, and 'leisure', including children's activities, pocket money, holidays and toys.

Facing this, combined with compulsory education, parents have therefore begun to limit the size of their families to secure for themselves and their children a higher standard of living. The move to a more child-centred society (discussed in Topic 4) has assisted in this restriction of family size, as smaller families mean parents can spend more money and time on and with each child.

The changing position of women   The changing position of women, particularly during the last century, has involved more equal status with men and greater employment opportunities, and many wish to, and do, pursue their own careers. Women today have different priorities from those in earlier generations, and many have less desire to spend long years of their lives bearing and rearing children. Sharpe (1976, 1994), for example, found the priorities of girls had changed from 'love, marriage, husbands, children, jobs, and careers, more or less in that order' in 1976, to 'job, career and being able to support themselves' in 1994. McRobbie (2008) argues that the once-common aspiration among many young women for marriage and motherhood has now been replaced by a desire for a degree qualification and an interesting and rewarding career. Many women who work in paid employment today have to combine this with childcare responsibilities, and will therefore either limit the number of children they have, often putting off having them until their careers are established, or choose to have none at all. This explains why for the last thirty years there have been decreases in **fertility rates** for women aged under 30, and increases for women aged 35–9, and 40+, and why the average age for giving birth has risen to 29.5 in 2010 – about one year older than ten years earlier.

While most women do eventually have children, there is a growing proportion who are choosing not to do so. For example, around 20 per cent of women born in 1964 were childless at age 45 in 2009, compared to about 12 per cent of those born in 1937. Nearly

The **fertility rate** is a general term whch is used to describe either the general fertility rate or the total fertility rate.

Most women work in paid employment today, and many will combine this with childcare responsibilities. Many wish to pursue careers and will therefore either limit the number of children they have, often putting off having them until their careers are established, or choose to have none at all

25 per cent of women born in 1973 are expected to be still childless at age 45. This trend towards childlessness can be expected to continue with women's growing position in paid employment.

The declining infant mortality rate   Until the 1940s, the absence of a welfare state meant that many parents relied on their children to care for them in old age. However, although more babies were beginning to survive infancy, it was still often uncertain whether children would outlive their parents. Parents therefore often had many children as a safeguard against some of them dying. The decline in the infant mortality rate and the death rate has meant that fewer people die before adulthood and old age, so parents no longer have more children as security against only a few surviving. In addition, the range of agencies which exist to help the elderly today means that people are less reliant on care from their children when they reach old age.

A geographically mobile labour force   Contemporary societies generally require a geographically mobile workforce – that is, a workforce that can easily move to other areas for work or promotion. This may have been a factor in encouraging smaller families, because they can more easily pack up and move elsewhere.

Changing values   Parenthood involves greater pressure on couples, a lifelong commitment, a loss of freedom and independence, and sacrifices like cuts in money to spend on consumer goods and the loss of time for leisure and pleasure. In the postmodern age, in which consumer values dominate and people seek to develop their identities through their consumer spending and leisure choices, couples are becoming more reluctant to have children.

Exam-style questions

1 Explain what is meant by the term 'net migration'. *(2 marks)*

2 Explain what is meant by an 'ageing population'. *(2 marks)*

3 Explain what is meant by the 'total fertility rate'. *(2 marks)*

4 Suggest **two** reasons why women may choose to postpone having children until they are older. *(4 marks)*

5 Explain the difference between the 'death rate' and the 'infant mortality rate'. *(4 marks)*

6 Suggest **three** reasons for the decrease in family size since 1900. *(6 marks)*

7 Examine the causes of an ageing population, and its consequences for family life and family diversity. *(24 marks)*

8 Examine the reasons for, and the consequences of, the fall in the birth rate since 1900. *(24 marks)*

CHAPTER SUMMARY AND REVISION CHECKLIST

After studying this chapter, you should be able to:

- describe the different forms of marriage, the family and household.

- identify arguments about the universality of the nuclear family.

- explain and criticize the functionalist, New Right, Marxist, and liberal, radical and Marxist feminist perspectives on the family, its role in society and how it might be changing.

- examine the arguments about whether or not the family has lost its functions.

- discuss reasons why the classic extended family is less common today.

- critically examine the links between the isolated nuclear family and contemporary society.

- outline postmodernist views of the family.

- explain what is meant by 'family ideology' and critically discuss its main features.

- discuss political views of the family, and government and other social policies and laws affecting families and households.

- describe and explain a range of changes in the family, including the rising divorce rate, the decline in marriage, the growth of cohabitation, changes in child-bearing and more births outside marriage, the increase in the number of lone parent families, and the growth of the reconstituted family.

- describe and explain why the 'cereal packet' family is a misleading myth, and identify the diversity of family and household forms in Britain, including extended and beanpole families, and cultural, social class, regional, and life cycle and life-course diversity.

- explain why there has been a growth in singlehood, and other alternatives to traditional family units.

- examine critically the view that roles in marriage and cohabiting relationships have become more equal.

- identify the features of domestic labour, and how these differ from paid work.

- describe and explain a range of inequalities in the contemporary family, including those in domestic labour, power and decision-making.

- examine the ways in which women's responsibilities for housework and childcare undermine their positions in paid employment.

- identify and explain some consequences of inequality in the family, including the darker side of family life.

- identify and explain the main features of childhood and how it is a social construction.

- describe a range of changes in the position of children in the family and society.
- critically examine the position of children in contemporary Britain, including some inequalities and problems they face, and assess how childhood might be changing or disappearing.
- describe and explain a range of demographic changes in the UK and how they affect the family, with some awareness of comparisons with other countries, including changing patterns in births,

deaths, infant mortality, life expectancy, net migration and family size.

- examine the significance of the ageing population for society and family life.
- discuss a range of reasons why average family size has decreased, and why more women are having fewer, or no, children.

KEY TERMS

(these are already defined in the text, and may also be found in the glossary at the end of the book)

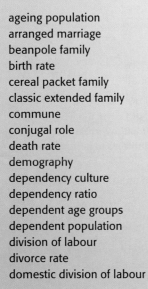

ageing population	domestic labour	life expectancy	privatized nuclear family
arranged marriage	emigration	marriage rate	reconstituted family
beanpole family	expressive role	meritocracy	scapegoat
birth rate	extended family	migration	secondary socialization
cereal packet family	family	modified extended family	secularization
classic extended family	family ideology	monogamy	segregated conjugal role
commune	fertility rate	moral panic	serial monogamy
conjugal role	general fertility rate	natural population change	sexual division of labour
death rate	household	net migration	social construction
demography	ideological state apparatus	nuclear family	stereotype
dependency culture	immigration	patriarchy	structural differentiation
dependency ratio	infant mortality rate	polyandry	symmetrical family
dependent age groups	instrumental role	polygamy	total fertility rate
dependent population	integrated conjugal role	polygyny	underclass
division of labour	kibbutz	population projection	
divorce rate	kinship	primary socialization	
domestic division of labour	life course	privatization	

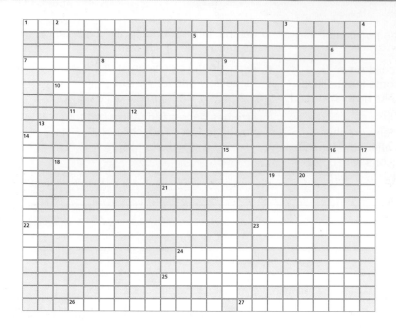

Across

1) Israeli alternative to the nuclear family (7)
5) The term used to describe an individual or group of people living under the same roof and sharing facilities (9)
7) She first identified the importance of social networks in understanding roles in the family (4)
8) An American functionalist writer who thought families were 'factories producing human personalities' (7)
9) The opposite to an instrumental role (10)
10) In marriage, one at a time, one after the other and they don't last long (6, 8)
12) The number of divorces per 1,000 married people (7, 4)
13) These families with same-sex parents have a happy name (3)
18) A family type involving the remarriage of one or both partners and the children of a previous marriage (13)
21) She was one of the first to study the sociology of housework (6)
22) One of the fastest-growing forms of family relationship and unlikely to be regarded as 'sinful' (12)
23) This legal bonding is in decline (8)
24) A writer who argued 'the family . . . is the source of all our discontents' – sounds like a bloodsucker (5)
25) A two-generational family (7, 6)
26) A family form usually arising from death of a partner, divorce or choice (4.6)
27) This approach challenged the male view of the family (8)

Down

2) Nearly half of these take place outside marriage (6)
3) The people we learn from by imitating their behaviour (4, 6)
4) These children are below working age and rely on their families to support them financially (9)
6) Relations of blood, marriage/civil partnership or adoption (7)
8) The process of learning the culture of society within the family (7, 13)
11) A type of family where there are similar roles performed by each partner (11)
12) Technical term for housework (8, 6)
14) Where males are dominant (10)
15) The traditional family stereotype (6, 6)
16) The term used to describe relationships between husband and wife (8, 5)
17) A nuclear family with vertical or horizontal extensions (8)
19) A male partner who takes an active role in housework and childcare (3, 3)
20) The legal termination of a marriage (7)

The solution to this crossword can be found on the teachers' pages of www.politybooks.com/browne

There are a variety of free tests and other activities that can be used to assess your learning at

www.politybooks.com/browne

EXAM QUESTION

SECTION B: FAMILIES AND HOUSEHOLDS

Time allowed: 1 hour   **Total for this section: 60 marks**

Read items **2A** and **2B** below and answer parts | 0 | 6 | to | 1 | 0 | that follow.

Item 2A

Functionalist writers suggest that the typical family in contemporary societies is the structurally isolated privatized nuclear family. This is because it is seen as well adapted to the needs of contemporary society. For example, this family unit is small and geographically mobile, and is not tied down by obligations to wider kin. Others suggest that there is no 'typical' family unit. Demographic changes, including declining birth rates, infant mortality and death rates, greater life expectancy and migration patterns, are some of the factors changing families and households, and creating a diversity of arrangements in which people now live.

5

Item 2B

There have been some major changes in the family in the last 30 or 40 years in Britain. One area of change is the dramatic increase in the number of marriages to end in divorce, with divorce numbers increasing around six times the number in 1961. The number of people who are cohabiting is now at an all-time high, and the number marrying is at an all-time low. One in four families with dependent children is now a lone parent family, and about four out of every ten children now grow up in either a lone parent or reconstituted family. Nearly half of births are now outside of marriage.

5

| 0 | 6 | Explain what is meant by a 'privatized nuclear family' (**Item 2A**, line 2)   *(2 marks)*

| 0 | 7 | Suggest **two** ways that greater life expectancy has changed families and households
         (**Item 2A**, lines 6–7)   *(4 marks)*

| 0 | 8 | Suggest **three** reasons for the decline in the birth rate since 1900.   *(6 marks)*

| 0 | 9 | Examine the contribution of feminist writers to the study of the family.   *(24 marks)*

| 1 | 0 | With reference to **Item 2B** and elsewhere, assess the view that the family in Britain is in
         decline.   *(24 marks)*

Wealth, Poverty and Welfare

Contents

Wealth, Poverty and Welfare

Topic 1

SPECIFICATION AREA

Different definitions and ways of measuring poverty, wealth and income

What is wealth?

> **Wealth** is property in the form of assets which can be sold and turned into cash for the benefit of the owner.

Wealth refers to property in the form of assets which can, in general, be sold and turned into cash for the benefit of the owner. The main forms of wealth are housing, land and factories, bank accounts and savings, shares in companies and private pension funds, and personal possessions, like household goods, vehicles and valuables like antiques or artworks. The main way of finding out about who has wealth in Britain in 2012 was through the Office for National Statistics *Wealth and Assets Survey*, which carries out a sample survey of all private households in Great Britain. This measures wealth through four components: property, financial assets, physical wealth (personal and household goods) and private pension wealth.

Within this general framework of what wealth is and how it is measured, there are different forms of wealth:

- **Marketable wealth**, is made up of assets that can be bought and sold and turned into cash for the owner's benefit, like a private car, a house, land, shares and other assets that can be sold.
- **Non-marketable wealth**, is wealth that cannot be sold or cashed in, like occupational and state pension rights.
- **Productive property**, is wealth which provides an unearned income (see below) for its owner, for example houses which are rented out, factories and land, or company shares which provide dividends.
- **Consumption property**, is wealth for use by the owner, such as consumer goods like fridges, cars, or a home that you own, which do not produce any income.

Topic 2 examines the patterns of inequality in wealth, and explanations for it.

What is income?

Income, refers to the flow of money which people obtain from work, from welfare benefits or from their investments in productive property.

- *Disposable income* is that which a person has left after paying taxes.
- *Discretionary income* is that which is left after taxes and all necessary household bills and expenses – like mortgage/rent, food, energy bills, travel costs, etc. – have been paid. This is what is left for people to spend as they choose.
- **Earned income** is income received from paid employment (wages and salaries).
- **Unearned income** is that received from productive property, like rent on buildings and land, dividends on shares, and interest on savings and other personal investments.

> ### Activity
>
> Classify each of the following situations as wealth, earned income or unearned income:
> - ownership of a chemical company.
> - royalties received from publishing a sociology book.
> - a boxer receiving £18 million for a boxing match.
> - receiving £435 million for writing the Harry Potter books.
> - the Queen receiving £7.9 million from the government to support the royal household.
> - ownership of the publishing rights to the Beatles songs.
> - an actor getting £20 million for making a film.
> - rent received from ownership of a string of flats in London.
> - dividends on shares held in a computer company.
> - £1.4 million received by a footballer for sponsoring football boots.
> - having £15 million worth of shares in a computer company.
> - profits received from owning a national daily newspaper.
> - £150 a week from working in a burger chain.

Topic 2 looks at the unequal distribution of income in contemporary Britain, and some explanations for these inequalities.

Marketable wealth consists of assets that can be bought and sold, and turned into cash for the owner's benefit.
Non-marketable wealth is that which cannot be sold or cashed in, like occupational and state pension rights.
Productive property is property that provides an unearned income for its owner, such as factories, land, and stocks and shares.
Consumption property is property for use by the owner which doesn't produce any income, such as owning your own car.

Income is a flow of money which people obtain from work, from their investments, or from the state.
Earned income is income received from paid employment (wages and salaries).
Unearned income is that received from productive property, like rent on buildings and land, dividends on shares, and interest on savings and other personal investments.

What is poverty?

Much of the early sociological research into poverty was a reaction against the idea that poverty was the poor's own fault – that they were simply idlers and scroungers, an undeserving group who were themselves to blame for their own poverty, and therefore nothing should be done to help them.

Two pieces of research showed the poor were in fact decent, hard-working families who were forced into poverty by circumstances beyond their control, such as irregular or low pay, ill-health or disability, unemployment or old age: the 'deserving poor'. These pieces of research were:

- Booth's *Labour and Life of the People in London* – a study of poverty in London in the 1880s.
- Joseph Rowntree's three studies of poverty in York, beginning with *Poverty, A Study of Town Life*, first published in 1901, with further studies published in 1941 and 1951.

These early researchers established the basis for much of the later research into poverty, including the debates over the definition and measurement of poverty which are discussed below.

DEFINING POVERTY (1): ABSOLUTE OR SUBSISTENCE POVERTY

A person in **absolute poverty**, lacks the minimum necessary for healthy survival. People in absolute poverty would be poor anywhere at any time – the standard does not vary much over time. The solution to absolute poverty is to raise the living standards of the poor above subsistence level.

Measuring absolute poverty

Various attempts have been made to measure absolute poverty. Rowntree, for example, used medical studies of nutrition to identify the cheapest costs of a standard basic diet needed to maintain life, coupled with minimum housing, heating and clothing costs.

The absolute conception of poverty has some advantages, as it makes it relatively straightforward to make national and international comparisons, since basic physical or subsistence needs seem fairly easy to identify (but see later for some problems). Such a view of poverty is generally the one most people consider when they think of poverty – the kind that is often found in less-developed countries, for example in Africa, where famines and starvation occur and people lack the basic subsistence needs for biological survival.

> **Absolute poverty** or subsistence poverty refers to a person's biological needs for food, water, clothing and shelter – the basic minimum requirements necessary to subsist and maintain life, health and physical efficiency. A person in absolute poverty lacks the minimum necessary for healthy survival.

Absolute poverty

> **Activity**
>
> 1 Keep a record of everything you consume in one week – food, drinks, leisure activities, rent if you pay it, an estimate of how much electricity and gas you use, travel expenses and so on.
> 2 Find out how much all these things cost, perhaps by visiting a local supermarket.
> 3 Then try to find out how much you would be entitled to in welfare benefits each week if you were unable to work. You may be able to find out from leaflets at a local Job Centre office or a community centre or from the Citizens' Advice Bureau website www. adviceguide.org.uk.
> 4 Discuss whether you could or would want to live on these benefit levels.

The weaknesses/disadvantages of the absolute conception of poverty

Difficulty in identifying basic subsistence needs   It is difficult to identify objectively what basic subsistence needs are. For example, Rowntree's minimum budget was based on a list of nutritional and other requirements essential for life. He was criticized for relying heavily on the values and opinions of those who drew up the list. In particular, his list involved a no-waste budget, in which everything was fully used and food didn't go off or not get eaten. The list reflected the nutritional, cooking and shopping skills of middle-class researchers rather than the reality of the choice of food and the resources of the poor.

Value judgements   Rowntree's views of food, clothing and shelter were those thought customary at the time. Even a basic budget may therefore reflect not simply minimal nutritional requirements, but value judgements of what an appropriate diet consists of.

It ignores the reality of people's lives   The views of experts about the contents and costs of a minimum diet make assumptions that the poor have the same knowledge of nutrition as the experts, and that the poor can shop around and get the cheapest goods. It doesn't really take into account the knowledge people have, their shopping habits, how they actually spend the money they have, and the social, cultural and psychological factors which may influence this. For example, having a Christmas pudding may not be necessary to maintain health, but most people in Britain, including the poor, would want to have one. Is this wasteful and does it make assumptions that the poor should deny themselves diets that most people would regard as perfectly normal? The poor are often unable to buy at the cheapest prices anyway. (See the box 'Trapped in poverty: the poor pay more' on page 252 later in this chapter.)

There is no clear subsistence minimum   There are wide differences between societies, and between groups in the same society, regarding what forms a subsistence minimum. Minimum diets will differ between men and women, by age, by the type of occupation a person has and so on. For example, an unskilled manual labourer doing heavy physical labour will require more calories each day than an office worker, and minimum nutritional and housing needs will be different in hot or cold climates.

It ignores social needs and cultural expectations   The absolute conception of poverty treats people as if they were nothing more than biological machines, and ignores the fact that people are social beings, who live in groups which create needs beyond just physical survival. This involves mixing with people, entertaining them, eating with them, participating in community life and leisure activities, and meeting social obligations, such as buying wedding or birthday presents, or giving children parties. This will also involve expectations of appropriate food – eating cats or rats is not something most of us in Britain would see as acceptable behaviour, even though they might be quite nutritious. Value judgements and cultural expectations therefore influence even a notion of a subsistence minimum.

These criticisms have led most sociologists and poverty researchers to adopt the idea of **relative poverty**.

> ### Activity
>
> Do you think poverty should be defined only in absolute terms? What other aspects, if any, of people's lives do you think should be considered in defining poverty?

> **Relative poverty** defines poverty in relation to a generally accepted standard of living in a specific society at a specific time. This takes into account social and cultural needs as well as biological needs, so that people can join in with the usual pattern of life in their society.

DEFINING POVERTY (2): RELATIVE POVERTY

The relative definition of poverty says that people are poverty-stricken when they lack things that wider society regards as the minimum necessary for a socially acceptable standard of living. Townsend (1979) has provided the classic definition of relative poverty:

> Individuals, families and groups in the population can be said to be in poverty when they lack the resources to obtain the types of diets, participate in the activities and have the living conditions and amenities which are customary, or at least widely encouraged or approved, in the societies to which they belong. Their resources are so seriously below those commanded by the average individual or family that they are, in effect, excluded from ordinary living patterns, customs or activities.

Relative poverty is a condition whereby individuals or families are deprived of the opportunities, comforts and self-respect which the majority of people in their society enjoy. Minimum needs are then related to the standard of living in any society at any one time, and will therefore vary over time and between societies, as standards of living change. For example, those living in squalid, damp and decaying housing in Britain would be regarded as poor in Britain, but their housing would appear as relative luxury to poor peasants in some developing countries. Similarly, running hot water and an indoor bathroom and toilet would have been seen as luxuries 100 years ago in Britain, but today are seen as basic necessities, and those without them would be regarded as poor by most people.

The solution to relative poverty necessarily involves a more equal distribution of wealth and income, so no section of society is deprived in relation to the average standard of living. The debate about poverty necessarily becomes a part of the debate about social inequality.

Dimensions of relative poverty apart from income: poverty as social exclusion

The relative definition of poverty is closely linked with the idea of **social exclusion**.

Social exclusion involves people being marginalized or excluded from participation in education, work, community life, access to services and other aspects of life seen as part of being a full and participating member of mainstream society. Those who lack the necessary resources are excluded from the possibility of joining in fully with society,

> **Social exclusion** is where people lack the resources which might enable them to participate fully in the community or society in which they live, excluding them – or cutting them off – from what most people would regard as a normal life.

and are denied the opportunities most people take for granted. It is about being cut off from what most people would regard as a normal life.

The ideas of relative poverty and social exclusion suggest there are wider social, cultural and psychological dimensions of poverty apart from just a low income. Poverty is not simply a matter of how much income people have, and consequently of going short of material things like food, clothing and heating, or being unable to afford to replace household goods or carry out household repairs and decoration. It can also involve a combination of other linked problems in their lives, such as discrimination, poor skills, poor housing, bad health, family breakdown, social isolation, a poor environment, high-crime neighbourhoods, and poor quality and availability of public services like transport, hospitals, libraries, schools and play areas for children. These problems are linked, and each one can make the others worse, and create a vicious cycle in people's lives which it is hard for them to escape from. Two people may have the same low income, but one may live in an isolated rural community with few facilities, no shop, no doctor's surgery, no car, irregular public transport, no local school and so on. The other may live in an urban area, with lots of facilities, easy transport or easy walking distances and so on. The poor may therefore live a deprived lifestyle apart from simply being short of money.

Figure 4.1 illustrates this range of linked dimensions of relative poverty, and how they can combine and overlap to create social exclusion.

Figure 4.1 Dimensions of relative poverty: poverty as social exclusion

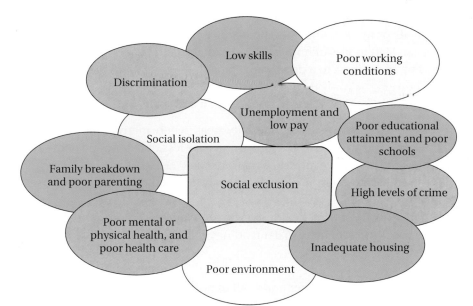

Activity

Refer to figure 4.1
1 Suggest two ways that high-crime areas and poor environments might be linked.
2 Suggest two ways that poor educational attainment and poor schools might be linked to poor parenting.
3 Suggest two ways that inadequate housing might be linked to poor health.
4 Suggest two reasons why poor health and a low income might contribute to social isolation.
5 Explain what is meant by 'social exclusion', and why relative poverty might be seen as social exclusion.

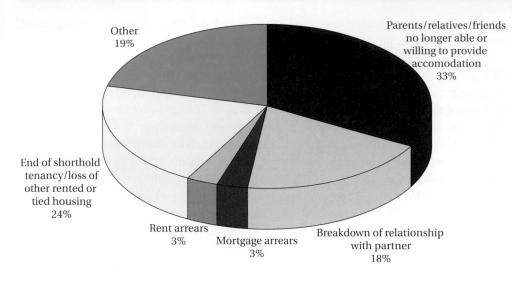

Figure 4.2 Reasons for homelessness: households officially accepted as homeless and in priority need, by reason of loss of last settled home, England, 2012

Source: Department of Communities and Local Government, 2012

Examples of poverty apart from low income include the following.

Homelessness   In the year to the end of March 2012, around 50,290 households were officially accepted as unintentionally homeless and in priority need by local authorities in England, though there were more homeless than this, such as those regarded as intentionally homeless, or not in priority need, or who simply don't come to the attention of local councils or other authorities. Breakdown of relationships, and mortgage and rent arrears can lead to loss of homes. This can make getting and holding down a job difficult, leading sometimes to a downward spiral.

Poverty in healthcare   Good health is important to an active life, but:

- There are fewer doctors practising in inner-city areas (where many of the poor live), and those who do are often overworked and have less time to spend with each patient, because the poor have more health problems.
- The poor are less likely to get time off work with pay to visit the doctor.
- The poor face longer hospital waiting lists.
- Many are not fully aware of what health services are available to them, and the poor tend to be less vocal and articulate in demanding proper standards of care from doctors.

Poverty at school   Education can offer a way out of poverty, but:

- Inner-city schools often have older buildings and poorer facilities.
- There is often a concentration of social problems in these schools, such as poor behaviour and lack of parental support, drugs and vandalism, and consequently a higher turnover of teachers.
- Parents are less able to help their children with their education, and have less money than better-off parents to enable the school to buy extra resources.

Poverty at work   Poor working conditions include a neglect of health and safety standards and a high accident rate; working at night and long periods of overtime because the pay is so low; lack of trade union organization to protect the workers' interests; lack of entitlement to paid holidays; insecure employment; and no employers' sick pay or pension schemes.

Why do you think people become homeless? Why do some become rough sleepers rather than staying in hostels for the homeless?

Environmental poverty   Environmental poverty refers to features of the environment in which people live, such as air quality, the quality of housing, proximity (closeness) to busy roads, and access to essential services like GP surgeries, shops and supermarkets, schools, post offices and public transport. These measures are used in England by the government to help in identifying deprived areas. The poor often live in neighbourhoods that lack access to many of the essential services identified above. They often live in poorly designed or maintained homes, which may be damp and expensive to heat, and they face higher levels of accidents in the home. They frequently live close to polluting industries and busy roads, where air quality is poor, with consequent health problems like breathing difficulties and asthma; living near busy roads, and without access to gardens, means poorer people, particularly children, face higher rates of accidents involving injury to pedestrians and cyclists.

Personal factors linked with poverty   These might include:

- *Poor health* Examples are respiratory problems, like asthma, and infectious diseases, as a result of poor diet, damp and overcrowded housing, and living in neighbourhoods with a poor environment.
- *Stress and depression* In the face of mounting bills and debts. Stress can lead to domestic violence, family breakdown, and mental and physical illness.
- *Social isolation and boredom* Making friends may be hard because there is no money to get involved in social activities.
- *Low self-esteem* This can be brought on by dependence on others, the lack of access to the activities and facilities others have, and difficulties in coping with day-to-day life.

Subjective poverty

Subjective poverty refers to people's own feelings and judgements about whether or not they are poor in relation to those other members of society with whom they compare themselves.

In addition to the wide range of factors discussed above in defining relative poverty, there is also a subjective dimension to the experience of poverty. **Subjective poverty**, refers to people's own feelings about whether or not they are poor – their own judgements about their situation and the resources they have compared to other members of their society. People generally compare themselves to their *reference group* – the group they identify themselves with. Many of those in relative poverty will see themselves as poor compared to others, but some may not experience subjective poverty as they see themselves in the same boat as the rest of the people in their neighbourhood or community. It is also possible that someone who is quite well-off and who would not be regarded as poor by most measures, such as a business executive or manager facing redundancy, may experience subjective poverty if they can no longer live up to their former high standards of living and lifestyle, as they can no longer afford to buy all the luxury consumer goods, foodstuffs, leisure activities and so on they were once accustomed to.

The conception of subjective poverty contrasts with other approaches, such as those based on experts' and sociologists' judgements about what poverty is, and is linked to the concept of **relative deprivation**, the sense of lacking things compared to the group with which people identify and compare themselves. Those with a sense of subjective poverty, even people most wouldn't regard as poor, may experience resentment and a sense of injustice at their condition, and become hostile to the society which they feel has deprived them of the lifestyle they once enjoyed, or to which they believe they are entitled in order to live a normal life.

> **Relative deprivation** is the sense of lacking things compared to the group with which people identify and compare themselves.

Measuring relative poverty

The idea of relative poverty is necessarily based on value judgements as to what constitutes a reasonable standard of living. How do you decide what the minimum standards are in relation to the expectations of a particular society? There have been a number of attempts to come up with various measures of relative poverty, using different kinds of **deprivation index**, and these are outlined below.

> A **deprivation index** is a list of items, lifestyle indicators or needs, such as food, health, housing, income, ownership of consumer goods, and access to transport, used to measure the level of deprivation experienced by an individual, group or geographical area.

Townsend's deprivation index   Townsend measured relative poverty in the UK using a deprivation index of sixty indicators of lifestyle considered to be customary for an acceptable standard of living. He reduced these to twelve which he saw as particularly important indicators of deprivation, clearly linked to low income, and then checked how many households lacked those items. This deprivation index is shown in the box below.

Townsend's deprivation index

1   Has not had a week's holiday away from home in the last twelve months.
2   (Adults only) Has not had a relative or friend to the home for a meal or snack in the last four weeks.
3   (Adults only) Has not been out in the last four weeks to a relative or friend for a meal or snack.
4   (Children only – under 15) Has not had a friend to play or to tea in the last four weeks.
5   (Children only) Did not have a party on last birthday.
6   Has not had an afternoon or evening out for entertainment in the last two weeks.
7   Does not have fresh meat (including meals out) as many as four days a week.
8   Has gone through one or more days in the past fortnight without a cooked meal.
9   Has not had a cooked breakfast most days of the week.
10 Household does not have a refrigerator.
11 Household does not usually have a Sunday joint (three in four times).
12 Household does not have sole use of four amenities indoors (flush WC; sink or washbasin and cold water tap; fixed bath or shower; and gas or electric cooker).

Source: Townsend (1979)

> ### Activity
> Study Townsend's deprivation index
> 1 Do you think the twelve items on Townsend's deprivation index provide useful indicators of poverty? Give reasons for your answers, with reference to each indicator.
> 2 Do you think such indicators provide an adequate view of poverty? Suggest ways of improving and updating Townsend's index, and suggest five additional or alternative indicators that you think might provide a better guide to poverty in contemporary society.
> 3 In what ways do you think Townsend's own values might have influenced his choice of indicators? How do you think your own values might have influenced your choice of indicators in the previous question?

Townsend's deprivation index was criticized heavily because:

- It was said to be measuring inequality not poverty.
- The choice of indicators was based on Townsend's own values and had more to do with taste than with poverty.
- It didn't allow for choice – for whether people lacked items because they couldn't afford them or because they simply didn't want them.
- It focused on people's individual behaviour, and ignored indicators of deprivation like the availability of and access to public services, such as public transport, hospitals, clinics and libraries, and environmental poverty.

The consensual measurement of relative poverty   The *Breadline Britain* studies in 1983 by Mack and Lansley (1985), and by Mack, Lansley and Frayman in 1990 (1992), whch were updated by Gordon et al.'s (2000) *Poverty and Social Exclusion in Britain* study in 1999, were attempts to overcome the criticisms of Townsend's deprivation index – particularly that it simply reflected his own preferences and values, and that it didn't allow for choice.

To avoid this, these surveys asked a representative sample of the public, not experts, to decide what items *they thought* were necessary for a minimum standard of living in Britain. The responses represented a consensus (widespread agreement) developed over a period of time on what ordinary people thought made up the minimum standards required for life in Britain at the beginning of the twenty-first century.

The *Poverty and Social Exclusion* survey included only items that 50 per cent or more thought necessities, and then calculated how many people lacked three or more of these items, asking them whether this was because of choice or because they couldn't afford them. This research provided a valuable insight into how the public measures relative poverty. The list is shown in the box below.

> ### The *Poverty* and *Social Exclusion* survey list
>
> 1 Beds and bedding for everyone.
> 2 Heating to warm living areas of the home.
> 3 Damp-free home.
> 4 Visiting friends or family in hospital.
> 5 Two meals a day.
> 6 Medicines prescribed by doctor.
> 7 Refrigerator.
> 8 Fresh fruit and vegetables daily.
> 9 Warm, waterproof coat.
> 10 Replace or repair broken electrical goods.
> 11 Visits to friends or family.
> 12 Celebrations on special occasions such as Christmas.
> 13 Money to keep home in a decent state of decoration.
> 14 Visits to school, for example on sports day.
> 15 Attending weddings, funerals.

16	Meat, fish or vegetarian equivalent every other day.	33	Replace worn-out furniture.
17	Insurance of contents of dwelling.	34	Dictionary.
18	Hobby or leisure activity.	35	An outfit for social occasions.
19	Washing machine.	36	New, not second-hand, clothes.
20	Collect children from school.	37	Attending place of worship.
21	Telephone.	38	Car.
22	Appropriate clothes for job interviews.	39	Coach/train fares to visit friends/ family quarterly.
23	Deep freezer/fridge freezer.	40	An evening out once a fortnight.
24	Carpets in living rooms and bedrooms.	41	Dressing gown.
25	Regular savings (of £10 per month) for rainy days or retirement.	42	Having a daily newspaper.
		43	A meal in a restaurant/pub monthly.
26	Two pairs of all-weather shoes.	44	Microwave oven.
27	Friends or family round for a meal.	45	Tumble dryer.
28	A small amount of money to spend on self weekly, not on family.	46	Going to the pub once a fortnight.
		47	Video cassette recorder.
29	Television.	48	Holidays abroad once a year.
30	Roast joint/vegetarian equivalent once a week.	49	CD player.
		50	Home computer.
31	Presents for friends/family once a year.	51	Dishwasher.
32	A holiday away from home once a year not with relatives.	52	Mobile phone.
		53	Access to the internet.
		54	Satellite television.

Source: Adapted from David Gordon et al., Poverty and Social Exclusion in Britain (York: Joseph Rowntree Foundation, 2000). Reproduced by permission of the Joseph Rowntree Foundation.

Activity

1 Either alone or through majority agreement in a group, go through the *Poverty and Social Exclusion* survey list shown in the box above, ticking those items which you think are necessities, which all adults should be able to afford, and no one should have to go without.

2 Compare your list with that of another person or group. How do your decisions compare with others? Were some items clear-cut and others borderline? Discuss the reasons for any differences of opinion about what count as necessities.

3 The Poverty and Social Exclusion in Britain national survey, conducted first in 2000, found that items 1–35 were considered necessities by 50 per cent or more of the population. At least two out of three members of the public classed items 1–25 as necessities which no one should have to go without. How far does your list agree or disagree with these national findings?

4 Do you think if you were in a very poor country you would have the same list of necessities? Give reasons for your answer.

5 What does this exercise tell you about the ways of measuring poverty in modern Britain?

6 Go to www.jrf.org.uk and look up the latest 'Monitoring Poverty and Social Exclusion' survey. Identify the main groups in poverty in Britain today and try to identify in each case two causes of their poverty.

A **poverty line** is the dividing point between those who are poor and those who are not. The poverty line used in Britain today, and by the European Union, is 60 per cent of average income.

Income measurements – the 'official' poverty line The **poverty line**, used in Britain in 2012, and by the European Union, was on or below 60 per cent of average income (or, strictly speaking, '60 per cent of contemporary median net disposable household income after housing costs'). This line dividing those who are regarded as poor and those who are not was adopted as it was thought that at or below this level of income people would be excluded from a minimum acceptable way of life in the society they were living in. This involves a clear relative conception of poverty, but you should note the limitations discussed above of using income alone as an indicator of poverty. Table 4.1 shows the strengths and weaknesses of the relative definition of poverty, and table 4.2 provides a summary of the main differences between the absolute and relative definitions of poverty.

Table 4.1 The strengths and weaknesses of the relative conception of poverty

(living below a generally accepted standard of living in a specific society at a specific time)

Strengths	Weaknesses
Recognizes poverty as a social construction – this means it recognizes that measures of social deprivation are influenced by how other members of society define what is a normal standard of living in any society.	It is not an indicator of poverty, but simply of social inequality. No matter how rich a society becomes, there will always be those who lack things that most people might want and have. Relative poverty will always exist as long as inequality exists.
Recognizes that what constitutes poverty can change between societies and over time in the same society.	It is riddled with value judgements. Relative poverty standards reflect the values of experts, as in Townsend's deprivation index, or of the public, as in the Breadline Britain and the Poverty and Social Exclusion surveys. Lacking three or more necessities was decided upon by the researchers as a significant indicator of poverty – but why not five, or six or seven or more?
Links poverty to wider issues of social exclusion.	The 60 per cent of average income poverty line means some people will always be relatively poor, even as society gets richer. The 60 per cent level is fairly arbitrary – why not 50 per cent or 70 per cent?
Recognizes the social, cultural and environmental dimensions of poverty.	

Activity

1 Go through each of the statements (A–G) below, and explain in each case which definition of poverty is being used. Give reasons for your answer.
2 Explain in your own words what Moore (statement B) meant when he said, 'The poverty lobby would, on their definition, find poverty in Paradise.'
3 With reference to the statements below, identify five aspects of poverty apart from a low income.
4 How do you think those who use a relative definition of poverty might respond to Moore's claim in statement B that 'It is hard to believe that poverty stalks the land when even the poorest fifth of families with children spend nearly a tenth of their income on alcohol and tobacco.'
5 Explain, with examples, the view in statement C that 'The notion of being able to measure what is necessary to live and fully participate in society is fraught with difficulty, as this will to some extent depend on how the person chooses to live and on the researcher's own values.'

Statement A
'Poverty curtails freedom of choice. The freedom to eat as you wish, to go where and when you like, to seek the leisure pursuits or political activities which others accept; all are denied to those without the resources . . . poverty is most comprehensively understood as a state of partial citizenship.'

(P. Golding, *Excluding the Poor*, London: Child Poverty Action Group, 1986)

Statement B

'Poverty in the old absolute sense of hunger and want has been wiped out, and it is simply that some people today are less equal. The lifestyle of the poorest 20 per cent of families represents affluence beyond the wildest dreams of the Victorians, with half having a telephone, car, and central heating and virtually all having a refrigerator and television set. It is hard to believe that poverty stalks the land when even the poorest fifth of families with children spend nearly a tenth of their income on alcohol and tobacco. It is absurd to suggest that a third of the population of Britain is living in or on the margins of poverty. Starving children and squalid slums have disappeared. What the poverty lobby is opposed to is simple inequality, and however rich a society becomes, the poor on their definition would never disappear. The poverty lobby would, on their definition, find poverty in Paradise.'

(Adapted from a speech by John Moore, a former social security minister)

Statement C

'Poverty cannot be defined simply in terms of survival. We need to look at whether individuals have the material resources to fully participate in society – this involves wider social needs (such as money to have a holiday, give children birthday parties, go to the cinema, etc.) and goes beyond mere biological or physical survival. The notion of being able to measure what is necessary to live and fully participate in society is fraught with difficulty, as this will to some extent depend on how the person chooses to live and on the researcher's own values.'

Statement D

'They can only be counted as "poor" in relation to contemporary British standards of affluence, but compared to Victorian times they are rich beyond the dreams of avarice. Their condition is only shocking because it is not as comfortable as that of those who are better off. What those who talk of poverty in modern Britain find offensive is not so much the existence of poverty but the existence of inequality.'

(Adapted from Peregrine Worsthorne in the *Daily Telegraph*, 27 Oct. 1979)

Statement E

'Living on the breadline is not simply about doing without things; it is also about experiencing poor health, isolation, stress, stigma and exclusion.'

(Adapted from C. Oppenheim, *Poverty: The Facts*, London: Child Poverty Action Group, 1988)

Statement F

'To have one bowl of rice in a society where all other people have half a bowl may well be a sign of achievement and intelligence . . . To have five bowls of rice in a society where the majority have a decent, balanced diet is a tragedy.'

(M. Harrington, *The Other America*, London: Macmillan, 1962)

Statement G

'Poverty should be seen in relation to minimum needs established by the standard of living in a particular society, and all members of the population should have the right to an income which allows them to participate fully in society rather than merely exist. Such participation involves having the means to fulfil responsibilities to others – as parents, sons and daughters, neighbours, friends, workers and citizens. Poverty filters into every aspect of life. It is about not having access to material goods and services such as decent housing, adequate heating, nutritious food, public transport, credit and consumer goods.'

(Adapted from C. Oppenheim, *Poverty: The Facts*, London: Child Poverty Action Group, 1988)

Table 4.2 Summary: comparing absolute and relative poverty

Feature	Absolute poverty	Relative poverty	Explanation
Concerned only with the minimum necessary for healthy survival	✔	✘	Relative poverty recognizes that what counts as poverty is not the subsistence minimum of absolute poverty, but what is regarded as an acceptable standard of living in a particular society.
Relatively easy to define and measure	✔	✘	Absolute poverty refers to a subsistence minimum broadly similar in most societies, but it is quite difficult with relative poverty to define both what counts as an acceptable standard of living and what cultural needs should be included.
Easy to make national and international comparisons	✔	✘	Absolute poverty standard is similar in most societies (subsistence), while the relative poverty standard changes between societies, and over time in the same society.
Involves value judgements	✔	✔	Both involve value judgements by experts and others about *either* the contents and costs of an appropriate minimum diet, and how people should spend their money (absolute poverty), *or* judgements about what constitutes a socially acceptable minimum standard of living (relative poverty).
Takes into account social, cultural and psychological needs and expectations, as well as biological needs	✘	✔	Only relative poverty involves social expectations of reasonable living standards and quality of life in specific societies, and wider dimensions of poverty like environmental poverty, healthcare, poverty at school and at work, and social exclusion.
Recognizes poverty as a social construction	✘	✔	Relative poverty recognizes that what constitutes poverty will depend on the perceptions of others, rather than simply basic subsistence needs.
Links poverty to wider issues of social exclusion	✘	✔	Relative poverty involves consideration of whether people have the resources to participate fully in the societies in which they live, rather than the mere biological existence of absolute poverty.

Exam-style questions

1 Explain what is meant by 'marketable wealth'. *(2 marks)*

2 Explain what is meant by 'disposable income'. *(2 marks)*

3 Explain what is meant by 'subjective poverty'. *(2 marks)*

4 Explain what is meant by the 'poverty line'. *(2 marks)*

5 Explain the difference between wealth and income. *(4 marks)*

6 Suggest **two** ways that values may influence the definition or measurement of poverty. *(4 marks)*

7 Suggest **three** reasons why income alone is an inadequate way of measuring relative poverty. *(6 marks)*

8 Suggest **three** reasons why poverty may lead to social exclusion. *(6 marks)*

9 Examine the problems sociologists face in defining and measuring poverty. *(24 marks)*

Topic 2

SPECIFICATION AREA

The distribution of poverty, wealth and income between different social groups

The distribution of wealth, income and poverty

Wealth and income are very unequally distributed in contemporary Britain, and one consequence of this is that there is also widespread relative poverty. It is worth emphasizing from the outset that these inequalities create and perpetuate inequalities in life chances. Not all social groups have the same chances of accumulating or inheriting wealth, or of achieving high incomes. Those in the richest groups benefit from often substantial inheritances from wealthy parents and other relatives, and those from better-off families benefit from financial help with the cost of weddings, cars, higher education and buying or maintaining a home, as well as a range of other social and cultural benefits arising from upper- and middle-class backgrounds. By contrast, those in the poorest groups receive very little or nothing by way of family inheritance of wealth or other financial help, and this contributes to wide inequalities of life chances. This means the poorest groups often fall farther behind and inequalities widen. This inequality also means that not all social groups face the same risks of poverty.

Figure 4.3 shows that in 2008–10 the share of wealth of the richest 50 per cent of households (90 per cent) was nine times greater than that of the poorest half (10 per cent), while the richest 10 per cent owned 44 per cent. One-fifth of households possessed nearly two-thirds of the nation's total household wealth. These are official figures, and they may underestimate the inequalities of wealth, as they do not include business assets, which are most likely to be owned by the most wealthy, and the wealthy also have an interest in concealing their wealth from the prying eyes of official government surveys and other bodies to avoid taxation.

As figure 4.4 shows, income is also unequally distributed, with the richest fifth (20 per cent) of the population getting 42 per cent of all income in 2010–11 – more than twice their fair share if income were equally distributed, and more than the bottom three-fifths of income-earners got between them. The poorest fifth got only 8 per cent, only two-fifths of their fair share if income was equally distributed. It should be noted that those with high incomes can convert some of their income into wealth, through purchasing productive property, like houses for rent or company shares, which will themselves generate additional unearned income for those who already have high incomes.

Activity

1 Describe the changes in the distribution of income between 1979 and 2010/11 shown in figure 4.4.
2 What do these changes suggest about the gap between the most and least well-off in the UK?

Figure 4.3 Distribution of household wealth: Great Britain, 2008–10

Source: Office for National Statistics, *Wealth in Great Britain Wave 2 2008–10 (2012)*

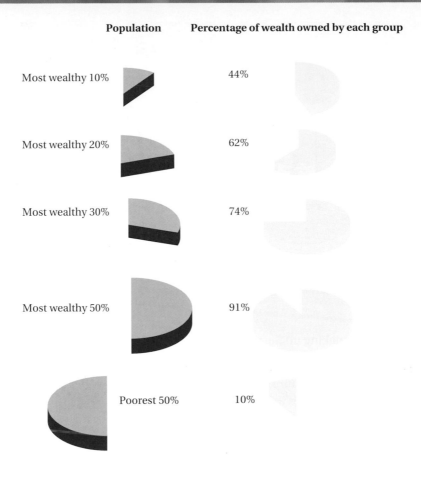

Population | Percentage of wealth owned by each group

Most wealthy 10%   44%

Most wealthy 20%   62%

Most wealthy 30%   74%

Most wealthy 50%   91%

Poorest 50%   10%

Figure 4.4 Changes in the distribution of income, by fifths of the population: United Kingdom, 1979–2010/11

Source: Department of Social Security, *Households Below Average Income* (1997), and Department for Work and Pensions (2012)

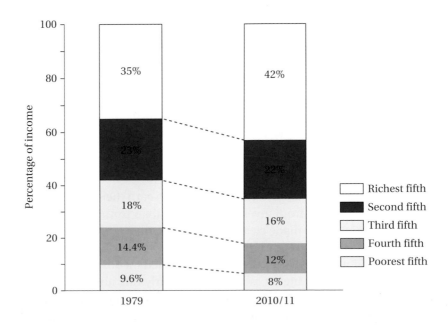

Richest fifth
Second fifth
Third fifth
Fourth fifth
Poorest fifth

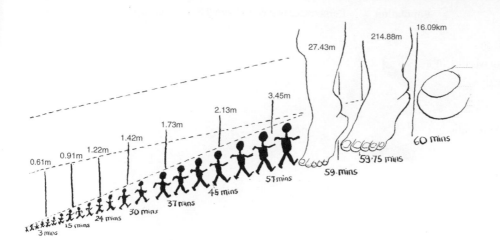

Imagine that everyone's height was based on their income, so the more you earned, the taller you were. Suppose the entire population of Britain marched past you in one hour, ranked in order of their income. This is what you might see.

For the first 30 minutes, you would be greeted by a parade of very small people, and you wouldn't see a person of average height (income) – 1.73m – go by until 37 minutes had passed. After 57 minutes, mini-giants of 3.45m appear. In the last minute, super-rich giants of 27.43m appear, but these are dwarfed by the unbelievably rich super-giants (214.88m tall) who go by in the final few seconds. The last person is so rich that his or her over-16 km height makes all the others look tiny.

Who are the rich?

There are three main groups making up the rich:

- *The traditional aristocracy* They are major landowners, such as the Duke of Westminster, who owns sizeable chunks of London, Cheshire, North Wales and Ireland, forests and shooting estates in Lancashire and Scotland, and properties in North America and the Far East. According to the 2012 Rich List published by the *Sunday Times*, the Duke of Westminster's wealth amounts to an estimated £7.35 billion (£7,350,000,000).

- *The owners of industry and commerce* – the corporate rich of the business world. This includes Britain's wealthiest person, Lakshmi Mittal, worth £12.7 billion; Sir Richard Branson of Virgin, Britain's 16th-richest person in 2012, with estimated assets of £3.41 billion; and Dame Mary Perkins of Specsavers, worth £850 million.

- *Stars of entertainment, sport and the media* These include Joanne Rowling, author of the Harry Potter books, on £560 million; former Beatle Sir Paul McCartney, and his wife Nancy Shevell (£665 million); Simon Cowell – the force behind TV shows *Pop Idol*, *The X-Factor*, *Britain's Got Talent* and *American Idol*, on £225 million; Sir Elton John (£220 million); Sir Mick Jagger (£190 million); David and Victoria Beckham on £190 million; and the relatively impoverished Robbie Williams on £100 million. Lewis Hamilton of Formula One is worth a modest £50 million, and Wayne Rooney of Manchester United gets by on just £37 million.

Most wealth is inherited, with those inheriting doing nothing to earn their wealth. Most of the rich live on unearned income from investments rather than from employment. The starkness of these inequalities is made clear by the Queen, one of Britain's richest women, with personal assets estimated at £310 million. If she were to pop this into her local high street bank, she would receive at least £14 in unearned income each minute of every day every year (after paying higher rate tax) – an hourly rate about 137 times greater than someone on the National Minimum Wage in 2012. Her unearned income each year after tax would take a full-time employee on average wages (after paying tax, and who was never ill) around 300 years to earn, and the Queen would still have her original £310 million.

The Queen is one of Britain's richest women, though there are other women and men who are *much richer*. She earns in interest on her wealth an hourly income, 24 hours a day, about 137 times greater than someone on the National Minimum Wage. Do you think such inequalities can be justified or the rich deserve their high incomes? Explain why or why not

High earners and the self-made rich do not necessarily put in more work than those who receive low pay; it is simply that society places different values on people in different positions, and rewards them more or less highly. A senior executive in a large company or a rock star will probably not have to work as hard for his or her high income as an unskilled manual worker working long hours in a low-paid job.

> ### Activity
> 1 Go to Google (www.google.uk) and search for the 'Rich List UK'. Have some fun finding out how rich your favourite celebrities are.
> 2 Do you agree or disagree with the view that it is wrong that the wealthy should be allowed to live off unearned income, and that large amounts of wealth should be able to be passed from parents to children? Do you think high earners really deserve their high rewards more than people who work in low-paid jobs? Give reasons for your answers.

Attempts to redistribute wealth and income

The massive inequalities in wealth and income which have existed over the last century, and the inequalities in life chances these have caused, have provoked various measures by governments to redistribute wealth and income more equally. Some of these measures include:

- *inheritance tax*, which is a tax payable when people give gifts of wealth either before or after death, and is intended to limit the inheritance of vast quantities of wealth from one generation by the next.
- *capital gains tax*, which is intended to reduce profits from dealing in property or shares, and is payable whenever these are sold.
- *income tax*, which is payable on earned and unearned income; this is generally progressive, as it rises as earnings increase.
- *social welfare benefits* from the state, which are generally seen as attempts to divert the resources obtained through taxation to the needy sections of society.

WHY HAVE ATTEMPTS TO REDISTRIBUTE WEALTH AND INCOME FAILED?

Despite these measures, attempts to redistribute wealth and income have been largely unsuccessful. Little real redistribution has occurred, and what redistribution has taken place has mainly been between the very rich and the lesser rich, and the gap between the richest and the poorest sections of society has actually grown wider in recent years.

Tax relief

The state allows tax relief, money normally used to pay income tax, on a wide variety of things such as business expenses, school fees and private pensions. These are expenses which only the better-off are likely to have. This means that they pay a smaller proportion of their income in tax than a person who is poorer but who does not have these expenses.

Tax avoidance schemes

These are schemes which are perfectly legal, often being thought up by financial advisers and accountants to find loopholes in the tax laws to beat the tax system, thereby saving the rich from paying some tax. Such schemes involve things like living outside Britain for most of the year, investing in pension schemes to avoid income tax, investing in tax-free or low-tax areas like the Channel Islands, giving wealth away to kin well before death to avoid inheritance tax, or putting companies or savings in other people's names, such as those of husband/wife, children or other kin.

Tax evasion

This is illegal, and involves people not declaring wealth and income to Her Majesty's Revenue and Customs (HMRC). This is suspected to be a common practice among the rich.

A failure to claim benefits

A final reason for the failure of attempts at wealth and income redistribution is that many people fail to claim the welfare benefits to which they are entitled. Some reasons for this are discussed later in this chapter.

The distribution and extent of poverty in the contemporary UK

In 2010–11 in the United Kingdom:

- 13 million people were living in poverty (below 60 per cent of average income) – 21 per cent of the population,
- 3,600,000 children (27 per cent of all children) were living in poverty.

For all the latest information on poverty go to www.poverty.org.uk

The identity of the major groups in poverty suggests that poverty is not caused by individual 'inadequacies', but by social circumstances beyond the control of the poor themselves.

Poverty does not affect all groups equally, and older retired people, children, the disabled, some minority ethnic groups and in some circumstances women have higher risks of poverty than others. However, what unites these groups is primarily their social class background, as poverty is essentially a problem of the working class: other classes have savings, employers' pensions and sick pay schemes to protect them and their children when adversity strikes or old age arrives, and people from better-off backgrounds often receive substantial benefits from their families, like help to rent, buy or maintain homes, buy cars, to pay for weddings or the costs of education; professional and managerial employees are also likely to receive better pay-offs, like redundancy pay and severance packages, if they are made redundant. These all help to provide a safety net not available to many working-class people, and particularly for those facing added disadvantages arising from racism, disability, age and gender. The groups who were living in low-income households (on the poverty line – 60 per cent of average income or below) in 2010–11 are shown below:

- *Those without work* – 51 per cent of those on low incomes were workless.
- *The low paid* – 48 per cent were self-employed or in full-time or part-time work. Many of the poor work long hours in low-paid jobs.
- *Pensioners* – 14 per cent were pensioners. Many elderly retired people depend on state pensions for support, and these are inadequate for maintaining other than a very basic standard of living.
- *Lone parents* – 16 per cent were lone parents. Lone parents with young children are often prevented from getting a full-time job by the lack of affordable childcare facilities, or only take part-time jobs, which generally get lower rates of pay. The costs of childcare often mean lone parents cannot afford to work. The majority of lone parents are women, who in any case get lower pay than men.
- *Children* – 27 per cent of all children lived in poverty. Children living in lone parent families, or with two parents who were unemployed or only working part-time, and in larger families with three or more children were the main groups. Families with young children are more likely to experience poverty because it may be more difficult for both parents to take up paid employment, especially given the high cost of childcare. Young children are expensive – with expenditure on nappies, bottles, foodstuffs and so on – and child benefit and inadequate maternity pay are barely enough to cover costs.
- *Minority ethnic groups* – about two-fifths of people from ethnic minorities were living in poverty: twice the rate for white people. More than half of people from Pakistani or Bangladeshi ethnic backgrounds were living in low-income households, and about two in every three Pakistani and Bangladeshi children.
- *The disabled* – 24 per cent of individuals living in families where someone is disabled were living in poverty. This compares with 20 per cent living in families with no disabled member. Disabled people are far more likely to be living in poverty than those who are not disabled, as disability often brings with it poorer employment opportunities, lower pay and dependence on state benefits.

Figure 4.5 illustrates which groups made up most of those living in poverty in 2010–11 by family type and by economic status. Figure 4.6 illustrates the risk of poverty facing those in particular social groups.

By family type

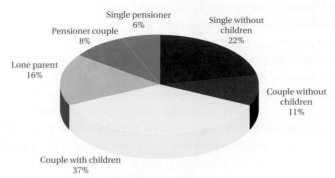

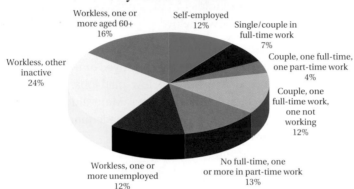

By economic status

Figure 4.5 Who are the poor? There were 13 million people living in low-income households (below 60 per cent of average income after housing costs) in the United Kingdom in 2010–11. This figure shows the family and economic features of those making up the total living on low incomes

Source: Department for Work and Pensions, Households below Average Income (2012)

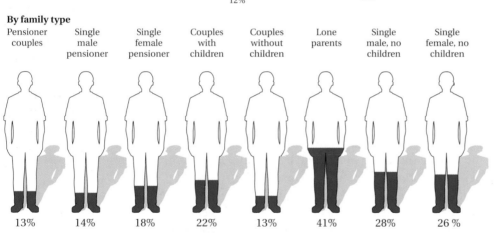

By family type

Pensioner couples	Single male pensioner	Single female pensioner	Couples with children	Couples without children	Lone parents	Single male, no children	Single female, no children
13%	14%	18%	22%	13%	41%	28%	26 %

Figure 4.6 The risk of poverty: proportion of individuals in particular groups living in poverty (below 60 per cent of average income after housing costs): United Kingdom, 2010-11

Source: Department for Work and Pensions, Households below Average Income (2011)

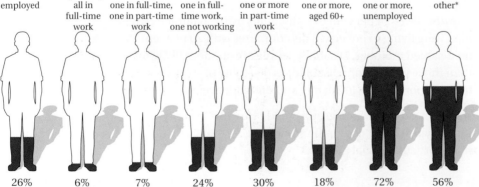

By economic status

Self-employed	Single/couple all in full-time work	Couple, one in full-time, one in part-time work	Couple, one in full-time work, one not working	No full-time, one or more in part-time work	Workless, one or more, aged 60+	Workless, one or more, unemployed	Workless other*
26%	6%	7%	24%	30%	18%	72%	56%

* Other = all those not included in previous groups, e.g. long-term sick, disabled people, and non-working lone parent

Activity

Refer to figure 4.5. In 2010–11:

1   What percentage of individuals in poverty were in pensioner couples?
2   What percentage of individuals in poverty were single without children?
3   What percentage of individuals in poverty were lone parents?
4   How many individuals in poverty were in households with no one working full-time but where one or more were in part-time work?

Refer to figure 4.6. In 2010–11:

5   Which family type had the greatest risk of individuals living in poverty?
6   Which family type had the lowest risk of individuals living in poverty?
7   Which group of individuals, by economic status, faced the greatest risk of poverty?
8   Which group of individuals, by economic status, faced the lowest risk of poverty?
9   What evidence is there in figure 4.6 that might be used to show that low pay is a cause of poverty?
10 Suggest how the evidence in figures 4.5 and 4.6 might be used to show that the poor are victims of unfortunate circumstances rather than being themselves to blame for their poverty. Could any of the evidence in the figures be used to support the opposite view?

ETHNICITY AND POVERTY

Kenway and Palmer (2007) found that people from minority ethnic groups are, on average, much more likely to be in poverty than White British people. Almost half of all children from ethnic minorities live in low-income households, compared to a quarter of White British children. Overall, poverty in minority ethnic groups is around double that of White British people. However, Kenway and Palmer noted there are substantial differences between ethnic groups. Bangladeshis, Pakistanis and Black Africans have the highest rates of poverty, with around two-thirds of Bangladeshis, over half of Pakistanis, and just under half of Black Africans (46 per cent) in poverty. This compares with around 33 per cent of Black Caribbeans, just over one in four Indians and one in five White British, who have the lowest rate. Minority ethnic groups are far more likely than white people to be in the poorest fifth of the population, as figure 4.7 shows. Pakistanis and Bangladeshis are the poorest groups in the UK.

Figure 4.7 Percentage of each ethnic group in the poorest fifth of the population: United Kingdom, 2010-11

Source: Department for Work and Pensions, Households below Average Income (2012)

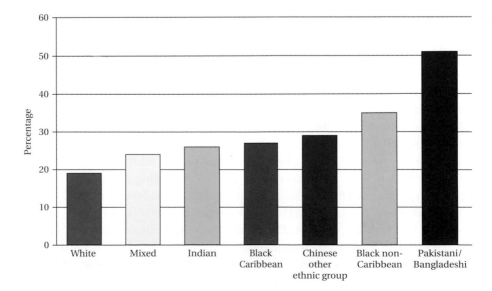

There are a number of possible explanations for this.

- *Low pay* is a significant factor, and many of those experiencing the highest rates of poverty are in low-paid jobs. This is particularly the case in Pakistani and Bangladeshi households where only one partner is in paid employment, with many women not in paid work.
- *Unemployment* tends to be higher among some minority ethnic groups, particularly among Bangladeshis, Pakistanis, Black Africans and Black Caribbeans.
- *Family type* is another factor. Pakistanis and Bangladeshis tend to have larger families and, combined with low-paid work, this increases poverty levels. Lone parent families are more common in the Black Caribbean and Black African ethnic groups, and lone parenthood is itself a factor contributing to poverty.
- *Racism* in employment means that some minority ethnic groups are often unable to obtain the best-paid jobs, and are relegated to low-paid employment or unemployment.
- *Underachievement in education*, particularly among Pakistanis, Bangladeshis and Caribbean boys means they often lack the qualifications needed for employment, and particularly for more secure and better-paid skilled jobs.

These explanations are all related to one another, and create multiple causes for poverty. Functionalist theories (discussed below) would suggest that such poverty among minority ethnic groups is functional for the system, as some minority ethnic groups will be motivated to take the low-paid jobs the White British don't want, as they often have little alternative; Weberian theories (see below) suggest that some minority ethnic groups have a weaker market situation, as a result of educational underachievement; Marxists might see racism and low pay contributing to divisions in the working class, by separating off the poor from the non-poor working class, and dividing black and white workers, preventing the development of working-class unity and a class consciousness that might threaten the stability of the capitalist system.

The New Right theories of the **dependency culture** and the **underclass**, which are discussed in the following topic, suggest that some members of some minority ethnic groups might be themselves to blame for their poverty, as they are part of a dependency culture and a work-shy underclass. However, Marxists might argue this may in itself be a response to racial disadvantage in education and employment, and consequent social exclusion.

AGE AND POVERTY

Older people – pensioners – are now no more likely, and perhaps less likely, to be living in low-income households than adults of working age, and are much less likely to be in poverty than children.

Children are much more likely to live in low-income households than either pensioners or working-age adults, and child poverty in the UK remains higher than in most of the other countries of the European Union. Around 27 per cent of all children in the UK were living in poverty in 2010–11, compared to 21 per cent of adults. Some groups of children are particularly vulnerable to severe hardship, including homeless children, those with disabled parents, children from Pakistani and Bangladeshi households, and children of marginalized groups like asylum seekers and Gypsies/Travellers.

Child poverty is a serious problem. Hirsch (2006) points out that poverty causes material and social hardships for children, affects their educational achievement, and has lasting effects on their health and psychological development, and leaves them

A **dependency culture** is a set of values and beliefs, and a way of life, centred on dependence on others, particularly benefits from the welfare state. The **underclass** is a social group right at the bottom of the social hierarchy, whose members are in some ways different from, and cut off or excluded from, the rest of society.

facing greater risks of poverty as adults. Child poverty can also generate wider social problems, such as crime and anti-social behaviour. Hirsch points out that poor children suffer because they cannot do or cannot afford to have the everyday things that their friends take for granted. For example, they cannot afford the toys and clothes others have, creating a stigma and possible consequences like the risk of bullying and ridicule at school.

Hirsch suggests the underlying factors influencing the high levels of child poverty in the UK include:

- *Lone parenthood*: a high number of children in poverty live with lone parents, a substantial proportion of whom are not in paid employment, and many have low qualifications, weakening their position in the job market.
- *Lack of work or low pay of parents* Unless all adults in the family are working, and at least one of them full-time and in a reasonably well-paid job, the risks of a child being in poverty are substantial. Many poor children live in working households where one or both parents have low pay.
- *Disability* undermines parents' ability to find employment, and particularly well-paid work. Around one in four children living in poverty has at least one disabled parent.
- *The inadequate help available through the tax and benefit system.*
- *Inadequate policies supporting childcare and flexible working*, making it difficult for those parents who both want to work to support their children.

DISABILITY AND POVERTY

Palmer (2006) showed that the poverty rate for disabled adults is around double that of non-disabled adults, and around 30 per cent of disabled adults of working age (aged 25 to retirement) are living in poverty. Around two-fifths of these are single adults without dependent children, and Palmer points out that because of this, many may lack day-to-day company and support, leading to social exclusion as well as poverty.

Palmer suggests the main reasons why people with a work-limiting disability are at a greater risk of poverty than those without such a disability include the following inter-related issues:

- *Inability to undertake paid employment.* Some disabled people have physical or mental impairments which make it difficult for them to take jobs. Even if all those wanting work found it, only about 60 per cent of disabled people would be in employment, leaving the rest unavoidably dependent on welfare benefits.
- *Unemployment.* Disabled people are around four times more likely to be out of work than the non-disabled with similar qualifications. Many of those who are not working say that they want to work, but have not been able to find jobs.
- *Low pay.* Disabled people who do find work are more likely to be low-paid than non-disabled people with similar qualifications.
- *Employer discrimination.* The fact that disabled people are more likely to be lower paid, and to be lacking but wanting work, than those who are not disabled points to discrimination against disabled people in the labour market. Palmer suggests this is because some employers have a poor attitude to disability and overtly or directly discriminate against disabled people (even though this is illegal). Other employers may not practise such overt discrimination, but still disadvantage

disabled people nonetheless, often because of ignorance. For example, they may worry about the risks of employing disabled people, the potential costs of work-place adaptations, about transport to and from work, and lack awareness about what disabled people can do, and what government support is available to help disabled people in work.

- *Inadequate welfare benefits.* Social security benefits are insufficient to keep many disabled people out of poverty, and increases in their benefit levels have not kept up with those available for children and pensioners, and are falling in relation to average household incomes.

GENDER AND POVERTY: THE FEMINIZATION OF POVERTY

Women overall are slightly more likely than men to experience poverty. In 2010–11, 20 per cent of all women lived in low-income households, compared to 19 per cent of men, with single female pensioners facing a higher risk of poverty than their male equivalents. Women of all ethnic groups have lower average individual incomes than men in the same ethnic group. Poverty rates for all groups of women are higher than those of White British men, but there are important variations by ethnic group. White British women have the lowest levels of poverty, followed by Chinese, Indian, Black Caribbean and Black African women, with Pakistani and Bangladeshi women having extremely high poverty rates of around 50 per cent, and their children are more likely to be poor and stay poor.

The higher poverty rates among women are because:

- *Women are more likely to be in low-paid and part-time work*, and therefore to miss out on work-related welfare benefits. This is because women are more likely to have the major responsibilities for housework and childcare. This means that many women are forced to combine paid employment with childcare, weakening their position in the labour market.
- *Women are the majority of homeworkers*, tied to the home by children or others dependent on them (such as the elderly). Many homeworking jobs are based on piecework (that is, payment for each product or part of a product made), are extremely low-paid, and rarely carry such basic employment rights as holidays, pensions, and compensation for industrial accidents.
- *Women are more likely than men to be lone parents* with sole responsibility for children, leading to reduced possibilities for employment, and dependence on state benefits.
- *Women are more likely to sacrifice their own standard of living to provide food, clothing and extras for the children.* As Middleton et al. (1997) found, in many low-income households, it is often mothers, rather than fathers, who bear the burden of trying to make ends meet, and who make the sacrifice, including going without food, new clothes and shoes, and holidays, in order to ensure that their children do not go without on a daily basis.
- *Women live longer than men and retire earlier* (until 2018 when their retirement age will be the same as men's), and therefore spend a greater proportion of their lives beyond retirement age. However, because of the time they have taken off work to care for children, combined with low pay throughout their lives, they are less likely than men to have savings for old age, or to be entitled to employers' pensions, and so they are more likely to experience poverty in old age.

Sociological theories explaining the unequal distribution of wealth, income and poverty

There are three main theoretical approaches to explaining the unequal patterns of wealth and income distribution, and the existence of poverty which is an aspect and consequence of these.

FUNCTIONALIST EXPLANATIONS

Functionalist writers like Davis and Moore (1967[1945]) argue that inequalities in wealth and income are necessary to maintain society. According to Davis and Moore:

- Some positions in society are more functionally important than others in maintaining society. These require specialized skills that not everyone in society has the talent and ability to acquire.
- Those who do have the ability to do these jobs must be motivated and encouraged to undertake the lengthy training often required for these important positions with the promise of future high rewards in terms of income and wealth. There must therefore be a system of unequal rewards to make sure the most able people get into the most important social positions.

Davis and Moore, and other functionalist writers like Gans (1973), argue that the existence of poverty also has important functions in contributing to the maintenance and stability of society. This is because:

- The existence of poverty ensures that the most undesirable, dirty, dangerous or menial low-paid jobs that most people don't want, but which are important to the smooth running of society, are performed. Poverty means some people have no other choice but to do these jobs.
- Poverty creates jobs in a range of occupations, such as for social workers, social security staff, debt advisers, the police, and so on.
- The threat of poverty provides necessary incentives and motivation for people to work, even when their rewards are low. The existence of the poor provides a living example to the non-poor of what not to be – an undesirable, deviant state to be avoided – and reinforces the mainstream values of honesty, hard work, seizing opportunities and planning for the future. As Gans said, 'The defenders of the desirability of hard work, thrift, honesty and monogamy need people who can be accused of being lazy, spendthrift, dishonest and promiscuous to justify these norms.'
- The existence of the low-paid keeps some industries and services running. Hospitals, catering, agriculture and the clothing industry all depend on low-paid workers.

These functionalist explanations for the unequal distribution of wealth, income and poverty have been subjected to a number of criticisms, such as the following:

1 There is no way of deciding which positions in society are more important, and this often rests on personal value judgements. There are many poorly rewarded occupations which can still be seen as vital in maintaining society. For example, a rich business executive can only become rich through the work of his or her employees, and low-paid workers like refuse collectors, hospital cleaners or roadsweepers are no less important than doctors in maintaining society's health.

2 Some people have high levels of wealth and income not because they have talent or occupy a position of functional importance, but because they have inherited their wealth. Having rich parents is still one of the major means of becoming wealthy.

3 Material rewards are not, as Davis and Moore suggest, the only means of motivating people to fill important social positions. People may be motivated by the prospect of job satisfaction, or by the attraction of giving service to others, as for example in teaching or nursing.

4 Poverty may not be functional in helping to maintain society through providing incentives and motivations for people to undertake the most undesirable jobs. While the poor may have no alternative to doing such jobs, they may well feel resentment and bitterness at the low pay, poor life chances, social exclusion and marginalization which scar their lives. This may create conflict and divisions in society, and provide a threat to social stability.

> **Activity**
>
> Do you think some jobs are more important than others in maintaining society? Do you think some jobs deserve higher rewards than others if people are to be motivated to train for them? Give examples of what you regard as important and unimportant jobs, giving reasons for your answer.

WEBERIAN EXPLANATIONS

Weber (1864–1920) was a social action theorist, who, along with Marx and Durkheim, is one of the key historical figures in the development of sociology. Those who follow Weber's theories are known as Weberian sociologists. Weber believed inequalities in wealth and income and the existence of poverty partly arise from the different **market situations** of individuals – the different skills that people have and the different rewards attached to them when they sell their labour in the job market.

Some people are able to get higher incomes when they sell their abilities and skills in the job market because they have rare skills, talents or qualifications that are in demand, such as those of doctors and lawyers. This might also happen because society values some skills and talents more highly than others and rewards them accordingly, as might be the case with business executives or company owners, or with football, film and music stars. Some celebrities receive high rewards simply for being famous and in public demand, even though they lack any obvious talents.

From a Weberian perspective, such as that adopted by Townsend, those in poverty have a weak market situation. They are marginalized because they lack the education and skills which might bring them higher rewards: they have very common easily acquired skills, or few skills at all, and the demand for unskilled and unqualified labour is declining. For many, such as the sick, lone parents, the disabled and the elderly, their circumstances often mean they are excluded from competing in the labour market at all, and so are dependent on inadequate state welfare benefits.

The difficulty with the Weberian approach is that it does not easily explain the position of those who inherit their wealth and do not sell their skills on the labour market, as they live on unearned incomes rather than those earned through employment.

> **Market situation** refers to the rewards that people are able to obtain when they sell their skills and talents on the labour market, with the rewards they get dependent on the scarcity of their skills and the power they have to obtain high rewards.

MARXIST EXPLANATIONS

Marxist explanations, such as those adopted by Miliband (1974) and Westergaard and Resler (1976), suggest that the main reason for inequalities in wealth and income and the existence of poverty lies in the private ownership of the means of production – the key resources like land, property, factories and businesses which are necessary to produce society's goods. The concentration of ownership of the means of production in the hands of a small upper class is the basis of the inequalities of wealth, and this generates similarly high levels of income inequality through unearned income on investments. Marxist approaches make the following points:

- Wealth and income is concentrated in the hands of the ruling class, and this generates class inequality. Poverty is the inevitable result of capitalism, and low-paid workers provide the source of profits, which enables the rich to achieve high incomes.
- The privileged position of the wealthy ultimately rests on working-class poverty. The threat of poverty and unemployment motivates workers, and provides a pool of cheap labour for the capitalist class.
- The existence of the non-working poor helps to keep wages down, by providing a pool of reserve labour which threatens the jobs of the non-poor should their wage demands become excessively high.
- Poverty divides the working class, by separating off the poor from the non-poor working class, and preventing the development of working-class unity and a class consciousness that might threaten the stability of the capitalist system.

The Marxist approach explains the wide inequalities in wealth and income and the existence of poverty that stem from the private ownership of the means of production, and which underpin the whole pattern of inequality in capitalist societies. However, the difficulty with this approach is that it does not easily explain the inequalities between men and women, the disabled and able-bodied, and between ethnic groups.

Activity

1. What assumptions and stereotypes do you have regarding the rich? Draw up your view of the features of rich people, such as their sources of wealth and income and their lifestyle. Where do you think your ideas and assumptions about the rich come from?

2. Do you think large inequalities in wealth and income are justified in society? Give reasons for your answer.

3. Which out of the functionalist, Weberian and Marxist explanations do you find the most convincing in explaining the distribution of wealth and income in our society? Give reasons for your answer.

4. Outline how *each* of the functionalist, Weberian and Marxist theories might explain the higher rates of poverty among: (a) disabled people, (b) some minority ethnic groups.

Exam-style questions

1 Explain what is meant by 'tax evasion'. *(2 marks)*

2 Suggest **two** reasons why some jobs get higher rewards than others. *(4 marks)*

3 Suggest **two** policies that might contribute to the redistribution of wealth and income. *(4 marks)*

4 Suggest **two** reasons why members of the working class face a higher risk of poverty than those in other social classes. *(4 marks)*

5 Suggest **three** ways in which poverty may have harmful effects on the lives of children. *(6 marks)*

6 Suggest **three** reasons why some minority ethnic groups are more likely to be in poverty than white British people. *(6 marks)*

7 Examine sociological explanations for the unequal distribution of wealth and income in contemporary Britain. *(24 marks)*

8 Examine the reasons why disabled people are more likely to experience poverty than the non-disabled. *(24 marks)*

Topic 3

SPECIFICATION AREA

The existence and persistence of poverty in contemporary society

Explaining the persistence of poverty

The previous topic reviewed the extent of poverty in contemporary Britain. This topic examines a range of explanations for the persistence of poverty, despite Britain being one of the richest countries in the world, and having an extensive welfare state. While the welfare state may have removed the worst excesses of absolute poverty, it has failed to solve the real problems of relative poverty. Why is this?

A good way to remember the various explanations of poverty is to think of them as 'blaming theories' – where is the blame placed for poverty? These can be grouped into cultural and material explanations.

CULTURAL EXPLANATIONS OF POVERTY

> The **culture of poverty** is a set of beliefs and values thought to exist among the poor which prevents them from escaping from poverty.

Cultural explanations focus on the behaviour and attitudes of the poor themselves. These are victim-blaming theories, which suggest poverty persists because of the existence of a **culture of poverty** among the poor, and a *dependency culture* (a set of values and beliefs, and a way of life, centred on dependence on others, particularly benefits from the welfare state) generated by the *generosity* of the welfare state.

The culture of poverty

Early work on the cultural attitudes of the poor was first developed by Oscar Lewis (1961), as a result of his research among the urban poor in Mexico and Puerto Rico in the 1950s. Lewis suggests that the poor have a culture of poverty with its own norms and values and way of life. This makes the poor different from the rest of society. He suggests the poor have the following cultural features:

- They are resigned to their situation, seldom taking opportunities to escape poverty when they arise.
- They have a sense of *fatalism* – that nothing can be done to change their situation.
- They are reluctant to work.
- They don't plan for the future.
- They make little effort to change their situation or take the initiative to try to break free of their poverty.
- They are marginalized, and don't see themselves as part of or involved in mainstream society.

Children grow up in this culture, which is passed on from generation to generation through socialization. This culture of poverty prevents those exposed to it from taking opportunities to escape from poverty when they arise, and the poor therefore remain poor because of their own values and behaviour.

This 'victim-blaming' approach was developed further by writers of the New Right.

The New Right: the dependency culture and the generosity of the welfare state

The New Right sees many of the poor as undeserving – a group of work-shy and lazy inadequates who are not deserving of support from the welfare state. New Right supporter David Marsland (1989) argues that poverty arises from the *generosity* of the welfare state. Marsland claims:

- The generosity of 'handouts' from the 'nanny' welfare state has created a dependency culture. This is where people abandon reliance on work, the family and the local community, and are content to live on welfare state 'handouts', rather than taking responsibility themselves for improving their situation. The more the welfare state provides benefits for people, the less they will do for themselves.
- Universal welfare benefits, which are payable to all regardless of income, such as education, healthcare and child benefits, take money away from investment in the economy and thus undermine the production of wealth.
- Universal welfare benefits should be withdrawn, and should be replaced by selective benefits targeted only at those who genuinely need them, such as the long-term sick and disabled, rather than given to those who are capable of supporting themselves. Benefits should therefore be targeted by *means testing*. This involves people having to pass a test of their income and savings (their 'means') before receiving any benefits, and only if these were low enough would they receive any assistance.

The underclass (New Right version) Charles Murray (1989), another New Right supporter, goes even further than Marsland. Murray has suggested that the attitudes and behaviour of the poor are responsible for their poverty, and that the poor form an anti-social, deviant underclass. This underclass is marked out by:

- high levels of illegitimacy, lone parenthood and family instability.
- drunkenness and 'yob culture'.
- crime, fiddling of the benefit system and drug abuse.
- exclusion from school and educational failure.
- work-shy attitudes leading to dropping out of the labour market and living off benefits.

Murray is particularly scathing about lone parenthood, which he says arises from the high level of benefits, which encourage women to have children they could not otherwise afford. Murray argues that the generosity of the welfare state has created, supports and encourages this underclass, and the solution is to cut benefits to encourage self-reliance, or marriage, or work.

New Right theories were very influential during the period of the Conservative governments in Britain between 1979 and 1997, and re-emerged in some forms after the Conservative – Liberal Democrat coalition formed the government in 2010. There was a strong sense of the poor being punished for their poverty, with cuts in benefits and all welfare state spending, and a growing stress on the need for everyone, including the poor, to take more responsibility for themselves, rather than relying on the state to help them out.

Activity

1 Suggest any ways in which you think the attitudes, beliefs and values of poor people might differ from those of the non-poor.
2 How might you carry out research to test whether the ideas of poor people are different from those of the non-poor? Work out a plan for carrying out research in this area.

Criticisms of cultural explanations of poverty

The differences between the attitudes of the poor and non-poor have been exaggerated   Kempson (1996), found that the poor were not an underclass with different attitudes and values to the rest of society, but wanted jobs, a decent home and an income that would cover their outgoings with a little to spare, much like the aspirations of the rest of the population. Walker et al. (2000) found there was 'no real indication that a social underclass actually exists', and said the evidence for benefit dependency is 'slight'. He said: 'Life on benefit is mean and harsh. Consequently, people are much more keen to avoid claiming benefits than to choose them as a way of life. Most claimants who are able to work are eager to do so and routinely look for jobs when they can.'

There is no clear-cut evidence that children inherit their parents' attitudes   There is some dispute over whether the cultural attitudes of parents get passed on to their children, and many parents often have higher ambitions for their children than they had for themselves. For example, Rutter and Madge (1976) found that 'At least half of children born into a disadvantaged home do not repeat the pattern of disadvantage in the next generation. Over half of all forms of disadvantage arise anew in each generation.' On the other hand, Blanden and Gibbons (2006) found poverty did get passed on between generations, with children growing up in poverty more likely to be poor as adults. However, they emphasize that there are many reasons poverty persists across generations, and parents' attitudes are only one among many other factors, including lack of skills and employment opportunities, lack of education, and shortage of material resources which affect the development, mental and physical health, educational attainment and motivation of children.

The poor want the same as everyone else   The poor want the same things as the rest of society, but factors like unemployment and social deprivation stop them from achieving them. For example, the poor cannot afford to save for a 'rainy day', planning for the future is difficult when the future is so hopeless or uncertain, and it is hard not to give up and become resigned to being unemployed after endless searching for non-existent jobs. It is the lack of resources that stops participation in society, not the culture of the poor or welfare state generosity. If there is any kind of dependency culture or culture of poverty, it is a *consequence* of poverty, not a *cause* of poverty.

Blaming the victims rather than the causes   Cultural explanations of poverty tend to blame the poor for their own poverty, and imply that if only the poor changed their values, then poverty would disappear. If these explanations are accepted, then the problem of poverty will be solved by policies such as cutting welfare benefits to the poor to make them stand on their own two feet, and job training programmes to get them used to working. However, in most cases it is economic circumstances, not attitudes, which made them poor in the first place. Cultural explanations are convenient ones for those in positions of power, as they put the blame for poverty on the poor themselves. As Westergaard and Resler (1976) put it: 'the blame for inequality falls neatly on its victims'.

MATERIAL EXPLANATIONS OF POVERTY

Material explanations blame material constraints, the cycle of deprivation, the *inadequacy* of the welfare state, and the unequal structure of power and wealth in capitalist society.

Material constraints

As seen in the criticisms of cultural explanations above, it is material or situational constraints, the economic and social position of groups like the low-paid, unemployed, sick and elderly, that influence the attitudes and behaviour of the poor. The hopelessness of the future undermines their ability and resolve to plan for the future. With a dead-end job or no job at all, and insufficient income to support a family, a person is unable to save and invest in the future or to support a stable family life. Resources are used up simply on week-by-week survival, concentrating the poor's attention on their immediate position. It is these factors that stop the poor from putting the mainstream values they share with everyone else into practice.

Any distinctive cultural features of the poor are therefore more likely to be a response to poverty than a cause of it. Once these material constraints are removed, by giving the poor decent housing, well-paid jobs, adequate benefits and some security in their lives, then any apparent culture of poverty or dependency culture will also disappear.

The cycle of deprivation

Coates and Silburn (1970), in their early study of the St Ann's area of Nottingham, emphasized the circumstances in which the poor are trapped, and how these circumstances combine to form a web from which, regardless of attitudes or ability, there is little chance of escape. This has been called the **cycle of deprivation**.

For example, a child born in a poor family may have poor-quality housing and diet. This may cause ill-health, and therefore absence from school. This means falling behind and failing exams, which in turn will mean a low-paid job or unemployment, and therefore poverty in adult life. It then carries on with their children. Figure 4.8 illustrates examples of possible cycles of deprivation.

> The theory of the **cycle of deprivation** suggests that poverty is cumulative, in the sense that one aspect of poverty can lead to further poverty. This builds up into a vicious circle of poverty from which the poor find it hard to escape, and it then carries on with their children.

What factors push people into a cycle of deprivation and prevent them escaping from poverty?

Figure 4.8 Cycles of deprivation

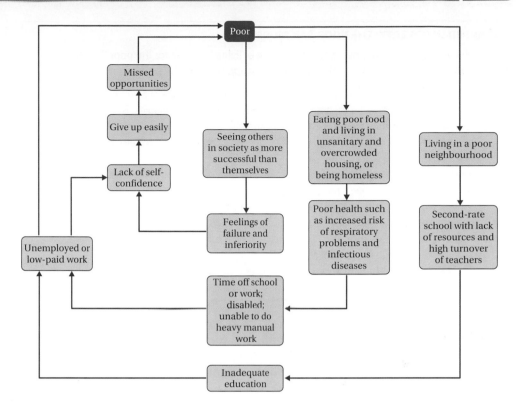

> ### Activity
>
> Refer to figure 4.8
> 1 Which of the cycles of deprivation suggested in this figure mainly consist of material factors, and which cultural?
> 2 Try to make up two further examples of such cycles of deprivation – one material, and one cultural.
> 3 Suggest three policies that a government might adopt to overcome these cycles of deprivation.

This cycle of deprivation is reinforced by the fact that poor people have to spend money in uneconomical ways – a matter in which they have little choice. The cost of living is higher for the poor than the non-poor, as illustrated in the box 'Trapped in poverty: the poor pay more'.

The problem with the cycle-of-deprivation explanation is that, while it explains why poverty continues, it does not explain how poverty begins in the first place.

The poverty trap and the inadequacy of the welfare state

While the welfare state has provided some important assistance to the poor, and has removed the worst excesses of absolute poverty, widespread deprivation remains and the welfare state has failed to reduce the inequalities between the rich and the poor. Poverty persists, some argue, because benefit levels are too low to lift people out of poverty. From this viewpoint, the welfare state is not generous enough, and the poor get trapped in poverty by an inadequate, means-tested benefit system from which they find it hard to escape.

This has led to an alternative view of the underclass to that suggested by Charles Murray.

TRAPPED IN POVERTY: THE POOR PAY MORE

One of the great ironies of poverty is that the cost of living is higher for the poor than the non-poor, and this hinders them in their attempts to escape poverty. The poor pay more because:

- They often live in poor-quality housing, which is expensive to heat and maintain.
- The cost of house and car insurance, and of other goods and services, is higher as a result of higher crime rates, like theft and vandalism, in poor areas.
- They have to buy cheap clothing, which wears out quickly and is therefore more expensive in the long run.
- They have to pay more for food as they can only afford to buy it in small quantities (which is more expensive) and from small, expensive corner shops as they haven't cars to travel to supermarkets. They also lack storage facilities like freezers for buying in bulk.
- They pay more for credit; banks and building societies won't lend them money because they consider them a poor risk. Loans are therefore often obtained from loan sharks at exorbitant rates of interest.
- They suffer more ill-health, and so have to spend more on non-prescription medicines, such as cold cures, pain-killers and vitamin supplements.

The underclass (social democratic version)   The social democratic view of the underclass is in keeping with the social democratic view of welfare discussed later in this chapter. This suggests the underclass consists of disadvantaged groups right at the bottom of the social class hierarchy whose poverty means they are excluded from taking part in society to the same extent as the non-poor.

Sociologists like Field (1989) and Townsend suggest this underclass consists of groups like the elderly retired, lone parents, the long-term unemployed, the low-paid, the disabled and the long-term sick. These groups are forced to rely on inadequate state benefits which are too low to give them an acceptable standard of living. More recently, we might include undocumented (illegal) migrant workers and asylum seekers in this group, who often have to work illegally in very low-paid jobs and are unable to claim benefits. These groups are frequently subject to horrendous exploitation by unscrupulous employers, as they lack the legal protection available to other workers. Many of these groups in the underclass are prevented from participating fully in society, and are left vulnerable to the **poverty trap**. This is when people are worse off if they get a low-paid job. This is because the money they lose in means-tested welfare benefits is more than they gain by working after paying tax. For example, the government suggested that, in 2011, in around 1.1 million workless households, a person would lose more than 70 per cent of their income if they worked for 10 hours a week. There is therefore little or no incentive to find work, or a better-paid job, because their poverty would be made worse, hence trapping them in poverty. The only solutions to this are either to make work pay more, by increasing wages and/or reducing tax or the amounts of benefit lost, or, in contrast, to punish the poor by making their lives even harder by reducing benefits.

This view of the underclass differs from that of Charles Murray and the New Right, as it is not the attitudes of poor people which are to blame for their poverty, but the difficulties and misfortune they face which are beyond their control (like unemployment, low pay, illness or disability). The poor live depressingly deprived lifestyles, and want many of the things most people in society already have, like secure and decently paid jobs and opportunities. As Field said, 'No one in their right mind believes that [the underclass] has volunteered for membership.' It is a lack of opportunities and jobs, low pay and inadequate benefits, not their attitudes, which leaves them excluded from full

The **poverty trap** is when people on means-tested benefits find themselves worse off if they get a low-paid job, as the benefits they lose are worth more than the money they gain through employment. This creates a disincentive for them to look for work or take low-paid jobs, trapping them in continuing poverty.

participation in society. This view suggests social policies should tackle unemployment and low pay, improve the living standards of those on benefits (for example, through higher pensions and child benefits), and give incentives to the poor to get off benefits through decently paid jobs, and a more generous National Minimum Wage. Only in this way will the excluded underclass disappear in our society.

Marxists such as Miliband (1974) and Westergaard and Resler are critical of the view that the poor are an underclass. They see the poor not as a separate, specially disadvantaged group, but simply as the most disadvantaged section of the working class, and argue that all working-class people face the risk of joining the ranks of the poor in circumstances of unemployment, sickness, disability, lone parenthood or old age.

Activity

Item A

'The underclass are a group who have developed a lifestyle and set of attitudes which means they are no longer willing to take jobs. They have developed a dependency culture, which means they are not prepared to help themselves but are prepared to live off the welfare state. Lack of morality, high crime levels, cohabitation and large numbers of lone parents are associated with this view of the underclass. Their 'sponging' attitudes and lack of social responsibility are to blame for their poverty. Most of the poor have only themselves to blame.'

Item B

'The underclass are a group whose poverty means they are excluded from taking part in society to the same extent as the non-poor, even though they want to. This group consists of people like the disadvantaged elderly retired, lone parent families, the disabled and the long-term sick and unemployed. Their attitudes are the same as those of the rest of society, but they are forced to rely on inadequate state benefits which are too low to give them an acceptable standard of living. This prevents them from participating fully in society, and gives them little opportunity to fulfil their ambitions and escape the poverty trap.'

Item C

'When I use the term "underclass" I am indeed focusing on a certain type of person defined not by his condition, e.g. long-term unemployed, but by his deplorable behaviour in response to that condition, e.g. unwilling to take the jobs that are available to him . . . Britain has a growing population of working-aged, healthy people who live in a different world from other Britons, who are raising their children to live in it, and whose values are contaminating the life of entire neighbourhoods . . .'

1 Compare the three views of the underclass which are considered above. Identify in each case one researcher who might support that view. Explain your reasons.
2 Using the items and elsewhere, identify four features of the 'deplorable behaviour' (Item C) of the underclass.
3 Identify and explain three criticisms of Charles Murray's view of the underclass.
4 Outline the evidence that the attitudes of the so-called 'underclass' are no different from those of the rest of society.
5 Identify the arguments and evidence you might use to show that the underclass is not a cause of poverty, but a result of poverty.
6 With reference to the items and elsewhere, identify and explain the solutions you would adopt to solve the problem of the underclass as identified in items A, B and C. Explain in each case how the policy adopted might solve the problem.
7 With reference to the items, discuss which view you think provides the most accurate picture of poor people.

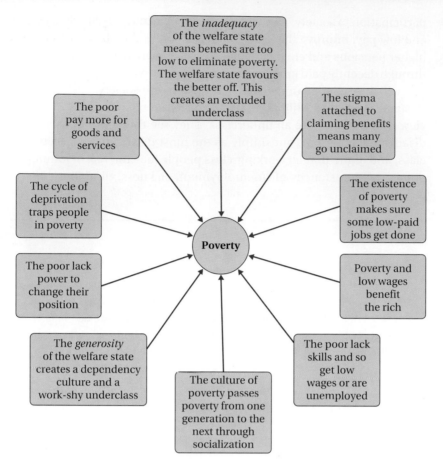

Figure 4.9 Why the poor remain poor

The diagram shows "Poverty" in a central circle with arrows pointing to it from the following boxes:

- The *inadequacy* of the welfare state means benefits are too low to eliminate poverty. The welfare state favours the better off. This creates an excluded underclass
- The poor pay more for goods and services
- The stigma attached to claiming benefits means many go unclaimed
- The cycle of deprivation traps people in poverty
- The existence of poverty makes sure some low-paid jobs get done
- The poor lack power to change their position
- Poverty and low wages benefit the rich
- The *generosity* of the welfare state creates a dependency culture and a work-shy underclass
- The culture of poverty passes poverty from one generation to the next through socialization
- The poor lack skills and so get low wages or are unemployed

Structural explanations: blaming the unequal structure of society

Structural explanations explain poverty as arising from the structures of inequality of capitalist society, with its unequal distribution of wealth, income and power.

Poverty is seen as an aspect of social inequality and not merely an individual problem of poor people. The problem of poverty is the same as the problem of riches, and the reason the poor remain poor is because they either are exploited by the rich (Marxist approach), lack skills and power (Weberian approach) or because they serve a necessary function in maintaining society (functionalist approach). These possible reasons were considered in the discussion of explanations for the unequal distribution of wealth and income, and the consequent poverty, in Topic 2 (see pages 243–5)

Structural approaches also suggest poverty remains because the poor lack the power to change their position. They don't have the financial resources to form powerful groups to change public opinion and get action taken to reduce inequality and end poverty, and they often lack the means to apply pressure on the rich, through strikes for example, as they are often not working or are in low-paid and poorly organized workplaces.

Activity

Make a chart in two columns. In the left column, very briefly summarize the main explanations for the persistence of poverty discussed in this topic. In the right column, suggest and briefly explain two solutions which might be adopted for each explanation.

Exam-style questions

1 Explain what is meant by an 'underclass'. *(2 marks)*

2 Explain what is meant by a 'dependency culture'. *(2 marks)*

3 Explain what is meant by the 'poverty trap'. *(2 marks)*

4 Explain the difference between cultural and material explanations of poverty. *(4 marks)*

5 Suggest **three** reasons why the poverty of parents may lead to poverty among their adult children. *(6 marks)*

6 Examine the reasons for the persistence of poverty in contemporary Britain. *(24 marks)*

7 Examine New Right explanations for the continued existence of poverty in the UK. *(24 marks)*

Topic 4

SPECIFICATION AREAS

The nature and role of public, private, voluntary and informal welfare provision in contemporary society.
Different responses to poverty, with particular reference to the role of social policy since the 1940s

Welfare provision in contemporary society

THE WELFARE STATE

A welfare state is one that is concerned with implementing social policies guaranteeing the 'cradle to grave' well-being of the whole population, and particularly the elimination of poverty, unemployment, ill-health and ignorance. Such policies are generally implemented using resources collected through taxation.

The welfare state in Britain mainly began with the Beveridge Report of 1942. This report, and the subsequent development of the welfare state in Britain, was based on four main principles and assumptions:

- full employment.
- universal welfare – cradle-to-grave provision.
- free healthcare and education.
- that women would be primarily housewives and mothers – as the Beveridge Report said, 'women would make marriage their sole occupation'.

The Beveridge Report recommended the development of state-run welfare services (backed up by voluntary organizations) aimed at the destruction of the 'five giants' of Want (poverty), Ignorance (lack of educational opportunity), Disease (ill-health and

The Beveridge Report of 1942 recommended tackling the 'five giants' of Want (poverty), Ignorance (lack of educational opportunity), Disease (ill-health and lack of healthcare), Squalor (poor housing) and Idleness (unemployment). These principles laid the basis for the state's role in tackling social problems that we see in today's welfare state

lack of healthcare), Squalor (poor housing) and Idleness (unemployment), and the creation of a society in which each individual would have the right to be cared for by the state from 'womb to tomb'. The welfare state as we know it today came into effect on 5 July 1948 – the date of the foundation of the National Health Service.

The welfare state provides a wide range of benefits and services, paid for by taxation. They include:

- A variety of welfare benefits through the social security and tax systems for many groups, such as the unemployed, those injured at work, the sick and disabled, widows, the retired, expectant mothers, lone parents and children. Some benefits, like Jobseeker's Allowance, Housing Benefit, Income Support, Pension Credit and Council Tax Benefit, are means-tested – related to people's income. In 2012 it was proposed that income-related benefits for those out of work should all be rolled up into a new single universal benefit system. Other benefits, like Child Benefit, are universal – available to all regardless of income.
- A comprehensive and largely free National Health Service, including antenatal and postnatal care, hospitals, local GPs, dentists and opticians (although some charges are payable – for example to dentists and opticians).
- A free and compulsory state education for all to the age of 17 (age 18 from 2015), and subsidies after that age.
- Social services provided by local councils, such as social workers, and residential and community care facilities for the mentally and physically impaired, the elderly and children. Local councils are also responsible for housing the homeless, for child protection, and for overseeing the adoption and arranging the fostering of children.

WHO PROVIDES WELFARE? THE MIXED ECONOMY OF PROVISION

Although welfare is generally seen as provided only by the state, private companies, voluntary organizations, charities, families and community groups are all involved in the provision of welfare, This range of provision is known as **welfare pluralism**.

Some suggest that welfare pluralism is better at meeting the population's welfare needs. This is because the diversity of providers of welfare services – what has been called a mixed economy of provision – and competition between them (such as private medicine competing with the NHS) – improves quality, and gives people more choice, enabling them to 'pick 'n' mix' what they most need. However, some argue that not everyone can afford to pay for private services, leading to unequal access to care, with two tiers of services for the rich and the poor.

> **Welfare pluralism** refers to the whole range of welfare provision, including informal provision by the family and community, welfare provided by the government, the voluntary sector and the private sector.

Informal welfare provision

Much welfare provision is provided informally, and free, by family, friends and neighbours. This may include things like caring for the sick, the elderly, providing childcare or emotional support, shopping, cooking meals and doing housework for the housebound elderly, and lending money on an informal basis. Feminist writers have emphasized that this often means care by women, as it is women who take on the main caring responsibilities in the family for the dependent elderly, the disabled and the sick. The Equal Opportunities Commission (now incorporated into the Equality and Human Rights Commission) has suggested around three times more women than men are involved in this informal care. As seen above, the Beveridge Report included the patriarchal assumption that women would be primarily housewives and mothers, concerned with housework, childcare and looking after the family, with men supporting them through paid employment. This meant it was assumed married women didn't need the same level of social security benefits as men, as these would go to their husbands to support their families in times of need. Much welfare provision today still rests on this assumption, despite the fact that many married women now also work outside the home in paid employment.

The voluntary sector

Voluntary organizations are non-official, non-profit-making organizations, often charities, which are 'voluntary' in the sense that they are neither created by, nor controlled by, the government. They are staffed by both salaried employees and voluntary helpers, and are funded by donations from the public and grants from, or sale of services to, central and local government. Voluntary organizations try to fill some of the gaps left by the safety net provided by the state, by providing help and information in areas where state assistance is too little or non-existent.

Voluntary organizations include groups such as the Salvation Army, which provides hostel accommodation and soup kitchens; Shelter, which campaigns for the homeless and helps with finding accommodation; Age UK; the Citizens' Advice Bureau (CAB); the NSPCC (the National Society for the Prevention of Cruelty to Children); and the Child Poverty Action Group, which promotes action for the relief of poverty among children and families with children. The churches also provide a range of welfare support, particularly to the elderly.

Voluntary organizations have the advantage of providing cheaper services than those provided by the state or private sectors, combined with high levels of expertise. They are often able to respond more quickly in meeting people's needs than the more centralized state sector, as they are less bureaucratic – tied up with 'red tape'. They often have a better understanding of people's needs and are better able to respond and provide support in specialized areas, like domestic violence, mental health, dementia care, housing and homelessness, debt, welfare rights or disability, where state provision may be under pressure, inadequate or non-existent. However, voluntary organizations often lack adequate funds to be as effective as they might otherwise be, and they do not exist in all the areas where they are needed. At the time of writing, many were under severe financial pressure as a result of funding cuts from local and national government.

Voluntary organizations also play important roles as **pressure**

Volunteer helpers play an important role in the voluntary sector of welfare provision

groups. Many voluntary organizations lead public campaigns to improve welfare benefits and services for the poor and socially excluded. They play a major role in highlighting the weaknesses of the welfare state, and keeping problems such as poverty, homelessness and the care of the mentally ill in the public eye. They frequently provide expert knowledge and make recommendations to governments for changes to improve social welfare.

The private sector

The private sector consists of both profit-making and not-for-profit private businesses, from which individuals or local and central government purchase welfare services. The private sector has been of growing importance in providing welfare since the 1980s, as the New Right, discussed below, tried to roll back the welfare state, and to encourage people to become more self-supporting by purchasing the services they need from private welfare businesses.

This sector provides welfare services such as private hospitals, schools, care homes for the elderly and the disabled, private pensions and medical insurance. Those with conservative views (see the New Right or market liberal approach, below) often see the private sector as more efficient and effective than state provision, and as providing services at lower costs and offering more choice. This is because it consists of businesses that have to compete for customers and provide a decent service if they are to survive in the face of competition. However, the need for some to make profits may mean cost-cutting takes a higher priority than the quality of services provided. Access to the private sector is only available to those who can afford it, and poor people may therefore not get services at all if the state doesn't provide or pay for them. This can mean that those who are able to afford it can 'queue jump', for example by seeing NHS consultants privately and paying, and then getting put at the top of their list for a free NHS operation.

Activity

1. Do you think the state should be the main provider of welfare for all? What are the advantages and disadvantages of welfare provision by the state compared to the informal, voluntary and private sectors?
2. Suggest reasons why informal welfare provision is mainly carried out by women. What consequences do you think this might have for women's lives and careers?
3. Suggest *two* ways in which private-sector welfare provision might create unequal access to welfare services.

Theoretical approaches to welfare

MARXIST APPROACHES

Marxist approaches tend to see the welfare state mainly as a way of buying off working-class protest, by reducing the risks to social order and political stability caused by unrest and protest against extreme inequality, ill-health and extensive poverty. By keeping the labour force healthy and efficient to the benefit of the capitalist class, the welfare state attempts to make a system based on inequality, exploitation and conflict appear caring and just. The welfare state is then a form of social control – an attempt to keep the workforce efficient and trained, and the capitalist system stable, by giving workers a stake in society.

FEMINIST APPROACHES

Feminist approaches emphasize the way the welfare state supports patriarchy, and the inadequacy of the welfare state in meeting the needs of women. They point to the way the benefit system is frequently based on contributions records built up by full-time workers, who are less likely to be women, and the way the founding principles of the welfare state, discussed earlier, were based on an assumption of women being financially supported by men, with important levels of care of the elderly, children, the sick and disabled being provided free by women.

The Marxist and feminist views of the welfare state provide general critical approaches to the welfare state, but the two main approaches to it are the social democratic approach (the welfare model) and the New Right or market liberal model. The main differences between these two are between those who think welfare should be the responsibility of individuals, provided by the private sector and with people buying services themselves, and those who think the state should provide welfare funded through taxation. Different governments have, at different times, adopted social welfare policies and attempts to tackle poverty linked to some degree to either the social democratic or New Right market liberal approaches. In more recent years – since around the late 1990s – the boundaries between these two approaches have become blurred, and contemporary social policies often combine elements of both approaches, and hover between them.

THE SOCIAL DEMOCRATIC APPROACH (THE WELFARE MODEL)

This approach has its origins in the 1940s, with the foundation of the welfare state based on the principle of universalism, with welfare available to all (universalism) at times of need, with cradle-to-grave support.

Social democratic approaches include the following beliefs:

- *The government should be responsible for social welfare*, and for action to eliminate problems such as unemployment and poverty, providing care for the disabled, children in need, the elderly and other vulnerable and socially excluded groups facing **marginalization**.
- *Social inequality threatens the stability of society*, and wealth and income should be redistributed through progressive taxation (the more you earn, the more tax you pay), with benefits and healthcare available to all to reduce social inequality and tackle poverty. Only the state has the power and resources to do this, and should provide 'womb to tomb' care.
- *Benefits should be available to all* (universal benefits), because selective, means-tested benefits, which are only payable to those whose income falls below a certain level, create a stigma on those claiming them. This stigma means those in greatest need often fail to claim benefits to which they are entitled (see box 'Unclaimed benefits'). Means testing also discourages people from taking low-paid work when it becomes available, catching them in a poverty trap (see table 4.3).
- *The need for more social cohesion* – universal provision, like free education, pensions, full employment and free healthcare, brings economic benefits through an employed, healthy and well-qualified workforce, and helps to promote a more cohesive, less divided, society.

> **Marginalization** refers to the process whereby some groups are pushed by poverty, ill-health, lack of education, disability, racism and so on to the margins or edges of society and are unable to take part in the life enjoyed by the majority of citizens.

UNCLAIMED BENEFITS

Many poor people do not claim the welfare benefits to which they are entitled, particularly those which are means-tested. According to the Department for Work and Pensions's own estimates released in 2012, between about 10 per cent and 40 per cent of those entitled to some income-related benefit were not claiming it, representing overall between £7.5 billion and £12.3 billion left unclaimed. This is between 18 per cent and 33 per cent of the money that was paid out. The failure to claim benefits is often because of:

- the complexity of the benefits and tax system.
- inadequate publicity.
- the obscure language of leaflets and complex means-testing forms, which mean people often do not know what their rights are or the procedures for claiming benefits.
- people's lack of confidence about whether or not they are entitled to receive anything, or because they regard the effort involved in claiming as too great for the amounts involved.

The bureaucratic hurdles are often so great that many people are deterred from claiming what they are entitled to. This is particularly important as the poor are among the least-educated sections of the population. The mass media periodically run campaigns about welfare 'fraudsters' and 'scroungers' – with headlines like 'Stuff the spongers' – which help to attach a stigma to claiming benefits which may deter some people from doing so. The establishment of the Department for Work and Pensions 'Targeting Benefit Thieves' website and campaigns (www.dwp.gov.uk/campaigns/benefit-thieves) may have further contributed to attaching such a stigma. A number of photos from these campaigns are shown below.

The Department for Work and Pensions's 'Targeting Benefit Thieves' campaign declares its aims to be 'to positively reinforce honest behaviour, create a climate of intolerance to fraud and to undermine its social acceptability'. By far the majority of benefits claimants are honest, but fraud (dishonest claims) is a serious problem, which cost the government an estimated £1.1 billion in 2011–12.

Do you think newspaper reports about welfare cheats and campaigns like 'Targeting Benefit Thieves' (examples of which are pictured here) might deter some people from claiming benefits to which they are entitled?

Activity

Refer to the box 'Unclaimed benefits'. Suggest answers to the questions below, and then discuss them.

1 Do you agree or disagree with the view that the media give the impression that people receiving benefits are 'scroungers'?
2 Do you think most people receiving welfare benefits are deserving?
3 Do welfare benefits discourage people from taking more responsibility for their own lives?
4 Should people be expected to take a job even if they will be worse off than if they received benefits?
5 Go to the 'Targeting Benefit Thieves' website, www.dwp.gov.uk/campaigns/benefit-thieves. How much does the government estimate benefit fraud costs each year? Study the advertising campaigns shown on the previous page, and discuss whether these might attach a stigma to all people claiming benefit. Do you think such advertising campaigns might stop people claiming benefits, even when they are entitled to them?

Table 4.3 Universal benefits and means testing

The case for means testing: the New Right or market liberal model	The case for universal benefits: the social democratic or welfare model
Means testing involves people having to pass a test of their income and savings (their 'means') before receiving any benefits: only if these are low enough will they receive any benefits.	Universal benefits are those available to everyone regardless of income, such as the basic state pension, Child Benefit and free healthcare and education.
Benefits are targeted only at those who really need them. People who are able to work should support themselves. Money is saved on universal benefits which most people don't need and shouldn't have. More money is available to invest in the economy, create jobs and cut taxes.	Means-tested benefits, which are received only by the very poor, may lead to some people being worse off if they take a low-paid job. They may lose means-tested benefits like housing or council tax benefits, and the extra they earn by working is not enough to compensate for the lost benefits. This 'poverty trap' discourages people from taking work. Universal benefits avoid this. Those who are well-off should still receive universal benefits, paid for through paying more taxes on their higher incomes gained through employment.
Means testing stops voluntary unemployment being an option for some people, and fights the welfare dependency culture.	Because of the poverty trap, means testing might drive people into a dependency culture and a reluctance to get a job.
Families, communities and voluntary organizations are strengthened as alternative sources of support.	Families and communities caught in the poverty trap are likely to be weakened by poverty and stress. Some will be encouraged to become 'benefit cheats' through concealing income and savings to get around means testing. Universal benefits keep everyone's standards up to an acceptable minimum level.
Selective means-tested benefits will enable more benefits for the most disadvantaged, by no longer wasting money on those who can afford to support themselves.	Often the most deprived do not take up or make full use of even universal benefits, as they're unsure of how to do so. Means-tested benefits attach a stigma to those who claim them, and make it even more unlikely they will claim benefits to which they are entitled.

THE NEW RIGHT OR MARKET LIBERAL MODEL

The New Right approach mainly developed in Britain first in the years of the Conservative governments between 1979 and 1997, when the aim was to 'roll back' the welfare state and make people more self-reliant. This approach is also known as a market liberal approach because it believes that individuals should have the freedom to choose welfare provision from all those competing in the welfare market, and should take responsibility themselves for obtaining it, mainly through the private sector. According to this approach:

- *The generosity of the 'nanny' welfare state is seen as undermining personal responsibility and self-help*, and people's willingness to work to support themselves. Writers like Murray (1989, 1990) and Marsland (1989) argue that the welfare state has created a dependency culture and a work-shy underclass – a social group right at the bottom of the social hierarchy, whose members are in some ways different from, and cut off or excluded from, the rest of society – which wants to avoid work by living off welfare benefits. The generosity of the welfare state has undermined the importance of support from families, and encourages lone parenthood, as women have children they could not otherwise have supported, knowing they can get help from state benefits. This approach is essentially victim-blaming, as it sees many of those in poverty as having only themselves to blame.
- *Welfare services are of better quality when they are not provided by the state*, but by private organizations, competing with each other, or provided through charities, voluntary organizations and families. Even state organizations are run better if they are in competition with the private sector, or with other state organizations – such as competition between NHS hospitals, or between NHS and private hospitals.
- *Taxation should be kept to the minimum*, and should not be wasted on providing welfare benefits or healthcare to those who are able to support themselves.
- *State benefits should be restricted only to the very poor*, and those unable to work through sickness or disability, and should be means tested (see table 4.3). The rest of the population should provide their own welfare services by buying them from the private sector, such as private medicine and private pension plans.

Activity

Refer to the following statements, and say in each case which model of welfare (Marxist, feminist, social democratic (welfare model) or New Right (market liberal)) it most closely matches. Give reasons for your answers.

1 'Those who are working resent seeing neighbours, apparently as fit as themselves, living on incapacity benefit. It has become known as "bad back" benefit.'
2 'If it wasn't for the safety net of the welfare state, there would be widespread discontent and protest by working-class people against the inequalities and exploitation they face.'
3 'The welfare state simply doesn't recognize the amount of unpaid work that women do in the home.'
4 'If you withdraw benefits, people will be forced to bear the consequences of their behaviour. Gradually a traditional morality will re-emerge, whereby the two-parent family becomes the norm again, and bastards and single parents are stigmatized.'
5 'A lot of unemployment is produced by the very policies we are talking about. It is avoidable. You have little boys growing up who literally do not know how to work. They have not been socialized to get up at 7 o'clock and go into work even if they don't feel like it.'

6 'Get the poor off our overtaxed backs.'

7 'Investment, investment, investment in health, education, pensions and other public services is what this country needs. The government has done a lot, but a lot more needs to be done and this government will do it.'

8 'The government should stop squandering money on a spending binge, and invest in the economy to raise the living standards of all.'

9 'The state's welfare services should be financed largely from the income of those who can most afford to pay. The state should ensure that resources are redistributed from the rich and top salary earners to those in our society who suffer ill-health, unemployment, poverty and deprivation.'

The solution to this activity can be found on the teachers' pages of www.politybooks.com/browne

Social policies on welfare and poverty since the 1940s

The social democratic or welfare model was that which underpinned the welfare state in Britain until 1979. This included policies to provide, as a right, welfare services, universal benefits, and social protection during periods of insecurity, at the best level possible. These included a minimum income, provision of free healthcare and education, housing (council housing) and a range of personal social services such as child protection and support. This pattern began to change in the late 1970s, when the market liberal model became more dominant.

THE NEW RIGHT AND THE CONSERVATIVE GOVERNMENTS OF 1979–1997: ROLLING BACK THE WELFARE STATE

The Conservative governments of 1979–97 were strongly influenced by the ideas of the New Right. This meant the government wanted to roll back the welfare state by cutting back welfare spending, privatizing some services (the state dentistry sector severely declined in these years, and private dentistry grew, and many council care homes were sold off to private and voluntary care organizations) and opening up competition in the provision of welfare services. These measures aimed to raise quality through competition, reduce inefficiency, eliminate the dependency culture, and develop the principles of self-help. It preferred to target benefits only on the 'deserving poor' – the sick, disabled and the elderly and others unable to help themselves. The rest of the population was encouraged to rely more on their own resources rather than expecting to be supported by the state.

These years were marked by serious cuts in welfare spending and the value of welfare benefits. Income taxes were reduced, more benefits were means tested, and grants to the poor were replaced with loans. Charges were either introduced or increased for eye tests and dentists, and prescription charges were increased. Student grants were replaced with loans, and the Child Support Agency was set up, so that absent fathers, rather than the state, could carry the financial costs of looking after their children. State education was starved of cash.

By 1997, Britain had the highest levels of poverty in the European Union, and the largest gap between the highest- and lowest-paid since records began in 1886. Britain was one of the most unequal countries in the Western world.

THE NEW LABOUR GOVERNMENT OF 1997–2010: A HAND UP NOT A HAND OUT

A Labour government – 'New Labour' – came to power in 1997, and began a process back towards a more social democratic model of welfare provision, while still retaining some elements of the previous New Right approach of using a range of private welfare providers and encouraging self-help. A stronger emphasis was placed on tackling the problems of those pushed to the margins of society and unable to participate fully in social life because of poverty, low pay, unemployment, lack of education, old age or ill-health. Rather than the victim-blaming approach of the New Right, the aim was to give people a hand up through the benefit system into becoming self-supporting citizens through well-paid and secure employment, rather than keeping them dependent on welfare state handouts. This became known as 'a hand up not a handout'. A large number of policies were implemented to tackle poverty and social exclusion, including:

- an increase in benefit and pension levels, a minimum income guarantee for pensioners, and big increases in spending on health and education.
- the introduction of Britain's first National Minimum Wage, and the introduction of a system of tax credits (allowances) to help the lowest-paid and the most disadvantaged, and overcome the poverty trap by making work pay more than could be obtained in benefits. This succeeded, and more than 1 million people were helped to move from a life on long-term benefit and back into work.
- the establishment of 'New Deals' to help the young, lone parents, the long-term unemployed and the disabled to move from welfare into work.
- an increase in childcare and nursery education, with all 3- and 4-year-olds guaranteed five half-days of nursery education a week, and the establishment of Sure Start Children's Centres to help especially the most disadvantaged children to get off to a better start in life.
- the introduction of the Family Intervention Project. This aimed to tackle the cycle of deprivation and the passing of poverty from one generation to the next by intervening in families where there were multiple problems of unemployment, disadvantage, illness and anti-social behaviour. This was the first attempt by any government to break the cycle of deprivation by getting a number of state agencies, like Jobcentres, social services and the police, to work together to tackle at the family level a range of interrelated problems both causing poverty and consequences of poverty.
- a Neighbourhood Renewal Strategy, to regenerate the most deprived communities, and to help improve the health and education of the most disadvantaged.
- a reduction in child poverty, with the aim of eliminating it within a generation.

CONDEM (CONSERVATIVE – LIBERAL DEMOCRAT) COALITION GOVERNMENT POLICIES: 2010 ONWARDS

The Conservative – Liberal Democrat (ConDem) coalition government, which came to power in May 2010, combined elements of both the New Right and the more social democratic and supportive New Labour approaches considered above, though there was generally more of a New Right emphasis.

- receive more spending per head on health.
- make better use of the health service, as they are more self-confident, effective and assertive in dealing with doctors, and therefore get longer consultations, ask more questions, receive more explanations from their doctors and are more likely to be referred for further treatment.
- receive more spending per person in education, as their children are more likely to stay in education after school-leaving age, and they have more knowledge and confidence in dealing with educational professionals to get the best deals in education for their children.
- benefit more from spending on roads and public transport (particularly rail travel), as they are more likely to be commuters and have cars.
- are more likely to be the biggest users of public services like public libraries, parks and local swimming pools.
- benefit more from tax relief on private pensions and business expenses.

Westergaard and Resler argue that the welfare system is largely concerned with transferring or redistributing resources within rather than between social classes, for example from one section of the working class to another, such as from those in work to those who are unemployed, and from the healthy to the sick. They see support for the old, the unemployed, the sick and disabled as being largely paid for by other working-class taxpayers, or through their own national insurance payments taken from their wages.

INEQUALITIES BETWEEN ETHNIC GROUPS

In chapter 7 on Health, there is a discussion of inequalities in health between ethnic groups. The weaknesses in healthcare discussed there are only part of the general pattern of disadvantage faced by some minority ethnic groups in the welfare state. Pakistani, Bangladeshi and African-Caribbean minority ethnic groups are marginalized, and encounter racism and discrimination in welfare provision. Literature is often not translated, and staff are often not trained in their cultural backgrounds. They are more likely to be unemployed, and so lose out on income-related benefits. Pakistani and Bangladeshi people are the poorest social groups in Britain.

GENDER INEQUALITY

Feminist views have already been mentioned earlier in the context of the patriarchal assumptions of women as primarily wives, mothers and carers which have traditionally underpinned the welfare state. There are a number of other inequalities where women are concerned.

Women are more likely to work part-time rather than full-time, and to interrupt their working lives for childrearing or caring for dependent elderly relatives. A lack of free childcare often makes it difficult for women to take full-time jobs. This means they often lose out on a range of income-related benefits, like the earnings-related state pension and the Jobseeker's Allowance. Poverty is more a problem for women than men, throughout their lives, but particularly in old age (the feminization of poverty was discussed in Topic 2 – see page 242). Feminists advocate making the welfare state more responsive to the needs of women, for example through the provision of better cancer screening, WellWoman clinics to meet women's health needs, and a recognition of women's unpaid work in the home.

Is the welfare state succeeding?

Huge sums of taxpayers' money are spent on the welfare state, and there are constant disputes about whether or not it is successful in tackling social problems like poverty and ill-health, and therefore whether more, or less, money should be spent on it. A few of these competing arguments are outlined in table 4.4 below.

Table 4.4 Is the welfare state succeeding?

Yes	No
State support has eliminated absolute poverty in childhood and old age, and in periods of ill-health, unemployment and disability throughout our lives. The standard of social (council and housing association) housing has massively improved, and slums have disappeared.	Many people still live a deprived lifestyle compared to most people, because of low pay and inadequate welfare benefits and the poverty trap. There remain huge inequalities in wealth, income, education, housing, health and employment. Relative poverty and social exclusion remain serious social problems.
All have access to free medical care, and the health of the nation has improved immeasurably.	The welfare state is failing to cope with the demands placed on it. For example, there are often delays for hospital treatment, and there remain huge inequalities in health and access to healthcare (see chapter 7).
All have free education from the ages of 3 to 18.	The middle class still benefit the most in education, and those from poorer families still suffer huge disadvantages (see chapter 6).
Many vulnerable groups have a range of state agencies and other organizations to assist them, such as social services, GP clinics and Age UK.	There are many vulnerable groups who slip through the safety net, or for whom there is inadequate or no state provision. They have to turn to a poorly funded voluntary sector, or just cope – or not cope – alone.
Everyone is guaranteed 'cradle to grave' security.	Generous welfare benefits create a nation of scrounging social misfits who are prepared just to live off benefits without ever working. The welfare state has undermined personal responsibility and self-help.

The future of the welfare state

The two competing political approaches to the welfare state, and related social policies, identified in the Social Democratic and New Right approaches discussed earlier, have become less of a divide between the political parties in recent years. This is because the views of all the mainstream political parties are changing. The soaring costs of the welfare state suggest the following will be the major concerns of all governments in the future:

- tackling dependency on welfare benefits, and reducing spending on them, by getting people off welfare benefits and moving them into paid employment through 'welfare to work' schemes.
- cutting the soaring levels of state spending on welfare provision, particularly the rising spending owing to the health and pension needs of the growing numbers of older people.
- making more people pay for the services they receive if they can afford it.
- putting greater emphasis on provision by the voluntary and private sectors.

- getting people to help themselves through the family and community, and encouraging people to save to pay for their own welfare services, particularly in later life.
- making welfare-state institutions like hospitals, surgeries, social services and schools more efficient, and introducing competition between them so they give clients better-quality services at lower costs, and offer them more choice. Welfare-state institutions are increasingly being run more like private businesses.

Poverty and value judgements

As seen throughout this chapter, defining and measuring poverty is inevitably a value-laden exercise. The definitions, measurement and explanations of poverty, and the social policies adopted to tackle the problem, rely to some extent on the value judgements of researchers and politicians. For example, if you adopt an absolute definition of poverty, then you will find very little in contemporary Britain. If you use the relative definition of 60 per cent of average income, you will find a lot (around a fifth of the population).

The solutions to poverty often reflect the political/ideological values of the researchers and their different interpretations of a similar range of evidence. The role of the welfare state in relation to poverty ultimately rests on judgements about what kind of society we should have. For example, New Right or conservative solutions to poverty frequently start with the assumption that the problem of poverty is primarily created by the nature of the poor themselves, and therefore the poor need harsh, punitive policies like cuts in benefits, or forms of resocialization and education, as an incentive for them to change their behaviour.

More liberal or left-wing researchers are less likely to blame individuals for their poverty. They are more likely to focus on the structural constraints on the poor arising from the unequal nature of society. Such researchers are likely to see solutions to poverty in providing opportunities for the poor to escape their poverty, through means like the National Minimum Wage, better education, better healthcare, more job opportunities, more childcare support and higher pensions.

These different analyses and policy solutions often rest on a similar base of evidence, but the different values of the researchers lead to different interpretations of that evidence.

Does this mean that poverty research is therefore so value-laden as to be pointless? The answer is no, because the intense sociological, political and media debates about the definition and measurement of poverty, and solutions to it, have overcome the value judgements of individual researchers. Poverty research, regardless of values, has certainly exposed the extent to which many people in our society face social exclusion, and are cut off from what most of us take for granted as a normal life. This alone makes it a worthwhile and productive research area.

Exam-style questions

1 Explain what is meant by a 'victim-blaming' approach to the problem of poverty. *(2 marks)*

2 Explain what is meant by 'welfare pluralism'. *(2 marks)*

3 Explain what is meant by the 'informal sector' of welfare provision. *(2 marks)*

4 Explain the difference between universal and means-tested benefits. *(4 marks)*

5   Suggest **two** contemporary government social policies designed to tackle the problem of poverty.   *(4 marks)*

6   Suggest **two** reasons why voluntary organizations may be better placed than the government to help those in poverty.   *(4 marks)*

7   Suggest **three** reasons why people may not claim welfare benefits to which they are entitled.   *(6 marks)*

8   Examine the ways in which government policies since the 1940s have attempted to tackle the problem of poverty.   *(24 marks)*

9   Examine different approaches to the role of the welfare state in society.   *(24 marks)*

10 Examine the view that social welfare is likely to be most effective when services are delivered by a range of providers rather than by the state alone.   *(24 marks)*

CHAPTER SUMMARY AND REVISION CHECKLIST

After studying this chapter, you should be able to:

- outline the different forms of wealth and income.

- identify and discuss the absolute, relative, subjective and consensual definitions and measurements of poverty, and the strengths and weaknesses of them.

- explain what is meant by social exclusion.

- identify a range of aspects of poverty apart from lack of income.

- describe the main inequalities in the distribution of wealth and income.

- identify measures to redistribute wealth and income, and why they have not been very successful.

- identify the major groups in poverty, and suggest reasons why these groups are in poverty.

- describe and explain the links between poverty and ethnicity, age, disability and gender.

- discuss functionalist, Weberian and Marxist explanations for the unequal distribution of wealth, income and poverty.

- identify and critically discuss a range of cultural and material explanations for the continuation of poverty, including the culture of poverty, the dependency culture, material constraints, the cycle of deprivation, the poverty trap, the generosity or inadequacy of the welfare state, and structural explanations.

- discuss different views of the underclass.

- identify and discuss the features of the welfare state.

- explain what is meant by the mixed economy of welfare provision, and outline welfare provided by the state, informally in the family and community, and by the voluntary and private sectors, and consider their relative strengths and weaknesses.

- identify and discuss a range of theoretical approaches to welfare provision, including the Marxist, feminist, social democratic (welfare model) and New Right (market liberal model) approaches to social welfare.

- identify the arguments for and against the means testing of welfare benefits.

- outline a range of government social policies on welfare and poverty since the 1940s, linked to different sociological theories of welfare provision.

- examine the role of the welfare state in tackling social inequality and poverty, and assess how successful it has been.

- discuss areas of inequality in the welfare state, including the inverse care law and inequalities based on ethnicity and gender.

- identify the links between poverty and the value judgements of researchers and social policymakers.

KEY TERMS

(these are already defined in the text, and may also be found in the glossary at the end of the book)

absolute poverty

consumption property

culture of poverty

cycle of deprivation

dependency culture

deprivation index

earned income

income

inverse care law

marginalization

market situation

marketable wealth

non-marketable wealth

poverty line

poverty trap

pressure groups

productive property

relative deprivation

relative poverty

social exclusion

subjective poverty

underclass

unearned income

wealth

welfare pluralism

There are a variety of free tests and other activities that can be used to assess your learning at

www.politybooks.com/browne

EXAM QUESTION

SECTION C: WEALTH, POVERTY AND WELFARE

Time allowed: 1 hour   **Total for this section: 60 marks**

Read **Items 3A** and **3B** below and answer questions 1 1 to 1 5 that follow.

Item 3A

The welfare state was set up to help those in the greatest need. Tudor-Hart suggested this was not happening, with the middle class – the least in need – benefiting most from welfare services like health care and education, and any universal or means-tested welfare benefits to which they might be entitled. This finding – those in greatest need of help from the welfare state get the fewest resources allocated to them, while those whose need is least get the most resources spent 5 on them – became known as the 'inverse care law'.

Item 3B

In contemporary Britain, poverty remains widespread. Around one-fifth of the population, and 27 per cent of children, were living in officially defined relative poverty in 2010–11. Some explanations of poverty take a 'victim blaming' approach. This suggests the poor have inadequacies in their own personalities and culture, and are themselves to blame for their poverty. This 'victim blaming' approach has been challenged by others who take a structural or 'system-blaming' 5 approach. They suggest that social inequalities are built into the structure of society, and the poor are kept in poverty by a cycle of deprivation and circumstances beyond their control. They therefore find it hard to escape from poverty.

---

1 1   Explain the difference between a universal and a means-tested benefit (**Item 3A**, lines 3–4).

(*4 marks*)

1 2   Suggest **two** reasons why the middle class 'benefits most from welfare services like health care and education' (**Item 3A**, lines 2–3).   (*4 marks*)

1 3   Explain the difference between voluntary sector and informal welfare provision.   (*4 marks*)

1 4   Examine the reasons given to explain the large inequalities in wealth and income in contemporary Britain.   (*24 marks*)

1 5   Using material from **Item 3B** and elsewhere, assess the view that 'the poor are kept in poverty by a cycle of deprivation and circumstances beyond their control' (**Item 3B**, lines 7–8).

(*24 marks*)

UNIT 2

Sociological Methods

Education

Health

Sociological
Methods

Contents

Sociological Methods

Introductory note

This chapter is a very important one. In Unit 2 of the AQA AS Sociology course – the one you are doing now – you are encouraged to use examples drawn from your own experience of small-scale social research. You are also required to answer a free-standing question on research methods, *and* to show how sociological research methods can be applied to the study of either education or health. This chapter should provide you with all the information you need to deal with these research methods questions, with some exercises which might provide examples of small-scale research. At the end of each of the Education and Health chapters, there is a further section on Methods in Context, which encourages you to think about how the research methods in this chapter might be applied to the topics of health and education. It would be wise to re-read this chapter after you have studied either education or health. It is also worth noting that, if you plan to do the second year of the A-level course, then research methods are required there as well. The message should be clear – make sure you know, understand and can apply and interpret the ideas and methods in this chapter.

Much of this book concentrates on what sociologists have already found out about society. But how do sociologists go about finding these things out in the first place? Sociological methods are the variety of tools or techniques sociologists use to collect evidence about an area which remains relatively unexplored, to describe some aspects of social life, or to discover the causes of some social event, such as the causes of educational underachievement or ill-health. This chapter will examine the various research methods, summarized in figure 5.1, sampling techniques that sociologists use to collect such evidence, and the practical, ethical and theoretical considerations that underpin their choice of research topic and the particular research methods they choose.

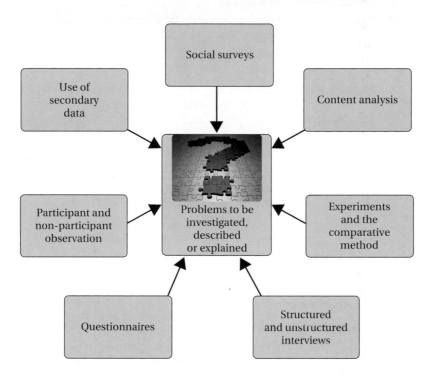

Figure 5.1 The range of research methods

Topic 1

SPECIFICATION AREA

The relationship between positivism, interpretivism and sociological methods; the nature of 'social facts'

Positivism is an approach in sociology that believes society can be studied using similar scientific techniques to those used in the natural sciences, such as physics, chemistry and biology.

Interpretivism is an approach emphasizing that people have consciousness involving personal beliefs, values and interpretations, and these influence the way they act. They do not simply respond to forces outside them.

Social facts are phenomena which exist outside individuals and independently of their minds, but which act upon them in ways which constrain or mould their behaviour. Such phenomena include social institutions like the law, the family, the education system and the workplace.

Quantitative data are anything that can be expressed in statistical or number form or can be measured in some way, such as age, qualifications, income or periods of ill-health. Such data are usually presented in the form of statistical tables, graphs, pie charts and bar charts.

Positivism, interpretivism and sociological methods

The main research methods in sociology broadly flow from two different theoretical or methodological approaches to the study of society. These two approaches are known as **positivism** and **interpretivism**. Positivists and interpretivists often choose different topics to explore, and use different research methods to investigate them, because they have different assumptions about the nature of society, which influences the type of data they are interested in collecting.

POSITIVISM AND RESEARCH METHODS

Positivists believe that, just as there are causes of things in the natural world, so there are external social forces, making up a society's social structure, that cause or mould people's ideas and actions. Durkheim, a positivist, called these external forces **social facts**.

Positivists believe social institutions create expectations of how individuals should behave and limit their choices and options, with social control making individuals behave in socially approved ways.

Durkheim said the aim of sociology should be the study of social facts, which should be considered as things, like objects in the natural world, and could in most cases be observed and measured quantitatively – in number/statistical form. The feelings, emotions and motives of individuals cannot be observed or measured, and should therefore not be studied. These are in any case the result of social facts existing outside the individual, such as the influences of socialization, the law, the mass media, family, the experiences of work and so on.

Examples of positivist approaches might be studies of whether people in some social classes achieve poorer exam results, suffer more illness or are more likely to commit crime than those in other classes, by looking at social facts like statistics on education, health and crime. Durkheim (2002 [1897]) used a positivist approach in his classic study of suicide in 1897, using suicide statistics to try to establish the social causes of suicide. Similarly, positivist research on relationships in the family might collect statistical data on who does what around the home, the length of time spent by partners on housework and childcare, and so on.

Positivists argue that, without quantification, sociology will remain at the level of insights and impressions lacking evidence, and it will be impossible to replicate (or repeat) studies to check findings, establish the causes of social events or make generalizations.

Just as the data of the natural sciences are drawn from direct observation and can be measured and quantified, so positivists use research methods which involve the collection of **quantitative** (statistical) **data** to test their ideas. Such quantitative methods are more likely to involve large-scale research – or a **macro approach** – on large numbers of people. These methods include:

- the experiment
- the comparative method
- social surveys
- structured questionnaires
- formal/structured interviews
- non-participant observation

INTERPRETIVISM AND RESEARCH METHODS

Interpretivists believe that, because people's behaviour is influenced by the interpretations and meanings they give to social situations, the researcher's task is to gain an understanding of these interpretations and meanings, and how people see and understand the world around them. Sociology should therefore use research methods which provide an understanding from the point of view of individuals and groups. This process is called **verstehen** (pronounced 'fair-shtay-en').

Instead of collecting statistical information, interpretivists suggest there is a need to discuss and get personally involved with people in order to get at how they see the world and understand it. Examples might be studies of whether people in some social classes tolerate or dismiss ill-health more than those in other classes, or are more likely to fail in education or be labelled as criminal because of the way teachers or the police see them. Atkinson's (1978) study of suicide involves an interpretivist approach which contrasts with Durkheim's study in arguing that suicide statistics are simply social constructions reflecting the behaviour of coroners, doctors, relatives, etc., and their definitions of suicide. They tell us more about the decision-making processes of the living than the intentions of the dead and the real number of suicides (see the activity on page 296). Similarly, interpretivist research on relationships in the family might carry out in-depth interviews with family members, to find out how they feel about doing jobs around the home, whether they see housework and childcare as shared out equally or not, and whether they'd want them to be.

The methods interpretivists use are therefore those which involve the collection of **qualitative data**. This consists of words, documents and images giving in-depth description and insight into the attitudes, values and feelings of individuals and groups, and the meanings and interpretations they give to events.

Such qualitative methods include:

- participant and (sometimes) non-participant observation.
- informal (unstructured/in-depth/open-ended) interviews.
- open-ended questionnaires.
- personal accounts, using personal documents like diaries and letters.

A **macro approach** is one which focuses on large numbers of people and the large-scale structure of society as a whole, rather than on individuals.

Positivist researchers are more likely to collect quantitative (statistical) data through questionnaires and interviews

Verstehen is the idea of understanding human behaviour by putting yourself in the position of those being studied, and trying to see things from their point of view.

Qualitative data are concerned with the feelings and meanings people associate with, and the interpretations they give to, some event, and try to get at the way they really see things. Such data are normally in the form of the sociologist's description and interpretation of people's feelings and lifestyles, often using direct quotations from the people studied.

> A **micro approach** is one which focuses on small groups or individuals, rather than on large numbers of people and the structure of society as a whole.

These are more likely to involve a **micro approach** to research, with in-depth small-scale research on small numbers of people.

Interpretivists question the value of the research methods used by positivists, such as structured questionnaires and interviews. This is because they impose a framework on research – the sociologist's own view of what is important, rather than what may be important to the individuals being researched.

Figure 5.2 shows the broad links which exist between the two different theoretical/methodological approaches of positivism and interpretivism, other wider theories of society identified with them, and the research methods most likely to be used.

Figure 5.2 The link between sociological theories and research methods: a summary

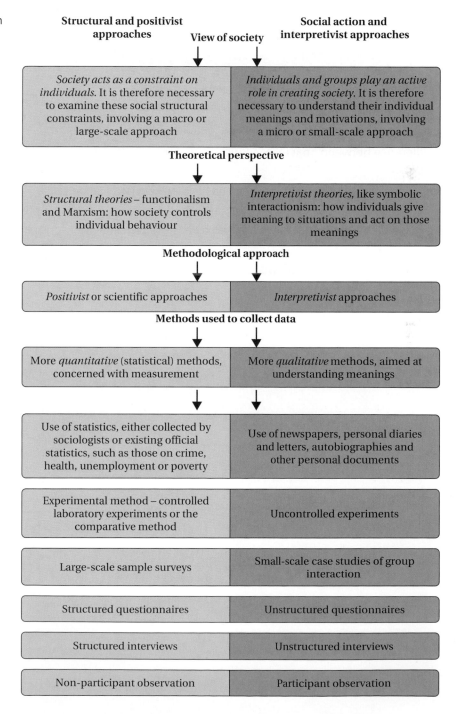

Structural and positivist approaches	Social action and interpretivist approaches
View of society	
Society acts as a constraint on individuals. It is therefore necessary to examine these social structural constraints, involving a macro or large-scale approach	*Individuals and groups play an active role in creating society.* It is therefore necessary to understand their individual meanings and motivations, involving a micro or small-scale approach
Theoretical perspective	
Structural theories – functionalism and Marxism: how society controls individual behaviour	*Interpretivist theories,* like symbolic interactionism: how individuals give meaning to situations and act on those meanings
Methodological approach	
Positivist or scientific approaches	*Interpretivist* approaches
Methods used to collect data	
More *quantitative* (statistical) methods, concerned with measurement	More *qualitative* methods, aimed at understanding meanings
Use of statistics, either collected by sociologists or existing official statistics, such as those on crime, health, unemployment or poverty	Use of newspapers, personal diaries and letters, autobiographies and other personal documents
Experimental method – controlled laboratory experiments or the comparative method	Uncontrolled experiments
Large-scale sample surveys	Small-scale case studies of group interaction
Structured questionnaires	Unstructured questionnaires
Structured interviews	Unstructured interviews
Non-participant observation	Participant observation

Activity

Imagine you wanted to do a study of how tasks are divided up between men and women in the home. You are interested in:

- housework and other household jobs.
- childcare (not just who does it, but who takes responsibility for making sure children have new clothes, shoes, the right gear for school, get food they like and so on).
- decision-making.
- dealing with family conflicts and emotions.

Suggest ways that positivists and interpretivists might approach these issues differently, and what types of methods they might use to obtain their information.

Exam-style questions

1   Explain what is meant by the term 'quantitative' data.   *(2 marks)*

2   Explain what is meant by the term 'social fact'.   *(2 marks)*

3   Explain the difference between 'quantitative' and 'qualitative' data.   *(4 marks)*

4   Explain the difference between 'macro' and 'micro' approaches to the study of society.   *(4 marks)*

5   Suggest **two** research methods that might be used by interpretivist sociologists.   *(4 marks)*

6   Suggest **two** research methods that might be used by positivist sociologists.   *(4 marks)*

7   Examine the differences between positivist and interpretivist approaches to sociological research.   *(20 marks)*

Topic 2

SPECIFICATION AREA

The theoretical, practical and ethical considerations influencing choice of topic, choice of method(s) and the conduct of research

Influences on the choice of research topic and method

A useful way to remember the various influences on the choice of research topic and method which are discussed below is by the word **PET**.

P – **P**ractical issues, like funding, ease of access to the place or group being studied, time available, and whether the researcher has the personal skills and characteristics to carry out the research.

E – **E**thical issues, like whether the research will have any harmful consequences, whether participants have given their consent, and whether research is reported accurately and honestly.

T – **T**heoretical issues, such as whether a Marxist, a functionalist, or a feminist approach is preferred, or a positivist or an interpretivist approach.

PRACTICAL AND ETHICAL ISSUES

Ethics concerns principles or ideas about what is morally right or wrong.

The theoretical and methodological issues considered later have important influences on the research topic sociologists choose to investigate, and the methods they use to investigate it. However, there are a range of non-theoretical and more practical factors, and considerations of the **ethics** of their research, that mean they do not have a completely free hand in what to investigate:

Informed consent is where those taking part in a sociological study have agreed to do so, and have given this consent based on a full appreciation and understanding of the nature, aims and purposes of the study, any implications or risks taking part might have, and the uses of any findings of the research.

- *How easy it is to access those being studied.* In *open settings*, which are public areas open to all, like streets, shopping malls or public buildings, access for research purposes may be easier than in *closed settings*, where access is restricted, such as hospital wards, doctors' surgeries, schools and classrooms, or meetings of educational or medical professionals. For example, access to hospitals and schools for research purposes would require permission from hospital management and headteachers and governors in schools, and researching the physically or mentally ill or school students would require their **informed consent**.

- *The time and funding that are available* to complete the research will influence the scale of the research and the types of method used. For example, large-scale research is expensive, and beyond the means of most sociologists. Research for military or defence purposes will attract funding more easily than research into help for disabled people. Government-backed research is likely to open more doors to researchers and produce more sponsorship than private individuals or small research departments are able to achieve by themselves. Government-backed research often favours quantitative data gathered through large-scale surveys, such as the Crime Survey for England and Wales funded by the Home Office.

- *The availability of existing data* on a topic may limit or decide the topic chosen and the research method adopted.
- *The values and beliefs of the researcher* will inevitably influence whether or not she or he thinks issues are important and therefore worthy of study, and what aspects should be investigated and how. Townsend (1979), for example, clearly believed the study of poverty was important, and particularly the investigation of relative poverty, and his values are reflected in his devotion to poverty research – and methods of exploring it – throughout his academic life.
- *Sociologists are professionals with careers and promotion prospects* ahead of them, and they face a constant struggle to get money to fund their research. There is therefore an understandable desire to prove their own ideas right. The desire for promotion may influence what topics are seen as useful subjects for research, and the choice of methods that might be most likely to produce speedy results. The current state of knowledge and what seems a cool topic at the time, or a lucrative research area, can also influence the choice of topic and enhance the careers of sociologists.
- *The pressure to publish findings* – publishing research articles and books is a very important requirement for university academic sociologists – and publishers' deadlines may mean research is not as thorough as it ought to be.
- *The personal safety of researchers* and whether the research topic or method chosen puts the researchers at risk in some way.
- *The personal skills and characteristics of the researcher.* For example, some topics, such as the investigation of the attitudes of women towards abortion or sexual health, might be better carried out by a female researcher, and participant observation would require the researcher to have personal characteristics and skills that would enable them to fit in and develop relationships with those being studied. Interviewing, particularly in unstructured interviews, requires the interviewer to have good inter-personal and conversational skills to keep the interview going and develop rapport with the interviewee (the person being interviewed).
- *The ethical issues involved in the choice of topic and the research methods chosen,* such as whether informed consent can be obtained, and whether confidentiality and the anonymity of those cooperating in research can be guaranteed (ethical issues are discussed further below).

THEORETICAL ISSUES

The theoretical/methodological issues related to positivism and interpretivism, which were discussed in the previous topic, will have important effects on:

- *how* something is investigated – the research *methods* sociologists choose to investigate and collect information about society.
- *what* is studied – the choice of research *topic*.

The sociological perspective held by a researcher will influence not only how she or he investigates a topic, but also the research topic that she or he sees as important and interesting to study.

Functionalists, for example, are likely to focus on those aspects which show how social institutions contribute to the maintenance of society as a whole, and their role in contributing to social stability. In education, this might involve research on topics like the roles of the overt and hidden curriculums (see glossary and chapter 6 on Education) in reinforcing social norms and values and producing responsible citizens;

in health, functionalists might look at the way the health service contributes to keeping the economy running smoothly, by maintaining the health of the workforce, and how doctors prevent people from avoiding their responsibilities by false claims of sickness.

Marxists are more likely to emphasize inequality, conflict and division, and to investigate research topics which highlight these areas, and to emphasize class inequality rather than, for example, ethnicity and gender. This might mean, in education, focusing on research showing how schools reproduce class inequalities from one generation to the next, and produce an obedient and passive labour force; or, in health, emphasizing the way doctors are agents of social control and focus on treating the symptoms of illness rather than the real causes rooted in social inequality.

Feminists are concerned with issues of gender inequality and this will guide their choice of research topic. Feminist research might focus, in education, on how boys and girls are treated differently in schools, and aspects of gender socialization which direct boys and girls into different subject choices and careers. In health, feminist research might focus on whether women face discrimination in the health service, or how child-bearing has become a medical process, designed to suit the needs of male doctors rather than of women themselves, and how this has been accompanied by a decline in the female profession of midwifery.

Figure 5.3 illustrates some of these theoretical, practical and ethical influences on the choice of research topic and the methods used.

Figure 5.3 Influence on choices of research topic and method

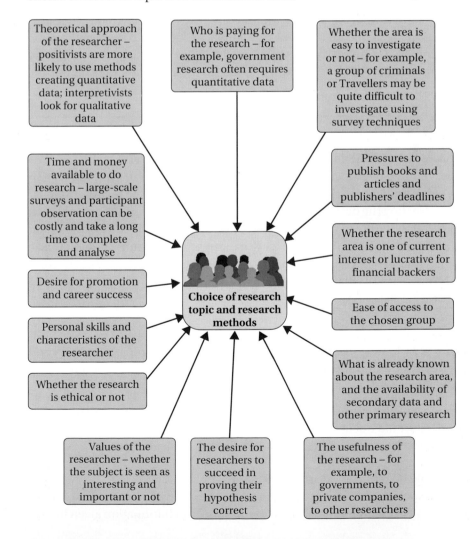

Theoretical approach of the researcher – positivists are more likely to use methods creating quantitative data; interpretivists look for qualitative data

Who is paying for the research – for example, government research often requires quantitative data

Whether the area is easy to investigate or not – for example, a group of criminals or Travellers may be quite difficult to investigate using survey techniques

Time and money available to do research – large-scale surveys and participant observation can be costly and take a long time to complete and analyse

Pressures to publish books and articles and publishers' deadlines

Desire for promotion and career success

Whether the research area is one of current interest or lucrative for financial backers

Choice of research topic and research methods

Personal skills and characteristics of the researcher

Ease of access to the chosen group

Whether the research is ethical or not

What is already known about the research area, and the availability of secondary data and other primary research

Values of the researcher – whether the subject is seen as interesting and important or not

The desire for researchers to succeed in proving their hypothesis correct

The usefulness of the research – for example, to governments, to private companies, to other researchers

> **Activity**
>
> Refer to figure 5.3.
> 1 Suggest two ways that sources of funding for research might influence that research.
> 2 Suggest two reasons why investigating some social groups may be much more difficult than others.
> 3 List three *practical* considerations in researching *either* educational settings like schools or colleges, *or* health settings like hospitals or GP surgeries, that might influence a researcher's choice of *topic* for research, giving examples to illustrate these.
> 4 Suggest two theoretical issues that might influence the researcher's choice of research method.

Key issues in social research

There are three key issues that should always be considered when carrying out or assessing research. These are the issues of **reliability**, validity and the ethics of research.

RELIABILITY

Reliability is concerned with replication: whether another researcher using the same method for the same research on the same or a similar group would achieve the same results. For example, if different researchers use the same questionnaire on similar samples of the population, then the results should be more or less the same if the techniques are reliable.

> **Reliability** refers to whether another researcher, if repeating research using the same method for the same research on the same or a similar group, would achieve the same results.

VALIDITY

Validity is concerned with notions of truth: how far the findings of research actually provide a true, genuine or authentic picture of what is being studied. Data can be reliable without being valid. For example, official crime statistics may be reliable, in so far as researchers repeating the data collection would get more or less the same results over and over again, but they are not valid if they claim to give us the full picture of the extent of crime, as such statistics don't include all the unreported and unrecorded crimes. Another example might be people responding untruthfully to questions, therefore not providing valid evidence of what is being investigated.

> **Validity** is concerned with notions of truth: how far the findings of research actually provide a true, genuine or authentic picture of what is being studied.

ETHICS

The ethics of research are concerned with morality – issues of right and wrong – and standards of behaviour, and when sociologists carry out research they should always consider the following points:

- They should take into account the sensitivities of those helping with their research. For example, it would not be appropriate to ask about attitudes to abortion in a hospital maternity ward where women may be having babies or have suffered miscarriages.
- Findings should be reported accurately and honestly.
- The physical, social and mental well-being of people who help in research should not be harmed by research – for example, by disclosure of information given in

confidence which might get the person into trouble, or cause them embarrassment. There may well be ethical concerns over using personal documents like letters and diaries if these were never meant to be made public, causing damage to a person's reputation, even if they are dead.

- The anonymity, privacy and interests of those who participate in their research should be respected. The participants should not be identified by name, and they (or an institution) should not be able to be easily identified.
- Whenever possible, research should be based on the freely given *informed consent* of those taking part in a sociological study. This means that they not only have agreed to take part, but have given their consent based on a full appreciation and understanding of the nature, aims and purposes of the study, any implications or risks that taking part might have for them, and the uses of any findings of the research. In short, researchers should make clear what they're doing, why they're doing it, and what they will do with their findings.

Activity

A useful discussion of ethical issues in social research can be found in the row surrounding *The Bookseller of Kabul*, a bestselling study of Afghan family life published in 2002 by Norwegian journalist Åsne Seierstad. Did she ignore ethical issues and exploit her subjects' privacy and trust in her portrayal of Afghan family life? Take a look at www.guardian.co.uk/theguardian/2010/jul/31/bookseller-of-kabul-interview-asne-seierstad or do a Google search on *The Bookseller of Kabul*, and decide for yourselves whether ethical guidelines were broken, and, if so, which ones.

Operationalizing concepts in social research

Cultural capital refers to the forms of knowledge, language, attitudes and values, and lifestyle which give those who possess them an advantage in a middle class-controlled education system.

A concept is an abstract idea or theory, like social class, **cultural capital**, educational achievement, health or disease. In order to explore concepts in any social research, but particularly for asking questions in social surveys (see later), it is necessary to convert a concept into something measurable. This is called operationalizing a concept. For example, if a sociologist wanted to investigate, through a survey, the links between social class and cultural capital (see chapter 6 on Education), or social class and health (see chapter 7 on Health), it would first be necessary to operationalize the concept of social class, and then the concepts of either cultural capital or health, and then devise questions to measure these.

An abstract concept like social class is often operationalized (converted into something measurable) by using people's occupation and income. The concept of cultural capital might be measured by the number of books people have in their homes, what newspapers they read, what their attitudes to education are, and the occupations and educational qualifications of parents. The concept of health might be operationalized by using measures like time off work or school because of illness, the number of visits to a GP surgery or hospital for treatment, the number of prescription medicines taken, people's weight, diets, levels of fitness or the amount of exercise they get. In these ways abstract concepts are broken down into various components and transformed into things that are fairly easy to measure and to devise questions about.

Exam-style questions

1 Explain what is meant by the term 'reliability' in sociological research. *(2 marks)*

2 Explain what is meant by the term 'validity' in sociological research. *(2 marks)*

3 Suggest **two** practical factors that may influence a sociologist's choice of research topic. *(4 marks)*

4 Suggest **two** ethical issues researchers should consider before carrying out a sociological study. *(4 marks)*

5 Examine the view that the main influences on a researcher's choice of research method are practical considerations. *(20 marks)*

6 Examine the extent to which theoretical issues are the most important influence when choosing a research topic and research methods to investigate it. *(20 marks)*

Topic 3

SPECIFICATION AREA

The distinction between primary and secondary data and between quantitative and qualitative data

Primary data
are those which are collected by sociologists themselves – they only exist because the sociologist has collected them.

Secondary data
are those which the sociologist carrying out the research has not gathered himself or herself, but which already exist.

Public documents are those which are produced for public knowledge
Personal documents are (usually) private documents for a person's own use, which record part of a person's life.

Primary and secondary data

Primary data are those which are collected by sociologists themselves, usually obtained by carrying out a social survey, using questionnaires and interviews, or by participant or non-participant observation.

Secondary data are those which already exist and are collected from secondary sources. Figure 5.4 shows a range of these sources that might be used by sociologists in carrying out research.

Both types of data can take either quantitative (statistical) or qualitative (non-statistical) forms. These may be either **public documents** or **personal documents.**

- *Personal documents* are (usually) private documents for a person's own use, which record part of a person's life. They include things like private diaries, personal letters, personal photographs or videos, pupils' school reports or personal medical files, and private bank statements.
- *Public documents* are those which are produced for public knowledge, and include a vast range of material like all manner of reports and statistics from government, councils, charities, voluntary organizations, businesses and the mass media. These include, for example, Ofsted reports on colleges, schools and nurseries; annual reports from the Department of Health; the Chief Medical Officer's Reports (which

Figure 5.4 Secondary sources of data

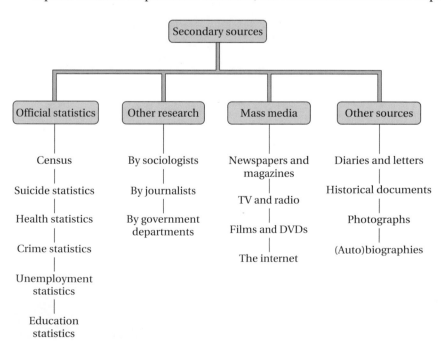

provide a record of the state of the nation's health); reports of the Care Quality Commission, which oversees care provided by the NHS, local authorities, private companies and voluntary organizations; and media news reports and documentaries, such as those about education or health matters.

Qualitative secondary sources

Qualitative secondary sources include newspaper, radio and TV reports, websites, novels, literature, art, autobiographies, letters, diaries, parish registers, historical documents, previous sociological studies, school records, social work files, police records, minutes of meetings, and some official government reports.

THE ADVANTAGES AND USES OF QUALITATIVE SECONDARY SOURCES

- Qualitative secondary sources may provide valuable, or the only, sources of information in an area. For example, historical documents are often the only way of investigating the past, and without them it would be very difficult to find out about history. Much historical work on the family would have been impossible without reference to records going back several centuries.
- They are useful for interpretivists who wish to gain insights into the worldview or ideologies of those who produced them. Some historical documents and personal documents like autobiographies and diaries can be particularly useful for these purposes.
- They may be very useful for assessing people's concerns or worries. For example, the letters pages and advice columns of newspapers and magazines may give valuable insights into the thinking of their readers (or the thinking of the editor on what

Secondary research

she or he chooses to print). Letters of complaint from patients to hospitals or parents to schools may provide valuable insights into people's views about the standards and quality they expect.

THE DISADVANTAGES AND LIMITATIONS OF QUALITATIVE SECONDARY SOURCES

Scott, in *A Matter of Record* (1990), suggests four criteria for judging secondary data in general, but his points are very useful in assessing secondary qualitative data.

Authenticity

Is the evidence genuine or a forgery? For example, diaries apparently by Adolf Hitler were purchased for millions of pounds and published in 1983 after being certified authentic by top historians. They were later found to be a complete forgery.

Credibility

Is the evidence believable, sincere and honest? Does it contain biases, distortions and exaggerations by the writers to deceive or mislead readers? Is the evidence reliable? Who was a document written for? Does it simply reflect the values and beliefs of those who produced it? The mass media, for example, are often seen as very biased (one-sided) sources of evidence, and material written for publication may be very different from material meant to be private. Published autobiographies and diaries of politicians should be treated with some scepticism, as they're likely to be very selective in the material included; at the same time, they may show how the politicians' minds worked, which might be useful for interpretivist research. Documents produced to promote a school or health services are likely to be biased as they may well exaggerate the good features and play down any negative issues.

Representativeness

Is the document typical of those appearing at the time? Is the evidence complete or merely a partial, biased account? Are other documents missing? Many historical documents have been destroyed, and governments often ban the publication of official records for a number of years after the events they relate to. What about those people in the past who couldn't read or write? Does the secondary data available simply reflect the views of the privileged minority in the past who were able to read and write well enough to produce diaries, letters and other documents?

Meaning

What do documents mean? Do they have the same meaning now as they did at the time they were first produced?

CONTENT ANALYSIS

Content analysis is a research method that produces primary *quantitative* data from the study of *qualitative* secondary sources: it is a way of analysing the content of documents and other qualitative material by quantifying it. This is done, for example, by sorting out categories, and then going through documents, books, magazines, television programmes and other qualitative material, and recording the number of times items in each category appear. For example, the Glasgow University Media Group has adopted this type of method in analysing television news. They video-recorded TV news bulletins for a year and then made a content analysis, categorizing reports on industrial unrest and evaluating them. Their research showed statistical evidence of television's biases towards management and against workers, with managers, for example, more often portrayed in calm, peaceful surroundings and workers in noisy conditions against a background of traffic noise. This gave the impression that managers were more rational and calm than workers. This research challenged the mass media's claims of impartiality and balance in news reporting.

The advantages of content analysis

- It is a relatively cheap means of research.
- There is no involvement with people, whose presence can sometimes lead to distorted results if their normal behaviour changes.
- It is a reliable research method, as it produces quantitative statistical data that other researchers can easily check.
- It enables the discovery of things that may not be obvious before the content analysis is carried out – for example, whether gender role stereotyping is really occurring in children's books.

The disadvantages of content analysis

- It depends on the categories chosen by the researcher and how he or she interprets what they see. For example, the researcher decides in analysing a children's comic to use the categories of 'male leader / female led', but these categories and what is happening depend on the researcher's personal judgements.
- It is mainly concerned with describing what is being studied, and is not very good at explaining it.
- The interpretation of what is being described may differ from one researcher to the next, and items may not fit neatly into one particular category.

Activity

1 Go through the following examples, marking each as primary or secondary *and* quantitative or qualitative data:
   - exam results of schools in your area published in a local newspaper.
   - newspaper stories from the 1930s.
   - information collected by you show*ing* the proportions of students doing different AS-level subjects.
   - teenage magazines.
   - statistics produced by the local NHS showing inequalities in health.
   - video-recordings of a week's news reports.
   - letters in a newspaper complaining about the risks to health of mobile phone masts.
   - the published diaries of a former prime minister.
2 Explain, with reasons, in what circumstances you might, or might not, consider each of the above pieces of data to be (a) reliable, and (b) valid, as sources of evidence.
3 Outline what ethical problems and problems with validity of the data collected, if any, there might be in each of the following situations:
   - a researcher joining a religious group to study it, concealing their role as a researcher.
   - a researcher taking on a temporary role as a teacher or classroom assistant to discover whether there was evidence of racism among teachers or pupils, and then publishing his or her research.

- standing outside a gay club and noting the car numbers of drivers using the club, then using a friend in the police force to get hold of their addresses for a follow-up questionnaire on what it's like being gay.
- pretending to be ill and going to the doctor to investigate how doctors decide whether someone is ill or not.

4 Do you consider there are ever any situations where a researcher might be justified in deceiving people to obtain research data? Explain your answer with examples of particular situations in *either* an educational *or* a health context.

Quantitative secondary sources

Quantitative secondary sources include a huge range of statistical data produced by groups like companies, charities and pressure groups. A major source of such data is the mass of official statistics collected by national and local government and other official agencies. These include census data, statistics on births, marriages / civil partnerships and deaths, and social services, unemployment, education, crime and health statistics.

Activity

Go to www.ons.gov.uk, the website of the Office for National Statistics, and identify (a) five government statistical publications, and (b) statistics for the current year (or the most recent year for which data are available) on some aspect, of your own choosing, of health, education, crime, divorce or marriage.

THE ADVANTAGES AND USES OF OFFICIAL STATISTICS

- Official statistics are important for planning and evaluating social policy, such as responding to housing needs, transport and education planning, and meeting the care needs of the elderly.
- They are frequently the only available source of data in a particular area.
- They are readily available and cheap to use. There is no need to spend time and money collecting data, and some data, such as census data, would be impossible for an individual to collect.
- They are often comprehensive in coverage, using either large samples – therefore, being more likely to be representative – or the whole population.
- They often cover a long timespan, and therefore allow the examination of trends over time, such as those on crime, unemployment, health and divorce. They can be used for 'before and after' studies, for example, to judge the effect of government policies on reducing inequalities in health or educational achievement.
- They allow intergroup and international comparisons to be made, such as between working-class and middle-class family sizes, or suicide, divorce and crime rates in different countries. They can therefore be used for the comparative method in sociology (discussed later in this chapter).
- They can provide useful background material when sociological researchers are deciding what issues should be studied, and can help in identifying a **hypothesis** for further investigation.

A **hypothesis** is an idea which a researcher guesses might be true, but which has not yet been tested against the evidence.

- They avoid any ethical issues, as they are publicly available, and unlikely to breach personal confidences or cause harm to individuals.

THE PROBLEMS AND LIMITATIONS OF OFFICIAL STATISTICS

If official statistics are basically accepted at face value as a true, or valid, record of events (as some researchers do with crime statistics and other official statistics), problems are likely to centre on their presentation, accuracy and completeness. For example, attempts have been made to overcome the inadequacy of the official crime statistics and make them more accurate by using **victim surveys** like the Crime Survey for England and Wales to discover the 'dark number' of unrecorded crimes.

Many sociologists would argue any statistics, and especially official statistics, can't be taken at face value as they are socially constructed and may be politically biased. For example:

> A **victim survey** is one that asks people to say whether they have been a victim of crime, whether they reported it to the police or not.

- Official statistics are collected for administrative purposes rather than for purposes of sociological research – so the definitions and classifications adopted may be unsuitable for that research.
- Official statistics are produced by the state. This means statistics made public may be 'massaged' – be not completely accurate or not provide a complete picture – to avoid political embarrassment to the government. The political process also affects which statistics are collected and which are not – for example, data on working days lost through strikes rather than industrial injuries; on welfare claimants rather than tax evaders; on house-building rather than homelessness; on the poor but not the rich, and so on. If the statistics are not accurate and complete, this may raise questions about the *validity* of some publicly available official statistics.
- Interpretivists argue that statistics are not objective facts but simply social constructions: the product of a process of interpretation and decision-making by those with authority. The following examples illustrate why sociologists should treat official statistics with some caution and pages 144–6 showed the limitations of official statistics on divorce.

Suicide statistics

Atkinson (1978) and other interpretivists argue that suicide statistics are simply social constructions reflecting the behaviour of coroners, doctors, relatives, etc., and their definitions of suicide. They tell us more about the decision-making processes of the living than the intentions of the dead and the real number of suicides (see the activity on page 296).

Health statistics

Health statistics can be inaccurate because:

- They depend on people persuading doctors they are ill, and are therefore simply a record of doctors' decision-making.
- Doctors may diagnose illnesses or the causes of death incorrectly, reflecting the state of the doctor's knowledge – and therefore recorded illnesses and cause-of-death statistics may not be accurate. For example, there may have been many AIDS deaths recorded as another disease, like pneumonia, before doctors discovered AIDS; many doctors still have difficulty in diagnosing ME (Myalgic Encephalopathy), also known as Chronic Fatigue or Post Viral Fatigue Syndrome,

as its symptoms are similar to those found in a range of other medical conditions. Many doctors don't even recognize ME as a genuine medical illness, even though it was first identified in the 1950s and an estimated 250,000 people suffer from it in the UK.

- Not all sick people go to the doctor and not all people who persuade the doctor they're sick are actually so – some may be malingerers or hypochondriacs.
- Private medicine operates to make a profit, and therefore is perhaps more likely to diagnose illness, as patients receiving treatment produce profits.

Crime statistics

Official crime statistics can be inaccurate for a number of reasons, and have to be treated very carefully by sociologists, because they do not show the full extent of crime in society. The following outlines some of these problems.

They only include crimes known to the police   Only around a quarter of all crimes are reported to the police, and even fewer are recorded by them as offences. There is a 'dark number' of undiscovered, unreported and unrecorded crimes.

Low clear-up rates   Only about one in four of all crimes reported to the police and recorded by them is 'cleared up', with an offender identified and action taken against them. This leaves open the possibility that the other 75 per cent of known offences are committed by very different criminal types from those who come before the courts.

Unreported crime   People may not report offences to the police. For example, they may think that the incident is too trivial to report, they may doubt the police could do anything about it; they may fear embarrassment or humiliation at the hands of the police or in court, as happens, for example, in cases of rape and domestic violence; or they may fear reprisals if the crime is reported, as in crimes of domestic violence.

Why might victims of crime not report it to the police?

Activity

1 Go to www.homeoffice.gov.uk/rds, find the latest Crime Survey for England and Wales, and look for the five main reasons included in the latest survey for why the public don't report crime, and the two offences or groups of offences that are most likely to go unreported.

2 Suggest one reason why sociologists might want to use each of the following sources of information, including the kind of information it may provide, and in each case suggest one problem in doing so (such as those relating to problems of validity, reliability, representativeness or ethical concerns):
   (a) surveys of parents' or patients' satisfaction carried out by schools or GP surgeries.
   (b) school or GP surgery websites.
   (c) school Ofsted inspection reports or reports on the performance of a local hospital.
   (d) pupils' school reports or patients' medical records.
   (e) letters from parents to schools, or from patients to doctors.
   (f) newspaper stories about a local school or hospital.

3 Read the following passage and then answer the questions beneath:
'Suicide is, by definition, the death of a person who intended to kill himself or herself. The problem for coroners is they can't ask dead people if they meant to kill themselves, so they can only guess at the truth by looking for "clues" in the circumstances surrounding the death. Atkinson has suggested there are four main factors which coroners take into account when deciding whether a death is a suicide or not:

• Whether there was a suicide note.
• The way the person died, for example by hanging, drowning or a drug overdose. Death in a road accident rarely results in a suicide verdict.
• The place the death occurred and the circumstances surrounding it; for example, a drug overdose in a remote wood would be more likely to be seen as a suicide than if it occurred at home in bed. A coroner might also consider circumstances such as whether the person had been drinking alcohol before taking the drugs, and whether the drugs had been hoarded or not.
• The life history and mental state of the dead person, such as her or his state of health, and whether the victim was in debt, had just failed exams, lost a job, got divorced and was depressed or not.

Coroners do not always agree on the way they interpret these clues. For example, Atkinson found one coroner believed a death by drowning was likely to be a suicide if the clothes were left neatly folded on the beach, but another coroner might attach little importance to this.'

   (a) How is suicide defined in the passage?
   (b) Why do you think coroners attach such importance to suicide notes?
   (c) Suggest two reasons why the presence or absence of a suicide note might be an unreliable 'clue' to a dead person's intention to die.
   (d) Suggest ways, with reasons, in which relatives and friends might try to persuade a coroner that a death was not a suicide but an accident.
   (e) On the basis of the evidence in the passage, suggest reasons why (i) some deaths classified as suicides may have been accidental, and (ii) some deaths classified as accidents may in fact have been suicides.
   (f) With reference to the evidence in the passage, suggest reasons why sociologists should be very careful about using official statistics on suicide as a record of the real number of suicides in society.

Exam-style questions

1 Explain what is meant by the term 'secondary data'. *(2 marks)*
2 Explain what is meant by the term 'primary data'. *(2 marks)*
3 Explain the difference between public and personal documents. *(4 marks)*
4 Suggest **two** problems of using secondary data in sociological research. *(4 marks)*
5 Examine the usefulness and problems of using content analysis in sociological research. *(20 marks)*
6 Examine the advantages of using official statistics in sociological research. *(20 marks)*

Topic 4

SPECIFICATION AREAS

- *Sources of data, including questionnaires, interviews, participant and non-participant observation, experiments, documents and official statistics; the strengths and limitations of these sources* (see Topic 3 for documents and official statistics)
- *Quantitative and qualitative methods of research; their strengths and limitations; research design*

The experimental (laboratory) method of research

The experiment is the main means of conducting research in the natural sciences. In natural science, experiments are used to test a *hypothesis* (an idea which a researcher guesses might be true, but which has not yet been tested against the evidence) in laboratory conditions in which all variables or causes are under the control of the researcher. By manipulating variables and studying and measuring the results, the researcher tries to test a hypothesis by isolating the causes of some phenomenon under investigation (such as, why pigs get fat).

The researcher will take two groups that are alike in every way: one is the *control group* and the other is the *experimental group*. The researcher will then alter some factor (the *independent variable*) in the experimental group to see whether the variable being investigated (the *dependent variable*) changes, compared to in the control group (for example, alter heat in pigsties to see whether this affects pigs getting fat). If nothing changes in the experimental group, then that variable can be dismissed as a cause of the thing being investigated, and other variables can be tested (for example, type of food). Through this experimental method, the researcher can eventually arrive at an explanation for the issue being investigated that has been tested against evidence, since any difference between the two groups after the experiment can only be because of the experimental variable, as the two groups were otherwise identical before the experiment.

Such laboratory experiments in the natural sciences have the advantages of:

- enabling scientists to test their hypotheses in controlled conditions.
- making it easy to isolate and manipulate variables to determine the causes of events.
- being repeatable (replicable) and therefore able to be checked by other researchers.
- enabling comparisons to be made with other similar experimental research.

PROBLEMS OF USING THE EXPERIMENTAL METHOD IN SOCIOLOGY

- In the social sciences, and sociology in particular, it is often difficult to isolate a single cause of a social issue like crime, or underachievement in school, and it is extremely difficult to isolate variables for testing. For example, crime and low achievement in school are the result of a range of causes.

Why might the laboratory experiment not be a suitable method for studying the behaviour of people in society?

- Experiments need to treat one group differently from another similar group and compare results. However, this poses ethical problems for sociologists, as it may have negative effects on the experimental group.
- People may object to being experimented on, and if they are deceived and don't realize they're involved in an experiment – for example, to avoid the **Hawthorne effect** (discussed below) – then the researcher will not have obtained the informed consent required in order to be acting ethically.
- Experiments are often only possible in small-scale settings with very limited, specific aims, but sociologists are often interested in wider settings like achievement in education and the causes of crime or ill-health, and such small-scale settings may be unrepresentative.

The **Hawthorne effect** is when the presence of a researcher, or a group's knowledge that it is the focus of attention, changes the behaviour of a group.

A particular problem is the Hawthorne effect.

The Hawthorne effect and the problem of validity

Sociologists want to study people in their normal social context, but the laboratory and experimental conditions are artificial situations. People, unlike chemicals and many animals, can and do know what is going on in an experiment. The knowledge that an experiment is taking place, even if it is not fully understood, may mean people behave differently from their usual, everyday behaviour. They may deliberately sabotage the experiment, or 'play up' for the researcher. The very presence of the observer may become the principal independent variable in social scientific experiments. The classic example of this is the Hawthorne effect, which is explained in the box below.

Such circumstances throw some doubt on the validity of using the experimental method for sociological research, and it is hardly ever desirable or possible to perform laboratory experiments in sociology. However, some experimental techniques have been used in sociology in the form of field experiments.

The Hawthorne effect

In 1927, a team of researchers led by Elton Mayo set up an experiment in the Hawthorne plant of the Western Electricity Company of Chicago, to try to find the factors affecting the productivity of workers. Using a control group and an experimental group, they set up a test area involving five workers who knew the experiment was taking place. Working conditions were matched with the rest of the factory, then the researchers varied factors such as room temperature, lighting, work hours, rest breaks, etc. They found output went up *even when conditions were made worse*. It turned out the most important variable affecting production was not environmental factors, etc., but the *presence and interest of the researchers themselves*: simply being the focus of interest and attention increased productivity. This influence of the researchers on research is known as the Hawthorne effect.

How do the cartoons show the Hawthorne effect, and how might this affect the validity of some kinds of sociological research?

No observer

Observer present

FIELD EXPERIMENTS

Field experiments are those conducted in the real world under normal social conditions, but following similar procedures to the laboratory experiment. They have similar advantages and disadvantages to the laboratory experiment, such as they may involve the researcher misleading research participants, changing their behaviour through the Hawthorne effect or failing to gain their informed consent, or research may potentially have negative consequences for them. Field experiments have mainly been carried out by interpretivists, who are interested in how meanings and labels, like 'bright' or 'mentally ill', get attached to people, and how others then react to them. This is illustrated in the work of Rosenthal and Jacobson and of Rosenhan, described in the box below.

EXAMPLES OF FIELD EXPERIMENTS

Rosenthal and Jacobson, *Pygmalion in the Classroom* (1968)

In the 1960s, Rosenthal and Jacobson wanted to test the hypothesis that teachers' expectations had important effects on pupils' academic performance. They told teachers that 20 per cent of children had been tested and shown to have high intelligence and were expected to make rapid progress in the next year compared to other students. In fact, the students had been chosen totally at random, and were no different from the others. Within a year, those students whom the teachers were told were bright made very rapid progress compared to other students. This was seen as evidence that

The **self-fulfilling prophecy** is where people act in response to predictions which have been made regarding their behaviour, thereby making the prediction come true.

pupil progress was affected by teacher expectation, and teachers' predictions of pupil progress could actually influence the progress they made – a **self-fulfilling prophecy**. This research posed ethical problems, as it may well have been that teachers' high expectations of the students labelled 'bright' were linked with low expectations of those labelled 'not bright', and had negative consequences on their progress – a self-fulfilling prophecy with negative effects on student progress.

Rosenhan, '*On being sane in insane places*' (1973)

Rosenhan was interested in discovering how the staff of mental hospitals made sense of, and labelled, people as mentally ill. He arranged for perfectly sane 'patients' to fake the symptoms of schizophrenia (hearing voices), and they were admitted to hospital, without staff knowing they were fakes. Once admitted to hospital, they behaved normally. All were diagnosed as schizophrenics, even though they were perfectly healthy. Rosenhan then reversed the experiment, telling hospital staff they could expect patients who would be faking illness. The staff eventually thought they had identified the fake patients, but all those they identified were actually genuine patients who wanted help.

Activity

1 Suggesting examples of your own drawn from the areas of *either* education *or* health, identify and explain three reasons why the experimental method may not be suitable for sociological research.
2 Refer to the examples of field experiments by Rosenthal and Jacobson, and Rosenhan:
   - What aims did Rosenthal and Jacobson have in carrying out their piece of research?
   - In what ways do you think their research might be useful to others?
   - Do you think there are any ethical difficulties in either piece of research?
   - To what extent do you think it might be possible to generalize these pieces of research to the whole of society? Would you need more information to answer this question?

The comparative method

The comparative method rests on the same principles as the experiment, and is an alternative to it. However, instead of setting up artificial experiments or situations, the researcher collects data about different societies or social groups in the real world, or the same society at different times (this is called the 'historical method'). The researcher then compares one society or group with another in an attempt to identify the conditions that are present in one society but lacking in the other, as a way to explain the causes of some social event.

This approach is most commonly used by positivists concerned with trying to isolate and identify the causes of social events and behaviour.

An example of the use of the comparative method is Durkheim's study of suicide. Durkheim could hardly experiment with people to see what kinds of factors made them commit suicide, and he couldn't control the social situations in societies whose suicide rates he wished to compare. All he could do was to compare official suicide statistics in various societies and examine what seemed to be the most frequent factors linked with high suicide rates. He collected suicide statistics from a number of European countries and, by comparing variables such as religion, marital status and geographical location, he concluded that differences in suicide rates could be partly explained by differences in religious belief between societies.

Surveys and sampling methods

Surveys are a means of collecting primary data from large numbers of people, and are most commonly carried out using questionnaires or structured interviews.

> **Surveys** are a means of collecting primary data from large numbers of people, usually in a standardized statistical form.

WHO USES THE SURVEY METHOD?

Because surveys mainly produce quantitative statistical data, they are the method most favoured by positivists.

Townsend used the survey method to produce a mass of statistical data, with questionnaires carried out by trained interviewers, about the causes and extent of poverty, in his classic study *Poverty in the United Kingdom* (1979). Many people use surveys, apart from sociologists – for instance, the government when it carries out the ten-yearly census, market researchers who want to test people's attitudes to products, and election pollsters trying to find out how people will vote in elections.

REPRESENTATIVENESS AND SAMPLING

In some cases, it may be possible to question or interview every member of the population under investigation because it is such a small group, such as a class of college students, or because the organization doing the research has the resources to investigate everyone. For example, the government surveys the entire population of the United Kingdom in the census every ten years.

Social surveys often use questionnaires on large numbers of people, carried out by post or online, and self-completed by those surveyed, or completed by interviewers, either in person (face-to-face) or over the telephone

A **sample** is a smaller *representative* group drawn from the survey population.

A **representative sample** is a smaller group drawn from the survey population, of which it contains a good cross-section, such as the right proportions of people of different ethnic origins, ages, social classes and sexes. The information obtained from a representative sample should provide roughly the same results as if the whole survey population had been questioned.

The **survey population** is the whole group being studied, and will depend on the hypothesis the researcher wishes to investigate

A **sampling frame** is a list of names of all those included in the survey population from which the sample is selected.

Sampling methods are the techniques sociologists use to select representative individuals to study from the survey population.

Sociologists rarely have the time or money to question everyone in large-scale and expensive surveys, so they usually collect information from a smaller group called a **sample**.

If it is a **representative sample**, containing all the relevant characteristics of the whole group under investigation (known as the **survey population**), such as the same proportions of age and gender groups, ethnic groups and social class, then the results obtained from the sample can be generalized or applied to the whole survey population. It is very important that a sample is representative, because if it is not, then it would not be valid to apply the results of a survey to the whole survey population, as the results would not provide a true, genuine or authentic picture of that whole survey population.

The representativeness of a sample can be affected by:

- *Sample size* Too small a sample may mean that it is not representative, and in general the larger the sample taken, the more representative it will be. However, a sample is at its ideal size when making it any larger won't produce much more accurate or representative results even if the entire survey population is questioned.
- *The sampling frame* A **sampling frame** is a list of names of all those in the survey population. A commonly used sampling frame is the Electoral Register, which includes the names and addresses of all adults over the age of 18 in Britain who are registered to vote in elections. Another nationwide sampling frame, which is now the most complete one available in Britain, is the Royal Mail's Postcode Address File, which lists all addresses in the UK. Doctors' lists of patients are also commonly used as sampling frames, as most people are registered with a doctor. In educational settings, sampling frames are readily available from lists of students like school registers. It is extremely important that a sampling frame should be complete: no individuals or particular groups of individuals should be missing. Otherwise, the sample drawn from the sampling frame may be unrepresentative of the entire survey population. For example, a telephone directory would be an unreliable sampling frame if the researcher wanted to select a sample which was representative of the entire adult population, as it only contains those who have a landline, and excludes those who may not be able to afford or want a telephone, or who are ex-directory and therefore not included in the phone book, or who only have a mobile.
- *The sampling method used* Careful **sampling methods** mean that often the information provided by the sample can be generalized with great accuracy to the whole survey population. For example, opinion polls on the voting intentions of electors often produce extremely accurate predictions of the outcome of general elections from questioning samples of only around 1,000 to 1,500 people, drawn from millions of adult voters. The problem for sociologists is how to obtain as representative a sample as possible, and this is achieved by various sampling methods.

SAMPLING METHODS

Figure 5.5 summarizes the main sampling methods discussed below, with examples.

Random sampling

Random sampling simply means that every individual in the survey population has an equal chance of being picked out for investigation. For example, all names are put in a hat and enough names picked out to make up the sample size required. This is most commonly done by numbering all the names in the sampling frame and then getting a computer to select numbers at random to fill the sample size. However, such a method

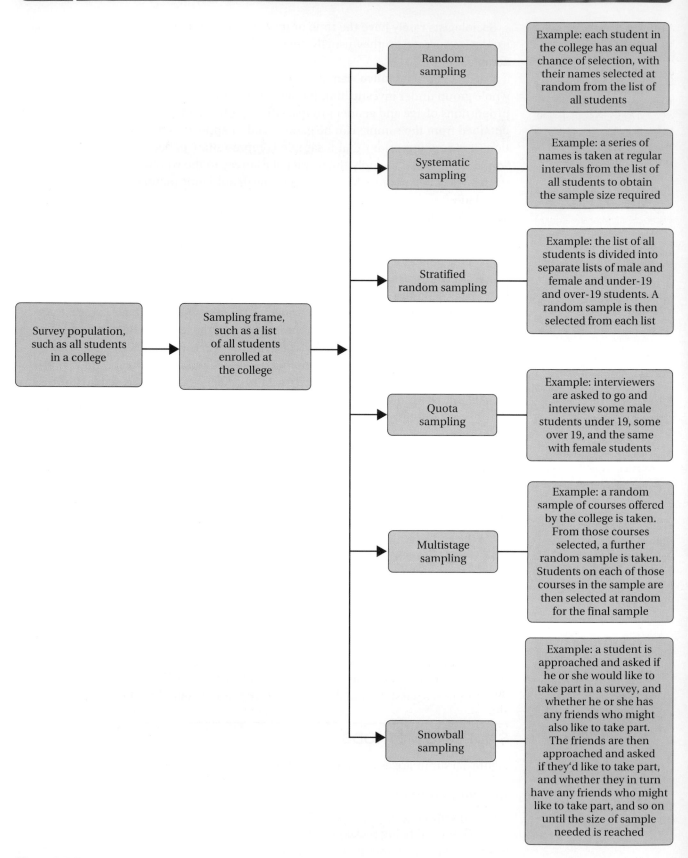

Figure 5.5 Examples of sampling methods

A random sample is a bit like a lottery draw – every person has an equal chance of being selected but, like the lottery, you've got to be in it to win it, or, in surveys, to be in the sampling frame to have a chance of being selected

is subject to the laws of chance, which may result in an unrepresentative sample – there may be too many people of one sex, age group or social class or who live in the same area. For example, a small survey of a school might by chance select only black females, and miss out black males and white males and white females.

Systematic sampling   Systematic sampling is where names are selected from the sampling frame at regular intervals until the size of sample is reached, for example by selecting every tenth name in the sampling frame. This has much the same risk of being unrepresentative as a random sample. For example, every tenth name might, purely by chance, happen to be a white and middle-class person.

Stratified random sampling   Stratified random sampling is a way of attempting to avoid the possible errors caused by simple random sampling. This is achieved by subdividing (stratifying) the sampling frame into a number of smaller sampling frames drawn up on particular bases, such as social class, age, sex, ethnic group or education, according to their proportions in the population under investigation. The criteria used will depend on the factors being investigated. Individuals are then drawn at random from each of these sampling frames. For example, in a survey of doctors, we may know from earlier research that 8 per cent of all doctors are Asian, and so the sociologist must make sure 8 per cent of the sample are Asian. To do this, the sociologist will separate out the Asian doctors from the sampling frame of all doctors, and then take a random sample from this list of Asian doctors to make up 8 per cent of the sample of all doctors in the survey population. In this way, the final sample is more likely to be representative of all doctors in the survey population. Stratified random sampling has the advantage over simple random sampling of being much more representative, because all the characteristics of the survey population are more certain to be represented in the sample. See the box 'Obtaining a stratified random sample' and figure 5.6, which shows an example.

Obtaining a stratified random sample

Suppose there were 400 students in a school. Of these, 50 per cent are male and 50 per cent are female. In each group, 75 per cent are white and 25 per cent are from minority ethnic groups. You want a 10 per cent representative sample (40 people). Figure 5.6 shows how you might obtain a stratified random sample by dividing up the sampling frame of 400 names, first into two sampling frames (by sex), and then by subdividing each again into two (by ethnic group). You then take a 10 per cent random sample from each of the final four sampling frames. This stratified random sample of 40 people (10 per cent of the original 400 students) should be representative of the sex and ethnic characteristics of the entire school population, as these features of the survey population are now certain to be included in the 10 per cent sample.

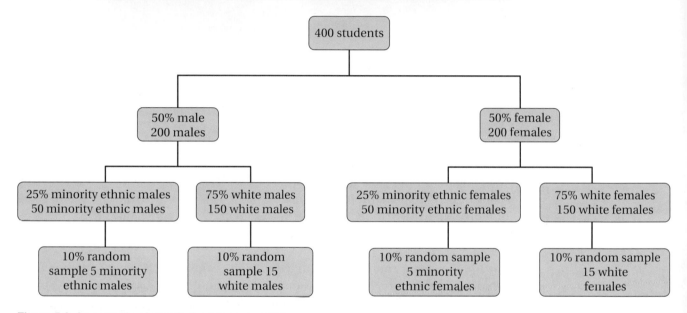

Figure 5.6 An example of stratified random sampling

Quota sampling In quota sampling, interviewers are told to go and select people who fit into certain categories according to their proportion in the survey population as a whole – such as, so many men and women over the age of 45. The choice of the actual individuals selected is left to the honesty of the interviewer (unlike other sampling methods where actual named individuals are identified). The problem with quota sampling is that it is not necessarily representative. For example, the quota might be filled by stopping people while shopping during the week, but this would exclude those not shopping or who are at work. The fact that the choice of person rests on the interviewer's discretion means there may be bias in the choices they make. For instance, they may not approach people who don't look very welcoming, even though they fit the category, or they might ignore those who refuse to cooperate and simply find another person who fits the quota. This could well lead to a bias in the sample.

Multistage or cluster sampling Multistage or cluster sampling involves selecting a sample in various stages, each time selecting a sample from the previous sample until the final sample of people is selected. For example, in a national survey of school students, you might first take a random sample of schools, then take a random sample of students in those sample schools.

Non-representative sampling

In some cases a non-representative sample might be useful in sociological research: for example, selecting a group for a particular purpose which is not representative, but because it has the particular characteristics you want to study. For example, in studying a hypothesis like 'roles in the family are more likely to be equal among younger middle-class couples', it might be useful to study a group that is young and middle class, to test or disprove the hypothesis, or gain insights into those couples.

Figure 5.7 Obtaining a sample: the example of the British Social Attitudes Survey

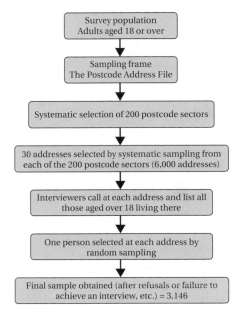

Snowball sampling   Snowball sampling is used when a sampling frame is difficult to obtain or doesn't exist, or when a sample itself is very difficult to obtain. The researcher may identify one or two people with the characteristics they're interested in, and ask them to introduce them to other people willing to cooperate in the research, and then ask these people to identify others. For example, Laurie Taylor, in *In the Underworld* (1984), used this technique to investigate the lifestyles of criminals. There was no readily available sampling frame of criminals. He happened to know a convicted criminal, who was willing to put him in touch with other criminals who were willing to cooperate in his research. These criminals in turn put him in touch with other criminals, and so his sample gradually built up, just as a snowball gets bigger as you roll it in the snow.

Such samples may be useful, but they are not random or representative. They rely on volunteers recommending other volunteers to the researcher, and the sample is therefore self-selecting, and this may create bias. For example, such volunteers may have particular views for or against a particular issue and that may be why they volunteered.

Figure 5.7 shows how a major national annual survey, the British Social Attitudes Survey, used a combination of multistage, systematic and random sampling to obtain a final sample of 3,146 individuals drawn from nearly all people over the age of 18 in Britain.

> **Activity**
>
> In each of the following cases, suggest both a hypothesis you might wish to test and how you might obtain your sampling frame and your sample:
> - the attitudes of family doctors (GPs) to changes in the National Health Service.
> - the reasons why few female school-leavers in a town go on to computer courses at a local college.
> - a survey of young mothers' experiences of hospital maternity services.
> - a survey of the health of old age pensioners.
> - a survey of school pupils involved in anti-social or criminal activity.
> - the opinions of adults in your neighbourhood about how they will vote in the next election.
> - the attitudes of gay men to the police.

THE STAGES OF A SURVEY

Any research always starts with some kind of hypothesis or question to investigate, and any survey needs to operationalize concepts (see page 287) to know who to investigate, what to question them about, and the form the questions should take.

Before carrying out a large-scale survey, it is important to carry out a **pilot survey**. Sometimes this is called a *pilot study*. Such studies are carried out not only in surveys, but in most kinds of primary research studying groups of people, to identify any unforeseen problems before beginning more detailed research.

The purpose of a pilot survey or a pilot study is to iron out any problems which the researcher might have overlooked, and avoid wasting time and money in the final survey. For example, some of the sample may have moved away or died, there may be problems with non-response or non-cooperation by respondents, or some questions may be unclear.

After the pilot survey is completed, the results are reviewed, any necessary changes are made, and the main survey can then proceed. The stages of a survey are shown in figure 5.8.

> A **pilot survey** is a small-scale practice survey carried out before the final survey to check for any possible problems.

PROBLEMS OF THE SOCIAL SURVEY

There are three major problems faced by social survey researchers in achieving what positivists might call 'scientific' accuracy:

- *Validity* Surveys need to be very carefully planned if they are to obtain data which are valid – which really provide a true, genuine or authentic picture of what they claim to represent. The statistical data produced by surveys are questioned by interpretivists, who would argue statistical data fail to describe accurately people's meanings and motives, and that they use categories which are imposed by the sociologists.
- *Generalization* This is concerned with representativeness: how far the findings of a piece of research can be generalized to other sections of the survey population rather than simply being restricted to the sample selected. For example, the sample selected may be too small, or unrepresentative, or people selected may have moved, died, etc., in which case the results may not be able to be generalized.
- *Reliability* Whatever the survey finds should be found by anyone else conducting the same survey again. This may be a particular problem where face-to-face interviews are used. This issue is discussed below under 'Interviewer bias' on pages 320–2.

Figure 5.8 The stages of a survey

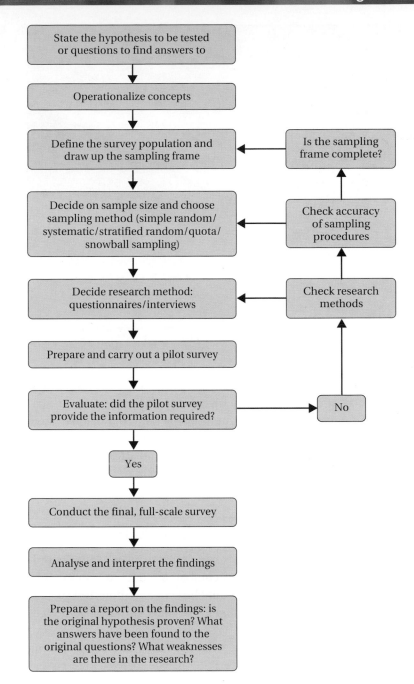

Questionnaires

THE NATURE AND USE OF QUESTIONNAIRES

Most surveys involve the use of a questionnaire of some kind. A questionnaire is a list of pre-set questions to which the *respondents* (the people answering the questions) are asked to supply answers – either by filling in responses themselves (a self-completion questionnaire) or by giving information to an interviewer, either face-to-face or over the telephone. When administered by an interviewer, these take the form of interviews.

Questionnaires are very commonly used in survey research to collect quantitative data

Researchers using questionnaires see them as a comparatively cheap, fast and efficient method (compared to other methods like unstructured interviews or participant observation) for obtaining large amounts of quantifiable data on relatively large samples of people.

The questionnaire is one of the main tools of measurement in positivist sociology, as data obtained by structured questionnaires are easily quantified and can be analysed more 'scientifically' and objectively than qualitative data.

QUESTIONNAIRE DESIGN: SOME PRINCIPLES AND PROBLEMS

Great care is needed in questionnaire design. Because the idea is to present all respondents with the same questions and therefore obtain comparable data, questionnaires can't be changed once a survey has begun. They should be kept as simple and clear as possible, otherwise those being interviewed or filling in the questionnaire themselves will be unlikely to complete it.

A pilot survey is therefore very important to clear up problems and avoid wasting time and money on a poorly designed questionnaire. Pilot studies are used to test questions, make sure their meaning is clear, and to ensure layout and wording are suitable for the intended sample.

The section below identifies some important issues in designing a questionnaire.

Designing a questionnaire

As short as possible, with clear layout and instructions   Completing the questionnaire should be made as easy as possible for the respondent.

- The questionnaire should be clearly laid out and well printed. Instructions for completing it should be easily understood by the respondent, and it should be easy to follow and fill in.
- The number of questions should be kept to the minimum required to produce the

information. Respondents may be unwilling to answer long lists of questions, or may stop giving serious thought to their answers.

- Start the questionnaire with the simplest questions and shortest answers first, leaving the more complicated questions or more detailed answers until the end. Otherwise people may be put off right from the beginning.
- There should be just enough alternative answers (including 'don't know') to allow respondents to express their views and to provide the information required.

Clear and neutral language, and the avoidance of 'leading questions'   The form of questions needs careful thought.

- Questions should be simple and direct – capable of being answered 'yes', 'no' or 'don't know', by a choice from fixed responses, or with short open-ended answers.
- Questions should be phrased in neutral terms – otherwise respondents might feel they are expected to give a particular answer. Questions which encourage people to give a particular answer are called 'leading questions', and they are likely to produce distorted or invalid (untruthful) results. A question like 'Why do you think promiscuous sex is wrong?' is a poor, leading question because the way the question is worded encourages people to accept that promiscuous sex is wrong.
- Questions should be clear in meaning and phrased in simple, everyday language, avoiding technical or unfamiliar words which people may not understand. For example, a question like 'Do you have joint conjugal roles in your household?' is a bad question because people are unlikely to understand what 'conjugal roles' are. Similarly, a question like 'Do you watch television a lot?' is a poor question, as people might interpret 'a lot' in different ways – it is better to specify actual time periods such as 1–2 hours, 3–4 hours a day, and so on.
- Only questions which the respondents are likely to be able to answer accurately should be asked – for example, requesting responses or opinions on things they might reasonably be expected to know about, or remember accurately.
- Questions should mean the same thing to all respondents. The researcher can't automatically assume that questions will have the same meaning to the respondent as they do to the researcher.
- Offensive questions should be avoided.

Confidentiality   Those being surveyed should be reassured that their answers will be kept confidential or anonymous.

Activity

1 Refer to the section 'Designing a questionnaire' above. Draw up a five-question questionnaire on attitudes to education or health (or some other sociological topic of interest to you).
2 Test your questionnaire on five people.
3 Identify and explain any difficulties you come across in your questionnaire, and amend your questions as necessary.
4 Suggest as many criticisms as you can of the following questions:
    - 'Do you think most teachers are any good? '
    - 'Have you been diseased recently?'
    - 'What do you think of recent changes to the National Health Service?'
5 In the light of your criticisms, write new questions, and a choice of answers, to overcome the difficulties you have identified.

DO YOUR CONJUGAL RELATIONSHIPS IN THE DOMESTIC DIVISION OF LABOUR ENCOMPASS SOME MEASURE OF ROLE INTEGRATION?

COME AGAIN?

Questionnaires should always be phrased in simple, everyday language

TYPES OF QUESTIONNAIRE

There are two main types of questions used in questionnaires: prc-coded or closed/ structured questions, and open-ended or open questions. Both types of question may be combined in the same questionnaire.

Pre-coded or closed questionnaires

Pre-coded or closed questionnaires, sometimes called structured or multiple-choice questionnaires, are highly structured, and involve individuals being asked a number of pre-set *closed* questions with the choice of a limited number of multiple-choice answers.

Advantages and strengths of pre-coded or closed questionnaires
- They are fairly quick to complete.
- They produce standardized data that are easy to classify and produce in quantitative statistical form.
- They are *reliable*, in the sense that they are likely to produce similar results if carried out by another researcher, and other researchers can check the findings, and repeat the research if they wish.
- They allow data to be collected to produce new theories or to test existing hypotheses.
- They enable comparisons to be made between different groups and populations. Since individuals are answering the same questions, and using the same choices of answers, their answers should show real differences between people rather than differences arising because of the way the questions were formulated or asked.

Disadvantages and problems of pre-coded or closed questionnaires
- The meaning of questions may not be clear to some respondents. Extra questions cannot be asked or added to get the respondents to expand or explain themselves more fully.
- The **imposition problem**. This is the risk that, when asking questions, researchers might be imposing their own views and framework on the people being researched,

> The **imposition problem** refers to the risk that the researcher, when asking questions, might be imposing their own views or framework on the people being researched, rather than getting at what they really think.

rather than getting at what they really think. The limited choice of answers imposes strict and artificial limits on what kind of information can be given or collected, as the constraints don't allow the respondent to develop or qualify their answers. The answer the respondent wants to give may simply not be there. This poses problems of *validity*, as the researcher may be imposing a choice of answers which may not really apply to that particular respondent.

Open-ended or open questionnaires

Open-ended questionnaires, sometimes known as unstructured questionnaires, are less structured than pre-coded questionnaires. Although open-ended questionnaires will still usually have a number of pre-set questions, there is no pre-set choice of answers. Open questions allow individuals to write their own answers or dictate them to an interviewer.

Advantages and strengths of open-ended/open questionnaires
- They produce more valid data, since the respondent is using his or her own words to express what they really mean rather than being given a pre-set choice of answers reflecting what the researcher thinks important. The *imposition problem* is less serious.
- They produce more detail and depth than pre-coded or closed questionnaires.

Disadvantages and problems of open-ended/open questionnaires
- The range of possible answers often makes it difficult to classify and quantify the results of such questionnaires. For example, the meaning of the answers may be unclear to the researcher.
- Because of the wide variety of answers, it may be difficult to compare results with other similar research.

Postal/mail or online self-completion questionnaires

This kind of questionnaire is either left with the respondent and picked up later, or sent through the post with a pre-paid addressed envelope for the reply, or posted on an internet site for people to reply to, or it may be sent and returned via email. The respondent will complete the questionnaire himself or herself (self-completion). Many surveys, including opinion polls and government surveys, are now using computerized and web-based self-completion questionnaires, sometimes recorded onto computer and played back with sound for those who are illiterate, and this can help in getting answers to embarrassing questions, like those on a person's criminal or sexual activity, that may otherwise remain unanswered if asked by a researcher in person. To ensure a good response rate, such questionnaires need to be well designed, with a limited number of simple/clear questions, and postal questionnaires often involve repeat mailings, or incentives like free entry to competitions to encourage people to return them.

Advantages and strengths of postal and other self-completion questionnaires
- They are a relatively cheap method compared to paying interviewers, particularly for collecting data from large numbers of people spread over a wide geographical area.
- Results are obtained quickly: most that get returned at all get returned within a couple of weeks.

- People can reply at their leisure and not just when an interviewer is present, so more precise answers may be obtained (especially if documents need to be consulted).
- Questions on personal, controversial, embarrassing or sensitive subjects, such as health and medical issues like depression or stigmatized diseases like HIV or AIDS, are more likely to get a better response in an anonymous questionnaire than if an interviewer is present.
- There is no problem of **interviewer bias** (see the later discussion on this).

> **Interviewer bias** refers to the answers given in an interview being influenced or distorted in some way by the presence or behaviour of the interviewer.

Disadvantages and problems of postal and other self-completion questionnaires

- There is a major problem of *non-response* in postal and other self-completion questionnaires (a 50 per cent response is very good), and of not getting representative responses in internet surveys. Those replying may be an unrepresentative sample of the survey population, for example in being more educated, or interested in the topic being researched, or having a particular axe to grind. This poses major problems for the *representativeness* and *validity* of the results.
- People may not give valid truthful replies, due to forgetfulness or dishonesty, or because of different interpretations or meanings attached to the questions. There is no interviewer present to prompt replies or explain questions.
- There is no way of knowing whether the right person completed the questionnaire – they may have let someone else do it.

IMPROVING RESPONSE RATES TO POSTAL AND OTHER SELF-COMPLETION QUESTIONNAIRES

Postal questionnaires are often the only financially viable option when collecting information from large, geographically dispersed populations. Edwards et al. (2002) point out that nonresponse reduces the effective sample size, and can affect the validity of studies and therefore pose a major threat to the quality of research. They found the response rates to postal questionnaires were improved when:

- a financial incentive was offered, whether or not a response was made.
- short questionnaires were used.
- questionnaires were personalized with accompanying letters.
- coloured ink was used.
- the questionnaires were sent by first-class post or recorded delivery, and stamped return envelopes were provided.
- participants were contacted before sending questionnaires.
- there was follow-up contact, and nonrespondents were provided with a second copy of the questionnaire.
- questionnaires were designed to appeal to the interests of participants.
- questionnaires originated from universities rather than from other sources, such as commercial organizations.

THE VALIDITY OF QUESTIONNAIRE RESEARCH

Interpretivists question whether questionnaires produce a valid picture of the social world and human behaviour. They make the following major criticisms of questionnaire research.

Imposition

Positivist-based questionnaires, particularly highly structured questionnaires, risk what has been called the *imposition problem* – whereby the researcher risks imposing their own views or framework on the people being researched. This is because they have already decided what the important issues are before the research and in drawing up the questions to actually ask people. Questionnaires don't really discover the way respondents see the world. Such researchers are therefore simply imposing their own structure (what they think is important) on what they are investigating, possibly affecting the *validity* of the research (see below). It is therefore difficult to develop hypotheses during research, and respondents cannot provide information they haven't been asked for. It is also impossible for respondents to express feelings and subtle shades of opinion in statistical form. It is, for example, impossible to measure subjective factors such as the nature and strength of religious belief.

Validity

There is no guarantee people will tell the truth in questionnaires. People may give answers they think are socially acceptable – what they think they ought to say, rather than what they really believe or how they behave in real life. This poses problems about the validity of the research. In 1983, for example, following major public concerns about children viewing unsuitable 'video nasties' (extreme horror, violent and sadistic films), questionnaire research was carried out, with results which suggested that 40 per cent of 6-year-old children had seen some of the famous video nasties. This had major repercussions in the press and Parliament, leading to legislation. The research was later repeated by other sociologists on another sample of 11-year-olds. They found 68 per cent claimed to have seen video nasties – but the researchers had named films which didn't even exist. In the 2001 census, 0.7 per cent of the population of England and Wales described their religion as 'Jedi' – fictional characters from the *Star Wars* films.

There may be different meanings attached to the wording of questions, which may influence the results. For example, many people prefer to call themselves 'middle class' when offered the choice of middle class or lower class, but when offered 'working class' more are prepared to put themselves in this category. Researchers need to be aware of how such meanings may differ between classes, ethnic groups, age groups and so on if their questionnaires are to produce valid data.

The scrounging Piresans

TÁRKI, a social research centre in Hungary, carried out a survey in that country in 2007, asking people about their opinion of immigrants from the nation of Piresa. Of those who responded, 68 per cent said that Piresans should not be let into the country under any circumstances. They were seen as scroungers, and most people said those who were already living in Hungary should be sent back immediately to Piresa. The survey was properly conducted, but there was one problem: there was no such place as Piresa, so there was no Piresa to stop immigration from, nor any Piresans to send back. Researchers had made up the country to test the tolerance of Hungarians. This was a perfectly reasonable research strategy, but it shows in a particularly stark way that questionnaires do not always get truthful replies.

Interviews

Questionnaires may also form the basis of interviews by social researchers. Interviews are one of the most widely used methods of gathering data in sociology. They may be conducted face-to-face, with either individuals or small groups of people, or via the telephone. There are two main types of interview: structured or formal interviews, and unstructured or in-depth, informal interviews.

STRUCTURED OR FORMAL INTERVIEWS

Structured or formal interviews are based on a structured, pre-coded questionnaire (the interview schedule). They are much like postal or other self-completion questionnaires except they are carried out by an interviewer. The interviewer asks closed questions set in the same order each time, and does not probe beyond the basic answers received: a formal question-and-answer session.

Advantages and strengths of structured interviews

- They are generally the most effective way of getting questionnaires completed and the problem of non-response found with postal and other self-completion questionnaires is much rarer. Skilled interviewers can persuade people to answer questions, and problems of illiteracy are overcome.
- Data so obtained are often seen as more *reliable*, since all respondents will be answering the same questions, so results can be compared with other groups. The research can, if necessary, be replicated by other interviewers to check the findings.
- They are useful for obtaining answers to questions about facts like the age, sex and occupation of those being interviewed.
- They usually involve pre-coded closed questions and answers which make them relatively easy to put into quantitative statistical form (note the *positivist* implication here).
- There is less of a problem with interviewer bias than in unstructured interviews, as there is little involvement of the interviewer with the interviewee beyond basic politeness (see the later discussion on interviewer bias).

Disadvantages and problems of structured interviews

- The interview schedule/questionnaire may impose limits on what the respondent can say, as the interviewer cannot probe beyond the basic questions asked. This means there is a limited depth of understanding of what the respondent may mean.

Interviewers may not always get the cooperation they hope for. . . especially if they choose the wrong moment

- They are more time-consuming and costly than postal and other self-completion questionnaires – interviews are often slow, and interviewers have to be paid. Many more people can be questioned with a postal or other self-completion questionnaire for the same cost. This may risk smaller, less representative samples being used.
- There is the possibility of interviewer bias.

UNSTRUCTURED OR INFORMAL (IN-DEPTH) INTERVIEWS

A **group interview** is an interview in which the researcher interviews several people at the same time, with the researcher controlling the direction of the interview, with responses normally directed to her/him.

A **focus group** is a form of group interview in which the group focuses on a particular topic to explore in depth, and people are free to talk to one another as well as the interviewer.

An unstructured interview is like a guided conversation. The interviewer has topics in mind to cover (the interview schedule) but few, if any, pre-set questions. If there is a questionnaire at all, it will be of the open-ended, unstructured variety. The interviewer will seek to put the respondent at ease, in a relaxed, informal situation, and will then ask open-ended questions which may trigger off discussions or further questions. The interviewer aims to obtain further depth or detail than is possible in a postal or other self-completion questionnaire or in a structured interview, and to draw out the respondent's feelings, opinions and confidences. This approach was used by Oakley (1981) in a study of the experience of becoming a mother in British society. Unstructured interviews may also be carried out with a group of people. This can help to trigger off discussions, encourage a dialogue to explore issues, and gain more detailed and in-depth qualitative information. These **group interviews** sometimes take the form of **focus groups**, when the group interview focuses on a particular topic, and people are free to talk to one another as well as the interviewer. In a group interview, the interviewer's role is to question, whereas in a focus group the researcher's role is to feed in ideas or questions for the participants to discuss and draw out their feelings, experiences and opinions. The researcher also has to make sure the group remains focused on the topic under discussion.

A group interview

A focus group

Group interviews and focus groups are both forms of in-depth interview. A group interview involves interviewing several people at the same time, with the interviewer controlling the direction the interview takes as he or she is seeking to obtain particular information; usually, responses will be to the interviewer rather than other members of the group. A focus group is a form of group interview, but which focuses on a single topic or group of related topics to discover people's views, such as what they think about abolishing fees for higher education, or providing maintenance grants for further education students. The researcher's role in a focus group is to get people discussing the issue and to draw out their opinions and ideas.

What are the advantages and disadvantages for sociologists of obtaining information in these ways, and how valid do you think the findings might be?

Advantages and strengths of unstructured interviews

- Their greater flexibility increases the validity of the data obtained compared to structured interviews. This is because they provide more opportunity for the respondent to say what they really think and feel about an issue (note the *interpretivist* implication). For example, Oakley found that unstructured interviews enabled her to develop close relationships of trust and openness with the mothers concerned which enabled them to speak for themselves openly and personally about motherhood.
- There is the possibility of probing much deeper than in a structured questionnaire, and gaining insights not otherwise available.
- Ambiguities in questions and answers can be clarified, and the interviewer can probe for shades of meaning.
- The ideas of the sociologist can develop in the course of the interviews. The interviewer can adjust questions and change direction as the interview is taking place if new ideas and insights emerge. It is possible a new hypothesis might emerge during the research (see the box below). By contrast, structured interviews have already decided the important questions.
- Interviewers may be able to assess the honesty and validity of replies during the course of the interview: this may be more difficult with structured interviews.
- Group interviews or focus groups can spark off discussions and ideas which can yield more in-depth information.

DEVELOPING A HYPOTHESIS IN UNSTRUCTURED INTERVIEWS

During the research which led to her theory of conjugal roles (the roles played by each partner in a married or cohabiting relationship) and social networks, Bott (1978[1957]) interviewed twenty couples in London. It was only because the link between social networks and conjugal roles emerged in the course of her interviews that Bott was able to develop her theory. This would have been impossible using questionnaires since she wouldn't have known what questions to ask, as she hadn't developed a hypothesis on social networks before she began interviewing.

Disadvantages and problems of unstructured interviews

- Unstructured interviews are time-consuming and costly, and this may mean fewer interviews are conducted, raising problems of representativeness.
- They may be less reliable than structured interviews as questions may be phrased in a variety of ways and the researchers are more involved with the respondents.

Differences between respondents may therefore simply reflect differences in the nature of the interview and the questions asked, rather than real differences between people.

- It is difficult to replicate such interviews. The success of an informal interview depends heavily on the personality and personal skills of the interviewer, such as in getting people to answer questions that produce useful information, and in keeping the conversation going. Another researcher repeating the interviews may therefore not get the same results again, so findings from such research may not be comparable with other groups (a criticism *positivists* might make).

- It is difficult to compare and measure the responses of different interviewees as they may be expressed in many different ways, and sometimes interviewees may contradict themselves during the same interview. Unstructured interviews are therefore more popular with *interpretivists*, who are concerned with increasing their understanding of respondents and obtaining qualitative data. *Positivists* don't often use this method, except for exploratory research to develop a hypothesis for further investigation (using other methods).

- Group interviews or focus groups may act as a form of peer pressure and individuals may conceal their true feelings in case others disapprove. They may be reluctant to reveal personal issues in such a group setting. They may also exaggerate or distort their views to impress others.

- *Interviewer bias* may be a particular problem in unstructured interviews, as these involve close involvement between the interviewer and the interviewee (see below).

Activity

1 Make up a short five-question structured questionnaire (with a choice of answers) to find out about attitudes to education or health (you might adapt the questionnaire you drew up in the earlier activity on 'Designing a questionnaire' on page 311).
2 Test this out on five people, using a structured interview, and record your findings.
3 Now, using the same questions as 'prompts', do unstructured interviews with two people. Be prepared to probe further and ask extra questions and enter discussions. Record your findings.
4 Compare the data collected by each type of interview, and the time it took to complete the interviews. Is there any difference between the information collected by these two types of interview, and the time taken to carry them out? Explain why you think this might be the case.
5 Suggest three ways in each case in which group interviews or focus groups might:
   (a) provide a greater depth of qualitative information than interviews with a single individual.
   (b) provide less valid information than interviews with a single individual.

Semi-structured interviews

The sections above have dealt with structured and unstructured interviews. However, in the real world of research, interviews are likely to include both structured and unstructured questions. These are called semi-structured interviews. For example, in a semi-structured interview, interviewers may ask some structured questions about the interviewee, to obtain some background information, such as about income, occupation and education, and then more unstructured questions to encourage the interviewees to open up and give their own accounts of what they think about the particular topics being researched. Any exam question on semi-structured interviews would need to consider the strengths and weaknesses of both types of question.

GENERAL PROBLEMS OF INTERVIEWS

The general problems of interviews centre on two main, and related, issues: the validity of the data obtained, and the problem of interviewer bias.

Validity

- Interview data are often taken by positivists as revealing the attitudes and behaviour of people in everyday life. However, interpretivists would argue that an interview is a very artificial situation, and what people say in an interview may have little to do with their real or normal behaviour. There is no guarantee people will give a true account in interviews, and they may lie, forget or otherwise mislead the interviewer. This may be particularly true in a group interview, when individuals may be concerned about what others may think, and therefore not tell the truth, or exaggerate or distort things. This poses problems for the validity of the data obtained by interviewing techniques.

- It is unlikely that many people in an interview situation will give honest answers to questions asked by a stranger that involve very personal or embarrassing issues.

- Interviews involve words and phrases, and meanings may vary between social groups. A structured interview, where there is little opportunity to qualify meaning, might not provide comparable data when administered to members of different social groups. For example, words like 'bad', 'wicked' and 'wasted' tend to be used in different ways by younger and older people.

- Members of different social groups may attach different importance to the content of questions. For example, mental illness carries less stigma among Puerto Ricans than among the Jews, the Irish or black people in the United States. This means Puerto Ricans are more willing to admit to the symptoms of mental illness – but this doesn't mean there is necessarily more mental illness among them than among other ethnic groups. This again raises doubts about the validity of some interview data, as it may simply reflect how much people are willing to admit to things to an interviewer, rather than real differences between people.

Interviewer bias

Interviewer bias refers to the way answers in an interview may be influenced or distorted in some way by the presence or behaviour of the interviewer. Interviews involve face-to-face social interaction between people, and the success of interviews often relies on the personal skills of the interviewer. The results of an interview will also partly depend on the way participants define the situation, and their perceptions of each other. For example, the interviewer's personality, sex, age, ethnic origin, tone of voice, facial expressions and dress (such as suit or jeans) all impose a particular definition of the situation on the respondent, and this may influence the responses given. Status differences, such as age and ethnicity, between the respondent and the interviewer can lead to bias too. For example, an adult carrying out interviews with school students may not be given honest answers. The interviewer may give the impression, however unwittingly or unintentionally, of wanting to hear a certain answer.

In such circumstances, it is possible that the interviewees might adapt their answers to impress the interviewer by giving answers they think the interviewer wants to hear and would approve of, rather than giving their real opinions. This is perhaps unsurprising, as nearly everyone likes to obtain the approval of the person they're talking to.

There is therefore a danger (particularly with unstructured interviews) that the interviewer and the interview context may unduly influence the interviewee (the person

Study the two photographs above and suggest possible sources of interviewer bias. In what ways might the interview on the right produce more (or less) valid information than the one on the left?

being interviewed). This may mean that differences between interviews reflect differences in the way the interviews were conducted rather than real differences in what the respondents were actually saying. This interaction situation can therefore affect the quality, validity and reliability of the data.

All the above suggests that in interview research it is very difficult for the researcher to avoid influencing what is obtained as data. It could therefore be argued that the data obtained by interviews are socially constructed – created and influenced by the presence, actions and behaviour of the interviewer, and the context in which the interview is conducted.

Overcoming interviewer bias To overcome interviewer bias and try to ensure that interviews produce valid data, interviewers are carefully trained to be *non-directive*. This means not to offer opinions, or show approval or disapproval of answers received. 'Be friendly but restrained', showing a polite indifference to the answers received, is often the advice given to interviewers to reduce the risks of interviewer bias. Another way is to try and match the social characteristics of the interviewer and the people being interviewed. For example, Nazroo's (1997b) research into the health of Britain's ethnic minorities involved translating questionnaires into six Asian languages, and, as often as possible, respondents were interviewed by someone from their own ethnic group who spoke the same language.

However, Becker (1970) suggests a more aggressive style of interviewing is more likely to squeeze information out of respondents which may not otherwise have been volunteered. This involves 'playing dumb', playing the devil's advocate by taking positions on issues, or deliberately trying to wind people up in the hope of prompting the respondent to say more. Another way of avoiding interviewer bias is to avoid face-to-face interviews altogether, and use telephone interviews instead.

CONCLUDING REMARKS ON INTERVIEWS

The more structured the interview, the more easily can results be quantified statistically and comparisons be made. However, the tighter the structure, the less the respondent can state and develop what she or he really means. The degree of structure of interviews will vary from highly structured to very unstructured depending on whether the researcher feels the need is for quantification, or for an understanding of meanings. This will depend on the theoretical perspective of the researcher – whether he or she adopts a more positivist or more interpretivist approach to understanding society. However, the other influences identified in figure 5.3 in Topic 2 earlier in this chapter (page 285) will also affect the type of interview approach adopted.

Activity

1 Consider the following situations, and in each case: (a) suggest possible ways in which interviewer bias might occur and distort the results of the interview, and (b) suggest what steps might be taken to help remove or reduce the bias:
- a white person being questioned by a black interviewer about her or his racial attitudes.
- an adult interviewing students in a school.
- an adult interviewer asking young people about their attitudes to illegal drug use.
- a female interviewer asking a married or cohabiting couple about how household tasks are divided up between them.
- an older woman asking questions of a young lone mother about the way children should be brought up.

Participant observation

Participant observation involves a researcher actually joining the group or community she or he is studying, and participating in its activities over a period of time. The researcher tries to become an accepted part of the group to see the world the way members of the group do. For example, American sociologist Venkatesh (2009) spent eighteen months, spread over a period of seven years, participating in the life of a Chicago crack-dealing gang (the 'Black Kings'), as part of his work on poverty in the United States. Through his participation, Venkatesh was able to gain insights into the lives of drug-dealing gang members, crackheads, squatters, prostitutes, pimps, police officers and others linked to the crack-selling business.

THE THEORETICAL CONTEXT OF PARTICIPANT OBSERVATION

Participant observation is typically used by interpretivists to develop an understanding of the world from the point of view of the subjects of the research. Interpretivists argue that a sociological understanding of society can only be gained by understanding people's meanings. They suggest the most effective way of doing this is for researchers to put themselves in the same position as those they are studying. The idea is to get 'inside' people's heads to see the world as they do and how they make sense of it. Rather than testing hypotheses against evidence and searching for the causes of social events, *verstehen* (an understanding developed through empathy or close identification) and qualitative research are what sociology should be about.

The problem for interpretivists who choose participant observation is not the positivist concern with scientific detachment, but how to become involved enough to understand what is going on as seen through the eyes of group members, and to avoid letting the researcher's own values and prejudices distort the observations.

THE STAGES OF PARTICIPANT OBSERVATION AND RELATED PROBLEMS

The stages of participant observation can be summed up in terms of *getting in*, *staying in* and *getting out* of the group concerned. These stages, and the success of participant observation in general, rely a great deal on the personality and personal skills of the researcher, as they have to be adaptable enough to be accepted into the group and get on with group members.

Getting in

Joining a group raises many questions about the researcher's role. The researcher may adopt an **overt role** whereby the researcher declares his or her true identity to the group and the fact he or she is doing research. Alternatively, the researcher may adopt a **covert role** (concealing his or her role as a researcher), or a *cover story* (partially declaring his or her role as a researcher, but concealing elements of it). To participate successfully, particularly if adopting a covert role, the researcher would need to share some of the personal characteristics of the group, such as age, gender or ethnicity.

A covert role A covert role is likely to be adopted when criminal or deviant activities or lifestyles are involved, when overt researchers may be seen as a threat and unwelcome, as in the research by Humphreys on gay men in *The Tea Room Trade* (1970). The researcher who called himself 'James Patrick' (not his real name) in *A Glasgow Gang Observed* (1973) had to keep even his name secret, as he feared for his personal safety when studying violent gangs in Glasgow. A covert role may also be adopted where there is a risk of people's behaviour changing if they know they are being studied.

If a covert role is to be adopted and maintained, the researcher has little choice but to become a full participant in the group, because there is a risk of the research being ruined if the covert researcher's real identity and purpose are discovered. This may involve participation in illegal or unpleasant activities. It is also difficult to ask questions and take notes without arousing suspicion, and there are also moral and ethical concerns over observing and reporting on people's activities in secret, without obtaining their consent first.

An overt role Adopting an overt role has the advantage that things might be hidden from a member of a group in a way that they might not be from a trusted and known outsider – since she or he will have nothing to gain in the group. The openness and honesty of the researcher about what she or he is doing may itself encourage and build trust with group members. Other advantages are that the researcher may be able to ask questions or interview people, take notes, and avoid participation in illegal or immoral

An **overt role** is one whereby the researcher reveals to the group being studied his or her true identity and purpose.

A **covert role** is one where the researcher conceals from the group being studied his or her true identity as a researcher, to gain access to the group and avoid disrupting its normal behaviour.

behaviour, without arousing suspicion. Ethically and morally, it is right that people should be aware they are being studied, and able to give their informed consent.

Adopting an overt role does have problems though. For example, there is always the possibility that the behaviour of those being studied may be affected, raising questions over the validity of the research. As Whyte admitted in *Street Corner Society* (1955), quoting the gang leader 'Doc': 'You've slowed me up plenty since you've been down here. Now when I want to do something, I have to think what Bill Whyte would want me to know about it and how I can explain it . . . Before I used to do things by instinct.'

After deciding the nature of the role, the next problem is getting access to the group. The presence of a stranger needs explanation, and researchers need to establish 'bona fide' credentials for getting access to the group. This may involve gaining friendships with key individuals. For example, Whyte was able to do his research because of his contacts with the gang leader 'Doc', and Patrick knew a gang member called 'Tim', who was able to get him into the gang and provide some protection for him. Venkatesh befriended a gang leader named 'JT', who provided him with protection as he documented what he saw in the dangerous world of crack-dealing.

Participant observation in some contexts may require permission from higher authorities. This may mean the researcher is identified with authority, which may affect the behaviour of those being observed. For example, participant observation by an adult of students in a school will require the permission of the headteacher. This may mean the researcher is identified with the staff rather than the students. Willis required permission to carry out his research in a secondary school in Wolverhampton, and on occasion found that the teachers expected him to take responsibility for disciplining the students, undermining his participant observer role.

Staying in

The observer has to develop a role which will involve gaining the trust and cooperation of those observed, to enable continued participation in and observation of the group. Initially this will involve learning, listening and getting a sense of what's going on: 'Initially, keep your eyes and ears open but keep your mouth shut' was Doc's advice to Whyte in *Street Corner Society*.

Problems of staying in the group involve issues such as the need for extensive note-taking, which may be disruptive of the behaviour of the group, and how far to involve yourself without either losing the trust of the group or the objectivity of a researcher. Maintaining the trust of the group may involve getting involved with acts that the

---

Activity

Refer to the five participant observation studies by Whyte, Humphreys, Patrick, Barker and Venkatesh in the box opposite

1 Suggest ways that the personal characteristics of the researcher may have been important in enabling him or her in each case to do the research.
2 What problems might there be in generalizing the findings of such studies to other similar social groups?
3 Suggest any difficulties you think the researchers might have found in each study in:
   • getting into the group
   • staying in the group
   • getting out of the group without damaging personal relationships
4 Write about one side of A4 paper on any (a) ethical difficulties and (b) problems of validity you think there might have been with any of these examples of research.

Five classic studies of participant observation research

William Foote Whyte, *Street Corner Society* (1955)

This is a study of an Italian-American street corner gang in Boston in the United States. Whyte spent three and a half years in the area as a participant observer, including living in an Italian house with the group he was studying, and he became a member of the gang.

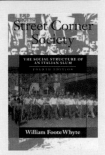

Laud Humphreys, *Tearoom Trade: Impersonal Sex in Public Places* (1970)

Humphreys wanted to study the gay subculture, and observed the sexual activity of gay men in ninety public toilets (the 'tearooms') in American cities in the 1960s. He initially adopted a covert role as a 'gay voyeur' (someone who liked watching sex between men) and 'watch-queen' – a lookout for other men in case of police interference. Humphreys became an accepted part of the gay scene in Chicago, through visiting gay bars and other parts of the gay scene. Adopting a more overt role, he also interviewed some men. Humphreys noted the car numbers of many gay men who used the 'tearooms' and, through police contacts, was able to get their addresses and background information for interview research a year later as part of a health survey. Humphreys had to disguise his appearance during this survey so he wouldn't be recognized by men he had met.

James Patrick, *A Glasgow Gang Observed* (1973)

James Patrick used a covert role to study a violent and delinquent teenage Glasgow gang over a period of four months between October 1966 and January 1967.

Eileen Barker, *The Making of a Moonie* (1984)

This is a study of members of the Unification Church, a controversial religious sect headed by the Revd Moon. Barker used overt participant observation over a period of six years, accepting the risk that this could mean the people she was studying could be affected by her presence.

Sudhir Venkatesh, *Gang Leader for a Day: A Rogue Sociologist Crosses the Line* (2009)

Venkatesh spent eighteen months, spread over seven years, participating in the life of the Black Kings – a Chicago crack-dealing gang – adopting an overt role. He lived with gang members, and slept on the couches and floors of people's apartments and of crack dens to gain insights into life in a poverty-stricken community. He observed much illegal and violent behaviour during his periods of participation.

researcher doesn't agree with. Barker (1984), for example, gave a talk to the Moonies which reinforced the beliefs of one Moonie, despite Barker's protests that she didn't believe a word of what she had said. Staying in might also involve the observer with unpleasant acts or people, and possibly criminal behaviour. For example, Whyte actually did some 'personating' – illegally voting twice in an election – as this was common practice in the group he was studying, and Venkatesh colluded in gang violence, when he took part in beating up the boyfriend of an abused teenager.

Getting out

Getting out of the group involves issues such as leaving the group without damaging relationships, becoming sufficiently detached to write an impartial and accurate account, and making sure members of the group cannot be identified. There may be possible reprisals against the researcher if criminal activities are involved. When Patrick's research on a Glasgow gang, using a covert role, was finally published, he faced threats to his personal safety.

ADVANTAGES AND STRENGTHS OF PARTICIPANT OBSERVATION

- The sociologist gains first-hand knowledge of the group being studied. By building a relationship of trust, more in-depth, valid data can be obtained than by other research techniques. It is the method least likely to impose the sociologist's own views on the group being studied, therefore providing a more valid understanding of a social group.
- It allows hypotheses and theories to emerge from the research as it goes along. This enables the researcher to discover things she or he may not even have thought about before. As Whyte noted in *Street Corner Society*, 'As I sat and listened, I learned the answers to questions that I would not even have had the sense to ask if I had been getting my information solely on an interviewing basis.'
- It is the best way to get at the meanings that a social activity has for those involved in it, through seeing the world through the eyes of members of the group.
- It may be the only possible method of research. For example, criminal and other deviant activities may be very difficult to investigate using other methods like interviews and questionnaires.
- People can be studied in their normal social situation over a period of time, rather than in the rather artificial and 'snapshot' context of a questionnaire or interview.
- There is less of a chance that the people being studied can mislead the researcher than there is using other methods. This might therefore produce more valid data.

DISADVANTAGES AND PROBLEMS OF PARTICIPANT OBSERVATION

- Positivists argue there are problems with the validity and reliability of participant observation studies. For example, there is no real way of checking the findings as there is no real evidence apart from the observations and interpretations of the researcher. What one researcher might regard as important may be missed or seen as unimportant by another. Even direct quotations from group members are often written down later, and may be only partially recalled – the researcher may remember what she or he *thought* was said. Rather than scientific detachment between the researcher and those being researched, positivists claim the method depends too heavily on the personal characteristics and personality of the researcher, creating in-built bias and making it almost impossible to check the findings of participant observation studies.

- The presence of a researcher, if she or he is known to the group, may in some ways change the group's behaviour simply because they know they are being studied. This *Hawthorne effect* may lead to problems for the validity of the research. For example, Whyte admits in *Street Corner Society* that knowledge of his presence and intentions may well have changed the behaviour of the gang.
- There is a danger of the researcher becoming so involved with the group, seeing the world only as the group does, and developing such loyalty to it, that she or he may find it difficult to stand back and report findings in a neutral way. 'Going native' – becoming so involved that all detachment is lost – is a possible problem. The researcher may then stop being a participant observer and become a non-observing participant.
- It is very time-consuming and expensive compared to other methods, as it involves the researcher being physically present in the group for long periods.
- Because only a small group is studied, it may not be representative, so it is difficult to make generalizations.
- There may be ethical issues if people do not know they are being observed, and therefore will not have the opportunity to give their informed consent to the research. Ethical issues also arise if knowledge is gained, during research, of activities harmful to others, and the researcher then faces the quandary of what course of action to follow. Telling the authorities might damage continuation of the research, but not telling them might cause harm to others. Venkatesh tried to overcome this

---

Activity

'Of course it was known that I was not a Moonie. I never pretended that I was, or that I was likely to become one. I admit that I was sometimes evasive, and I certainly did not always say everything that was on my mind, but I cannot remember any occasion on which I consciously lied to a Moonie. Being known as a non-member had its disadvantages, but by talking to people who had left the movement I was able to check that I was not missing any of the internal information which was available to rank-and-file members. At the same time, being an outsider who was "inside" had enormous advantages. I was allowed (even, on certain occasions, expected) to ask questions that no member would have presumed to ask either his leaders or his peers. Furthermore, several Moonies who felt that their problems were not understood by the leaders, and yet would not have dreamed of being disloyal to the movement by talking to their parents or other outsiders, could confide in me because of the very fact that I was both organisationally and emotionally uninvolved.'

(Barker (1984))

1 With reference to the passage above, explain in your own words the advantages Barker found in adopting an overt role.
2 What ethical problems are involved in Barker's admission that she was 'sometimes evasive'?
3 Barker says, 'Being known as a non-member had its disadvantages.' What disadvantages do you think she might have come across (either read the research, or think and guess!).
4 Do you consider there are any circumstances in which adopting a covert role in research might be justified? Explain your answer.
5 Humphreys took car numbers of gay men who used public toilets to obtain gay sex and, through police contacts, was able to get their addresses and background information for interview research a year later as part of a health survey. What ethical difficulties do you think this poses?

by avoiding situations where he might overhear the planning of criminal activity so he then wouldn't have to report it to the police.

- In personal terms, such research may be difficult for the researcher – for example, mixing with people they would rather not be with, getting involved in distasteful or illegal activities (in order to fit in) or even facing personal danger – as Patrick did in *A Glasgow Gang Observed*. Humphreys was actually arrested during his research on gays. Venkatesh had a gun put to his head and was kept captive for 24 hours because the crack-dealing gang initially thought he was a rival gang member. As well as illegal drug dealing, Venkatesh also witnessed a lot of beatings, drive-by shootings and other episodes of violence. His overt role and protection by the gang members and the wider community enabled him to avoid actively participating in such criminality, but he himself admitted that simply observing such activity was very unpleasant.

RELIABILITY AND VALIDITY IN PARTICIPANT OBSERVATION

Positivists tend to be critical of participant observation because they argue the data obtained are rarely quantified and are unreliable. Participant observation depends heavily on the sensitivity, skills, personality and personal characteristics of the observer, and this makes it very difficult to replicate a participant observation study in order to check the findings. As Whyte said in *Street Corner Society*: 'To some extent my approach must be unique to myself, to the particular situation, and to the state of knowledge existing when I began research.'

Participant observation is always to some extent selective observation – the researcher's interpretation of the significant and important things happening in a group. What one participant observer reports or interprets as significant may not be seen as such by another. Positivists would ask how interpretivists can prove they have interpreted the attitudes and experiences of others correctly. Participant observers use devices like extensive note-taking to accumulate evidence to help to ensure that their research is reliable as well as valid and can be checked by others. Other sociologists are, though, ultimately left to rely on the memory, observational and interpretive skills of the researcher, and this raises problems for the validity and reliability of the research that are difficult to resolve.

Activity

1 Identify and explain two criticisms positivists might make of participant observation as a research method.

2 Identify and explain two reasons why interpretivists might argue that participant observation is the most effective method of understanding and explaining social life.

3 Suggest two reasons sociologists who employ participant observation might give to claim their work is as 'scientific' as any positivist research.

4 Suggest three ways that the social characteristics of the researcher might make it difficult to conduct participant observation in a primary or secondary school classroom.

5 With examples, explain the advantages of adopting (a) a covert role and (b) an overt role in participant observation.

6 What are the ethical and moral issues which make participant observation difficult, particularly if using a covert role?

7 Explain what is meant by the risk in participant observation that 'the researcher may stop being a participant observer and become a non-observing participant'.

8 Look at the weaknesses and disadvantages of participant observation listed earlier. Suggest ways that a skilled participant observer might be able to overcome the problems identified.

9 Much participant observation research has been done on deviant groups. Suggest reasons why this might be the case.

Exam-style questions

1 Explain what is meant by the term 'sampling frame'. *(2 marks)*

2 Explain what is meant by the term 'hypothesis'. *(2 marks)*

3 Explain what is meant by the term 'representative sample'. *(2 marks)*

4 Explain what is meant by the term 'case study'. *(2 marks)*

5 Suggest **two** reasons why sociologists might undertake a pilot study. *(4 marks)*

6 Suggest **two** reasons why sociologists might use a sample when doing a survey. *(4 marks)*

7 Suggest **two** advantages that sociologists might find in using postal questionnaires. *(4 marks)*

8 Examine the advantages of using structured interviews in sociological research. *(20 marks)*

9 Examine the advantages of using participant observation in sociological research. *(20 marks)*

10 Examine the problems of using experiments in sociological research. *(20 marks)*

CHAPTER SUMMARY AND REVISION CHECKLIST

After studying this chapter, you should be able to:

- explain the difference between positivism and interpretivism, and how these two approaches use different research methods.

- discuss a range of practical, ethical and theoretical (PET) issues that a sociological researcher might consider when choosing a research topic, a research method and conducting research.

- explain what is meant by the issues of reliability, validity and ethics in social research.

- explain what is meant by 'operationalizing concepts' in social research, and why sociologists might need to do this.

- distinguish between quantitative and qualitative data, and the advantages and limitations of each.

- identify the difference between primary and secondary sources, and the strengths and limitations of the different types of quantitative and qualitative data obtained from each.

- explain the difference between public and personal documents.

- outline the features, and strengths and weaknesses, of content analysis and how it might be used in sociological research.

- explain, with examples, the uses, advantages and limitations of official statistics.

- explain the uses and problems of the experimental/laboratory method in sociology, including field experiments.

- explain how the comparative method might be used as an alternative to the experimental one.

- explain the main features, stages and problems of the social survey, and the various sampling methods sociologists use to gain representative samples.

- explain the uses, strengths and weaknesses of different types of questionnaires and interviews, including the problems of imposition and the validity and reliability of these methods.

- explain fully the problem of interviewer bias.

- explain the uses, strengths and weaknesses of participant observation as a research method, including practical, ethical and theoretical (PET) problems, and the issues of validity and reliability.

- examine the uses, strengths and limitations of non-participant observation.

- discuss the strengths and weaknesses of longitudinal studies, case studies and life histories.

- explain what is meant by methodological pluralism and triangulation, and why sociologists might want to use a range of methods in sociological research.

- carry out small-scale research of your own, drawing on the various methods outlined in this chapter.

KEY TERMS

(these are already defined in the text, and may also be found in the glossary at the end of the book)

covert role	interpretivism	primary data	secondary data
cultural capital	interviewer bias	public documents	social facts
ethics	macro approach	qualitative data	survey population
focus group	methodological pluralism	quantitative data	surveys
group interview	micro approach	reliability/replication	triangulation
Hawthorne effect	overt role	representative sample	validity
hypothesis	personal documents	sample	verstehen
imposition problem	pilot survey	sampling frame	victim survey
informed consent	positivism	sampling methods	

There are a variety of free tests and other activities that can be used to assess your learning at

www.politybooks.com/browne

CHAPTER

6 Education

Contents

CHAPTER

6 Education

Topic 1

SPECIFICATION AREA

The role and purpose of education, including vocational education and training, in contemporary society

The role and purpose of education in contemporary society

Education is a major social institution, and around 13 per cent of total public spending (spending by central and local government) goes on education – around £86 billion a year in 2012. Schools in Britain command a captive audience of virtually all children between the ages of 5 and 17 (age 18 from 2015). During this period of compulsory education, young people spend about half of the time they are awake at school or college during term time – a major time commitment – and the education system is therefore a major agency of secondary socialization in advanced contemporary societies. This topic examines a range of sociological explanations of why such importance is attached to education.

Full-time education is compulsory in the UK from ages 5–17 (age 18 from 2015), though many children start younger in reception classes at primary and infant schools, or at pre-schools, nurseries and playgroups. About 13 per cent of everything national and local government spends goes on education. Why do you think such importance is attached to education?

Sociological perspectives on the role of education in society

THE FUNCTIONALIST PERSPECTIVE ON EDUCATION

The functionalist perspective on education follows the same principles as all functionalist approaches to the study of society. It is concerned with the links between education and other social institutions, such as the family and the workplace, and the functions or role of education for society as a whole. Functionalists see education as an important agency of socialization, helping to maintain social stability through the development of value consensus, social harmony and **social cohesion**. Education is seen as playing a key role in preparing young people for adulthood, citizenship and working life, providing them with the means for improving their lives and life chances through upward **social mobility**, and preparing them for a rapidly changing society.

The two most important writers on education from a functionalist perspective have been Émile Durkheim (1858–1917) and the American functionalist Talcott Parsons. They identified four basic functions of education.

1 Passing on society's culture and building social solidarity

Education meets a key **functional prerequisite** by passing on to new generations the central or core values and culture of a society. This is achieved by both the **hidden curriculum** and the actual subjects learnt at school (the overt curriculum), for example through subjects like Citizenship and Personal, Social and Health Education (PSHE). This unites or 'glues' people together and builds **social solidarity** by giving them shared values (a value consensus) and a shared culture.

2 Providing a bridge between the particularistic values and ascribed status of the family and the universalistic values and achieved status of contemporary advanced societies

Durkheim argued that schools are a 'society in miniature' – a small-scale version of society as a whole that prepares young people for life in the wider adult society.

Parsons sees schools as important places of secondary socialization, increasingly taking over from the family as children grow older. He argues schools provide a bridge

Social cohesion refers to the bonds or 'glue' that bring people together and integrate them into a united society.
Social mobility refers to movement of groups or individuals up or down the social hierarchy.

Functional prerequisites refer to the basic needs that must be met if society is to survive.
The **hidden curriculum** concerns not so much the formal content of subject lessons and examinations (the overt curriculum) as the way teaching and learning are organized. This includes the general routines of school life which influence and mould the attitudes and behaviour of students, such as the school rules and discipline, dress codes, school organization, and so on.
Social solidarity refers to the integration of people into society through shared values, a common culture, shared understandings and social ties that bring them together and build *social cohesion*.

Particularistic values are rules and values that give a priority to personal relationships.
Universalistic values are rules and values that apply equally to all members of society, regardless of who they are.
A **meritocracy** (or meritocratic society) is a society where occupational positions (jobs) and pay are allocated on the basis purely of people's individual talents, abilities, qualifications and skills – their individual merits. In Britain today, this nearly always means educational qualifications.

between the **particularistic values** and ascribed status of the family, and the **universalistic values** and achieved status of contemporary societies which are based on the values of **meritocracy**.

Children's status in the family is ascribed and they are judged in terms of particularistic values. For example, their status is ascribed as a child and not an adult, or as a younger rather than an older brother or sister, and they are treated as special individuals and judged differently from everyone else outside the family. However, wider contemporary adult society is meritocratic. People have to earn their status positions according to their individual achievements, such as talent, skill or educational qualifications.

In this situation of achieved status, the same universalistic values or rules apply to everyone, regardless of who they are. For example, a teacher marking student essays might reasonably be expected to mark every essay by the same criteria (universalistic values), not give different marks depending on whether they liked the student or not (particularistic values), and those same students might be expected to achieve a place at university because of their exam grades, not because they knew someone who worked there.

Activity

1 Identify those features which make school life like a 'society in miniature', preparing people for wider society.
2 Parsons suggests that schooling provides a bridge between the family and wider adult society. Think about your own schooling, and the way that, as you moved from infant school through to the end of secondary schooling, teacher attitudes and the experience of schooling changed. Can you identify any evidence of a move from particularism to universalism?
3 Identify all the features of both the formal curriculum and the hidden curriculum, with examples, which transmit values and culture from one generation to the next. To what extent do you think those things learnt in school actually unite people in society?

Human capital refers to the knowledge and skills possessed by a workforce that increase that workforce's value and usefulness to employers.

The **division of labour** is the division of work or occupations into a large number of specialized tasks, each of which is carried out by one worker or a group of workers.

3 Developing human capital – a trained and qualified labour force

Schultz (1971) originally developed the theory of **human capital**, which suggests that high levels of spending on education and training are justified as these develop people's knowledge and skills, and this investment is an important factor in a successful economy.

Functionalists see this development of human capital through the expansion of schooling and higher education as necessary to provide a properly trained, qualified and flexible labour force to undertake the wide range of different jobs which arise from the specialized **division of labour** in a modern economy. They argue the education system prepares this labour force, and makes sure the best and most qualified people end up in the jobs requiring the greatest skills and responsibilities. This is discussed further in a later section on vocational education (see pages 349–51).

4 Selecting and allocating people for roles in a meritocratic society, and legitimizing social inequality

For functionalists, like Davis and Moore (1967 [1945]), the education system is a means of selecting or sifting people for different levels of the job market, and ensuring the most talented and qualified individuals are allocated to the most important jobs. By grading people through streaming and test and exam results, the education system is a major method of role allocation – fitting the most suitable people into the hierarchy of unequal positions in society.

In a meritocratic society, access to jobs, and to positions of wealth, status and power, depend mainly on educational qualifications and other skills and talents. Davis and Moore suggest that in this educational race for success there is **equality of educational opportunity**, and everyone who has the ability and talent and puts in the effort has an equal chance of coming out ahead. Inequalities in society are therefore legitimized – made to seem fair and just. Those who succeed deserve their success, and those who fail have only themselves to blame.

> **Equality of educational opportunity** is the idea that every child, regardless of his or her social class background, ability to pay school fees, ethnic background, gender or disability, should have an equal chance of doing as well as his or her ability will allow.

Activity

To what extent do you think the school work you are doing, or did, and the qualifications you obtain(ed) at school might be preparing, or did prepare, you for doing a job? Identify, with examples, the links between your school subjects and exams and earning a living.

Table 6.1 Criticisms of the functionalist view of education

Functionalist view	Criticism
Education passes on society's culture from one generation to the next, including shared norms and values underpinning value consensus. These provide the 'social glue' which creates social solidarity and social cohesion.	*Marxists* would argue that this view ignores the inequalities in power in society. There is no value consensus, and the culture and values passed on by the school are those of the dominant or ruling class. *Feminists* might argue the school passes on patriarchal values, and disadvantages girls and women.
Education provides a bridge between the particularistic values and ascribed status of the family and the universalistic values and achieved status of wider society.	There is some doubt about how far contemporary society is really based on universalistic values and achieved status. Many in the upper class inherit wealth, and there are many elite jobs where ascribed status characteristics such as social class, gender and ethnic background still have a very important influence.
Education provides a trained and qualified labour force.	The link between educational qualifications and pay and job status is a weak one, and certainly much weaker than functionalists assume. The content of what people learn in schools often has very little to do directly with what they actually do in their jobs. Most occupational skills are learnt 'on the job' or through firms' own training schemes. The demand for educational qualifications for many occupations is simply an attempt to raise the status of the occupation, rather than providing the knowledge and skill requirements necessary for performing the job.
Effective role selection and allocation. Education selects the most suitable and qualified people and matches them with the right jobs in a meritocratic society.	The education system does not act as a neutral 'sieve', simply grading and selecting students according to their ability. Social class particularly, but also ethnicity and gender seem to be the major factors influencing success or failure in education. There is no equality of opportunity in education – everyone does not start at the same point, and not everyone has the same chance of success in education, even when they have the same ability.
Education legitimizes social inequality.	Bowles and Gintis (2011 [1976]) (discussed later) argue that the education system simply disguises the fact that there is no equality of opportunity in education, and that it is social class particularly, but also ethnicity and gender that are the main influences on educational success.

THE NEW RIGHT

The New Right approach to education policy reflects many of the ideas of the functionalist perspective. The New Right argues education should be concerned not with promoting equality or equality of opportunity, but with training the workforce, making sure the most able students have their talents developed and are recruited into the most important jobs, while others are prepared for lower-level employment. Education should socialize young people into collective values and responsible citizenship, and thereby build social cohesion and social solidarity to ensure a stable and united society.

New Right theorists like Chubb and Moe (1990, 1992) believe an education system controlled by state and local authorities (local councils) is not the best means of achieving these aims, as it imposes a single type of school regardless of the wishes and needs of parents or local communities. They argue there should be a free market in education, with a range of different types of independently managed schools and colleges, run like private businesses, tailored to, answerable to and shaped by the wishes and needs of local communities of parents and students. Competition for students and funding, combined with a free choice of school for parents/students, will lead to a more efficient education system delivering better value for the taxpayer who funds education. This **marketization** of education, discussed in Topic 4, is seen as producing benefits for both the taxpayer and the consumers of education, such as a higher quality of education and educational standards, and a more skilled and qualified workforce. The New Right therefore sees education operating much like supermarkets, which are forced to supply cheaper and better-quality products as they compete for customers.

Marketization is the process whereby services, like education or health, that were previously controlled and run by the state, have government or local council control reduced or removed altogether, and become subject to the free market forces of supply and demand, based on competition and consumer choice.

MARXIST PERSPECTIVES ON EDUCATION

Marxists see education primarily as a means of social control, encouraging young people to be conformists, to accept their social position and not to do anything to upset the current patterns of inequality in power, wealth and income. Marxists emphasize the way the education system reproduces existing social class inequalities, and passes them on from one generation to the next. At the same time, it does this by giving the impression that those who fail in education do so because of their lack of ability and effort, and have only themselves to blame. In this way, people are encouraged to accept the positions they find themselves in after schooling, even though it is disadvantages arising from social class background that create inequalities in educational success.

The work of Althusser: education as an ideological state apparatus

The French Marxist Althusser (1971) saw the main role of education in a capitalist society as the reproduction of an efficient and obedient labour force. This involves two aspects:

False consciousness is a failure by members of a social class to recognize their real interests.

- the reproduction of the necessary technical skills.
- the reproduction of ruling class ideology (the dominant beliefs and values) and the socialization of workers into accepting this dominant ideology (this is known as **false consciousness**).

Althusser argues that, to prevent the working class from rebelling against their exploitation, the ruling class must try to win their hearts and minds by persuading them to accept ruling class ideology. This process of persuasion is carried out by a number of **ideological state apparatuses**, such as the family, the mass media, the law, religion and the education system. Althusser argues that in contemporary Western societies the main ideological state apparatus is the education system, which:

Ideological state apparatuses are agencies which serve to spread the ideology, and justify the power, of the dominant social class.

- passes on ruling class ideology justifying the capitalist system.
- selects people for the different social classes as adults, developing the right attitudes and behaviour; for example, workers are persuaded to accept and submit to exploitation, and managers and administrators to rule.

Schooling, repression and hegemonic control: Illich and Freire

The Marxist idea of education reproducing inequality and a conformist, submissive and obedient working class is reflected in the work of Illich (1995). Illich argues schools are repressive institutions which promote conformity and encourage students into passive acceptance of existing inequalities and the interests of the powerful, rather than encouraging them to be critical and to think for themselves. Illich suggests schools do this by rewarding those who accept the school regime with qualifications and access to higher levels of the education system and better jobs. Those who don't conform, or who question the authority of teachers or the value of the education provided by schools, are excluded from further progress in education, and end up in lower-level jobs. Illich suggests the solution to this is to abolish schooling altogether – what he calls deschooling.

Freire (1996) sees schools as repressive institutions, where learners are conditioned to accept oppressive relations of domination and subordination, and to listen to their betters, for example through obeying teachers and deferring to their superior knowledge.

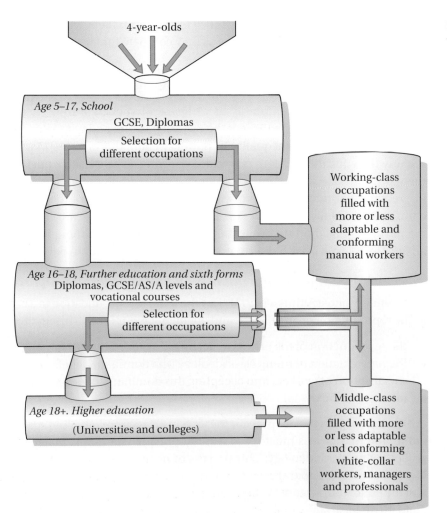

Figure 6.1 Education and the class structure

Activity

1 Refer to figure 6.1. Suggest the attitudes and values that might be required by those leaving the education system at different stages for different levels of employment.
2 Can you think of values or ideas that are passed on through the education system which might be in the interests of the dominant groups in society rather than in the interests of all?

Hegemony refers to the dominance in society of the ruling class's set of ideas over others, and acceptance of and consent to them by the rest of society. **Hegemonic control** is where control of the working class is mainly achieved through the hegemony and acceptance of ruling class ideas

The work of Althusser, Illich and Freire suggests that the education system plays an important role in producing the **hegemony** and **hegemonic control** of the ruling class – convincing the rest of society to accept the truth and superiority of the ruling class's set of ideas over others, and winning their consent to continued control by the dominant class.

Bowles and Gintis: schooling and the 'long shadow of work'

Bowles and Gintis (2011 [1976]) argue, like Althusser, that the major role of education in capitalist societies is the reproduction of labour power – a hard-working, submissive and disciplined workforce. Bowles and Gintis argue that such a workforce is reproduced in two main ways:

1 Through the hidden curriculum of schooling and the correspondence, or very close similarity, between the social relationships at school and at work – in particular, the way schooling operates in the 'long shadow of work'.
2 Through the role of the education system in legitimizing or justifying inequality.

Schooling and the 'long shadow of work'   Bowles and Gintis argue that the world of work influences the organization of education. They suggest this is like work casting a long shadow over education, with the hidden curriculum in schools corresponding closely to many features of the workplace. Table 6.2 on the next page illustrates some elements of this correspondence between the hidden curriculum at school and relations at the workplace.

Activity

1 Describe in detail five features of the hidden curriculum found in your school, or the one you once attended, which reflect the expectations of employers and the demands of the workplace after school.
2 Drawing on your own experiences at school, what features of your education do you think prepared / will prepare you most for life after school? Think of particular subjects studied and activities undertaken, and the features of the hidden curriculum in table 6.2 which were/are found in your school.
3 Using examples from your own school life, to what extent do you agree with Bowles and Gintis that 'schooling operates in the long shadow of work'?
4 The features of the hidden curriculum shown in table 6.2 are mainly influenced by Bowles and Gintis's Marxist approach. The functionalists also see the hidden curriculum as an important means of teaching students the culture and values of society so that a value consensus can be built and society can be kept stable and harmonious. Suggest ways that functionalist writers might alter the second column in table 6.2 ('What is being taught') to give it more of a functionalist than a Marxist 'flavour'.

Table 6.2 The hidden curriculum

Features of the hidden curriculum	What is being taught
Privileges and responsibilities given to sixth formers	Respect for elders and superiors/managers
School rules, detentions and exclusions, rewards like merit badges, prizes, good marks, etc.	Conformity to society's rules and laws, whether you agree with them or not
School assemblies	Respect for religious beliefs and the dominant moral values
Males and females often playing different sports, having different dress rules, and being counselled into different subjects, further education courses, and careers; many teachers having different expectations of boys and girls	Males and females being encouraged to conform to gender stereotypes and work in different jobs; for example, women being encouraged into taking primary responsibility for housework and childcare
Competitive sports and competition against each other in class rather than cooperating together; students being tested individually – being encouraged to rely on themselves rather than others	Workers having to compete for jobs and wages, and individuals having to stand on their own two feet – not joining with other workers to take action
Respecting authority of teachers regardless of what they say or do; pupils always having to justify where they're going and why, and do as they're told	Respect for those in authority, such as bosses at work and the police
Punctuality/being on time – time belonging to the school, not the pupil	Good time-keeping at work – the employer pays for the worker's time, so it belongs to the firm, not the worker
Concentrating on schoolwork, whether or not it's boring and whether or not you want to do it	Workers having to accept boring, menial and repetitive jobs
Value being placed on hard work and getting on	Everyone being able to make it to the top if she or he tries hard enough
Grading by ability, and exam success/failure	The differences in pay and status between social classes being natural and justified – those higher up are more intelligent and better qualified
Rewarding (by high grades) qualities of dependability, punctuality and acceptance of authority	Workers' duty to be dependable, be punctual and accept bosses' authority
Different streams and bands	Getting used to accepting the different levels of the job market, such as professional, managerial, skilled, semi-skilled and unskilled manual occupations, which are seen to be based on ability
Pupils lack power and control about the subjects taught or how the school is run or the school day organized	Workers' lack of power and control at work
The authority hierarchy of the school, involving pupils fitting into a complex organization of heads, deputies, heads of department, year heads, etc.	Messages about being placed in the hierarchies of power and control in society and accepting it – for example, in the authority hierarchy at work
The school curriculum being broken up into separate subjects which are clearly separated from one another	Work is divided into many separate jobs (the division of labour) which keeps the workforce from having knowledge of the whole process
Schools aim to motivate pupils by marks, grades and qualifications	Working for pay in unfulfilling and powerless jobs

The legitimation of inequality   Bowles and Gintis argue that the educational system:

- helps to maintain, justify and explain (legitimate or legitimize) the system of social inequality in capitalist society.
- helps people to come to terms with their own position in it.
- therefore helps to reduce discontent and opposition to inequality.

Bowles and Gintis reject the functionalist view that social class inequalities in capitalist society arise from fair competition in education, in which everyone stands an equal chance. In contrast, they argue that social class background, ethnicity and gender are the main factors related to success or failure in education and the job market. People from upper and upper middle-class backgrounds (and who are white and male) tend to obtain higher qualifications and better jobs than working-class children of similar ability. Bowles and Gintis see both equality of opportunity and meritocracy as myths that promote the idea that failure in education arises from lack of ability or hard work, when in most cases it arises because of social class and family background. Education is therefore seen as acting as a kind of confidence trick, that hides the fact that it maintains and reproduces the existing pattern of social class inequalities between generations, and in most cases simply confirms individuals' class of origin (the one they were born into) as their class of destination (the one they end up in as adults).

Criticisms of Althusser, Illich, Freire, and Bowles and Gintis

These theorists have been criticized on two main fronts:

- There is a lack of detailed research into schools. Althusser, and Bowles and Gintis, for example, assume the hidden curriculum is actually influencing pupils, but pupils are often not passive recipients of education, and, despite what Illich and Freire suggest, pupils often have little regard for teachers' authority and school rules and discipline (as Willis's research below shows).
- Bowles and Gintis, Illich and Freire ignore some influences of the formal curriculum. This does not always seem designed to promote the ideal employee for capitalism, and to develop uncritical, passive and unquestioning conformist behaviour. The humanities and subjects like sociology produce critical thinkers, while work-related courses remain of relatively low status. Employers often complain that the education system does *not* produce the well-qualified and conformist workers with suitable skills that Marxist writers suggest it does.

The work of Willis

Paul Willis's work, *Learning to Labour: How Working Class Kids Get Working Class Jobs* (1977), helps to overcome some of the weaknesses of more traditional Marxist approaches like those of Althusser and Bowles and Gintis. Willis adopts a Marxist approach, but also draws on the interactionist perspective.

Willis recognizes that schools do not produce a willing and obedient workforce – a quick glance at almost any secondary school provides evidence that students do not always obey teachers, that they can be disruptive and challenge the school. Willis says it is easy to understand why middle-class young people willingly go into secure and well-paid middle-class career jobs, but what is more difficult to explain is why working-class young people go so willingly into dead-end, low-paid and boring manual working-class jobs.

Willis studied a group of twelve working-class male pupils he referred to as 'the lads' in a school on a working-class housing estate in Wolverhampton in the 1970s. The lads developed an **anti-school** or **counter-school subculture** opposed both to the main aims of the school, and to the 'ear 'oles' – conformist pupils who generally conformed to school values. 'The lads' attached little value to the aims of the school, such as gaining qualifications, and their main priority was to free themselves from control by the school, to avoid or disrupt lessons, to have a 'laff' and to get into the world of work as soon as possible.

Rejecting schooling and wanting to leave school as soon as they could and escape from the 'pen-pushing' of the 'ear 'oles', the lads did not see school as relevant to them.

A **subculture** is a smaller culture held by a group or class of people within the main culture of a society, in some ways different from the main culture, but with many aspects in common.

An **anti-school** or **counter-school subculture** is a group organized around a set of values, attitudes and behaviour in opposition to the main aims of a school.

Their priorities were to get their hands on money, to impress their mates, to keep up with older drinkers in the pub, to impress the girls, and to show they could 'graft' in male manual jobs as well as the next man.

In this context, school was boring, pointless and irrelevant to their lives, and stopped them smoking, drinking, going out at night, getting a job and cash, and involving themselves in the 'real' world of male, manual work.

Willis found a similarity between the counter-school culture and the workplace culture of male lower working-class jobs, such as **sexism**, a lack of respect for authority and an emphasis on 'having a laff' to escape the boring and oppressive nature of both school and work.

Willis's research suggests that schools are not directly preparing the sort of obedient and docile labour force required by capitalism which Althusser and Bowles and Gintis suggest. Young, working-class males are not forced or persuaded by the school to leave and look for manual jobs, but actively reject school through the counter-school culture and willingly enter male semi-skilled and unskilled work the minute they leave school.

> **Sexism** refers to prejudice or discrimination against people, especially women, because of their sex.

Activity

1 To what extent do you think Willis's research might be true of all schools? Do you think there are any reasons why there might be uncertainty about this given the size of Willis's study?

2 What evidence is/was there at your own school of an anti-school or counter-school subculture like that of 'the lads'? Give examples of the types of behaviour displayed by such students, and suggest reasons for it.

A COMPARISON OF FUNCTIONALIST AND MARXIST PERSPECTIVES ON EDUCATION

Similarities between functionalist and Marxist views of education

- Both see schools playing a role in legitimizing (justifying and explaining) social inequality.
- Both are macro (large-scale) theories concerned with the structural relationship between education and other parts of the social system, such as the economy and social inequality.
- Both see education as serving the needs of industrial and/or capitalist society.
- Both see the education system as a powerful influence on students, ensuring they conform to existing social values and norms.

But they have differences, too, summarized in table 6.3.

Criticisms of both Marxist and functionalist perspectives

- They both place too much emphasis on the role of education in forming students' identity, and they pay too little attention to the influences of other agencies of socialization, such as the family, the mass media and work.
- They don't fully consider the way students react to schooling in ways that aren't necessarily 'functional' for the social system or capitalism. For example, pupils disrupt schools, play truant and don't learn, and workers' earlier experience of schooling does not stop them from going on strike. (However, note the exception of Willis's work here.)

Table 6.3 Differences between functionalist and Marxist views of education

Functionalism	Marxism
• Education serves the needs of an *industrial* society with an advanced division of labour.	• Education serves the needs of a *capitalist* society divided into social classes.
• Education serves the needs of the social system by socializing new generations into society's culture and shared norms and values, leading to social harmony, social cohesion, stability and social integration.	• Education serves the needs of capitalism by socializing young people into the dominant ideology (ruling-class norms and values), leading to an obedient workforce and the stability of capitalism.
• The hidden curriculum helps to prepare society's future citizens for participation in a society based on value consensus.	• The hidden curriculum helps to persuade society's future citizens to accept the dominant ideology and their position in a society based on inequality, exploitation and conflict.
• Education provides a means for upward social mobility for those who have the ability.	• With the exception of a few individuals, education confirms individuals' class of origin (the one they were born into) as their class of destination (the one they end up in as adults). Education therefore contributes to the reproduction of present class inequalities between generations, and does not provide a means of upward social mobility for most people.
• Education justifies and explains (legitimizes) social inequality, as roles are allocated according to meritocratic criteria such as educational qualifications, in a society in which all have equality of opportunity.	• Education legitimizes social class inequality by persuading working-class individuals to accept that their lack of power and control at work and in society generally is due to their lack of academic ability, effort and achievement, when in fact they do not have the same opportunities as those who are more advantaged.

- They both see too tight a link between education and the economy, and exaggerate the extent to which schools provide a ready, willing and qualified labour force. The new emphasis on vocational education and pressure to drive up school standards are a direct response to employers who criticized schools for not providing a suitably disciplined and qualified labour force.

Activity

1. Suggest three ways in which schooling prepares young people for the world of work.
2. Explain what is meant by the legitimization of social class inequality, and suggest two ways in which schooling might achieve this.
3. Identify and explain two ways in which the educational system contributes to the economy.
4. Explain what is meant by the 'hidden curriculum', and suggest two ways this might prepare children for adult life.

Vocational education and the development of human capital

The emphasis on developing what Schultz called *human capital*, by preparing young people for work and making education meet the needs of the economy, is known as vocational education. Functionalists and the New Right see this in a beneficial way, as helping to boost the economy. Marxists tend to view vocational education largely as a second-rate education for those from working-class backgrounds, concerned with producing passive and conformist workers to support a profit-making capitalist society, while the middle class enjoy a more academic education leading to well-paid positions of power and influence in society.

A key focus of vocational education in contemporary Britain has been on improving the quality of the basic skills of the workforce, and in particular those of 14- to 18-year-old young people. It was thought that, by making the education system produce a more skilled and flexible labour force, this would better meet the needs of employers and would enable Britain to maintain a successful position in the world economy. Measures to achieve this have included:

- Work experience programmes for pupils in school years 10 and 11 to ease the transition from school to work, and help/encourage them to get jobs successfully and carry them out well, with a better understanding of work and the economy.
- More educational courses, and government training schemes for those leaving school, which are closely related to the world of work, and concerned with learning work-related skills. For example, school-/college- and work-based NVQs (National Vocational Qualifications), Diplomas, BTECs, City and Guilds and OCR Nationals were developed to provide nationally approved and recognized qualifications for vocational courses. Vocational GCSEs and Applied GCEs (vocational A levels) were intended as vocational alternatives to academic GCSEs and A levels.
- An expansion of post-16 education and training.
- A stronger emphasis on key skills in the use and application of number, and in communication and information technology, as well as basic literacy and numeracy skills. These are the skills that most employers find that school leavers lack.

All these changes were designed to produce a more flexible labour force, fitting education to the needs of employers.

CRITICISMS OF VOCATIONAL EDUCATION

Work experience is often seen by school students as boring and repetitive, involving little development of their skills and having little to do with their future ambitions. Post-school training schemes are often similarly criticized for providing little development of skills, for being used as a source of cheap labour by employers, and for not leading to 'proper' jobs at the end of the training. Such schemes are sometimes seen as having more to do with reducing politically embarrassing unemployment statistics, reducing the proportion of NEET 16- to 18-year-olds (NEET means 'not in education, employment or training') and thereby keeping young people away from crime and other forms of deviance, than with producing a skilled labour force.

Vocational education and qualifications, like NVQs and vocational GCSEs and Applied GCEs (vocational A levels), are often seen as having lower status than more traditional academic subjects and courses. Vocational qualifications are, in general, less likely to lead to university entry, and are more likely to lead to lower-status, lower-paid jobs as adults. Parents, teachers and students themselves therefore often see vocational qualifications as an inferior or second-rate option compared to more traditional academic subjects and courses. Those from working-class backgrounds are more likely to find themselves taking vocational subjects and courses, reinforcing divisions between social classes.

Birdwell et al. (2011) suggested that secondary schools in England and Wales routinely neglect pupils with vocational aspirations, and focus on brighter children destined to go on to higher education. Schools failed to help teenagers prepare for the

Do you think work experience programmes at school are useful? Do you think vocational courses are more or less valuable to students compared to doing more academic courses like traditional GCSEs and AS and A levels?

world of work, offering them little careers advice or help in finding jobs that would suit them. The report found that many of the vocational qualifications that young people are encouraged to aim for turn out to be worthless, that work-related training was found to be of low quality, and that schools undervalued the importance of part-time work, after-school clubs and volunteering in building up young people's skills and experience.

Activity

1. Should schools and colleges be concerned mainly with meeting the needs of business and industry, and fitting people into the job market? Or should they be concerned with the development of free-thinking, creative and critical individuals, allowing them to pursue and develop their interests? Suggest two advantages and two disadvantages of each view.
2. Think back over your school work experience programmes. Were they very useful to you? Give reasons for your answer.
3. Do you think AS and A levels have the same status as vocational qualifications, such as NVQs, BTEC, Diplomas and applied GCEs? Explain your answer.
4. Is offering the option of vocational GCSEs at age 14 a sensible idea? How might this affect the future career prospects of young people who choose them, compared to those doing traditional academic GCSEs? Do you think this might have any effect on equal opportunities for all in education?

Exam-style questions

1 Explain what is meant by the term 'vocational education'. *(2 marks)*

2 Explain what is meant by the term 'meritocracy'. *(2 marks)*

3 Suggest **three** ways in which schooling might contribute to social stability. *(6 marks)*

4 Suggest **three** ways in which the education system contributes to the economy. *(6 marks)*

5 Outline the ways that Marxists see education producing a passive and conformist labour force. *(12 marks)*

6 Assess the view that the main function of education is to prepare and select young people for their future roles in employment. *(20 marks)*

Topic 2

SPECIFICATION AREA

Relationships and processes within schools, with particular reference to teacher/ pupil relationships, pupil subcultures, the hidden curriculum, and the organisation of teaching and learning

School organization, school processes and the teaching and learning context

Underachievement is the failure of people to fulfil their potential – they do not do as well in education (or other areas) as their talents and abilities suggest they should.

Research has suggested that how well students perform in school, or other educational institutions, and in particular social patterns of **underachievement** in education, which are discussed in the next topic, are affected by school processes and organization, and the teaching and learning context. These include all the things that go on in schools and school classrooms, and the student experience of education: factors like the quality of teaching and the headteacher's leadership, school ethos, teacher attitudes and expectations, school discipline, the curriculum offered, the choices available to students, and the way students are organized into ability groups.

THE INTERACTIONIST PERSPECTIVE

Much of the material in this topic is based on the interactionist perspective. Interactionist approaches tend to use micro or small-scale detailed studies of what actually happens within schools and classrooms, in contrast to the macro or large-scale structuralist approaches of functionalism and Marxism. By using qualitative research methods like unstructured interviews or participant or non-participant observation, interactionists seek to discover how, through interaction with others, teachers or pupils experience education and come to interpret and define situations, and develop meanings which influence the way they behave and the educational progress they make. This is shown by issues like teacher expectations and stereotyping, streaming, labelling and the self-fulfilling prophecy, how students react to these and how they affect their learning and educational progress.

SCHOOL ETHOS AND THE HIDDEN CURRICULUM

The *ethos* of a school refers to the character, atmosphere or 'climate' of a school. This might include things like whether:

- all pupils, whatever abilities they may have, are valued, rewarded, praised and encouraged to fulfil their potential in every way.
- there is an emphasis mainly on academic success, and/or artistic and/or sporting achievements.
- there is an emphasis on the social, moral and spiritual/religious development of students.
- there is an emphasis on equal opportunities, with intolerance of racism and sexism, the promotion of multicultural education, and support and encouragement for students with special educational needs.

- parents are actively encouraged to get involved in their children's learning and the life of the school, through parent–teacher associations (PTAs), as voluntary helpers in the classroom and on school trips.
- a school keeps in close touch with parents through newsletters and school reports.
- a school has friendly, happy and respectful relationships between students and between staff and students.
- a school participates in cultural activities outside school, like school recreational and cultural trips, and involvement in local community activities.
- a school encourages pupils to participate actively in school life, like taking part in decision-making through school councils.

The hidden curriculum

The ethos of a school is normally reflected in and supported by the hidden curriculum, as well as the formal programme of subjects and lessons making up the overt curriculum, which a school designs to promote the educational achievement of students.

Students learn attitudes and values reflected in the school ethos and hidden curriculum simply by participating in the daily routines of school life. For example, a school with a sports specialism might have displays of athletic trophies, rather than other achievements, in the hallway near the school's entrance, or a Catholic faith school might display religious artifacts like crosses or statues, communicating things valued by the school and encouraging respect for them by the students. Things underpinning the ethos, like punctuality, respect for authority, school rules, uniforms, school assemblies, prize giving, an emphasis on academic achievement and exam success, the organization of students into grouping by ability (see 'Banding, streaming and setting' below), students standing in line, raising their hands to answer questions, opening doors for teachers, or giving way to them in corridors, and so on all seek to instil certain values, attitudes and behaviour among students.

In contemporary Britain, many parents will assess a school's suitability for their children in terms of its ethos, put into practice through the hidden curriculum, and whether these combine to produce high educational standards. For many parents today, a good school is one that has high-quality teaching, good discipline and an ethos promoting high achievement and that succeeds in getting the best results in NCTs (National Curriculum Tests, commonly still referred to by their previous name of Standard Assessment Tests, or SATs), and GCSE and AS-/A-level examination results in the area.

Do schools make a difference?

Rutter et al. in their book *Fifteen Thousand Hours: Secondary Schools and their Effects on Children*, reported research they had carried out in twelve schools. This study attempted to show, in the face of much previous research suggesting the opposite, that good schools can make a difference to the life chances of all pupils. Rutter et al. suggest that it is features of the school's organization which make this difference. These features are summarized below.

- Teachers are well prepared for lessons.
- Teachers have high expectations of pupils' academic performance, and set and mark classwork and homework regularly.
- Teachers set examples of behaviour; for example, they are on time and they use only officially approved forms of discipline.
- Teachers place more emphasis on praise and reward than on blame and punishment.
- Teachers treat pupils as responsible people, for example by giving them positions of responsibility looking after school books and property.

- Teachers show an interest in the pupils and encourage them to do well.
- There is an atmosphere or ethos in the school which reflects the above points, with all teachers sharing a commitment to the aims and values of the school.
- There is a mixture of abilities in the school, as the presence of high-ability pupils benefits the academic performance and behaviour of pupils of all abilities.

Activity

Refer to the box 'Do schools make a difference?'

1 Explain how you think each of the features of a good school which Rutter et al. describe might or might not help pupils of all backgrounds and abilities to make more progress.

2 Do you agree or disagree with Rutter's features of a good school? Are there any other features that you would expect to find in a good school or college? Give reasons for your answer.

3 List at least three characteristics, based on your own opinions and reading, of a good teacher.

4 Outline three features of the ethos of your school, or the one you last attended.

5 How important do you think the role of the school and teachers is in the educational progress of pupils compared to material and cultural factors outside of school?

Teacher stereotyping and the halo effect

Teachers are constantly involved in judging and classifying pupils in various ways, for example as bright or slow learners, as troublemakers or ideal pupils, or as hardworking or lazy. This process of classification or **labelling** by teachers has been shown to affect the performance of students. The stereotype held by the teacher (good/bad or thick/bright student, and so on) can produce a **halo effect**. This means that a teacher who has formed a good impression of a student in one way, for example seeing them as cooperative, polite and helpful, may see that student more favourably in other unrelated ways too – for instance, as being bright and hard-working (even if they're not) – and therefore encourage and support them. The opposite halo effect may also occur, whereby a poor impression in one area, for example for being stroppy and difficult, may affect other unrelated impressions too, with the student also being seen as lazy or not very bright (even if this isn't true).

Labelling refers to the process of defining a person or group in a certain way – as a particular 'type' of person or group.

A **halo effect** is when pupils become stereotyped, either favourably or unfavourably, on the basis of earlier impressions, and these impressions colour all future teacher–student relations.

TEACHER STEREOTYPES OF THE 'IDEAL PUPIL'

Long-established research by writers such as Rist (1970), Hargreaves (1976), Cicourel and Kitsuse (1971), Becker (1971) and Keddie (1971) has repeatedly shown that teachers initially evaluate pupils in relation to their stereotypes of the 'ideal pupil'. A whole range of non-academic factors such as speech, dress, personality (how cooperative, polite, and so on), enthusiasm for work, conduct and appearance make up this stereotype of the ideal pupil, and influence teachers' assessments of students' ability. The social class of the student, and sometimes also their ethnic background and sex, has an important influence on this evaluation, and can positively or negatively affect students' later academic achievement.

An American study by Harvey and Slatin (1975) showed photographs of children from different ethnic and social class backgrounds to a sample of ninety-six primary school teachers, and they found white, middle-class children were identified as more likely to be successful students, while teachers had lowered expectations of those from poorer and non-white backgrounds. Gillborn (2011) found that this 'ideal pupil' stereotype held by teachers also favours those who are white, and that many teachers simply do not see black children as likely academic successes. He found teachers were denying opportunities to black children, especially Black Caribbean pupils, regardless of their social class or gender, their ability and achievements, their subject choices or their drive and ambition. They were more likely to be placed in lower teaching groups, denied access to the most sought-after subjects, and were less likely to be entered for the top exams because of not fitting the stereotype of the ideal pupil likely to succeed. Hartley and Sutton (2011) suggest the ideal pupil stereotype is also more likely to be applied to girls, including Indian Asian girls, than to boys. The reasons for this are explored more fully in the next topic.

Research into teacher stereotypes of the ideal pupil therefore suggests students – particularly male students – from lower-working-class homes, and from some ethnic groups, are often seen as being poorly motivated and lacking support from the home, and liable to be disruptive in the classroom. This may mean they are perceived by teachers as lacking ability, even if they are very able. By contrast, those from middle-class and white backgrounds most closely fit the teacher's ideal pupil stereotype, and teachers may assume that children who enter school already confident, fluent and familiar with learning, who are more likely to be from middle-class homes, have greater potential and will push them to achieve accordingly. In short, the evidence suggests that the ideal pupil stereotype in general fits most closely the profile of white, middle-class and Indian Asian girls, and the expectations arising from these teacher stereotypes and evaluations may well lead to the **self-fulfilling prophecy** discussed below.

> The **self-fulfilling prophecy** is where people act in response to predictions which have been made regarding their behaviour, thereby making the prediction come true.

In what ways might attitudes and behaviour of teachers affect a student's progress?

LABELLING AND THE SELF-FULFILLING PROPHECY

The way teachers assess and evaluate students affects achievement levels, as pupils may gradually bring their own self-image in line with the one the teacher holds of them. Those labelled as 'bright' and likely to be successful in education are more likely to perform in line with the teachers' expectations and predictions, while those labelled as 'slow', 'difficult' or of 'low ability' and unlikely to succeed are persuaded not to bother ('what's the point in trying – the teacher thinks I'm thick anyway'). In both cases, the teachers' predictions may come true. This suggests the difference between 'bright' and 'slow' or 'good' and 'bad' students, and the progress they make in school, is created by the processes of stereotyping and labelling. This is the self-fulfilling prophecy, which is illustrated in figure 6.2.

Classic research by Rosenthal and Jacobson (1968) in California provided useful evidence of the self-fulfilling prophecy. They found that a randomly chosen group of students whom teachers were told were bright and could be expected to make good progress, even though they were no different from other students in terms of ability, did in fact make greater progress than students not so labelled.

The previous section on the 'ideal pupil' suggests the self-fulfilling prophecy is likely to have the most negative effects on working-class and black boys. Recent research into

Figure 6.2 The self-fulfilling prophecy: two examples

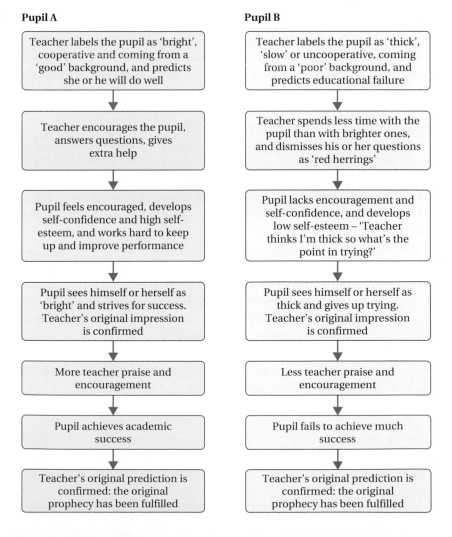

Pupil A

Teacher labels the pupil as 'bright', cooperative and coming from a 'good' background, and predicts she or he will do well

↓

Teacher encourages the pupil, answers questions, gives extra help

↓

Pupil feels encouraged, develops self-confidence and high self-esteem, and works hard to keep up and improve performance

↓

Pupil sees himself or herself as 'bright' and strives for success. Teacher's original impression is confirmed

↓

More teacher praise and encouragement

↓

Pupil achieves academic success

↓

Teacher's original prediction is confirmed: the original prophecy has been fulfilled

Pupil B

Teacher labels the pupil as 'thick', 'slow' or uncooperative, coming from a 'poor' background, and predicts educational failure

↓

Teacher spends less time with the pupil than with brighter ones, and dismisses his or her questions as 'red herrings'

↓

Pupil lacks encouragement and self-confidence, and develops low self-esteem – 'Teacher thinks I'm thick so what's the point in trying?'

↓

Pupil sees himself or herself as thick and gives up trying. Teacher's original impression is confirmed

↓

Less teacher praise and encouragement

↓

Pupil fails to achieve much success

↓

Teacher's original prediction is confirmed: the original prophecy has been fulfilled

the self-fulfilling prophecy by Hartley and Sutton suggests this may apply to gender too, with labelling, stereotypes and the expectations of teachers, as well as peers, parents and the media, generating a self-fulfilling prophecy with negative effects on the performance of boys. In Hartley and Sutton's study of 140 children in three Kent primary schools, children were assigned to two groups, with the first group told that boys do not perform as well as girls, and the other not told this. They were then tested in maths, reading and writing. Boys in the first group performed significantly worse than those in the second, while girls' overall performance was similar in both groups. Hartley and Sutton's research suggested that boys' relatively poor performance nationally could be explained in part by negative gender stereotypes, including those held by teachers, generating a self-fulfilling prophecy; this was fuelled further by adults, including teachers, and wider society routinely using phrases like 'silly boys', 'school boy pranks' and 'why can't you sit nicely like the girls?'

Banding, streaming and setting

Banding, **streaming** and **setting** are ways of grouping students according to their actual or predicted ability. 'Banding' is used in two ways. It is sometimes used to describe the situation in which comprehensive schools try to ensure their intakes have a spread of pupils drawn from all bands of ability. More commonly, it is used as an alternative word for streaming. Streaming is where students are divided into groups of similar ability (bands or streams) in which they stay for all subjects. Setting is where school students are divided into groups (sets) of the same ability in particular subjects. For example, a student might be in a top maths set, with the most able maths students, but in a bottom set for English. Being placed in a low stream or set may undermine pupils' confidence and discourage them from trying, and teachers may be less ambitious and give less knowledge to lower-stream children than they would with others.

This was confirmed by Ball's research in Beachside Comprehensive (1981). Ball found that top-stream students were 'warmed up' by encouragement to achieve highly and to follow academic courses of study. On the other hand, lower-stream students were 'cooled out' and encouraged to follow lower-status vocational and practical courses, and consequently achieved lower levels of academic success, frequently leaving school at the earliest opportunity.

Smyth et al. (2006) found that students in lower-stream classes have more negative attitudes to school, find the teaching pace too slow, spend less time on homework and are more likely than other students to disengage from school life, and become disaffected with school. Such evidence suggests streaming has a negative impact on the educational aspirations and attainment of children labelled as of low ability, as well as damaging effects on their self-esteem and self-confidence.

Streaming, and to a lesser extent setting, are often linked to the stereotypes of the ideal pupil discussed above, and teacher expectations may lead to the positive or negative self-fulfilling prophecy. Research conducted for the Sutton Trust (Sutton Trust/Ipsos MORI (2010)) found that, while setting was a good way of stretching bright pupils from poor backgrounds, not enough of them were reaching top sets. It also found streaming put poorer pupils at a disadvantage and favoured those from the middle class. The evidence suggests that, in general, the higher a pupil's social class, the greater their chance of being allocated to a top stream, for reasons which will become clearer later in this chapter.

Streaming therefore contributes to the underachievement of working-class pupils,

Banding either is where schools try to ensure their intakes have a spread of pupils drawn from all bands of ability, or, more commonly, is used as an alternative word for *streaming*.
Streaming is where, in schools, students are divided into groups of similar ability (bands or streams) in which they stay for all subjects.
Setting is where students are divided into groups (sets) of the same ability in particular subjects.

Figure 6.3 Social class divisions and streaming/banding

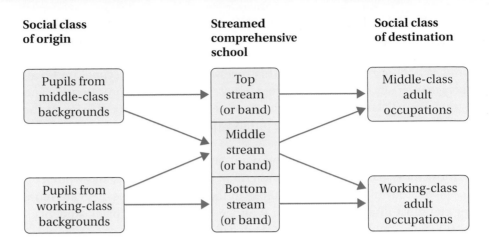

Social class of origin → Streamed comprehensive school → Social class of destination

- Pupils from middle-class backgrounds
- Pupils from working-class backgrounds

- Top stream (or band)
- Middle stream (or band)
- Bottom stream (or band)

- Middle-class adult occupations
- Working-class adult occupations

and affects the occupation and social class they may eventually achieve. This is illustrated in figure 6.3.

UNEQUAL ACCESS TO CLASSROOM KNOWLEDGE

One of the consequences of streaming and setting is that not all children are given access to the same knowledge. Keddie found that teachers taught those in higher-stream classes differently from those in lower streams. Pupils were expected to behave better and do more work, and teachers gave them more, and different types of, educational knowledge, which gave them greater opportunities for educational success. Lower-stream working-class pupils might therefore underachieve in education partly because they have not been given access to the knowledge required for educational success.

Educational triage

The term '**educational triage**' is derived from medical triage whereby, on a battlefield or in the Accident and Emergency Department of a hospital, doctors and nurses treat patients in a priority order of those who might survive if they get immediate treatment, those likely to survive who don't need immediate attention, and those who have little chance of survival whatever is done.

Gillborn and Youdell (2000) found schools were undertaking a similar process of educational triage, dividing students into three groups: those who they thought were most likely, with little additional help, to get 5 GCSE A*–C grades or more recently the 6 GCSEs A*–C grades necessary for the **English Baccalaureate (EBacc)** (this includes GCSEs in English, maths, two sciences, a foreign language and a humanity, such as history or geography); those on the grade-C/D borderline, who with a bit of extra help, might get a C grade or better; and a third group of hopeless cases who were unlikely to achieve a C grade or above, whatever was done. Schools focus their attention on the first two groups, as this will improve their position in the league tables (discussed later in this chapter) and give the impression of a good and successful school. The third group are basically written off as no-hopers and left to die an educational death.

In 2011, the government announced that, to end what it saw as a culture of low expectations in some schools, every secondary school in England would be expected to increase the proportion of all pupils achieving five A*–C grades at GCSE, including

Educational triage refers to the way schools divide pupils into three groups – those who are likely to succeed in exams (mainly concerning GCSEs A*–C) whatever happens, those who have a chance of succeeding if they get some extra help (mainly those around the C/D-grade boundary) and those who have little chance of succeeding whatever is done. Schools concentrate on the first two groups, and particularly the second group, and basically write-off those who have little chance of success.

The **English Baccalaureate (EBacc)** is a certificate (not a qualification) awarded to pupils, who achieve at least 6 GCSEs A*–C in maths, English, two sciences, a foreign language and a humanity, like history or geography. The EBacc is also used to measure a school's performance.

English and maths, from the 35 per cent in 2011 to at least 40 per cent by 2012 and 50 per cent by 2015. Schools not achieving this standard would be regarded as underperforming, and would risk being taken over by the headteacher of a higher-performing neighbouring school or by an academy. This renewed emphasis on school improvement is likely to intensify the process of educational triage, as even more attention and school resources are diverted onto those who stand at least some chance of reaching the 5 GCSEs A*–C target, and away from those pupils who seem highly unlikely to achieve this standard, whatever schools do.

The school processes and teacher stereotypes and expectations described above mean that those most likely to be in the third group seen as no-hopers, and written off and left to die an educational death, are those in the bottom streams, who are more likely to be the most disadvantaged lower-working-class white and black students – predominantly boys – and those with special educational needs.

Student responses to the experience of schooling: school subcultures

Students experience, and react and adapt in a wide variety of ways to schools' label and categorize them, in accordance with the various features of school life considered so far in this topic. These adaptations or responses frequently take the form of *pupil subcultures*, which can influence students' motivation in school and their levels of achievement.

Pupil subcultures are groups of students who share some values, norms and behaviour, which give them a sense of group identity and belonging, and provide them with support and peer-group status during the schooling process. These subcultures take a variety of forms, ranging from pro-school to anti-school subcultures, with a variety of other responses between these, and these may themselves vary according to social class, gender and ethnicity.

DIFFERENTIATION AND POLARIZATION

Lacey's (1970) study of a middle-class grammar school found that there were two related processes at work in schools – differentiation and polarization. Most schools generally place a high value on things such as hard work, good behaviour and exam success, and teachers judge students and rank and categorize them into different groups – streams or sets – according to such criteria. This is what Lacey called *differentiation*. One of the consequences of differentiation through streaming, setting and labelling is *polarization*. This refers to the way students become divided into two opposing groups or 'poles': those in the top streams who achieve highly, who more or less conform, and therefore achieve high status in terms of the values and aims of the school, and those in the bottom streams who are labelled as failures and are therefore deprived of status. Studies by Hargreaves (1967, 1976) in a secondary modern school, Ball (1981) in a streamed comprehensive school, and Abraham (1989) in a comprehensive school using setting found that teachers' perceptions of students' academic ability and the processes of differentiation and polarization influenced how students behaved, and led to the formation of pro- and anti-school (or counter-school) subcultures.

THE PRO-SCHOOL SUBCULTURE

A **pro-school subculture** consists of groups of pupils who generally conform to the academic aims, ethos and rules of a school, and tends to be linked to students in upper streams and sets who are valued and rewarded and given status as they fulfil the school's ambition for good behaviour and academic success. 'The lads' in Willis's study of a Wolverhampton comprehensive school (see below and pages 347–8) called this conformist group the 'ear 'oles'. Mac an Ghaill (1994) found a conformist pro-school subculture emerged in two male groups, which he called the 'Academic Achievers' and 'New Enterprisers', who were skilled manual working-class white and Asian students who were aspiring to middle class careers, through either academic success (the Academic Achievers) or success in vocational subjects like technology and computers (the New Enterprisers). Sewell (1998) found a pro-school subculture among some black pupils ('the conformists'), who sought to achieve academic success and avoid racist stereotyping and labelling by teachers by conforming to school values.

Belonging to such a pro-school subculture is likely to encourage peer-group support for success in education. Such students are, in general, more likely to be from middle-class or skilled working-class backgrounds.

> A **pro-school subculture** is a group organized around a set of values, attitudes and behaviour which generally conforms to the academic aims, ethos and rules of a school.

THE ANTI-SCHOOL (OR COUNTER-SCHOOL) SUBCULTURE

An anti-school subculture, sometimes called a counter-school subculture, consists of groups of pupils who rebel against the school for various reasons, and develop an alternative set of delinquent values, attitudes and behaviour in opposition to the academic aims, ethos and rules of a school. In this subculture, truancy, playing up teachers, messing about, breaking the school rules, copying work (or not doing any) and generally disrupting the smooth running of the school become a way of getting back at the system and resisting a schooling which has denied students status by labelling them as failures by putting them in lower streams and sets. This is a **subculture of resistance** and an *anti-learning subculture*, and provides a means for pupils to improve their own self-esteem, by giving them status in the eyes of their peer group which has been denied them by the school. Participation in such subcultures contributes further to poor educational performance, and in many cases contributes to the self-fulfilling prophecy of underachievement.

> A **subculture of resistance** is one that not only has some differences from the dominant culture, but is also in active opposition to it.

For the reasons considered above, and explored further in the following topic, anti-school or counter-school subcultures are more likely to be comprised of pupils who are Black Caribbean and White British working-class males. Typical of the anti-school subculture was that found by Willis among the working-class 'lads' in a Wolverhampton comprehensive school (see pages 347–8), who were opposed to the main aims of the school and the pro-school 'ear 'oles' , and sought to free themselves from what they saw as a boring and oppressive schooling by making 'having a laff' the main purpose of their school day. Both Mac an Ghaill's and Sewell's research also identified groups of Black Caribbean working-class boys in the bottom streams or sets – the 'Macho lads' and 'the rebels' – who were similarly hostile to schooling. They tried to achieve status and identity denied by the school through aggressive masculinity and peer-group support available through the formation of an anti-school subculture. Their rejection of school was an act of rebellion against racist stereotypes and labelling by teachers, who saw them as anti-school, anti-authority macho boys.

Jackson's (2006) research among 13- to 14-year-old boys and girls, based on interviews and questionnaires with pupils and teachers from six comprehensive schools, suggests that some girls may be increasingly becoming part of anti-school subcultures,

The anti-school, or counter-school, subculture

as they adopt 'ladette' behaviour – the female equivalent of the assertive, boisterous and crude 'laddish' culture found among boys – and an 'it's uncool to work' approach to school, and a similar confrontational approach, and attempt to make teachers' lives hell. Jackson's evidence, though, also suggested that many girls still tried to achieve academic success, working clandestinely by hiding their work and effort, at the same time as adopting ladette behaviour.

BETWEEN PRO- AND ANTI-SCHOOL SUBCULTURES: A RANGE OF RESPONSES

Woods (1979) suggested that dividing the responses of pupils to the experience of schooling into just the two 'poles' of conformity or opposition through pro- and anti-school subcultures is too simple. While Woods's research is now old, his framework is still relevant today as it does suggest there is a wide variety of possible responses and adaptations to school, each of which will influence what students achieve in school, and students may change their responses over time as they move through schooling. These responses may also affect individual pupils rather than whole groups, as implied by the term 'subculture', and may span social class, gender and ethnic differences at different stages of the schooling process. For example, students' response may change from rebellion to ingratiation or compliance as they grow older and subject options, exams and post-school career or education choices loom. Woods identified eight responses ranging from pro-school to anti-school, as shown in figure 6.4 opposite.

Activity

1 List all the reasons you can think of to explain why pupils from lower-working-class homes are more likely to be placed in lower streams than those from middle-class backgrounds.
2 Have you had any experience of the self-fulfilling prophecy in your own schooling? How do teachers communicate impressions of whether they think you are 'bright' or not, and how do you think this might have affected your progress?
3 In what ways do you think students in lower streams are treated differently and given different knowledge from those in higher streams? Give examples to illustrate your answer.

4 How do you think schools and teachers 'warm up' or 'cool out' students?
5 Is there any evidence of an anti-school subculture in your own school, or the school you once attended? What do you think membership of an anti-school subculture might mean to those who belong to it? Draw on examples from your own schooling.
6 Drawing on Woods's research in figure 6.4, try to identify some subcultures or individual responses in your own school (or the one you once attended), and explain the various ways that such subcultures or individual responses might affect educational achievement.

Figure 6.4 Woods and pupils' adaptations to schooling

PRO-SCHOOL

- *Ingratiation*: pro-school conformity as in the pro-school subculture, with eagerness to please teachers and win favour with them.

- *Compliance*: conformity, but basically for what they can get out of schooling, like exam success, not because they necessarily like or enjoy school.

- *Opportunism*: those who try to gain both teacher and peer group approval, who move between both, depending on which response seems most beneficial to them at the time.

- *Ritualism*: lack of interest and engagement with schooling, but appearing to conform by going through the motions and avoiding trouble.

- *Retreatism*: not actively opposed to school values, but indifferent to them – messing about in class, distracted and lacking concentration, daydreaming, indifferent to exam success, and dropping out from involvement in school, including any school subcultures.

- *Colonization*: those who generally accept school for what it offers them, but reject school for things it forbids. Such pupils take opportunities as they arise to have fun, express aggression and hostility so long as they avoid getting into trouble.

- *Intransigence*: troublemakers who are indifferent to school, and who aren't that bothered about the consequences of non-conformity.

- *Rebellion*: outright rejection of schooling and its values, and involvement in anti-school activity, as in the anti-school subculture.

ANTI-SCHOOL

An evaluation of explanations for student progress focusing on school organization, school processes and the teaching and learning context

THEY RECOGNIZE THE IMPORTANCE OF WHAT HAPPENS INSIDE SCHOOLS

Explanations for educational achievement which focus on school organization, school processes and the teaching and learning context, and interactionist approaches which examine stereotyping, streaming, labelling and teacher expectations and how they affect pupils' learning, recognize the importance of what happens inside schools and classrooms. This avoids putting the whole blame for educational failure on deficiencies in the pupil, their family, their cultural values and attitudes, or material circumstances arising from their social class background.

THEY ARE TOO DETERMINISTIC

Interactionist theories can be too deterministic, in the sense that they suggest that once a negative label is applied, it will always have a negative effect, with the self-fulfilling prophecy coming into effect. In fact, a negative label like 'thick' or 'waster' may have the opposite effect, and encourage those so labelled to prove the label wrong via hard work and academic success. Fuller (1980), for example, found in a study that, although most black girls were subject to negative labelling and stereotyping and placed in low streams, some of them consciously chose to reject such labels and strived to prove the teachers wrong by achieving educational success, while still seeming not to conform to the ethos and rules of the school. This showed that negative labelling does not always lead to failure.

THEY DO NOT PAY ENOUGH ATTENTION TO THE DISTRIBUTION OF POWER IN SOCIETY

Such explanations do not explain why so many teachers seem to hold similar views on what counts as an 'ideal pupil', what constitutes 'proper' educational knowledge and ability, and why these appear to be related to social class, gender or ethnicity. They therefore do not take enough account of the distribution of power in society, which means some definitions of knowledge, culture and ability are given more importance than others (as Bourdieu's theory of **cultural capital** and **habitus** discussed in the next topic suggests).

THEY DO NOT PAY ENOUGH ATTENTION TO FACTORS OUTSIDE THE SCHOOL

The interactionist approach is very helpful in drawing attention to the factors inside schools, particularly teacher–pupil interaction through the labelling process, which explain why some social groups underachieve in education. However, such explanations do not take enough account of the structural, material and cultural factors *outside* the school, discussed in the following topic, and the role of parents and the contribution of the media to forming stereotypes, which influence what happens *inside* the school. Teachers and schools cannot be held solely responsible for what happens in schools, and they certainly cannot be blamed for problems which have their roots outside the school in the structure of inequality in the wider society. A full explanation of why some social groups consistently do better than others in education, even if some individuals break out of the mould, needs to take account of factors both outside the school and inside the school, both material and cultural factors and interaction in the classroom. In other words, a full account of achievement and underachievement needs to look at both structural and interactionist explanations – not just what happens to pupils in schools, but what happens to them outside school, and frequently before they even start school. These issues are discussed in the following topic.

> **Cultural capital** is the knowledge, language, manners and forms of behaviour, attitudes and values, taste and lifestyle which give middle-class and upper-class students who possess them an in-built advantage in a middle-class-controlled education system.
> A **habitus** is the cultural framework and set of ideas possessed by a social class, into which people are socialized, and which influences their cultural tastes and choices.

Exam-style questions

1 Explain what is meant by the term 'school ethos'. *(2 marks)*

2 Explain what is meant by the term 'halo effect'. *(2 marks)*

3 Explain what is meant by the term 'self-fulfilling prophecy'. *(2 marks)*

4 Suggest **three** factors inside schools that may affect the educational progress that pupils make. *(6 marks)*

5 Suggest **three** reasons why pupils may form an anti-school subculture. *(6 marks)*

6 Outline some of the ways stereotyping and labelling in schools might influence the educational achievements of pupils. *(12 marks)*

7 Outline some of the ways pupils might respond to their experiences in schools. *(12 marks)*

8 Assess the claim that schools are mainly responsible for what pupils achieve in education. *(20 marks)*

Topic 3

SPECIFICATION AREA

Differential educational achievement of social groups by social class, gender and ethnicity in contemporary society

Is contemporary Britain a meritocracy?

Functionalist writers like Parsons have suggested that social inequality in contemporary societies is based on the principles of meritocracy and equality of opportunity. In a meritocracy, social inequality is based on the different abilities, talents and skills individuals have. For most people today, their abilities and talents are demonstrated by their educational qualifications, and everyone should have an equal opportunity to develop and achieve these educational qualifications, regardless of their social class background, ethnicity, gender or disability.

However, there is substantial evidence that Britain is not meritocratic, and the link between educational qualifications and pay levels is relatively weak. Most sociologists argue that not everyone has the same chance of developing their talents and skills, and that there is no real equality of opportunity in education. Marxists argue that what the education system really does is to maintain and reproduce existing social class, ethnic and gender inequalities from one generation to the next.

The evidence for this lack of equality of opportunity in education is that, even for students of the same ability, there are wide differences in educational achievement which are closely linked to the social class origins of students, and their gender and ethnic characteristics.

The following sections look at the evidence for these inequalities in educational opportunity and achievement, and seek explanations for them.

Social class differences in educational achievement

Free school meals as a proxy or substitute for social class

In educational research, there is often no easily available data on the social class of the parents of children in school. To overcome this problem in school-based research and data collection, eligibility for receipt of free school meals[1] is often used as an indicator of economic disadvantage and as a proxy or substitute way of measuring social class. This is because those children who are entitled to free school meals are those whose parents' incomes are so low that they qualify for a range of income-related welfare benefits.

[1] Many of those entitled to free meals do not claim them for fear of being stigmatized or ridiculed by their peers, so this indicator may underestimate the extent of disadvantaged pupils in schools.

As Perry and Francis (2010) point out, social class is the strongest predictor of educational achievement in the UK, and the key factor influencing whether a child does well

Many children from disadvantaged backgrounds are already up to a year behind more privileged youngsters educationally by the age of 3, according to 2007 research by the Centre for Longitudinal Studies at the London University Institute of Education

or badly at school. In blunt terms, as the Conservative Secretary of State for Education, Michael Gove, put it in 2010, 'Rich, thick kids do better than poor, clever children', even before they start school. There are major differences between the levels of achievement of the working class and middle class and, in general, the higher the social class of the parents, the more successful a child will be in education. Waldfogel and Washbrook (2010), using data from the Millennium Cohort Survey (a nationally representative longitudinal study of 12,644 children), found many children from disadvantaged backgrounds were already up to a year behind more privileged children educationally by the age of 3 – before many had even started school. The degree of social class inequality in education begins even before children enter primary school and becomes greater as children move upward through the education system, with the higher levels of the education system dominated by middle-class and upper-class students.

A comparison of social class differences in educational achievement

When students from the lower working class have been compared to middle-class children of the same ability, it has been found that:

- They are more likely to start school unable to read.
- They do less well in tests like the National Curriculum Tests (NCTs or SATs).
- They are less likely to get places in the best state schools. In 2005, only 3 per cent of those attending state schools which were in the top 200 for performance received free school meals – the standard poverty indicator used in schools – compared to 17 per cent nationally.
- They are more likely to be placed in lower streams.
- They generally get poorer exam results. For example, around three-quarters of young people from upper-middle-class backgrounds get five or more GCSEs A*–C, compared to less than a third from lower-working-class backgrounds.

- They are more likely to leave school at the minimum leaving age of 17 (from 2013), many of them with few or no qualifications of any kind. Only about half of young people from unskilled manual families stay on in post-17 full-time education, compared to about nine in every ten from managerial and professional families.
- They are more likely to undertake vocational or training courses if they stay in education after 17, rather than the more academic AS- and A-level courses, which are more likely to be taken by middle-class students.
- They are less likely to go into higher education. In 2008 at least 70 per cent of those accepted for higher education came from middle-class backgrounds, even though only about half of the population was middle-class. Young people from unskilled backgrounds made up only around 5 per cent of those accepted. Just 4 per cent of those eligible for free school meals at age 15 go on to university, compared with 33 per cent of their peers.

EXPLAINING SOCIAL CLASS DIFFERENCES IN EDUCATIONAL ACHIEVEMENT

There is a range of factors that sociologists have identified in explaining the pattern of differences in educational achievement (summarized in figure 6.5). These can be grouped into three main categories:

- *material explanations*, which put the emphasis on social and economic conditions outside school.
- *cultural explanations*, which focus on values, attitudes and lifestyles outside school.
- *factors within the school itself.*

The following sections mainly focus on social class differences, though some of these explanations will also be referred to later in discussing gender and ethnic group differences.

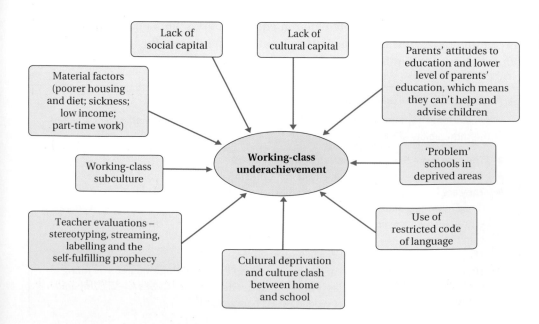

Figure 6.5 Social class and educational achievement

Material explanations

Although schooling and further education are free to the age of 19 (though there are fees for higher education), material factors outside school like poverty and low wages, diet, health and housing can all have important direct effects on how well individuals do at school. Indicators of social deprivation like these make an important contribution to explaining the pattern of working-class underachievement in education.

Poverty and home circumstances   These are some of the factors in a child's background that can affect their chances in education:

- Waldfogel and Washbrook (2010) point out that children from low-income families are more likely to live in crowded or damp accommodation than other children, are less likely to have access to a garden, and are more likely to have a home that is dark, unclean or unsafe. Poor housing conditions such as overcrowding and insufficient space and quiet can make study at home difficult. They suggest these factors link with poorer health, as well as educational development. Poorer diets and higher levels of sickness in disadvantaged homes may mean tiredness at school, making learning more difficult, and more absence and falling behind with lessons.
- Poorer parents are less likely to have access to pre-school or nursery facilities, which may affect their children's development compared to those who have such access.
- Low income or unemployment may mean that educational books and toys are not bought, and computers and/or internet access are not available in the home. This may affect a child's educational progress before or during her or his time at school. There may also be a lack of money for out-of-school trips, sports equipment, calculators and other hidden costs of free state education (see the box below), as well as inability to afford any extra private tuition needed.

THE HIDDEN COSTS OF 'FREE' STATE SCHOOLING

The hidden costs of sending a child to a state school amounted to nearly £700 a year for a primary school child, and £1,200 for a secondary school child in 2009. These are the costs parents are expected to pay for things like school uniform, PE kit, school trips, class materials, stationery, swimming lessons, school lunches, travel, photographs, charity contributions and other school activities. Even when these costs are voluntary, some schools still pressure parents to pay up, even if they have difficulty in affording them.

Source: The Cost of Schooling (British Market Research Bureau, for the Department of Children, Schools and Families, 2009)

- Young people from poorer families are more likely to have part-time jobs, such as paper rounds, babysitting or shop work. This becomes more pronounced after the age of 17, when students may be combining part- or full-time work with school or college studies or training. This may create a conflict between the competing demands of study and paid work.
- Schools themselves in poorer areas may suffer disadvantages compared to those in more affluent middle-class areas. For example, many schools today rely on support from parents to finance extra resources for the school, and parents in poorer areas are less likely to be able to raise as much as those in more middle-class areas. This will mean schools in poorer areas will have less to spend on pupil activities.

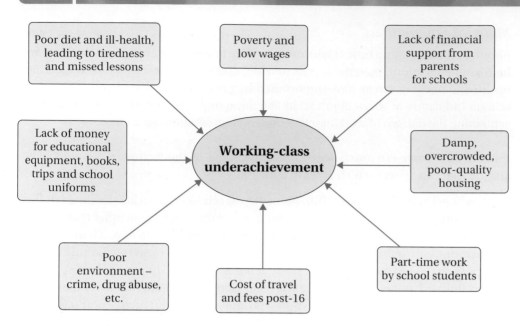

Figure 6.6 Material factors explaining class differences in educational achievement

- It may be financially difficult for parents on a low income to support students in education after school-leaving age. This is particularly the case in further education, where there are few grants available and there may be travel costs involved. In higher education, the potential debts arising from student loans to cover tuition fees and living costs while studying are likely to be a source of anxiety to those from poorer backgrounds, deterring them from going to university.

The effects of these material factors tend to be cumulative, meaning that social deprivation gradually builds up, as one aspect of deprivation can lead to others. For example, poverty may mean overcrowding at home *and* ill-health *and* having to find part-time work, making all the problems worse. The cartoon illustrates this.

Activity

Explain in your own words how the cartoon shows the effects of social deprivation on educational achievement are cumulative.

The catchment area Catchment areas (or priority areas) are the areas from which primary and secondary schools draw their pupils. In deprived areas, where there may be a range of social problems such as high unemployment, poverty, juvenile delinquency, crime and drug abuse, there are often poor role models for young people to imitate. The accumulated effects of the environment on children's behaviour mean schools in such areas are more likely to have discipline problems that prevent students from learning, and a higher turnover of teachers. This may mean children from the most disadvantaged backgrounds have the worst schools. In contrast, schools in middle-class neighbourhoods will probably have stronger and more conformist role models for young people, have fewer discipline problems and therefore offer a better learning environment.

Research has repeatedly confirmed that material explanations like those above have a major impact in explaining the underachievement of many children from poorer backgrounds. For example, Gibson and Asthana (1999) found that the greater the level of family disadvantage, measured in terms of lack of parents' qualifications, unemployment, and not owning a car or house, the smaller was the percentage of students gaining five or more GCSEs at grades A* to C. The National Equality Panel (2010) confirmed this, pointing out that the highest achievers in schools come from the most advantaged areas, with very few coming from the most deprived areas, and very few of the lowest achievers coming from the most advantaged areas. More than 85 per cent of teachers responding to a 2011 survey by the ATL teachers' union said they believed that poverty had a negative impact on the well-being and attainment of pupils they taught, with disadvantaged students coming to school tired, hungry and wearing worn-out clothes or lacking the proper uniform. Teachers reported that such students often lacked confidence, missed out on activities outside school such as music, sports or going to the cinema or theatre, and faced problems like not having a quiet place to study at home, and lack of access to computers and the internet.

Cultural explanations and cultural deprivation

Cultural explanations of underachievement in education suggest that the values, attitudes, language, and other aspects of the cultural life of some social groups are deficient or deprived in various ways in relation to the white, middle-class culture of the education system. This is known as **cultural deprivation**, and places the blame for educational underachievement on factors outside the school, such as young people's socialization in the family and community, and on the cultural values with which they are raised. Sodha and Margo (2010) suggest the range of cultural factors discussed below combine

> **Cultural deprivation** is the idea that some young people fail in education because of supposed cultural deficiencies in their home and family background, such as inadequate socialization, failings in pre-school learning, inadequate language skills and inappropriate attitudes and values.

Figure 6.7 Cultural factors explaining class differences in educational achievement

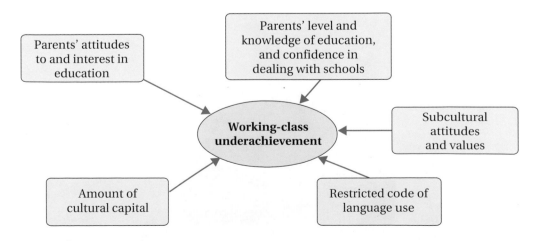

to create *disengagement* from education for the most disadvantaged sections of the working class. This involves a cultural barrier of low expectations and low aspirations, in which education is seen by parents with scepticism and fatalism – a view that their position in life can't be changed and that education is for other people, not for them.

Parents' attitudes to education   Douglas (1964) found, fifty years ago, that the single most important factor explaining educational success and failure was the degree of parental encouragement, interest and involvement in their children's education. Feinstein and Symons (1999) showed that this remains true today, with very high parental interest leading to much better exam results than for children whose parents show no interest, and that children's progress can be hindered by lack of parental involvement.

Middle-class parents, compared to working-class parents, on the whole:

- take more interest in their children's progress at school, as indicated by more frequent visits to the school to discuss their children's progress.
- become relatively more interested and encouraging as the children grow older, when exam options are selected and career choices loom.
- are more likely to want their children to stay at school beyond the minimum leaving age and to encourage them to do so.

Parents' level of education   Because they are generally themselves better educated, middle-class parents tend to understand the school system better than working-class parents. Lower-working-class parents may feel less confident in dealing with teachers at parents' evenings, and in dealing with subject options and exam choices. Middle-class parents know more about schools, the examination system and careers and so are more able to advise and counsel their children on getting into the most appropriate subjects and courses. They can hold their own more in disagreements with teachers (who are also middle-class) about the treatment and educational progress of their child; they know more about complaints procedures, and fighting sex discrimination

In what ways might parents influence success or failure in their children's education?

against their daughters; they know which educational toys, games and books to buy, or cultural events to go to, to stimulate their children's educational development both before and during schooling (and they have the money to pay for them); and they can help their children with school work generally. As a consequence, even before they get to school middle-class children may have learnt more as a result of their socialization in the family. These advantages of a middle-class home may be reinforced throughout a child's career in the education system.

Subcultural explanations – attitudes and values   These explanations suggest that different social classes have some different values, attitudes and lifestyles, or different subcultures, and that these affect the performance of children in the educational system. Two main researchers developed these subcultural explanations: the British sociologist Sugarman (1970) and the American H. H. Hyman (1967). Table 6.4, based on the work of Hyman and Sugarman, shows how the different values and attitudes of the middle class and working class might influence children's progress in school. While Sugarman's and Hyman's research is now very old, Perry and Francis's 2010 review identifies evidence, such as that by Sodha and Margo, that similar attitudes and values are still found today and have an impact on aspirations and achievements in education.

Table 6.4 Class subcultures and educational achievement

Class	Subculture	Effects on educational achievement
Middle class	In middle-class jobs, the promise of career progress through individual effort and educational qualifications leads to a *future orientation* (planning for the future) and *deferred gratification* (putting off today's pleasures for future gains). *Individual effort* and intelligence are seen as the key to success.	Children are socialized into values and attitudes which encourage ambition and educational success. A *future orientation* and *deferred gratification* creates a recognition of the need for individual hard work, staying in and doing homework, and staying on in further/higher education in order to get the qualifications needed for career success. *Individual effort* is seen as providing the key to educational success.
Working class	In working-class jobs, educational qualifications are often not very important for work. The lack of promotion opportunities leads to a *present-time orientation* (a lack of emphasis on long-term goals and future planning), *immediate gratification* (getting pleasures now, rather than putting them off for the future), and *fatalism* (an acceptance of the situation rather than attempts to improve it). Working together (*collectivism* through trade unions) provides more gains than individual effort.	Children are socialized into general sets of values and attitudes which don't encourage ambition and educational success. Immediate gratification, a present-time orientation and fatalism discourage effort for future rewards, such as exam success. Leaving school and obtaining a skill/getting a job and money are seen as more important than educational qualifications. Loyalty to the group (collectivism) discourages the individual effort and achievement which success at school demands.

Activity

Look at table 6.4 and explain briefly what is meant by each of the following terms and how each one affects educational achievement: future orientation; deferred gratification; individual effort; present-time orientation; immediate gratification; fatalism; collectivism.

Language use and educational achievement: Bernstein and the restricted and elaborated codes   Success in education depends very heavily on language – for reading, writing, speaking and understanding. The ability to read and understand books, to write clearly, and to be able to explain yourself fully in both speech and writing are key language skills required for success in education. If these skills are not developed through discussion, negotiation and explanation in the family, then such children will be disadvantaged in education.

Bernstein (1971) has argued that there are two types of language use, which he calls the **elaborated code** and the **restricted code**. It is middle-class young people's familiarity with the elaborated code that gives them a better chance of success in education.

- The *restricted code* is the sort of language which is used between friends or family members – informal, simple, everyday language (such as slang), sometimes ungrammatical and with limited explanation and vocabulary. The restricted code is quite adequate for everyday use with family or friends because they generally know what the speaker is referring to – the context is understood by both speakers and so detailed explanation is not required. The restricted code is used by both middle-class and working-class people, but Bernstein argues lower-working-class people are mainly limited to this form of language use.

- The *elaborated code* is the sort of language which is used by strangers and individuals in some formal context, where explanation and detail are required, such as that used by teachers in the classroom when they are explaining things, or in an interview for a job, writing a business letter, writing an essay or an examination answer, or in a school lesson or textbook. It has a much wider vocabulary than the restricted code. According to Bernstein, the elaborated code is used mainly by middle-class people. Bernstein argues that the language used in schools is the elaborated code of the middle class. It is this that gives the middle-class student an advantage at school over working-class students, since understanding textbooks, writing essays and examination questions, and class discussions require the detail and explanation which are found mainly in the formal language of the elaborated code. Middle-class young people who are used to using the elaborated code at home will therefore find school work easier and learn more than those working-class students whose language experience is limited only to the restricted code. The cartoon illustrates these two different types of language use.

Bernstein's work has been subject to a number of criticisms:

The **elaborated code** is the sort of formal language used by strangers and individuals in some formal contexts where explanation and detail are required, and uses a much wider vocabulary than the restricted code.

The **restricted code** is the informal, simple, everyday language, sometimes ungrammatical and with limited explanations and vocabulary, which is used between friends or family members.

> **Activity**
>
> 1 With reference to the cartoon opposite, explain the difference between the elaborated and restricted codes of language use.
> 2 Explain *two* ways that having access to the elaborated code might provide advantages in education.

- Bernstein tends to put all the middle class together as having equal use of the elaborated code, but there are wide differences between the higher and lower sections of the middle class. A similar point can be made about higher and lower sections of the working class and the use of the restricted code. It is difficult to generalize about all working-class and middle-class families, and there is likely to be a diversity of arrangements in the way language is used in the family.
- Rosen argues that Bernstein gives few examples to back up his claims of the existence of restricted and elaborated codes. He accuses Bernstein of creating a myth of the superiority of middle-class speech.
- Labov (1973) is very critical of the notion that working-class speech is in any way inferior to that of the middle class. Based on his research in Harlem, in New York, Labov claims they are simply different, and that in many ways working-class speakers are more effective in making their points, and that middle-class speakers frequently get bogged down in a mass of irrelevant detail.

Bourdieu's theory of cultural capital   Bourdieu (1971) was a French Marxist, who saw the culture of the school as giving an inbuilt advantage to middle-class children. He argues that each social class possesses its own cultural framework or set of ideas, which he calls a **habitus**.

> A **habitus** is the cultural framework and set of ideas possessed by a social class, into which people are socialized, and which influences their cultural tastes and choices.

This cultural framework contains ideas about what counts as good and bad taste, good books, newspapers, TV programmes and so on. This habitus is picked up through socialization in the family. The dominant class has the power to impose its own habitus in the education system, so what counts as educational knowledge is not the 'culture of society as a whole', but that of the dominant social class.

Those who come from better-off middle- and upper-class backgrounds have more access to the culture of the dominant class. Bourdieu calls this advantage **cultural capital**.

Robson (2003), for example, found that possession of cultural capital in the form of activities like going to museums, zoos, exhibitions, the theatre, the opera or a (classical music) concert, reading books for pleasure and participating in artistic or music-related activities gives greatly improved chances of success in education. Such cultural capital can be turned into educational capital (educational qualifications), which can in turn lead to possession of economic capital (material advantages like a high income).

> **Cultural capital** is the knowledge, language, manners and forms of behaviour, attitudes and values, taste and lifestyle which give middle-class and upper-class students who possess them an in-built advantage in a middle class-controlled education system.

Upper- and middle-class children are more successful in education because they possess more cultural capital and consequently feel more comfortable in the education system and are more familiar with what they have to do at school. Those from the working class are more likely to fail exams, to be pushed into lower-status educational streams or courses, or to drop out or be pushed out of the educational system, because they lack cultural capital.

Bourdieu therefore suggests that, while the schooling process appears to be 'neutral' and fair, since schools measure all pupils against the same culture and knowledge, it is not really neutral at all because the culture of the educational system is that of the dominant class, which middle-class children already possess – and working-class children lack – through socialization in the family.

Bourdieu also refers to **social capital**, which is linked to cultural, economic and educational capital.

Social capital refers to the social networks of influence and support that people have through involvement and cooperation with neighbours, community life, and social and professional groups, such as knowing the right people, who to talk to, who to get advice from, who is in a position to help them (or their children) in times of difficulty or need and to influence others in their favour. Possession of social capital is highest in the middle and upper classes, and can provide a network of support and influence to help their children's education. Examples of this might include knowing people who can provide extra help to their children with specialist subjects, knowing teachers who can give them inside information about the best schools – and which to avoid – or knowing teachers or university admission tutors who can brief them on what their children should say at interviews.

It is the possession of economic, educational, cultural and social capital by middle-class parents that gives their children in-built advantages in the education system.

> **Social capital**
> refers to the social networks of influence and support that people have.

Cultural and social capital in action

Activity

1 How do you think your family background helped or didn't help you in making progress in education?
2 Refer to the cartoon. Identify all the cultural features you can which might encourage success in education, and explain how the cartoon illustrates the concepts of cultural and social capital.
3 What cultural capital and skills do you think are important for success in education? Draw up a list of these, and explain in each case how they might help in schooling.
4 Through a questionnaire given to a sample of middle-class and working-class students, investigate whether they have the cultural factors you have identified in the previous question. Discuss this in the framework of explanations for social class differences in educational achievement.

The culture clash

Cultural explanations suggest that schools are mainly middle-class institutions, and they stress the value of many features of the middle-class way of life, such as the importance of hard work and study, making sacrifices now for future rewards (deferred gratification), the elaborated code of language, good books, good TV programmes, quality newspapers, and so on. Archer et al. (2007) suggest that the middle-class child is therefore more likely to experience a smooth transition between home and school, as school may appear like an extension of earlier home experiences; by contrast, the working-class child is more likely to experience a break or a clash between home and school, resulting in a sense of alienation or disaffection and distance from school. Middle-class children therefore arrive at school with the cultural capital enabling them to be more tuned in to the demands of schooling, such as  the subjects that will be explored there, seeking good marks, doing homework, showing good behaviour and a cooperative attitude to teachers, and other features of middle-class culture. Consequently, they may appear to teachers as more intelligent and more sophisticated, promising students. By contrast, working-class children may face a difference and conflict between the values of the home and those of school. This is known as the **culture clash**.

> **Culture clash** is a difference and conflict between the cultural values of the home and those of educational institutions.

Criticisms of cultural explanations

Reay (2009) points out that cultural explanations involve a 'blame the victim' approach, which places the blame for educational underachievement on the home and family background, with the culture of the lower working class seen as deficient or deprived in various ways compared to that of the middle class – for example, the working class lacks the ambition and aspirations, attitudes and values, the necessary language skills or the cultural capital which are important for educational success. However, there have been a number of criticisms of these cultural explanations of working-class underachievement.

Exaggeration   They tend to exaggerate the differences and downplay the similarities between the attitudes and beliefs of the different social classes.

Overlooking practical difficulties and lack of self-confidence   Many working-class parents are very concerned and ambitious for their children's success in education. Douglas, for example, used measures of 'parental interest' based on teachers' comments about parents' attitudes, and the number of times parents visited schools. However, many working-class people work longer hours, have less flexibility and choice in their working hours, do more shift work, get less time off with pay, and are less educated than teachers and many other members of the middle class. Not visiting a school may be evidence not of a lack of interest or encouragement among working-class parents, but of the material constraints of their jobs. Reay points out that working-class people often lack the same degree of confidence and assertiveness that the middle classes possess in their interactions with teachers and schools. These factors can prevent working-class people from turning parental interest into practical support in the way middle-class parents can.

Ignoring the role played by schools themselves Schools do not simply 'process' children whose attitudes and ambitions are pre-formed in the family, but play an active part in forming those attitudes and ambitions. Middle-class students may perform better because they receive more praise and encouragement from teachers, as they are more in tune with teachers. Blaming social class background and the family as irresponsible and, in Reay's words, as 'unmotivated, unambitious and underachieving', can attach a stigma to such families, and may lead to low expectations by teachers. This may encourage some teachers and schools to label lower-working-class children as 'born to fail', and they may therefore neglect their needs, such as by not giving them the best teaching, particularly if, as Cassen and Kingdon (2007) suggest, they are unlikely to contribute to their school's achieving a high position in the educational league tables. This 'not worth bothering' approach and the resulting self-fulfilling prophecy, rather than so-called 'cultural deprivation', may lead to the poor performance of some children in school. These issues were considered in Topic 2.

The need for schools to change If there is a culture clash for working-class children going to school, then, rather than blaming their family and social class background, schools should be pressed to improve the situation. Keddie (1973) argues that there is no cultural deprivation, but merely a cultural difference. She suggests that the idea of cultural deprivation fails to recognize the cultural strengths of those said to be deprived. The problem arises because education is based mainly on white middle-class culture, which disadvantages those from other backgrounds. It is not that the working class is in some ways deficient, but that the school is failing to meet the needs of working-class children and to recognize their culture as worthwhile. Explanations for class differences in educational achievement should therefore focus more on the nature of what happens inside the school, and the cultural values it promotes.

Compensatory education and positive discrimination

Cultural deprivation theories suggest that, for all young people to have an equal chance in the educational system, those from culturally deprived backgrounds need extra assistance and resources to help them compete on equal terms with other children. This idea of extra help is known as **compensatory education**, and involves **positive discrimination**.

Positive discrimination is when schools in disadvantaged areas, where home and social class background are seen as obstacles to success in education, are singled out for extra-favourable treatment, such as more and better-paid teachers, and more money to spend on buildings and equipment, to help the most disadvantaged succeed in education.

The idea of positive discrimination is based on the idea of equality of educational opportunity. In this view, children from disadvantaged backgrounds and poor homes can only get an opportunity in education equal to those who come from non-disadvantaged backgrounds if they get unequal and more generous treatment to compensate.

Education Action Zones and Excellence in Cities In Britain, an attempt at compensatory education was the setting-up in the late 1990s of *Education Action Zones* in socially disadvantaged areas, where unemployment, poverty, poor housing and overcrowding, ill-health and lack of self-confidence and aspiration contributed to poor educational performance. This initiative was rebranded as *Excellence in Cities* in 2005. Schools in these areas were given extra money and teachers to help them become better schools,

Compensatory education is extra educational help for those coming from disadvantaged groups to help them overcome the inequalities they face in the education system and the wider society.
Positive discrimination involves giving disadvantaged groups more favourable treatment than others to make up for the inequalities they face.

and to improve the educational performance of the most disadvantaged young people, by raising their levels of educational achievement and boosting their aspirations, confidence and self-esteem.

However, Power and Whitty (2008) pointed out that, though some individual schools, teachers and individuals benefited, the evidence suggested that the reforms did not work, and failed to make a significant impact on the achievement gaps between advantaged and disadvantaged schools and their students. Kerr and West (2010) conclude that, while the evidence shows that schooling can lessen the impact of deprivation on children's progress, its influence is limited by factors beyond the control of the school system, and that children's performance at school cannot be divorced from what happens to them outside school – in their families, communities and neighbourhoods.

There are many attempts being made to overcome the disadvantages that young people from deprived communities face in achieving success in education. Material and cultural disadvantages have many complex causes, and solutions are likely to take a number of years, and involve a wide range of social policies to reduce the poverty, low income and ill-health that underlie much educational failure. However, previous experience would suggest, as Bernstein put it, that 'education cannot compensate for society': that schools alone cannot solve the problem of working-class underachievement and that it is unrealistic to expect schools to compensate for inequalities of educational opportunity arising from the problems of a deeply unequal society.

Activity

1 Go to the Department for Education website, www.education.gov.uk/ and search for two policies which are currently being implemented to improve educational opportunities in the most disadvantaged communities. Explain in each case how these might improve educational opportunities.
2 Suggest three material factors in pupils' home and family background that may affect how successful they are in education, explaining carefully how these factors might affect educational achievement.
3 Explain what is meant by 'immediate gratification' and 'fatalism', and how these might affect working-class pupils' educational achievements.
4 Explain, with examples, what is meant by a 'culture clash' between the home and the school.
5 Identify three cultural factors that may affect pupils' educational achievements, explaining carefully how these factors might have these effects.
6 Identify two ways in which a school's catchment area might influence the education of pupils from the area.
7 Suggest three criticisms of cultural explanations for underachievement in education.

Factors inside the school influencing working-class underachievement

The explanations of working-class underachievement discussed so far have centred largely on the material and cultural factors *outside* the school that shape children before and during schooling. It is almost as if those from upper- and middle-class backgrounds are born to succeed in education, while those from the most disadvantaged, poor backgrounds are born to fail.

However, many would argue that schools can make a difference to the life chances of students whatever their backgrounds, and much research has suggested that social patterns of underachievement in education are affected not simply by material and cultural factors outside school, but also by what goes on in school classrooms. The previous topic showed how the meanings constructed in schools – how teachers and students come to see each other – affect student progress. From this interactionist perspective, pupils are not seen simply as passive victims of structural, material or cultural forces outside the school which cause underachievement. On the contrary, the emphasis is on the way, through interaction with others, teachers or pupils come to interpret and define situations, and develop meanings which influence the way they behave. The sociological evidence demonstrating a link between working-class origin and underachievement may have led teachers to expect working-class pupils to perform poorly, and these low expectations may actually be an important factor contributing to their failure.

Figure 6.8 illustrates a range of factors *inside* the school, discussed earlier in Topic 2, that sit alongside material and cultural factors arising *outside* the school, which provide further explanations for social class differences in educational achievement. This interactionist approach is very helpful in drawing attention to the factors inside schools which explain working-class underachievement. However, a full explanation of underachievement in education needs to take account of factors both outside the school and inside the school, both material and cultural factors and interaction in the classroom. In other words, a full account of working-class underachievement needs to look at both structural and interactionist explanations.

Activity

Read the passage below and answer the questions that follow.

The brutal truth

. . .but what do we mean by a good school? Examination results are the only criteria we accept, and politicians imply these have something to do with quality of teaching, sound leadership, strong discipline, clarity of aims and so on. And these can all make a difference. The brutal truth, however, is that the surest way to turn a bad school into a good one is to change the pupils who attend it . . . Parents, particularly middle-class parents, look at exam results and choose [schools] accordingly. Some don't bother with the results: they see well-scrubbed, nicely dressed and well-behaved pupils, and say that's the one for their child. They are right: home background, as you'd expect when you think how much more time children spend at home than at school, is another guide to attainment . . . A school can change the head, sack teachers, crack down on truancy and bad behaviour . . . these things may make the school happier, more peaceful, more businesslike. They may even improve exam results. They will make no long-term difference at all unless the intake changes . . . Rebranding the school may make a difference . . . a bright new wrapper always helps, for schools as well as chocolate bars, . . . but as long as schools have differing pupil intakes, some will be deemed 'good' and some 'bad'.

Source: adapted from Peter Wilby, Parents' admissions trauma is down to gross inequality outside school gates, *Guardian*, 5 March 2009

1 Describe in your own words what Wilby means by the 'brutal truth' in the passage above.
2 How do you think Peter Wilby might respond to the view that good schools can make a difference to the life chances of all pupils?
3 Suggest what Wilby seems to think are the main factors that affect whether or not a school is judged good or bad.
4 What does Wilby suggest might be the main factor influencing educational achievement?

The double test for working-class students

A combination of factors in the home, social class background and the school help to explain why working-class young people do less well at school than their middle-class peers of the same ability. Schools test all pupils when doing subjects like mathematics, English or science. However, for the working-class student there is a double test. At the same time as coping with the academic difficulties of school work which all pupils face, working-class students must also cope with a wide range of other disadvantages and difficulties. These problems, on top of the demands of academic work, explain working-class underachievement in schools. These disadvantages start even before they begin at primary school and become more and more emphasized as young people grow older, as they fall further and further behind and become more disillusioned with school. In this context, it is perhaps not surprising that a large majority of those who leave school at age 17 every year, with few or no qualifications, come from lower-working-class backgrounds.

Figure 6.8 Factors inside the school explaining class differences in educational achievement

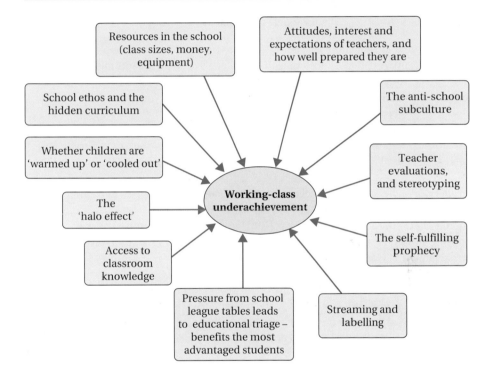

Gender and educational achievement: the underachievement of boys . . . but don't forget the girls

While the educational achievements of both males and females have improved in recent years, there are still big differences between them. Until the 1980s, the major concern was with the underachievement of girls. This was because, while girls used to perform better than boys in the earlier stages of their education, up to GCSE, after this they tended to fall behind, being less likely than boys to get the three A levels required for university entry, and less likely to go into higher education. However, in the early 1990s girls began to outperform boys, particularly working-class boys, in all areas and at all levels of the education system. The main problem today is with the underachievement of boys, though by 2011 this was beginning to change, with boys starting to catch up with, and sometimes marginally outperform, girls in some subjects. There are still concerns about the different subjects studied by boys and girls, and there are also

Activity

Refer to figure 6.8 and, if necessary, refer back to Topic 2 (pages 353–64)

1 Explain carefully how each of the factors identified in figure 6.8 might explain why working-class students are less likely to succeed in education than those from middle-class backgrounds.

2 Complete the following summary of explanations for social class differences in educational achievement, filling in the gaps from the word list below. Each dash represents one word.

'cooled out'	ability	Bourdieu
meritocratic	dominant class	deprivation
anti-school	poverty	functionalist
streaming	Marxist	legitimize
material circumstances	deficient	interactionist
'warmed up'	self-fulfilling prophecy	evaluations
compensatory	social class stereotypes	restricted
intelligence	educational qualifications	

___ theories argue that education selects and allocates the most talented people to the most functionally important roles according to ___ criteria like ability, talents and skills as shown by ___ ___ and achievement. Achievement reflects ___, and middle-class young people are more intelligent and harder-working than working-class young people.

___ theories argue that schools ___ social class inequality by making it appear that working-class students fail because of their lack of ___ , when in fact it is a consequence of their home and social class background, and the culture and ideology of the school.

___ explains working-class underachievement as a consequence of the lack of cultural capital, and the fact that the culture of the school is the culture of the ___ ___. ___ ___ of the home affect educational achievement, with factors such as ___ and low wages, poor housing and overcrowding, poorer health and more sickness all contributing to the underachievement of working-class pupils.

Cultural ___ theories suggest that the culture of the lower working class is ___ or deprived. Their different values and attitudes, the lack of parental interest and encouragement, their use of the ___ code of language and their lack of cultural capital undermine their chances of success in education, though positive discrimination and ___ education might help.

___ theories emphasize the importance of what goes on inside schools and classrooms. Teachers' ___ through typing, labelling, banding and ___ generate the ___-___ ___. Middle-class pupils are ___ ___ to succeed, and working-class pupils are ___ ___ to fail. Teachers give different knowledge to, and make different demands on, pupils depending on the stream the students are in. Streaming often reflects ___ ___ ___. These factors can lead to the formation of ___-___ subcultures with opposition to and rejection of educational success.

The solution to this activity can be found on the teachers' pages of www.politybooks.com/browne.

concerns that girls could do even better if teachers spent as much time with girls as they are obliged to do with boys.

The sections that follow provide a general picture of gender and achievement in education, but it is important to note that not *all* boys are underachieving, and neither are *all* girls doing well. The social class differences discussed above are generally more

Girls are generally much more successful in education than boys

important than gender (or ethnicity) in explaining differences in achievement, and girls generally only outperform boys with the *same* social class and ethnic characteristics. Perry and Francis (2010) point out, for example, that girls entitled to free school meals – those in the poorest social groups – continue to do less well in education than both girls and boys not on free school meals, and middle-class boys, even if they are outperformed by middle-class girls, are likely to achieve more highly than working-class girls.

THE FACTS ON GENDER DIFFERENCES IN EDUCATIONAL ACHIEVEMENT

- Girls do better than boys at every stage in National Curriculum Tests (NCTs or SATs) in English and science, and outperform boys in language and literacy.
- Girls are more successful than boys in most GCSE subjects, outperforming boys in every major subject, though boys are catching up with girls in more subjects each year. In English at GCSE, the gender gap is huge, with 73 per cent of girls getting an A*–C, compared to 59 per cent of boys in 2011. In 2011, 83 per cent of girls got five or more GCSEs (grades A*–C) compared to 75 per cent of boys, and girls were more likely to be entered for and achieve the six A*–C grades in the subjects making up the English Baccalaureate.
- A higher proportion of females stay on in sixth form and further education, and post-18 higher education.
- Female school leavers are now more likely than males to get three or more A-level passes, and achieve higher average point scores than males.
- More females than males get accepted for full-time university degree courses: in 2011, over half (55 per cent) of those accepted on degree courses were female, and 58 per cent of all undergraduate students, and 54 per cent of all postgraduates, were female.
- Female students are more likely to get top 1st-class and upper 2nd-class degrees.

PROBLEMS REMAINING FOR GIRLS

Despite the general pattern of girls outperforming boys, problems do still remain for girls. The attention given to girls outperforming boys and the underachievement of boys can draw attention away from the fact that large numbers of girls are also low-attainers and are underachieving. It is also important to remember that social class differences, rather than gender, remain the most significant influences on educational achievement, so, for example, as Perry and Francis point out, although girls outperform boys at literacy within each social class, middle-class boys outperform working-class girls, and girls taking free school meals continue to underperform in relation to girls and boys not on free school meals. Girls still tend to do different subjects from boys, which influences future career choices. Broadly, arts subjects are more likely to be chosen by females, and science and technology subjects by males. This exists at GCSE, but becomes even more pronounced at A level and above. Girls are therefore less likely to participate after 16 in subjects leading to careers in science, engineering and technology.

Girls tend to slip back between GCSE and A level, with girls achieving fewer high-grade A levels than boys with the same GCSE results. There is little evidence that the generally better results of girls at 16 and above lead to improved post-school opportunities in terms of training and employment. Women are still less likely than men with similar qualifications to achieve similar levels of success in paid employment, and men still hold the majority of the positions of power in society. Among people in the 16–59 age group in the population as a whole who are in employment or unemployed, men tend to be better qualified than women. However, this gap has decreased among younger age groups, and can be expected to disappear if females keep on outperforming males in education.

EXPLAINING GENDER DIFFERENCES IN EDUCATION

What follows are some suggested hypotheses and explanations, based on the framework provided by Mitsos and Browne (1998), for the huge improvement in the performance of girls, the underperformance of boys and the subject choices that continue to separate males and females. The explanations are summarized in figure 6.9.

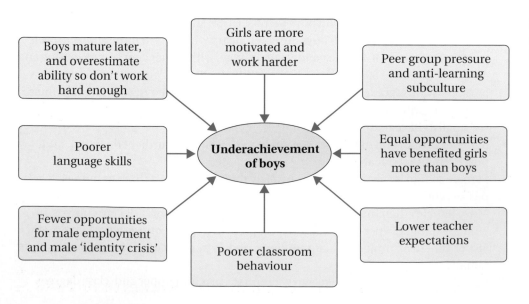

Figure 6.9 Gender and educational underachievement

Why do females now do better than males?

The women's movement and feminism   The women's movement and feminism have achieved considerable success in improving the rights and raising the expectations and self-esteem of women. They have challenged the traditional stereotype of women's roles as housewives and mothers, and more people have become aware of the problems of patriarchy, gender role stereotyping and sex discrimination. This means many women now look beyond being a housewife/mother as their main role in life.

Equal opportunities   The work of sociologists in highlighting the educational under-performance of girls in the past led to a greater emphasis in schools on equal opportunities, in order to enable girls to fulfil their potential more easily. These policies included, among others, monitoring teaching and teaching materials for gender bias to help schools to meet the needs of girls better, encouraging 'girl-friendliness' not only in male-dominated subjects but across the whole range of the experience of girls in schools. Initiatives such as WISE (Women into Science, Engineering and Construction – www.wisecampaign.org.uk) have aimed to inspire girls and to attract them into studying and following careers in subjects like science, technology, IT, engineering and mathematics. Teachers are now much more sensitive about avoiding gender stereotyping in the classroom, and this may have overcome many of the former academic problems which girls faced in schools.

Growing ambition, more positive role models and more employment opportunities for women   There has been a decline in recent years in the number of what were traditionally regarded as 'men's jobs', particularly in semi- and unskilled manual work, while there are growing employment opportunities for women in the **service sector**.

As a consequence, girls have become more ambitious, and they are less likely to see having a home and family as their main role in life. Many girls growing up today have mothers working in paid employment, who provide positive role models for them. Many girls now recognize that the future involves paid employment, often combined with family responsibilities. Sharpe (1976, 1994) found in 1976 that girls' priorities were 'love, marriage, husbands, children, jobs, and careers, more or less in that order'. When she repeated her research in 1994, she found these priorities had changed to 'job, career and being able to support themselves'. Francis (2000) carried out research involving observation of twelve classes of 14- to 16-year-olds and interviews with students in three London secondary schools in 1998–9. Her interviews with girls confirmed Sharpe's findings, and she found many girls were very ambitious, aiming for higher professional occupations like doctors and solicitors, rather than the traditional female occupations like clerical work, hairdressing or beauty therapy. McRobbie (2008) argues that changes in the job market have meant more and more young women now expect to gain a degree qualification as a requirement for an interesting and rewarding career – an aspiration which in many ways has replaced marriage and motherhood. These factors may all have provided more incentives for girls to gain qualifications.

Girls work harder, are better motivated and have more peer-group support   There is evidence that girls work harder, are more conscientious and are better motivated than boys. Girls put more effort into their work, and spend more time on doing their homework properly. They take more care with the way their work is presented, care more than boys about the opinion of their teachers, and they concentrate more in class and have better concentration over a longer period of time (some research has shown the

> The **service sector** of the economy, sometimes referred to as the tertiary sector, is concerned with the production of services instead of actual products. It is concerned with administration, information, communication, catering, the leisure industry, sales, finance and insurance, transport and distribution, and the running of government services such as the health, welfare and education services.

typical 14-year-old girl concentrating for about three to four times as long as her fellow male students). Girls are generally better organized: they are more likely to bring the right equipment to school and meet deadlines for handing in work. Some suggest these factors may help girls to perform better than boys in qualifications involving course-work, which often requires good organization and sustained application, and girls do better than boys in these respects.

Francis suggests the development of feminine identity in school settings involves cooperative and conciliatory attitudes to teachers, other pupils and authority in general. This femininity is linked to a supportive attitude to schoolwork, reinforced and enhanced by a consequently more pro-school peer group. This all reinforces girls' working habits in school and higher levels of achievement, and contrasts sharply with the anti-school stance of many boys (see below), characterized by active resistance to authority and disengagement from school.

Girls mature earlier   By the age of 16, girls are estimated to be more mature than boys by up to two years. Put simply, this means girls are more likely to view exams in a far more responsible way, and recognize their seriousness and the importance of the academic and career choices that lie ahead of them.

Why do boys underachieve?

Many of the reasons given above also suggest why boys may be underachieving. However, there are some additional explanations.

Lower expectations   There is some evidence that staff are not as strict with boys as with girls. They are more likely to extend deadlines for work, to have lower expectations of boys, to be more tolerant of the disruptive, unruly behaviour often found more com-monly from boys in the classroom and to accept more poorly presented work. These lower expectations could create a self-fulfilling prophecy contributing to boys' lower achievement, as they perform less well than they otherwise might.

Boys are more disruptive   Boys are generally more disruptive in classrooms than girls. The male peer group often devalues schoolwork (see the anti-learning subculture below) and boys may achieve peer-group status by aggressive and dominating disrup-tive classroom behaviour. They may lose classroom learning time because they are sent out of the room or sent home. Boys are around four times more likely to be permanently excluded from schools, and three times more likely to be excluded for fixed terms, than girls; most of these exclusions are for disobedience of various kinds, and usually come at the end of a series of incidents.

Masculinity and the anti-learning subculture   Forde et al. (2006) suggest peer-group pressure encourages boys to maintain a dominant masculine identity, which is partly developed through resistance to school and is therefore largely incompatible with aca-demic success. This often involves rejecting academic work as feminine, and adopting disruptive classroom behaviour. Boys, especially working-class boys, appear to gain 'street cred' and peer-group status by not working, and some develop a laddish, anti-education, anti-learning subculture, where schoolwork is seen as 'girly' and 'unmacho', and where it's not 'cool' to work hard or to achieve at school. This was shown by Epstein et al. (1998), who found that working-class boys risked harassment, bullying and being labelled as 'gay' if they appeared to be hard-working at school. This may explain why boys are often less conscientious and lack the persistence and application required for exam success. This anti-learning subculture is like that adopted by 'the lads' in Paul Willis's *Learning to Labour*, discussed earlier in this chapter, where aspiring for academic success is seen to conflict with adolescent conceptions of masculinity. Francis's (2000) research confirmed this view of boys achieving more peer-group macho status by resisting teachers and schools, through laddish behaviour like messing about in class and not getting on with their work, contributing to their underachievement. As seen in the last topic, boys are more likely than girls to develop anti-school subcultures.

Teaching is often seen as a mainly female profession, and there is a lack of positive male role models, especially in primary schools. This may be a further reason why learning comes to be seen by some boys, from an early age, as a 'feminine' and 'girly' activity. This may further contribute to a negative attitude to schools and schooling.

Declining traditional male employment opportunities and the male identity crisis Mac an Ghaill (1994) suggests the decline in traditional male working-class jobs is also a factor in explaining why many boys, and particularly working-class boys, are underperforming in education. They may lack motivation and ambition because they feel that they have only limited prospects, and getting qualifications won't get them anywhere anyway, so what's the point in bothering? These changing employment patterns have resulted in a number of (predominantly white and working-class) boys and men having lowered expectations, a low self-image and a lack of self-esteem. The collapse of the traditional male breadwinner role in the family brought about by poor job prospects has led to a crisis of masculinity – an identity crisis for men who feel insecure about their masculine role and position. This insecurity is reflected in schools, where boys don't see the point in working hard and trying to achieve. The future seems bleak and to lack a clear purpose for many working-class boys, and this curbs their ambition, and education just seems like a pointless waste of time. This leads boys to attempt to construct a positive self-image through laddish behaviour, aggressive macho posturing and anti-school activity, in attempts to draw attention to themselves, while at the same time contributing further to their underachievement.

Feeling and behaving differently Boys and girls feel differently about their own ability, with most boys overestimating their ability, and girls underestimating theirs. Stanworth (1983) and Licht and Dweck (1987) found girls lacked confidence in and underestimated their ability, and felt undervalued in the classroom. Renold and Allan's (2006) research suggests this still remains true today. Their research on highly achieving girls in two primary schools in South Wales found that such girls were torn between being seen as academically bright and being attractive to boys. Consequently, in order to continue to be attractive to boys, girls played down their academic abilities.

Research by Michael Barber (1996) at Keele University's Centre for Successful Schools showed 'that more boys than girls think that they are able or very able, and fewer boys than girls think that they are "below average"'. Yet GCSE results show these perceptions to be the reverse of the truth. Boys feel that they are bright and capable but at the same time they say they don't like school and they just coast along rather than rise to the challenge of academic work, and they don't work hard enough to get the results they think they're capable of. This was confirmed by Francis's research in three London secondary schools in 1998–9, which found that some boys thought it would be easy to do well in exams without having to put in much effort. When they do fail, boys tend to blame either the teachers or their own lack of effort – not their ability.

Different leisure – doing not talking   More research is coming to the conclusion that the differences in the achievement of girls and boys is due to the differing ways in which the genders behave and spend their leisure time. To simplify and generalize: while boys run around kicking footballs, playing sports or computer games, and engaging in other aspects of laddish behaviour, girls are more likely to read or to stand around talking. Girls relate to one another by talking, while boys often relate to their peers by doing things. The value of talking, even if it is about the heart-throb of Year 11, is that it tends to develop the linguistic and reasoning skills needed at school and in many non-manual service sector jobs. Most school subjects require good levels of comprehension and reading and writing skills, but many boys view these crucial reading and linguistic skills as 'girly' and 'uncool'.

Boys don't like reading   Girls like reading while boys don't: boys see reading as a predominantly feminine activity, which is boring, not real work, a waste of time and to be avoided at all costs. Reading is 'feminized' in our culture: women are not only the main consumers of reading in our society, but they are also the ones who read, talk about and 'spread the word' about books, and they are more likely to be the ones who read to their children (and they are more likely to read to their daughters than to their sons). Girls are therefore more likely to have positive role models of their own sex than boys, regarding education. Research has shown that boys tend to stop being interested in reading at about 8 years old.

   Girls and boys also tend to read different things: girls read fiction while boys read for information. Schools tend to reproduce this gendered divide: fiction tends to be the main means of learning to read in the primary school years and this puts girls at an early advantage in education. Oakhill and Petrides (2007) found that boys' interest in the content of what they read influences their ability to understand a text, and

Girls relate to one another by talking, while boys are more likely to relate to each other by doing things. Do you think this is true in your own experience?

therefore their grasp of, motivation and development in that subject, while girls' understanding and performance is far less influenced by the content of what they read. In effect, this means girls are better than boys at handling and understanding reading in those subjects, or bits of any subject, which don't have much personal interest for them.

Activity

Drawing on your own experience, and giving examples, do you think:
- Boys overestimate their ability, while girls underestimate theirs?
- Boys and girls behave differently in school, particularly in relation to how they behave with their peer group?
- Boys don't read as much as girls, and when they do, read different things?
- Boys are more likely to show an anti-education, anti-learning subculture than girls?
- Girls work harder than boys?

Why do males and females still tend to study different subjects?

There is still a difference between the subjects that males and females do at GCSE and above, as figure 6.10 shows.

Traditionally, science subjects have been seen as masculine, and arts and humanities subjects, like English literature, foreign languages and sociology, as feminine. Skelton et al. (2007) point out that young males still typically pursue technical/ technological and science-oriented subjects, while young women typically pursue caring, or arts / humanities / social science subjects. Skelton suggests that the science subjects, more often taken by males, are seen as more difficult and of higher status than what are regarded as the lower-status 'soft' or easier subjects taken by girls. These subject differences exist despite the National Curriculum, which makes maths, English and science compulsory for all students. However, even within the National Curriculum, there are gender differences in option choices. For example, girls are more likely to take home economics, textiles and food technology, while boys are more likely to opt for electronics, woodwork or graphics. How can we explain these differences?

Gender socialization   Pupils' aspirations and subject choices have their roots in the primary and secondary socialization processes whereby the social and cultural norms linked to stereotyped gender roles are learnt. From an early age boys and girls are encouraged to play with different toys and do different activities at home, and they very often grow up seeing their parents playing different roles around the house. Research in 1974 by Lobban found evidence of gender stereotyping in children's books, with women more clearly linked to traditional domestic roles. Research by Best in 1993 found that little had changed since Lobban conducted her research. (You can read more about the gender role socialization process on pages 65–9 in chapter 2.)

Such socialization may encourage boys to develop more interest in technical and scientific subjects, and discourage girls from taking them. These socialization factors may be reinforced by peer pressure to opt for particular subjects, and also by gendered perceptions of subjects and future career choices which are considered below.

Subject counseling   In giving subject and career advice, teachers and career advisers may be reflecting their own socialization and expectations, by counselling or

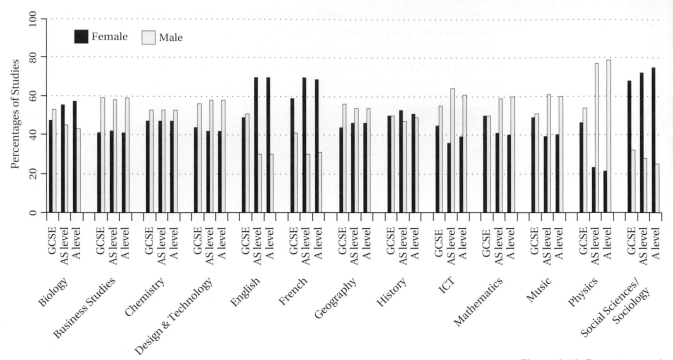

Figure 6.10 Percentages of male and female students entering for different subjects at GCSE, AS and A level: United Kingdom, 2011

Source: Joint Council for Qualifications, 2011

Activity

Refer to figure 6.10

1 In which three A-level subjects was the gap between the percentages of male and female entries the greatest?

2 In which three GCSE subjects was the gap between the percentages of male and female entries the greatest?

3 In which (a) A-level and (b) AS-level subjects were there more male than female entries in 2011?

4 Which two subjects showed the greatest gap between the percentages of male and female entries at GCSE, AS and A level?

5 Which two subjects had more male entries at GCSE, but more female entries at A level?

6 Why do you think the gap in subject entries between males and females tends, in general, to be smaller at GCSE than at A level?

7 Drawing on the data in figure 6.10, outline the main gender differences in subject choices at GCSE, AS and A level, and suggest reasons for them, with reference to specific subjects.

channelling boys and girls into choosing different gendered subject options, in accordance with their own gender stereotypes of suitable or appropriate subjects. Such gendered subject choices will have clear consequences for what happens after school, in higher education course options and future career opportunities.

Subject images, gender identity and peer pressure Research by Colley (1998) suggested that the gender perceptions of different subjects are important influences on subject choice, with the arts and humanities seen by students as feminine, and science and technology as masculine.

Skelton et al. (2007) suggest that males and females may tend to be drawn to different subject areas due to their own ideas of what is appropriate for their gender identity. For example, they suggest literacy and English are often seen as feminine subjects, and girls therefore find this subject choice confirms their conception of femininity, while boys find the opposite, and that it challenges their view of masculinity. Mitsos (1995–6), in her interview research with Year 11 boys and girls at a Coventry inner-city comprehensive school, found boys' unfavourable responses to English were often voiced in the context of stereotypical male and female behaviour and boys' differences from girls (see, for example, the activity taken from her research at the end of this section). Paechter (1998) illustrated this gendering of subject images with the example of physical education (PE). She found that sport was seen as primarily a masculine activity, which encouraged some girls to opt out of the subject. Female athletes who did choose PE and sport had to cope by working hard in other ways to express their femininity. Those who didn't risked being marginalized by both their male and female peers for appearing 'unfeminine', and stigmatized by being called names such as 'butch' or 'lesbian'.

Science and the science classroom are still seen as mainly 'masculine'. As Kelly (1987) found, and subsequent research has repeatedly confirmed, boys tend to dominate science classrooms – grabbing apparatus first, answering questions aimed at girls, ridiculing girls' questions and answers and so on, which all undermine girls' confidence and intimidate them from taking up these subjects. Gender stereotyping is still found in science, with the 'invisibility' of females particularly obvious in maths and science textbooks, where examples are often more relevant to the experience of males than of females. This reinforces the view that these are 'male' subjects.

Colley (1998) noted that, like science, ITC (Information and Communication Technology) is seen as part of the masculine domain, with the use of machines (computers) accompanied by a more individual style of learning appealing more to boys than the group work preferred by girls.

The choices of girls and boys may therefore reflect their desire to select subjects which they see as having an image appropriate to their gender. This is reinforced by peer-group pressure to conform to gender-appropriate behaviour, rather than risking ridicule or name-calling. This may be further reinforced by the expectations that schools have of gender-appropriate options, as considered above.

Colley suggested that the changing content of the curriculum of some subjects can alter its gender identity, and therefore the gender of those who choose to study it. For example, she found that music, which was once traditionally seen as a feminine subject, with girls making up the majority of those taking it, was becoming more popular with boys. Colley's research suggested that this change was largely because the subject had become more computer- and electronics-based, with the application of technology to music production contributing to the 'masculinization' of the subject's content, making it more appealing as a subject option for boys, and reducing its appeal for girls. By 2011, the masculinization of music had developed to such an extent that it had become a more popular option among boys than among girls. For example, in 2001, boys made up 42 per cent of GCSE music entries, 47 per cent of AS entries, and 43 per cent of A-level entries. By 2011, this had increased to 52 per cent at GCSE, and 61 per cent at both AS and A level.

Activity

The following comments are from Year 11 boys talking about doing English and science:

'I hate it! I don't want to read books.'

'Science is straightforward. You don't have to think about it. There are definite answers. There are no shades to it.'

'In science, everything is set out as a formula, and you have the facts. All you have to do is apply them to the situation.'

'When you read a book, it's like delving into people's lives. It's being nosey.'

English is about understanding, interpreting . . . you have to think more. There's no definite answer . . . the answer depends on your view of things.'

'I don't like having discussions – I feel wrong . . . I think that people will jump down my throat.'

'That's why girls do English, because they don't mind getting something wrong. They're more open about issues, they're more understanding . . . they find it easier to comprehend other people's views and feelings.'

'You feel safe in science.'

(Adapted from Mitsos (1995 and 1996))

1   What points are being made above about why females are more likely to choose to study English than males?
2   Identify all the ways you can think of in which gender differences in subject choices might be linked to gender role socialization in society as a whole.

Activity

Applying the research methods studied in the previous chapter:
1   Observe classroom activities and try to see whether boys and girls behave differently in class or are treated differently by teachers. For example, do they sit separately? Are boys or girls asked more questions? Are boys more disruptive? Does this vary between different subject classes and between male and female teachers? (If you plan to do classroom observation, applying Flanders Interaction Analysis might be useful – see page 433 later in this chapter.)
2   Interview a sample of male and female students, asking them about what influenced them in making subject and exam choices.

Schooling and gender identity

Much of this section, and the previous topic on factors inside the school, suggest that the schooling process reinforces and reproduces gender identities, and particularly reinforces elements of patriarchal control of males over females. There is more on this in chapter 2, on the ways the school and the peer group contribute to the social construction of gender identities, and you should refer to this (see page 67).

Francis (2005) points out that gender is an important part of our social identity, and fitting in at school often means adopting behaviour which conforms to gender stereotypes, with boys and girls frequently adopting different gender-appropriate behaviours, with those failing to do so risking peer-group marginalization and possibly bullying. Skelton et al. (2007) point out that boys and girls act out their gender roles as opposites, with acting as a boy meaning behaving in ways that are the exact opposite of acting as a girl. Skelton says children act out these deep-seated gender roles often without being consciously aware of them, and what is seen as appropriate boy or girl behaviour can take different forms at different stages of education, according to the school ethos, and in different social classes and ethnic groups. Peer groups are of central importance in forming gender identities in school settings, as these normally involve same-sex friendship groups, who sit together, and such groups 'police' the gendered behaviour of their peers, and punish failure to conform to traditional gender norms. While clearly not all boys or all girls conform to the stereotypes, most do, leading to different experiences for males and females at school. Francis (2005) picks out the following key elements in this process of creating and reinforcing gender identities and patriarchal relations through schooling:

- *Gendered verbal behaviour* – boys dominate talk in mixed-sex classrooms, drowning out girls' talk and often interrupting and ridiculing girls' contributions. Boys thereby gain greater proportions of the teachers' time and attention, though a lot of this is to do with discipline rather than learning, unlike with girls, who are more focused on learning. Boys are also frequently verbally abusive in ways that reinforce their masculinity, such as denigrating (belittling) behaviour they see as gay or girly, and showing contempt for all things female, often using terms of abuse relating to women or female body parts. This reinforces male identity as well as patriarchy, as it defines men as better than and superior to women.

- *Gendered physical behaviour* – boys and girls tend to sit in separate groups in the classroom. While girls might resist schooling, it is likely to be in more passive ways, like reading magazines, chatting or doing their make-up, instead of working; boys are more likely to get into confrontations with the teacher. This creates a sense of girls being 'invisible' in the classroom. Boys also dominate physical space, through playground behaviour, sprawling at desks, and literally taking up more room when they boisterously move around the classroom. Research suggests this is, consciously or unconsciously, an exercise of patriarchal power and control by some boys over girls.

- *Gendered pursuits* – girls' classroom talk and activity involve pursuits that focus on their appearance and the construction of femininity, like hair, make-up and diet, and efforts to make themselves 'look nice' to please boys – attractive to what Mac an Ghaill (1994) called the 'male gaze'. Boys' focus mirrors this, involving constructing their masculinity through boasting about their alleged sexual conquests, and how far girls would let them go (see page 67 for how boys have a double standard when they talk about their own and girls' sexual exploits – with promiscuous boys seeing themselves as 'studs', yet at the same time seeing similarly promiscuous girls as slags or sluts). In this way, boys and girls are constructing their different but related gender identities.

- *Gendered classroom behaviour and power* – research shows that in the mixed-sex classroom, girls often help in supporting boys, such as clearing up after them and helping them with homework, and girls defer to boys in classroom interaction. Girls may also find themselves silenced, ridiculed, or physically or sexually abused or harassed by boys. This happens most often to the most assertive or self-confident girls, who risk challenging boys and undermining their masculinity, and whom boys feel they have to punish to show them who's boss. Girls may also face ridicule by other girls if they don't conform to mainstream conceptions of femininity. Such things reinforce the patriarchal power of boys over girls, as well as reinforcing stereotypes of masculinity and femininity.

- *The role of teachers* – Francis suggests teachers also contribute to creating and perpetuating gender stereotypes. She points out that teachers often have different expectations of pupils according to their gender, with girls expected to be relatively quiet, conformist, obedient and conscientious compared to boys. Because of these expectations, girls who don't conform to what is seen as appropriate gender behaviour and behave badly are penalized more heavily than boys, whose bad behaviour is seen as 'natural high spirits' and 'boys will be boys'.

SOME CONCLUDING COMMENTS ON GENDER AND UNDERACHIEVEMENT: WHAT ABOUT THE GIRLS?

Educational research has repeatedly shown that teachers focus more attention and spend more time on boys. Spender (1982) first showed that teachers' time is spent mostly on the troublesome boys, rather than on the girls who are keen to learn and to get on with their schooling. Stanworth (1983) found students themselves thought boys got more than twice the amount of attention from teachers that girls did, in terms of getting help, being asked questions and being encouraged to get involved in class discussions. Francis's (2000) research in 1998–9 found classrooms were still dominated by boys, and girls were getting less attention. Girls therefore see teachers spending more time with the boys than with them. Francis (2005) suggests that, while improvements have been made, education policy, the school's overt and hidden curriculum, interaction with boys and teacher expectations continue to have negative effects on girls' self-esteem and experiences at school.

Feminist researchers like Jackson et al. (2010) have become increasingly angry at the way educational policy in recent years has ignored girls and been almost exclusively concerned with boys' underachievement. They point out a range of ways in which attempts to raise boys' attainment can have negative consequences for girls. They point out that concerns about girls' achievement and their experiences of schooling are largely neglected or ignored, and girls remain marginalized, as boys' needs are given greater priority. They suggest there needs to be a new focus on issues like how peer pressures and demands for femininity can be damaging to girls' self-concepts and social networks, particularly for those girls who strive for academic excellence. They emphasize the continuing problems of gendered subject choices, of the educational underachievement of many girls, and of boys' domination of school space and teacher time.

In the face of girls' marked disadvantages, such as underrating themselves and a lack of confidence in their ability, getting less of teachers' time, and having to tolerate the dominance of boys in the classroom, it is perhaps surprising that they generally tend to do much better at school than boys. This suggests that girls may still be underachieving, even if they are not doing so in relation to the boys.

It is still men who hold most of the highly paid, powerful positions in society – it is still mainly men who pull the strings and run our society. Women go out to work more than they used to, and they now make up about half the workforce. However, as seen in chapter 3, research has shown that in the home gender roles have not changed that much: women now not only go out to paid work a lot more, but also still have the majority of the burden of housework, childcare and managing family emotions.

Activity

1 Go through the reasons suggested in the sections above for why girls often outperform boys in education. List the explanations in what you think is their order of importance, and explain/justify your reasons.
2 Using your answer to question 1, suggest measures that might be taken to improve the educational performance of boys.
3 Drawing on your own experience of schooling, can you identify ways in which boys and girls are treated differently by teachers? Do boys behave differently in class from girls? Are they more disruptive in the classroom? Do boys have a different attitude to school work and to different subjects? Were/are there some subjects in your school which attracted more of one sex than another? Why do you think this might be?
4 Do you think girls, even though they are doing better than boys, are still underachieving in education?

Ethnicity and educational achievement

Alongside social class and gender differences, there are also identifiable differences in educational achievement linked to the ethnic group to which people belong, some of which are shown below. Although there are important differences between minority ethnic groups, the overall statistics disguise wide variations between individuals – some minority ethnic group children may be very successful in the education system, even if they come from a group that generally underachieves. Conversely, some children may perform badly in education even if they come from an ethnic group that generally has high levels of attainment.

THE EVIDENCE ON ACHIEVEMENT AND UNDERACHIEVEMENT AMONG MINORITY ETHNIC GROUPS

The highest-achieving groups

Chinese and Indian Asian pupils consistently have higher levels of attainment than other ethnic groups, and they make the greatest progress in school. They are more likely to achieve five or more GCSE grades A*–C, to get better AS/A-level results, to stay in education after the end of compulsory schooling, and to enter university than all other ethnic groups, including the White British ethnic majority.

The lowest-achieving groups

Black Caribbean, Pakistani, Bangladeshi and the small number of Gypsy/Roma and Traveller-of-Irish-Heritage pupils consistently have lower levels of attainment than all other ethnic groups, and most pupils from such backgrounds do less well than they should, given their ability. A range of evidence from Gillborn and Gipps (1996), Gillborn and Mirza (2000), Bhattacharyya et al. (2004) and the DfES* (2005, 2006) identified the main evidence on these underachieving groups as follows:

---

* The DfES refers to the Department for Education and Skills, whose name was changed to the Department for Children, Schools and Families (DCSF) in 2007, and changed again in 2010 to the present Department for Education (DfE).

- Taken overall, they appear to have below-average reading skills.
- At the beginning of primary school (Key Stage 1), most ethnic minority pupils (with the exception of Chinese pupils) lag behind White British-born pupils. However, most ethnic groups, particularly Indian Asians, make greater progress than White British pupils throughout compulsory schooling and this narrows the original pre-school gap. The exception to this is Black Caribbean boys, whose performance deteriorates between Key Stage 1 and Key Stage 4, most clearly at secondary school, compared to White British children with similar levels of ability.
- Black Caribbean, Pakistani and Bangladeshi pupils, and Gypsy/Roma and Traveller-of-Irish-Heritage pupils, consistently have lower levels of attainment than other ethnic groups across all National Curriculum Key Stages and are less likely to attain higher grade (A*–C) GCSE results than children of Chinese, White British or Indian origin.
- Black Caribbean young people are overrepresented (there are more than there should be, given their numbers in the population as a whole) in special schools for those with learning difficulties. They are one and a half times as likely to be categorized as having emotional, behavioural or social difficulties as White British students.
- Despite rising standards of achievement for all ethnic groups, the gap between Black Caribbean and Pakistani pupils and their White British peers is little different from what it was in the 1990s.
- Black Caribbean school students are between three and six times more likely to be permanently excluded from schools than White British students of the same sex, and to be excluded for longer fixed terms than white students for the same offences.
- Where schools are streamed by ability, minority ethnic groups are overrepresented in the lower streams. Evidence suggests they are placed in lower streams even when they get better results than some students placed in higher streams.
- They are more likely than other groups to leave school without any qualifications.
- They are less likely to stay on in education after the end of compulsory schooling, and, when they do, they are more likely to follow vocational courses rather than the higher-status academic courses, like AS and A levels.

EXPLANATIONS FOR ETHNIC GROUP DIFFERENCES IN EDUCATION

There is no single factor that explains the differences between ethnic groups – a range of factors, both inside and outside the school, work together to produce the lower levels of achievement of some minority ethnic groups.

It is important to remember that the influence of ethnicity on educational achievement works alongside the influences of social class and gender discussed above, which can make untangling the patterns of achievement quite complex. Social class remains the single most important influence on educational achievement, but ethnic and gender differences arise within the same social classes. For example, Black Caribbean girls generally make more progress throughout compulsory schooling and perform better in education than Black Caribbean boys of the same social class, who lose ground as they progress through the education system, and working-class Black Caribbean girls generally do better than working-class White British girls. These influences of social class and gender are considered and intermeshed among the explanations below.

Social class and material factors

Minority ethnic groups are far more likely than white people to live in low-income households and to be in the poorest fifth of the population. About two-fifths of people from ethnic minorities were living in poverty in 2010 – twice the rate for White British people. More than half of people from Pakistani or Bangladeshi ethnic backgrounds, and around a third of Black Caribbeans, compared to one in five of White British people, were living in poverty, and higher-than-average proportions of pupils from these groups are eligible for free school meals (an indicator of the poorest social classes). Black Caribbean, Pakistani and Bangladeshi people are more likely to be unemployed, and to live in the poorest areas with the greatest concentrations of social problems.

This means some ethnic minority groups face problems like poor-quality housing, overcrowding, higher levels of unemployment (partly due to racism) and general material disadvantage, which may affect achievement levels in school. Such material disadvantage means they face a similar range of problems to those of the poorest sections of the working class to which they belong. This means all the explanations discussed above explaining working-class underachievement, such as material deprivation, language differences, cultural deprivation, lack of cultural and social capital, teacher attitudes, teacher expectations/labelling and the self-fulfilling prophecy may also contribute to explaining the differences between ethnic groups.

In contrast, the percentage of Indian Asian and Chinese pupils who are eligible for free school meals is below the average for all pupils, and they are more likely to come from business and professional middle-class family backgrounds, thereby gaining all the benefits that being middle-class confers in education.

The variation in social class background may mean that some of the differences between ethnic groups, in terms of educational achievement, may have less to do with ethnicity as such, and more to do with social and economic disadvantage.

However, Gillborn and Mirza (2000) point out that, while social class remains the main influence on educational attainment, social class factors do not completely override the influence of ethnic inequality. This is shown by the fact that pupils from the *same* social class background but from different ethnic groups still show marked inequalities in attainment. For example, White British students from middle-class homes will often perform much better than Black Caribbean students from the same class background; and Indian Asian and Chinese students are doing better, and Black Caribbean, Pakistani and Bangladeshi students are doing worse, than White British students from the same social class background (the exception to this is White British students from the most deprived social groups, who have the lowest levels of educational attainment).

Language

Around 12–17 per cent of pupils in primary and secondary schools (with much higher proportions in some areas – as high as 78 per cent in some primary schools in parts of London) did not have English as their first language or the main language used in their homes, according to official statistics published in 2011. Pupils for whom English is an additional language often have lower levels of attainment on starting school than pupils whose first language is English.

Language differences may cause difficulties in doing some schoolwork and communicating with the teacher, and white, middle-class teachers may mistake language difficulties for lack of ability in general, and therefore have lower expectations of some of their pupils.

Some Black Caribbean homes use Caribbean English, a different form of English, and its use may be unconsciously penalized in the classroom, because most teachers are white and middle-class. The active discouragement of children from using their mother tongue in school, and negative labelling, may provide obstacles to learning and motivation in school, as the self-fulfilling prophecy takes effect.

The Swann Report (1985) found that, while language factors might hold back some children, for the majority they were of little importance, and the DfES (2005) found any impact of language declines as children get older, and that pre-school language differences are rapidly overcome. Gillborn and Mirza (2000) point out that the very high attainment of Indian pupils suggests that language differences in the home do not form a barrier to success.

Family life and parental support

Parental involvement in their children's education has been shown to be a key factor in pupils' attainment. While many ethnic minority parents have high aspirations for their children and see education as a route to upward social mobility, the Swann Report (1985) and Pilkington (1997) suggested that pupils from some minority ethnic groups enjoy greater parental support than others. Asian family life has been characterized as consisting of close-knit extended families, which have high aspirations for their children and very supportive attitudes to education, combined with wider cultural values which encourage higher levels of achievement than, for example, working-class Black Caribbeans. Lupton (2004) suggests that lower working-class White British families in the most disadvantaged areas have a fairly indifferent or negative attitude towards learning and towards school, and low aspirations for their children. These family cultures may contribute to differences in attainment between ethnic groups.

Bhatti's (1999) research, discussed further below, of the relationship between home and school for Pakistani, Bangladeshi and Indian Asian pupils, found parents were very supportive and had a high level of interest in their children's education, though they often didn't know much about the daily processes and organization of schools, and their children's experience of schooling, and many didn't know how to approach the school or teachers, so avoided doing so unless it was essential. Many of those who did visit found school unwelcoming. Their own level of education meant they were sometimes unable to help their children with schoolwork as much as they would have liked to.

Black Caribbean communities have a high level of lone parenthood, and this may pose financial and practical problems for such parents in supporting their children's education, no matter how much concern they may have about their children's progress. For Black Caribbean girls, who display higher levels of achievement than Black Caribbean boys, the fact that women are often the primary breadwinners in many Black Caribbean families may provide positive role models for girls and encourage higher levels of achievement – a recognition that they themselves will in future be major breadwinners.

Vincent et al. (2011) found black middle-class parents were particularly concerned with and actively involved in their children's schooling, often making particular efforts to meet teachers, insisting on high standards, and carrying out research to actively demonstrate their knowledge about education to teachers and to support their children's education. However, they often found teachers treated them as if they knew less about their children's education than white middle-class parents, despite having similar qualifications, and expected black middle-class parents and pupils to be far less interested in education than their white peers.

Moon and Ivins (2004), in a telephone survey of a representative sample of over 1,500 parents/carers of minority ethnic children, found parental involvement with their children's education was greater in minority ethnic groups than in the population as a whole, and a higher proportion saw their children's education as mainly the parents' responsibility rather than the school's, and this was particularly true of Black Caribbean and Bangladeshi parents. A very high proportion (82 per cent) went to parents' evenings whenever there was an opportunity, although Pakistani and Bangladeshi parents were less confident about helping their children with homework, largely because they lacked the cultural capital to which Bourdieu referred (see pages 375–6).

One further indicator of the high levels of parental aspiration and interest among many minority ethnic parents is the fact that working-class Black Caribbean and Asian parents are more successful than their White British equivalents in getting their children, including those who are relatively unsuccessful at GCSE, to stay on in education at the end of compulsory schooling, and to enter higher education. Modood (2006) showed that this parental aspiration, support and encouragement was an important factor in explaining why ethnic minority students are now more likely to enter higher education than White young people. In 2010, for example, 22 per cent of accepted applicants to UK universities were from ethnic minorities, about double their proportion in the population as a whole.

Racism

Racism is believing or acting as though an individual or group is superior or inferior on the grounds of their racial or ethnic origins.

Barnard and Turner (2011) note that the complex relationships between social class, gender and ethnicity create a wide variation between and within ethnic minority groups. This makes it difficult to make generalized statements about minority ethnic groups as a whole. Nevertheless, they point out that many share some common experiences, particularly in terms of discrimination and **racism**.

Racism among pupils   Research by Cline et al. (2002) found racism was common among pupils in schools. A significant proportion of minority ethnic pupils reported race-related name-calling, such as 'big lips', 'Paki', 'chocolate boy', 'little browny boy', 'chimpanzee' and 'Malteser', other unkindness or rudeness because of their ethnicity, or verbal abuse at school or while travelling to and from school, and often such racial harassment continued over an extended period of time. Traveller/Gypsy children also often face bullying and harassment at school. Such behaviour may contribute to lowering the self-esteem of minority ethnic pupils, and certainly makes their experience of schooling a more distressing one than that of White British pupils. Other dimensions of racism and race-motivated behaviour are considered below.

Teacher expectations, stereotyping, labelling and conflict in the classroom   The Swann Report found only a small minority of teachers were consciously racist, but there is evidence of a good deal of unintentional racism, which can affect progress at school. Green, in an appendix to the Swann Report, found that some teachers with racist attitudes favoured and gave more time, individual attention and praise and encouragement to white pupils than to Black Caribbean boys and girls.

Bhatti (1999) carried out a study of Bangladeshi, Pakistani and Indian students in a comprehensive school in the south of England which she called 'Cherrydale' (not its real name). Using multiple research methods including interviews, questionnaires and participant observation in classrooms, Bhatti identified pupils' own views of racist behaviour by teachers. This included being ignored, not being given the chance to answer questions in class, not being helped, not being given responsibility, and being unfairly picked on for punishment or a telling-off.

As seen in Topic 2, teachers often hold stereotypes of particular groups of students. Classroom research by Wright (1992) and by Connolly (1998) in inner-city primary schools found some teachers hold ethnic-based stereotypes, with more positive expectations of Asians, particularly of Asian girls, generally seeing them as relatively quiet, well behaved and highly motivated. In contrast, they found Black Caribbean pupils, particularly boys, were often seen by teachers as having low academic potential, and were often expected to be, and labelled as, disruptive trouble-makers. This may mean teachers take swift action against them, causing further conflict with teachers. These teacher stereotypes may not be consciously or deliberately racist, but permeate into teacher consciousness through the general **racial prejudice** and racial stereotypes generated through the mass media, and perceptions by Black people that schools are racist institutions may affect the way they respond to them (see the section below).

Gillborn (2008) found low teacher expectations continued into secondary education, and were fuelled by teacher perceptions of behaviour-related issues concerning Black Caribbean young people. Strand (2012) found that teachers' judgements of pupils' academic potential were distorted by perceptions of their behaviour, and that pupils whose behaviour was challenging, or who behaved badly/inappropriately, may also be seen as being poorer academically, though the two are not necessarily related. These processes mean black pupils consequently get placed into lower-ability groups early in their schooling, and this contributes to explaining the decline in achievements of many Black Caribbean boys during their years of compulsory education.

Gillborn and Youdell (2000) suggested racism still plays an important role in disadvantaging black students, and if teachers hold negative stereotypes, with consequent negative labelling, and have low expectations of black pupils ('slow learners' / 'lack concentration' / 'difficult to control'), this may lead to the development of low self-esteem among such pupils, and the self-fulfilling prophecy of failure. Such processes of stereotyping, labelling and low expectations may fuel the resentments of black pupils, and drive them into a cycle of disruption and low achievement.

Research in primary and secondary schools has found an unusually high degree of conflict between white teachers and Black Caribbean children, who, unlike whites and Asians, are often punished not for any particular offence but because they have the 'wrong attitude'. A London Development Agency Education Commission report in 2004 said that relationships between Black Caribbean students and white teachers were characterized by 'conflict and fear'. A Black Caribbean student in this report pinpointed teacher stereotyping when he said: 'When it is white boys it is a group, but when it is black boys, it is a gang.' Black Caribbean (especially male) pupils are more likely to fight racism at school, and form anti-school subcultures (see below). These factors might explain the high level of exclusions among Black Caribbean students, since most permanent exclusions are for disobedience of various kinds, such as refusing to comply with school rules, verbal abuse or insolence to teachers.

The perception of some pupils, particularly Black Caribbean students, that schools are racist institutions is also fuelled by the lack of black role models in the teaching profession. In 2010, Black Caribbeans or Black Africans made up just 0.7 per cent of headteachers and 1.5 per cent of all teachers in England's state schools, reinforcing the perception many people have that headteachers are typically white males in secondary schools, and white females in primary schools.

> **Racial prejudice** involves a set of assumptions about a racial or ethnic group which people are reluctant to change even when they receive information which undermines those assumptions.

Teacher expectations and educational triage Gillborn and Youdell suggested the process of educational triage discussed in Topic 2 (see pages 359–60) reinforces the failure of black students, as they are allocated to lower streams and sets and their needs get neglected as they are seen as unlikely to achieve the 5 A*–C GCSEs on which a school's performance is judged. Gillborn (2011) suggested the introduction of the EBacc in 2010 as a means of measuring school performance was likely to make it even harder for black pupils to succeed. This is because black pupils are likely to be placed in lower teaching groups and denied the opportunity to study and/or achieve the required grades in the EBacc subjects, because teachers do not see black children as likely academic successes.

Pupil responses and subcultures of resistance Topic 2 looked at the various ways that pupils may respond to the experience of schooling, teacher expectations, streaming, labelling and stereotyping, often through the formation of various types of school subculture. There are similarly a range of possible responses to the experiences of negative labelling, low teacher expectation and racism among ethnic minority students.

Stuart Hall, from a Marxist point of view, has discussed a 'culture of resistance' among Black Caribbean youth, leading to a rejection of schooling and to conflict within it when they are compelled to attend.

Sewell (1996, 1998) found some Black Caribbean students ('the rebels') responded to the denial of status and respect by what they saw as a racist schooling by forming a subculture of resistance, which gave them status through the assertion of a black macho masculinity. Sewell found teachers often held stereotypes of *all* Black Caribbean boys as anti-school, anti-authority macho boys, even though only a minority fitted this stereotype. The largest group (the 'conformists') tried to escape teacher stereotypes by accepting school, while the 'innovators' maintained an anti-school and anti-teacher stance, but wanted the benefits education could offer them. A small group, the 'retreatists', basically dropped out of both school and black subculture.

However, the low expectations of teachers and negative labelling might not be accepted by those labelled. Mac An Ghaill (1992) found that racism and negative labelling do not necessarily have the negative effects on student progress that the self-fulfilling prophecy suggests. Students may adopt various survival strategies, like resisting schooling by breaking rules and dress and behaviour codes, while at the same getting on with their work. Research by Fuller (1980) among Black Caribbean girls in a London comprehensive school found that they combined a subculture of resistance to schooling with the hard work needed to overcome the obstacles placed before them and to achieve educational success. This partly arose because black girls recognized their future roles as key breadwinners in black families. This demonstrates that negative labels do not always have negative effects and lead to a self-fulfilling prophecy, and Fuller's research might also explain why Black Caribbean females in general do better than their male counterparts in education.

The ethnocentric school curriculum

Many schools have strong equal opportunities policies to tackle racism and **multicultural education** to try to include minority ethnic group cultures within the school curriculum. This multiculturalism was described by Troyna and Williams (1986) as a means of making the educational experience of minority ethnic groups more palatable by using the 3 Ss (saris, samosas and steel bands) to overcome the 3 Rs (resistance, rejection and rebellion).

Despite attempts at multicultural education, many aspects of school life and the school curriculum continue to show signs of **ethnocentrism**.

Multicultural education involves a recognition of the diversity of cultures in society, and teaching about the culture of other ethnic groups besides that of the majority culture.

Ethnocentrism is a view of the world in which other cultures are seen through the eyes of one's own culture, with a devaluing of the others.

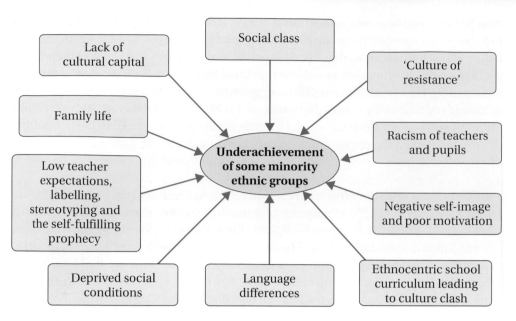

Figure 6.11 Ethnicity and educational achievement

Ethnocentrism and an ethnocentric curriculum in education involve things like the subjects taught, activities and the hidden curriculum at school being biased towards one particular culture – such as concentrating on white British society and culture, rather than recognizing and taking into account the cultures of other ethnic groups. For example, role models are frequently white; 'white' is good and 'black' is evil (as in the white knight versus the black knight); history is white, Christian and European; foreign languages taught in schools are primarily European, rather than those from the main minority ethnic groups who live in the UK. History and other textbooks still frequently carry degrading stereotypes of people from non-white races – portrayed often in sub-servient or 'primitive' roles, or as people needing constant help and assistance to run their lives and countries; positive role models from the history, music, literature, art and culture of black and other minority ethnic groups are frequently absent from the curriculum.

It has been suggested that this ethnocentrism, along with the other factors discussed above, contributes to the low self-esteem of some minority ethnic children, and it means the school curriculum may be more attractive and culturally acceptable to some ethnic groups than others.

Combining all the factors above may mean there is a culture clash between some minority ethnic groups and the white middle-class culture of the school. To apply Bourdieu's theory of cultural capital, while it might appear that all have an equal opportunity in education since they are assessed against the same culture and knowledge, the education system is not really neutral at all because its culture is predominantly white British, middle-class culture. These factors would contribute to explaining patterns of underachievement in education between ethnic groups.

SOME WORDS OF CAUTION

Explaining the underachievement of some minority ethnic groups is no easy task. It is likely to be a combination of several of the factors outlined above, with the different factors having different significance for particular groups in particular circumstances. However, all the explanations need to be treated with caution. For example, while some teachers may hold racist beliefs, this does not necessarily mean they behave in a racist way in the classroom, and they may not allow the negative stereotypes of ethnic minorities they may hold to disadvantage children from minority ethnic groups. It should not be assumed all teachers are racist, and many make great and successful efforts to overcome any feelings of racial prejudice they hold and do all they can for all students. Racism is not as widespread in teaching as in some professions, like the police and legal professions, and teachers and schools have often been among the first to tackle racism and promote equal opportunities for all.

Activity

1 Go through the reasons suggested in the sections above for the underachievement of some minority ethnic groups, and refer to figure 6.11. List the explanations in what you think is their order of importance. Explain and justify your reasons, and then suggest steps that might be taken in each case to overcome the obstacles you have listed.
2 Drawing on your own experience of schooling, can you identify any ways in which ethnic minority and white students were/are treated differently by teachers or by other students? Is/was there any evidence of racism in your own school or college?
3 How ethnocentric is/was the curriculum in your school or college? Is/was there any evidence of knowledge of other cultures being taught in your school, appearing in textbooks and so on?

Bringing it all together: social class, gender and ethnicity – the achievement hierarchy

The links between social class, gender and ethnicity are complex and fluid as they change over time. All sociologists agree that these factors have important influences on educational achievement, with most agreeing social class is the most significant, but there is no clear agreement on how these influences interact, nor on what the exact hierarchy of achievement is. Much depends on what measures of achievement are used, such as attainment at starting school, progress made, achievements at different Key Stages, five GCSEs A*–C, six GCSEs A*–C forming the EBacc, AS/A levels, university admissions and so on.

Figure 6.12 attempts to provide a *rough* guide to how social class, gender and ethnicity intersect to form an overall hierarchy of achievement to the end of compulsory schooling. This suggests that social class remains overwhelmingly the main factor influencing achievement, but that within each class there is a further hierarchy related to ethnicity and gender. It is worth remembering that some *individuals*, even if they come from a group that generally underachieves, may overcome disadvantages arising from their gender, ethnicity or the social class into which they were born, and be very successful in the education system. For some, but not for many, success in education may provide an escape route from disadvantage, and a means of improving life chances and for achieving upward social mobility.

Activity

Study figure 6.12. Drawing on all you have learnt in this topic on social class, gender and ethnicity and educational achievement, discuss whether you think the diagram gives a fair or unfair picture of the pattern of educational achievement. Suggest explanations for the position of some of the groups, and/or any reasons why you think the hierarchy of achievement might be wrong or need amending.

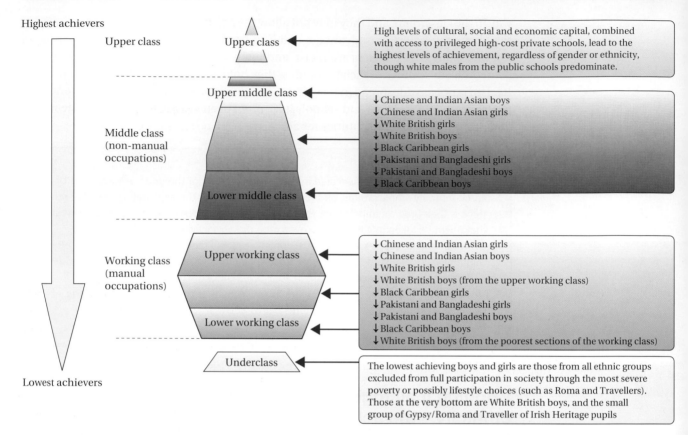

Highest achievers

Upper class

Middle class (non-manual occupations)

Working class (manual occupations)

Lowest achievers

Upper class — High levels of cultural, social and economic capital, combined with access to privileged high-cost private schools, lead to the highest levels of achievement, regardless of gender or ethnicity, though white males from the public schools predominate.

Upper middle class / Middle class / Lower middle class:
↓ Chinese and Indian Asian boys
↓ Chinese and Indian Asian girls
↓ White British girls
↓ White British boys
↓ Black Caribbean girls
↓ Pakistani and Bangladeshi girls
↓ Pakistani and Bangladeshi boys
↓ Black Caribbean boys

Upper working class / Lower working class:
↓ Chinese and Indian Asian girls
↓ Chinese and Indian Asian boys
↓ White British girls
↓ White British boys (from the upper working class)
↓ Black Caribbean girls
↓ Pakistani and Bangladeshi girls
↓ Pakistani and Bangladeshi boys
↓ Black Caribbean boys
↓ White British boys (from the poorest sections of the working class)

Underclass — The lowest achieving boys and girls are those from all ethnic groups excluded from full participation in society through the most severe poverty or possibly lifestyle choices (such as Roma and Travellers). Those at the very bottom are White British boys, and the small group of Gypsy/Roma and Traveller of Irish Heritage pupils

Figure 6.12 The achievement hierarchy – how social class, gender and ethnicity overlap in influencing educational achievement

Exam-style questions

1 Explain what is meant by the term 'underachievement'. *(2 marks)*

2 Explain what is meant by the term 'cultural capital'. *(2 marks)*

3 Explain what is meant by the term 'educational triage'. *(2 marks)*

4 Suggest **three** reasons why girls generally achieve more highly in education than boys. *(6 marks)*

5 Suggest **three** cultural factors that might cause working-class educational underachievement. *(6 marks)*

6 Outline some of the reasons why some minority ethnic groups underachieve in education. *(12 marks)*

7 Outline some of the ways in which teacher labelling and stereotyping may lead to the educational under-achievement of some pupils. *(12 marks)*

8 Assess the claim that social class differences in educational achievement are primarily the result of school factors. *(20 marks)*

Topic 4

SPECIFICATION AREA

The significance of educational policies, including selection, comprehensivization and marketization, for an understanding of the structure, role, impact and experience of education

Admissions and selection in education

OPEN ENROLMENT AND PARENTAL CHOICE

In the UK, what is called *open enrolment* means a parent can apply for a place for their child at any state-funded school in any area, and if the school is under-subscribed – that is, it is not full – then it must accept that child. This is often described as a system of parental choice, where the parents choose their child's school, but often the most popular schools fill up quickly and are over-subscribed – that is, there are more applicants than places. This means not all parents are able to get their first choice of school, and so really it is a case of parents expressing a *preference* for a particular school or schools, rather than having a real free choice. Every year, thousands of parents appeal against not getting their chosen school: for example, in 2009–10, in England alone, there were around 85,000 appeals by parents against being refused places at their chosen primary and secondary schools, of which only about one-fifth were successful.

ADMISSIONS POLICY IN OVER-SUBSCRIBED SCHOOLS

If a school is over-subscribed, then pupils are admitted according to over-subscription criteria, which should comply with a government Schools Admissions Code. This gives priority to, for example, children in care, those who already have brothers and sisters at the school, those who live in the school's catchment area (the area from which it draws its pupils), those who live closest to the school, and religious faith (but only in Faith Schools – those of a religious character).

Over-subscribed schools (excluding grammar schools) are not allowed to include academic ability or aptitude as a basis for deciding which pupils to accept and which to reject. They are also forbidden from selecting children using means that might disadvantage some social groups compared to others or deny parents a choice. These might include social factors like parents' educational level, social class, ethnicity or the particular area in which people live (like a working-class council housing estate).

The most popular, highest-performing schools, which are nearly always over-subscribed, tend to be found in the wealthiest middle-class neighbourhoods. These schools generally produce good results because they contain children from middle-class homes, who do better in education for reasons considered in the previous topic. The over-subscription criteria discussed above often mean that middle-class parents have the best chances of securing places for their children in what are seen as the best, highest-performing schools, as they live in the middle-class residential areas in which the schools are located. Working-class parents therefore often lose out on getting places at the most popular schools because they live in the wrong catchment areas and in the poorest areas, and this contributes to perpetuating the social class inequalities in education discussed in the previous topic.

SELECTIVE SCHOOLING

A *selective school* is a school which chooses the pupils it admits, rather than parents having this choice, on the basis of some selection criteria, usually general academic ability or aptitude for particular subjects. The opposite to this is a *comprehensive school*, a secondary school which accepts all students regardless of ability (comprehensive education is discussed below)

There are three main types of selection:

1   *Selection by ability.* This is where the intake of a school is selected on the basis of their academic ability, assessed by their performance in an intelligence test at the age of 11 (the 11+ exam). This used to be the main form of selection for secondary education for all pupils in the UK (see the tripartite system below), but selection by ability is now forbidden for all state-funded schools, except for a few remaining state-funded grammar schools (though selection by ability is still commonly used for places at private, fee-paying schools).

2   *Selection by aptitude.* This is where pupils are selected on the basis of their 'aptitude' or potential to be good in certain subjects. Specialist Schools, which now include nearly all state secondary schools, are allowed to select up to 10 per cent of students on the basis of their aptitude in some specialist subjects, though many schools have chosen not to use such a selection process.

3   *Selection by faith.* Faith schools – those of a religious character – may select a proportion of their pupils on the basis of the religious beliefs and commitment of their parents (this form of selection may also take place in primary schools).

THE CONTROVERSY OVER SELECTION

Selection by ability for secondary education, and whether this is necessary to give young people the most suitable form of secondary education, has been a long-standing controversial issue in education. Many schools prefer to select, if given the opportunity, the brightest, best-behaved and best-motivated pupils. They prefer pupils with well-off and well-educated parents who can support the school financially and as volunteer helpers, who can provide educational support to their children, and thereby enable the school to be seen as the best in the area, and to gain high positions in the school Performance Tables (league tables), which will be discussed later. For the reasons discussed in the previous topic, such pupils are generally those from middle-class homes. Selection therefore benefits the middle class and disadvantages those from poorer working-class homes, and therefore reinforces social class inequalities in education. Selective schools, particularly grammar schools which select all their pupils by ability, are seen by many as the best schools, but the underlying reason for this is because they contain the brightest students from predominantly middle-class homes.

Selection has also been attacked, not only for reinforcing social class inequalities, but for labelling children as successes and failures at age 11.

The debate over selection really began with the tripartite system established by the 1944 Education Act, which based the entire system of state secondary education on selection by ability at age 11.

THE TRIPARTITE SYSTEM: SELECTION BY ABILITY

Before 1944, young people only had free access to a basic form of elementary education to the age of 14. This was roughly similar to a basic primary education today. Secondary schooling involved paying fees, and many poorer parents therefore could not afford it.

The 1944 Education Act changed this. It provided free secondary education for all pupils, thereby removing the inequalities in access to secondary education, and raised the school leaving age to 15. The 1944 Education Act established three types of secondary school – grammar, technical and secondary modern schools. These three types of secondary school became known as the tripartite system. It was thought that children had three different sorts of ability, which were fixed by the age of 11, were unlikely to change, and could be reliably and accurately measured at age 11 by a special intelligence quotient test (IQ test). This became known as the 11+ exam.

Until the 1960s, all children went first to primary schools (as they do now) but then were selected by whether they passed or failed the 11+ examination to go to one of the three types of secondary school. The 15–20 per cent of children with the best 11+ exam results went to grammar schools, with most children going to secondary modern schools. There were hardly any technical schools established.

During the 1960s the tripartite system came under increasing attack. The 11+ exam was seen as an unfair, unreliable and inaccurate selection test, which disadvantaged children from working-class homes and damaged the self-esteem and educational opportunities of children who failed to win a place at a grammar school. Secondary modern schools were seen as inferior, second-rate schools, with grammar schools having higher status and offering better life chances to their pupils. Figure 6.13 shows the tripartite system, and the social classes young people were being prepared for as adults.

Research in the 1950s and 1960s suggested that the talent, ability and potential of many children in the secondary modern schools were being wasted. It was felt that this wasted talent could be better developed in comprehensive schools, which accept pupils of all abilities. As a result, in the 1960s the tripartite system was abolished in most of the country, and since the 1970s most children have attended comprehensive schools of some kind.

Figure 6.13 The tripartite system after the 1944 Education Act

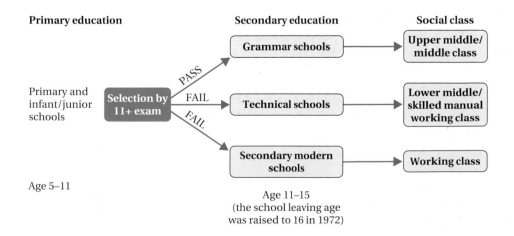

COMPREHENSIVE EDUCATION AND SELECTION

Comprehensive education abolished both selection at age 11 by the 11+ exam and the three types of secondary school. Most children now, regardless of their ability, generally transfer to secondary school at the age of 11 with no selection by examination. Nearly all young people in the UK in 2012 were attending some form of comprehensive school, with only 164 state grammar schools remaining.

Fully comprehensive schools have no selection by ability at all, and children of all abilities are admitted to the same types of school and taught in mixed-ability classes. While most schools are now comprehensive schools in that they do not formally select the pupils they admit by ability, there are different types of comprehensive school, and selection by aptitude in particular subjects is allowed in some specialist comprehensive schools. Selection by ability continues in those few remaining areas that still have grammar schools and the 11+ exam. However, there is some evidence of continuing selection by ability in comprehensives through hidden or covert selection.

Comprehensive schools and covert selection

Tough and Brooks (2007) have identified a form of selection in comprehensive schools that they call covert (hidden) selection, which they argue reinforces social class divisions in education. Covert selection is where comprehensive schools, and sometimes primary schools as well, use backdoor selection to cherry-pick those pupils who they think are likely to be of higher ability and/or from a higher social class, with well-off and well-educated parents, even though this is forbidden by the Schools Admissions Code. Tough and Brooks suggest covert selection aims to 'select in' or cream off the pupils who are most likely to behave well, achieve good results and cost less to teach, while 'selecting out' the pupils who are most likely to be disruptive, difficult to teach and to achieve poor results. Covert selection involves discouraging parents from low-achieving backgrounds (usually those from poorer working-class backgrounds) from even applying in the first place, by generally giving the impression of the school as more suited and having more appeal to middle-class than working-class parents. Examples of this discouragement include: making school literature difficult to understand for parents with poor literacy; having expensive school uniforms or other kit; not publicizing or promoting the school in poorer neighbourhoods, like working-class housing estates, or to primary schools in such neighbourhoods. Faith schools have sometimes covertly selected by ability and/or social class by gaining information about family circumstances and potential pupil characteristics through letters from spiritual leaders about a family's religious background and commitment.

As seen in the previous topic, covert selection is, in effect, about 'selecting in' the middle class, and 'selecting out' the poor and disadvantaged by giving poorer families a perception that some schools 'are not for the likes of them'.

THE CASE AGAINST SELECTION: THE ADVANTAGES OF COMPREHENSIVE EDUCATION

Opportunities remain open

In comprehensive schools, the possibility of educational success and obtaining qualifications remains open throughout a child's school career, since moving between streams and classes within one school is easier and more likely to happen than moving between different types of school in a selective system.

Late developers benefit

Late developers, whose intelligence and ability improve later in life, can be catered for better in the comprehensive system, rather than having their opportunities limited at an early age. Middle-class parents are generally better placed to coach a less bright child, who might therefore have once got a grammar school place at age 11, than parents from a less well-off background with a late-developing bright child, who might have failed to get a grammar school place. Comprehensives cater for both, and disadvantage neither.

More get better qualifications

Fewer students leave school without any qualifications in the comprehensive system, and more obtain higher standards than under selective systems, such as where grammar schools continue to exist or where there are covert forms of selection by ability.

More social mixing and fewer social divisions

As all children attend the same type of school, there is more social mixing between students from homes of different social class and ethnic backgrounds, and this helps to overcome divisions between different social groups. Selection by ability in education often benefits the middle class, which dominates selective schools and the top streams in streamed comprehensive schools. The reasons for this were discussed in the previous topic.

Reduced risk of the self-fulfilling prophecy

Children are less likely to be labelled as failures at an early age, lowering their self-esteem (how they feel about themselves and their ability) and avoiding the damaging effects of the self-fulfilling prophecy (see pages 357–8 for a discussion of this).

Benefits of mixed-ability teaching

Where all pupils of the same age, regardless of their ability, are taught in the same type of school and in the same classroom (mixed-ability teaching), the more intelligent pupils can have a stimulating influence on the less able, and the problems created by the self-fulfilling prophecy are easier to avoid. Recent research, like that by Smyth

Selection by ability can have harmful effects on the self-esteem of students, and create a self-fulfilling prophecy

et al. (2006), has shown that mixed-ability teaching has beneficial effects on the 'high flyers', improves the performance of the less able, and makes no difference to a school's overall examination performance.

More choice and opportunity

The large size of many comprehensive schools, designed to contain all pupils in an area, means there are more teachers teaching a wider range of subjects to meet the needs of pupils of all abilities, with a great variety of equipment and facilities. This benefits all pupils and gives them greater choices and opportunities to develop their talents, to reach their full potential and to gain some educational qualifications.

Benefits for working-class students

Selective schools, comprehensives using covert selection, and streamed comprehensives can be much like the tripartite system, with working-class students less likely to gain places in selective schools and the best-performing, most popular comprehensives, and more likely to be placed in the bottom streams. True comprehensive education avoids this.

No negative impact on social mobility

Despite claims that selective education offers greater opportunities for upward social mobility, particularly for bright working-class students who manage to get selected, Boliver and Swift (2011), using data from the National Child Development Study, found selective schooling as a whole yields no mobility advantage of any kind to children from any particular origins. Any gains provided by grammar schools for the few working-class children selected were cancelled out by the obstacles to mobility suffered by those who attended secondary moderns. Overall, they found that comprehensive schools were as good for social mobility as the selective schools they replaced.

THE CASE FOR SELECTION: CRITICISMS OF COMPREHENSIVE EDUCATION

Inadequate comprehensives and 'creaming off'

Some argue so-called 'comprehensive' schools in some areas lack the brightest students and are not true comprehensives at all, and have much the same negative impact on their pupils' opportunities as the secondary moderns of the tripartite system. This occurs where selective (grammar) schools continue to exist alongside so-called 'comprehensive' schools, or where the best-performing most popular comprehensives practise covert selection, and 'cream off' the most able students. Critics argue that, in such circumstances, it may be better to have a transparent and open selective education, based on clear meritocratic IQ (ability) tests.

'High flyers' are held back

Because comprehensive schools contain pupils of all abilities, some suggest brighter children are held back by the slower pace of learning of the less able. Critics argue this wouldn't happen with selection, as 'high flyers' are taught in the same school or streams within a school.

Overlooked talents and discipline problems

The large size of some comprehensives, containing all students in an area, may make it impossible for staff to know all pupils personally, and this may create discipline problems and the talents of individuals may not be noticed and developed.

Stretching the most able

Selection by ability through streaming or setting (rather than mixed-ability teaching) in the same school means brighter students can be 'stretched', rather than being held back by slower learners who take up the teacher's time, and who may be disruptive because they are unable to cope with the work. To overcome this, many so-called 'comprehensive'schools stream or set pupils (or practise covert selection), but they then cease to be true comprehensives, as this is really a form of selection in the same school.

Activity

1 Do you think young people should be selected by ability for secondary schools? What arguments would you put forward both for and against the idea of selection by ability?
2 Do some people develop their talents and abilities later in life? Can you think of examples from your own experience of people who seem to have become 'more intelligent' as they grew older?
3 Do you have any evidence of covert selection being carried out by any schools in your area, for example by them giving the impression that they'd prefer applications from those from some social class and family backgrounds or residential areas than others?

The marketization of education

While the comprehensive system succeeded in improving overall educational standards compared to the tripartite system that preceded it, the comprehensive system itself came under increasing criticism in the 1980s and 1990s for not reaching sufficiently high standards, particularly among the most disadvantaged social groups, for not giving parents enough choice about the school their child attended, and for not providing the well-qualified school leavers needed by employers so Britain could compete successfully in the world economy. Since the 1980s, these criticisms have led to repeated attempts to raise educational standards, improve schools, give parents more choice in schools and extend educational opportunities, particularly for those from the poorest social groups so they have greater opportunities for upward social mobility to escape disadvantaged backgrounds.

Marketization is the process whereby services, like education or health, that were previously controlled and run by the state, have government or local council control reduced or removed altogether, and become subject to the free market forces of supply and demand, based on competition and consumer choice.

The means of achieving these aims was seen in the **marketization** of education, whereby schools become more independent, self-governing institutions, competing with one another for students in an educational market based on consumer (parent) choice. It was believed that such an approach would lead to a more efficient, constantly improving education system, delivering higher standards, better exam results and better value for the taxpayer who funds education.

Marketization as a means of improving educational standards was originally an idea of New Right theorists like Chubb and Moe (1990, 1992) (see also Topic 1, page 343), and the policy first developed in Britain under Conservative governments between 1979 and 1997, but now appears to be a policy accepted by all the main political parties.

THE FEATURES OF MARKETIZATION IN EDUCATION

The main features of marketization of education can be summarized as

- *independence* – make schools (including sixth-form colleges and colleges of further education) more independent, controlling their own affairs and run like private businesses.
- *competition* – make schools and colleges compete with one another for customers (students).
- *choice* – give customers (parents and students) a choice of schools, enabling them to choose whatever education they think best suits their needs.

These features are backed up by quality control, through school and college inspections by Ofsted (The Office for Standards in Education, Children's Services and Skills), a National Curriculum, or recommended government-approved subjects (like the subjects making up the EBacc), testing, and the publication of Performance Tables to provide information for parents on the best and weakest schools.

Marketization and parentocracy

Underpinning marketization was the emphasis on 'parent power', with parents having more rights and choice of schools than ever. This parent power has been described by Brown (1990) as a **parentocracy**, in which a child's education is increasingly dependent upon the wealth and wishes of parents, rather than the ability and efforts of pupils. The wealth element relates to parents who choose private education, but also to how parental wealth (social class) means more affluent people are able to make more effective choices in the state system than others (this is examined shortly). The wishes of parents now drive which schools their children attend, whereas before the 1980s many children just attended the local comprehensive school to which they were allocated, or a grammar or secondary modern school allocated after testing for ability. Parents now also have guaranteed places as parent governors on school governing bodies, and access to appeal procedures if they don't get the school of their choice.

> A **parentocracy** is where a child's education is dependent upon the wealth and wishes of parents, rather than the ability and efforts of pupils (Brown (1990))

Marketization and school diversity

To satisfy consumer (parent) choice, since the 1980s there has been a growing diversity (or range of different types) of state-funded schools, offering parents more choice of schools than ever before. The promotion of school diversity is often accompanied by greater independence of schools from local authorities, and encouraging 'partners' like private businesses, universities and colleges, community and parent groups and educational charities to become more involved in running schools, and to help to raise standards by using their expert knowledge or enthusiasm. The range of state-funded schools currently available (2012) is shown in figure 6.14. It should be noted that not all of these schools are found in every area of the country, and many exist only in England, and the schools mentioned do not always exist in a pure form, but may involve elements of different types. For example, an Academy may also be a Faith School (with a religious character) and a Specialist School (specializing in certain subjects). As mentioned earlier, there is also no guarantee that parents will necessarily get their first choice of school, particularly if it is very popular and over-subscribed.

Figure 6.14 School diversity (You can find out more about these schools by going to the Department of Education website (www. education.gov.uk) and using the search box)

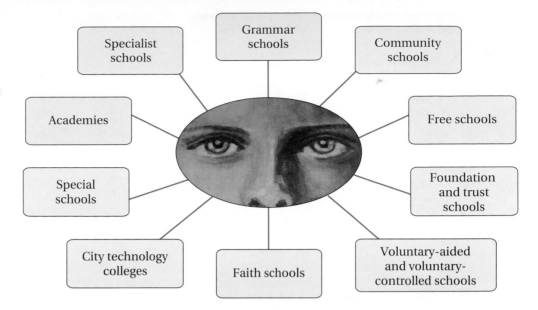

- Specialist schools
- Grammar schools
- Community schools
- Academies
- Free schools
- Special schools
- Foundation and trust schools
- City technology colleges
- Faith schools
- Voluntary-aided and voluntary-controlled schools

The free market in education has made schooling a bit like supermarket shopping, where parents can 'read the labels' and pick and choose the type and quality of school they want. However, middle-class parents and young people have gained the most benefits from the marketization of education. Why do you think this is?

Marketization and raising standards

Marketization was designed to raise education standards. As consumers of education in a free market, parents could choose between a diversity of competing schools, rejecting some in favour of others, in the same way that people choose between competing supermarkets or products. Schools would be forced to improve standards to attract students (and money), and sell or market themselves to parents through glossy school brochures, open days, and other devices to show off their achievements and facilities compared to other schools. Schools or colleges that performed well would grow and improve even more, and poorly performing schools or colleges would risk losing money as student numbers fell, and would be forced to improve, or face being taken over by another better neighbouring school, or face closure. It was therefore thought these marketization processes would lead to improvement of all schools, more satisfied parents and students, and a more efficient and effective education system, with higher standards.

Table 6.5 illustrates some of the main features and policies linked to the marketization of education, and a number of these are explained and discussed in the pages that follow.

Table 6.5 The marketization of education

Policy	Aim
Target setting (for example, ensuring at least 35 per cent of pupils get five GCSEs at grades A*–C) *National testing* (NCTs/SATs, GCSEs, GCEs and other exams) with publication of the results *National Performance Tables ('league tables')* of school performance, showing test and exam results of all schools *Ofsted inspections*, with reports on the strengths and weaknesses of schools and colleges, and recommendations for improvements, or special measures / closure for poorly performing schools	• to drive up standards by encouraging competition between schools and colleges for the best results and good positions in the school league tables, therefore attracting students and money • to identify the best schools, and shame the worst into improving their standards or face closure • to give parents and students the information to choose the best schools and colleges
More independence for schools and colleges, with Local Management of Schools (schools mainly run by headteachers and school governors) and less control by local councils. Independence for state-funded Academies and Free Schools and further education and sixth-form colleges.	• to give schools and colleges more independence to control their own affairs, so they can respond to parents' wishes, improve quality, standards and exam results as they compete for students in the education marketplace
Formula funding (money allocated per student enrolled) and a *pupil premium* (extra money per head for pupils eligible for free school meals from poorer homes)	• to reward popular schools and colleges that succeed in attracting customers (students) – those that succeed in the education market get the most money and are able to expand and improve further. Those that don't attract students will risk going out of business (being closed). The *pupil premium* aims to encourage the best schools to attract pupils from the poorest homes, and to provide extra money to help improve the education of the most disadvantaged
School diversity – a diversity of school types, like Specialist Schools, Faith Schools, Academies and Free Schools (see figure 6.14) *Parental choice / parentocracy* – parents as consumers, with more parent power in education, and parental wishes driving the choice of school children attend *Open enrolment* – schools have to accept students if they have vacancies	• to enable consumers (parents and students) to have a choice of different schools, and therefore to choose the best products in the education marketplace – the schools they consider best for their children – rather than just having to go to the local one • to allow the most popular schools to expand and fill every place they have, which further encourages competition between schools and colleges to attract students
Business sponsorship of schools, and private financing in building, maintaining and running of some state schools	• to bring in more money for successful schools • to use private business money and expertise to help schools compete in the education market, with better buildings and facilities and improved standards

GOVERNMENT POLICIES FROM 1988 ONWARDS ON MARKETIZATION AND RAISING STANDARDS

Since the 1980s, all political parties have appeared to agree on the main features and principles of marketization and raising standards, and education policy more generally, and any disagreement seems to focus mainly on matters of detail. In general, the process since the 1980s has been one of continuing and developing the same or similar policies established by previous governments, rather than major new policy changes.

Conservative Party government policies 1979–1997

The marketization of state education in Britain began during the period of Conservative government between 1979 and 1997, influenced by the ideas of the New Right, like those of Chubb and Moe discussed above. A series of Education Acts in this period, and most importantly the 1988 Education Reform Act, established the following features of the education system in England (some features differ in Wales, Scotland and Northern Ireland), and nearly all these are still features of the education system today.

Growing independence and Local Management of Schools (LMS)

LMS transferred control of school budgets, and of a wide range of other aspects of the school, to school governors, headteachers and the consumers of education – parents and students – and away from the local authority (county and city councils, in most areas). Further education and sixth-form colleges also became completely independent of the local authority. Schools were also encouraged to opt out of local authority control altogether, and become independent self-governing Grant Maintained Schools funded directly by central government. Joint state- and private-funded independent City Technology Colleges were established in some cities. These changes were designed to make schools and colleges more responsive to local needs and the wishes of parents, and to enable them to compete with one another for students and therefore funds.

Formula funding

Schools and colleges were funded by a formula which was largely based on the number of students they attract. It was thought this would drive up standards by rewarding successful schools that attracted students (and hence money), and giving less successful schools the incentive to improve.

Parental choice and open enrolment

Before 1981, and particularly 1988, children were allocated to schools within their area and parents had little choice of school. After 1988, parents were allowed a free choice of school, and under the open enrolment regulations any school with vacancies had to accept them. Schools which are unpopular with parents, where exam and test results and standards of behaviour are poor, run the risk of losing pupils and therefore money. As suggested earlier in this topic, in most cases parents don't really have much choice of school, as places in the most popular, highest-performing schools are usually filled up by those living in the school's catchment area (the area from which children are admitted first).

The National Curriculum and national testing

To improve standards across the country, and ensure all students had access to the same high-quality curriculum, the 1988 Education Reform Act set up the National Curriculum, a range of subjects and set programmes of study that were to be followed by all school students in England (there were, and are now, different requirements in Scotland, Wales and Northern Ireland). There are attainment targets (goals which all teachers are expected to enable students to reach), with formal teacher assessment at the end of Key Stages 1–3, and National Curriculum Tests (NCTs), in English, maths and science at the end of Key Stages 2 and 3 (ages 11 and 14) to ensure these targets are met.

Testing through National Curriculum Tests (NCTs, commonly still referred to by their previous name of Standard Assessment Tests, or SATs), even for young children, has been one method used to improve and check on the quality and standards of education

The Office for Standards in Education, Children's Services and Skills (Ofsted)*

The 1992 Education Act established the Office for Standards in Education (Ofsted), renamed in 2007 as the Office for Standards in Education, Children's Services and Skills, to conduct regular inspections of all state schools, sixth-form and further education colleges. This aimed to ensure these institutions were doing a good job, by publishing their inspection reports and requiring action to be taken on any weaknesses identified. Ofsted reports are often used by some parents to help them in their choice of school.

School Performance Tables (league tables)

In the early 1990s, the Conservative government established parents' right to know about comparative school performance through the publication of Performance Tables, including information about test and exam results and absence rates for all schools and colleges. These tables became known as 'league tables', ranking schools like football league tables, and were designed, together with school prospectuses, to help parents to decide how well schools are doing so they can choose the best for their children. By encouraging competition for students between schools and colleges, these league tables aimed to raise overall standards.

Activity

Go to www.education.gov.uk/rsgateway/DB/PER/index.shtml. Follow the links and explore what information is available in the School Performance Tables about your school (or the one you once attended).

1 How easy do you think it is to tell how well your school (or the one you once attended) is performing from the information given?
2 How much understanding of the education system do you think you need to interpret the information provided?
3 Do you think parents from all social backgrounds have real equality of opportunity to use this information to identify the best schools when choosing a school for their children? Explain your answer.

Labour Party government policies 1997–2010

The Labour government between 1997 and 2010 continued with many of the marketization policies that were begun in the Conservative years, and continued the drive to increase school diversity and parental choice and to raise standards, though with a new emphasis on the most disadvantaged areas. The main Labour policies are outlined below.

More money for schools, more nursery education and smaller primary school classes

The Labour government established a national maximum class size of thirty for all 5-, 6- and 7-year-olds, and allocated huge amounts of extra money to schools to enable them to provide the staff, materials, buildings and facilities necessary to provide a high-quality learning environment for children, and thereby improve standards.

Labour emphasized the importance of early learning to ensure children had the best start in life, and all children aged 3 and 4 were given a guarantee of five half-days (fifteen hours) of free nursery education a week. SureStart Children's Centres were established, especially in the most disadvantaged areas, to provide a variety of advice and support for parents and carers of pre-school children.

Helping the most disadvantaged

There was an emphasis on the need to create equality of educational opportunity for all, particularly focusing on the most deprived and most disadvantaged areas where educational results were poor. As well as the measures above, there were attempts to raise standards in schools in poorer areas through extra money and better-paid teachers, through schemes such as Education Action Zones and Excellence in Cities Action Zones (see pages 378–9).

One of the main Labour policies to tackle educational underachievement in some of the country's most disadvantaged communities was the establishment in 2000 of City Academies, but this name was soon changed to simply 'Academies'. Academies are independent publicly funded schools, found only in England, which were originally set up as new schools to replace and give a fresh start to under-performing schools in deprived areas, with the aim of raising the achievements of disadvantaged pupils.

The Academies programme, when it began under Labour, was highly controversial, and the controversy continues today. Parents often get the impression through publicity and new buildings and equipment that Academies are the best schools in an area. This means there often aren't enough places in Academies for all those who want them. Even though they were originally meant to be helping the most disadvantaged, there was some evidence that rising educational standards compared to the schools they replaced were achieved by a process of *excluding* the disadvantaged through covert selection (see page 408). Some independently managed Academies reduced the proportion of children eligible for free school meals (the standard indicator of deprivation) and creamed off the better pupils in the area, who were easier to teach and often came from better-off social backgrounds. This covert selection process made it harder for neighbouring schools, who had to take the more difficult or disadvantaged students the Academies didn't want.

Specialist Schools

Specialist Schools originally began in 1994, but Labour massively extended the programme. These schools have a special focus on their chosen subject area, such as technology, languages, business and enterprise, or music. These were an attempt to move away from what Labour leaders called 'bog standard' comprehensives. These schools originally had to raise money from private business, but they then got extra money from the government and were allowed to select up to 10 per cent of their pupils by 'aptitude' (ability) in the specialist subject. It was thought that, by specializing, these schools would raise standards in their specialist subjects, and that selection by aptitude would raise standards, not just in the specialist subjects, but across the whole school curriculum. Nearly all secondary schools now have a specialism of some kind.

ConDem (Conservative – Liberal Democrat coalition) government policies 2010 onwards

Ball and Exley (2011) describe Conservative policies – the Conservatives were the dominant party in the ConDem coalition government formed in 2010 – as a mixture of 'something old, something new'. The 'something old' refers to the traditional Conservative emphasis on parental choice and independence for schools from local authorities, which first emerged as Conservative policy in the late 1980s as Grant Maintained Schools and City Technology Colleges, and which took the form of Academies in deprived areas under Labour. It also refers to a return to an emphasis on traditional subjects and teaching methods. The 'something new' mainly refers to the new form that these traditional policies took, such as the EBacc and new-style Academies and Free Schools. There was also 'something new' in the Conservative-led coalition's continuing emphasis on the previous Labour government's attempts to tackle educational inequality and the underachievement of the most disadvantaged – something that Conservative governments previously paid little attention to. At the time of writing (2012), the main ConDem policies have been:

New-style Academies

In 2010, the focus for Academies changed from raising standards in deprived areas by replacing poorly performing schools, to encouraging *all* state schools (including primary and special schools) that were performing well to become independent Academies, free from local authority control and the National Curriculum. Poorly performing schools could be forced into becoming Academies, under the leadership of a high-performing neighbouring Academy. Academies are the fastest-growing type of school, and, at the time of writing, nearly half (about 45 per cent) of England's secondary schools were Academies.

Free Schools

Free Schools are all-ability state-funded independent schools, very similar to Academies, but set up in response to what local people say they want and need in order to improve education for children in their community. They were generally presented as a way of improving standards and meeting parents' wishes in disadvantaged areas where existing schools were seen by parents as providing inadequate education. They were designed to be run by groups of teachers, parents, charities or education experts to satisfy local demand.

The Pupil Premium

The *pupil premium* is extra money per head allocated for pupils who come from poorer homes, defined as those eligible for free school meals. This aimed to encourage schools to attract and work harder for poorer pupils, with the aim of reducing social inequalities in education.

The English Baccalaureate (EBacc)

Ball and Exley suggest that ConDem policy was underscored by Conservative beliefs in 'real subjects' and that 'the old methods are the best' when it comes to teaching, discipline and curriculum. This was shown, for example, by detailed instruction over what should be taught in schools, with the original establishment of the National Curriculum back in 1988. This was further reinforced by making the proportion of students achieving the EBacc a feature of school league tables in 2010, thereby encouraging schools to put an emphasis on teaching the core EBacc subjects of maths, English, the sciences, foreign languages and the humanities, like history and geography. A survey of schools conducted for the DfE in 2011 estimated that by 2013 nearly half of those taking GCSEs would be studying the subjects making up an EBacc.

Activity

1   Identify and explain four ways in which the educational reforms from the late 1980s to the present have introduced market forces into the education system.
2   Is competition between schools and colleges a good thing? Identify and explain its advantages and disadvantages.
3   Do you think the changes in education since the 1980s will succeed in raising standards? Go through each of the changes, and explain why they might or might not improve standards.
4   Do you think schools alone can be held responsible for their exam results and other aspects of their pupils' performance (like truancy, the EBacc results, and work and higher education after school)? What other factors might influence a school's performance?

CRITICISMS OF THE MARKETIZATION OF EDUCATION

The free market in education, with more independence for schools and competition between them, as a means of raising standards and increasing parental choice has been very controversial. The main criticisms are outlined below.

The myth of parentocracy: the middle class has gained the most

Ball et al. (1996) argue that parents are now encouraged to see themselves as consumers of education, with good parenting seen, at least in part, as taking on the responsibilities of school choice. However, they point out that parental choice follows a pattern related to social class differences, and contributes to the reproduction of the social class inequalities in education which were discussed in the preceding topic. Tough and Brooks (2007) point out that better-educated middle-class families with higher incomes are more likely to make choices based on a school's performance, while those from more disadvantaged working-class families are more likely to choose schools that are near to their homes and which their child's friends attend, rather than because of its position in the school Performance Tables (league tables).

While marketization is said to create a parentocracy in which all parents have a free choice of school, this is a myth, and disguises the fact that not all parents have the same freedom to exercise this choice. Some of the highest-performing schools carry out covert selection, as discussed earlier (see page 408), and deliberately try to dissuade poorer parents from applying by giving the impression that their school 'is not for the likes of them'.

Machin and Vernoit (2010) found evidence that the ConDem coalition government's new-style Academies that opened from September 2010 onwards were significantly more advantaged than the average secondary school, contained far lower proportions of pupils who were eligible for free school meals and were likely to reinforce advantage and make worse existing inequalities in schooling.

Middle-class parents have been able to make the greatest use of parental choice and open enrolment, and it is they who are better placed to make the most effective use of the education system and exploit the new system to their children's advantage. The educational system remains socially selective, and the higher the social class of the parents, the better are the schools to which they send their children, and these schools stay better because they are supported by advantaged middle-class parents whose children take up most of the places. Because of their higher levels of income, education, and social and cultural capital, middle-class parents know more about how to work the system to get the schools they want. For example, Toynbee (2011) suggests that the middle-class alternative to paying (for private education) is praying, 'so parents get on their knees at the birth of a child' and begin to attend religious services just to get their children into good Faith Schools. The middle class are better placed than many working-class parents to:

- shop around and find the best schools.
- understand and compare schools in the league tables.
- know more about how to assess Ofsted school inspection reports and what constitutes a 'good school'.
- afford more easily to move into the catchment areas of the highest-performing schools.
- afford higher transport costs, giving their children a wider choice of schools.
- know more about how popular schools allocate places, and to make more effective use of appeals procedures should they be refused a place at their chosen school.

This means that, in the educational marketplace, those who have already benefited from education the most will gain more, while those who are more disadvantaged may become further disadvantaged.

Student needs at risk and social divisions increased

As Whitty et al. (1998) have pointed out, in a free market, 'the advantaged schools and the advantaged parents gravitate toward each other and the disadvantaged families are left in schools with falling enrolment, falling funding, and, as a result, more difficulty in climbing out of the spiral of decline'.

The free market has therefore opened up further the gap between the educational achievements of working-class and middle-class young people, as schools compete to achieve high results to keep up the image of the school or college for parents and achieve high positions in the league tables of results. Weaker students, who are more likely to come from working-class backgrounds (as is explained in Topic 3), may find their needs are neglected as they are covertly selected out of the best schools because of the risk of them getting poorer results and therefore undermining the position of the school/college in the league tables.

Educational triage The process of educational triage discussed earlier (see pages 359–60) can make these divisions worse. The competitive climate and the importance of school league tables may mean brighter students, or those, for example, on the C/D-grade borderline at GCSE, are likely to get more resources and teacher time spent on them, disadvantaging weaker students who are less likely to deliver the prestige five GCSE A*–C results or the six GCSEs A*–C making up the EBacc.

A report of the House of Commons Education Committee of MPs (2011) suggested the introduction of the EBacc would lead to teachers devoting more time to pupils who have a chance of achieving this certificate, who are more likely to come from middle-class homes, and that there was a 'serious risk that schools will simply ignore their less academically successful pupils', who are more likely to come from working-class homes. There was also evidence emerging in 2012 of schools allocating less time on the timetable to non-EBacc subjects, which are more likely to be taken by more disadvantaged students.

As a result of these processes, social divisions between the middle class and the working class, and between ethnic groups, are likely to be widened.

Difficulties in improving schools and colleges

Competition between schools and colleges for students, and therefore for money, the emphasis on exam results, a good position in the league tables and presenting a good image to parents in the free market may make it harder for poorer schools and colleges to improve, as students go elsewhere. While popular schools get more money which enables them to have better facilities and employ more experienced and better-qualified teachers (who are more expensive) and thereby maintain and further improve their standards, less successful schools and colleges lose income and may therefore lack the resources to improve their performance to attract more students to match their more successful rivals – the opposite of the improved standards marketization was intended to achieve.

The pupil premium – extra money for poorer students – may not be enough to encourage higher-performing schools to try to attract poorer students, who are often the hardest to teach, and the money available may not be enough to provide the extra help such students need to help them to perform at a level which doesn't undermine the position of the best schools in the league tables. Such schools may seek to reject such pupils through covert selection of various kinds, and this means the poorest students in the most disadvantaged areas may then continue to find themselves going to the worst schools.

'Dumbing down'

As school students, and particularly post-16 further education and sixth-form students, now have a choice of institutions, this may lead to a 'dumbing down' of teaching and subject content. The need for schools and colleges to retain students – and the money they bring with them – means that if students have too much work to do or find the work difficult, they may go to another course or educational institution where things seem easier and less demanding. Retaining (keeping) students may mean not pushing students too hard for fear of losing them.

Problems with the National Curriculum and testing

The National Curriculum has been criticized for not giving teachers enough opportunity to respond to the needs of their pupils, as teachers are told what they have to teach and when they have to teach it. Testing, either by external tests (the NCTs/SATs) or teacher assessment has been criticized, particularly at Key Stage 1 (age 7), for putting too much pressure on young children, and possibly giving them a sense of failure early in their schooling. More generally, teaching may become too focused on the content of the tests as a way to get the good test results needed for a high position in the league tables, at the expense of the wider school curriculum.

Academies and Free Schools are exempt from the National Curriculum, so it is difficult to ensure a suitable standard is being set. As the number of Academies and Free Schools grow – as the Department for Education wants to turn all schools into Academies – then, once over half of schools are exempted, it is difficult to see how there will any longer be a truly National Curriculum.

Private education: the independent schools

Around 7 per cent of the school population have exercised a choice in the education market to opt out of the free, state-funded school system altogether and attend the fee-paying private sector of education – the independent schools. As Walford (2003) points out, there is a wide diversity of schools in the independent sector, some of which are so small that they are almost 'better thought of as parents home schooling their children'. As Walford says, there are 'schools that practise Transcendental Meditation and Buddhism; others that serve Seventh Day Adventists (a religious sect), Sikhs or Jews. There are more than 60 evangelical Christian schools and more than 50 Muslim schools.' Many of these schools start up because of parents expressing their choice of school, and while such schools may meet parental wishes, they do not necessarily lead to the **elite** careers associated with some of the most prestigious independent schools, which are the focus of attention here.

> An **elite** is a small group holding great power and privilege in society.

THE PUBLIC SCHOOLS

Most research and discussion of the private sector of education has been about what are known as the 'public schools', which, despite their name, are not in fact 'public' at all, but very expensive private schools. The reason for this attention is because, as Walford says, 'Entry to such schools has been seen as a passport to academic success, to high-status universities and to prosperous and influential careers.' The public schools are a small group of independent schools belonging to what is called the 'Headmasters' and Headmistresses' Conference' (HMC). Pupils at these schools are largely the children of wealthier upper- and upper-middle-class parents. These are long-established private schools, many dating back hundreds of years, which charge fees running into thousands of pounds a year. For secondary age students in 2011–12, annual fees for day students averaged around £12,000, and for boarders (living in) £25,000. The two most famous boys' public schools are probably Eton and Harrow (boarding fees around £32,000 a year, plus extras, in 2011–12), and many of the 'top people' in this country have attended these or other public schools. A public school education means parents can almost guarantee their children will have well-paid future careers bringing them power and status in society.

Eton College, one of Britain's most famous public schools, with fees of £32,067 a year plus extras in 2011–12, counts among its former students nineteen British prime ministers, numerous princes, kings, archbishops, judges, generals, admirals and other members of Britain's elite

THE CASE FOR INDEPENDENT SCHOOLS

The defenders of private education point to the smaller class sizes and better facilities of the public schools, compared to those found in the state system, which means children have a much better chance of getting into university, and particularly the top universities like Oxford and Cambridge. The Sutton Trust (2011) found that independent school pupils are nearly 7 times as likely as pupils in comprehensive schools to be accepted into Oxford and Cambridge, rising to 55 times more likely than the most disadvantaged students who qualify for free school meals (FSM), and more than twice as likely to be accepted into the thirty top-ranked British universities (and 22 times more likely than those on FSM).

Many public schools are also selective schools, with selection through entrance examinations, so the average ability of students tends to be higher than in state schools, helping to maintain high academic standards, which is reinforced by high levels of parental interest (particularly as they are paying customers). Many defend private education on the grounds that parents should have the right to spend their money as they wish, and improving their children's life chances through choosing for their children to be educated outside the state system is a sensible way of doing so, particularly if they regard their local state schools as inadequate or ineffective for their children. Teachers' salaries also tend to be higher in the private sector, especially in the public schools, and this may mean they attract better-qualified and more experienced teachers than the state sector.

THE CASE AGAINST INDEPENDENT SCHOOLS

Many remain opposed to private education, arguing that most people do not have the money to purchase a private education for their children, and it is wrong that the children of the well-off should be given more advantages in education than the poor. Despite many of the schools catering only for the well-off, they have traditionally had the same tax subsidies and benefits through charitable status as charities helping those in poverty or need. This charitable status has been estimated to be worth about 5–10 per cent on the average school fee (Palfreyman, 2003), or up to about £3,000 per pupil each year – an amount so generous that in 2006 the Charities Act was amended so that charities providing education had to demonstrate wider public benefit, such as offering more access to those who could not afford high fees, and clear evidence of support to neighbouring state schools, in order to continue to qualify as charities. The taxpayer also pays the cost of training the teachers in these schools, since they attend state-run universities and colleges.

The quality of teaching in independent schools is often no better than in state-run comprehensives. However, classes tend to be smaller than in state schools, allowing more individual attention, and the schools often have better resources and facilities. Eton College in 2010 had assets estimated at £229 million, with the added advantage of charitable status. These investments and fee income allow Eton to spend in the region of £25–30,000 per year on each student, compared to the sum of around £6,000 spent on the average state school student in 2010–11. The opponents of private education argue more money should be spent on improving the state system so everyone has an equal chance in education.

Research has shown that, even when children who go to private schools, especially the public schools, get worse examination results than children who go to comprehensive schools, they still get better jobs in the end. This suggests that the fact of attending a public school is itself enough to secure them good jobs, even if their qualifications are not quite as good as those of students from comprehensives.

Elite education and elite jobs

A public school education remains a prime qualification for the elite jobs in society – that small number of jobs in the country which involve holding a great deal of power and privilege. Although only about 7 per cent of the population have attended independent schools (and public schools are only a proportion of those schools), many of the top positions in government, in the civil service, medicine, the law, the media, the Church of England, and industry, banking and commerce are held by privately educated school students, as shown in table 6.6.

Table 6.6 Some UK elites educated at private schools (percentages)

All pupils attending private schools (2010/11)	7
Top barristers[a] (2004)	68
Top judges[b] (2007)	70
Top solicitors[c] (2004)	55
Top 100 media personnel[d] (2006)	54
Top doctors (2007)[e]	51
Leaders of FTSE 100 top companies (2007)	54
All Members of Parliament (2010)	35
Conservative MPs	54
Liberal Democrat MPs	40
Labour MPs	15
Conservative / Lib Dem MPs holding government office as ministers (2010)	60
Bishops in House of Lords (2005)	60

[a] Barristers at eight leading corporate and commercial chambers

[b] Law Lords and Appeal and High Court Judges

[c] Partners at the City's five 'magic circle' law firms

[d] Newspaper editors, newspaper columnists, broadcast presenters and editors who have the power to decide the stories that are given most prominence, and how they are presented to the public through newspapers, magazines, radio and TV

[e] Doctors with positions on the Councils of the Medical Royal Colleges or other national representative bodies

Source: Sutton Trust

Figure 6.15 The old boys' network

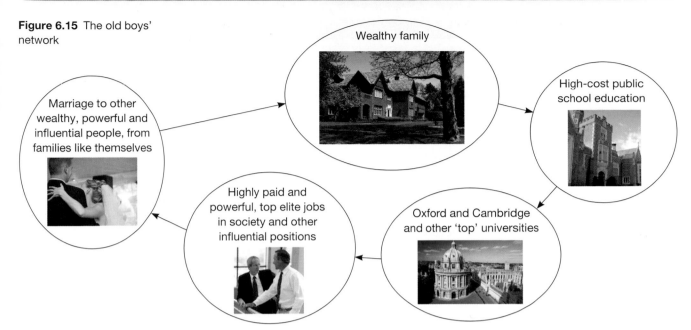

In many cases, even well-qualified candidates from state schools will stand a poor chance of getting such jobs if competing with public school pupils. The route into the elite jobs is basically through a public school and Oxford and Cambridge universities, where around 40 per cent of students come from private schools. This establishes the 'old boys' network', a social network providing valuable social capital, where those in positions of power recruit others who come from the same social class background and who have been to the same public schools and universities as themselves (this is shown in figure 6.15). This shows one aspect of the clear relationship which exists between wealth and power in modern Britain, and how being able to afford a public school education can lead to a position of power and influence in society.

A public school education therefore means well-off parents can almost guarantee their children will have well-paid future careers bringing them levels of power and status in society similar to those of their parents. This undermines the principle of equality of educational opportunity, and any idea that Britain might be a meritocracy. This is because social class background and the ability to pay fees, rather than simply academic ability, become the key to success in education. Not all children of the same ability have the same chance of paying for this route to educational and career success. This would seem to demonstrate in a particularly stark way Bowles and Gintis's Marxist idea that the education system simply confirms and legitimizes social class of origin as social class of destination.

Activity

1 Go to www.etoncollege.com, the website of Eton College, or www.harrowschool.org.uk (Harrow School) and explore how the educational facilities and lifestyle at these schools differ from those of the school you go/went to (unless you went to one of these schools).

2 Discuss the arguments for and against the following view:
The existence of private schools undermines the principle of equality of educational opportunity, because social class background rather than simply ability becomes the key to success in education. They only exist to help the wealthy and powerful pass on their wealth and power from one generation to the next. Private education should therefore be abolished.

Exam-style questions

1   Explain what is meant by the term 'parentocracy'.   *(2 marks)*

2   Explain what is meant by 'school diversity'.   *(2 marks)*

3   Suggest **three** educational policies that have attempted to raise standards in education in the last twenty-five years in the UK.   *(6 marks)*

4   Suggest **three** ways in which middle-class parents may be more effective in achieving better schooling for their children than those from more disadvantaged backgrounds.   *(6 marks)*

5   Outline some of the policies introduced by governments since 1988 to create an education market in the United Kingdom.   *(12 marks)*

6   Outline some of the reasons why selection by ability in education may have harmful effects on some young people.   *(12 marks)*

7   Assess the view that reforms in education since 1988 have not benefited all children equally.   *(20 marks)*

8   Assess the view that the marketization of education may lead to increased inequality in education.   *(20 marks)*

Topic 5

SPECIFICATION AREA

The application of sociological research methods to the study of education

---

Note to students

This topic assumes that chapter 5, on sociological research methods, has already been studied. If you haven't yet covered chapter 5, you are advised to return to this topic once you have done so.

   The aim of this topic is to get you to think about how to apply your knowledge and understanding of the research methods and types of data discussed in chapter 5 to researching *particular* issues in education, and to consider some of the practical, ethical and theoretical (PET) issues that might arise in educational research.

   You should be aware that, for the Methods-in-Context question, you will not gain many marks if you simply discuss methods in general, such as the strengths or weaknesses of interviews. You must apply what you know to the specific educational context, characteristics of the people or situation involved, and to the particular research topic that the question asks about.

Methods in context: researching education

THE RESEARCH CONTEXT OF EDUCATION

Access to closed settings

Research in education settings, and particularly schools, poses particular practical problems because schools are *closed settings* where access is restricted. Obtaining access to schools for research purposes would require permission from headteachers and possibly school governors and teachers. Obtaining such access and informed consent may not be easy.

Ethical issues

The duty of care and confidentiality

- Schools have a *duty of care* to their pupils, which means they have a legal obligation to take reasonable care to ensure their safety and welfare, and avoid acts that might harm them. This responsibility for the safety and welfare of children and young people might well involve protecting vulnerable young children from sociological researchers, and particularly protecting the confidentiality of private information in school records about their educational progress, health or family circumstances.
- Teachers have to maintain professional standards and a professional image, and this may mean they are reluctant to discuss or disclose what they regard as confidential or potentially damaging information about pupils, parents or the educational institutions in which they work.
- A possible related obstacle may be that adults working regularly in an establishment that is wholly or mainly for children may need a Criminal Records Bureau (CRB) check, to ensure they have no criminal record that might pose a threat to young people.

- Sociological researchers too have a moral or ethical duty of care, if not a legal one, and ethical issues are always of great concern in education-related research, especially with younger children. It is important, for example, to exercise a duty of care by avoiding any possible labelling of students which might have negative effects on their progress and self-esteem. As in most sociological research, care and sensitivity are needed.

Informed consent   Any research involving pupils would require the informed consent of their parents, and of course the pupils themselves and their teachers. The younger the child, the more difficult it will be to explain the nature of the research and for them to fully understand this, and therefore to obtain their meaningful informed consent. Young children may also lack the skills or maturity required to take part in research, such as completing questionnaires or giving honest, rather than fanciful, replies to interviewer questioning.

Intrusive and harmful effects   Some issues may be very sensitive or personal, such as social deprivation in the home, or questions about free school meals. People may find researchers' questions or observations intrusive and threatening, and even raising the issues may have harmful consequences. For example, parents may feel guilty if they do not or cannot fulfil a school's expectations about the level of support they should provide for their children's education. Confidentiality and the protection of the identity of individual parents, pupils, teachers and educational institutions are particularly important in such circumstances.

School hierarchies

Schools are hierarchical institutions, with a top-down authority structure, and even if access is granted by headteachers, it doesn't necessarily mean that any classroom teachers involved will have agreed to cooperate. This hierarchy also means that teachers and children may not necessarily be willing to risk their positions by a free expression of opinion, such as by divulging information about how the school operates, or children talking about their teachers.

Schools are busy workplaces

Schools are very busy institutions. They are constantly being asked for information by government, and teachers have to work hard in classrooms, dealing with many different students of all ages every day, and they may well be unwilling to take on the additional commitment involved in being the subject of sociological research. Children and young people are also there to work, and it is important any research should not disrupt the daily routines and relationships of school or classroom life, or undermine disciplinary codes or other aspects of the school ethos designed to make schools educationally productive institutions.

Public image and the Hawthorne effect

Schools and colleges have to maintain a particular 'image' to parents and students if they are to retain and attract them, and this means they may try to put on an act to impress researchers. Parents may also feel they have to maintain a public image as 'good parents', who are supportive and involved in their children's education (even if they are not). Teachers, too, have to maintain professional standards and their professional role, as well-prepared and effective teachers, who are caring, considerate and respectful of their pupils (even if they're sometimes not). These matters, and the school hierarchy issues considered above, may create a *Hawthorne effect* that raises potential problems with the validity of any findings.

Activity

1 Suggest three ethical issues that sociological researchers may face if they wished to conduct research in a primary school.
2 Suggest two research methods that sociological researchers might regard as effective for obtaining valid information from very young children, and explain in each case why they might be effective.

USING EXPERIMENTS

- The use of the experimental method to show how teacher expectations affect pupil progress, as in the example of Rosenthal and Jacobson (see page 300) risk undermining the professional roles and responsibilities of teachers and their duty of care to students – for example, by misleading them by planting false information about pupils' ability.
- The experimental method involves treating one group differently from another. When dealing with issues of pupil progress, this can create ethical issues over whether such experiments may have harmful effects on those involved in them.
- The ethics of sociological research should involve informed consent. There is the question of whether young children are really able to give informed consent to experimental research. Even if such informed consent can be obtained, the very fact of obtaining such consent may change the behaviour of school pupils, parents or teachers involved in the experiment, undermining the validity of any findings. Not obtaining such consent, or misleading participants into giving it, breaches ethical guidelines.
- The Hawthorne effect may arise through the very presence of researchers in an educational setting. The researchers may be seen as a threat by teachers or by pupils, which may alter their normal behaviour.
- Experiments in education research are in varying degrees artificial situations, so the findings of a classroom experiment, for example, may not reflect situations, experiences or behaviour in everyday schooling.
- Experimental situations generally involve testing hypotheses by attempting to isolate one or two variables. However, education issues involve a complex range of factors, and the experiment risks over-simplifying causes and thereby undermining the validity of research. Teacher expectation, for example, is only one factor among many others affecting student progress.

USING CONTENT ANALYSIS

- Content analysis in education may be used to establish the extent of gender stereotyping in school textbooks. Examples might include feminist researchers analysing reading books for children and seeking evidence of gender-role stereotyping: they might use categories such as male leader / female led, female works or plays indoors / male outdoors, and so on.
- Content analysis of letters of complaint to schools may reveal an underlying pattern, showing there are similar problems affecting a number of parents or pupils, enabling the identification of wider problems affecting the institutions concerned.

USING OFFICIAL STATISTICS AND OTHER SECONDARY SOURCES

This chapter has already referred to a range of quantitative data used to analyse education, like statistics on examination results, subject choices, those staying on in education post-16, and acceptances to university. These form part of an enormous amount of data collected from sources such as:

- the examination results of schools, colleges and universities.
- applications by students to higher education, and their gender, ethnicity and social class.
- the number of school leavers entering education, training or employment.
- the School Census, which is conducted up to three times a year and collects a wide range of information from all schools.
- pupil absence rates.
- pupils' characteristics, such as gender, ethnicity, eligibility for free school meals, special educational needs and English as an additional language, linked to test and examination results.
- surveys on education, either very large-scale surveys like the School Census, which covers all schools, or smaller surveys that cover more specialized areas, such as the Further Education (FE) Learners Longitudinal Survey (2007) which looked at the experiences of around 7,000 further education students over two years.
- government surveys like the General Lifestyle Survey and the Labour Force Survey collect data on a range of issues, including educational qualifications.
- longitudinal surveys: most of the significant quantitative data on education is collected at least every year. As such data are collected on a regular basis, it is possible to carry out longitudinal studies and build up a picture of changes in education over time.

Uses

- Official statistics like exam results, statistics on gender or ethnicity and achievement, and school attendance are collected on a regular (usually annual) basis from all schools. They are therefore usually representative and reliable, and this can save sociological researchers time and money.
- Comparisons between different institutions or groups and identification of changes over time are possible.

Problems and limitations

- The categories used to collect these statistics may not be those required by sociologists. For example, statistics are not often collected on the basis of social class, and there may be difficulties in the measurements used, such as social deprivation measured by free school meals.
- There may be issues about the validity of indicators used, such as whether school league tables and exam results really provide a valid measure of how effective a school is.
- There may be ethical issues relating to the use of personal documents on education, such as pupils' school reports, or reports on home circumstances of families. There needs to be constant vigilance to ensure ethical guidelines are followed, and informed consent is given.

Activity

1 Suggest two reasons in each case why the following statistics might or might not provide completely valid and representative information about what is happening in education in the UK:
   (a) pupil sickness absence statistics.
   (b) the reasons for pupils being excluded from schools.
   (c) the number of times parents attend parents' evenings.
   (d) the number of post-16 students who are in education, training, employment or unemployed / not working.
2 In the light of your answers to the activity above, in each case suggest one step social researchers might take to improve the validity of the statistics, explaining carefully why the steps you suggest might achieve this.

USING SURVEYS

Surveys are the main means of collecting education data, and much of this is collected by the government, which has the resources and legal powers to carry out large-scale, national research into schools and colleges, either with large and representative samples, or complete coverage of schools like the School Census. Depending on whether the aim is to collect quantitative or more qualitative data, these surveys use various forms of questionnaire and interview, and a range of different ways of collecting the data – such as group discussions, structured, semi-structured and unstructured face-to-face or telephone interviews, and postal or internet-based questionnaires.

As discussed in chapter 5, there are always questions to be raised about the reliability, validity and representativeness of quantitative data derived from surveys. While data derived from very large surveys like the School Census might provide comprehensive and representative data, smaller surveys may not necessarily do so.

USING QUESTIONNAIRES

Uses

Questionnaires might be used on a wide range of educational issues: to explore how home background affects educational achievement, by looking at matters like the income, educational qualifications and attitudes to education of parents; pupils' subject choices or what pupils and parents think about their local school. The anonymity and detachment of questionnaires, particularly if identity protection and confidentiality can be guaranteed, may be of benefit in overcoming embarrassment or apprehensiveness when exploring highly personal or sensitive issues, like any experiences of bullying in school, or teacher and peer-related racism.

Problems and limitations

- Schools are busy places, and they have a duty of care to pupils and parents. They may therefore be reluctant to grant permission for questionnaires to be distributed, given the time and disruption they may involve and the need to protect the interests of those in their care.
- Sensitivity is needed with the language used in questionnaires. Younger pupils, or people with poor literacy skills, will need to have very simple language used, with short questions, which may limit the amount and depth of information obtained.

- English may not be the home language of parents. This may make it necessary to use a variety of languages in questionnaires, or to adopt an alternative method, like interviews using interviewers of the same ethnic group as the interviewee.
- School-based questionnaires may be seen as 'official', with pupils or parents feeling obliged to fill them in, or seeing them as a nuisance, or not taking them seriously. Pupils may treat them only light-heartedly, get bored quickly (particularly younger pupils) or sabotage them with dishonest or silly answers, or discuss their answers first, so possibly undermining their validity.
- While those managing institutions like schools are often able to provide informed consent for questionnaire research to take place, this doesn't necessarily mean those actually asked to complete the questionnaires have similarly consented. Many people, especially younger pupils or the less educated, may simply not have a sufficient grasp of what the research is about, or enough interest in it, to give proper *informed* consent.
- Professionals like teachers often have stressed and busy working lives, and may simply not have the time or inclination to fill in questionnaires, particularly as they often have a lot of other required paperwork to complete. This may mean voluntary questionnaires get a low response rate.

USING INTERVIEWS

Uses

Interviews, particularly unstructured interviews, can be useful to gain the trust and confidences of parents, pupils and teachers in school settings. This is particularly the case when exploring sensitive issues, like material deprivation in the home, parental discipline and support for their children's education, or issues like bullying at school.

This building of trust may lead to more honesty and openness in replies, providing more valid information than with other methods, and interpretivists would see this as providing opportunities to develop hypotheses and explore meanings. Interviews may also help to overcome difficulties using self-completion questionnaires with young children, or with those having literacy difficulties or whose main language is not English.

Problems and limitations

- Education settings require permission before conducting research. This means interviewers may be identified with authority figures like teachers, with consequent risks to the validity of the responses, as people may not wish to give too honest or critical answers to those they associate with authority.
- The personal characteristics of interviewers may influence the success and validity of interviews. For example, adults interviewing school students may be identified as on the side of the teachers; white people interviewing students from minority ethnic groups may not get as much cooperation or have as much of a shared understanding of the issues as an interviewer from the same ethnic group, who may also be able to conduct interviews in the respondents' first language; male researchers may not be able to develop the same rapport with female students as a female interviewer might.
- Interviews on sensitive issues may be seen as intrusive or threatening by those being interviewed. For example, parents may feel threatened by interviewers asking about how much support they provide for their children's education, and see such research as intrusive and unwarranted prying into their personal lives.

USING NON-PARTICIPANT AND PARTICIPANT OBSERVATION

Observational research methods like non-participant and participant observation are less commonly used in government-funded research, but have been used to great effect by education researchers wishing to adopt a more interpretivist approach. This enables them to gain insights which are not achievable by quantitative methods. Flanders's research (see box) provides a useful example of how non-participant observation might be used in a classroom setting.

AN EXAMPLE OF NON-PARTICIPANT OBSERVATION

Flanders's Interaction Analysis

Flanders (1970) studied interaction in classrooms. He produced a list of ten categories of interaction, and he then observed lessons and ticked the category that best described what was happening at particular times. These categories, with explanations, are listed below. Categories 1–7 are concerned with what the teacher is saying or doing, and categories 8 and 9 with what students are saying or doing.

1 Accepts feelings (teacher accepts an attitude or feeling of a student).
2 Praises or encourages (teacher praises/encourages student behaviour, including jokes, smiles, nods of the head and similar teacher responses).
3 Accepts/uses idea of student (teacher accepts and uses / builds on / develops ideas suggested by a student).
4 Asks question (teacher uses own ideas to ask questions of a student, to which an answer is expected).
5 Lecture (teacher gives own facts, opinions and explanations – the teacher, not student, makes the first move).
6 Gives direction (teacher gives commands or orders to student).
7 Criticizes or justifies authority (teacher criticizes student to make student behaviour more acceptable, or justifies teacher's own behaviour/actions).
8 Student response (student responds to teacher's questions or ideas).
9 Student initiated (student makes the first move to express his or her own ideas/ opinions, asks teacher questions or introduces a new topic).
10 Silence or confusion (a category to describe times when interaction can't be easily understood or categorized by the observer, such as periods of silence or confusion).

The observer then produces a tally chart to show what type of interaction (1–10) is going on in the classroom in particular time periods, for example every minute of a lesson. This produces a quantitative account of teacher–student interaction during the course of a lesson, which can then be used for comparison with other teachers and lessons.

Willis's research (1977) (see pages 347–8) used participant observation in a Wolverhampton school to gain insights into how young working-class lads experienced school and the transition to work, and to try to understand how and why they resisted schooling. Wright's classroom research (1992), undertaken over three years in four inner-city primary schools, used a range of methods, including participant observation and unstructured interviews, to explore the relationships between black children, their white peers, and teachers and school staff, during the earlier years of schooling. Wright examined the classroom setting and teacher–pupil interaction, interactions in the playground between children, and children and auxiliary staff, home–school relations, and the academic performance of the different groups of children. Using such methods, she gained insights into black and Asian students' experience of schooling that would not have been uncovered by more quantitative methods. Bhatti's study of Bangladeshi, Pakistani and Indian students (1999) used participant observation in classrooms at 'Cherrydale' school to gain similar insights.

However, there are problems associated with observational techniques:

- Teachers and other educational professionals will experience pressure to maintain a professional image, when being observed, meaning they may not behave as they normally do when they are not being observed. This *Hawthorne effect* may affect the validity of any findings.

- The personal characteristics of the researcher, such as their age, ethnicity and gender, are likely to influence the practical possibility of being able to carry out participant observation in school settings. For example, Willis found during his participant observation that teachers expected him, as an adult, to take some responsibility for disciplining those pupils he was meant to be participating with, posing a threat to his acceptance by the pupils concerned. An adult white male is unlikely to be able to observe or participate with a group of Asian girls, or even with young white females or males.

- As in interviews, researchers may be identified by pupils as authority figures, undermining the validity of any findings.

- School classrooms may pose the practical problem of being difficult to access – gaining access will require permission, and issues of pupil confidentiality, as well as the interruption of busy everyday routines, may mean this is refused.

- There may well be difficulties surrounding informed consent by those being observed, particularly for covert observation, and such consent, even if it was given, may create a Hawthorne effect, undermining the validity of any findings.

- While non-participant observation, like that conducted by Flanders, can fairly easily be repeated and checked by other researchers, and therefore be quite reliable, participant observation in educational settings, as in any location, is dependent very much on the personal observations and interpretations which are recorded by the observer, and cannot easily be checked by other researchers, and therefore lack reliability.

Activity

How would you set about a participant observation study of a primary school classroom? Make a list of things you would need to consider. For example, what kind of observer role might you adopt (overt or covert)? How would you get in and stay in? What steps would you take to ensure your research was valid? What ethical issues would you need to consider?

Activity

A good way to understand how research methods apply to education issues is to carry out your own small piece of research, perhaps on no more than five or six people.

1   Form a hypothesis or a question you wish to find answers to.
2   Devise a suitable sample and a research method appropriate to your aim or hypothesis.

3 Draw up a short questionnaire, interview schedule or whatever else is needed.
4 Carry out your research.
5 Do a careful analysis of the strengths and weaknesses of your research, including your findings. If you are in a group, you could criticize one another's surveys. Topics could be anything related to education, such as:
   - identifying a range of factors that might make up what Bourdieu calls 'cultural capital' and exploring whether a sample of students have the cultural factors you have identified.
   - seeing whether boys and girls behave differently in class and are treated differently by teachers by observing classroom behaviour. (If you plan to do classroom observation, applying Flanders's interaction analysis might be useful – see the box on page 433).
   - asking a sample of female and male students about what influenced them in making subject and exam choices.
   - interviewing some students who identify with an anti-school or other type of school or college subculture, and find out about what they get out of it.
6 Suggest a suitable method for studying each of the following topics, and explain in each case why it might be suitable:
   (a) the relationship between people's educational qualifications and the employment they get.
   (b) whether different styles of teaching influence student exam results.
   (c) what students' ideas are about the 'perfect teacher'.
   (d) whether ethnic minority students feel they are treated unfairly in schools.
   (e) which ICT-based resources are most frequently used in your school or college.

EXAMPLES OF RESEARCH

The following examples of research and research methods, and the activities relating to them, aim to get you thinking about how research methods are applied to some real-world issues in educational research.

National Child Development Study (Centre for Longitudinal Studies)

The National Child Development Study (NCDS) examines the factors affecting people throughout their lives. It is a continuing longitudinal study of a cohort of all 17,634 children who were born in one particular week in March 1958, and living in Britain. By 2012, there had been eight 'sweeps' (individual surveys) to 'sweep up' or collect data on the physical, educational, social and economic development of this birth cohort. The first sweep was carried out in 1965, when respondents were aged 7, then in 1969 (aged 11), in 1974 (aged 16), in 1981 (aged 23), in 1991 (aged 33), in 1999–2000 (aged 41–2), in 2004–5 (aged 46–7), with the eighth sweep carried out in 2008 when the respondents hit the age of 50. The eighth sweep used CAPI interviews (computer-assisted personal interviews, where questions are completed on a computer, either by an interviewer or by the respondent) and self-completion postal questionnaires. The survey asked questions about a range of topics, including housing, personal and family relationships, family income, employment status / employment history, academic education, vocational training and other courses, access to and use of computers, basic skills and health. In common with all longitudinal studies, the number of people participating in the NCDS has declined as the cohort grows older. For example, the eighth sweep managed to contact 9,790 people. This was about 56 per cent of the original 17,634 cohort, compared to about 97 per cent in the first sweep in 1965.

Activity

1 Identify the research methods used in the eighth sweep of the National Child Development Study.
2 Explain two advantages and two disadvantages of this method of investigating the lives of the birth cohort.
3 Suggest three possible reasons why the number of people who participated in the eighth sweep was so much less than the first sweep in 1965.
4 Do you think the findings from the eighth sweep in the NCDS survey could be generalized to represent the lives of people across the country? Explain your answer.
5 Identify and explain four pieces of information that the NCDS might produce that might help sociologists understand the factors influencing educational achievement.
6 Suggest two methods other than that used in the eighth sweep of the NCDS that sociologists might use in a future sweep to collect qualitative information about the birth cohort's experience of their own and their children's schooling.

Perspectives of One-to-One Laptop Access (research by Danny Doyle, presented to the National Teacher Research Panel)

The details below are derived from the summary presented to the Teacher Research Conference, 2004.

Doyle carried out a case study of Les Landes Primary School in Jersey, where all Year 5 and Year 6 children had one-to-one access to a laptop computer. This qualitative insider research sought to explore the children's knowledge, views, understandings, interpretations and experiences of using laptop computers one-to-one, and to gauge the effectiveness of the laptop use for the children's learning. The study explored the

How might sociologists go about researching children's experiences of using laptops at school?

perceptions of twenty-three Year 6 children during the 2001–2 school year. Interviews and participant observation were the main methods used for this interpretive research, which included forty-five participant observations, fifteen taped interviews of children in pairs, twelve focus group interviews with five or six children, twenty-five non-participant observations, and seventy-three informal interviews. The analysis of the taped interview data became a starting point for the participant and non-participant observations and informal interviews. One of the research findings was that the children felt that they were more independent, more organized and produced better work because of their one-to-one access to a laptop computer.

Activity

1 Suggest two reasons why Doyle's research may have provided a more valid picture of children's attitudes to using laptops at school than a large-scale national questionnaire.
2 Identify two methods that were used in the case study above to gain insights into children's experiences of using laptops and their effectiveness in children's learning.
3 Suggest two difficulties that Doyle may have faced in carrying out participant observations in a primary school.
4 Suggest two reasons why interviewing children in pairs might produce less valid information than informal interviews with children on their own.
5 Suggest three reasons why the twelve focus group interviews with five or six children may have produced a greater depth of understanding of children's experiences with laptops in schools than interviews conducted with children either singly or in pairs.
6 Suggest two ways in which the analysis of the taped interviews may have provided an essential starting point for the participant and non-participant observations and informal interviews.
7 Suggest two reasons why sociologists should be careful before applying the findings of the Laptop study to all schools in Britain.

Longitudinal Study of Young People in England (LSYPE), also known as Next Steps (DfES; renamed the Department for Education (DfE) in 2010)

This longitudinal study uses annual interviews with the same group of young people and (in the first four waves only) their parents to explore a wide range of factors influencing young people's education. The study began in spring 2004, with interviews completed with 15,770 households from an original sample of just over 21,000 young people in Year 9 (aged 13–14). The first four waves (2004–7) used structured face-to-face interviews with both parents and the young people. Waves 5 and 6 (2008–9) also used telephone interviews, as well as face-to-face interviews and online interviews with only the young people, whereas previously their parents or guardians had also been interviewed. In the first wave in 2004, the interviewers asked most of the questions, which they read from a laptop computer on which they recorded their answers. The interviewer had to record who else, if anyone, was present in the room during the interviews, apart from the person being interviewed.

There were some questions which the respondents themselves had to complete, so their responses could be kept private. In such cases, the computer was turned to the parent or young person, and they were asked to fill in their own answers on the screen, with help from the interviewer if needed. These self-completion sections involved questions about things like arguments between parents and young people; sex and sexual orientation; prolonged absences from school, such as through illness, exclusions and truancy; bullying (including abuse, violence and theft); police involvement because of the young person's behaviour; and the young person's experiences of their truancy, smoking, alcohol, illegal drug use and doing graffiti.

Activity

1 Identify *two* research methods that are used in the survey of young people above.
2 Suggest *three* reasons why some questions about the experiences of young people were recorded via a self-completion questionnaire on a laptop rather than by the interviewer.
3 Suggest *two* reasons why it might have been important for the interviewer 'to record who else, if anyone, was present in the room during the interviews, apart from the person being interviewed'.
4 Suggest *three* possible problems with the validity of young people's responses to questions about their truancy, smoking, alcohol, illegal drug use and doing graffiti.
5 Identify all the people who might have to give their consent for this research to be carried out.
6 Identity *two* ethical issues that researchers should be aware of when conducting research like that above.
7 Suggest at least *three* pieces of information you would need to know in order to evaluate whether the survey above was representative.
8 Suggest two factors, apart from those given in your answer to question 4 above, that may influence the validity of the findings of the research above.

Exam-style question

The Methods-in-Context question, included in the Section A: Education with Research Methods question in Unit 2, involves a stimulus item, followed by a question about the strengths and limitations of one of two research methods for exploring the issue. The following is a typical example.

Item B

Investigating gender and attitudes to science

Murphy and Whitelegg (2006) were interested in why girls choose not to start or continue to study physics. They found that at the beginning of secondary school students had less interest in science than for other subjects, and this declined further as they went through secondary schooling. Although both boys and girls had negative views regarding the relevance, appeal and interest of chemistry and physics, boys were much more likely than girls to study physics, particularly after age 16. Prior achievement influenced student subject choices, with more girls than boys seeing themselves as becoming less competent in physics as they went through secondary school. Girls studying physics saw it as a means of doing good and helping people, and preferred physics content related to social and human concerns.

Using material from **Item B** and elsewhere, assess the strengths and limitations of **one** of the following methods for investigating gender differences in students' views about studying physics or other science subjects:

EITHER self-completion questionnaires

OR group interviews.   *(20 marks)*

CHAPTER SUMMARY AND REVISION CHECKLIST

After studying this chapter, you should be able to:

- critically discuss the main purposes of education, including vocational education, as identified by the functionalist, New Right and Marxist perspectives.

- explain what is meant by the hidden curriculum, and how it reflects and reinforces values and ideology from outside schools.

- explain what is meant by equality of educational opportunity.

- outline the features of the interactionist perspective on education.

- critically discuss the effects of a range of issues concerning relationships and processes within schools, for students' progress and their experiences of schooling. These include school ethos, the hidden curriculum, teacher stereotyping, labelling, the self-fulfilling prophecy, the organization of teaching and learning through banding, streaming and setting and their consequences, including educational triage.

- discuss a variety of ways students react to the experience of schooling, including a range of pupil subcultures, and how these influence the progress they make at school.

- explain what is meant by a meritocracy, and why Britain is not a meritocracy.

- describe the facts about, and discuss a range of explanations for, social class, gender and ethnic group differences in educational achievement.

- examine the ways that the schooling process reinforces and reproduces gender identities.

- describe and explain the features of admissions and selection policies in education, including covert selection and selection by ability, and the strengths and weaknesses of the tripartite and comprehensive systems of education.

- identify and explain the main changes in education policy since the 1980s, and discuss the aims, consequences and criticisms of these reforms, and particularly the meaning, features, consequences and criticisms of the marketization of education.

- discuss the significance of, and the arguments for and against, private education.

- apply research methods to the study of particular issues in education.

KEY TERMS

(these are already defined in the text, and may also be found in the glossary at the end of the book)

anti-school subculture
banding
compensatory education
counter-school subculture
cultural capital
cultural deprivation
culture clash
division of labour
educational triage
elaborated code
elite
English Baccalaureate (EBacc)

equality of educational opportunity
ethnocentrism
functional prerequisite
habitus
halo effect
hegemonic control
hegemony
hidden curriculum
human capital
ideological state apparatuses
labelling

marketization
meritocracy
multicultural education
parentocracy
particularistic values
positive discrimination
pro-school subculture
racial prejudice
racism
restricted code
self-fulfilling prophecy
service sector
setting

sexism
social capital
social cohesion
social solidarity
streaming
subculture
underachievement
universalistic values

There are a variety of free tests and other activities that can be used to assess your learning at

www.politybooks.com/browne

EXAM QUESTION

Answer **all** the questions from this Section

Section A: Education with Research Methods

You are advised to spend approximately 50 minutes on Questions | 0 | 1 | to | 0 | 4 |

You are advised to spend approximately 30 minutes on Question | 0 | 5 |

You are advised to spend approximately 40 minutes on Questions | 0 | 6 | to | 0 | 9 |

Time allowed: 2 hours   **Total for this section: 90 marks**

Education

Read **Item A** below and answer questions | 0 | 1 | to | 0 | 4 | that follow.

Item A

Recent changes have tried to create a free market in education. Parents now have some choice in their children's school, with Ofsted reports and school and college league tables to help them find the best schools. Schools have much more control of their own affairs, and some schools, further education and sixth-form colleges and universities are completely independent and entirely manage their own affairs. In the educational marketplace, they compete with each other to raise income by attracting students. The government thought this would make educational institutions more responsive to parents' and students' needs, and raise standards of teaching and learning. Like supermarkets competing for customers, educational institutions producing good results would be popular with parents and students, and thrive. Institutions that were failing to produce good quality 'products' would lose students and money, and would either improve or be closed.

| 0 | 1 | Explain what is meant by the term 'cultural capital'   *(2 marks)*

| 0 | 2 | Suggest **three** reasons why some minority ethnic groups underachieve in education.

(6 marks)

| 0 | 3 | Outline some of the reasons why there is sometimes said to be a 'culture clash' between the home and the school for those from working-class backgrounds.   *(12 marks)*

| 0 | 4 | Using material from **Item A** and elsewhere, assess the view that the 'marketization' of education has mainly benefited middle-class parents and students.   *(20 marks)*

Methods in Context

This question requires you to **apply** your knowledge and understanding of sociological research methods to the study of this **particular** issue in **education**.

Read **Item B** below and answer the question that follows.

Item B
Investigating teacher attitudes and ethnic minority achievement
Gillborn was interested in exploring how teacher attitudes and expectations influenced the opportunity for ethnic minority pupils to achieve success at school. He did this by observing interaction between teachers and pupils. His study of an inner city comprehensive school in the Midlands described how teachers perceived a threat to their authority in their daily interactions with African-Caribbean pupils. When teachers acted on this perception, it created conflict with African-Caribbean pupils. African-Caribbean pupils responded by asserting their ethnic identity as young black people, which teachers interpreted as a threatening attitude. Such research suggests there is a considerable gap between policies promoting equal opportunities in schools and the daily experiences of many black pupils.

| 0 | 5 | Using material from **Item B** and elsewhere, assess the strengths and limitations of one of the following methods for investigating the study of teacher attitudes and ethnic minority achievement:

EITHER participant observation
OR structured interviews. *(20 marks)*

Research Methods

These questions permit you to draw examples from **any areas** of sociology with which you are familiar.

| 0 | 6 | Explain what is meant by the term 'sample'. *(2 marks)*

| 0 | 7 | Suggest **two** sampling methods that sociologists might use, **apart from** random sampling. *(4 marks)*

| 0 | 8 | Suggest **two** reasons why sociologists might use official statistics. *(4 marks)*

| 0 | 9 | Examine the problems sociologists may find when using postal questionnaires in their research. *(20 marks)*

Contents

CHAPTER

7 Health

SPECIFICATION TOPICS

- **Topic 1** Health, illness, disability and the body as social and as biological constructs
- **Topic 2** The unequal social distribution of health and illness in the United Kingdom by social class, age, gender, ethnicity and region, and internationally
- **Topic 3** Inequalities in the provision of, and access to, healthcare in contemporary society
- **Topic 4** The sociological study of the nature and social distribution of mental illness
- **Topic 5** The role of medicine and the health professions
- **Topic 6** The application of sociological research methods to the study of health

Topic 1

SPECIFICATION AREA

Health, illness, disability and the body as social and as biological constructs

The social construction of the body

> **Social construction** means that the important characteristics of something, such as statistics, health, illness, disability or crime, are created and influenced by the attitudes, actions and interpretations of members of society.

When sociologists talk of the **social construction** of something, they mean it only becomes real because it is created and influenced by the attitudes, actions and interpretations of members of society. As will be seen in this chapter, even apparently natural or biological events or categories like disease and the human body are the results of social influences and activity, and the interpretations of people.

The human body may appear to be a wholly natural phenomenon, which exists in a more or less unchanging form everywhere, regardless of social circumstances and the society in which people live. However, this would be an incorrect assumption, as the human body is very much subject to social influences and is a social as well as a biological construction. For example, there are wide differences between societies in ideas about the most desirable size, shape and appearance of bodies, and these differ

444

in what is seen as appropriate for men and for women. In different cultures and sub-cultures today, the human body is constantly being reinvented in different ways. In a globalized society, there is no clear view of what a desirable body is like, as body images are increasingly drawn from different cultures across the world. Societies have always been involved in constructing bodies, and people try actively to control and remould their bodies to conform to what they think they should look like, and to create their sense of **identity** in the society to which they belong. For example, artificially elongating necks, binding feet and waists, extending lower lips, scarring, tattooing, body-piercing, body-building, cosmetic surgery, dentistry, tanning, dieting, sex-change operations and hormone treatment have all been used at different times to form bodies in their social context.

In contemporary British society, which postmodernists argue is a consumer-led culture, the human body and health are often design projects for people to work on in forming their identities. The body has become a central focus of cultural activity, and

> **Identity** is concerned with how individuals see and define themselves and how other people see and define them.

Activity

1 With reference to the pictures above, explain what is meant by 'the social construction of the body'.
2 Suggest *three* ways in contemporary Britain in which the human body is used as a way for individuals to present particular images, feelings or identities (whether positive or negative) to people they meet.
3 Suggest *three* ways that people's attitudes to their bodies might influence how they define good health.

postmodernists argue we are now living in a sort of what Turner (1996) calls a 'somatic society', in which people seek to express themselves through and take control of all aspects of their bodies. Modern technology means people today have a greater ability to alter their bodies. Men and women now often go to great lengths to maintain and construct or shape their bodies in accordance with the identity they wish to project, through consuming goods and services around their bodily images such as health foods and diet products, fitness clubs and equipment, cosmetics and cosmetic surgery, breast implants and reduction, tattoos, hair extensions and tanning salons. Even apparently natural phenomena like pregnancy and childbirth are socially constructed. For example, new reproductive technologies, such as contraception, fertility drugs, artificial insemination and the storage of embryos for future use, mean that women can now choose whether and when to have children, the sex of their baby and whether to have it independently of sexual relations with a man. Organ transplants now enable deteriorating and disintegrating bodies to be reassembled and renewed.

The social construction of the body is also increasingly tied up with health in contemporary Britain, and health is increasingly seen in terms of body maintenance. The commercial and advertising pressures which promote and sell fitness products of all kinds are wrapped up in the message that people should take control of their bodies and their health, and that adopting a healthy lifestyle means good-looking bodies, feeling good and being healthy. For example, Gill et al. (2005), in a study of body projects and masculinity, found many men saw using skin-care products like moisturiser and hand cream in terms of the health of their skin (rather than its appearance) and male gym users often saw working out as concerned with their health rather than their appearance, for example through cardiovascular exercises, strengthening otherwise flaccid muscles, and staying fit and healthy as they got older.

The social construction of health, illness and disease

Activity

1 Think of some people you know whom you consider to be very healthy. Explain carefully what makes you think of them as healthy. For example, is it because they never appear to be ill, because they seem to be physically fit and have strong bodies, because they seem healthy for their age, because they have no disease or anything 'wrong' with them, or because they have healthy habits and lifestyles? Consider these factors and others of your own.

2 Now write your own definitions, with examples, of 'health', 'illness' and 'disease'. Discuss, with examples, what your definitions might mean for promoting health and eliminating disease.

3 What factors do you consider when deciding whether you are ill? How do you decide when you are ill enough to seek out medical attention from a doctor? Discuss your reasons with others if you are in a group, and see if there are any differences between you.

4 How do you think your definitions of health and illness might differ between different countries, between different age groups, and between rich and poor people?

As you may have found from the activity at the beginning of this topic, the definitions of **health**, **illness** and **disease** are not simple matters. What counts as health and illness varies between individuals, between different social groups within a single society –

Health is probably easiest to define as 'being able to function normally within a usual everyday routine'.

Illness refers to the subjective feeling of being unwell or in ill-health – a person's own recognition of lack of well-being. It is possible both to have a disease and not feel ill, and to feel ill and not have any disease.

Disease generally refers to a biological or mental condition, such as high blood pressure, a faulty heart or chemical imbalances in the body, which usually involves medically diagnosed symptoms.

such as between men and women – and between societies. Views of acceptable standards of health are likely to differ widely between the people of a poor African country and those of Britain. Even in the same society, views of health change over time. At one time in Britain, mental illness was seen as a sign of satanic possession or witchcraft – a matter best dealt with by the church rather than by doctors. Similarly, what were once seen as personal problems have quite recently become seen as medical problems, such as obesity, alcoholism and smoking.

There is no simple definition of illness, because, as interactionist sociologists would say, for pain or discomfort to count as a disease it is necessary for someone to diagnose or label it as such. Interactionist sociologists also point to the subjective influences on health, and how the way we define health and illness is partly dependent on our own experiences and perceptions of illness, rather than simply physical symptoms: some of us can put up with or ignore pain more than others; some feel no pain; and many of us will have different notions of what counts as 'feeling unwell'. Individuals will define and respond to health in different ways. For example, older people may define good health as not having too many aches and pains, and having energy levels that enable them to go about their daily tasks, or being well enough to run their own homes. Younger people may define good health as being well enough to go clubbing or take part in sport. Dubos and Pines (1980) point out the physical demands of work mean that what counts as good health or a disease may have different meanings to an astronaut, an athlete, a roadsweeper and a fashion model. We can also change our views of the state of our

How might the definition of 'good health' differ between an astronaut, an athlete, a fashion model and a roadsweeper?

health depending on our choices and situations. For example, we might be too ill to go to school or college, but well enough to go clubbing.

This means health is a relative concept, which will vary according to age, lifestyle, personal circumstances, culture and the environment in which people live. There are strong subjective (personal) influences on health, and whether a person sees himself or herself as healthy or not will depend on how well they are able to function within their own everyday routines.

So what counts as health and illness can be considered as a social construction – a result of individual, social and cultural interpretations and perceptions.

Activity

The United Nations World Health Organization defines health as 'a state of complete physical, mental, and social well-being, and not merely the absence of disease or infirmity'. Some have argued that this definition goes far beyond a realistic definition of health, as it implies not simply the absence of disease, but also a personally fulfilling life.

1 Discuss how the World Health Organization's definition of health might apply to the health of the long-term unemployed in Britain.
2 Using the World Health Organization's definition, how might the definition of 'good health' differ between:
    (a) people who live in a poor African country and those who live in modern Britain?
    (b) people in Britain who live in an isolated village in the country and those who live in a town?
3 How do you think the society we live in influences people's ideas of what counts as health and illness?
4 Discuss the view that 'good health is simply a state of mind'.

The social construction of disability

The idea that what counts as health and illness is a social construction, and a creation of and response to people's interpretations and perceptions, is shown by **disability**.

Disability is often linked with health, and associated, often incorrectly, with symptoms of illness, helplessness and weakness. Most of us learn about disability as part of the socialization process, rather than as a result of personal experience. Media images of disability are often linked with what some see as abnormal, socially unacceptable behaviours, or suggest we have good reasons to fear people with disabilities, especially those with mental or behavioural difficulties, or who display violent or inexplicable behaviour. Disability then is often not seen simply as being different, as some having impairments or health issues others don't have, but frequently has a **stigma** attached to it – a demeaning mark of shame, that can create a **stigmatized identity** – an undesirable or demeaning identity which stops people being fully accepted in society.

There are clearly some physical or mental impairments, such as loss of use of limbs or sight, or brain damage, that will mean some people will find more difficulty in carrying out everyday tasks than others.

However, impairment is not the same as disability. Shakespeare (1998) suggests that disability should be seen as a social construction – a problem created by the attitudes of society and not by the state of our bodies. Shakespeare argues that disability is created by societies that don't take into account the needs of those who do not meet with that society's ideas of what is 'normal'. Whether someone is disabled or not is then a social product – it is social attitudes which turn an impairment into a disability,

Disability is defined by the Disability Discrimination Act 1995 as 'a physical or mental *impairment* which has a substantial and long term adverse effect on [your] ability to carry out normal day-to-day activities'.
An **impairment** is some abnormal functioning of the body or mind, arising from birth or from injury or disease.

Stigma Any undesirable physical or social characteristic that is seen as abnormal or unusual in some way, that is seen as demeaning and stops an individual being fully accepted by society.
Stigmatized identity An identity that is in some way undesirable or demeaning, and excludes people from full acceptance in society.

because society discriminates against those with some impairments. For example, people parking on pavements makes it difficult for those in wheelchairs or the blind to get by; design of buildings may make access difficult or impossible for those who have lost the use of their lower limbs and need wheelchairs to aid their mobility. People who are short-sighted only become disabled if they have no access to glasses to correct their sight, or if documents are printed in small type or colours which people with visual impairments find hard to read. Workplaces can be disabling if adjustments to the working environment are not made to enable people with impairments to perform their jobs successfully. With the ageing population (a growing proportion of elderly people in the population), all of us will, if we live long enough, eventually become disabled unless social attitudes change and society adapts to the needs of those with physical or mental impairments.

Important further reading

There is a further section on disability on pages 89–92 dealing with the social construction of disability, stereotypes of disability, and disability and identity. You are advised to read it now to gain a fuller understanding of disability as a health issue.

Activity

'People become disabled, not because they have physical or mental impairments, but because they have physical or mental differences from the majority, which challenges traditional ideas of what counts as "normal". Disability is about the relationship between people with impairment and a society which discriminates against them. People are disabled by society, not by their bodies. Disability is about discrimination and prejudice . . . Understanding disability is about flexing the sociological imagination – turning personal troubles into public issues.'

(Adapted from an unpublished paper by Tom Shakespeare, 26 Jan. 2001)

1 Do you agree with the view that people are disabled by society and the attitudes of others rather than by the state of their minds or bodies? What evidence can you think of for and against this view?
2 Explain in your own words what you think Shakespeare means when he says: 'Understanding disability is about . . . turning personal troubles into public issues.'
3 What kinds of impairments in our society create disadvantages for those who have them? What steps might be taken to remove these disadvantages facing people with some impairments, in order to prevent them becoming disabilities?

The biomedical model of health

As seen above, there are different meanings attached to 'health'. There are two main approaches to health arising from different views of what the causes of ill-health are, and the policies needed to solve it. These two competing models of health are often referred to as the biomedical (or medical) and social models of health.

The biomedical model of health is the one which underlies the development of Western medicine, and is the main approach found in the National Health Service. This model sees health in terms of the absence of disease, with ill-health arising from identifiable biological or physical causes. The main aim of medicine, and modern healthcare systems like the NHS, is therefore to diagnose and tackle these physical symptoms.

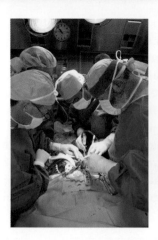

The biomedical (or medical) model of health views the human body as working like a machine that occasionally breaks down, with doctors like mechanics, fixing it in 'body shops' like surgeries and hospitals

MAIN FEATURES OF THE BIOMEDICAL MODEL

- Disease is seen as mainly caused by biological factors, together with the recent emphasis on personal factors such as smoking and diet. Health is defined as the absence of disease or disability.
- The human body is seen as working like a machine which occasionally breaks down. In the same way as with a car that has broken down, 'body mechanics' (doctors) apply their expert medical knowledge to diagnose the biological or chemical processes that have caused the sickness. Doctors are then able to treat and cure the disease they have identified, through medical or surgical treatments in 'body shops' – clinical situations like doctors' surgeries and hospitals.
- The causes of ill-health are seen as arising either from the moral failings of the individual (such as smoking too much, not eating the right food or not getting enough exercise) or from random attacks of disease. This is a bit like blaming car breakdowns on poor maintenance and lack of proper servicing, or on faulty parts and bad luck.
- Scientific medicine is seen as the way to identify and solve health problems. This means good health depends on the availability of trained medical personnel, medical technology, operating theatres, drugs and so on. Medicine and medical technology is seen as in itself a good thing, and the more of it there is, the better people's health will be.

THE BIOMEDICAL MODEL AND THE MEDICAL GAZE

Foucault (2003 [1973]) points out that, before the advent of modern scientific medicine and the biomedical approach to the understanding of disease, doctors often based their diagnosis and treatments on patients' own accounts of their illness, including their life-style, moral attitudes and beliefs, and the environment in which they lived. There was little, if any, direct analysis of their bodies, and treatment was based on a fairly intimate doctor–patient relationship. Foucault suggests that, over time, medicine became more scientific and practical, with a growing arsenal of new techniques, surgical skills, and medical technology enabling doctors to conduct more careful and thorough physical examinations of their patients. Doctors began to develop their diagnosis and uncover the truth about disease by gazing on or observing their patients' bodies, and the importance attached to their patients' own accounts of their symptoms diminished.

The **medical gaze** refers to the way doctors look upon a patient merely as a body, an object like a piece of meat or a machine, rather than as a whole person with a conscious mind and individual identity. Doctors search for the existence and causes of a disease through detached and sophisticated analysis obtained by gazing at a patient's body, rather than relying on that individual's accounts of her or his symptoms.

Foucault used the term **medical gaze** to describe the way the biomedical model meant that patient diagnosis changed from being based on patients' accounts to examination of their bodies. The biomedical model and the advent of scientific medicine meant doctors became experts who alone understood how the body worked, and had the knowledge and power to define what counts as health and illness, and to treat the sick. Doctors' search for the scientific truth about disease was separated from the individual's mind. Rather than seeing a patient as a whole person with an identity and conscious mind, doctors came to gaze upon a patient merely as a body, an object, like a piece of meat or a machine, or like a zombie – a body without a mind, consciousness or feelings. They then treat that body through drugs, surgery, diet, medical technology and other tools of scientific medicine.

Activity

1 Suggest three ways those adopting the biomedical model might tackle the issue of improving a society's health.
2 Do you think there are any problems with an approach to improving health which concentrates only on the medical treatment of individuals? What other factors might also be important in influencing the state of our health?

CRITICISMS OF THE BIOMEDICAL MODEL

- *It suggests that health can be defined objectively, as the absence of disease.* However, what counts as disease or illness and good health is, as shown above, socially constructed – it is a product of people's interpretations and social influences, which can vary by time, place and culture, and is not simply a biological fact. What counts as good health will vary over time and between individuals, groups and societies.

- *It does not take account of the cultural and social context which influences health and well-being, and the wider social conditions that may have created ill-health.* Marmot (2010) suggested health and well-being were shaped by a wide range of factors in daily life, including material circumstances, such as hazardous work environments, poor-quality food, poverty or environmental pollution, and social position, education, occupation, income, gender and ethnicity. Illness and disease do not strike at random, out of the blue. They follow consistent social patterns. Ill-health is not simply a matter of fate or bad luck, but very much a product of the society and social circumstances in which a person lives. White (2005) and his colleagues stress that health and illness, and people's well-being, are influenced by a combination of biological, psychological and social factors. Dubos (1966) and Dubos and Pines (1980) explored the interplay of environmental, physical, mental and spiritual dimensions of health, and stressed that individuals were not just biological units but thinking individuals living in a social context. They pointed out that, while people are more or less the same biologically, people usually have diseases characteristic of the society, the social groups and the social conditions in which they live their lives. These factors can all influence health, and are important considerations in maintaining health, and diagnosing and treating disease.

- *It focuses on treating sick individuals*, rather than looking at health education, preventive measures and the social causes which make people sick in the first place.

- *It exaggerates the role and effectiveness of medicine.* Researchers like McKeown (1976) and Szreter (2003) have shown that doctors are not (solely) responsible for improving **life expectancy** and health. Improvements in social conditions led by government intervention and support – such as public sewers and clean water – are far more important than the application of scientific medicine. Szreter stresses that such improvements are only possible when governments make political choices to intervene to improve public health and social conditions. For example, biomedical approaches to improving health are unlikely to be effective in developing countries if governments choose to invest in military equipment rather than safe water supplies, waste disposal and food safety regulation.

- *It serves the interests of doctors and the medical establishment, and gives them a great deal of power as agents of social control* (this is discussed in Topic 5). Doctors have a legal monopoly over treatment, and other alternative approaches, like acupuncture or homeopathy, have traditionally been downgraded and dismissed as ineffective.

- *It leads to growing medicalization.* The identification of healthcare with medical care has led to a 'pill for every ill' syndrome, and there is a growing trend towards defining in terms of the biomedical model a range of issues that were once regarded as non-medical matters, which are then diagnosed and treated as medical disorders or illnesses under the authority of doctors and other health professionals. This process is called **medicalization**, and is discussed shortly in considering the medicalization of pregnancy, childbirth and motherhood, and in Topic 5 in the medicalization of deviance. The medical profession increasingly prescribes drugs for all sorts of ailments; new diseases are constantly being discovered and ever more conditions are being labelled as diseases, which may be primarily social rather than biological in character. Examples might include stress, anxiety and depression arising from difficulties at work or unemployment, eating disorders like bulimia or anorexia, and the way some 'naughty children' are now labelled as suffering from emotional and behavioural difficulties (EBD) or attention deficit disorder (ADD) or hyperactivity disorder.

- *It over-emphasizes treatment and cure rather than care.* The biomedical model suggests disease has an identifiable biological cause, and that measures can be taken to treat and cure it. However, modern medicine has often proved unable to provide cures for the new degenerative diseases, such as cancer and heart disease, which are the main killers of people in the developed world in the twenty-first century. Medicine is almost completely ineffective in curing some new diseases like AIDS (Acquired Immune Deficiency Syndrome) or vCJD (variant Creutzfeldt–Jakob Disease), and ME (Myalgic Encephalopathy – also known as Chronic Fatigue or

> **Life expectancy**
> is an estimate of how long people can be expected to live from a certain age.

> **Medicalization**
> is the process whereby previously non-medical social issues and problems come to be seen and defined in medical terms, and treated as medical disorders or illnesses under the authority of doctors and other health professionals.

The identification of health care with medical care has led to a pill for every ill, with health problems that have social causes being treated medically

Post-Viral Fatigue Syndrome). There is still no cure for the common cold or flu. Bury (2001) points out that, in many ways, contemporary medicine is faced less with the treatment and cure on which the biomedical model is based, and more with the management and care of chronic and degenerative illnesses which have no cure. This means the doctor's role is now less likely to involve the medical gaze of diagnosis, treatment and cure, but has a growing emphasis on care, and listening to patients' own accounts of their illnesses and providing whatever professional practical help and guidance they can to help people maintain quality in their lives as they live with their illnesses.

- *It is just one more metanarrative.* Postmodernists see the biomedical model as just one more metanarrative – a big story claiming to provide the only universal truth and solution to ill-health, when really it is just a story that mainly serves the interests of doctors and benefits the medical establishment and the pharmaceutical industry, and dismisses other equally valid explanations of and solutions to ill-health, such as those found in the vast range of complementary medicines and treatments (this is discussed on pages 532–4).

- *It diverts attention away from health education and preventive medicine.* It suggests resources are best channelled into medical science, new drugs and medical technology, and state-of-the-art high-tech hospitals. The focus on cure means prevention is not given the resources needed. As the cartoon below suggests, this is like standing by a river bank and constantly hauling people out of the water, without asking who is throwing them into the river in the first place.

- *It underestimates iatrogenesis and exaggerates the extent to which medical intervention always produces beneficial results.* It suggests there is a steady march of medical progress, with the medical and nursing professions generally doing a good job in promoting good health and preventing or curing ill-health. Marxist writers like Illich (1976) have argued that medical intervention, surgery and drugs can actually have more harmful effects than the condition they are meant to be curing. Illich calls this **iatrogenesis.** Some tranquillizers, for example, are addictive,

Iatrogenesis
is any harmful mental or physical condition induced in a patient through the effects of treatment by a doctor or surgeon.

The biomedical model of health tends to concentrate on rescuing sick individuals, rather than looking at health education, preventive measures and the social causes which make people sick in the first place

and feminists have been particularly critical of mastectomy (the surgical removal of breasts) as a treatment for breast cancer. The development of antibiotics – the 'wonder drug' of the 1940s – has led to the emergence of antibiotic-resistant organisms, like MRSA.

Iatrogenesis in Britain

The harmful effects of medical treatment, with incompetent or unnecessary surgery, inadequate care after surgery, side-effects from drugs, infections caught in hospital, and missed diagnoses, are reported widely in the media. Media headlines are formed from horror stories of people having the wrong legs amputated or healthy kidneys removed, patients dying or being brain-damaged because of wrongly prescribed or overdoses of medicines, or their side-effects, or septicaemia occurring as a result of transfusions of contaminated blood, GPs failing to identify tumours, children dying after incompetent heart surgery, wrongly administered injections causing death and disability, and people dying from general anaesthetics in dental surgeries. A Department of Health report in 2000, *An Organisation with a Memory*, admitted that every year:

- More than 400 people die or are seriously injured in 'adverse' events involving medical devices.
- Nearly 10,000 people experience serious adverse reactions to drugs. At least 13 patients had died or been paralysed since 1985 because a drug was wrongly administered by spinal injection.
- Hospital-acquired infections (HAI) like MRSA – the 'superbug' immune to antibiotics – and others, like MSSA, affect thousands of hospital patients every year, and 5,000 of them die in England alone.
- Around 1,150 people who have been in recent contact with mental health services commit suicide.

The National Patient Safety Agency estimated in 2007 that there were around 850,000 'adverse events' in the NHS each year, in which patients are harmed through things like unnecessary or incompetent medical and surgical treatments, the effects of prescribed drugs or hospital-acquired infections. Kafetz (2010) reported that, in 2009–10, tens of thousands of patients were harmed in NHS hospitals, when they developed avoidable blood clots or blood poisoning, suffered from obstetric tears during childbirth, had objects left inside them after operations or were not given immediate treatment after a stroke. A 2011 report by the Royal College of Surgeons said that of 170,000 patients having major emergency surgery each year, 100,000 would develop significant complications following surgery, resulting in more than 25,000 deaths.

Statistics such as these almost certainly underestimate the scale of the problem because of inaccuracies in the recording of data, but estimates suggest poor aftercare, accidents, errors and mishaps in hospital affect as many as 1 in 10 in-patients.

Activity

Do you believe you are safe in the hands of doctors and other medical professionals? Do you have any personal experience of medicine being of little help to you or harming you in some way? Are there currently any stories of medical negligence around that you are aware of? Collect together information, and discuss it in your group.

The social model of health

Sociological approaches to health and medicine generally adopt the social model of health, which highlights the way that social factors are involved in both defining health and the causes of ill-health, and that health is a social construction. This model is the main alternative to the biomedical model, and recognizes there are important social influences on health which the biomedical model neglects. The *Acheson Report* (1998) and the *Marmot Review* (2010), for example, made powerful cases that many of the factors causing ill-health are rooted in social inequality (discussed in the next topic), and therefore recognized the importance of the social dimensions of health.

FEATURES OF THE SOCIAL MODEL OF HEALTH

- Health and illness are not seen simply as medical or scientific facts. Health is a relative condition. What is defined as health depends on what is regarded as 'normal' in a particular society, and this will vary over time and between cultures, and between individuals in the same culture.
- A choice exists as to whether someone sees himself or herself as ill or not, and those with power can choose whether or not to classify someone as ill. In most cases, 'those with power' means doctors and other medical experts. What counts as health and sickness is as much about the power of medical professionals as it is about biology.
- Medical science is not the detached objective science the biomedical model implies. It is influenced by wider social and economic considerations, rather than simply the treatment of biological disease. Drug companies and medical technology manufacturers are likely to have important influences on the way doctors go about their work.
- A strong emphasis is placed on the social causes of health and ill-health, and on how society influences health. Patterns of health and illness cannot simply be explained and treated individually, but should be understood within the social and economic environment in which they occur. It is not just random individuals who become sick through bad luck, but whole groups of people who are more at risk of ill-health. There is a pattern of social class, gender and ethnic inequalities in health. This suggests that it is social and environmental factors that make some groups of people more vulnerable to disease than others, and not simply lightning bolts from the blue hurled out by nature at unfortunate and randomly chosen individuals.

Activity

1. List six social and environmental factors you think influence health, and identify in each case how they do so.
2. How would you set out to improve society's health if you were particularly concerned with tackling the social and environmental causes of ill-health?
3. Go to www.dh.gov.uk (the Department of Health) and search for three policies being followed by the government to improve the health of Britain. Explain how each of the policies you identify might improve health.

LIMITATIONS OF THE SOCIAL MODEL OF HEALTH

It is important to recognize the social dimensions of health, and the ways conceptions of health and illness are socially constructed. However, there is a danger of overemphasizing these social aspects at the expense of the biomedical approach. Medicine has contributed to improvements in health, even if not as much as some doctors might claim. Childhood immunization against diseases such as tuberculosis, polio, smallpox, measles, mumps and rubella (German measles) have contributed to reducing these diseases, and in some cases wiped them out in modern Britain. Antibiotics have proved very effective in treating many infections, medicine has effective treatments for broken bones, and surgical procedures can often improve the quality of people's lives and sometimes save those lives. Most of us therefore derive some benefit from medical cures and surgical interventions, and knowledge through health education about preventing disease, which come from scientific medicine.

How society influences health

That health is the product of society rather than simply of biology or medicine is shown by historical evidence that patterns of disease change over time. While the message has been that medicine can cure us, all the major advances in health have occurred before medical intervention. In Britain, the elimination or substantial reduction of the killer infectious diseases of the past, such as tuberculosis (TB), pneumonia, cholera, typhoid and diphtheria, all took place before the development of modern medicine. It was social changes such as better diet, clean water supplies, sewage disposal, improved housing and general knowledge about health and hygiene that contributed to the greatest improvements in health, rather than simply medical improvements like antibiotics and vaccines.

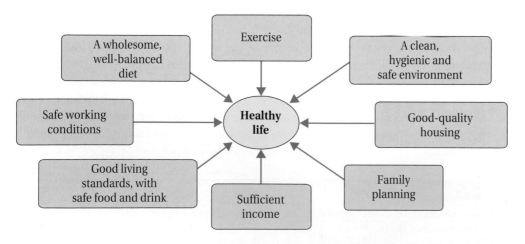

Figure 7.1 Some key social influences on health

> **Activity**
>
> Make a list of as many environmental, political, social and economic factors affecting health as you can think of, such as unemployment, pollution or poor housing. Explain in each case how the factors you identify might influence health. Refer to figure 7.1 to help you in this.

This is shown especially in the developing countries today, where the major advances in health have come about as a result of simple preventive measures such as clean water and sewage control, where vaccines have been less effective because of malnutrition, and where medicines are often not affordable because of the high prices charged by international drug companies. Doctors and medical treatment have therefore not had the impact on health they often claim, and it is incorrect to assume that medicine has been largely responsible for the most significant improvements and promotion of health. Improvements in health are due to wider social, economic and environmental factors, and not simply medical ones.

Changes which occurred in Britain during the nineteenth century and the first half of the twentieth century illustrate this well.

IMPROVEMENTS IN HEALTH IN THE NINETEENTH AND EARLY TWENTIETH CENTURIES

Mortality refers to the number of deaths in a population.

Morbidity refers to the extent of disease in a population, including either the total number of cases or the number of new cases of a disease in a particular population at a particular time.

Mortality rate refers to the number of deaths per year scaled to the size of a population group, such as the number of deaths per thousand of the population each year (the crude *death rate*).

In the nineteenth century, adult and child **mortality** (death rates) started to fall, and this was accompanied by a large and rapid population increase. For a long time this was thought to be due to the development of medicine. However, McKeown (1976) showed that the role of medicine in reducing **morbidity** (the extent of disease) and **mortality rates** in the nineteenth and twentieth centuries had been massively exaggerated. It is now agreed that these changes were due to a number of social and economic changes and the general improvement in living standards. These included:

- *Public hygiene* The movement for sanitary reform and public hygiene in the nineteenth century helped to develop a clean and safe environment and higher standards of public hygiene. Pure drinking water, efficient sanitation and sewage disposal, paved streets and highways all helped to reduce deaths from infectious diseases.
- *Better diet* Being well fed is the most effective form of disease prevention, as is shown in less-developed countries today where vaccination programmes are not as successful as they should be because children are poorly nourished. The high death rates of the past were mainly due to hunger or malnutrition, which led to poorer resistance to infection. The nineteenth and early twentieth centuries saw improved communications, technology and hygiene enabling the production, transportation and import of more and cheaper food. Wages improved, and higher standards of living meant better food and better health.
- *Safer and more effective contraception* This led to smaller families, enabling a better diet and healthcare for children. It also improved the health of women, who spent less time child-bearing.
- *Housing legislation* This increased public control over standards of rented housing, which helped to reduce overcrowding and the spread of infectious diseases between family members and in the close community.
- *The war effort* During the First World War (1914–18) unemployment was virtually eliminated. As part of the war effort, rents were controlled, food rationing was introduced and minimum wages were established in agriculture. The resulting decline in poverty cut childhood deaths, especially among the families of unskilled workers in urban areas.
- *General improvements in living standards* Higher wages, better food, clothing and housing, laws improving health and safety at work, reduced working hours,

and better hygiene regulations in the production and sale of food and drink all improved health.

All the above suggest that good health is more the result of government policy decisions and of economic development than simply of individual initiative or medical intervention.

The new disease burden: diseases of affluence

The infective diseases of the nineteenth century were often called the '**diseases of poverty**' – diseases arising because victims were malnourished and poor. These have been replaced in the developed world by '**diseases of affluence**' – diseases arising from growing wealth in a society, as a result of eating too much poor-quality food, a lack of exercise, and smoking and drinking too much.

A well-balanced diet is necessary for good health, and the lack of one makes people more vulnerable to disease. Despite the wealth of contemporary developed Western societies, there is a problem of malnutrition, in the form not of too little food, as you find in less-developed countries, but too much of the wrong sort. As a result, contemporary developed societies experience health problems rarely found in simpler, less-developed rural societies. The new disease burden includes obesity and degenerative (worsening) diseases like cirrhosis of the liver, certain cancers, heart disease, respiratory diseases and diabetes. These kill or disable more people than they did in the past, and many more people are becoming chronically ill for longer periods in their lives than ever before.

> **Diseases of poverty** are those arising from poverty and malnutrition.
> **Diseases of affluence** are those arising from lifestyles and social conditions in societies as they get richer.

WHAT ARE THE CAUSES OF THESE NEW DISEASES?

It is generally accepted that the causes of these new diseases of affluence are mainly social and environmental, and therefore preventable. Public concerns over the food supply have been rising. There were major scares over BSE ('Mad cow disease') in beef in the 1990s, and the linked human equivalent vCJD (variant Creutzfeldt–Jakob Disease) had killed 176 people in the UK up to July 2012. The Food Standards Agency estimates there are 5.5 million cases of food poisoning in Britain each year. Between 1982 and 2008, cases of food poisoning serious enough to be reported to a doctor rose by 500 per cent in England and Wales, and there were around 70,000 such cases

Adult obesity rates have almost quadrupled in the last twenty-five years, and the number of obese children has tripled in twenty years. In 2009 around a quarter of adult (over age 16) men and women, and one in six young people (aged 2–15) in England (with similar proportions in Scotland, Wales and N. Ireland) were officially classified as obese, and more than 30,000 deaths a year are caused by obesity in England alone. The UK has more obese women than any other country in Europe, according to the 2011 European Union's European Health Interview Survey. By 2030, estimates in the *Lancet* medical journal (27/08/2011) suggested more than four in ten British adults (48 per cent of men and 43 per cent of women) could be obese if present trends continue. The World Health Organization predicts that almost 50 per cent of children could be obese by 2025 through a combination of junk food and lack of exercise.

Obesity is much more common among the most deprived and least-educated sections of society. How might sociologists explain this?

To what extent does the food we eat and drink pose a threat to our health? Is the food we eat a result of individual lifestyle choices or of social pressures?

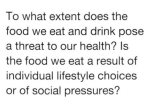

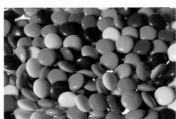

each year in 2002–9, and around 450 deaths in that period, with an average of around 55 people dying each year from food poisoning. Some doctors have linked the rise of asthma to poor diet, with insufficient fruit and vegetables. The rise in heart disease has been blamed on factors such as smoking, stress, an inactive lifestyle and a diet high in sugar, salt and fats but low in fibre. In 2010, the Faculty of Public Health, which represents 3,000 leading public health specialists in the UK and around the world, called for the removal of artificial trans fats – found in many cakes, pastries, pies, chips and fast foods – from British food, to reduce the risk of heart attacks, strokes and diabetes. The *Lancet* medical journal reported in 2003 that women eating too much food high in fat, such as butter, milk, meat, burgers, crisps, biscuits and cakes, were more likely to get breast cancer than others whose fat intake was low. A World Cancer Research Fund (WCRF) report in 2011 suggested increasingly sedentary (inactive) lifestyles, junk food, smoking and alcohol are key factors in around a quarter of all cancers. The WCRF estimated around 2.8 of the 12 million cancers diagnosed worldwide could be prevented each year if people adopted healthier lifestyles, with more exercise, staying slim and abstaining from too much fast food, alcohol, red meat and preserved meats like ham, bacon and salami.

The British are now eating a more highly processed diet than at any time in history. We consume a whole range of factory-produced food, which is often low in nutritional value and may well be harmful to health because of additives making up chemical cocktails of flavourings, colourings, preservatives and various drugs. For example, trans fats (mentioned above) have no nutritional value, but are added to foods to bulk them up and increase their supermarket shelf life. In 2007, the *Independent on Sunday* reported research suggesting that a common food preservative (E211 – Sodium Benzoate), found in a range of fizzy soft drinks like Fanta and Sprite, had the ability to 'switch off' vital parts of DNA, risking cirrhosis of the liver and other degenerative diseases such as Parkinson's and Alzheimer's. A 2007 Food Standards Agency study on 300 randomly selected children found that hyperactivity rose after a drink containing additive combinations. This may explain why between 5 and 10 per cent of school-age children suffer some degree of ADHD (Attention Deficit Hyperactivity Disorder), with symptoms such as impulsiveness, inability to concentrate and excessive activity.

Highly processed junk food reinforces the trend towards a high-sugar, high-salt and high-fat diet which is low in vitamins, minerals, protein and fibre, and generates obesity as a growing health problem. The spread of Western-style fast-food diets around the world has contributed to a large increase in obesity globally, and a huge surge in diabetes.

Becoming a health statistic

Another way of thinking about the social construction of health and illness, and the social influences on health, is to look at some of the ways in which health is measured, and how the statistics we use to assess the state of a country's health are themselves social constructions.

The main ways used to measure the extent of health and illness are *morbidity* (the extent of disease) and *mortality* (death) statistics. Major concerns have been raised over the *validity* (or truthfulness) of these statistics. Morbidity statistics are collected from sources such as the number of consultations with GPs, absence from work and self-reported illness surveys. Self-reported illness and absence from work statistics rely on the honesty of those claiming to be ill or absent from work due to illness. The types of disease recorded based on GP consultations will depend on the diagnostic skills of doctors, since their decisions will affect how the symptoms are classified (e.g. as pneumonia or AIDS). Statistics on the causes of death are derived from death certificates. What cause is put on these certificates will depend on the doctor's interpretation of what the cause of death is, and analysis of these statistics will depend on the level of explanation provided.

Health statistics must therefore be treated with considerable care, and many sociologists argue health statistics are simply social constructions, rather than being valid in providing a true picture of the pattern of health.

THE SOCIAL CONSTRUCTION OF HEALTH STATISTICS

- Health statistics depend on people persuading doctors they are ill, and are therefore simply a record of doctors' judgements and decision-making.
- Doctors may diagnose illnesses incorrectly, reflecting how patients describe their symptoms and the state of the doctor's knowledge. Records of illnesses may not be accurate. For example, there may have been many AIDS deaths recorded as pneumonia or other diseases before AIDS was discovered in the 1980s; many doctors still have difficulty in diagnosing ME (Chronic Fatigue Syndrome), as its symptoms are similar to those found in a range of other medical conditions. Many doctors don't even recognize ME as a genuine medical illness, even though it was first identified in the 1950s and an estimated 250,000 people suffer from it in the UK.
- Not all sick people go to the doctor, and not all people who persuade doctors they are ill are really sick.
- Private medicine operates to make a profit, and therefore is perhaps more likely to diagnose symptoms as a disease.

Official health statistics have been described as a 'clinical iceberg', as it is estimated that only about 10 per cent of illness is reported to doctors, with most concealed beneath the surface.

INTERACTIONIST APPROACHES TO THE SOCIAL CONSTRUCTION OF HEALTH AND HEALTH STATISTICS

The process of becoming ill is not as simple and straightforward as it might seem. People often have choices over whether to report themselves sick or not. People may respond to the same symptoms in different ways. While some may seek medical help, others may choose to ignore their symptoms. They may look for alternative non-medical or less serious explanations for them: bronchitis may become simply a 'smoker's cough', and possible brain tumours may be dismissed as headaches. Often, whether an individual goes to the doctor or not, and becomes officially labelled as sick and hence a health statistic, will depend on the interactions of individuals with other people, such as whether they can put up with a person's moaning any longer, or whether the individual's friends can continue to play sport with them or not. It may be difficulties experienced with looking after children while feeling unwell, pressures from friends and family, or health scare stories in the media, the costs of taking time off work and so on which finally persuade people to go to the doctor. These examples suggest it may be difficulties in coping with an illness, rather than the illness itself, which bring people to seek medical attention.

Doctor–patient interaction

Interactionists emphasize how becoming classified as sick involves a range of interactions with other people, like those considered above. A key element in this process is the interaction involved in the meeting between a doctor and a patient, in which the patient establishes through discussion and persuasion with the doctor whether he or she is really ill, and the outcome of this negotiation will affect whether or not access to the **sick role** is permitted (see pages 524–6 in Topic 5).

> The **sick role** refers to the pattern of behaviour which is expected from someone who is ill.

Labelling of the sick

For people to be labelled as 'sick' – and to be recorded as a health statistic – there are at least four stages involved:

Stage 1: Individuals must first recognize they have a problem.
Stage 2: They must then define their problem as serious enough to take to a doctor.
Stage 3: They must then actually go to the doctor.
Stage 4: Patients, in their interaction with the doctor, must persuade the doctor that they have a medical or mental condition capable of being labelled as an illness requiring treatment.

How might interactions between patients and doctors influence statistics on health and illness?

Activity

1 List all the factors you can which might influence each of the four stages involved in labelling someone 'sick', and which lead some people to visit the doctor and others not to. For example, in stage 1, you might consider a person's ability to continue his or her responsibilities to friends and family, pressure from relatives, friends and employers, etc. Draw on your own experiences of what makes you decide whether you are ill, and whether or not to go to see the doctor.
2 Devise a short questionnaire, and interview a sample of people, about what they consider to be the most important things influencing whether they go to the doctor or not.

Sociological approaches to health

Sociological approaches to health all concern themselves with the social dimensions of health, including the social model of health and social influences on health and illness discussed in this topic. The main functionalist, Marxist, feminist and interactionist approaches are discussed below and in the topics that follow, with some interactionist and postmodernist approaches already referred to in this topic (see pages 447, 453 and 461). The following sections summarize the main features of these sociological approaches and refer to where they are explored further.

FUNCTIONALIST APPROACHES

Functionalist approaches mainly consider health and illness in the context of their role in either maintaining or threatening social stability and cohesion. The functionalist approach is mainly considered in Topic 5, where the role of the medical profession and the definitions of health and illness are considered through a discussion of professionalism and the sick role.

MARXIST APPROACHES

Marxists like Navarro (1976) argue:

- The biomedical model of health suggests ill-health is caused by either random attacks of disease or the failure of individuals to follow a healthy lifestyle. This puts the blame on individuals when ill-health is really a result of social class inequality, caused by social influences in an unequal capitalist society, such as low pay, unemployment and poverty, unhealthy food, environmental pollution and hazardous workplaces. Improving health in the biomedical model is seen as depending on medical advance rather than reducing inequality. The state doesn't tackle the real social causes of ill-health, and allows companies to continue making profits out of health-damaging products, like tobacco, alcohol and junk food.
- The medical profession and the National Health Service help to keep the workforce fit, and this caring face of capitalism conceals the exploitation of the working class by the owning class.
- Doctors are agents of social control – **gate-keepers** who control access to the sick role and therefore keep the workforce at work in the interests of capitalists.
- The definition of health and the provision of healthcare are concerned with

Gate-keeping is the power of some people, groups or organizations to limit access to something valuable or useful. For example, doctors act as gate-keepers as they have the power to allow or refuse entry to the sick role.

protecting the interests of the dominant class in an unequal capitalist society. Medicine is mainly concerned with providing capitalists with a healthy workforce.

- The focus on medical treatment, rather than the prevention of ill-health, supports big business in the form of drug and medical technology companies. These companies are mainly concerned with making profits out of ill-health, not reducing it.

Marxist approaches have been criticized for a rather crude analysis which sees medicine and healthcare as a means only of making profits and social control, and keeping workers fit for employers, while failing to recognize that doctors, medical technology, and the medical and pharmaceutical industry can all make major contributions to improving the length and quality of people's lives. Marxist approaches are considered further in Topics 4 and 5 and the Marxist concern with social inequality links to much of the discussion of social inequality and health in Topic 2.

FEMINIST APPROACHES

Feminist writers, like Oakley (1984), Hart (1985) and Graham (1993), have been very critical of the biomedical approach to health and the patriarchal nature of the medical profession – what has been called 'malestream' science and medicine. Feminists have focused on the following main issues.

The medicalization of pregnancy, childbirth and motherhood

Feminists have been very critical of the way pregnancy and childbirth have come to be defined as medical problems, dealt with as an illness or a medical procedure, and treated clinically with medical technology, rather than as a natural process. For example, pregnancy and childbirth are now associated with regular medical check-ups, vaginal examinations, ultrasound monitoring, and births in hospital. Births may be induced by drugs, or babies delivered by major surgical procedures, like caesarean births, at times to suit the working hours of hospitals and doctors rather than the needs of the mother and baby. Oakley (1992) suggests childbirth has quite literally been taken out of women's own control, and that many maternity services are more to do with control over women rather than caring for them. A survey for *Mother and Baby* magazine in 2005 found that just 43 per cent of the 96 per cent of expectant mothers giving birth in hospital had the same midwife throughout their labour, and half described their postnatal care as 'not kind or compassionate'.

Jebali (1993), from a feminist perspective, has been very critical of the biomedical approach to post-natal depression (PND). She argues that the biomedical approach to

Feminist writers have been very critical of the way childbirth has become medicalized, and seen as a medical problem to be treated clinically with medical technology at times suited to doctors

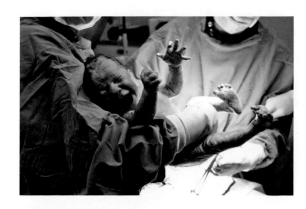

this mental illness, which is estimated to affect 1 in 10 of all new mothers, is based on the patriarchal assumption that childbirth, child-rearing and the motherhood role are natural processes which should be seen as satisfying and enjoyable by all women. Any other feelings are seen as abnormal, and any emotional problems related to motherhood must therefore be due to some biological malfunctioning of the individual, which should be corrected by medically prescribed treatment. Jebali, by contrast, suggests PND has social roots in society's double standards on motherhood. On the one hand, motherhood is idealized and seen as central to female identity, and, on the other, it is trivialized and undervalued, creating feelings of confusion, inadequacy and depression in some new mothers. Those who do not experience the transition to the motherhood role and the unrelenting demands of infant care as a happy and fulfilling experience face a sense of disappointment, guilt, loss of independent identity and freedom which generates PND. This is seen as a problem exclusive to women, reflecting the patriarchal assumptions on which motherhood is based.

The policing of motherhood

Douglas and Michaels (2004) suggest that, in contemporary motherhood, there is an intensive process of what Foucault (1991) called surveillance. This means everyone is watching and judging how mothers parent their children, and mothers are watching and judging their own parenting, and comparing themselves with, and judging, how others mothers raise their children. Douglas and Michaels suggest motherhood has become a 'psychological police state', with mothers policing themselves, and policing and being policed by other mothers. Medical professionals like doctors and health visitors play a role in this surveillance and policing of motherhood, in the sense of making assessments about whether women are 'good' or 'bad' mothers. Mothers may experience reproach and judgement if their parenting practices and their children's behaviour do not conform to what is often a middle-class stereotype held by medical professionals of what the ideal family, and the ideal mother, should be like.

Patriarchy in healthcare

Feminist writers point to patriarchy in the medical profession and the drug and medical technology industries, with women marginalized in many aspects of healthcare. Witz (1992) shows how in the nineteenth and twentieth centuries, up to about the 1930s, there was a long struggle by men to exclude or marginalize women in the medical professions, including female doctors, midwives, nurses and radiographers. These attempts were not always successful, but the male-dominated medical professions (like doctors) succeeded in securing the highest professional status over female-dominated professions like nursing. For example, today midwives (nearly all women) are supervised by mainly male obstetricians and gynaecologists, around 59 per cent of whom, in 2010–11, were men. Nurses, around 90 per cent of whom are women, have lower status than doctors – around 65 per cent of whom are men – and there is a large body of research evidence which suggests that, despite their lesser numbers, men have greater career success, and are more likely to earn more and be promoted into leadership roles in the nursing profession than women. Women dominate in the lower levels of every aspect of the National Health Service.

Feminists also point out, for example, that contraception is mainly aimed at women rather than men. What male contraception there is has few side-effects. In contrast to this, contraception for women does have harmful effects, with worries, for example, that certain contraceptive pills might be linked to higher risks of cancer, and IUDs (intrauterine devices) and caps might leave women vulnerable to infections. Is this because men dominate the development of contraceptive technologies?

Feminists also point to the ways women and men are treated differently by doctors, and some illnesses are more likely to be diagnosed and labelled as women's illnesses. This is often the case with mental illnesses like depression and anxiety, which are more likely to be diagnosed among women than men, and these are often not recognized among men, who try to avoid the challenge to their masculinity that such a diagnosis might pose.

The impact of social inequality on women's health

Feminist writers are also concerned with the general issues of women's health arising from women's unequal position in society. Marxist feminists focus more closely on the particular impact of social inequality in general on the health of the lives of women in the working class and minority ethnic groups. These issues are discussed in the following topic.

INTERACTIONIST APPROACHES

Interactionist approaches to health are concerned with the following interrelated issues:

- *The subjective experience of health and illness* This is about how people can give different definitions and meanings to health, and the different ways they experience health and illness, depending on their social situations and interaction with others, as considered earlier in this topic.
- *The social construction of health and illness* This is about how interaction between people, such as doctors and patients, contributes to the social construction of health and illness – for example, the significance of doctor–patient interaction in the social construction of health statistics that was considered on page 461. Topic 5 considers doctor–patient interaction in the discussion of professionalism and the sick role.

- *The labelling process*, such as the way people become labelled as sick through interaction between doctors and patients, and the consequences that follow from the attachment of such a label, especially if that label carries a social stigma, such as sexually transmitted diseases, HIV/AIDS or mental illness. Interactionists suggest that if people are defined as physically or mentally ill, or as disabled, then people may come to see themselves in terms of the label and act accordingly. This is considered further in the discussion of labelling and the social construction of mental illness in Topic 4 (see pages 514–18), including the chain of interactions that may occur as patients labelled as mentally ill enter psychiatric hospitals, and the consequences for individuals of being labelled as mentally ill.

POSTMODERNIST APPROACHES

These approaches to health involve the following features:

- *The rejection of health metanarratives* Postmodernists reject the biomedical model, and scientific thinking in general, as simply metanarratives or big stories claiming to provide the only universal truths and solutions to ill-health. Postmodernists suggest there are a range of other equally valid explanations and solutions for ill-health, such as those found in the vast range of complementary and alternative medicines and treatments (this is discussed on pages 532–4).
- *Growing consumer culture in health* Postmodernists argue we now live in a consumer-led culture, where, as considered earlier in this topic, the human body and health are often design projects for people to take control of and to work on to form and express their identities. This consumer culture in health is often reflected in talk of 'patient choice' in NHS healthcare (see Topic 3) and in people choosing a whole host of complementary medicines and treatments.

Exam-style questions

1   Explain what is meant by the term 'diseases of poverty'.   *(2 marks)*

2   Explain what is meant by the term 'iatrogenesis'.   *(2 marks)*

3   Explain what is meant by the term 'medicalization'.   *(2 marks)*

4   Identify **three** features of the social model of health and illness.   *(6 marks)*

5   Suggest **three** material factors that might affect a person's health chances. *(6 marks)*

6   Suggest **three** examples of ways in which the body can be seen as a social construction.   *(6 marks)*

7   Outline some of the criticisms sociologists make of the biomedical model of health. *(12 marks)*

8   Outline some of the criticisms feminists make of the role of the medical professions in women's healthcare.   *(12 marks)*

9   Assess sociological explanations for the view that health statistics may not provide a true picture of the type and extent of disease in society.   *(20 marks)*

10   Assess sociological contributions to our understanding of what is meant by health and illness.   *(20 marks)*

Topic 2

SPECIFICATION AREA

The unequal social distribution of health and illness in the United Kingdom by social class, age, gender, ethnicity and region, and internationally

Inequalities in health chances

> **www.sochealth.co.uk**
>
> The website of the Socialist Health Association is one of the most useful for exploring all aspects of health and health policy, including inequalities in health and a wide range of other issues relevant to those studying the sociology of health. Clicking on the 'Poverty and Inequality' tab at the top of the homepage will take you to the extensive page on health inequalities. The website also contains many of the complete documents referred to in this topic, or links to them.

> **Health chances** refer to the chances people have of enjoying good health, and avoiding ill-health and disease.

Health chances are one element of life chances, and refer to the chances people have of enjoying good health and a long and healthy disease-free life, and avoiding ill-health and disease. There are important differences in health chances based on social class, gender and ethnicity, and between regions in the UK and countries internationally. Underpinning all these differences in health chances is social inequality, and it is these issues that are considered in this topic.

Health and social inequality

HEALTH, INEQUALITY AND SOCIAL COHESION

The importance of the social causes of ill-health, discussed in the last topic, is illustrated well by Wilkinson (1996, 2005). Wilkinson recognizes the importance of social deprivation in affecting health, but he argues that health differences between social groups cannot be explained simply by material deprivation, such as poverty. He suggests that **social cohesion** is a significant factor – the extent to which people stick together and identify with each other in a sense of community. Wilkinson suggests that large income differences between social groups divide people from one another, and lead to a lack of social cohesion. Social inequalities, and the social divisions they create, can in themselves have poor effects on health, even among those who are not especially poor in income terms. He concludes that 'societies with narrower income differences are likely to be more socially cohesive and consequently more healthy'. In other words, the more equal a society is, the healthier it is, because a sense of community and social cohesion can in themselves improve health.

> **Social cohesion** refers to the bonds or 'glue' that bring people together and integrate them into a united society.

Wilkinson and Pickett (2010) suggest the health of *all* members of society tends to be worse in an unequal society, and emphasize that, however rich a country is, health (as well as a range of other things) will be worse where the gap between social classes grows too wide. People are healthier and happier in more equal societies than they are in unequal ones. They suggest reducing social inequality is the best way to improve everyone's health and reduce overall health inequalities.

> **Activity**
>
> Go to www.equalitytrust.org.uk/ (the Equality Trust)
> 1 Identify three ways in which income inequality may be damaging to health.
> 2 Identify three ways in which income inequality may be harmful to societies *apart from* health.
> 3 Find three reasons for the harmful effects of inequality you have identified above.

THE SOCIAL GRADIENT IN HEALTH AND STATUS SYNDROME

The clearest inequalities in health are between the richest at the top and the poorest at the bottom of the social hierarchy, but there is a social gradient in health, with obesity, smoking, alcohol, morbidity and mortality all getting gradually worse as you move down the social hierarchy. Marmot (2004) argues, following two longitudinal studies of the health of London civil servants begun in 1967 and repeated in 1985 (commonly known as the *Whitehall I* and *Whitehall II* studies), that there is a social gradient in society – a status hierarchy – that runs, like a ladder, from top to bottom. Everyone has a position in it and wherever we are in the social hierarchy, that spot affects our quality of life, health and life expectancy. Our health is likely to be better than those below us in this status hierarchy, and worse than those above us. This social gradient is illustrated in figure 7. 2.

Each ascending rung on the social gradient is accompanied by an improvement in health and increased life expectancy, and a decrease in the chance of developing many diseases, such as stroke or heart disease. Marmot suggests health differences can be explained by what he calls **status syndrome**.

Status syndrome concerns how status, or people's social standing, is influenced by things such as money, education, career position, influence and involvement in work and the community, and the amount of control people have over their lives. These affect

> **Status syndrome** refers to the harmful effects on an individual's health caused by stress and anxiety about their status situation (social standing), and consequently their self-esteem, or view of their own social worth.

Figure 7.2 The social gradient in health

people's self-esteem, or their view of their own social worth, which in turn influences their health. Marmot suggests that those with the highest status usually have more opportunities to achieve these, and as you move down the status hierarchy, people have less respect from others, less security, and less control in their work and over their daily lives. This sense of insecurity, disrespect, lack of self-esteem, and lack of control leads to stress, which affects people's health, happiness and how long they live. Marmot in effect suggests that people get worn-out by the stress of living with status inequality, even if they are relatively well-off. The greater the degree of social inequality, the worse are the effects of status syndrome, and it affects everyone's health, and not only that of the poor.

As suggested above, social and economic inequality has major influences on the patterns of illness and death. In any country, region or city in the world, it is generally the poor who experience the greatest inequalities in health and have the worst health chances, and these inequalities can be made worse by the effects of gender and ethnic group. It is these dimensions of social and economic inequalities in health which will now be examined.

Social class inequalities in health chances

STATISTICAL EVIDENCE FOR SOCIAL CLASS INEQUALITIES

Official statistics reveal massive social class inequalities in health, which are often referred to as the 'health divide'. Poverty is the major driver of ill-health, and poorer people tend to get sick more often, to suffer more years in poor health and to die younger than richer people. Those who die youngest are people who live on benefits or low wages in poor-quality housing and who eat cheap, unhealthy food. Lifestyle factors associated with poor health, like smoking, alcohol misuse, obesity, poor diets and lack of exercise, are all more common among the most deprived sections of society.

In 2005, the Office for National Statistics reported that people in the most prosperous neighbourhoods of England enjoyed seventeen more years of fit and active life than those in the poorest, and a 2010 report, *Fair Society, Healthy Lives* (the Marmot Review), calculated that if everyone were as healthy as university graduates (mainly from the middle class), with everyone without a degree having their death rate reduced to that of people with degrees, there would be 202,000 fewer early deaths each year among those aged over 30.

Figures 7.3 and 7.4, table 7.1 and the box on p. 471 show some of these social class inequalities, which provide strong evidence that it is society and the way it is organized that influence health, rather than simply our biological make-up.

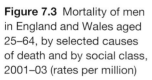

Figure 7.3 Mortality of men in England and Wales aged 25–64, by selected causes of death and by social class, 2001–03 (rates per million)

Source: Office for National Statistics, Health Statistics Quarterly 38, 2008

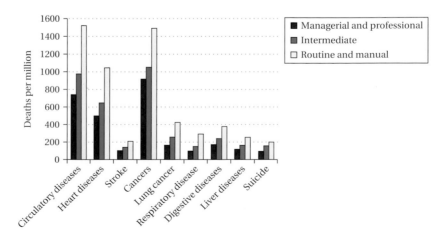

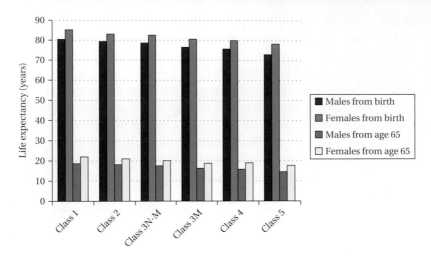

Figure 7.4 Life expectancy at birth and at age 65 by social class, men and women in England and Wales, 2002–6

Source: Office for National Statistics, Health Statistics Quarterly 49, 2011

Table 7.1 Infant mortality[a]: by socio-economic classification, England and Wales, 2007

	Rates per 1,000 live births	
	Inside marriage	Outside marriage[b]
Large employers and higher managerial	2.7	3.3
Higher professional	3.1	3.9
Lower managerial and professional	3.3	3.5
Intermediate occupations	4.5	3.9
Small employers and self-employed	3.9	4.0
Lower supervisory and technical	3.8	4.1
Semi-routine occupations	6.0	6.0
Routine occupations	6.3	5.5
All	4.2	5.0

[a] Deaths within one year of birth

[b] Jointly registered by both parents

Source: Office for National Statistics

Activity

Study figure 7.3

1. Which disease shows the greatest difference in deaths between the managerial and professional class and the routine and manual class?
2. Which disease shows the smallest difference in deaths between the managerial and professional class and the routine and manual class?
3. Which social class shows the lowest deaths from lung cancer?
4. dentify two patterns shown in figure 7.3.
5. Suggest two possible social explanations for the social class differences shown in heart disease.
6. Suggest **two** reasons for the differences in the suicide rate shown.

Refer to figure 7.4

7 What does figure 7.4 show about the differences in life expectancy between males and females?

8 What is the approximate difference in the life expectancy of women in class 2 compared to women in class 5 from (a) birth (b) age 65?

9 After the age of 65, approximately how much longer can a typical man in class 1 be expected to live compared to a man in class 5?

10 Suggest **three** reasons for the social class differences in life expectancy shown.

Refer to table 7.1

11 Which social class (socio-economic group) has the lowest level of infant mortality for births both within and outside of marriage?

12 Which two social classes have the highest rates of infant mortality, both within and outside marriage?

13 Suggest **three** reasons for the differences in infant mortality shown in table 7.1.

The extent of social class inequalities in health in contemporary Britain

- People living in the poorest areas will, on average, die seven years earlier than people living in richer areas and spend up to seventeen more years living with poor health.
- The death rate in class 5 (unskilled manual workers) is about twice that of class 1. A person born into social class 1 (professional) lives, on average, about seven years longer than someone in social class 5.
- In the first year of life, for every five children who die in class 1, around eight die among unskilled workers. The risk of dying before the age of 5 is twice as great for a child born into social class 5 as for social class 1, and children from poorer backgrounds are five times more likely to die as a result of an accident than children from better-off families.
- Men and women in class 5 have twice the chance of dying before reaching retirement age than people in class 1. About 90 per cent of the major causes of death are more common in social classes 4 and 5 than in other social classes.
- Lung cancer and stomach cancer occur twice as often among men in manual jobs as among men in professional jobs, and death rates from heart disease and lung cancer – the two biggest causes of premature death – are about twice as high for those from manual backgrounds. Four times as many women die of cervical cancer in social class 5 as in social class 1.
- Working-class people, especially the unskilled, go to see doctors far more often and for a wider range of health problems than do people in professional jobs.
- For the majority of cancers, there is a five-year gap in the survival rates between the best- and worst-off.
- Semi-skilled and unskilled workers are more likely to be absent from work through sickness than those in professional and managerial jobs. Long-standing illness is around 50 per cent higher among unskilled manual workers than for class 1 professionals.
- All of the above are worse for the long-term unemployed and other groups in poverty.

These social class inequalities in health have been reported time and again in a series of official reports and policy documents, described below. These provided so much evidence of the link between social class and the 'health divide' in Britain that it is doubtful whether any rational person could seriously deny it.

OFFICIAL EVIDENCE FOR SOCIAL CLASS INEQUALITIES IN HEALTH

The Black Report (1980) and The Health Divide (1987)

Evidence for social class inequalities in health was first most clearly revealed in a British government report in 1980, which became commonly known as the *Black Report*. This report was so contentious and carried such a strong condemnation of health inequalities that the government made available only 260 duplicated copies, and it was released just before August Bank Holiday weekend – when it was guaranteed to get the absolute minimum of publicity. The *Black Report* was followed up in 1987 by *The Health Divide*, which confirmed yet again the pattern of social inequalities in health. As with the *Black Report*, there was strong evidence of official connivance in suppressing the findings of *The Health Divide*; as Townsend and his colleagues noted (1990), there was 'an attempted cover-up of unpalatable information about the nation's health'.

The Acheson Report (1998)

Both the *Black Report* and *The Health Divide* were based on the social model of health, and emphasized the importance for health of social conditions throughout the life course. The *Acheson Report* followed in their footsteps in confirming earlier findings of wide social class inequalities in health, and in recommending more help for the poor as a means of improving health. The *Acheson Report* helped to establish the framework for future health policies.

These policies were unveiled in the 1998 Department of Health paper *Our Healthier Nation*, and *Saving Lives* a year later.

Our Healthier Nation (1998) and Saving Lives (1999)

Although overall trends show an improvement in health since the 1970s, with life expectancy increasing and infant mortality falling, these overall trends mask the fact that the health of the poor has failed to keep up with the improvements of the most prosperous sections of society, and the health gap between those at the top and those at the bottom of the social scale has been widening since the last quarter of the twentieth century. The Labour government, in its 1998 paper *Our Healthier Nation*, and *Saving Lives* a year later, finally officially recognized these social class inequalities in health, and the social, environmental and economic causes of ill-health. These documents laid the basis for government health policy for the years ahead.

Our Healthier Nation pointed out that:

> The poorest in our society are hit harder than the well off by most of the major causes of death. Poor people are ill more often and die sooner. The life expectancy of those higher up the social scale (in professional and managerial jobs) has improved more than those lower down (in manual and unskilled jobs). This inequality has widened since the early 1980s.

The Marmot Review: Fair Society, Healthy Lives (2010)

To inform future strategy after 2010, the Labour government in 2008 commissioned a major review on health inequalities. This was led by Professor Sir Michael Marmot, and was asked to propose the most effective strategies for reducing health inequalities. The report, *Fair Society, Healthy Lives*, known as the *Marmot Review*, recommended that policy to reduce health inequalities should focus on the **life course**. – the events people experience as they make their way through life. This was because it recognized health disadvantage begins even before birth, with higher risks of still births, premature births

The **life course** refers to the various experiences of individuals and their choices as they make their way through the whole course of their lives.

and underweight babies among the poorest social groups. These early health disadvantages are cumulative, in the sense that early health disadvantages in childhood often build up and get worse as people become older, and the gap between the richest and the poorest social groups gets wider. This life-course approach is illustrated in figure 7.5.

The *Marmot Review* recommended six areas for action to reduce health inequalities, shown in table 7.2

Figure 7.5 The life-course approach to health inequalities

Source: Adapted from Marmot (2010)

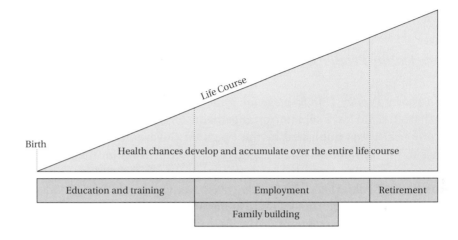

Life Course

Birth

Health chances develop and accumulate over the entire life course

| Education and training | Employment | Retirement |

Family building

Table 7.2 Recommendations of the *Marmot Review*

Recommendation	Examples
1 Give every child the best start in life	Antenatal and postnatal programmes, development of parenting skills, Children's Centres and early years education, especially focusing on the most disadvantaged families
2 Enable all children, young people and adults to maximize their capabilities and have control over their lives	Reduce social inequalities in educational attainment; extend the role of schools in supporting families and communities; increase access to and use of learning and employment opportunities throughout the life course
3 Create fair employment and good work for all	Improve access to good jobs and reduce long-term unemployment; make it easier for people who are disadvantaged in the labour market to obtain and keep jobs, and improve the quality of jobs, with wages enabling people to have a reasonable standard of living, and with more control over their work
4 Ensure a healthy standard of living for all	Establish a minimum income for healthy living for people of all ages; reduce the social gradient in the standard of living through progressive taxation – the more you earn, the more you pay in tax
5 Create and develop healthy and sustainable communities and places to live	Ensure everyone has access to good-quality air, water, food, sporting, recreational and cultural facilities and green space
6 Strengthen the role and impact of ill-health prevention	Give priority to the prevention and early detection of those conditions most strongly related to health inequalities, such as cancer, heart disease and strokes, which are associated with smoking, alcohol, drug use and obesity; ensure availability of funding for ill-health prevention and health promotion

Activity

Look at the six recommendations on the previous page from the *Marmot Review*, and the examples given. Drawing on what you have learnt so far in this chapter, suggest in each case two ways that the policies recommended might reduce social inequalities in health.

(If you have the time or interest, all the recommendations and how they might reduce health inequalities are explained in detail in chapter 4 of the *Marmot Review*, available at www.marmotreview.org/).

Healthy Lives, Healthy People: Our Strategy for Public Health in England (2010)

Healthy Lives, Healthy People: Our Strategy for Public Health in England (Scotland, Wales and Northern Ireland have separate arrangements for health, but will probably adopt similar proposals) was published by the Coalition Government in November 2010 in response to the *Marmot Review*. It set out a long-term vision for the future of public health, adopting a life-course framework for tackling the social determinants of health and reducing health inequalities. The stated aim was to create a 'wellness' service – Public Health England. This followed some of the recommendations of the *Marmot Review*, such as improving maternal health to give children a better, healthier start in life, improving educational attainment, reducing working-age ill-health, and changing adults' behaviour to reduce risks to their health. Underpinning these was also a desire to save money, through reducing the high costs of healthcare that avoidable diseases incur.

How successful these policies prove to be, and whether social class inequalities in health will be reduced, will only be revealed over future years.

EXPLANATIONS FOR SOCIAL CLASS INEQUALITIES IN HEALTH

The causes of ill-health are complex, and there are clearly some influences on health which go beyond social factors. The ageing process and our genetic inheritance do have important influences on our health, though health education awareness, access to health, leisure and social services and a range of other social factors have an impact on how effectively we cope with them.

There are four main types of explanation for social class inequalities in health:

- artifact explanations
- natural or social selection explanations
- cultural or behavioural explanations
- material or structural explanations

The artifact explanation

This suggests that health inequalities between social classes are artificial rather than real – a manufactured explanation arising only because of distortion and bias in the way statistics are used, and the way the link between social class and health is measured. The apparent link between poor health and social class is simply because the number of lower-working-class occupations is getting smaller, and those left in these occupations tend to be older than those in other social classes, with younger people going into new skilled or non-manual occupations. It is therefore only to be expected that those in such occupations will suffer poorer health, because the people left are older. This explanation is rejected by sociologists, since social class inequalities in health remain even after using a number of different methods of measurement.

The natural or social selection explanation

This explanation suggests that people in lower social classes are there because of their poor health, with their lack of physical strength, vigour and fitness stopping them getting into, and hanging on to, higher social class jobs. Poor health acts as a 'filter', with poor health causing their low social class, rather than their social class causing their ill-health. Society is seen as based on 'survival of the fittest', with the most unhealthy people inevitably ending up in the lowest social classes, while those in good health succeed in society and achieve the highest rewards. This explanation is rejected by sociologists, because most adult health problems seem to arise among those coming from already deprived backgrounds, and there is significant evidence to show that poor health is a result of deprived circumstances rather than a cause of them. There are also some people in higher social classes who suffer poor health, and people in lower social classes who enjoy good health, so good or poor health cannot by itself explain a person's social class position.

The following two types of explanation for social class inequalities in health are those firmly rooted in society itself.

Cultural or behavioural explanations – blaming the victims

Cultural explanations suggest that those suffering from poorer health have different attitudes, values and lifestyles which mean they don't look after themselves properly. For example, they have a fatalistic attitude to life – a view that whatever happens will happen regardless of what they do – and put an emphasis on immediate gratification (enjoyment) without thinking or caring about the longer-term consequences of their behaviour for their health. Cultural explanations see health inequalities as rooted in the unhealthy behaviour and lifestyles of individuals, and individuals can and should tackle them themselves by making voluntary efforts to change. Examples might include smoking too much, consuming too much alcohol, using too much salt or sugar, eating junk food and not enough fresh fruit and vegetables, or not bothering to take any exercise.

These types of factors are linked to a variety of conditions, including heart disease, cancer, strokes, diabetes, bronchitis and asthma. *Our Healthier Nation* estimated that alcohol abuse, for example, leads to around 40,000 deaths a year, and that a third of all cancers are the result of a poor diet.

Cultural explanations for social class inequalities in heath tend to place the blame for ill-health on the victims themselves for having unhealthy lifestyles. To what extent do you think people are themselves responsible for their poor health? Or do unhealthy lifestyles arise from the material circumstances of people's lives, like social deprivation?

Cultural explanations essentially place the blame on individuals themselves, in what are called 'victim-blaming' theories. However, as Townsend and his colleagues (1990) pointed out:

> While some of the links between deprivation and ill-health are still very poorly understood, lifestyle is clearly far from being the whole answer . . . some people have more freedom than others by virtue of their individual situation and circumstances to choose a healthy lifestyle, the unlucky ones being restrained from adopting a healthier life, even when they would wish to do so, by income, housing, work and other social constraints.

The way material factors can influence lifestyles and health choices was well illustrated in *Our Healthier Nation*:

> Low income, deprivation and social exclusion all influence smoking levels. It's harder to stop smoking when you're worrying about making ends meet . . . If the nearest supermarket is miles away or the bus doesn't go there when you can, it can be difficult to buy food which is cheap and healthy; if the street outside your home is busy with traffic or there are drug dealers in the park, then it's safer to keep the kids in front of the TV than let them out to play.

The *Black Report* and *The Health Divide* both pointed out that class differences in health remained even when lifestyle factors were taken into account, and many class differences were not related to factors such as smoking, drinking and other lifestyle choices. The *Marmot Review* pointed out that 'such systematic differences in health do not arise by chance, and they cannot be attributed simply to genetic makeup, "bad" behaviour, or difficulties in access to medical care, important as these factors may be. Social and economic differences in health status reflect, and are caused by, social and economic inequalities in society.' It is for all these reasons that sociologists have generally given more emphasis to material, social and economic explanations rather than cultural explanations for social class inequalities in health.

Activity

1 Do you agree or disagree with the view that health and illness are the responsibility of individuals and the lifestyle choices they make? Give three reasons to support your answer.
2 Suggest three problems there might be for an approach to improving a society's health which focused only on the behaviour and choices of individuals.

Material or structural explanations – blaming social conditions

Material or structural explanations suggest that those suffering poorer health do so because of the inequalities of wealth and income in Britain. Those who suffer the poorest health are those who are the most materially disadvantaged and lack enough money to eat a healthy diet, who have poor housing, dangerous or unhealthy working conditions, live in an unhealthy local environment, and so on.

These conclusions have been reconfirmed time and again in official reports, including the latest *Marmot Review*, in which poverty and income inequality are recurring themes. Health policy in the first decades of the twenty-first century has finally recognized that, as long as inequalities of wealth, income, education, occupation, opportunity and social privilege continue, so will inequalities in health.

Figure 7.6 on page 478 identifies a range of possible factors which might explain health inequalities, and figure 7.7 shows that multiple disadvantage can create a cycle of disadvantage – including ill-health – which can be very hard to break out of.

Activity

1 Go to www.dh.gov.uk and find three policies the government, through the Department of Health, is currently implementing to tackle health inequalities, and explain how each of them might achieve this. (Try searching on 'inequalities' or 'health improvement' to start).

2 Go through the list of possible health policies below. Take five of them, and explain in each case not simply how the policy might help in improving health, but specifically how and why it might reduce social class inequalities in health. The first is already done for you, as an example.

Policy	How it might help to reduce social class inequalities in health
1 Eradicate child poverty	Poverty is a major cause of ill-health. Tackling child poverty is likely to improve the health of the most disadvantaged children, making them healthier as adults and giving them more opportunities to be successful in society
2 Develop health education in schools	
3 Encourage people to stop smoking	
4 Improve educational attainment and skills among disadvantaged groups	
5 Improve access to, and the quality of, antenatal care, and early years support for children and families in disadvantaged areas	
6 Improve the physical activity of the population	
7 Improve environmental health and reduce the risk of accidents in the home and on the road	
8 Improve the quality and energy efficiency of housing, particularly in social (council and housing association) housing in the most disadvantaged areas	
9 Tackle alcohol misuse	
10 Provide more information about the health risks of obesity, poor diet and lack of exercise, and action that people can take themselves to improve their health	
11 Develop better labelling on the nutrition content of packaged food, showing which foods can make a positive contribution to a healthy diet (and which don't)	
12 Reduce crime, the fear of crime, and drug misuse	
13 Reduce unemployment, and improve the income of the most disadvantaged groups	

What other material or structural factors create social class inequalities in health, apart from living in poor housing or areas with high levels of environmental pollution?

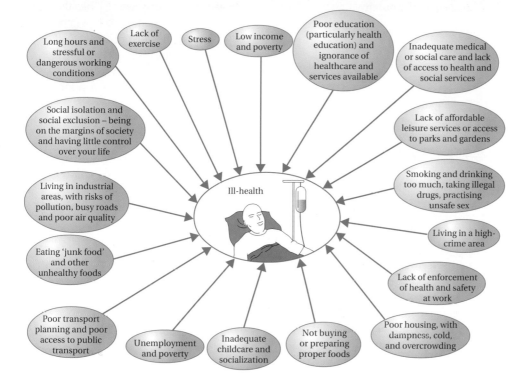

Figure 7.6 Cultural and structural/material influences on health

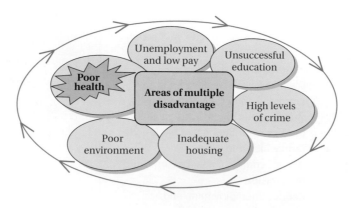

Figure 7.7 Areas of multiple disadvantage and the cycle of disadvantage. In areas experiencing multiple disadvantage, one aspect of deprivation can make others worse, creating a cycle of disadvantage that can be very hard to break out of

Activity

Study figure 7.6 and answer the following questions

1 Suggest ways each factor might explain social class inequalities in health.
2 Try to divide the explanations into 'cultural' and 'structural/material' explanations.
3 Identify and explain three cultural factors that may affect a person's health.
4 Identify and explain three material explanations for social class inequalities in health.
5 Suggest ways the cultural explanations might be influenced by structural/material factors.
6 Do you think cultural or structural/material explanations (or a bit of both) are better in explaining health inequalities? Give reasons for your answer.
7 Which of the factors in figure 7.6 do you think society can help to tackle, and which do you think are individual problems which only individuals themselves can solve?

Refer to figure 7.7 and

8 Explain how each of the six issues identified might impact on and feed the others.
9 Explain why breaking out of a cycle of disadvantage and improving health might be very difficult if all the issues are not tackled together.

The importance of material disadvantage in causing ill-health was summed up by Dr John Collee in the *Observer* newspaper in 1992:

> Forget everything else I have written on the subject. There is one piece of health advice which is more effective than all the others. One guaranteed way to live longer, grow taller, avoid chronic illness, have healthier children, increase your quality of life and minimize your risk of premature death. The secret is: be rich.

Gender differences in health chances

Payne (2006) has shown there are differences between men and women in their health, in how they respond to ill-health and in their access to healthcare. These differences are found across the world.

In Britain, men are much more likely than women to die from heart disease and cancer. At all ages, women's death rates are much lower than men's. Men's overall death rates are more than 40 per cent higher than those of women, and on average women live around four years longer than men. Almost two-thirds of deaths before the age of 65 are male. After age 65, there are around 40 per cent more women than men in the population, and by age 85, women outnumber men by more than two to one.

ARE WOMEN HEALTHIER THAN MEN?

The answer to whether women are healthier than men is 'yes' if we use only the indicators of death rates and life expectancy. However, statistics show that men, who in general die younger, don't seem to experience as much ill-health during their lives as women. Women are the major users of healthcare services and apparently get sick more often than men. Though women might expect to live longer than men, they are also more likely to spend more years in poor health or with a disability.

Compared to men, women:

- go to the doctor about 50 per cent more often over the age of 16, though, as Nettleton (2006) points out, this may be more for health reasons, such as infertility or pregnancy, than because of illness.
- report more head and stomach aches, high blood pressure and weight problems.
- consume more prescription and non-prescription drugs.
- are admitted to hospital more often and have more operations.
- go to see doctors about conditions like insomnia, tension headache and anxiety and depression (which are often labelled as 'mental illness') about twice as often, and receive far more prescriptions for tranquillizers, sleeping pills and anti-depressants. In 2007–8, 56 per cent of those over age 16 in England using NHS specialist mental health services for adults were women.
- are off work with reported sickness more often and spend more days in bed.
- have a much higher rate of arthritis and rheumatism in the 65–74 age group.

EXPLAINING GENDER DIFFERENCES IN HEALTH

There is some evidence that boys are the weaker sex at birth, and male babies have a higher infant mortality rate – that is, they are more likely to die in the first year of life. Women seem to have a better genetic resistance to heart disease than men. However, Arber and Thomas (2005) suggest the different health experiences of women and men primarily reflect gender roles. Men's demonstrations of masculinity, and women's of femininity, expose men and women to particular health conditions relating to the different circumstances in which they live their lives, and the different ways they think and behave, and access health services. For example, men often assert their masculinity through shrugging off illnesses and risk-taking behaviour. These differences are examined below.

Why do women live longer than men?

- The process of gender role socialization means men are more likely to be brought up to shrug off illnesses, and are less likely to visit GPs. Mackenzie et al. (2006) found men are not socialized to show their emotions as much as women, so are less open in talking about emotions and seeking help. They are more likely to be socially isolated and have fewer support networks, and so have fewer outlets for stress. Yet they are less likely to admit to this, and use mental health services, and this may explain why men have higher suicide rates than women. Men's higher death rates may simply be because they deny or dismiss symptoms of disease, or bottle everything up until it is too late.

- Women are socialized to take care of themselves more than men, such as by consuming healthier diets with more fruit and vegetables, and they are more likely to visit doctors, which may mean they receive better healthcare. Sometimes working fewer hours means women have more opportunity to visit doctors.

- Women are more involved in family health, as they are more likely to be involved in nurturing and caring roles in the family, and sensitive to illness. Women are the biggest users of the health service, both for themselves and because it is generally women who organize the rest of the family going to the doctor's.

- Scambler (2008) emphasizes greater risk-taking behaviour by men. All forms of substance abuse are higher among men – they are more likely to drink, smoke and take illegal drugs (with all the consequences for health), are more aggressive and take more risks, are less careful in what they eat and are more likely to find healthy food unappetizing. Men generally live more hazardous lives than women, including participation in more dangerous sports. The more dangerous occupations are more likely to be done by men – such as construction work, and those involving toxic chemicals or other environmental hazards – and therefore men are more at risk of industrial accidents and diseases. In the home, men are more likely to do the dangerous and risky jobs, such as jobs using ladders or climbing on the roof. Men also make up the majority of lorry and car drivers and of motor-cyclists, and are therefore more at risk of death through road accidents.

- Men are more likely to work full-time and to work longer and more unsociable hours, such as overtime working and shift work, which can be harmful to health.

- Men have traditionally retired later than women (age 65 compared to 60), and this later retirement age could have been an important factor in reducing their life expectancy. The significance of this in explaining the *differences* between men and women will reduce as the compulsory retirement age has been abolished, and the minimum age at which both men and women can take their state pensions is due to become the same (age 66) by 2020, though this state pension age may rise further.

Activity

1 Which of the reasons given for women living longer than men do you think is most important? Put them in order of importance, giving your reasons.
2 Do you think men's 'macho' behaviour is an important factor in shortening their lives? Suggest evidence for or against this from your own experiences.

Why do women apparently suffer more sickness?

As suggested above, there are differences in male and female gender roles that make men more vulnerable to earlier deaths than women. These same gender roles also contain particular features in women's lives that may make them more vulnerable to sickness than men during their lives, even though on average they live longer than men.

Stress Many women suffer a triple burden of being low-paid workers, carrying responsibilities for housework and childcare, and managing family emotions. In many cases this involves having to manage limited household budgets with pressure to make ends meet, and working long days with little time to relax.

Patriarchy and domestic violence As Payne points out, men's demonstration of masculinity through dominant behaviour like the greater risk-taking discussed above not only affects men's health, but also that of women. Patriarchy, with men's dominance in family and other relationships, may contribute to women's stress referred to above, and the assertion of male power through domestic violence and abuse, which is overwhelmingly carried out by men against women, is accompanied by heavy physical and mental costs to women's health.

Poverty Women are more likely to experience poverty than men, because they are more likely to be lone parents, and because they live longer than men while being less likely to have employers' pensions or savings for old age. As Kempson and Bryson (1994) found in a study of seventy-four low-income families, it is usually women who go without to ensure other family members get enough to eat. Nettleton (2006: 191) showed that women also 'spend more of their income on household goods – especially food – than do men, and are more likely to be responsible, in Graham's words, for "maintaining the material and psychosocial environment of the home and well-being of those who live there"'. Women are therefore likely to suffer the effects of poverty more directly than men.

Domestic labour Domestic labour (housework) is rarely fulfilling (for further discussion on this, see pages 175–80 in chapter 3). Depression may be linked to the unpaid, repetitive, unrewarding and low-status nature of housework in a society where only paid employment is really respected. The high accident rates at home might be influenced by the isolated nature of housework.

Socialization and higher recorded illnesses As Mackenzie et al. suggest, women are socialized to express their feelings and talk about their problems more than men, and are therefore more willing to discuss them with doctors when they feel necessary. Since women are generally the ones who 'manage' family health matters, and have greater childcare responsibilities, they go to the doctor's more with their children, and themselves have greater health needs relating to pregnancy. This means they are often more aware of health and healthcare matters. Women may therefore be more willing than men to admit to and report physical and mental health problems to GPs. The higher rates of recorded illnesses among women could then be due not necessarily to greater health problems than men, but to women's greater willingness to admit to them and to take them to doctors, where their illnesses are then recorded in official statistics, while men's are not. While women go to doctors for prescribed drugs like tranquillizers, men opt for non-prescribed drugs like alcohol.

Different diagnoses Busfield (1996) shows that women are overrepresented in data on mental illness, with some mental disorders of various kinds seen as female maladies, such as anxiety, depression and anorexia. Until recently, women had a much higher chance than men of being institutionalized in mental hospitals. Busfield suggests these apparent differences may be explained by men being less likely to visit the doctor, particularly for stigmatized illness like mental disorders. Due to gender roles, it may be that women are more willing to report symptoms of mental illness, and doctors are more likely to see symptoms reported by women as mainly mental, while men's are seen as physical. Women are therefore more likely to be diagnosed as depressed or suffering from anxiety than men.

Activity

1 Refer to the activity on page 462 about the four stages involved in being labelled as 'sick', and becoming a health statistic, and suggest reasons why women might be more likely to end up as a health statistic than men.
2 Discuss the explanations suggested above for women apparently suffering more sickness than men. Do you think women really do suffer more ill-health, or do you think they are simply more open and honest about it than men?
3 'The growing equality of women with men is a threat to women's health.' Explain this statement. Do you agree? How might this situation be avoided (apart from stopping women becoming more equal)?

Ethnic inequalities in health chances

Social class and gender are not the only important social inequalities in health; there are also differences between ethnic groups.

Although ethnic minority groups broadly experience the same range of illnesses and diseases as others in the UK, some minority ethnic groups tend, in surveys, to report worse health than the general population. Many of the health differences below are derived from Balarajan (1996) and Sproston and Mindell (2006). Sproston and Mindell obtained data on minority ethnic groups from the large-scale *Health Survey for England*. This used a large representative sample of adults and children from minority ethnic groups across England, using interviews as well as physical measurements of health, such as blood, urine and saliva analysis (you can read more about the *Health Survey for England* on page 546).

Balarajan and Sproston and Mindell found there were wide variations in health among different minority ethnic groups, which means that it is difficult to make generalizations about all minority ethnic groups. For example, Sproston and Mindell found that Bangladeshi men were more than twice as likely as the general population to describe their health as 'bad or very bad'. On the other hand, they also found that Black African and Chinese men reported better health than average. Parry et al. (2004) found that the small minority ethnic group of Gypsies and Travellers had significantly poorer health and more self-reported symptoms of ill-health than other UK-resident, English-speaking ethnic minorities and economically disadvantaged white UK residents.

SOME FINDINGS ON MINORITY ETHNIC GROUP INEQUALITIES

Compared to the White British majority ethnic group:

- *Ill-health* Black and minority ethnic groups are more likely to report themselves as being in ill-health. African Caribbeans, Pakistanis and Bangladeshis are between 30 and 50 per cent more likely to suffer ill-health.
- *Diseases* AfricanCaribbeans seem more biologically vulnerable to developing sickle cell anaemia (a blood disease); they are more likely to suffer from hypertension (high blood pressure) and to die from strokes. South Asians (Indians, Pakistanis and Bangladeshis) suffer more heart disease, are 50 per cent more likely to have a heart attack, and are more likely to die from it. Those from South Asian and African and Caribbean backgrounds are all more likely to suffer and die from TB, liver cancer and diabetes.
- *Mental illness* Those from ethnic minorities are much more likely to receive a diagnosis of mental illness, and one in five patients in hospital for mental illness comes from a black and minority ethnic group background – around twice their proportion in the population as a whole. They are more likely to be diagnosed as schizophrenics, and have high rates of admission to hospital with severe mental disorders (psychosis). African-Caribbean men are up to ten times more likely than white people to be compulsorily committed (sometimes called 'sectioned') to psychiatric hospitals under the compulsory powers of the Mental Health Act.
- *Death rates* Most ethnic minority groups have generally higher adult and child mortality (death) rates. This includes still births of babies, deaths at birth or within the first week of life (perinatal deaths,) or within a month (neo-natal deaths) or within a year of birth (infant mortality). The most disadvantaged group is the Gypsy and Traveller community, in which infant mortality is three times higher than the

national average, and a mother is nearly twenty times more likely to lose her child before their eighteenth birthday than the rest of the population.

EXPLANATIONS FOR ETHNIC INEQUALITIES IN HEALTH

As with social class, the social and economic contexts in which people from minority ethnic groups live their lives, rather than biology, are the main factors explaining their poorer health chances in Britain. Black and minority ethnic groups are more likely than White British people to live poorer lives in the worst housing and in more deprived areas, where there are fewer, and less easily accessible, healthcare services available. As shown in the following topic, they are often less successful in taking up those services that are available than the white majority population, and this often contributes further to their poorer health chances.

Material factors: social deprivation and poverty

Nazroo (1997b) found many people from ethnic minority backgrounds experience poor housing and high levels of poverty, and analysis of self-reported ill-health data has shown that deprivation explains a large amount of the ill-health experienced by minority ethnic groups. Evidence suggests that health inequalities arise from many of the same cultural and material reasons as the social class inequalities discussed earlier, though the cultural explanations are contributed to by specific ethnic subcultural factors (see below), and poverty is greater than in the majority population. For example, in 2010–11, ethnic minorities were twice as likely to be living in poverty as the White British majority, and more than half of people from Pakistani or Bangladeshi ethnic backgrounds were living in low-income households, and they are among the poorest groups in society.

Davey Smith et al. (2002) suggest social disadvantage, such as poverty, does not fully explain the differences in health between ethnic groups, and between ethnic minorities and the majority population, and they suggest other explanations include language and cultural factors, the effects of racism, and cultural insensitivity in the provision of healthcare.

Cultural/subcultural factors

The cultural explanations for poor health suggested earlier for social class inequalities also apply to the poorest minority ethnic groups, but there are some additional subcultural factors that contribute to the poorer health of some minority ethnic groups.

- *Diet and lifestyle* Black Caribbean and Bangladeshi men have higher rates of cigarette smoking than the general population, with subsequent health consequences. Higher levels of heart disease may arise from aspects of the high-fat Asian diet, which also generates higher levels of obesity – itself a cause of heart disease. The national shortage of sites and the pressures of being constantly moved on have a huge impact on the health of Gypsy and Traveller communities.
- *Language* Many older Asian women, and some older men, speak poor English, possibly creating difficulties for awareness of health promotion messages and health risks, and in taking up screening services for things like breast or cervical cancer, and in obtaining treatment, advice and guidance from doctors and other health professionals. Many asylum seekers and refugees will also have poor levels of literacy in the English language, but often no information in their languages is available. Despite big improvements in translation services in the NHS, there is still

a lack of information available in minority ethnic group languages. Gypsies and Travellers often have low literacy levels, and therefore lack access to a lot of health information.

- *Beliefs and values.* Latif (2010) suggests that family values and the idea of families supporting one another may create some reluctance to accept care from someone from outside of their own community. However, there is often no health staff of that ethnic group with suitable skills available. There may be variations in interpretation of what conditions need medical attention. Some groups may think they should not seek healthcare until their conditions are serious, which means that they may not be caught early enough to treat effectively. Moriarty (2008) points out that Asian and Black Caribbean families may sometimes interpret changes that may be a result of dementia as just a normal part of ageing, rather than as an illness, which means that they are less likely to consider asking for help at an earlier stage. Cultural beliefs may also influence whether or not they follow the recommendations of health professionals. Asian women, and Gypsy and Traveller women, often prefer to see female doctors, and many find it difficult talking to white or male doctors. However, the number of female GPs is lowest in those areas with the largest concentrations of Asian households. Such factors contribute to poorer health chances, and may partly explain, for example, why Asian women are less likely to visit ante- and postnatal clinics, which helps explain their higher levels of infant mortality.

Racism and discrimination

Racism in society means some minority ethnic groups are more likely than white people to find themselves living in the worst housing, and to be unemployed or working for long hours and doing shift work in low-paid manual jobs, in hazardous and unhealthy environments. Nettleton showed that racism – both the experience and the fear of racist harassment – affects health adversely. Such conditions create stressful, unhealthy lives, as people live day to day in fear of racist harassment and abuse. Those who worry about racial harassment are more likely to report themselves as having poorer health than those who don't have these worries. Racism and poverty are the twin planks of ill-health in minority ethnic groups.

Research suggests that racism may also explain the higher rates of *recorded* mental illness in some ethnic minorities. This is for two main reasons. First, it arises because of the more stressful lives they lead as a result of racism, as described above. Second, there is some evidence that psychiatrists vary their diagnosis of the symptoms of mental illness depending on the ethnicity of the patient, which may partly explain why one in five patients in hospital for mental illness comes from a black and minority ethnic group background – around twice their proportion in the population as a whole.

There is also evidence of differences in treatment. For example, Black Caribbean and African people are more likely to enter psychiatric care through the criminal justice system than through contact with the health services.

Regional inequalities in health chances

Within the United Kingdom, there are wide differences in the health of people living in different parts of the country. There is a clear North–South divide in health, and a difference in life expectancy at birth, and other health indicators, between those growing up in the most affluent and the most deprived areas of the country.

Table 7.3 Some regional inequalities in health in the United Kingdom, 2007–2009

Region	Life expectancy 2007–9		Still births (rate per 1,000 live births) 2009	Perinatal mortality[a] (rate per 1,000 live births) 2009	Infant mortality[b] (rate per 1,000 live births) 2009	Prescription items dispensed per person 2006	Deaths from circulatory diseases (heart disease and strokes) (rate per 100,000 of the population) 2009	Deaths from cancer (rate per 100,000 of the population) 2009	Deaths from all causes (rate per 100,000 of the population) 2009
	Males	Females							
England	78.3	82.3	5.2	7.6	4.6	15.1	165	169	548
North-east	76.8	80.9	4.8	6.9	3.8	17.8	177	197	616
North-west	76.6	80.8	5.1	7.6	4.9	17.8	190	185	624
Yorkshire and the Humber	77.4	81.5	5.6	8.2	5.5	17.0	178	178	584
East Midlands	78.1	82.1	5.6	8.4	5.1	15.3	166	169	558
West Midlands	77.5	81.9	5.8	9.1	6.0	15.5	168	172	566
East	79.3	83.0	4.9	7.2	4.0	14.5	155	160	508
London	78.6	83.1	5.4	7.7	4.5	11.6	162	163	524
South-east	79.4	83.3	4.6	6.5	3.9	13.8	149	158	501
South-west	79.2	83.3	4.8	6.7	4.0	15.4	150	159	505
Wales	77.2	81.6	5.1	7.4	4.8	19.9	183	177	589
Scotland	75.4	80.1	5.3	7.4	4.0	15.4	194	198	667
Northern Ireland	76.8	81.4	4.8	7.8	5.1	16.8	177	173	591
United Kingdom	77.9	82.0	5.2	7.6	4.6	..........[c]	169	173	563

[a] Still births and deaths of infants under 1 week of age

[b] Deaths of infants under 1 year of age

[c] Data not applicable or not available

Source: Office for National Statistics;; The Information Centre for Health and Social Care; General Register Office for Scotland; Information and Statistics Division, NHS Scotland; Northern Ireland Statistics and Research Agency; Central Services Agency, Northern Ireland; Welsh Assembly Government. Released on Regional Trends Online, ONS, 3 March 2011

Table 7.4 Some international inequalities in health: the ten most-advantaged and ten least-advantaged countries, ranked on health spending per head (PPP international dollars). The United Kingdom and Cuba are included for comparison

Country	Total health expenditure per head (PPP inter-national dollars[a]) 2009	Life expectancy at birth (years)		Adult mortality rate (Probability of dying between 15 and 60 years of age per 1,000 population)		Infant mortality rate (Probability of dying by age 1 per 1,000 live births)	Under-5 mortality rate (Probability of dying by age 5, per 1,000 live births)	Maternal mortality ratio (Number of women dying while pregnant or within 42 days of giving birth per 100,000 live births)
		Males 2009	Females 2009	Males 2009	Females 2009	Both sexes 2009	Both sexes 2009	Females 2008
10 highest-spending countries per head								
USA	7,164	76	81	134	78	7	8	24
Luxembourg	5,996	78	83	95	57	1	2	17
Monaco	5,750	78	85	112	51	3	4	...[b]
Norway	5,207	79	83	83	50	3	4	7
Switzerland	4,815	80	84	74	43	4	4	10
Netherlands	4,233	78	83	75	56	4	5	9
Malta	4,197	78	82	76	44	6	7	8
Austria	4,150	78	83	102	50	4	5	5
Belgium	4,096	77	83	105	59	4	5	5
Germany	3,922	78	83	99	53	3	4	7
UNITED KINGDOM	3,222	78	82	95	58	5	5	12
CUBA	495	76	80	120	78	5	6	53

10 lowest-spending countries per head

Country								
Guinea-Bissau	48	47	51	431	369	115	193	1000
Liberia[c]	46	54	57	339	337	80	112	990
Madagascar[c]	46	63	67	273	198	40	58	440
Bangladesh	44	64	66	246	222	41	52	340
Niger	40	57	58	229	224	76	160	820
Mozambique[c]	39	47	51	557	434	98	142	550
Comoros[c]	39	58	62	284	229	75	104	340
Ethiopia	37	53	56	445	379	67	104	470
Central African Republic	32	49	48	461	470	112	171	850
Myanmar (Burma)	27	61	67	275	188	54	71	240
Democratic Republic of the Congo	23	47	51	442	331	126	199	670
Eritrea	18	64	68	249	179	39	55	280

[a] Purchasing Power Parity (PPP) international dollars is a way of measuring the amount of goods and services in that country as a US dollar would buy in the United States, or how much what is spent in local currency will actually purchase. This minimizes the consequences of differences in price levels between countries. For example, a dollar spent in Sierra Leone will buy around five times more healthcare than a dollar spent in the UK. The international dollar measure recognizes this, making comparisons between countries more accurate.

[b] Data not applicable or not available.

[c] Liberia and Madagascar, and Mozambique and Comoros, are separate countries but spending per head on health is the same, and they therefore share the positions of 9th and 6th from the bottom in the world in terms of total health spending per head.

Source: World Health Organization, *World Health Statistics 2011*

Hacking et al. (2011), in a study of death rates from 1965 to 2008, found the chances of dying early – below the age of 75 – are a fifth higher in the north of England compared with the south, with men affected more than women. Some 37,000 people a year die in the north earlier than they might if they had enjoyed the same life chances as those in the south. Boys' life expectancy at birth in Glasgow is 13 years less, and girls' 10 years less, than those living in Kensington and Chelsea in London.

Table 7.3 shows that women in the east, south-east and south-west of England can expect to live around two and a half to three years longer than women in the north-east and north-west of England and in Scotland, and these regional inequalities persist across a range of other health indicators, such as infant mortality and cancer deaths.

These differences can generally be explained by differences in the social class, age, gender or ethnic make-up of different areas of the UK, or different industries in different areas. For example, there are more upper- and middle-class people in the south, who enjoy the best health and life chances. Hacking et al. found that there were still health inequalities even between people in the north and the south from the same social classes, and the research suggested this was because people in the south, even if they had low incomes, had greater access to resources, such as better education, more transport, more GPs and other health resources. Hacking et al.'s research suggested that the underlying and most significant causes of the divide were social and economic, rather than cultural explanations like people in the north not looking after themselves properly. What is clear, though, is that the areas where social deprivation is highest also have the poorest health, and regional differences can be explained using the kind of explanations for social class, gender and ethnic inequalities in health discussed throughout this topic.

International inequalities in health chances

Internationally, inequalities in health are huge – with different amounts of money spent on healthcare as a proportion of national income, and huge differences in the causes, type and extent of disease and death between the richest and poorest countries. Table 7.4 illustrates some international inequalities in health and healthcare spending. The highest-spending nations spend on average around 150 times more per head than the poorest nations, even though their immediate healthcare needs are far less. The highest-spending United States spends nearly 400 times more per head than Eritrea, and men and women in the USA can on average expect to live around 13 years longer than their equivalents in Eritrea. Overall, life expectancy in the poorest countries is about a third less than that in the richest countries. It is worth noting that the lowest spenders are the poorest countries, and, except for Bangladesh and Myanmar, they are all in Africa – the poorest continent on the planet.

While there is a broad general link between the amount of money spent on health and the health of the population, with the richest and poorest countries respectively having the best and worst health in general, there is not a direct link. Higher spending on healthcare does not necessarily mean longer lives or better health. For example, the United States has by far the largest spending per head among the richest nations, but ranks the lowest among the richest countries in all of the indicators of health shown in table 7.4. It comes only 38th in the world in terms of life expectancy. Many countries outperform the United States with approximately half the spending. The most dramatic example is that of Cuba (see box, and also table 7.4) which spends about 7 per cent of what the United States spends, and yet matches or beats the United States in most health outcomes. Cuba's health outcomes, including life expectancy, are generally more in line with those of the richest countries who spend much more on health. Similarly, as table 7.4 shows, Liberia and Madagascar, and Mozambique and Comoros, in each case spend the same amount per head on health, but there are some quite large differences in the health outcomes shown in the table, such as life expectancy.

Cuba – it's not what you spend but the way that you spend it

Cuba spends a fraction of what many countries spend on healthcare. Nonetheless, Cuba achieves health outcomes as good as or better than many countries that spend much more (see table 7.4). For example, Cuba spends about 7 per cent of what the United States, and 15 per cent of what the UK, spend on healthcare, but achieves world-class health outcomes with some as good as or better than both countries. This shows that health policy, the priorities governments attach to health and the ways they deliver healthcare are more important than simply health spending.

In Cuba, these better health outcomes arise because:

- There is greater social equality, and, as seen at the beginning of this topic (see pages 467–9), this means there is greater social cohesion and fewer health risks arising from status syndrome.
- Healthcare spending is shared more equally between people, so more benefit from that spending. Health spending statistics are expressed as spending per head of population, but this disguises the fact that in many richer countries health spending is not spread equally among the population. Huge inequalities mean poorer people have far less spent on them and die younger and have poorer health, while a smaller proportion of richer people spend huge amounts on their healthcare.
- Healthcare and well-being are a national political priority, with free universal healthcare for all. The policy focus is on preventive care, with health education, vaccination programmes, and annual medical check-ups for everyone, to prevent potential health problems and the outbreak of diseases before people get ill, and to address diseases in their earliest stages.
- Healthcare is delivered through easily accessible primary care services, provided by neighbourhood community clinics, backed up by a network of free hospitals and plentiful medical personnel. According to the World Health Organization (2011), in the decade between 2000 and 2010, Cuba had the highest doctor–patient ratio in the world (with very high dentist– and nurse–patient ratios), with 1 doctor for every 156 residents, compared with 1 for every 375 residents in the United States, and 1 for every 365 in the UK.
- The preventive approach also includes health education and high literacy levels, and tackling the wider causes of ill-health, such as the various environmental, social and cultural causes discussed throughout this chapter.

Activity

Refer to tables 7.3 and 7.4 on regional and international inequalities in health.

1 What evidence, if any, is there in table 7.4 of a direct link between health spending per head and the health of the population?

2 Suggest three ways in which the causes of the difference in the life expectancy of males and females in every country of the world might change between the richest countries and the poorest countries.

3 There are growing concerns among some people in the richest countries about the size and shape of their bodies and about the ageing process. Consequently, some seek to define their own bodies and view of health through non-essential surgery and other

medical treatments. Suggest three additional demands that might be placed on medical professionals and health services by this concern with body image and identity.

4 Suggest three ways that the demands on healthcare services in the activity immediately above might differ from those in the poorest countries.

5 Either individually or in a group, imagine yourself as a nuclear family – mum, dad, and two twin children, one boy and one girl, aged 3, with a baby on the way. You should take on the role of the mum and dad (or, if you're working in a group, you could adopt the roles of mum, dad, boy and girl – and the unborn baby, of your chosen sex – in which case the 3-year-olds and the unborn baby can represent their own interests). Because of changing circumstances, you've got to move from the area, and even have the option of moving to another country. You're all completely obsessed with having a healthy and long life, and the mum and dad both want as long and as healthy a life as possible for all of the family. With reference to tables 7.3 and 7.4, and considering all the evidence and indicators of health inequalities, work out the following and decide which option is the 'healthiest fit' best suiting all your family members:

(a) which region of the United Kingdom you would be most likely to move to, and which one you would most want to avoid. Clearly explain your reasons.

(b) which country of the world you would be most likely to move to, and which one you would most want to avoid. Clearly explain your reasons.

6 Suggest three other factors apart from those given in tables 7.3 and 7.4 which might also influence your choice of where to live for a healthy long life.

7 Suggest three reasons in each case below for inequalities in health and healthcare:

(a) between different regions of the United Kingdom, and (b) between different countries of the world.

Death and disease often have different causes in poorer countries. The diseases of poverty – infectious diseases like typhoid, cholera, malaria and TB – are more common than the diseases of affluence found in the more developed countries – degenerative diseases such as heart disease, strokes, cancer and diabetes.

The explanations for these international inequalities are generally related to the issues that have been considered throughout this and the previous topic, such as poverty, poor hygiene, lack of proper sanitation and safe waste disposal, poor diet / malnutrition and lack of safe drinking water, polluting and dangerous industries, lack of healthcare facilities and health education, and other social, cultural and environmental factors.

These are added to by exploitation of the poorest countries by the richest, most developed countries. For example, there are huge inequalities in trade between the more developed and least developed countries, and the poorest countries are burdened with debts. Interest repayments on loans from the most developed countries far exceed the amounts the poorest countries receive in aid each year.

Poorer countries cannot afford to provide the health infrastructure necessary to deliver a healthy population. This infrastructure would include things like facilities to train doctors, nurses, midwives and other health professionals, hospitals and clinics, medical technology and affordable drugs, and resources for health education and health promotion campaigns. This runs alongside the problems created by the social, cultural, material and environmental dimensions of health and healthcare which have been discussed throughout this chapter.

This is the way many people in the world get water every day, and poor health often arises from a lack of such basic facilities as clean running water, and safe waste disposal and sanitation

Exam-style questions

1 Explain what is meant by the term 'social cohesion'. *(2 marks)*

2 Explain what is meant by the term 'health chances'. *(2 marks)*

3 Suggest **three** reasons why women, in general, live longer than men. *(6 marks)*

4 Suggest **three** ways in which social inequality may pose a threat to good health. *(6 marks)*

5 Outline some of the reasons for inequalities in health and healthcare between richer and poorer countries of the world. *(12 marks)*

6 Outline some of the ways in which material factors may affect social class differences in health chances. *(12 marks)*

7 Assess sociological explanations for differences in health between ethnic groups. *(20 marks)*

8 Assess sociological explanations for gender differences in health and illness. *(20 marks)*

Topic 3

SPECIFICATION AREA

Inequalities in the provision of, and access to, healthcare in contemporary society

Inequalities in the provision of, and access to, healthcare

Inequalities in healthcare have two main aspects:

- *Issues of provision* are about whether the services people need, such as GPs, specialist clinics, health screening services and hospitals, are provided in the areas in which they live, and whether these services are freely available to all.
- *Issues in demand and access to healthcare* are about whether everyone has equality of opportunity to make full use of the services they need, or whether there are obstacles such as cultural barriers or lack of awareness that means some are more assertive and effective in accessing healthcare than others, and therefore place greater demands on the healthcare system.

Figure 7.8 below summarizes the main factors influencing these two aspects of healthcare provision, which are discussed throughout this topic.

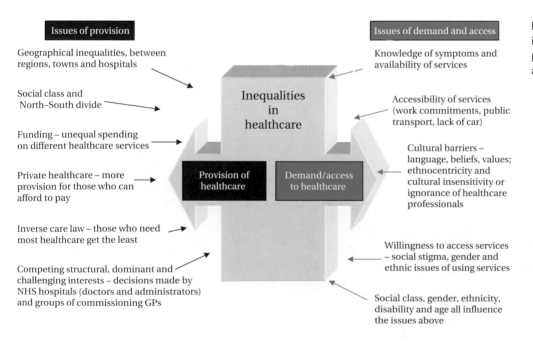

Issues of provision

Geographical inequalities, between regions, towns and hospitals

Social class and North–South divide

Funding – unequal spending on different healthcare services

Private healthcare – more provision for those who can afford to pay

Inverse care law – those who need most healthcare get the least

Competing structural, dominant and challenging interests – decisions made by NHS hospitals (doctors and administrators) and groups of commissioning GPs

Inequalities in healthcare

Provision of healthcare

Demand/access to healthcare

Issues of demand and access

Knowledge of symptoms and availability of services

Accessibility of services (work commitments, public transport, lack of car)

Cultural barriers – language, beliefs, values; ethnocentricity and cultural insensitivity or ignorance of healthcare professionals

Willingness to access services – social stigma, gender and ethnic issues of using services

Social class, gender, ethnicity, disability and age all influence the issues above

Figure 7.8 Inequalities in healthcare: issues of provision and demand/access

The provision of healthcare

Commissioning in the NHS is the process of assessing the health needs of the local population, and organizing the delivery of health services from NHS or private healthcare companies to meet these needs.

NHS HEALTHCARE

In the UK, the majority of formal clinical healthcare is provided free at the point of use through the NHS* (National Health Service) which is funded by public money raised through taxation. Before 2012 NHS healthcare in England (funding and organization differ slightly in Wales, Scotland and Northern Ireland) was organized mainly through local Primary Care Trusts (PCTs), each covering on average around 330,000 people. These were responsible for **commissioning** (organizing and paying for) health services, tailored to the needs of local communities, from NHS hospitals, GPs, dentists and other public and private providers. Between them they were responsible for spending around 85 per cent of the total NHS budget in 2011. PCTs were overseen by larger Strategic Health Authorities (SHAs).

INEQUALITIES IN HEALTHCARE PROVISION

Despite the National Health Service, this does not mean that healthcare services are provided equally for everyone, and services do vary from location to location and in the quality of care provided. There are four main areas of inequality in the provision of healthcare: geography, social class, funding, and private medicine.

Geography

NHS provision of healthcare facilities varies between different locations, such as between regions, towns and hospitals. For example, there are differences in waiting times to see a consultant after being referred by a GP, and, within hospitals, from one specialism to another.

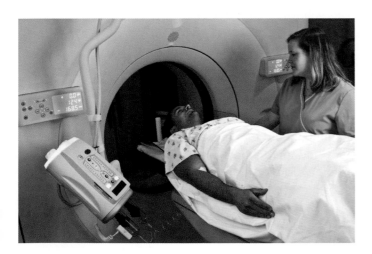

Healthcare facilities are not spread equally across the country. For example, there are more modern high-tech NHS hospitals, with more medical technology, as well as private healthcare provision in the affluent south of England than in the more disadvantaged areas of the north

---

* The term *National Health Service* only applies in England; in Scotland it is called *NHS Scotland*; in Wales, *NHS Wales*; and in Northern Ireland, *HSC* (Health and Social Care). Although slightly different funding and organizational arrangements apply in each case, most discussion regarding the NHS in England in this chapter is equally applicable to the other health services too.

Modern high-tech hospitals, with a wide range of advanced medical technology, and the highest numbers of GPs are concentrated in urban areas, disadvantaging people living in the countryside. Specialist hospitals and units, such as heart and cancer units, are not spread equally across the country.

Social class and the North–South divide

There are differences in healthcare provision for different social classes, and the evidence suggests that this inequality has not been significantly reduced since the introduction of the National Health Service. Health services in working-class areas are often less accessible and of poorer quality. Healthcare provision is better in the more affluent south of England than the disadvantaged areas of the north, producing a North–South divide in healthcare. The more disadvantaged industrial areas of northern England and Wales have fewer and older hospitals, fewer and less adequate specialized facilities, such as for cancer or kidney treatments, fewer hospital beds per head of population, and higher patient–doctor ratios. Those in the south get faster access to diagnostic tests, scans, anti-cancer drugs and chemotherapy.

In deprived areas, there are fewer GP practices and GPs per head of population than in wealthier areas. This means GPs have less time to spend with their patients, despite them having greater health needs and higher levels of sickness. This is partly because many GPs themselves prefer to work in more middle-class areas, where the workload is less and living conditions are more congenial, and they find it easier to deal with and respond to the concerns of middle-class people. Tudor-Hart (2009) compared the challenges facing GPs in delivering care to deprived, as opposed to more affluent, populations with the deep and shallow ends of a swimming pool. At the deep end are the more disadvantaged communities, where the GPs and their staff cannot even get their feet on the bottom of the pool, they have to swim all the time in order to avoid drowning, and they also have the task of stopping the patients drowning. They tend to save themselves first, which is understandable, because they will not save any patients if they do not. At the shallow end are the more affluent communities. GPs still work hard, but their workloads are lighter, and they can put their feet on the bottom when they need to, and their patients do not drown so much.

Funding

Despite the shift in health policy away from the curative medicine of the biomedical model towards a greater emphasis on preventive medicine based on the social model of health, the 'acute' sector (hospitals) still gets the most attention and funding. This is often at the expense of other services, such as chiropody and mental health, and services geared towards the particular needs of groups like the disabled, adults with learning difficulties and minority ethnic groups. Standards of care are therefore not as good, nor as responsive, as they should be.

Private healthcare

Though the NHS dominates healthcare provision, private healthcare makes up around 18 per cent of health spending in the UK. Private healthcare is expensive, and is only really available to those who are very well-off. About one tenth of the population are covered by private health insurance, with most financed by employers for those in upper-middle-class jobs that provide private medical insurance as part of their jobs package.

Private healthcare duplicates NHS provision in many areas, plus providing a range of alternative and complementary treatments not readily available on the NHS for those willing and able to pay. These include things like non-essential cosmetic surgery, homeopathy, chiropractic, colonic irrigation and massage.

Private care offers some advantages over the NHS, as appointments may be obtained more quickly and at more convenient times, such as outside normal working hours. Treatment is often faster, there is a choice of doctor or surgeon, and accommodation in hospital is better (private rooms, better food, etc.). However, if something goes wrong in a private hospital, it might not have the emergency facilities and junior medical staff on call to deal with it that large NHS hospitals have.

The NHS, private healthcare and inequality

NHS services already involve a mix of public- and private-sector provision. For example, some non-emergency and non-urgent operations, such as hip and knee replacements, cataract operations and other treatments, are carried out by private hospitals and paid for by the NHS. Around 200,000 NHS patients were treated this way in 2010. In some clinical areas, such as mental health and medically based residential provision for elderly and physically disabled people, the private or independent sector is dominant. There are also private 'pay beds' and private-patient units in NHS hospitals, and some NHS hospitals are run by private health companies.

Private healthcare creates inequality in healthcare provision, as the middle class have more money and so they are better able than the more disadvantaged to choose private medical care. Being able to afford private healthcare can also create inequalities *within* the NHS, as people may choose to pay for private consultations with consultants, most of whom work for the NHS as well, and they are then given priority by those consultants for free NHS treatment, enabling them to queue-jump NHS waiting lists.

CHANGES TO THE NHS IN 2012

In 2012, there were controversial new changes to the NHS, which were the most extensive ever made to the National Health Service in England. These changes abolished SHAs and PCTs, with commissioning of healthcare provision handed to smaller consortiums (or groups) called Clinical Care Groups (CCGs), consisting of (mainly) GPs, along with some hospital doctors and nurses. It was thought this would give more power to GPs – the primary care providers who are the first point of contact for most patients, and who really know what healthcare their patients need.

These changes were seen as part of improving patient choice (see box). CCGs were obliged to increase patient choice by allowing private healthcare companies to become more involved in delivering healthcare, rather than exclusively favouring existing NHS publicly owned hospitals and similar public services.

Criticisms of the 2012 changes

The changes to the NHS in 2012 were made in the face of very strong opposition from the medical profession, public health officials, patient groups and many members of the public. The main reasons for this opposition lay in their concerns that:

- there would be a growing **privatization** and **marketization** of healthcare, with more services provided by private companies and a growing consumer market in healthcare, where the most well-off would gain more access to healthcare than the more disadvantaged.

Privatization is where services that were once provided by the state are transferred to private companies, as, for example, with healthcare services once provided by publicly owned NHS hospitals becoming provided by privately owned hospitals.

Marketization refers to the process whereby services, like education or health, that were previously controlled and run by the state, have government or local council control reduced, and become subject to the free market forces of supply and demand, based on competition and consumer choice.

Ken Pyne

Do most patients really have any meaningful choice in the healthcare they receive?

Patient choice

Patient choice in healthcare aims to give to patients more involvement in and control over their treatment, and where and when it takes place. Patients can already choose between hospitals for treatment, and patient choice has been presented by politicians of all political parties for many years as a reason for changes in the NHS. However, making healthcare choices is often difficult for patients, and can create inequalities. Calnan (2010) suggests this is because of:

- *Lack of knowledge and expertise* Most patients, and particularly the most socially disadvantaged, lack the specialist scientific and medical knowledge and diagnostic skills and expertise of doctors needed to make informed choices. They are in most cases unaware of what drugs or medical treatments are most suitable or available, or what other medical experts or hospitals they might be referred to. This makes it difficult for them to compare different forms of treatment and different hospitals without relying on the advice of medical professionals like GPs. Dixon et al. (2010) found that seven in ten patients, when offered a choice, still opted for their local hospital, and most people tended to rely on the advice of their GP when deciding where to go.

- *Unequal opportunity* Richer and more educated patients are better placed to access and make sense of the high-quality information (such as through the mass media and internet) needed to take advantage of patient choice. They also have more opportunities to pay for private care, though even then they often consult their GPs first about how to access these services and for information on their quality.

- *Uncertainty and unpredictability* There is not always a clear-cut choice in health matters, and patients are vulnerable and may not be well enough to exercise choice. They may be uncertain about the nature of their conditions and the treatments needed, and outcomes may be unpredictable. Patients may not trust their own judgements in choosing between alternatives. This increases their dependency and reliance on the expertise of medical professionals to make the choices for them, and most people hold doctors in high esteem and trust them to choose the best options.

The above points mean that, while most people say they welcome more patient choice in healthcare provision, most are happy to see that choice made for them by doctors.

- there would be competition between NHS hospitals and private hospitals for patients.
- the private sector would only take on the most straightforward, simplest cases, which are easiest, cheapest and most profitable to treat, leaving NHS hospitals with the more complex and more expensive operations.
- NHS hospitals would no longer be offering a full range of services, as some would only be available in private hospitals or clinics, which might not be in the local area.
- local NHS hospitals might have to close, as they would face higher running costs and less income as they got fewer patients, and only the more expensive cases.
- NHS hospitals would be free to treat private paying patients first, and there would no longer be a limit on the number of private patients in NHS hospitals. This could lead to NHS hospitals concentrating on profitable areas of private work rather than those where health needs were the greatest – for example, giving higher priority to private patients who want cosmetic surgery for vanity reasons, or to affluent patients prepared to pay extra for private heart operations, rather than less-profitable NHS patients needing heart surgery.
- there would be longer waiting lists for NHS treatment, as more well-off private patients take up beds currently used for NHS patients.
- there would no longer be a comprehensive and free health service across the country, with growing inequality in healthcare and a two-tier health service: speedy private healthcare for the well-off, and slower NHS treatment for the more disadvantaged, who may be in greater need but lack the cash to access faster services.
- there would be growing inequality of provision, as some NHS services might disappear altogether in local communities.

Whether the concerns above prove justified will only become clear as changes begin to be implemented in the years that lie ahead. However, they do appear to threaten to disadvantage the poorest the most, as they have no option but to use the NHS, as they can't afford private treatment.

There were fears in 2012 that the NHS would increasingly be taken over by profit-making private healthcare companies, at the expense of publicly-run NHS hospitals and other healthcare services

SOCIOLOGICAL EXPLANATIONS FOR THE DISTRIBUTION OF HEALTHCARE

Marxist approaches

Marxist approaches suggest:

- *Inequalities in healthcare provision reflect social inequality* Like all other life chances under a capitalist system, the distribution of healthcare provides the most benefits for the richest and most powerful groups. This view would support the social class inequalities and the North–South divide discussed above. There is what Tudor-Hart (1971) called the '**inverse care law**'. This suggests that healthcare resources tend to be distributed in inverse proportion to need. This means that the most advantaged gain the most from healthcare, even though their needs are least, while those in greatest need of healthcare get the least.

- *Healthcare provision supports big business* The focus on the provision of medical treatment, GP surgeries and hospitals, rather than the prevention of ill-health, supports big business in the form of drug, medical technology and private healthcare companies. Clinical care produces huge profits for the pharmaceutical industry, and such companies are mainly concerned with making profits out of ill-health, not reducing it.

- *Healthcare through the NHS is for the benefit of capitalism and to buy off social protest* Navarro (1976) suggests healthcare benefits capitalists by keeping the working class fit enough to work, and is an instrument of social control to stop people from malingering and feigning sickness to avoid work. The working class get just enough healthcare to stave off social protest by giving the impression of fairness and caring in a society riddled by inequality and conflict.

- *Healthcare through the NHS protects the capitalist system* Marxists like Navarro suggest that healthcare provided by the NHS focuses on treating seemingly individual illnesses. This disguises the social causes of illness rather than challenging a capitalist system that produces ill-health through dangerous and unhealthy working conditions, unhealthy foods, poverty and other effects of unequal capitalist societies.

> The **inverse care law** is the suggestion that those in the greatest need of help from the welfare state (including health services) get the fewest resources allocated to them, while those whose need is least get the most resources.

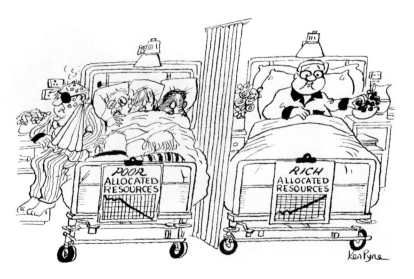

The inverse care law suggests that those with the least healthcare needs get the most resources allocated to them, while those in greatest need get the least

Marxist approaches have been criticized for a rather crude analysis which sees medicine and healthcare as a means only of making profits and social control, and keeping workers fit for employers. Others argue that the medical profession, and the medical technology and pharmaceutical industries, have made major contributions to improving the length and quality of people's lives. The NHS, despite its shortcomings and inequalities like those suggested by the inverse care law, still provides world-class healthcare for everyone, including the most disadvantaged.

Pluralist approaches

Pluralism is a view that sees power in society spread among a wide range of interest groups and individuals, with no group or individual having a monopoly of power. Applied to health, this pluralist approach suggests the distribution and allocation of healthcare resources is not decided by any single dominant group. It is a result of bargaining between many competing groups, such as the medical professional associations, like the British Medical Association and the various Royal Colleges (professional bodies for medical groups like the Royal College of GPs, and others like Surgeons, Anaesthetists, Obstetricians and Gynaecologists, and Nursing), groups of commissioning GPs like Clinical Care Groups, health administrators, the government, political parties, trade unions, private healthcare companies, patient groups and so on. These groups may all have different priorities for the way NHS resources get allocated – for example, GPs may give priority to patient care, while health administrators may want to keep costs down, and some political parties may wish to promote publicly provided NHS healthcare, while others may wish to promote private healthcare. The distribution of healthcare will reflect a compromise reached after bargaining between these different groups.

> **Pluralism** is a view that sees power in society spread among a wide range of interest groups and individuals, with no group or individual having a monopoly of power.

Structuralist approaches

Structuralist approaches draw on both the Marxist emphasis on the significance of social inequality in the allocation of healthcare, and the pluralist view of conflicting interests.

Alford (1975), in a study of the New York healthcare system in the 1960s, suggested there were different and competing interests among those who work within the healthcare system, which often overrode the interests of those who used it. Alford identified three structural interest groups in healthcare provision in New York in the 1960s:

- *Dominant interests* The final decision-makers, who ultimately decided the allocation of healthcare resources.
- *Challenging interests* Those who challenged the interests of the dominant group.
- *Repressed interests* Those whose interests were least likely to have their needs met by the existing structure of healthcare organization. In New York, the system of private medicine meant the interests of the poor and unemployed were often overlooked entirely and they lacked healthcare resources.

Alford suggested how healthcare is distributed in society will reflect the outcome of struggles between these three groups, and particularly an eventual compromise between the dominant and challenging interests.

Dominant, challenging and repressed interests in the NHS Checkland et al. (2009) applied Alford's framework to the NHS in England in the 2000s. They found the distribution of healthcare provision in the NHS showed the following interests:

- *Dominant interests* NHS hospitals, including hospital consultants and administrators, dominated the system of healthcare, and their interests lay in maximizing their income, and reducing their costs, often at the expense of medical practitioners outside the hospitals, like GPs.
- *Challenging interests* Groups of GPs whose interests lay in achieving the best for their patients, particularly outside of expensive hospital settings. These challenged the power of hospitals by providing some diagnostic and therapeutic services, formerly provided by hospital outpatient departments, in GP surgeries, thereby saving GPs money that could be reinvested in patient care. This challenge was resisted by the hospitals, since it threatened to remove some of their business and the income it generated.
- *Repressed interests* Checkland et al. do not have much to say about repressed interests. However, they point out that, in the context of the NHS, which provides universal healthcare services, mostly without charge, to all UK residents, it is difficult to identify repressed interests in the sense of a group not having their healthcare needs met, although there may be inequalities in the distribution of resources and access to healthcare, as considered above. Checkland et al. do emphasize though that NHS organization leaves little scope for public/patient participation, and patients and clients of the NHS are the least powerful group, and have the least control over the allocation of healthcare.

Like Alford, Checkland et al. see the distribution of healthcare reflecting a compromise between the dominant NHS hospitals and the challenging interests of GPs. Patients, who rarely exercise their patient choice, generally accept the decisions of the other two groups, unless they opt to pay for private healthcare. The 2012 changes in the NHS discussed above suggest that, over time, the commissioning Clinical Care Groups (CCGs) may replace NHS hospitals as the new dominant interests in the NHS, with the challenging interests coming from NHS hospitals and private healthcare companies.

Activity

1 Outline how Marxists, pluralists and structuralists might each view the following inequalities in the provision of healthcare:
   - geographical differences
   - social class and the North–South divide
   - funding
   - private healthcare
2 Suggest three reasons why middle-class areas might have more healthcare provision than more disadvantaged areas.
3 Suggest three ways that private healthcare might contribute to inequalities in health chances.

Inequalities in demand for, and access to, healthcare

Access to healthcare will partly depend on the availability of services, which was considered above, but here the main issue is with the differences between groups of people seeking help from whatever services are available. These differences provide further evidence for Tudor-Hart's inverse care law discussed above, because, in many cases, those whose need for healthcare services is greatest use them the least, while those whose need is least access them the most.

Whether people are able or choose to access healthcare will depend on factors like:

- their ability to recognize and accept that they have a health problem.
- their knowledge of what healthcare services and treatments are available. This may depend on levels of education, or whether healthcare organizations are making all population groups equally aware of the services available.
- their willingness to accept help from healthcare services, and whether they regard those services as offering valuable or appropriate treatment.
- whether healthcare services are readily accessible, including factors like travel distance, availability and costs of public transport or whether people have their own cars, waiting times for treatment, and whether people can afford any charges, as for example in NHS dental treatment or private medical care. Some may experience problems getting time off work for things like hospital appointments.
- cultural barriers, such as those created by gender socialization, education or ethnicity, or lack of understanding by healthcare services of the needs of their clients.

Social factors like social class, gender, ethnicity, disability and age all influence these, as considered below.

SOCIAL CLASS AND ACCESS TO HEALTHCARE

Poor access to healthcare services is a contributing factor to the social class inequalities in health chances discussed in the previous topic. As Tudor-Hart's inverse care law suggests, people in poorer social classes not only face some inequalities in the provision of healthcare discussed above, but they also use (access) those services less on average, relative to their need, than those from higher social classes. For example, working-class children, even though they suffer more illnesses and accidents, are less likely to be taken to the doctor than those from the middle class, or for dental checks and treatment. Access to health services may be difficult for those in poorer social classes who may lack their own transport and so spend greater time travelling to hospitals and GPs, or find it difficult to take time off work to attend. The poorest social groups also don't have the luxury of being able to afford private healthcare when the NHS or social services let them down.

Dixon et al. (2007) found that, in general, use of general practitioners (GPs) was fairly equal across most social groups, though unemployed individuals and individuals with low income and poor educational qualifications used GPs less, relative to need, than those who were more affluent and better educated.

Although most people may visit their GPs when they become aware of their need to do so, this does not mean they get equal treatment once there. In general, middle-class patients, compared to the more deprived:

- are more educated, and know more about illness and how to prevent it, and have a better knowledge of the healthcare system and the services available.
- are more self-confident, effective and assertive in dealing with doctors and other health professionals. They are better able to express their health needs and describe their symptoms, and therefore have a better chance of achieving an accurate diagnosis and appropriate treatment; they demand, and get, longer consultations with their doctors, ask more questions and get more detail and explanation about their illnesses.

- are more vigorous and successful in persuading GPs that they should be referred for further specialist advice and treatment, such as hospital appointments with consultants.
- are more likely to fight against inadequate medical services, and use complaint procedures if they are dissatisfied with their treatment.

This means working-class people may not get the same quality of consultation and treatment as the middle class, even if they visit the same GP practice.

Dixon et al. found that those from the better-educated and more affluent higher social classes were more likely to access specialist services for a range of treatments and conditions including cardiac, diagnostic and surgical care, diabetes clinics, cancer care, preventive care (like immunizations), and non-urgent surgical procedures (elective surgery). This was despite their need for such services being less than that of people from lower social classes. Such inequalities point to an inverse care law in access to healthcare just as there is in the provision of healthcare.

GENDER AND ACCESS TO HEALTHCARE

The discussion of gender and health in the last topic contains a range of reasons why men might be less likely to access healthcare than women, and particularly why women access it more than men. These include women's role in managing family health, and the gender socialization process. You should review that section again in relation to gender differences in *accessing* healthcare (see pages 480–3). The main focus here is on why men don't access healthcare as much as women, and not nearly as much as they should, given their shorter lives.

Wilkins et al. (2008) found that men and women tend to use health services differently. Men are less likely than women to recognize a wide range of symptoms, such as those of hypertension (high blood pressure), cancer, heart disease and mental disorders, and are therefore less likely than women to seek out medical consultations and treatment with their GPs, or to recognize the need for emergency treatment. Mackenzie et al. (2006) found this is particularly the case with mental illnesses, like anxiety and depression, where men are less willing to recognize they have a problem, to seek help from their GPs, and to use mental health services, and they have less positive attitudes towards the usefulness of the services available.

Smith et al. (2005) found, in relation to cancer – though it also applies in wider health matters – that men had a greater fear of consulting doctors, and considered help-seeking as emasculating in terms of their masculine identity, especially if they appeared to be consulting doctors for what they might think were trivial matters that might suggest they worried too much about their health.

Wilkins et al. noted that men thought women were better at using healthcare services because they had to use them more often. This suggests that men's under-use of healthcare services might partly be because of their lack of familiarity with them, and this in itself becomes a barrier to accessing healthcare services even when they are in need of them.

One particular barrier to women accessing healthcare may be that many women, and particularly Asian women, prefer to see a female doctor, as they may find they experience greater empathy with women doctors, especially for gender-specific complaints. However, female doctors may not always be available, particularly in smaller GP practices.

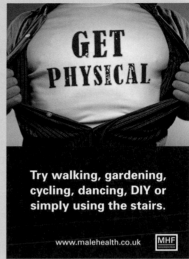
Men have shorter life expectancy partly because they are less likely to access healthcare services than women, and campaigns like this are aimed at encouraging more men to take care of their health, and access health services.

Go to www.menshealthforum.org.uk/ and identify six measures that are being taken to encourage men to improve their health and access healthcare services.

ETHNICITY AND ACCESS TO HEALTHCARE

The NHS has not catered well to Britain's diverse population. Minority ethnic groups report higher levels of dissatisfaction with NHS services, and those from Pakistani, Indian and Bangladeshi backgrounds report significantly poorer experiences as hospital inpatients than their White British counterparts in Care Quality Commission patient surveys. Sproston and Mindell found some ethnic minority groups experience not only poorer health chances than the White British population, but that this can be made worse by poorer access to healthcare. This includes:

- poorer access to services, such as hospital care and screening services.
- poorer take-up of whatever healthcare is available.
- poorer quality of services.

Some of the reasons for minority ethnic communities having less access to healthcare services are similar and related to some of those considered earlier explaining ethnic inequalities in health chances (see pages 485–6). One of the key reasons may be that poorer levels of education and the social marginalization of some minority ethnic groups, particularly the most marginalized group of Gypsies and Travellers, mean they are simply not aware of, or don't know how to take advantage of, whatever healthcare services are available.

Latif (2010) suggests that the underlying reason why some minority ethnic groups do not access health services as effectively as the White British population, and express less satisfaction with their care, is that there is a poor level of engagement and understanding between ethnic minority patients and healthcare staff. Moriarty, in relation to older people, and Latif suggest this is for the following interrelated reasons:

Language, communication and culture

Messages about health risks and healthcare services addressed to minority ethnic groups are often most effective when they are communicated in their own languages and within the context of the everyday lives and cultures of their communities. However, there is still a lack of interpreters, health information, counselling and materials designed to communicate and promote healthcare services within such communities.

Latif suggests patients from some ethnic groups may have different views and interpretations to those of many doctors and other health professionals regarding health, which may lead them to describe their symptoms in ways that are unfamiliar to medical professionals. She suggests some NHS staff lack cultural competence and are ethnocentric, focused on White British culture and operating with assumptions based on a White British majority view of the world. The King's Fund (2006) suggests that health professionals and the NHS are often not sufficiently familiar with the religious, cultural and dietary practices of different ethnic groups. They therefore do not have enough sensitivity towards the healthcare needs or the religious, cultural and social beliefs, norms and values held by patients from black and minority ethnic communities.

This may give rise to stereotyped assumptions by health professionals, such as the belief that those from ethnic minorities don't like to talk about depression, or that Asian families prefer to 'look after their own' and don't want outside intervention.

This range of issues means those from minority ethnic groups, especially older people and those recently arrived in the UK, tend to be less aware of what services are available and how to access them. Messages about health risks may not be received, and the health concerns and needs of some minority ethnic groups may not be understood. Consequently medical diagnoses may be inadequate, unsuitable quality of care provided, or proper medical advice not given or followed, and there may be unconscious discrimination on the part of healthcare professionals. This lack of cultural sensitivity may mean that some conditions may not be reported to or recognized by doctors, and therefore not be treated.

A lack of diversity in the healthcare workforce

There is evidence to show that some of those from minority ethnic groups prefer to see healthcare professionals of similar ethnic background, with a language and culture like their own. When there is a shared language and culture, there is greater empathy between doctor and patient, more patient satisfaction and higher quality of care. The lack of diversity in the healthcare workforce has been seen as a barrier to culturally competent care, and this may discourage access to healthcare services. As mentioned above, Asian women often prefer to see female doctors, and many find it difficult talking to white or male doctors. However, the number of female GPs is lowest in those areas with the largest concentrations of Asian households, and this may deter some Asian women from going to visit their GP.

Stigma and a lack of trust

Many people from all ethnic groups view mental disorders as stigmatized illnesses, as shameful and to be concealed. In the Asian community, the stigma attached to mental illness may mean those suffering from it may not recognize it as such, or be unwilling to admit to it and to access help to treat it. For example, dementia is often seen as a normal part of the ageing process in ethnic minorities, rather than as a disease needing treatment.

Many black people mistrust and fear mental health services because they associate them less with treatment than with punishment, thereby deterring those who need psychiatric care from seeking such help. African-Caribbean men, for example, are around ten times more likely to be compulsorily admitted to psychiatric hospitals under the Mental Health Act than their white counterparts, and this is more likely to happen through the criminal justice system (police, courts and prisons) than through GPs.

In the Gypsy and Traveller community, centuries of discrimination and harassment and constantly being moved on have generated a fear and distrust of 'authority', which means that some people will put up with pain or emotional distress rather than seek help.

DISABILITY AND ACCESS TO HEALTHCARE

'A disability can make you invisible to the health service and normal medical care.' This is how Peter Cardy of the MS (Multiple Sclerosis) Society in 2000 described the way many disabled people do not have adequate access to medical treatment or equipment. Disabled people are also regularly excluded from routine treatment because of difficulties in travelling to a health centre or dentist.

The Royal College of Physicians has recommended that people with learning disabilities have annual health checks, but in many cases this is not happening, even though such people are more vulnerable to hearing problems, heart disease and epilepsy. *Death by Indifference*, a 2007 report by Mencap, a charity supporting those with learning disabilities, found that people with a learning disability often die younger than other people, and suggested part of the reason for this was because many of them get poorer health services than other people. People with a learning disability are seen to be a low priority within the NHS, and many healthcare professionals do not understand much about learning disability. Among GPs, 90 per cent said they found it harder to diagnose people with a learning disability, and 75 per cent said they had received no training in treating such patients. In 70 per cent of GP surgeries, there is no information that those with learning disabilities could easily understand. Some GPs do not understand the needs of disabled people, and think that all the health problems people with a disability have are a result of their disability, and so they do not take their health problems as seriously as they would if they were presented by someone without such a disability.

AGE AND ACCESS TO HEALTHCARE

Older people, particularly the most socially disadvantaged, tend not to get the same access to healthcare as do younger people, even though they generally have greater need for it. This may be due partly to cultural reasons, with older people simply not wishing to bother the doctor, or playing down their illnesses and not seeking treatment for what they dismiss as symptoms of old age. On the other hand, doctors may sometimes dismiss what may be quite serious conditions as simply part of the wear-and-tear of the ageing process, and therefore not undertake thorough tests, or be slow in referring older patients to specialists for further investigation, or prescribing effective medication. For example, Foot and Harrison (2011) found older people faced age bias in access to cancer treatment and were under-treated. They were more likely to die of cancer than younger patients, not simply because of their age, but because they received less investigation and late diagnosis, and delays in having their cases referred to specialists and the commencement of treatment. Breast and bowel cancer screening programmes are still not extended upwards to the maximum ages at which people can achieve health gains.

In 2011, the Equality and Human Rights Commission found evidence of a 'systematic failure' in the care and treatment of some older people, and the Care Quality Commission found some older hospital patients did not have their care needs properly assessed, and did not receive help to eat and drink, and were not treated in a dignified way.

Age UK suggests that the majority of chronic illnesses affecting the lives of older people can be either prevented or postponed, mainly through the adoption of healthier lifestyles, but that services and public health initiatives sometimes exclude older people, and sometimes older people receive insufficient support from GP services, including those living in care homes, and those suffering from depression.

Charities dealing with ageing, like Age UK, report **ageism** – stereotyping, prejudice and discrimination – in regard to the health and social care of older people, which means they face a range of disadvantages not encountered by those who are younger.

> **Ageism** is stereotyping, prejudice and discrimination against individuals or groups on the grounds of their age.

For example, geriatric medicine, which specializes in the treatment and care of older people, generally has low status in the medical profession. It has poorer funding and staffing levels, in relation to the rising numbers and needs of older people, than other areas. It therefore doesn't get the allocation of staff expertise and other resources that are needed to give the best care to older people.

Age UK reports that older people:

- feel they have had second-class treatment and care simply because of their age.
- are sometimes not referred by doctors to a consultant because of their age.
- face inappropriate comments about their age and patronizing attitudes while in hospital.
- lack transport to access healthcare services.
- lack NHS specialized services, such as help with podiatry (foot care), leaving them in pain, housebound and at increased risk of falls.
- have little help with the difficulties they may face in interpreting and understanding instructions on medication and other aspects of their treatment, perhaps because of confusion or depression, or their visual or hearing impairments.

Older people often don't get the help and support they may need in taking medication and understanding their treatment

Exam-style questions

1   Explain what is meant by the term 'inverse care law'.   *(2 marks)*

2   Explain what is meant by the term 'ageism'.   *(2 marks)*

3   Suggest **three** reasons why some minority ethnic groups make less use than the general population of some healthcare services.   *(6 marks)*

4   Suggest **three** reasons why males are less likely than females to make use of healthcare services.   *(6 marks)*

5   Suggest **three** reasons why disabled people may have poorer access to healthcare than those who are not disabled.   *(6 marks)*

6   Outline some of the reasons for social class differences in access to healthcare.   *(12 marks)*

7   Outline some of the reasons for inequalities in the provision of healthcare in the UK.   *(12 marks)*

8   Outline some of the reasons why middle-class people are in general more successful in accessing healthcare than those from more disadvantaged backgrounds.   *(12 marks)*

9   Assess sociological explanations for differences in the use of healthcare services between social classes and between age groups.   *(20 marks)*

10   Assess sociological explanations for gender differences in health chances and healthcare.   *(20 marks)*

Topic 4

SPECIFICATION AREA

The sociological study of the nature and social distribution of mental illness

Mental illness

An estimated one in six people of working age suffers some form of mental illness, ranging from depression, through disabling anxiety disorders, to schizophrenia and, for a tiny minority, dangerous and severe personality disorder (DSPD – these are popularly known as 'psychopaths'). GPs say that there is a mental health component to at least half of all the cases they see, and one in four of us uses specialist mental health services at some time in our lives. Yet, despite being relatively common, mental illnesses are often seen and treated quite differently from physical ones. The mentally ill often face discrimination at every level of society, because mental illness is among the most stigmatized and misunderstood of illnesses. This is because it involves behaviour we find very hard to understand, and because it does not have any obvious physical symptoms. There's a stigma attached to mental illness, and it is often associated in the popular imagination with people talking to themselves or others who aren't there, ranting and raving about people out to get them, hallucinations, and all manner of weird behaviour and violence. This might explain research findings like that by the Mental Health Foundation charity in April 2001, *Is Anybody There? A Survey of Friendship and Mental Health*. This found that four in ten people with mental health problems were worried about telling friends about their problems, and one in three felt friendships had become strained, or lost, because of their mental illness. They felt their friends would not understand, or were likely to react negatively, because of the continuing stigma attached to mental illness. Philo (1999) of The Glasgow Media Group (GMG) found that media reporting portrayed a high level of violence as associated with mental illness, especially schizophrenia. Philo et al. (2010) of the GMG, in a study of TV drama and entertainment, found nearly half of peak-time programmes with mental illness storylines portrayed people with mental health problems as posing a threat to others, and 63 per cent of references to mental health were negative, in the sense of being critical, flippant or unsympathetic. The 2006 British Social Attitudes survey revealed widespread prejudice against people with a mental illness, with fewer than one in five British adults saying they would be happy for a close relative to marry someone with schizophrenia.

People are likely to see mental illness as less 'real' than physical illness. There is, as a consequence, frequently a greater reluctance by other people to accept the legitimacy of the sick role, even though some mental illness, like some kinds of depression, does have a biological basis.

What is mental illness?

Mental illness has been defined as 'a state of mind which affects the person's thinking, perceiving, emotion or judgement to the extent that she or he requires care or medical treatment in her or his interests or in the interests of other persons'.

Mental illness might therefore be seen as any mental disorder affecting the behaviour and personality of an individual so as to prevent him or her functioning adequately within their society. Mental illnesses can range from anxiety and mild depression, through behavioural and emotional problems like eating disorders, to personality disorders and severe neurotic and psychotic disorders.

The biomedical approach to mental illness

In the past, mental illness was often explained as being the result of possession by evil spirits or the Devil, or the work of witches. In contemporary societies, the biomedical model treats mental illness as a real disease – a medical problem with observable symptoms that can be diagnosed, treated or cured by the use of drugs or other medical or surgical treatments, and as something affecting individuals rather than whole groups of people.

There are a range of possible explanations for the causes of what is defined as mental illness, with some psychiatrists suggesting biologically based explanations for some conditions, like clinical depression or schizophrenia, while others may point to stress-producing social factors in the lives of individuals, such as family breakdown, racism, poor housing and poverty as the more likely triggers of mental illness.

The social model of mental illness 1: social realist and structuralist approaches

Social realists agree with the biomedical approach that mental illness is a real and treatable condition. However, they challenge the biomedical approach that mental illness is a clearly recognizable medical condition affecting individuals. Social realists point out that what is defined as mental illness varies over time and between cultures, and that mental illness is not simply an individual matter, and there are social causes and a social pattern of mental illness.

Laing (2010[1960], 1970) was one of the first psychiatrists to challenge the biomedical approach to mental illness held by the medical establishment. Laing developed the social realist view of mental illness and pointed to structuralist explanations, suggesting that the causes of mental illness are located in the structure of society and in patients' relationships with others, rather than in the individual. Structuralists point out there is a social pattern of mental illness, similar to the general health differences based on social class, gender and ethnicity discussed earlier in this chapter, and with a similar range of cultural and material explanations. This social pattern suggests mental illness cannot stem simply from biological or individual factors, where a more random pattern would be expected.

THE SOCIAL PATTERN OF MENTAL ILLNESS

Some aspects of the social patterns of mental illness and their explanations were considered earlier in Topics 2 and 3 on differences in health chances and access to healthcare, so the following mainly summarizes the points made earlier.

Social class

The working class is diagnosed as suffering more mental illness than the middle class, and working-class mothers report more depression than middle-class mothers. Suicide and depression are more common among young unemployed males. These differences may reflect higher levels of poverty and consequently more stressful everyday lives and family relationships. Class differences in the treatment given, such as admittance to NHS psychiatric hospitals (where they will become a health statistic) rather than unrecorded private psychotherapy or psychiatric treatments at home or in private clinics, may also explain this difference in the pattern shown in statistics on mental illness.

Gender

Busfield (1996) shows that women are overrepresented in data on mental illness, with some mental disorders of various kinds seen as female maladies, such as anxiety, depression and anorexia. Women are much more likely than men to use specialist mental health services. Busfield suggests these apparent differences may be explained by men being less likely to visit the doctor for stigmatized illness like mental disorders. Due to gender roles, women generally suffer more stressful lives than men. It may also be that women are more willing to report symptoms of mental illness, and doctors are more likely to label symptoms reported by women as mainly mental, while men's are seen as physical. Women are therefore more likely to be diagnosed as depressed or suffering from anxiety than men. Mackenzie et al. (2006) found men are less willing to recognize they have a mental health problem, to seek help from their GPs, and to use mental health services, and they have less positive attitudes towards the usefulness of the services available. Some men often try to avoid a diagnosis of mental illness as they see it as a challenge to their masculinity.

Ethnicity

Ethnic differences in mental health are controversial. Most of the data are based on treatment rates, which show that those from black and minority ethnic groups are much more likely to receive a diagnosis of mental illness than the White British. One in five patients in hospital for mental illness comes from a black and minority ethnic group background – around twice their proportion in the population as a whole. People from minority ethnic groups are more likely to be diagnosed as schizophrenics, and have high rates of admission to hospital for severe mental disorders (psychosis). African-Caribbean men are up to ten times more likely than white people to be 'sectioned' – admitted, detained and treated in psychiatric hospitals against their wishes under the compulsory powers of the Mental Health Act.

Explanations of these differences include more stressful lives brought about by the combined effects of racism and social deprivation. Other explanations suggest that GPs and psychiatrists diagnose potential symptoms of mental illness differently depending on the ethnicity of the patient. This seems to be particularly the case with Black Caribbean young men, amongst whom behaviour that might pass unnoticed in other groups is often labelled as mental illness. This may explain why they are more likely to receive a diagnosis of mental illness, and to be compulsory committed to mental hospitals.

These social patterns of mental illness have led some researchers to suggest that not only is mental illness caused by social factors, like racism, stress, unemployment and poverty, but also these patterns may reflect the decision-making and labelling

An estimated one in six people suffers from some form of mental illness. The World Health Organization (WHO) found that those suffering from depression had the worst health, with a more disabling condition than angina, arthritis, asthma or diabetes. By the year 2020, WHO estimates suggest depression will be the world's second leading cause of years of productive life lost due to disability, for all ages and both sexes

processes of medical professionals rather than real differences in the pattern of mental illness. Doctors may simply be labelling and responding in different ways to similar symptoms depending on the social characteristics, like the social class, gender and ethnicity, of those they examine.

The social model of mental illness 2: labelling and the social construction of mental illness

Social constructionists suggest that there is no general or universal definition of mental illness. What is defined as mental illness is not an absolute, scientific fact, but is created by society – a *social construction*. Mental illness is simply a label attached to some forms of behaviour that people disapprove of, and reflects constantly changing interpretations in particular societies.

Foucault (2001 [1964]) argues that what is defined as mental illness – or what was called 'madness' in the past – and how it is treated depends on how a particular society interprets some kinds of deviant, abnormal behaviour. What is seen as madness is not therefore a natural, unchanging thing, but depends on the society in which it exists. For example, 'madness' was once associated with visions of the end of the world, with evil or demonic possession, but by the nineteenth century it had come to be seen as a treatable disease, with the mentally ill put in asylums, where they could be kept under control, observed and diagnosed. The medical gaze of observation and scientific analysis was applied to mental illness, with the biomedical approach of doctors and psychiatrists used to treat the mentally ill in psychiatric hospitals, with their treatment justified by the authority and expertise of science and medicine.

THE MEDICALIZATION OF PERSONAL AND SOCIAL PROBLEMS

This view of mental illness as a product of how a particular society responds to and interprets deviant or abnormal behaviour, and how this changes over time, is shown in the medicalization of society, and the way ever more conditions and life experiences are being labelled as 'mental illness'. Appignanesi (2011) points out that, over the last forty years, *The Diagnostic and Statistical Manual of Mental Disorders* (DSM) published by the American Psychiatric Association – the bible of the psychiatric professions in the United States, and used around the world – has invented ever more disorders, thereby reducing the range of what can be regarded as normal or sane, while drug companies make huge profits from treating these alleged disorders. The 5th edition of the DSM, due out in May 2012, was proposing to label as new mental disorders shyness in children, uncertainty over gender identity, loneliness, and unhappiness following bereavement. This could mean many thousands of people could be labelled as mentally ill for behaviour most people would consider normal. Appignanesi points to a 2011 survey which suggests 38 per cent of the adult population of Europe – 164.8 million people – suffer from a mental disorder in any year. This includes a range of behaviour that might well be regarded as mental illness, but also includes things like panic attacks and anxiety, shyness, mild depression, alcoholism and 'conduct disorder' in childhood, with symptoms like disobedience, tantrums, fighting, lying and stealing. Appignanesi suggests such surveys point to a growing tendency to label all our problems and unhappiness as a 'mental disorder'.

THE LABELLING OF MENTAL ILLNESS

The interactionist approach and labelling theory suggest that the definition of mental illness rests on what people see as normal and socially acceptable behaviour. Whether or not the label is applied will depend on how society defines normal behaviour, and involves other people – such as partners, family, friends, workmates and doctors – making judgements about whether someone's behaviour is so outside the boundaries of normal and socially acceptable behaviour, so strange, unusual, bizarre or frightening, that it presents a problem for either the individual concerned or other people.

Medical professionals, particularly psychiatrists, have the power to define and label abnormal behaviour as an illness, and to treat people so labelled in a different way from those not so labelled. This obviously prompts the question of how the notions of normal and abnormal behaviour are established, and therefore what is and isn't classed as mental illness. This is no easy matter, since what is regarded as abnormal or 'mad' in one society or group may be seen as perfectly normal in another, and notions of normality and deviance change over time. For example, agoraphobia (fear of open spaces) is only seen as a mental illness because other people don't regard staying indoors all the time as normal behaviour.

Certainly, the label of 'mental illness' has been used to condemn deviant (non-conformist) behaviour. For example, some young women were once put in mental hospitals simply because they were unmarried mothers, and opponents of the former communist regime in the Soviet Union (now Russia and its neighbouring countries) were once seen as 'mad' to oppose the government and put in mental hospitals for 'treatment'. Homosexuality was once commonly seen as a mental disorder, with gay men subjected to conversion therapy, using drugs and electric shocks to 'cure' them of their homosexuality. Such treatments are still occasionally found today, despite being condemned by most psychiatrists.

Even today in Britain, we find an increasing medicalization of non-conformist behavior, so that, for example, badly behaved children are often labelled as suffering from Emotional and Behavioural Difficulties or Attention Deficit Disorder, or political protesters become labelled as mentally ill, 'feral' (or wild), anti-social, unsocialized people. How often do many of us dismiss people whom we think of as strange, with odd views or bizarre behaviour, as 'crazy'? The following topic discusses further how there is a growing medicalization of all forms of deviance (see page 527).

THE WORK OF SCHEFF

These issues have led researchers, such as Scheff (1966) and Szasz (1972), influenced by labelling theory and Marxism, to claim that what we call mental illness is a social construction – simply a label applied by those with power, such as doctors, politicians and the mass media, to those who display forms of rule-breaking and unacceptable forms of deviant behaviour they cannot make sense of, or dislike, or which they disapprove of, or feel threatened by. In this view, those exhibiting such behaviour, a group Becker (1997[1963]) described as 'outsiders', may be defined as mentally ill because they are deviant and go against the dominant norms of a specific society.

Scheff sees what is called mental illness as a label – 'a dustbin of bizarre behaviour' – to explain away, and justify treatment of, behaviour that cannot be explained or made sense of in any other way. The label 'mental illness' is applied to rule-breaking and odd behaviour which takes place in unapproved contexts, and which might pose a threat to the smooth running of society.

Scheff argues that most people at some time go through stages of stress, anxiety or depression, or show signs of odd or bizarre behaviour. In the majority of cases, other people do not label this as evidence of mental illness, and it is dealt with through the normal sick role. A few days off work, a change in social circumstances or a holiday is often enough to deal with these problems. It is only when others label this behaviour as evidence of mental illness that it begins to have important consequences for individuals.

Scheff argues that, once others begin to see behaviour as so bizarre, frightening or intolerable that it is seen as a sign of mental illness, then stereotypes of mental illness we have all learnt since childhood – like the 'nutter' or the 'loony' – come into play. The patient then acts according to the stereotype she or he has learnt to expect of the mentally ill. Others react in terms of the same stereotyped expectations. Psychiatrists confirm the 'insane' label, psychiatric treatment begins, and the deviant label of 'mentally ill' is firmly established. People labelled in such a way are thus thrown into the 'insanity role'. Those labelled as mentally ill often have little choice but to accept the label, as refusal of it and of the treatment ('there's nothing wrong with me') is interpreted by others as yet further confirmation of their illness.

THE WORK OF SZASZ

The **self-fulfilling prophecy** refers to people acting in response to predictions of their behaviour, thereby making the prediction come true. For example, people's response to being labelled as mentally ill can make their condition worse.

Szasz, like Scheff, argues that mental illness is not really an illness at all, but a label used by powerful or influential people to control those who are seen as socially disruptive or who challenge existing society or the dominant ideas in some way. Szasz says that it is the views and reactions of others that lead to the mental illness label being applied, and not the abnormal behaviour itself that makes us 'mad'. What we define as mental illness or 'madness' cannot therefore be treated or cured, as the problem lies with the attitudes of other people, not with the behaviour itself. Szasz also points to the way in which society's reactions to those labelled as 'mentally ill' can actually make their condition worse – a **self-fulfilling prophecy** which Goffman (see below) explores. As Szasz himself put it, 'It takes one person to develop a real disease. But it takes two people to develop a mental illness.'

Researchers like Scheff and Szasz suggest that what we call 'mental illness' is simply a label applied by others to those whose behaviour they simply cannot make sense of, because it is so bizarre or odd. The 'Hatman', pictured above, stands harmlessly every day for long periods of time on a busy main road wearing a range of bizarre headgear, wigs and masks. Why is such behaviour sometimes seen simply as an expression of individuality, personal eccentricity or oddness, and other times labelled as a sign of mental illness needing treatment?

Source: With permission of Peter Moulder

THE WORK OF GOFFMAN

Goffman is an interactionist who is concerned with how the attachment of the label of 'mentally ill' can become a self-fulfilling prophecy, through the consequences that follow for those individuals whose behaviour has been labelled as a mental illness. In *Asylums* (1991 [1961]), Goffman suggests that, once a person is labelled as mentally ill and chooses or is forced to enter a psychiatric hospital as a patient, then the insanity role is confirmed and the career of the psychiatric patient begins.

Goffman argues that psychiatric hospitals develop their own subculture, in which people don't get cured but learn to 'act mad' according to the label that has been attached to them. This reduces their chances of release and makes it difficult for them to re-enter normal society successfully. He therefore suggests that hospitals for the treatment of mental illness are more likely to reinforce and create the behaviour they are supposed to be curing, making release and a return to normality even more difficult.

Entering a mental hospital – mortification

Entering a mental hospital involves what Goffman calls a process of **mortification**, whereby the patient's own identity is replaced by one defined by the institution. This is to encourage the patient to conform to the hospital regime. It involves things like removing personal clothing and possessions, lack of privacy, making the patient follow hospital routines, obeying staff and so on.

In these circumstances, Goffman suggests, patients may respond to the institution and the label applied to them in various ways:

- *Withdrawal* Patients keep themselves to themselves – behaviour which is interpreted as part of the illness, confirming the label.

> **Mortification** is a process whereby a person's own identity is replaced by one defined and imposed by an institution, such as a psychiatric hospital or a prison.

- *Rebellion* Patients challenge the institution – which is interpreted as part of the illness, but suggests more treatment is needed.
- *Institutionalization* Patients accept they are mentally ill, feel more secure in hospital and scared of the outside world, and want to remain in hospital.
- *Conversion* Patients accept their new identities and hospital rules, and creep to staff as a 'model patient'.
- *Playing it cool* Patients keep their heads down and don't break rules so they can hang on to what's left of their own identity.

> A **master status** is the dominant status of an individual which overrides all other characteristics of that person, such as that of an 'ex-con', a druggie or mentally-ill.

Goffman argues that the label of 'mentally ill' carries with it a stigma – a sign of social disapproval, exclusion, rejection, blame and inferiority – that has severe consequences for people so labelled, even when they have been cured. It can take on the form of what Becker (1997[1963]) called a **master status** – a dominant status that overrides all other aspects of that person's identity. For example, some employers are reluctant to employ people who have a history of mental illness, no matter how good they might be at their job. This means that, even if patients are released, they are likely to face the social stigma attached to being a former mental patient. Figure 7.9 illustrates this 'career' of a mental patient.

Figure 7.9 The career of a mental patient

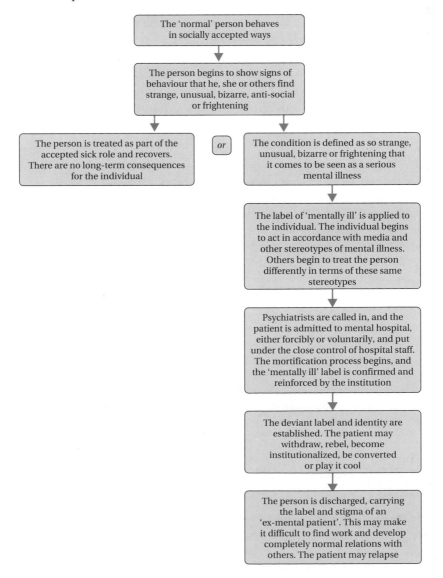

THE WORK OF ROSENHAN

Rosenhan's research 'On being sane in insane places' (1973) showed how unreliable diagnoses of mental illness were. This research confirmed the views of Scheff, Szasz and Goffman that mental illness is basically a label placed on behaviour by others.

Rosenhan in 1972 was interested in discovering how the staff of mental hospitals in the United States made sense of perfectly sane 'patients' who, unknown to staff, faked the symptoms of schizophrenia by claiming to hear a voice saying 'thud'. Nine people (including Rosenhan himself) prepared themselves by not washing, shaving or cleaning their teeth for five days before going to the hospitals. All were diagnosed as schizophrenics and admitted to hospital. Once admitted, they behaved normally, and said the voice wasn't bothering them any more. All the pseudopatients were perfectly healthy, but were nonetheless kept in hospital for periods ranging from 7 to 52 days, and aspects of their perfectly normal lives before being admitted to hospital were reinterpreted as signs of their apparent illness. Rosenhan took many notes while in hospital, and this was also interpreted by staff as part of his illness, labelled as 'writing behaviour'.

Rosenhan then reversed the experiment, telling hospital staff they could expect an undisclosed number of patients who would be faking illness. The staff eventually thought they had identified forty-one fake patients, but all those they identified were actually genuine patients who wanted help, and Rosenhan had in fact not sent any fake patients at all.

Rosenhan's work illustrated very clearly that the attachment of the label 'mentally ill' is a fairly arbitrary and inaccurate process. This is a matter of concern given the stigma that is attached to mental illness, and the consequences that may flow once the label is applied.

Rosenhan revisited

Rosenhan's experiment hit the world of psychiatry like a bombshell, and resulted in changes in the way diagnoses of mental illness were made. Contemporary psychiatrists are convinced that what happened with Rosenhan and his fellow pseudopatients could not happen in the twenty-first century. However, in 2002, the experiment was repeated by the psychologist Lauren Slater. She followed the same procedures as Rosenhan, not washing and so on for five days before going to the hospital, and claimed, like Rosenhan, that 'I'm here because I'm hearing a voice and it's saying "thud".' Like Rosenhan's pseudopatients, Slater had no other symptoms of mental illness or physical ill-health. She was initially diagnosed as having post-traumatic stress disorder, and then as suffering psychosis and depression. She visited eight hospitals, and, while she was not admitted, she was prescribed a total of twenty-five antipsychotic and sixty antidepressant drugs. Like Rosenhan thirty years earlier, her non-existent condition was misdiagnosed and mislabelled.

For further information, see 'Into the cuckoo's nest', *Guardian*, 31 Jan. 2004, an edited extract from *Opening Skinner's Box: Great Psychological Experiments of the Twentieth Century* by Lauren Slater (London: Bloomsbury, 2004).

CRITICISMS OF THE SOCIAL CONSTRUCTION APPROACH TO MENTAL ILLNESS

The work of writers like Scheff, Szasz, Goffman and Rosenhan has been criticized for the small scale of their studies, which may therefore not be representative of all institutions involved with mental health.

The view that mental illness is simply a social construction – a response to the interpretations of other people – ignores the fact that for many people it is a real illness, often causing a great deal of distress for both individuals and their families and friends. In such circumstances, psychiatric help and medical treatment can sometimes be effective. Nonetheless, the views of writers like Scheff, Szasz, Goffman and Rosenhan do raise serious questions about the way we think about, define and label mental illness. The study of mental illness shows yet again that there are significant social aspects to health which are as important as biological or physical causes.

Primary deviance is deviant behaviour which is not publicly labelled as deviant.

Secondary deviance is deviant behaviour which is labelled as such by others.

Activity

1. Do you agree or disagree with the view that mental illness is simply a social construction? Give three arguments or pieces of evidence to support your answer.

2. Do you think the media present negative stereotypes of those with mental illness? Try to find evidence from recent media reporting.

3. **Primary deviance** is the type of deviant behaviour we might all display from time to time with few, if any, social consequences, because other people either don't know about it or don't see it as very important. **Secondary deviance** is when that behaviour is seen as worrying by others, and labelled as deviant or unacceptable behaviour, with a need for action to be taken. Suggest how the concepts of primary and secondary deviance might be applied to the cases of those displaying symptoms of mental illness.

4. Identify and explain *three* reasons why people might try to conceal their mental illness from others.

5. Suggest *three* ways in which the label of 'mentally ill' might affect the identity of a person so labelled.

6(a) Conduct a small survey in your school or college, exploring attitudes to mental illness. Ask about things that interest you, but you might consider some of the following issues:
   - whether the welfare state should provide the best possible care for people with mental illness.
   - whether the people in your survey think the mass media give unfair treatment to those with mental illnesses.
   - whether they believe anyone can become mentally ill.
   - what they think the causes of mental illness are.
   - whether anyone with a history of mental health problems should be excluded from taking up some jobs.
   - whether care units for people with psychiatric problems should be located in residential neighbourhoods.
   - whether people with mental illness should live as part of a normal community.

6(b) Analyse and discuss your findings. What do these show about public attitudes to mental illness?

Exam-style questions

1 Explain what is meant by the term 'stigma' in relation to mental illness. *(2 marks)*

2 Explain what is meant by the term 'self-fulfilling prophecy'. *(2 marks)*

3 Suggest **three** reasons why women are more likely to be recorded as suffering from mental illness than men. *(6 marks)*

4 Suggest **three** consequences that may follow for someone labelled as mentally ill. *(6 marks)*

5 Outline some of the criticisms of the biomedical approach to mental illness. *(12 marks)*

6 Outline some of the ways in which mental illness is socially defined. *(12 marks)*

7 Assess the view that mental illness is primarily a social construction. *(20 marks)*

8 Assess the view that mental illness is simply a label that has successfully been applied to some forms of deviant behaviour. *(20 marks)*

Topic 5

SPECIFICATION AREA

The role of medicine and the health professions

The power of the medical profession

As seen earlier, the medical gaze accompanying the biomedical model of health has brought considerable power and prestige to the medical profession. Doctors are seen as possessing expert knowledge; they are the only people legally allowed to practise medicine, and they alone have the power and authority to label conditions as genuine illnesses. This gives doctors and other medical professionals a great deal of power to control and treat patients.

This power relationship is present throughout doctor–patient interactions. For example, doctors have a substantial amount of control over their patients' intimate lives, such as the right to medically examine their patients' bodies and to obtain very personal details about their lives. The power of the medical profession is increasingly spreading into new areas, with the growing medicalization of society discussed below.

Doctors often have a great deal of power and authority over patients. What factors might contribute to this unequal relationship?

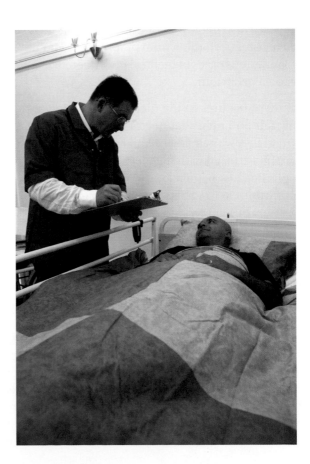

The functionalist view of the medical profession: protecting patients and benefiting society

Functionalist writers like Parsons argue that there is a high level of trust involved in the doctor–patient relationship, and the patient's interests must be protected.

Functionalists suggest that the following features of professionalism apply to the medical profession (and similar points apply to other professions like lawyers) and establish and maintain trust in the doctor–patient relationship, and protect the interests of patients by ensuring confidentiality of their conditions and high standards of treatment.

- Doctors have a long period of theoretical and practical training, giving them the specialized and expert knowledge (biomedical science) and the wide range of diagnostic skills necessary to treat their patients effectively.
- **Altruism** Doctors work with an unselfish concern for patient care, and act in the best interests of patients rather than for personal gain.
- **Universalistic values** Doctors act in terms of universalistic values, which are rules and values that apply equally to everyone. All patients are treated equally and fairly on the basis of their medical needs alone and regardless of issues such as their wealth, gender, social class or ethnicity.
- Doctors have a legal monopoly and only those who are qualified can legally practise medicine. This monopoly protects the patient from unqualified 'cowboy' doctors.
- Doctors are controlled and regulated by a code of professional and medical ethics. This is a set of rules about how they should behave, which includes putting the interests of the patient first and protecting the confidentiality of the doctor–patient relationship. If doctors breach this code of ethics, and fail in their duty to patients, they may face disciplinary action. Some doctors are occasionally 'struck off' the medical register (forbidden from practising medicine) by the General Medical Council in serious cases of medical incompetence or breaches of appropriate professional behaviour.

Because of these features of the medical profession and their expert knowledge, it is seen as only fair and right that doctors should have authority over their patients and expect them to follow their advice and recommended treatments. Doctors should also be – and can be – trusted with high levels of independence to get on with their work of curing people. Because of their long periods of training, often on relatively low incomes, and their contribution to society's well-being, doctors are consequently and justifiably given high status in society, with high salaries to match.

These functionalist views have not gone unchallenged.

Altruism is behaviour that is motivated by an unselfish concern for the welfare of others.

Universalistic values are rules and values that apply equally to all members of society, regardless of who they are.

Criticisms of the medical profession: protecting patients? Or benefiting and protecting themselves?

- *Professionalism is about maintaining the high rewards of doctors* Weberian sociologists suggest medical professionalism is part of a strategy to maintain and protect the high status, rewards and power of doctors and other medical professionals. The control of doctors over the training and qualifications needed to practise medicine ensures they control entry to their profession, and restricting entry limits the numbers of those qualified so there is continued high demand for their services and high salaries. The monopoly that doctors have over medical treatment protects their high status and salaries, by preventing competition from practitioners of complementary and alternative medicine (CAM), discussed below, of which the British Medical Association does not approve. Such alternative practitioners are presented as giving inferior treatments, even though these might benefit patients.

- *Doctors do not always act altruistically* As suggested above, the professionalism of medicine may be interpreted as doctors acting out of self-interest to maintain their high pay and status. Certainly private doctors carrying out cosmetic surgery for patient vanity reasons and for a high price are no more altruistic than anyone else selling a product or service for profit, like Tesco or Boots. Marxist writers like Navarro, and McKinlay (1977), argue that most doctors work within the framework of publicly funded healthcare, in large organizations like the National Health Service, in which doctors have become salaried employees, or self-employed like GPs. Medical practice and decision-making is driven not simply by concern with patients, but also by concerns over the costs of treatment. This may mean doctors do not always provide the best care or prescribe the most effective drugs, but may go for cheaper, less effective treatments. Navarro emphasizes that doctors are more concerned with social control of the sick, and getting them back to work as labour power in a capitalist society.

- *Doctors do not always operate with universalistic values* Doctors do not treat all patients fairly and equally. Doctors give preferential treatment to their private patients, in whom they have a personal financial interest. As seen earlier in this chapter, middle-class patients tend to get more out of their doctors and the NHS than the more disadvantaged, in terms of things like the length of consultations, explanations given and referral to consultants. Doctors react less favourably to patients with conditions that they might see as of their own creation, like obesity arising from overeating, unhealthy foods and inactive lifestyles, or heart and liver disease arising from smoking or drinking. They may also regard less favourably patients they see as time-wasting hypochondriacs, those who complain a lot, or those they simply do not like or who do not follow their advice. This chapter has shown numerous examples of how doctors diagnose and treat patients differently according to their social class, gender, ethnicity, disability and age.

- *Doctors reinforce patriarchy* As seen earlier (see pages 463–5) feminist writers suggest that doctors reinforce patriarchy, through the policing of motherhood and their control over women through the medicalization of pregnancy and childbirth.

- *There is little control over the quality and competence of diagnosis and treatment by doctors* Because of their long training, and specialized knowledge and skills, doctors have high levels of independence in their work. This means there is little control by others over what they do, and often incompetent doctors remain undiscovered and unchallenged. Dr Harold Shipman achieved notoriety as Britain's worst serial killer, killing at least 215 patients between 1975 and 1998, though the number is probably much higher. While Shipman was something of an exception in the medical profession, and he is the only doctor in the history of British medicine ever to have been found guilty of murdering his patients, the Shipman public inquiry was told the independence given to doctors undermined safeguards for patients against an incompetent doctor or, as in this case, a determined killer, or other doctors whose crimes have never been uncovered.

- *Medical professionals may not always provide the best patient care* As seen earlier when discussing iatrogenesis (see pages 453–4), doctors and nurses don't always do a good job, and may occasionally do more harm than good to patients' health. For example, in 2011, Jane Maher of Macmillan Cancer Support suggested that

GPs were failing to spot long-term side-effects caused by cancer treatments, such as osteoporosis, heart disease and bowel trouble. This affected up to 500,000 people who had survived cancer, often causing unnecessary disruption to their work, health, relationships and home lives, which could have been avoided if doctors had identified their symptoms.

- *It is hard for patients to complain* The professional code of ethics means doctors are not meant to criticize the work of other doctors publicly, and in any event doctors and nurses do not like to criticize their fellow professionals. This makes it very difficult for patients to complain about and expose medical incompetence. This code of ethics also protects doctors, as it suggests that their behaviour is largely beyond criticism.

Medicine and social control

Social control is concerned with maintaining order and stability in society. Parsons, writing from a functionalist perspective, argues that sickness is really a form of deviance, which threatens the stability of society. This is because those who are classified as sick are able to avoid their normal social responsibilities, like going to work, school or college, or looking after the family. If too many people did this, then society would collapse – imagine a school or factory where the teachers, students, managers or workers were always off ill. Ill-health is therefore something that needs to be kept within careful limits to avoid undermining social order and the smooth functioning of society. This means there have to be controls over those who claim to be sick, so they can be encouraged to return to taking on their usual social responsibilities again as quickly as possible. One way in which the power of the medical profession, and particularly doctors, is shown is the key role they play in controlling the sick and legitimizing (justifying) sickness by their gate-keeping function in relation to the sick role.

THE SICK ROLE

Parsons sees doctors playing a key role in this social control of the sick through their control over access to the *sick role* – the pattern of behaviour which is expected from someone who is ill. The sick role provides an escape route for individuals from everyday responsibilities. This is because, when people are sick, they can reasonably abandon normal everyday activities, and often others will take over their responsibilities so that they are able to recover.

Features of the sick role

Parsons suggests the sick role involves both rights and obligations for those who are sick.

Rights
- Depending on the illness, individuals are excused normal social activities, such as going to school or work, or looking after the family. This requires approval by others such as teachers, employers and family members. The doctor often plays a key role in this process, by diagnosing the person as genuinely ill, and issuing sick notes.
- Individuals are not seen as personally to blame for their illness: relatives, friends and doctors are often very critical of those they see as responsible for their own

illness. For example, those who smoke tobacco, eat and drink too much or overdose on drugs often don't get much sympathy from the medical profession.
- There is a recognition that individuals cannot be expected to be solely responsible for their recovery by a sheer act of will, and that they will need help, often professional help from doctors, to recover.

Obligations
- The sick person must see his or her sickness as an undesirable state, and individuals have an obligation to want to get well, and ensure their sickness state is only a temporary one.
- When necessary, sick people are expected to seek and accept medical help and cooperate in their treatment to get well. In other words, sick people are expected to do what the doctor orders, and they cannot expect sympathy and support if they don't try to get well. Those refusing medical treatment are unlikely to have their illnesses recognized as genuine sickness or get much sympathy if they are suffering. Even if people don't want to call in the doctor because they don't see their illness as serious enough to do so, they are still expected to stay in bed, take non-prescription medicines, or take it easy in an effort to recover.

Parsons argues these obligations are necessary to stop people getting into a subculture of sickness, where sickness, dependence on others and apathy are seen as a normal and desirable state. Such a subculture would disrupt the smooth running of society. People must therefore be obliged to get well and resume their everyday responsibilities as quickly as possible.

Activity

1 Most people have some understanding of the rights and obligations of the sick role simply by living (and occasionally being sick) as a member of society. Outline: (a) the circumstances which have led you to adopt the sick role; (b) any ways in which you have manipulated the sick role for your ends, such as faking sickness or playing it up to get time off school or college or work.
2 Do you think everyone who is ill can or should adopt the sick role? Try to think of individuals or groups whose circumstances might make it difficult for them to do so. Give reasons for your answers.

Doctors as gate-keepers of the sick role

Gate-keeping is the power of some people, groups or organizations to limit access to something valuable or useful. Doctors and other medical professionals play a key role in the social control of the sick by acting as gate-keepers for entry to the sick role – doctors are the ones who legitimize (justify) sickness by officially classifying it as such, and aim to cure the sick as quickly as possible to stop them evading their normal responsibilities for any longer than necessary. Interactionists emphasize how the interaction between a doctor and a patient is essentially a negotiation, in which the doctor is involved in assessing whether or not a patient is really sick, and therefore whether or not access to the sick role should be permitted.. For example, doctors can stop people taking more than a few days off work on the grounds of illness by refusing to issue sick notes. Doctor–patient interaction therefore involves a process of sorting out those who are really sick from hypochondriacs, malingerers and skivers who try to evade their responsibilities by faking illness.

Doctors play an important part in social control of the sick and access to the sick role

Criticisms of Parsons and the sick role

- Not everyone who is ill goes to the doctor, maybe because they lack knowledge or awareness of their condition, or they don't regard it as sufficiently serious, or are afraid of doctors, so people may be sick but do not actually become an officially classified patient entitled to access to the sick role.

- Not everyone who feels ill is able to adopt the sick role, perhaps because they cannot afford to have time off work, or because they have other responsibilities. For example, lone parents may not be able to afford the luxury of adopting the sick role as they have to continue looking after their children.

- Not everyone who is ill gets the sympathy of others and avoids the personal blame implied in the rights of the sick role. For example, AIDS, heart disease brought on by smoking or obesity, drug abuse and alcohol poisoning often bring little sympathy from others, including some doctors, as they are seen as self-inflicted.

- Some diseases, like STDs (sexually transmitted diseases), mental illness and HIV/AIDS, involve high degrees of stigma (social disapproval, rejection and inferior status), and sufferers may wish to avoid public knowledge of their illness. They may therefore wish to avoid adopting the sick role because of the consequences of doing so.

- Some illnesses or disorders are not curable, and it may be better for both the individual and society for people with such conditions to avoid entering a permanent sick role and to try to carry on with normal life as much as possible. This might well apply to those with terminal illnesses, various forms of impairment, such as blindness or loss of limb functions, or conditions like heart disease or diabetes.

- The sick don't always act as the well-behaved, passive and obedient patients implied by the sick role. They may well refuse to cooperate with doctors, challenge diagnoses and the doctor's authority, and ask for second opinions. The relationship between doctors and patients is changing, and patients now have access to much more information about medical treatments through the internet, and services such as NHS Direct. This means doctors no longer have the monopoly of medical knowledge they once enjoyed.

THE MEDICALIZATION OF SOCIETY AND SOCIAL CONTROL

Another way in which the medical profession has become an increasingly significant agency of social control is through the growing medicalization of society. This is the process whereby what were not previously regarded as medical issues come to be defined, diagnosed and treated as medical disorders or illnesses under the authority of doctors and other health professionals. This medicalization of society means the medical gaze of doctors has extended over an ever-widening range of social issues and problems as they become 'experts' on issues that once had nothing to do with them, such as the ageing process, childhood behaviour and all manner of personal behaviour and lifestyle choices. Some of these issues of medicalization were discussed earlier – see pages 463–4 (pregnancy, childbirth and the policing of motherhood) and pages 513–14 (personal and social problems).

The medicalization of deviance

The medicalization of society and the power of doctors is shown by the growing medicalization of deviance. Conrad and Schneider (1992 [1980]) suggest that behaviour that was once defined as immoral, sinful or criminal has been given medical meanings. Definitions of deviance have been transformed from 'badness to sickness', with medical treatments becoming, in some cases, new forms of punishment and social control. Increasingly, 'badness' and all manner of non-conformist appearance, behaviour and belief are treated as physical or mental problems needing medical treatment – for example crime, being overweight, excessive drinking and gambling, recreational drug use, sexual promiscuity, racism, some political beliefs, and beliefs in UFOs or bizarre religious cults. For example, we hear stories of drug treatments for hyperactivity in children, gastric bypass surgery and jaw wiring for obesity, cognitive behaviour therapies for eating disorders, medical treatments for excessive drinking, methadone treatments for heroin addiction, and drugs for the treatment of all kinds of what are seen as personality disorders, such as violent behaviour, compulsive criminal behaviour, depression, mood swings, anger, impulsive behaviour, irritability, anxiety, or believing in things that suggest a loss of touch with reality. A number of these conditions, many of which are socially caused and socially defined, are seen as forms of mental illness. The issue of this medicalization in relation to what is defined as mental illness was discussed in Topic 4.

That issues such as these become medicalized means that doctors and other medical professionals become ever more agents of social control, with their alleged medical knowledge and expertise in these areas giving them power and moral authority to police what are often either simply people's lifestyle choices, or products of the social circumstances in which they live their lives.

Contemporary changes in the role of medicine and the power of the medical profession

THE EROSION OF MEDICAL POWER IN FAVOUR OF THE PATIENT?

In contemporary Britain, some suggest the power of the medical profession is being eroded to some degree, with more power shifting in favour of the patient. Some of the reasons for this include:

- *Degenerative diseases* Many of the new diseases in contemporary society are degenerative diseases for which there are no medical cures. In such circumstances, doctors are of less use to patients.

- *Patient doubts* Many people have growing doubts about the alleged superiority of conventional medical treatment, with more of them turning to alternative therapies, medicines and treatments, such as acupuncture and homeopathy. The rise of these alternatives was given extra force when the House of Lords recognized in 2000 that there was scientific evidence that some, such as acupuncture and herbal medicine, could be effective, and the British Medical Association has now accepted the usefulness of certain alternative treatments.

- *Erosion of public confidence* Public confidence in the medical profession is being eroded by unprecedented interest in medical scandals and misjudgements of various kinds. The 'Doctor Death' Shipman case referred to earlier raised major concerns over lack of proper supervision of doctors. There was a wave of public revulsion and distrust arising from the scandal at Alder Hey hospital in Liverpool in 2001, when the organs of dead children were routinely removed during post-mortem examinations and stored for research purposes, without the prior consent of the parents. In 2009–10, there were widespread warnings and near-panic in the medical profession over what was described as a looming swine flu pandemic (an epidemic of infectious disease spreading across large regions or many countries), with estimates suggesting as many as 750,000 could die from it. Many were vaccinated, yet very few were affected by the disease, even among the many who weren't vaccinated, and flu deaths were little different from those in any normal year. Further lack of confidence in medicine arises from the return of diseases which were once thought to be nearly extinct in Britain. For example, tuberculosis has returned as a significant disease, particularly among the most disadvantaged, and in England and Wales cases of TB have increased by around 30 per cent over about the last twenty years, and around 350 people in England and Wales now die each year from the disease, according to the Health Protection Agency.

- *More knowledgeable and demanding patients* Patients are demanding much more from their doctors and nurses, and have growing knowledge of medically based ideas, which medical treatments are effective and what they should be entitled to. Diagnosis is no longer a one-way process, with the doctor as the only expert. The sick are increasingly knowledgeable about health and disease, and the diagnoses doctors make, and knowledge which was once almost exclusively the preserve of doctors is now available to every member of the public who has access to a computer. More patients are questioning the knowledge, decision-making, authority and competence of doctors, and losing confidence in them. This is reflected in rising numbers of complaints against medical professionals, with an all-time record high of nearly 9,000 complaints about GPs to the General Medical Council in 2011. Patients now have the right to see their medical records, and doctors are facing growing threats of legal action when care is inadequate or when mistakes are made.

- *Declining role of doctors in medical care decisions* In the National Health Service, managers and administrators, rather than doctors, often make the major decisions about the types and costs of medical care provided.

These factors are changing the balance of power between patients and doctors in the patient's favour, giving patients more rights through complaints procedures, and undermining the status of doctors. Reforms in the National Health Service through the 2000s, reinforced by changes in 2012, aimed to provide more personalized health services for people, with the healthcare system fitting the needs of individuals rather than the other way round, giving patients more control and choice over their medical treatment.

A SHIFT FROM THE BIOMEDICAL TO SOCIAL MODEL OF HEALTH

The unanswerable weight of sociological evidence has meant there is a growing recognition among health professionals that poor health is a result of a combination of individual and structural material, social and cultural factors, as well as the biological causes which form the core explanation of the biomedical model. Many now recognize that lifestyle choices, such as smoking cigarettes, what foods you eat and drink (and how much), the amount of exercise and relaxation people get, as well as structural factors like low pay, poverty, poor housing and unhealthy environments, all influence health.

There has also been a growing trend within medicine to treat patients more as individuals with identities made up of social and psychological characteristics, rather than as simply biological machines. This has been accompanied by greater attention focused on patients' own accounts and interpretations of their symptoms and illnesses, and their choices in the medical care they receive.

There have, in other words, been some moves away from the biomedical model to a more social model of health. Although the biomedical model is still a strong influence among health professionals, this change has reduced the power and influence of medical professionals, and of the medical gaze and medical expertise derived from the biomedical approach to health.

There's a growing emphasis on patient choice in the National Health Service

CONSUMER CHOICE

In postmodern society, there is a growing emphasis on the consumer lifestyle and on meeting the demands and choices of consumers. People are more likely to take control of their health and fitness, to consume health and fitness products, and to see their health and fitness as important parts of their identities. Consequently, people now expect more choice* (but see page 498 on the limits of patient choice) – for example, which hospital or GP to go to; whether to be treated at home, in hospital or at the GP surgery; what treatments to follow; and when the treatment should take place. They expect more information about their diagnosis and treatment, are more likely to question them and expect to be able to see their medical records. They can now easily obtain information about their condition and treatment from the internet, with access to a vast range of specialist support groups, giving them more control in their dealings with doctors, and reducing the power and authority of doctors over their patients.

Table 7.5, which is derived from work by Nettleton (2006), identifies the main changes that have occurred and are still occurring, in the approaches to health and healthcare. Nettleton suggests a range of possible reasons for some of these changes. These include:

Activity

Consider the following extract from a speech by a former Health Minister in 2001:
'In this country we can no longer accept the traditional paternalistic attitude of the NHS, that the benefits of medicine, science and research are somehow self-evident regardless of the wishes of patients or their families . . . the health of the patient belongs to the patient, not to the health service. I want the balance of power in the NHS to shift decisively in favour of the patient, not to pitch patients against doctors but to put the relationship between patients and the health service on a more modern footing.'

1 What changes would you recommend to be introduced to shift the balance of power in favour of the patient, rather than doctors?
2 Go to www.dh.gov.uk, do a search on 'choice' or 'patient choice' and identify three steps the government has taken to implement such changes.
3 Devise and carry out a small piece of research among a sample of adults (who will probably have more experience of the health service) to find out how they see health and healthcare. You should think of a suitable research method, and explain why you think this is appropriate for what you are investigating. You might explore things like what people want from the NHS, how important choice is to them in terms of the treatments they get, the doctors they see, and the timing and location of both; whether they have faith in their doctor, or modern medicine in general; and what they like or dislike about their treatment by their doctors.
4 Compare your findings with others in your group, and discuss to what extent your findings confirm or otherwise the changes suggested in table 7.5.

---

* Though people *expect* more choice, they in most cases don't exercise any choice at all and follow the advice of their GP and other doctors, who in effect make the choice for them. See the box on patient choice on page 498.

Table 7.5 Changing approaches to health and healthcare

Traditional healthcare	New approaches
(based on a biomedical model of health) $\longrightarrow$	(based more on a social model of health)

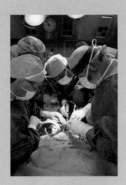 

Disease $\longrightarrow$	*Health*
Emphasis on treating acute life-threatening and infectious diseases.	Emphasis on preventing ill-health. Health promotion campaigns.
Hospital $\longrightarrow$	*Community*
Care is provided in hospitals, which are seen as centres of medical or psychiatric expertise and treatment.	Care is provided in the community, such as by nurses and GPs, 'halfway' houses for the mentally ill, and home care for older people.
Intervention and cure $\longrightarrow$	*Monitoring, prevention and care*
The focus is on medical intervention to protect health, and treating and curing acute illnesses where possible.	The focus is on individuals, either alone or working with their doctors, monitoring their own health and fitness, preventing them developing chronic illnesses, and caring for those with chronic illnesses for which there is no cure.
Patient $\longrightarrow$	*Person*
The individual is seen through the medical gaze as a 'patient' – a malfunctioning biological object requiring treatment, which is directed by medical professionals ('experts') in terms of location and type of treatment. Medical records are secret, and there is hardly any patient choice, as 'the doctor knows best'.	The individual is seen as a combination of biological, social and psychological characteristics. In a consumer-oriented society, medical professionals need to respond to the wishes and needs of patients, who have more choice, information and control over what type of treatment they receive, and where and when, and have means of complaining if they don't get what they want.

- *The need to limit the financial costs of NHS healthcare* Increasing investment in 'high-tech' medicine has not produced equivalent success rates in terms of patients treated and cured. Rising expectations of the NHS, escalating costs of new drugs and medical technology, along with a growing elderly population, mean costs have been spiralling out of control, and demand needs to be limited, and money spent more effectively.

- *The changing disease burden* Acute illness (diseases with an abrupt onset, a short course and that can generally be treated and cured), like infectious diseases, has declined, and there has been an increase in chronic diseases. These are diseases that last a long time, with many modern diseases caused by social and environmental factors, which can be prevented, but which are often not capable of being cured, only controlled.

- *Consumer culture and postmodern society* There has been a loss of faith in the ability of the science and medicine metanarratives to cure diseases, together with an undermining of the role of medical professional 'experts', and the distinction between medical experts and ordinary people has become more blurred. Postmodern societies involve consumers taking control, and there is a growing emphasis on the patient as a consumer of healthcare. This involves the patient exercising a more dominant role in their healthcare and in the patient–doctor relationship, with the expectation of many elements of patient choice in picking and mixing treatments as they wish. No longer can medical experts alone simply decide what happens to patients.

Complementary and alternative medicine (CAM)

The issues of the changing power of the medical profession, the shift from the biomedical to a more social model of health, growing consumer choice in health matters, and postmodernist views of health all come together when looking at competing views of complementary and alternative medicine (CAM).

CAM refers to non-orthodox medicines and treatments which are outside the evidence-based biomedical approach of conventional scientific medicine. CAM takes a more holistic approach – treating the whole person – than conventional medicine, and frequently deals with spiritual dimensions of patients' lives, as well as mainstream healthcare features like the importance of diet and exercise in preserving health. Such therapies include herbal medicine, aromatherapy, homeopathy, acupuncture/acupressure, massage (various kinds, from head to toes), reflexology, osteopathy, chiropractic, Reiki, hypnotherapy and yoga.

The use of CAM by the public is increasing in the United Kingdom, despite little scientific evidence to support the effectiveness of many treatments or therapies. Estimates suggest between 20 and 75 per cent of all adults in developed countries use at least one type of complementary medicine or treatment each year.

CAM AND THE BIOMEDICAL MODEL

CAM represents a challenge to the evidence-based biomedical model. Ernst (2009) refers to CAM as pseudo medicine, and sees it as unscientific nonsense, using pseudo-scientific language such as vitalism, energy, integrative medicine, balance, toxins and detoxification, and immune-boosting to give a scientific gloss to sell unproven CAM

More and more people are turning to alternative and complementary medicines and treatments, such as (shown here) Reiki, yoga, spiritual healing, and acupuncture. How might sociologists explain this?

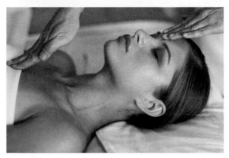
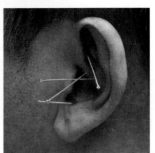

therapies to the public. He suggests clinical trials provide little evidence that CAM works or cures diseases, and that judgements on the safety and effectiveness of treatments should be based on scientific evidence. Ernst suggests that any positive effects of CAM arise because of the placebo effect – whereby patients are given drug-free tablets or sham surgery or other therapies with no real treatment, and their medical condition improves only because they believe their condition will improve. Ernst suggests CAM involves, as Toynbee (2004) put it, 'trusting to remedies from days when children died in droves, women were ripped apart in labour and no one lived long' (cited in Ernst, p. 300). Despite this, CAM is being taken more seriously by some of the medical profession. For example, according to a survey of GPs by the General Medical Council (GMC), nearly half of GPs arrange acupuncture for their patients, while 79 per cent think it should be available on the NHS. There are currently five NHS homeopathic hospitals, and over 400 medical GPs are also members of the Faculty of Homeopathy. The House of Commons Science and Technology Committee (2010) and the Department of Health (2010) have both considered the usefulness of CAM, and there are clinical trials being conducted on the effectiveness of homeopathy and other CAM treatments. Increasingly, there is a blurring of the distinction between the science-based biomedical model and the social model of health of which CAM is a part.

CAM AND POSTMODERNISM

Ernst sees the emergence and growing popularity of CAM as a product of postmodernist thinking, in particular postmodernist dismissals of science and the biomedical approach as metanarratives or grand theories. Postmodernists argue that scientific evidence is just one among other competing types of evidence, which are all of equal value although they can be interpreted in different ways and are based on different assumptions. Ernst argues that those who practise and use CAM clearly have different beliefs about health, illness and the body, and about the nature of the healing process, from those of scientific medicine, but these beliefs do not identify effective cures for diseases.

CAM AND THE POWER OF THE MEDICAL PROFESSION

The power and status of doctors has rested on their scientific and medical expertise and control over decisions about healthcare, approved treatments and medicines, but this power is being challenged as more people are choosing either to reject scientific medicine or to opt for additional unproven CAM. There are many common diseases, mostly chronic, for which new drugs and surgical interventions have failed to provide outcomes that are satisfactory for many patients. This partly reflects the fact that the medical gaze of doctors using the biomedical approach cannot cure some conditions, such as various forms of arthritis, lower back pain, asthma, allergies, depression, irritable bowel syndrome, stress and some forms of cancer. Some conventional treatments can also have distressing side-effects. People are becoming less trusting of doctors' treatments and decision-making, and turning to CAM to replace or supplement conventional medical treatments.

CAM AND CONSUMER CHOICE

Although CAM often lacks or has only limited scientific evidence to back up its claims, and most of the mainstream medical profession is fairly scathing about its benefits, more people are exercising their choices as consumers of health and opting for CAM. The House of Lords Science and Technology Committee (2000) reported a series of surveys showing that consumer choice of CAM is often based on a mixture of the points considered above. For example, some choose it because they have exhausted orthodox medical treatments, and find CAM helps or relieves injuries or conditions when conventional medicine has failed. Some choose it because they do not believe conventional medicine works, and no longer have faith in scientific solutions, or have anxiety about their health and choose CAM as a preventive measure. Others use it as part of lifestyle choices – because they like it, find it relaxing, want to explore other ways of life or medical systems, or the more spiritual/paranormal dimensions of life. Some may choose CAM because it's fashionable, and having an alternative therapist (for those who can afford it) is seen as cool, for example having massages and aromatherapy to treat stress in their daily lives. Whatever the reasons, CAM is growing in popularity. Swayne (2009), in a response to Ernst, notes that there is some shaky evidence for much conventional medicine as well as CAM, and using the biomedical approach may not always be appropriate in patient care. Swayne suggests that something can be learned by medical practitioners from CAM's unorthodox approaches, which may complement the achievements of scientific medicine and enhance patient well-being.

Exam-style questions

1 Explain what is meant by the term 'sick role'. *(2 marks)*

2 Explain what is meant by the term 'altruism'. *(2 marks)*

3 Suggest **three** reasons why the medical profession may be losing power and influence over its patients. *(6 marks)*

4 Suggest **three** ways in which there is growing consumer choice in healthcare. *(6 marks)*

5 Outline some of the ways in which the medical profession might be seen as agents of social control. *(12 marks)*

6 Outline some of the reasons for the superior incomes, power and status of doctors. *(12 marks)*

7 Assess the functionalist view of the medical profession. *(20 marks)*

8 Assess the view that there is a growing medicalization of society, including deviance. *(20 marks)*

Topic 6

SPECIFICATION AREA

The application of sociological research methods to the study of health

---

Note to students

This topic assumes that chapter 5, on sociological research methods, has already been studied. If you haven't yet covered chapter 5, you are advised to return to this topic once you have done so.

The aim of this topic is to get you to think about how to apply your knowledge and understanding of the research methods and types of data discussed in chapter 5 to researching *particular* issues in health, and to consider some of the practical, ethical and theoretical (PET) issues that might arise in health research.

You should be aware that for the Methods-in-Context question, you will not gain many marks if you simply discuss methods in general, such as the strengths or weaknesses of interviews. You must apply what you know to the specific health context, characteristics of the people or situation involved, and to the particular research topic that the question asks about.

Methods in context: researching health

Activity

Suggest one research method that might produce *quantitative* information and one that might produce *qualitative* information, in each of the following cases. In each case, give two reasons for choosing that method, and explain how valid and reliable you think the information provided might be in relation to the specific topic mentioned.

a) the relationship between gender and access to healthcare
b) ethnic inequalities in health
c) how satisfied patients are with their GP
d) the interaction between doctors and patients in a hospital ward
e) the distribution and nature of mental illness
f) the stigma attached to some health conditions

THE RESEARCH CONTEXT OF HEALTH

Access to closed settings

Research in health settings, and particularly hospitals, nursing homes, clinics and GP surgeries, poses particular practical problems because these are *closed settings* where access is restricted. Obtaining access to these and similar locations for research purposes would require permission from managers, administrators, medical professionals and possibly patients. Obtaining such access and informed consent may not be easy. It is difficult to conduct research within health self-help groups, such as Alcoholics

Anonymous, mainly because of the anonymity and confidentiality upon which these insist, and consequent difficulties of identifying suitable comparison groups.

Ethical issues

Ethical issues are always of great concern in health-related research, as the state of people's health is often a very personal and private matter. Unhealthy people are often quite vulnerable and may find that questions about their own or their family's health cause them anxiety. So care and sensitivity is needed in such research.

The duty of care, confidentiality and professional code of ethics

- Medical professionals, such as doctors and nurses, have to maintain proper ethical standards, and have a *duty of care* to their patients. This means they have a legal obligation to take reasonable care to ensure their safety and welfare, and avoid acts that might harm them, both physically and psychologically. This responsibility might well involve protecting vulnerable patients from sociological researchers. As discussed in the previous topic, medical professionals, particularly doctors, have a professional code of ethics, which includes protecting the confidentiality of private information about the health status of patients. Medical staff are very likely to face disciplinary action, both by their employers and by their regulatory bodies, such as the General Medical Council (GMC) for doctors, or the Nursing and Midwifery Council (NMC) for nurses and midwives, and may potentially face the risk of losing their jobs and being banned from practising if they reveal patient information to unauthorized personnel.
- Sociological researchers too have a moral or ethical duty of care, if not a legal one, and ethical issues are always of great concern in health-related research, especially with people who are very vulnerable because of their illnesses.

Informed consent   Any research involving medical staff or patients would require their informed consent. This may be difficult to obtain from seriously ill patients, who may be too ill either to understand the nature of the research or to be bothered with any involvement, and to give their informed consent. Vulnerable patients may feel pressured to participate to please medical professionals, or those suffering from mental illnesses or mental disability may not be able to reasonably give informed consent.

Intrusive and harmful effects   Issues like the health of patients may be very sensitive or personal. People may find researchers' questions or observations intrusive and threatening, and even raising the issues may have harmful consequences, causing stress and feelings of guilt and anxiety. For example, patients having stigmatized or sensitive illnesses like HIV, sexually transmitted diseases or mental illnesses may be very reluctant to discuss them, or have them revealed to others. Confidentiality and the protection of the identity of individuals and institutions is particularly important in such circumstances.

Medical hierarchies

Clinical settings tend to have hierarchical arrangements, with a top-down authority structure, ranging from hospital consultants down to junior doctors, hospital matrons down to nursing auxiliaries, or GPs down to nursing assistants, with similar hierarchies in administration. Even if access is granted by senior staff, it doesn't necessarily mean that any junior staff involved will have agreed to cooperate, let alone patients. This hierarchy also means that medical or administrative staff may not necessarily be willing to risk their positions by a free expression of opinion, such as by divulging information about the 'darker side' of hospital care, or medical practices. 'Whistleblowers' in the NHS, who reveal clinical shortcomings and failings, or dishonesty, risk disciplinary action and possibly dismissal. Such factors might well influence the validity and extent of some kinds of sociological research. An example of the consequences of such whistle-blowing was consultant paediatrician Dr Kim Holt, who blew the whistle in 2006 on St Anne's clinic in Haringey, in north London. She pointed out that unsafe practices, such as understaffing and poor record keeping, posed a serious risk to patients' safety. Bosses ignored her warnings and removed her from the clinic, with tragic consequences months later. You can read more about this case and whistleblowing in the NHS at www.patientsfirst.org.uk/.

Medical settings are busy workplaces

Many medical settings are very busy institutions. Medical staff have to work hard in patient care, often dealing with many conditions that are distressing for them as well as the patients, and they may well be unwilling to take on the additional commitment involved in being the subject of sociological research.

Public image, professionalism and the Hawthorne effect

In a growing climate of competition in healthcare, healthcare institutions have to maintain an image of high-quality care and a strong professional ethos, if they do not wish to risk losing patients and the income they provide. This means they may try to put on an act to impress researchers. Doctors and nurses, particularly, have to maintain a professional image, such as being caring, sensitive, patient and listening and responding to patient needs – summed up perhaps as having a good bedside manner. No doubt doctors and nurses get as irritated and annoyed with patients as we all do at times in all walks of life, but they are unlikely to show this in front of researchers. These matters, and the medical hierarchy issues considered above, may create a *Hawthorne effect* that raises potential problems with the validity of any findings.

Activity

1 Suggest three ethical issues that sociological researchers might face if they wished to conduct research in a psychiatric hospital.
2 Suggest two features of the professional role of medical personnel that might influence the validity of sociological research. In each case explain carefully how the features you identify might have this affect.

USING EXPERIMENTS

- The use of the experimental method to show, for example, how medical staff come to label mental illness, as in the example of Rosenhan's research (see pages 518 and 547–8) risks undermining the professional roles and responsibilities of medical staff, and their duty of care to patients – for example by misleading them by suggesting some patients were faking their illnesses. Rosenhan's research showed that some people suffering from real mental illness were wrongly identified as faking their illnesses, undermining potential treatment.
- The experimental method involves treating one group differently from another. When dealing with people suffering from health problems, this can create ethical

issues over whether such experiments may have harmful effects on those involved in the experiments.

- The ethics of sociological research should involve informed consent. There is the question of whether vulnerable sick patients are really able to give informed consent. Even if such informed consent can be obtained, the very fact of obtaining such consent may change the behaviour of patients involved in the experiment, undermining the validity of any findings. Not obtaining such consent, or misleading participants into giving it, breaches ethical guidelines.
- The Hawthorne effect may arise through the very presence of researchers in a medical setting. The researchers may be seen as a threat by medical professionals, or by patients, altering their normal behaviour.
- Experiments in health research are in varying degrees artificial situations, so the findings of an experiment may not reflect situations, experiences or behaviour in real-life health contexts, or how people deal with health matters in their daily lives.
- Experimental situations generally involve testing hypotheses by attempting to isolate one or two variables. However, health issues involve a complex range of factors, and the experiment risks over-simplifying causes and thereby undermining the validity of research. For example, people's health may be influenced by a wide range of genetic, environmental and social factors.

USING CONTENT ANALYSIS

- Content analysis of publications like newspapers and magazines, or television news and entertainment shows, can give medical professionals insight into public knowledge of, or attitudes towards, a health topic, and can help in designing methods to tackle public health problems.
- This may assist health researchers in assessing whether public health education has succeeded in changing the public's thinking or approach to a problem.
- Many people become aware of health-related information through the media, and content analysis might be used to study systematically health-related information – for example by analysing the space in print media, or TV time, related to health issues; by studying what messages and information readers and viewers are given about health, and whether such information is accurate; by examining whether media content is used to inform people, or to provide sensationalized health scare stories aimed at attracting readers and viewers.
- Content analysis of letters of complaint to hospitals or GPs may reveal an underlying pattern, showing there are similar problems affecting a number of patients, enabling the identification of wider problems affecting the institutions concerned.

USING OFFICIAL STATISTICS AND OTHER SECONDARY SOURCES

This chapter has already referred to a range of quantitative data used to analyse health, for instance morbidity statistics, such as those on the extent of heart disease, and mortality (death) statistics, like the infant mortality rate or deaths from cancer. These are collected from sources such as:

- the number of consultations with GPs.
- hospital admissions.
- sickness absence from work.

- death certificates (which also record causes of death).
- national surveys on health, such as the *Health Survey for England*, the *GP Patient Survey*, the *National Survey of NHS patients*, and other national surveys that include health-related questions, like the *General Lifestyle Survey* and the ten-yearly census.
- longitudinal surveys, like those mentioned above, which are repeated on a regular basis to build up a picture of how health and related issues are changing over time.

Uses

Official statistics on measures of health, like morbidity (extent of disease), mortality (deaths), vaccinations, flu cases and accidents are collected on a regular annual or more frequent basis from hospitals and GP surgeries, and deaths are legally required to be registered. Such statistics are therefore usually representative and reliable, and this can save sociological researchers time and money. Comparisons between different groups and identification of changes over time are possible.

Problems and limitations

- The categories used to collect these statistics may not be those required by sociologists. For example, statistics are not often collected on the basis of social class, and there may be difficulties in the measurements used, such as health measured by absence from work due to (alleged) illness.
- There may be issues about the *validity* of indicators used, such as whether health statistics are really just social constructions arising through doctor–patient interaction, and other limitations of health statistics (see pages 460–1). These raise more general questions about the *validity* of some quantitative data derived from surveys in providing a true picture of the health of the population.
- There may be ethical issues relating to the use of personal documents on health, such as personal medical records. There needs to be constant vigilance to ensure ethical guidelines are followed, and informed consent is given.

Activity

1 Suggest two reasons in each case why the following statistics might not provide completely valid information about the health of a country:
   (a) the number of times people consult their GPs
   (b) the number of cases of self-reported illness
   (c) the number of deaths from heart disease (or other causes)
   (d) the number of days lost at work due to sickness
   (e) the number of incidents of food poisoning in different areas
   (f) the number of people suffering from a mental illness
2 In the light of your answers to the above activity, in each case suggest two steps that social researchers might take to improve the validity of the statistics, explaining carefully why the steps you suggest might achieve this.

USING SURVEYS

Surveys are the main means of collecting health data, and much of this is gathered by the government, which has the resources and legal powers to carry out wide-scale, national research, with large and representative samples. Depending on whether the aim is to collect quantitative or more qualitative data, these surveys use various forms of question-

Some sources of quantitative data on health: extract from 2011 Census form; Health Survey for England; GP Patient Survey

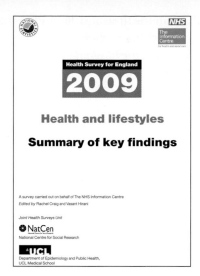

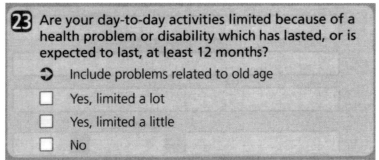

naires and interviews, and a range of different ways of collecting the data – such as group discussions, focus groups, structured, semi-structured and unstructured face-to-face or telephone interviews, and postal or internet-based self-completion questionnaires.

As discussed in chapter 5, there are always questions to be raised about the reliability, validity and representativeness of quantitative data derived from surveys. While data derived from large surveys like the *Health Survey for England*, or the *GP Patient Survey*, might provide comprehensive and representative data, smaller surveys may not necessarily do so.

USING QUESTIONNAIRES

Uses

Questionnaires might be used on a wide range of health issues, such as the public's attitudes to health matters, and patients' attitudes to healthcare and services provided by GP surgeries and hospitals. The anonymity and detachment of questionnaires, particularly if identity protection and confidentiality can be guaranteed, may be of benefit in overcoming embarrassment or apprehensiveness when exploring highly personal or sensitive issues, such as stigmatized illnesses like sexually transmitted diseases, HIV or mental illness.

Problems and limitations

- Health settings are busy places, and medical professionals have a duty of care to patients. They may therefore be reluctant to grant permission for questionnaires to be distributed, given the time and disruption they may involve and the need to protect the interests of those in their care.

- Sensitivity is needed with the language used in questionnaires. Health matters relate to a wide diversity of people, some of whom will have poor literacy skills, and will need to have very simple language used, with short questions, which may limit the amount and depth of information obtained.

- English may not be the home language of patients seeking access to healthcare. This may make it necessary to use a variety of languages in questionnaires, or to adopt an alternative method, like interviews using interviewers of the same ethnic group as the interviewee.

- Questionnaires in health contexts will often need official approval, and vulnerable patients may feel obliged to complete them, even if they regard them as an unwanted imposition, intrusive or threatening, and may therefore not treat them seriously; others may feel they should be very positive in their responses, as they feel indebted to those looking after them. Such factors may undermine the validity of responses to health questionnaires in some contexts.

- While those managing institutions like hospitals are often able to provide informed consent for questionnaire research to take place, this doesn't necessarily mean those actually asked to complete the questionnaires have similarly consented. Some people, especially the less educated, may simply not have a sufficient grasp of what the research is about, or enough interest in it, to give proper *informed* consent.

- Professionals like doctors and nurses often have stressed and busy working lives, and may simply not have the time or inclination to fill in questionnaires, particularly as they often have a lot of other required paperwork to complete. This may mean voluntary questionnaires get a low response rate.

Activity

Postal questionnaires on children's dental health

Postal questionnaires were used in a 2003 Department of Health 'Children's Dental Health' survey. This was based on a representative sample of 12,698 children aged between 5 and 15, attending schools in the UK. The sample was first asked to take part in a dental examination at school, and then questionnaires were sent by post to parents to collect background data on their children's oral hygiene and dental care, with a response rate of 61 per cent.

What problems might there be with the validity of parents' answers to questions about their children's oral hygiene and dental care?

USING INTERVIEWS

Uses

Interviews, particularly unstructured interviews, can be useful to gain the trust and confidences of doctors and patients in health settings. They can be used to gain insights into the private views of medical professionals. They are useful for exploring how far people really adopt healthy lifestyles or to get them talking about their experiences of ill-health and disease. Interviews may also help to overcome difficulties with using self-completion questionnaires to ask questions about health matters of those having literacy difficulties or whose main language is not English.

Unstructured interviews, particularly, can be a useful method to explore sensitive and private issues with vulnerable patients, by seeking to put them at ease in a relaxed, informal situation. By developing empathy with the respondent, it may be possible to draw out their feelings, opinions and confidences, and get them talking more honestly and openly about issues like the nature of their illnesses and how they cope with them, how they affect their relationships with others, and their feelings about the healthcare they receive. The building of trust in well-executed unstructured interviews can be particularly useful for gaining insights when exploring sensitive issues, like stigmatized illnesses such as mental illness or sexually transmitted diseases.

Problems and limitations

- Health settings require permission before research can be conducted. This means interviewers may be identified with authority figures like medical staff, with consequent risks to the validity of the responses, as people may not wish to give too honest or critical answers to those they associate with authority, or about those who may be providing their care.
- The personal characteristics of interviewers may influence the success and validity of interviews. For example, white interviewers investigating health matters in minority ethnic groups may not get as much cooperation or have the same perception of what counts as health and illness in an ethnic group as an interviewer from the same ethnic group, who may also be able to conduct interviews in the respondents' first language. Male researchers may not be able to develop the same rapport with women as a female interviewer might, and this could be particularly significant in relation to health matters.
- Interviews on sensitive issues may be seen as intrusive or threatening by those being interviewed. For example, parents may feel threatened by interviewers asking about their children's diet or dental hygiene. Patients may see questions about their health, asked by someone other than a medical professional, as intrusive and unwarranted prying into their personal lives, and they may experience embarrassment or fear exposure and a breach of confidentiality if they have stigmatized diseases like mental illness, sexually transmitted diseases or AIDS.

USING NON-PARTICIPANT AND PARTICIPANT OBSERVATION

Observational research methods like non-participant and participant observation are less commonly used in government-funded research, but have been used to great effect by health researchers wishing to adopt a more interpretivist approach. Rosenhan's research, discussed on pages 518 and 547–8, used participant observation in psychiatric hospitals to gain insights into how medical professionals labelled and responded to symptoms of mental illness. This was also a form of field experiment, as it involved patients faking their symptoms.

Some problems associated with observational techniques in health settings might include:

- Doctors and other medical professionals will experience pressure to maintain a professional image when being observed, meaning they may not behave as they normally do when they are not being observed. This *Hawthorne effect* may affect the validity of any findings.
- The personal characteristics of the researcher, such as their age, ethnicity and gender, and professional qualifications, are likely to influence the practical

possibility of being able to carry out participant observation in health settings. For example, a white male investigating women's health is unlikely to be able to observe or participate with a group of women, particularly Asian women. An observer wishing to investigate stress among junior hospital doctors by becoming a participant observer and passing him- or herself off as a doctor is unlikely to have the skills or qualifications to do so, and there are also the ethical and criminal implications involved in pretending to be a doctor, particularly if involved with patient care.

- As in interviews, researchers may be identified by patients as authority figures, especially if adopting an overt role, undermining the validity of any findings.
- Medical settings like hospitals or GP surgeries may be difficult to access – gaining access will require permission, and issues of patient confidentiality, as well as the interruption of busy everyday routines, may mean this is refused.

Activity

How would you set about a participant observation study of a hospital ward? Make a list of the things you would need to consider. For example, what kind of observer role might you adopt (overt or covert)? How would you get in and stay in? What steps would you take to ensure your research was valid? What ethical issues would you need to consider?

Activity

A good way to understand how research methods apply to health issues is to carry out your own small piece of research, perhaps on no more than five or six people.

1 Form a hypothesis or a question you wish to find answers to.
2 Devise a suitable sample and a research method appropriate to your aim or hypothesis.
3 Draw up a short questionnaire, interview schedule or whatever else is needed.
4 Carry out your research.
5 Do a careful analysis of the strengths and weaknesses of your research, including your findings. If you are in a group, you could criticize one another's surveys. Topics could be anything health-related, such as:
   - whether there are any differences between men and women in how they experience health and illness (or you could do differences between social class, ethnic or age groups).
   - whether there are differences in the health of people from richer and poorer areas of your town or city.

- how social class, gender, lifestyle, people's occupations, poverty, ethnicity or other material and cultural factors affect health.
- people's attitudes to mental illness.

6 Suggest a suitable method for studying each of the following topics, and explain in each case why it might be suitable:
- the relationship between people's work and their state of health.
- the effects of 'healthy food' labelling on people's choice of food.
- what people expect from their GP.
- whether government health promotion campaigns, like '5-a-Day', 'Couch to 5k', 10,000 steps, and other physical fitness campaigns, Alcohol Awareness and Stop Smoking, are effective in improving the health of the nation (see some campaigns below, but the whole range of campaigns can be explored at www.nhs.uk/LiveWell).

How might researchers find out whether health promotion campaigns like these are effective?

EXAMPLES OF RESEARCH

The following examples of research and research methods, and the activities relating to them, aim to get you thinking about how research methods are applied to some real-world issues in health research.

Food Scares and Food Safety, 2005 (Food Standards Agency)

This research explored changing consumer attitudes and perceptions towards food, food risks and food scares, who consumers would trust to provide reliable information and advice on food and food scares, and other food-related matters.

Eight group discussions and twenty short qualitative open-ended interviews were conducted among members of the public who had sole or joint responsibility for buying food. The discussions were held in Birmingham, London and Leeds, with groups made up from different social class, age and ethnic groups, with both single and mixed-sex groups. The interviews were held in Luton with seven men and thirteen women, from different age groups, social class and ethnic backgrounds.

The Health Survey for England (The NHS Information Centre)

The Health Survey for England is a series of annual surveys that began in 1991. It aims to provide regular information on various aspects of the nation's health. The first surveys used a nationally representative sample of those aged 16 and over living in private households in England. Children aged 2–15 were first included in 1995, and since 2001 infants under 2 have also been included. The survey therefore covers a complete cross-section of the whole population, including people of different ages and states of health, living in different areas and from differing backgrounds.

Clinical measurements, like blood pressure, blood samples, saliva and urine samples are taken by specially trained nurses from selected people who have given their consent, and they also ask additional clinical-based questions. In 2009, individual face-to-face computer-assisted interviews were held with 4,645 adults aged over 16, and 3,957 children aged 0–15. Parents of those under 11 were asked about their children's health, with the children present where possible so they could comment if they wished.

Questions were asked on a range of topics, such as general health, alcohol consumption, smoking, fruit and vegetable consumption, and use of complementary and alternative medicine. All those over the age of 8 were also asked to fill in a booklet (a self-completion questionnaire) on health issues related to their age group.

The Mental Health of Children and Young People in Great Britain, 2004 (Department of Health and the Scottish Executive)

This survey explored the type and extent of mental illness among 5- to 16-year-olds in Britain. There were 7,977 interviews conducted, covering 76 per cent of the children contacted. Teachers nominated by the parents were contacted via a postal questionnaire, with 83 per cent returning them. Face-to-face structured interviews with parents were used, but these were supplemented by open-ended questions to parents when symptoms of mental illness in children had been identified in the structured questions. This enabled parents to describe the problem in their own words. Additional information was collected by a five-minute self-completion questionnaire. Parents, mostly mothers, were interviewed first, and then, if they and their children gave their permission, their 11- to 16-year-old children were interviewed face-to-face. Questions about the young people's smoking, drinking and drug-taking experiences were recorded via a self-completion questionnaire on a laptop. It was thought by the researchers to be very important for children and parents to be interviewed separately and alone.

Activity

1 Identify *three* research methods that are used in the mental health survey above.
2 Suggest *two* reasons why questions about the young people's smoking, drinking and drug-taking experiences were recorded via a self-completion questionnaire on a laptop rather than by the interviewer.
3 Suggest *two* reasons why the researchers thought 'it was . . . very important for children and parents to be interviewed separately and alone'.
4 Suggest *three* possible problems with the use of postal questionnaires sent to teachers to find out about the mental health of their pupils.
5 Identify all the people who might have to give their consent for this research to be carried out.
6 Identity *two* steps taken that show the researchers were aware of ethical issues in conducting this research.
7 Suggest at least *two* further pieces of information you would need in order to evaluate whether the survey above was representative.
8 Suggest *two* factors that may influence the validity of the findings of the research above.

Being Sane in Insane Places' (Rosenhan, 1973)

Rosenhan, in 1972, was interested in discovering how the staff of twelve mental hospitals in the United States made sense of perfectly sane 'patients' who, unknown to staff, faked the symptoms of the mental illness schizophrenia. Eight sane people prepared themselves by not washing, shaving or cleaning their teeth for five days before going to the hospitals. All were diagnosed as schizophrenics and admitted to hospital. None of the pseudo-patients really believed that they would be admitted so easily. Once there, they behaved normally, for instance speaking to patients and staff as they would ordinarily, and doing what they were told and taking (though secretly not swallowing) prescribed medicines. They told the staff they were feeling absolutely fine whenever they were asked, and that they experienced no symptoms. All the pseudo-patients were perfectly healthy, and their main worry was over whether they would be embarrassed at being exposed as frauds. They were nonetheless kept in hospital for many days.

Exam-style question

The Methods-in-Context question, included in the Section B: Health with Research Methods question in Unit 2, involves a stimulus item, followed by a question about the strengths and limitations of one of two research methods for exploring the issue. The following is a typical example.

Item D

Investigating gender and mental health

Around one in six British adults is thought to have a common mental disorder or illness, such as depression, stress, panic attacks or anxiety, though official statistics and surveys suggest these affect women more than men.

Gender differences in recorded mental illness may be because men wish to present a strong masculine identity, demonstrating things like strength, independence and lack of vulnerability, and are reluctant to undermine this by admitting to mental illness, and so are more likely than women to conceal symptoms from doctors and researchers.

This assertion of masculinity can make use of qualitative research methods to explore men's mental health difficult. For example, focus groups, group interviews or one-to-one interviews may not uncover valid information, especially if those participating think others are monitoring or judging their masculinity.

Using material from **Item D** and elsewhere, assess the strengths and limitations of **one** of the following methods for investigating gender differences in mental health:

EITHER self-completion questionnaires

OR unstructured interviews   *(20 marks)*

CHAPTER SUMMARY AND REVISION CHECKLIST

After studying this chapter, you should be able to:

- explain what is meant by 'the human body is a social construction'.

- explain what is meant by health, illness, disease and disability, and how they are socially constructed.

- describe and explain the differences between the biomedical and social models of health, and assess both.

- explain what is meant by iatrogenesis.

- identify and explain a range of social factors which influence health and disease.

- explain what is meant by 'diseases of affluence' and why they have emerged.

- identify some problems with health statistics, their social construction and their limitations for measuring the extent of health and illness.

- outline functionalist, Marxist, feminist, interactionist and postmodernist contributions to the study of health.

- explain how inequality may affect health, including the social gradient in health, social cohesion and status syndrome.

- describe and explain social class, gender and ethnic inequalities and differences in health chances, including artefact, natural/social selection, cultural and material/structural explanations, and identify some policies to tackle health inequalities.

- identify and explain some regional and international inequalities in health.

- identify and explain a range of inequalities in the provision of healthcare, including those related to geography, social class, funding, private healthcare, the effects of changes in the NHS, and Marxist, pluralist and structuralist explanations.

- explain what is meant by the 'inverse care law'.

- identify and explain a range of inequalities in demand for and access to healthcare, including the reasons why some people may seek medical or psychiatric help while others may not, and differences based around social class, gender, ethnicity, disability and age.

- describe and assess different sociological approaches to the study of mental illness, including social realist, structuralist and labelling approaches, and the view that it might be seen as a social construction.

- identify and explain the social pattern of mental illness relating to social class, gender and ethnicity.

- examine the variety of ways in which the medical profession has power in society, including the functionalist view of professionalism, and criticisms of it, and the role of medicine and medical professionals in social control.

- explain and assess the 'sick role', and identify its rights and obligations.

- describe and explain what is meant by the medicalization of society, including deviance.

- outline and explain a range of ways in which the power and influence of doctors in society are being eroded.

- outline the ways in which the approach to health and healthcare is moving away from the biomedical model towards a more consumer-centred and social model, including competing views of complementary and alternative medicine.

- apply research methods to the study of particular issues in health.

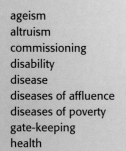

KEY TERMS

(these are already defined in the text, and may also be found in the glossary at the end of the book)

ageism	health chances	medical gaze	secondary deviance
altruism	iatrogenesis	medicalization	self-fulfilling prophecy
commissioning	illness	morbidity	sick role
disability	impairment	mortality	social cohesion
disease	inverse care law	mortality rate	social construction
diseases of affluence	life course	mortification	status syndrome
diseases of poverty	life expectancy	pluralism	stigma
gate-keeping	marketization	primary deviance	stigmatized identity
health	master status	privatization	universalistic values

There are a variety of free tests and other activities that can be used to assess your learning at

www.politybooks.com/browne

EXAM QUESTION

Answer **all** the questions from this Section

Section B: Health with Research Methods

You are advised to spend approximately 50 minutes on Questions ☐1☐0 to ☐1☐3

You are advised to spend approximately 30 minutes on Question ☐1☐4

You are advised to spend approximately 40 minutes on Questions ☐1☐5 to ☐1☐8

Time allowed: 2 hours   **Total for this section: 90 marks**

Health

Read **Item C** below and answer questions ☐1☐0 to ☐1☐3 that follow.

Item C

The biomedical model of health sees good health as the absence of disease. Ill-health is seen as individuals having random attacks of disease with identifiable biological or physical causes. Doctors apply their expert medical knowledge and technology to diagnose the disease, and treat and cure it through medical or surgical treatments. The main aim of medical professionals and health care systems, like the National Health Service, is therefore to diagnose and tackle these physical symptoms. Scientific medicine is seen as the way to solve health problems, with intervention by trained medical personnel, medical technology, operating theatres, drugs and so on. Medicine is seen as in itself a 'good thing', and the more of it there is, the better people's health will be. Some criticize the medical model for not recognising that social factors are involved in both defining health and the causes of ill-health.

---

1 0   Explain what is meant by the term 'life expectancy'.   *(2 marks)*

1 1   Identify **three** reasons why health statistics may not provide a true picture of a country's health.   *(6 marks)*

1 2   Outline some of the reasons why not all sections of society have equal access to health care in the UK.   *(12 marks)*

1 3   Using material from **Item C** and elsewhere, assess the approach of the biomedical model to improving a country's health.   *(20 marks)*

Methods in Context

This question requires you to **apply** your knowledge and understanding of sociological research methods to the study of this **particular** issue in **health**.

Read **Item D** below and answer the question that follows.

Item D

Investigating what patients want from their GPs

The Department of Health's GP Patient Survey in 2012 surveyed about three million patients. Those surveyed were selected at random from a list of all patients who were registered with a GP in England in the six months before the survey.

The survey used a postal questionnaire, and asked about patients' experience of access to GPs at their practices and practice opening hours, how often they attended their GP practice, the quality of care received, and patients' age, gender and ethnicity. Although the GP Patient Survey questions provided detailed information, the questions were not comprehensive and some had a yes/no-style format. This meant that the results did not always provide GP practices with all the information they may have needed to know about patient preferences or needs.

| 1 | 4 | Using material from **Item D** and elsewhere, assess the strengths and limitations of one of the following methods for investigating what patients want from their GPs:

EITHER   postal questionnaires
OR   unstructured interviews   *(20 marks)*

Research Methods

These questions permit you to draw examples from **any areas** of sociology with which you are familiar.

| 1 | 5 | Explain what is meant by the term 'primary data'.   *(2 marks)*

| 1 | 6 | Suggest **two** sampling methods that sociologists might use, **apart from** random sampling.   *(4 marks)*

| 1 | 7 | Suggest **two** reasons why sociologists might use official statistics.   *(4 marks)*

| 1 | 8 | Examine the problems sociologists may find when using face-to-face structured interviews in their research.   *(20 marks)*

Glossary

Words in blue within entries refer to terms found elsewhere in the glossary.

absolute poverty   Poverty defined as lacking the minimum requirements necessary to maintain human health. *See also* relative poverty.

achieved status   Status which is achieved through an individual's own efforts. *See also* ascribed status.

ageing population   A population in which the average age is getting higher, with a greater proportion of the population over retirement age, and a smaller proportion of young people.

ageism   Stereotyping, prejudice and discrimination against individuals or groups on the grounds of their age.

altruism   Behaviour that is motivated by an unselfish concern for the welfare of others.

anti-school subculture   A group organized around a set of values, attitudes and behaviour in opposition to the main aims of a school.

arranged marriage   A marriage which is arranged by the parents of the marriage partners, with a view to compatibility of background and status. More a union between two families than between two people, and romantic love between the marriage partners is not necessarily present.

ascribed status   Status which is given to an individual at birth and usually can't be changed. *See also* achieved status.

banding   A means of ensuring the pupil intake of schools has a spread of pupils drawn from all ability bands. It is also commonly used as an alternative word for streaming in schools, whereby students are divided into groups of similar ability (bands or streams) in which they stay for all subjects. *See also* streaming.

beanpole family   A multi-generation extended family, in a pattern which is long and thin, with fewer aunts, uncles and cousins, reflecting fewer children being born in each generation, but people living longer.

birth rate   The number of live births per 1,000 of the population per year.

bisexuality   A sexual orientation or sexual attraction towards people of both sexes.

bourgeoisie   In Marxist theory (see Marxism), the class of owners of the means of production.

bricolage   The use of readily available ordinary objects to create something new. For example, in the study of youth culture, it refers to the use of everyday items like bin liners, safety pins and toilet chains, and habits like spitting, to create a new distinctive Punk identity.

capitalists   The social class of owners of the means of production in industrial societies, whose primary purpose is to make profits.

cereal packet family   The stereotype of the ideal family found in the mass media and advertising. It is generally seen as involving first-time married parents and their own natural children, living together, with the father as the primary breadwinner and the mother as primarily concerned with the home and children.

class conflict   The conflict that arises between different social classes. It is generally used to describe the conflict between the bourgeoisie and proletariat in Marxist views of society (*See also* Marxism).

class consciousness   An awareness in members of a social class of their real interests. *See also* false consciousness.

classic extended family   A family where several related nuclear families or family members live in the same house, street or area. It may be horizontally extended, where it contains aunts, uncles, cousins, etc., or vertically extended, where it contains more than two generations. *See also* modified extended family.

commissioning   In the National Health Service, the process of assessing the health needs of the local population, and organizing the delivery of health services by the NHS or private healthcare companies to meet these needs.

commubes   Self-contained and self-supporting communities, where all members of the community share property, childcare, household tasks and living accommodation.

communism   An equal society, without social classes or class conflict, in which the means of production are the common property of all.

compensatory education   Extra educational help for those coming from disadvantaged groups to help them overcome the inequalities they face in the education system and the wider society.

conjugal roles   The roles played by a male and female partner in marriage or in a cohabiting couple.

consumption property   Wealth for use by the owner, such as consumer goods like fridges, cars, or a home that you own, which do not produce any income. *See also* productive property.

counter-school subculture   A group organized around a set of values, attitudes and behaviour in opposition to the main aims of a school.

covert role   Where the researcher in a participant observation study keeps her or his identity as a researcher concealed from the group being studied. *See also* overt role.

cultural capital   The knowledge, education, language, attitudes and values, and network of social contacts and lifestyle possessed by the upper and upper middle class which give students who possess them an in-built advantage in a middle-class-controlled education system. Associated with the French Marxist Bourdieu (*see* Marxism). *See also* habitus.

cultural deprivation   The idea that some young people fail in education because of supposed cultural deficiencies in their home and family background, such as inadequate socialization, failings in pre-school learning, inadequate language skills and inappropriate attitudes and values.

culture   The language, beliefs, values and norms, customs, roles, knowledge and skills which combine to make up the way of life of any society.

culture clash   A difference and conflict between the cultural values of the home and those of educational institutions. *See also* culture.

culture of hybridity   A culture that is a 'mix' of two or more other cultures, creating a new culture (a hybrid).

culture of poverty   A set of beliefs and values thought to exist among the poor which prevents them escaping from poverty.

customs   Norms which have existed for a long time.

cycle of deprivation   An explanation of how one aspect of poverty, such as poor housing, can lead to further poverty, such as poor health, building up into a cycle which makes it difficult for the poor to escape from poverty.

death rate   (sometimes referred to as the crude death rate) The number of deaths per 1,000 of the population per year. *See also* mortality rate.

demography   The study of the characteristics of human populations, such as their size and structure and how these change over time.

dependency culture   A set of values and beliefs, and a way of life, centred on dependence on others. Normally used by New Right writers in the context of those who depend on welfare-state benefits.

dependency ratio   The relationship between the proportion of the population who are working and those who are dependent or not working.

dependent age groups   Those under age 17 (age 18 from 2015) in compulsory education, and over retirement age.

dependent population   That section of the population which is not in work and is supported by those who are, such as the under-18s (who are still at school or in training), pensioners, the unemployed and others living on welfare benefits.

deprivation index   A list of items, lifestyle indicators or needs, such as food, health, housing, income, ownership of consumer goods, and access to transport, used to measure the level of deprivation experienced by an individual, group or geographical area.

determinism   The idea that people's behaviour is moulded by their social surroundings, and that they have little free will, control or choice over how they behave.

deviance   Failure to conform to social norms.

diaspora   The dispersal of an ethnic population from its original homeland, and its spreading out across the world, while retaining cultural and emotional ties to its area or nation of origin.

disability   A physical or mental impairment which has a substantial and long-term adverse effect on a person's ability to carry out normal day-to-day activities.

disease   A biological or mental condition, which usually involves medically diagnosed symptoms.

diseases of affluence   Diseases arising from lifestyles and social conditions in societies as they get richer.

diseases of poverty   Diseases which primarily arise from poverty and malnutrition.

division of labour   The division of work or occupations into a large number of specialized tasks, each of which is carried out by one worker or group of workers.

divorce rate   The number of divorces per 1,000 married people per year.

domestic division of labour   The division of roles, responsibilities and work tasks within a household.

domestic labour   Unpaid housework, including cooking, cleaning, childcare and looking after the sick and elderly.

dominant culture   The main culture in a society, which is shared, or at least accepted without opposition, by the majority of people.

dominant ideology   The set of ideas and beliefs of the most powerful groups in society, which influence the ideas of the rest of society. Usually associated with Marxist ideas (*see* Marxism) about the ruling class and how the ruling class can impose its own ideas on the rest of society.

earned income   Income received from paid employment (wages and salaries). *See also* income, unearned income.

educational triage   The way schools divide pupils into three groups – those who are likely to succeed in exams (mainly concerning GCSEs A*–C) whatever happens, those who have a chance of succeeding if they get some extra help (mainly those around the C/D-grade boundary), and those who have little chance of succeeding whatever is done. Schools concentrate on the first two groups, and particularly the second group, and basically write-off those who have little chance of success.

elaborated code   A form of language use involving careful explanation and detail. The language used by strangers and individuals in some formal context, like a job interview, writing a business letter, or a school lesson or textbook. Associated with the work of Bernstein. *See also* restricted code.

elite   A small group holding great power and privilege in society.

emigration   Leaving the usual country of residence for another country for a period of at least a year, so that the country of destination becomes the one of usual residence.

English Baccalaureate (EBacc)   A certificate awarded to pupils who achieve at least 6 GCSEs A*–C in maths, English, two sciences, a foreign language and a humanity, like history or geography.

equality of educational opportunity   The principle that every child, regardless of her or his social class background, ability to pay school fees, ethnic background (*see* ethnicity), gender or disability, should have an equal chance of doing as well in education as her or his ability will allow.

ethics   Principles or ideas about what is morally right and wrong.

ethnicity   The shared culture of a social group which gives its members a common identity in some ways different from that of other groups.

ethnocentrism   A view of the world in which other cultures are seen through the eyes of one's own culture, with a devaluing of the others. For example, school subjects may concentrate on White British society and culture rather than recognizing and taking into account the cultures of different ethnic communities (*see* ethnicity).

expressive role   The nurturing, caring and emotional role, often seen by functionalists (see functionalism) as women's natural role in the family, linked to women's biology. *See also* instrumental role.

extended family   A family grouping including all kin (see kinship). There are two main types of extended family: the classic extended family and the modified extended family. *See also* beanpole family, nuclear family.

false consciousness   A failure by members of a social class to recognize their real interests. *See also* class consciousness.

family   A social institution consisting of a group of people related by kinship ties: relations of blood, marriage / civil partnership or adoption. Cohabiting couples not linked by kinship are also often regarded as a family unit.

family ideology   A dominant set of beliefs, values and images about how families ought to be.

feminism   The view that examines the world from the point of view of women, coupled with the belief that women are disadvantaged and their interests ignored or devalued in society. *See also* liberal feminism, Marxist feminism, radical feminism.

fertility rate   A general term which is used to describe either the general fertility rate or the total fertility rate.

focus group   A form of group interview in which the group focuses on a particular topic to explore in depth and people are free to talk to one another as well as the interviewer.

folk culture   The culture created by local communities that is rooted in the experiences, customs and beliefs of the everyday life of ordinary people.

functional prerequisites   The basic needs that must be met if society is to survive.

functionalism   A sociological perspective and structural theory which sees society as made up of parts which work together to maintain society as an integrated whole. Society is seen as fundamentally harmonious and stable, because of the agreement on basic values (value consensus) established through socialization. *See also* Marxism, structuralism.

fundamentalism   A return to the literal meaning of religious texts and associated behaviour.

gate-keeping   The power of some people, groups or organizations to limit access to something valuable or useful. For example, doctors act as gate-keepers as they have the power to allow or refuse entry to the sick role.

gender   The culturally created differences between men and women which are learnt through socialization.

gender identity   How people see themselves, and how others see them, in terms of their gender roles and biological sex.

gender role   The pattern of behaviour which is expected from individuals of either sex.

general fertility rate   The number of live births per 1,000 women of child-bearing age (15–44) per year. *See also* total fertility rate.

global culture   The similarity of cultures in different countries of the world, sharing increasingly similar consumer products and ways of life. This has arisen as globalization has undermined national and local cultures.

globalization   The growing interdependence of societies across the world, with the spread of the same culture, consumer goods and economic interests across the globe.

group interview   An interview in which the researcher interviews several people at the same time, with the researcher controlling the direction of the interview, and responses directed to her or him. *See also* focus group.

habitus   The cultural framework (*see* culture) and set of ideas possessed by each social class, into which people are socialized (*see* socialization) and which influences their tastes in music, newspapers, films and so on. Bourdieu, a French Marxist (*see* Marxism), argued the dominant class has the power to impose its own habitus in the education system, giving those from upper-class and middle-class backgrounds an inbuilt advantage over those from working-class backgrounds.

halo effect   When pupils become favourably or unfavourably stereotyped (*see* stereotype) on the basis of earlier impressions by the teacher, and are rewarded and favoured or penalized in future teacher–student encounters.

Hawthorne effect   When the presence of the researcher, or a group's knowledge that it has been specially selected for research, changes the behaviour of the group, raising problems with the validity of social research.

health   Being able to function normally within a usual everyday routine.

health chances   The chances people have of enjoying good health, and avoiding ill-health and disease.

hegemonic control   Control of the working class achieved mainly through the hegemony and acceptance of ruling-class ideas.

hegemonic identity   An identity that is so dominant that it makes it difficult for individuals to assert alternative identities.

hegemony   The acceptance of the dominant ideology by the working class, as a result of the power of the ruling class to persuade others to accept and consent to its ideas.

heterosexuality   A sexual orientation towards people of the opposite sex.

hidden curriculum   Attitudes and behaviour which are taught through the school's organization and teachers' attitudes but which are not part of the formal timetable.

high culture   Cultural products (*see* culture), mainly media-based, seen as of lasting artistic or literary value, aimed at small, intellectual, predominantly upper-class and middle-class audiences, interested in new ideas, critical discussion and analysis. *See also* low culture, mass culture, popular culture.

homophobia   An irrational fear of or aversion to homosexuals (*see* homosexuality).

homosexuality   A sexual orientation towards people of the same sex, with lesbian women attracted to other women, and gay men attracted to other men.

household   An individual or group living at the same address and sharing facilities.

human capital   The knowledge and skills possessed by a workforce that increases that workforce's value and usefulness to employers.

hybrid identity   An identity formed from a mix of two or more other identities.

hypothesis   An idea which a researcher guesses might be true, but which has not yet been tested against the evidence.

iatrogenesis   Any harmful mental or physical condition induced in a patient through the effects of treatment by a doctor or surgeon.

identity   How individuals see and define themselves and how other people see and define them.

ideological state apparatuses   Agencies which serve to spread the dominant ideology and justify the power of the dominant social class.

ideology   A set of ideas, values and beliefs that represent the outlook, and justify the interests, of a social group.

illness   The subjective feeling of being unwell or unhealthy (*see* health) – a person's own recognition and definition of a lack of well-being.

immigration   Entering another country for a period of at least a year, so that country becomes the one of usual residence.

impairment   Some abnormal functioning of the body or mind, either that one is born with or arising from injury or disease.

imposition problem   When asking questions in interviews or self-completion questionnaires, the risk that the researcher might be imposing their own views or framework on the people being researched, rather than getting at what they really think.

impression management   The way individuals try to convince others of the identity they wish to assert by giving particular impressions of themselves to other people.

income   A flow of money which people obtain from work, from their investments, or from the state. *See also* earned income, unearned income, wealth.

infant mortality rate   The number of deaths of babies in the first year of life per 1,000 live births per year.

informed consent   The ethical requirement (*see* ethics) that those taking part in a sociological study have agreed to do so, and have given this consent based on a full appreciation and understanding of the nature, aims and purposes of the study, any implications or risks taking part might have, and the uses of any findings of the research.

instrumental role   The provider/breadwinner role in the family, often associated by functionalists (*see* functionalism) with men's role in family life. *See also* expressive role.

integrated conjugal roles   Roles in marriage or in a cohabiting couple where male and female partners share domestic tasks, childcare, decision-making and income earning.

interpretivism   A sociological perspective that suggests that, to understand society, it is necessary to understand the meanings people give to their behaviour, and how these are influenced by the behaviour and interpretations of others. The focus of research is therefore on individuals or small groups rather than on society as a whole. *See also* positivism, social action theory.

interviewer bias   The answers given in an interview being influenced or distorted in some way by the presence or behaviour of the interviewer.

inverse care law   The suggestion that those in the greatest need of help from the welfare state (including health services) get the fewest resources allocated to them, while those whose need is least get the most resources.

Islamophobia   An irrational fear and/or hatred of or aversion to Islam, Muslims or Islamic culture.

kibbutz   A community established in Israel, with the emphasis on equality, collective ownership of property and collective childrearing.

kinship   Relations of blood, marriage / civil partnership or adoption.

labelling   Defining a person or group in a certain way – as a particular 'type' of person or group.

labour power   People's capacity to work. In Marxist theory (*see* Marxism), people sell their labour power to the employer in return for a wage, and the employer buys only their labour power, not the whole person.

laws   Official legal rules, formally enforced by the police, courts and prison, involving legal punishment if the rules are broken.

liberal feminism   A feminist approach (*see* feminism) which seeks to research the inequalities facing women, and to enable women to achieve equal opportunities with men, without challenging the system as a whole. *See also* Marxist feminism, radical feminism.

life chances   The chances of obtaining those things defined as desirable and of avoiding those things defined as undesirable in a society.

life course   The various significant events individuals experience as they make their way through life, and the choices they make and the meanings they give to events such as marriage or cohabitation, parenthood, divorce and retirement.

life expectancy   An estimate of how long people can be expected to live from a certain age.

low culture   A derogatory (critical and insulting) term used to describe mass culture or popular culture, suggesting these are of inferior quality to the high culture of the elite. *See also* high culture, mass culture, popular culture.

macro approach   A focus on large numbers of people and the large-scale structure of society as a whole, rather than on individuals. *See also* micro approach.

male gaze   Where men look (gaze) at women as sexual objects.

marginalization   The process whereby some people are pushed by poverty, ill-health, lack of education, disability, racism and so on to the margins or edges of society, and are unable to take part in the life enjoyed by the majority of citizens. *See also* social exclusion.

market situation   The rewards that people are able to obtain when they sell their skills and talents in the labour market, depending on the scarcity of the skills they have and the power they have to obtain high rewards.

marketable wealth   Assets that can be bought and sold and turned into cash for the owner's benefit, like a private car, a house, land, shares and other assets that can be sold. *See also* non-marketable wealth.

marketization   The process whereby services, like education or health, that were previously controlled and run by the state, have government or local council control reduced, and become subject to the free market forces of supply and demand, based on competition and consumer choice.

marriage rate   The number of men or women marrying per 1,000 unmarried men or women aged 16 or over each year.

Marxism   A structural theory of society which sees society divided by conflict between two main opposing social classes, due to the private ownership of the means of production and the exploitation of the non-owners by the owners.

Marxist feminism   A Marxist approach (*see* Marxism) to the study of women, emphasizing the way they are exploited both as workers and as women. *See also* feminism, liberal feminism, radical feminism.

mass culture (sometimes called popular culture or low culture)   Commercially produced culture, involving cultural products produced for sale to the mass of ordinary people. These involve mass-produced, standardized, short-lived products, often media-based, which many see as of little lasting value and which demand little critical thought, analysis or discussion. *See also* high culture, low culture, popular culture.

master status   The dominant status of an individual which overrides all other characteristics of that person, such as that of an 'ex-con', a druggie or someone who is mentally ill.

means of production   The key resources necessary for producing society's goods, such as factories and land.

medical gaze   The way doctors look upon a patient merely as a body, an object like a piece of meat or a machine, rather than as a whole person with a conscious mind and individual identity. Doctors search for the existence and causes of a disease through detached and sophisticated analysis obtained by gazing at a patient's body, rather than relying on that individual's accounts of her or his symptoms.

medicalization   The process whereby previously non-medical social issues and problems come to be seen and defined in medical terms, and treated as medical disorders or illnesses under the authority of doctors and other health professionals.

meritocracy (or a *meritocratic society*)   A society in which occupational and other status positions are achieved on the basis of individual merit like talent, skill and educational qualifications, rather than who you know or the family you were born into.

metanarrative   A broad all-embracing 'big theory' (literally, a 'big story') or explanation for how societies operate.

methodological pluralism   The use of a variety of methods in a single piece of research.

micro approach   A focus on small groups or individuals, rather than on large numbers of people and the structure of society as a whole. *See also* macro approach.

middle class   Those in non-manual work – jobs which don't involve heavy physical effort, are usually performed in offices and involve paperwork or computer work of various kinds. *See also* social class, upper class, working class.

migration   Changing the country of usual residence for a period of at least a year, so that the country of destination effectively becomes the country of usual residence.

minority ethnic group   A social group which shares a cultural identity (*see* culture) which is different in some respects from that of the majority population of a society.

modified extended family   A family type where related nuclear families, although living apart geographically, nevertheless maintain regular contact and mutual support through visiting, the phone, email and letters. *See also* classic extended family.

monogamy   A form of marriage in which a person can only be legally married to one partner at a time. *See also* polyandry, polygamy, polygyny, serial monogamy.

moral panic   A wave of public concern about some exaggerated or imaginary threat to society, stirred up by over-blown and sensationalized reporting in the mass media.

morbidity   The extent of disease in a population, including either the total number of cases or the number of new cases of a disease in a particular population at a particular time.

mortality   The number of deaths in a population, usually measured as a rate (mortality rate) per 1,000 of a population group, such as the number of deaths per thousand of the total population each year. *See also* death rate, infant mortality rate.

mortality rate   The number of deaths per year scaled to the size of a population group. *See also* death rate, infant mortality rate.

mortification   A process whereby a person's own identity is replaced by one defined by an institution, such as a hospital or prison.

multicultural education   Education which involves teaching about the culture of other ethnic groups (*see* ethnicity) besides that of the majority culture.

nation   A particular geographical area with which a group of people identify, sharing among themselves a sense of belonging based on a common sense of culture, history and usually language.

nationalism   A sense of pride and commitment to a nation, and a very strong sense of national identity.

nationality   Having citizenship of a nation-state, including things like voting rights, a passport and the right of residence.

nation-state   A nation which has its own independent government controlling a geographical area.

natural population change   Changes in the size of a population due to changes in the number of births and deaths, excluding migration. Expressed as a *natural increase* (+) or *decrease* (–) in population.

negative sanctions   Punishments of various kinds imposed on those who fail to conform to social norms. *See also* positive sanctions, sanction.

neo-tribalism   Groups with very loose, fluid boundaries and an ever-changing floating membership, that only exist when they come together for particular lifestyle rituals (like clubbing and dancing). They are not the cohesive and fixed social groups, with clear identities, styles and lines of division between them, associated with the concept of a subculture.

net migration   The *difference* between immigration and emigration, and therefore whether the population of a country or area has gone up or gone down when both emigration and immigration are taken into account. Usually expressed as a net gain or increase (+) or a net loss or decrease (–) of population.

New Right   A political philosophy and approach found in the work of some sociologists, mainly associated with the years of Conservative government in Britain between 1979 and 1997. This approach stresses individual freedom; self-help and self-reliance; reduction of the power and spending of the state; the free market and free competition between private companies, schools and other institutions; and the importance of traditional institutions and values.

non-marketable wealth   Wealth that cannot be sold or cashed in, like occupational and state pension rights. *See also* marketable wealth.

norms   Social rules which define correct and approved behaviour in a society or group.

nuclear family   A family with two generations, of parents and children, living together in one household. *See also* extended family.

objectivity   Approaching topics with an open mind, avoiding bias, and being prepared to submit research evidence to scrutiny by other researchers.

overt role   Where the researcher in a participant observation study reveals her or his identity as a researcher to the group being studied. *See also* covert role.

parentocracy   Where a child's education is dependent upon the wealth and wishes of parents, rather than the ability and efforts of pupils.

particularistic values   Rules and values that give a priority to personal relationships. *See also* universalistic values.

patriarchy   Male dominance, with men holding power and authority.

peer group   A group of people of similar age and status, with whom a person often mixes socially.

personal documents   Documents, which are usually private, for a person's own use, which record part of a person's life. *See also* public documents.

perspective   A way of looking at something. A sociological perspective involves a set of theories which influences what is looked at when studying society.

pilot survey   A small-scale practice survey carried out before the final survey to check for any possible problems. Sometimes referred to as a *pilot study*.

pluralism   A view that sees power in society spread among a wide range of competing interest groups and individuals, with no group or individual having a monopoly of power.

polyandry   A form of marriage in which a woman may have two or more husbands at the same time. *See also* monogamy, polygamy, polygyny, serial monogamy.

polygamy   A form of marriage in which a member of one sex can be married to two or more members of the opposite sex at the same time. *See also* monogamy, polyandry, polygyny, serial monogamy.

polygyny   A form of marriage in which a man may have two or more wives at the same time. *See also* monogamy, polyandry, polygamy, serial monogamy.

popular culture   The cultural products liked and enjoyed by the mass of ordinary people. It is sometimes referred to as mass culture or low culture.

population projections   Predictions of future changes in population size and composition based on past and present population trends.

positive discrimination   Giving disadvantaged groups more favourable treatment than others to make up for the inequalities they face.

positive sanctions   Rewards of various kinds to encourage people to conform to social norms. *See also* negative sanctions, sanction.

positivism   An approach in sociology that believes society can be studied using similar scientific techniques to those used in the natural sciences, such as physics, chemistry and biology. *See also* interpretivism.

postmodernism   An approach that stresses that society is changing so rapidly and constantly that it is marked by chaos, uncertainty and risk, and is fragmented into many different groups, interests and lifestyles. Social structures are being replaced by a mass of individuals making individual choices about their lifestyles. Societies can no longer be understood through the application of general theories or grand stories (metanarratives), like Marxism or functionalism, which seek to explain society as a whole.

poverty line   The dividing point between those who are poor and those who are not. The poverty line used in Britain today, and by the European Union, is 60 per cent of average income.

poverty trap   When people on means-tested benefits find themselves worse off if they get a low-paid job, as the benefits they lose are worth more than the money they gain through employment. This creates a disincentive for them to look for work or take low-paid jobs, trapping them in continuing poverty.

pressure groups   Organizations which try to put pressure on those with power in society to implement policies they favour.

primary data   Information which sociologists have collected themselves. *See also* secondary data.

primary deviance   Deviant behaviour which is not publicly labelled (*see* labelling) as deviant. *See also* secondary deviance.

primary socialization   Socialization during the early years of childhood carried out in the family and close community. *See also* secondary socialization.

privatization   Either: the process whereby households and families become isolated and separated from the community and from wider kin (*see* kinship), with people spending more time together in home-centred activities; or: where services that were once provided by the state are transferred to private companies, as, for example, with healthcare services once provided by publicly owned NHS hospitals becoming provided by privately owned hospitals.

privatized nuclear family   A self-contained, self-reliant and home-centred family unit that is separated and isolated from its extended kin, neighbours and local community life.

productive property   Wealth which provides an unearned income for its owner, such as houses which are rented out, factories and land, or company shares which provide dividends. *See also* consumption property.

proletariat   The social class of workers who have to work for wages as they do not own the means of production.

pro-school subculture   A group organized around a set of values, attitudes and behaviour which generally conforms to the academic aims, ethos and rules of a school.

public documents   Documents which are produced for public knowledge. *See also* personal documents.

qualitative data   Information concerned with the feelings and meanings people associate with, and the interpretations they give to, some issue or event.

quantitative data   Information that can be measured and expressed in statistical or number form.

racial prejudice   A set of assumptions about an ethnic group (*see* ethnicity) which people are reluctant to change even when they receive information which undermines those assumptions.

racism   Believing or acting as though an individual or group is superior or inferior on the grounds of their racial or ethnic (*see* ethnicity) origins.

radical feminism   A feminist approach (*see* feminism) which focuses on the problem of patriarchy. For radical feminists, the main focus of research is on the problem of men and male-dominated society. *See also* liberal feminism, Marxist feminism.

reconstituted family   A family in which one or both partners have been previously married, or living as a cohabiting couple, and bring with them children of a previous relationship. Also known as a *stepfamily* or a *blended family*.

reflexive self   The way an individual's identity is formed and develops through a process of reflecting on, or thinking about, her or his identity in interaction with other individuals and the agencies of socialization.

relations of production   The relationships between those people involved in production, such as in cooperation or private ownership and control.

relative deprivation   The sense of lacking things compared to the group with which people identify and compare themselves.

relative poverty   Poverty defined in relation to a generally accepted standard of living in a specific society at a particular time. *See also* absolute poverty.

reliability   Whether another researcher, if repeating or replicating research using the same method for the same research on the same or a similar group, would achieve roughly the same results.

replication   *see* reliability.

representative sample   A smaller group drawn from the survey population, of which it contains a good cross-section. The information obtained from a representative sample should provide roughly the same results as if the whole survey population had been surveyed.

resocialization   The learning of appropriate new norms and values to enable people to operate in a changed social environment when they enter a new and different society or social situation, or when their life circumstances otherwise change.

restricted code   A form of language use which takes for granted shared understandings between people. Colloquial, everyday language used between friends, with limited explanation and use of vocabulary. *See also* elaborated code.

role conflict   The conflict between the successful performance of two or more roles at the same time, such as those of worker, student and mother.

role models   People's patterns of behaviour which others copy and model their own behaviour on.

roles   The patterns of behaviour which are expected from individuals in society.

ruling class   The social class of owners of the means of production, whose control over the economy gives them the power to rule over all aspects of society.

ruling-class ideology   The set of ideas and beliefs of the ruling class.

sample   A smaller representative group drawn from the survey population for studying. *See also* representative sample.

sampling frame   A list of names of all those in the survey population from which a representative sample is selected.

sampling methods   The techniques sociologists use to select representative individuals to study from the survey population.

sanction   A reward or punishment to encourage social conformity. *See also* negative sanctions, positive sanctions.

scapegoats   Individuals or groups who get blamed for things that aren't their fault.

secondary data   Data which already exist and which the researcher hasn't collected her- or himself. *See also* primary data.

secondary deviance   Deviant behaviour which is labelled (*see* labelling) as such by others. *See also* primary deviance.

secondary socialization   Socialization which takes place beyond the family and close community, such as through the education system, the mass media and the workplace. *See also* primary socialization.

secularization   The process whereby religious thinking, practice and institutions decline and lose influence in society.

segregated conjugal roles   A clear division and separation between the roles of male and female partners in a marriage or in a cohabiting couple.

self-fulfilling prophecy   People acting in response to predictions of their behaviour, thereby making the prediction come true. Often applied to the effects of streaming in schools, and how people respond to being labelled as mentally ill.

serial monogamy   A form of marriage in which a person keeps marrying and divorcing a series of different partners, but is only married to one person at a time. *See also* monogamy, polyandry, polygamy, polygyny.

service sector   The section of the economy, sometimes called the *tertiary sector*, concerned with the production of services instead of actual products, such as administration, information, communication, catering, the leisure industry, sales, finance and insurance, transport and distribution, and the running of government services such as the health, welfare and education services.

setting   A system of dividing school students into groups (or sets) of the same ability in particular subjects.

sex   The biological differences between men and women.

sexism   Prejudice or discrimination against people (especially women) because of their sex.

sexual division of labour   The division of work into 'men's jobs' and 'women's jobs'.

sexual orientation   The type of people that individuals are either physically or romantically attracted to, such as those of the same or opposite sex.

sexuality   People's sexual characteristics and their sexual behaviour.

sick role   The pattern of behaviour which is expected from someone who is classified as ill.

social action theory   A perspective which emphasizes the creative action which people can take, and that people are not simply the passive victims of social forces outside themselves. Social action theory suggests it is important to understand the motives and meanings people give to their behaviour. *See also* interpretivism, structuralism.

social capital   The social networks of influence and support that people have.

social class   A broad group of people who share a similar economic situation, such as occupation, income and ownership of wealth. *See also* middle class, upper class, working class.

social cohesion   The bonds or 'glue' that bring people together and integrate them into a united society.

social construction   The important characteristics of something, such as statistics, health, childhood, old age or what is regarded as deviance, are created and influenced by the attitudes, actions and interpretations of members of society. They only exist because people define them as such. Official statistics, notions of health and illness, deviance and suicide are all examples of social phenomena that only exist because people have constructed them and given these phenomena particular labels.

social control   The process of persuading or forcing individuals to conform to values and norms.

social exclusion   The situation in which people are marginalized (*see* marginalization) as they lack the resources which might enable them to participate fully in education, work and community life, and lack access to services and other aspects of life seen as part of being a full and participating member of the community or society in which they live. This excludes some people – or cuts them off – from what most people would regard as a normal life, and denies them the opportunities most people take for granted.

social facts   Social phenomena which exist outside individuals but act upon them in ways which constrain or mould their behaviour. Such phenomena include social institutions such as the family, the law, the education system and the workplace.

social institutions   The organized social arrangements which are found in all societies, such as the family and the education systems.

social mobility   Movement of groups or individuals up or down the social hierarchy.

social policy   The packages of plans and actions adopted by national and local government or various voluntary agencies to solve social problems or achieve other goals that are seen as important.

social problem   Something that is seen as harmful to society in some way, and as needing something doing to sort it out.

social solidarity   The integration of people into society through shared values, a common culture, shared understandings, and social ties that bind them together.

social structure   The network of social institutions and social relationships that form the 'building blocks' of .society.

socialization   The process of learning the culture of any society. *See also* primary socialization, secondary socialization.

sociological perspective   A set of theories which influences what is looked at when studying society.

sociological problem   Any social issue that needs explaining.

status   Sometimes refers to the position someone occupies in society, but more commonly refers to the amount of prestige or social importance a person has in the eyes of other members of a group or society. *See also* achieved status, ascribed status.

status frustration   A sense of frustration arising in individuals or groups because they are denied status in society.

status syndrome   The harmful effects on an individual's health caused by stress and anxiety about their status situation (social standing), and consequently on their self-esteem, or view of their own social worth.

stereotype   A generalized, oversimplified view of the features of a social group, allowing for few individual differences between members of the group.

stigma   Any undesirable physical or social characteristic that is seen as abnormal or unusual in some way, that is seen as demeaning, and stops an individual being fully accepted by society.

stigmatized identity   An identity that is in some way undesirable or demeaning, and excludes people from full acceptance in society.

streaming   A system of dividing school students into groups of similar ability (streams or bands) in which they stay for all subjects. *See also* banding.

structural differentiation   The way new, more specialized social institutions emerge to take over functions that were once performed by a single institution. An example is the way some once traditional functions of the family have been transferred to the education system and the welfare state.

structuralism   A perspective which is concerned with the overall structure of society, and sees individual behaviour moulded by social institutions like the family, the education system, the mass media and work. *See also* functionalism, Marxism.

structuration   A sociological perspective between structuralism and social action theory which suggests that, while people are constrained by social institutions, they can at the same time take action to support or change those institutions.

subculture   A smaller culture held by a group of people within the main culture of a society, in some ways different from the main culture, but with many aspects in common.

subculture of resistance   A subculture that not only has some differences from the dominant culture, but is also in active opposition to it.

subjective poverty   People's own feelings and judgements about whether or not they are poor in relation to those other members of society with whom they compare themselves.

surplus value   The extra value added by workers to the products they produce, after allowing for the payment of their wages, and which goes to the employer in the form of profit.

survey   A means of collecting primary data from large numbers of people, usually in a standardized statistical form.

survey population   The section of the population which is of interest in a survey.

symbolic interactionism   A sociological perspective which is concerned with understanding human behaviour in face-to-face situations, and how individuals and situations come to be defined in particular ways through their encounters with other people.

symmetrical family   A family where the roles of husband and wife or cohabiting partners have become more alike (symmetrical) and equal.

total fertility rate (TFR)   is the average number of children women will have during their child-bearing years. *See also* general fertility rate

tourist gaze   The viewing and experiencing of objects and locations with curiosity and interest, organized by professional tourism experts to provide pleasurable experiences for tourists that are different from everyday life.

triangulation   The use of two, or usually more, research methods in a single piece of research to check the reliability and validity of research evidence.

underachievement   The failure of individuals or groups to fulfil their potential – they do not do as well in education (or other areas) as their talents and abilities suggest they should.

underclass   A social group right at the bottom of the social class hierarchy, whose members are in some ways different from, and cut off or excluded from, the rest of society.

unearned income   Income received from productive property, like rent on buildings and land, dividends on shares, and interest on savings and other personal investments. *See also* income, earned income.

universalistic values   Rules and values that apply equally to all members of society, regardless of who they are. *See also* particularistic values.

upper class   A small social class who are the main owners of society's wealth. It includes wealthy industrialists, landowners and the traditional aristocracy. *See also* middle class, social class, working class.

validity   The extent to which the findings of research actually provide a true, genuine or authentic picture of what is being studied.

value consensus A general agreement around the main values of a society.

value freedom The idea that the beliefs and prejudices of the sociologist should not be allowed to influence the way research is carried out and evidence interpreted.

values General beliefs about what is right or wrong, and about the important standards which are worth maintaining and achieving in any society.

verstehen (pronounced 'fair-shtay-en') The idea of understanding human behaviour by putting yourself in the position of those being studied, and trying to see things from their point of view.

victim survey A survey which asks people if they have been victims of crime, whether or not they reported it to the police.

wealth Property in the form of assets which can, in general, be sold and turned into cash for the benefit of the owner. *See also* consumption property, income, marketable wealth, non-marketable wealth, productive property.

welfare pluralism The range of welfare provision, including informal provision by the family and community, and welfare provided by the government, the voluntary sector and the private sector.

white mask Non-white minority ethnic groups seeking to overcome prejudice and racism and gain acceptance in white society by playing down their own ethnicity and culture, and adopting the features (the 'white mask') of majority white culture.

working class Those working in manual jobs – jobs involving physical work and, literally, work with their hands, like factory or labouring work. *See also* middle class, social class, upper class.

Bibliography

Abel-Smith, B. and Townsend, P. (1965) *The Poor and the Poorest.* London: G. Bell & Son.

Abraham, J. (1989) 'Testing Hargreaves' and Lacey's differentiation–polarisation theory in a setted comprehensive', *The British Journal of Sociology* 40/5.

Acheson Report (1998) *Independent Inquiry into Inequalities in Health.* London: Stationery Office.

Alford, R. (1975) *Health Care Politics.* Chicago: University of Chicago Press.

Allan, G. and Crow, G. (2001) *Families, Households and Society.* Basingstoke: Palgrave Macmillan.

Allan, G., Crow, G. and Hawker, S. (2011) *Stepfamilies.* Basingstoke: Palgrave Macmillan.

Althusser, L. (1971) *Lenin and Philosophy and Other Essays.* London: New Left Books.

Anwar, M. (1998) *Between Cultures: Continuity and Change in the Lives of Young Asians.* London: Routledge.

Appignanesi, L. (2011) 'The mental illness industry is medicalising normality'. *The Guardian* 6 September.

Arber, S. and Thomas, H. (2005) 'From women's health to a gender analysis of health', in W. C. Cockerham (ed.) *The Blackwell Companion to Medical Sociology.* Oxford: Blackwell.

Archer, L., Halsall, A. and Hollingworth, S. (2007) '"University's not for me — I'm a Nike person": urban working-class young people's negotiations of "style", identity and educational engagement, *Sociology* 41/2.

Ariès, P. (1973) *Centuries of Childhood.* Harmondsworth: Penguin.

Atkinson, J. M. (1978) *Discovering Suicide.* Basingstoke: Macmillan.

Balarajan, R. (1996) 'Ethnicity and variations in the nation's health', *Health Trends* 27/4.

Ball, S. J. (1981) *Beachside Comprehensive: A Case Study of Secondary Schooling.* Cambridge: Cambridge University Press.

Ball, S. J. and Exley, S. (2011) 'Something old, something new . . . understanding Conservative education policy', in H. Bochel (ed.) *The Conservative Party and Social Policy.* Bristol: Policy Press.

Ball, S. J., Bowe, R. and Gewirtz, S. (1996) 'School choice, social class and distinction: the realization of social advantage in education', *Journal of Education Policy* 11/1.

Ballard, R. (1982) 'South Asian families', in R. N. Rapoport, M. P. Fogarty and R. Rapoport (eds.) *Families in Britain.* London: Routledge & Kegan Paul.

Barber, M. (1996) *The Learning Game.* London: Victor Gollancz.

Barker, E. (1984) *The Making of a Moonie.* Oxford: Blackwell.

Barnard, H. and Turner, C. (2011) *Poverty and Ethnicity: A Review of Evidence.* York: Joseph Rowntree Foundation.

Barnes, C. (1992) *Disabling Imagery and the Media.* Halifax: Ryburn Publishing.

Barrett, M. and McIntosh, M. (1982) *The Anti-Social Family.* London: Verso.

Baudrillard, J. (2001) *Selected Writings*, ed. M. Poster, Cambridge: Polity Press.

Bauman, Z. (1996) 'From pilgrim to tourist – or a short history of identity', in S. Hall and P. du Gay (eds.), *Questions of Cultural Identity.* London: Sage Publications.

Bauman, Z. and May, T. (2004) 'Identity, consumerism and inequality', *Sociology Review* February.

Beck, U. (1992) *Risk Society: Towards a New Modernity.* London: Sage Publications.

Beck, U. and Beck-Gernsheim, E. (1995) *The Normal Chaos of Love.* Cambridge: Polity Press.

Becker, H. S. (1970) *Sociological Work.* Chicago: University of Chicago Press.

Becker, H. S. (1971) 'Social class variations in the teacher–pupil relationship', in School and Society Course Team, Open University (ed.), *School and Society.* London: Routledge & Kegan Paul.

Becker, H. S. (1997 [1963]) *Outsiders: Studies in the Sociology of Deviance.* New York: Free Press / Simon & Schuster.

Bennett, A. (1999) 'Subcultures or neo-tribes? Rethinking the relationship between youth, style and musical taste', *Sociology* 33/3.

Bennett, A. (2001) *Cultures of Popular Music.* Buckingham: Open University Press.

Bernstein, B. (1971) 'Education cannot compensate for society', in School and Society Course Team, Open University (ed.), *School and Society.* London: Routledge & Kegan Paul.

Berthoud, R. (2001) *Family Formation in Multi-cultural Britain: Three Patterns of Diversity.* ISER working paper 2000-34. Colchester: Institute for Social and Economic Research, University of Essex.

Best, L. (1993) 'Dragons, dinner ladies and ferrets: sex roles in children's books', *Sociology Review* 3/3.

Bhattacharyya, G., Ison, L. and Blair, M. (2004) *Minority Ethnic Attainment and Participation in Education and Training: The Evidence.* Research Topic Paper RTP01-03. London: Department for Education and Skills.

Bhatti, G. (1999) *Asian Children at Home and at School: An Ethnographic Study.* London: Routledge.

Birdwell, J., Grist, M. and Margo, J. (2011) *The Forgotten Half*. London: Demos.

Blanden, J. and Gibbons, S. (2006) *The Persistence of Poverty across Generations: A View from Two British Cohorts*. Bristol: Policy Press.

Bocock, R. (2004) *Consumption*. London: Routledge.

Boliver, V. and Swift, A. (2011) 'Do comprehensive schools reduce social mobility?' *The British Journal of Sociology* 62/1.

Bott, E. (1978 [1957]) 'Conjugal roles and social networks', in P. Worsley (ed.), *Modern Sociology* (2nd edn). Harmondsworth: Penguin.

Boulton, M. G. (1983) *On Being a Mother*. London: Tavistock.

Bourdieu, P. (1971) 'Systems of education and systems of thought' and 'Intellectual field and creative project', in M. F. D. Young (ed.), *Knowledge and Control*. London: Collier-Macmillan.

Bourdieu, P. (2010[1979]) *Distinction: A Social Critique of the Judgement of Taste*. London: Routledge [originally published 1979 as *La distinction: Critique sociale du jugement (Le sens commun)*. Paris: Les Éditions de Minuit].

Bowles, S. and Gintis, H. (2011 [1976]) *Schooling in Capitalist America*. Chicago: Haymarket Books [London: Routledge & Kegan Paul, 1976].

Bradford, B. (2006) *Who are the 'Mixed' ethnic group?* London: Office for National Statistics.

Bradley, H. (1995) *Fractured Identities: Changing Patterns of Inequality*. Cambridge: Polity Press.

Brake, M. (1985) *Comparative Youth Culture: The Sociology of Youth Culture and Youth Subcultures in America, Britain and Canada*. London: Routledge.

Brannen, J. (1996) 'Discourses of Adolescence: Young People's Independence and Autonomy within Families', in J. Brannen and M. O'Brien (eds.) *Children in Families: Research and Policy*. London: Falmer Press.

Brannen, J. (2003) 'The age of beanpole families', *Sociology Review* 13/1.

Brannen, J., Dodd, K., Oakley, A. and Storey, P. (1994) *Young People, Health and Family Life*. Buckingham: Open University Press.

Brown, P. (1990), 'The "Third Wave": Education and the Ideology of Parentocracy', *British Journal of Sociology of Education* 11/1.

Bryan, M. L. and Sevilla Sanz, A. (2008) *'Does Housework Lower Wages and Why?' Evidence for Britain*, ISER Working Paper 2008-3. Colchester: University of Essex, based on data from the UK Time Use Survey.

Burdsey, D. (2004) 'One of the lads? Dual ethnicity and assimilated ethnicities in the careers of British Asian professional footballers', *Ethnic and Racial Studies* 27/5.

Bury, M. (2001) 'Illness narratives: fact or fiction?' *Sociology of Health & Illness* 23/3.

Busfield, J. (1996) *Men, Women and Madness: Understanding Gender and Mental Disorder*. Basingstoke: Palgrave Macmillan.

Butler, C. (1995) 'Religion and gender: young Muslim women in Britain', *Sociology Review* February.

Calnan, M. (2010) 'Consumerism and the provision of health care', *British Journal of Healthcare Management* 16/1.

Cassen, R. and Kingdon, G. (2007) *Tackling Low Educational Achievement*. York: Joseph Rowntree Foundation.

Chagnon, N. A. (1996) *Yanomamö: The Fierce People*. Case Studies in Cultural Anthropology. London: Thomson Learning.

Charles, N. (2008) *Families in Transition: Social Change, Family Formation and Kin Relationships*. Bristol: The Policy Press.

Charlesworth, S. (2000) *A Phenomenology of Working-Class Experience*. Cambridge: Cambridge University Press.

Checkland, K., Harrison, S. and Coleman, A. (2009) '"Structural interests" in health care: evidence from the contemporary National Health Service', *Journal of Social Policy* 38/4.

Chubb, J. E. and Moe, T. M. (1990) *Politics, Markets and America's Schools*. Washington DC: Brookings Institute.

Chubb, J. E. and Moe, T. M. (1992) *A Lesson in School Reform from Great Britain*. Washington DC: Brookings Institute.

Cicourel, A. V. and Kitsuse, J. I. (1971) 'The social organisation of the high school and deviant adolescent careers', in School and Society Course Team, Open University (ed.) *School and Society*. London: Routledge & Kegan Paul.

Clarke, J. (1976) 'The skinheads and the magical recovery of community', in S. Hall and T. Jefferson (eds.) *Resistance through Rituals: Youth Subcultures in Post-War Britain*. London: Hutchinson.

Clarke, J. and Critcher, C. (1995) *The Devil Makes Work: Leisure in Capitalist Britain*. Basingstoke: Palgrave Macmillan.

Clarke, J. and Saunders, C. (1991) 'Who are you and so what?', *Sociology Review* September.

Clarke, J., Hall, S., Jefferson, T. and Roberts, B. (1976) 'Subcultures, cultures and class', in S. Hall and T. Jefferson (eds.) *Resistance through Rituals: Youth Subcultures in Post-war Britain*. London: Hutchinson.

Cline, T., de Abreu, G., Fihosy, C., Gray, H., Lambert, H. and Neale, J. (2002) *Minority Ethnic Pupils in Mainly White Schools*. London: DFES Research Report No 365.

Coard, B. (1971) *How the West Indian Child is Made Educationally Subnormal in the British School System*. London: New Beacon Books.

Coates, K. and Silburn, R. (1970) *Poverty: The Forgotten Englishmen*. Harmondsworth: Penguin.

Cohen, P. 1972. *Subcultural Conflict and Working Class community*. Working Papers in Cultural Studies 2. University of Birmingham.

Cohen, S. (2002 [1972]) *Folk Devils and Moral Panics*. London: Routledge & Kegan Paul.

Colley, A. (1998) 'Gender and subject choice in secondary education', in J. Radford (ed.) *Gender and Choice in Education and Occupation*. London: Routledge & Kegan Paul.

Connell, R. W. (1995) *Masculinities*. Cambridge: Polity Press.

Connolly, P. (1998) *Racism, Gender Identities and Young Children: Social Relations in a Multi-ethnic, Inner-city Primary School*. London: Routledge.

Conrad, P. and Schneider, J. W. (1992 [1980]) *Deviance and Medicalization: From Badness to Sickness*. Philadelphia: Temple University Press.

Cooley, C. H. (1998) *On Self and Social Organization*, ed. H.-J. Schubert. London: University of Chicago Press.

Cooper, D. (1972) *The Death of the Family*. Harmondsworth: Penguin.

Critcher, C., Bramham, P. and Tomlinson, A. (1995) *The Sociology of Leisure*. London: Chapman & Hall.

Cunningham, H. (2005) *Children and Childhood in Western Society since 1500*. London: Longman.

Davey Smith, G., Chaturvedi, N., Harding, S., Nazroo, J. and Williams, R. (2002) 'Ethnic inequalities in health: a review of UK epidemiological evidence', in S. Nettleton and U. Gustaffson (eds.) *The Sociology of Health and Illness Reader*. Cambridge: Polity Press.

Davis, K. and Moore, W. E. (1967 [1945]) 'Some principles of stratification', in R. Bendix and S. M. Lipset (eds.) *Class, Status and Power* (2nd edn). London: Routledge & Kegan Paul.

Deem, R. (1986) *All Work and No Play*. Milton Keynes: Open University Press.

Deem, R. (1990) 'Women and leisure – all work and no play', *Social Studies Review* 5/4.

Delphy, C. and Leonard, D. (1992) *Familiar Exploitation: A New Analysis of Marriage in Contemporary Western Societies*. Cambridge: Polity Press.

Department of Health (1998) *Our Healthier Nation*. London: Stationery Office.

Department of Health (2010) *Government Response to the Science and Technology Committee Report 'Evidence Check 2: Homeopathy'*. London: The Stationery Office.

DfES (2005) *Ethnicity and Education: The Evidence on Minority Ethnic Pupils*. Research Topic Paper: RTP01-05. London: Department for Education and Skills.

DfES (2006) *Ethnicity and Education: The Evidence on Minority Ethnic Pupils aged 5–16*. London: Department for Education and Skills.

Dixon, A., Le Grand, J., Henderson, J., Murray, R. and Poteliakhoff, E. (2007) 'Is the British National Health Service equitable? The evidence on socioeconomic differences in utilization', *Journal of Health Services Research and Policy* 12/2.

Dixon, A., Robertson, R., Appleby, J., Burge, P., Devlin, N. and Magee, H. (2010) *Patient Choice: How Patients Choose and How Providers Respond*. London: King's Fund.

Dobash, R. E. and Dobash, R. P. (1992) *Women, Violence and Social Change*. London: Routledge.

Douglas, J. W. B. (1964) *The Home and the School*. London: MacGibbon & Kee.

Douglas, S. J. and Michaels, M. W. (2004). *The Mommy Myth: The Idealization of Motherhood and How It Has Undermined Women*. New York: Free Press.

Dubos, R. (1966) *Man and his Environment: Biomedical Knowledge and Social Action*. Scientific Publication No. 131. Washington DC: Pan American Health Organization.

Dubos, R. and Pines, M., (1980) *Health and Disease*. Time-Life Books.

Duncombe, J. and Marsden, D. (1995) 'Women's "triple shift": paid employment, domestic labour and "emotion work"', *Sociology Review* 4/4.

Durkheim, E. (2002 [1897]) *Suicide: A Study in Sociology*. London: Routledge and Kegan Paul.

Edgell, S. (1980) *Middle-Class Couples*. London: Allen & Unwin.

Edwards, P., Roberts, I., Clarke, M., et al. (2002) 'Increasing response rates to postal questionnaires: systematic review', *British Medical Journal* 324/1183.

Eisenstadt, S. N. (1956) *From Generation to Generation*. Chicago: Free Press.

Elston, M. (1980) 'Medicine: half our future doctors', in R. Silverstone and A. Warde (eds.) *Careers of Professional Women*. London: Croom Helm.

Epstein, D., Elwood, J., Hey, V. and Maw, J. (1998) *Failing Boys? Issues in Gender and Achievement*. Buckingham: Open University Press.

Ernst, E. (2009) 'Complementary/alternative medicine: engulfed by postmodernism, anti-science and regressive thinking', *British Journal of General Practice* 59/561.

Eversley, D. and Bonnerjea, L. (1982) 'Social change and indications of diversity', in R. N. Rapaport, M. P. Fogarty and R. Rapoport (eds.) *Families in Britain*. London: Routledge & Kegan Paul.

Fanon, F. (2008 [1952]) *Black Skin, White Masks*. Editions de Seuil, France; new edition 2008, London: Pluto Press.

Featherstone, M. (2007) *Consumer Culture and Postmodernism*. London: Sage Publications.

Feinstein, L. and Symons, J. (1999) 'Attainment in Secondary School', *Oxford Economic Papers* 51/2.

Field, F. (1989) *Losing Out: The Emergence of Britain's Underclass*. Oxford: Blackwell.

Flanders, N. A. (1970) *Analysing Teaching Behaviour*. New York: Addison Wesley.

Fletcher, R. (1966) *The Family and Marriage in Britain*. Harmondsworth: Penguin.

Foot, C. and Harrison, T. (2011) *How to Improve Cancer Survival: Explaining England's Relatively Poor Rates*. London: King's Fund.

Forde, C., Kane, J., Condie, R., McPhee, A. and Head, G. (2006). *Strategies to Address Gender Inequalities in Scottish Schools: A Review of the Literature*. Scottish Executive Social Research. Edinburgh: Information and Analytical Services Division, Scottish Executive Education Department.

Foucault, M. (1991) *Discipline and Punish: The Birth of the Prison*. London: Penguin Books.

Foucault, M. (2001[1964]) *Madness and Civilization*. Abingdon: Routledge.

Foucault, M. (2003 [1973]) *The Birth of the Clinic: An Archaeology of Medical Perception*. First published in English, London: Tavistock (1973); published as a Routledge Classic (London: Routledge, 2003).

Fox Harding, L. (1995), *Family, State and Social Policy*. Basingstoke: Palgrave Macmillan.

Francis, B. (2000) *Boys, Girls and Achievement: Addressing the Classroom Issues*. London: Routledge/Farmer.

Francis, B. (2005) 'Not/knowing their place: girls' classroom behaviours', in G. Lloyd (ed.) *Problem Girls*. London: Routledge.

Freire, P. (1996) *Pedagogy of the Oppressed*. London: Penguin.

Fuller, M. (1980) 'Black girls in a London comprehensive school', in R. Deem (ed.) *Schooling for Women's Work*. London: Routledge & Kegan Paul.

Ganley, A. L. and Schechter, S. (1995) *Domestic Violence: A National Curriculum for Family Preservation Practitioners*. San Francisco: Family Violence Prevention Fund, www.endabuse.org.

Gans, H. J. (1973) *More Equality*. New York: Pantheon.

Garfinkel, H. (1984) *Studies in Ethnomethodology*. Cambridge: Polity Press.

Gatrell, C. J. (2004) *Hard Labour: The Sociology of Parenthood, Family Life and Career*. Maidenhead: Open University Press.

Gatrell, C. J., Burnett, S. B., Cooper, C. L., Sparrow, P. and Swan, J. A. (2011) *Working and Fathers: Combining Family Life and Work*. London: Working Families. Available at www.workingfamilies.org.uk.

Gershuny, J. (1994) 'The domestic labour revolution: a process of lagged adaptation', in M. Anderson, F. Bechhofer and J. Gershuny (eds.) *The Social and Political Economy of the Household*. Oxford: Oxford University Press.

Ghuman, P. A. S. (1999) *South Asian Adolescents in the West*. Leicester: British Psychological Society.

Gibson, A. and Asthana, S. (1999) 'Schools, markets and equity: access to secondary education in England and Wales', presentation to American Educational Research Association Annual Conference, Montreal, reported in the *Guardian*, 6 July.

Gibson, C. (1994) *Dissolving Wedlock*. London: Routledge.

Giddens, A. (1991) *Modernity and Self-identity: Self and Society in the Late Modern Age*. Cambridge: Polity Press.

Giddens, A. (1993) *The Transformation of Intimacy: Sexuality, Love and Eroticism in Modern Societies*. Cambridge: Polity Press.

Giddens, A. (2005), 'Modernity and self-identity revisited', speech at ESRC Identities and Social Action Programme Launch, available at www.open.ac.uk/socialsciences/identities/pdf/modernity_and_selfidentity_revisited.pdf.

Giddens, A. (2006) *Sociology* (5th edn). Cambridge: Polity Press.

Giddings, A. (2010) *Cultural Differences: High, Low and Mass Culture*, Journoblog, www.journoblog.com/2010/05/cultural-differences/.

Gill, R., Henwood, K., and McLean, C. (2005). *Body Projects and the Regulation of Normative Masculinity*. London: LSE Research Articles Online. Available at: http://eprints.lse.ac.uk/archive/00000371/.

Gillborn, D. (2008), *Racism and Education: Coincidence or Conspiracy?* Abingdon: Taylor and Francis.

Gillborn, D. (2011) 'No black in a baccalaureate'. *Guardian* 13 June.

Gillborn, D. and Gipps, C. (1996) *Recent Research on the Achievements of Ethnic Minority Pupils*. London: Office for Standards in Education.

Gillborn, D. and Mirza, H. S. (2000) *Mapping Race, Class and Gender: A Synthesis of Research Evidence*. London: Office for Standards in Education.

Gillborn, D. and Youdell, D. (2000) *Rationing Education: Policy, Practice, Reform and Equity*. Buckingham: Open University Press.

Gilmore, D. (1991) *Manhood in the Making: Cultural Concepts of Masculinity*. London: Yale University Press.

Gilroy, P. (1993) *The Black Atlantic: Modernity and Double Consciousness*. London: Verso Books.

Gilroy, P. (2002) *There Ain't No Black in the Union Jack*. London: Routledge.

Goffman, E. (1990a) *Stigma: Notes on the Management of Spoiled Identity*. Harmondsworth: Penguin.

Goffman, E. (1990b) *The Presentation of Self in Everyday Life*. Harmondsworth: Penguin.

Goffman, E. (1991 [1961]) *Asylums: Essays on the Social Situation of Mental Patients and Other Inmates*. London: Penguin.

Goode, W. J. (1971) 'A sociological perspective on marital dissolution', in M. Anderson (ed.) *Sociology of the Family*. Harmondsworth: Penguin.

Gordon, D., Levitas, R., Pantazis, C., et al. (2000) *Poverty and Social Exclusion in Britain*. York: Joseph Rowntree Foundation.

Graham, H. (1993) *Hardship and Health in Women's Lives*. Hemel Hempstead: Harvester Wheatsheaf.

Green, E., Hebron, S. and Woodward, D. (1990) *Women's Leisure, What Leisure?* Basingstoke: Macmillan.

Greer, G. (2007) *The Whole Woman*. London: Black Swan.

Hacking, J. M., Muller, S. and Buchan, I. E. (2011) 'Trends in mortality from 1965 to 2008 across the English north–south divide: comparative observational study', *British Medical Journal* www.bmj.com/content/342/bmj.d508.

Hakim, C. (2011*)* *Feminist Myths and Magic Medicine: The Flawed Thinking behind Calls for Further Equality* Legislation. London: Centre for Policy Studies.

Hall, S. (1992) 'The question of cultural identity', in S. Hall, D. Held and T. McGrew (eds.) *Modernity and Its Futures*. Cambridge: Polity Press.

Hall, S. and Jefferson, T. (eds.) (1976) *Resistance through Rituals: Youth Subcultures in Post-War Britain*. London: Hutchinson.

Hargreaves, D. (1967) *Social Relations in a Secondary School*. London: Routledge & Kegan Paul.

Hargreaves, D. (1976) 'Reactions to labelling', in M. Hammersley and P. Woods (eds.) *The Process of Schooling*. London: Routledge & Kegan Paul.

Harkness, S. (2005) *Employment, Work Patterns and Unpaid Work: An Analysis of Trends since the 1970s*. Swindon: Economic and Social Research Council.

Hart, N. (1985) *The Sociology of Health and Medicine*. Ormskirk: Causeway Press.

Hartley, B. and Sutton, R. (2011) 'Failing boys: A stereotype threat account of the gender gap in children's academic performance'. Paper presented at the April meeting of The Society for Research in Child Development (SRCD), Montreal, Canada.

Harvey, D. G. and Slatin, G. T. (1975) 'The relationship between a child's SES and teacher expectations: a test of the middle-class bias hypothesis', *Social Forces* 54/1.

Heath, S. (2004) 'Transforming friendship – are housemates the new family?', *Sociology Review* September.

Hebdige, D. (1976). 'The meaning of Mod', in S. Hall and T. Jefferson (eds.) *Resistance through Rituals: Youth Subcultures in Post-war Britain.* London: Hutchinson.

Hebdige, D. (1979) *Subculture: The Meaning of Style.* London: Methuen.

Henderson, A. C., Harmon, S. M. and Houser J. (2010). 'A new state of surveillance? An application of Michel Foucault to modern motherhood', *Surveillance & Society* 7/3–4.

Her Majesty's Government (2010) *Healthy Lives, Healthy People: Our Strategy for Public Health in England.* London: The Stationery Office. Available at www.official-documents.gov.uk/ .

Hirsch, D. (2006) *What Will It Take to End Child Poverty? Firing on All Cylinders.* York: Joseph Rowntree Foundation.

Hobson, A. (2000) 'Multiple methods in social research', *Sociology Review* 10/2.

Hoggart, R. (1969) *The Uses of Literacy.* Harmondsworth: Penguin.

Hollands, R. G. (1995) *Friday Night, Saturday Night: Youth Cultural Identification in the Post-Industrial City.* Originally published (March 1995) as 'Department of Social Policy Working Paper No. 2', University of Newcastle.

House of Commons Education Committee (2011) *Education Committee – Fifth Report of Session 2010–12: The English Baccalaureate.* London: House of Commons and The Stationery Office (available at www.parliament.uk/education-committee).

House of Commons Science and Technology Committee (2010) *Science and Technology Committee – Fourth Report. Evidence Check 2: Homeopathy.* London: The Stationery Office.

House of Lords Science and Technology Committee (2000) *Science and Technology Committee – Sixth Report.* London: The Stationery Office. Available at www.publications.parliament.uk/ .

Humphreys, L. (1970) *Tearoom Trade: Impersonal Sex in Public Places.* London: Duckworth.

Hyman, H. H. (1967) 'The value systems of different classes', in R. Bendix and S. M. Lipset (eds.) *Class, Status and Power* (2nd edn). London: Routledge & Kegan Paul.

Illich, I. (1976) *Limits to Medicine.* London: Marion Boyars.

Illich, I. (1995) *Deschooling Society.* London: Marion Boyars.

Jackson, C. (2006) *Lads and Ladettes in School: Gender and a Fear of Failure.* Maidenhead: Open University Press.

Jackson, C., Paechter, C. and Renold, E. (eds.) (2010) *Girls and Education 3–16: Continuing Concerns, New Agendas.* Maidenhead: Open University Press / McGraw-Hill.

Jacobson, J. (1990) *Islam in Transition: Religion and Identity among British Pakistani Youth.* London: Routledge.

Jebali, C. (1993) 'A feminist perspective on postnatal depression', *Health Visitor* 66/2, February.

Jenkins, R. (1996) *Social Identity.* London: Routledge.

Johal, S. (1998) 'Brimful of Brasia', *Sociology Review* November.

Jones, O. (2011) *Chavs: The Demonization of the Working Class.* London: Verso.

Kafetz, A. (ed.) (2010) *Dr. Foster Hospital Guide 2010.* London: Dr Foster Research, www.drfosterhealth.co.uk/ .

Kan, M. Y., Sullivan, O. and Gershuny, J., (2011) 'Gender convergence in domestic work: discerning the effects of interactional and institutional barriers in large-scale data', *Sociology* 45/2.

Keddie, N. (1971) 'Classroom knowledge', in M. F. D. Young (ed.) *Knowledge and Control.* London: Collier-Macmillan.

Keddie, N. (ed.) (1973) *Tinker, Tailor . . . the Myth of Cultural Deprivation.* Harmondsworth: Penguin.

Kelly, A. (1987) *Science for Girls.* Milton Keynes: Open University Press.

Kempson, E. (1996) *Life on a Low Income.* York: Joseph Rowntree Foundation.

Kempson, E. and Bryson, A. (1994) *Hard Times: How Poor Families Make Ends Meet.* London: Policy Studies Institute.

Kenway, P. and Palmer, G. (2007) *Poverty among Ethnic Groups: How and Why Does It Differ?* York: Joseph Rowntree Foundation.

Kerr, K. and West, M. (ed.) (2010) *Insight 2 – Social Inequality: Can Schools Narrow the Gap?* Macclesfield: British Educational Research Association.

King's Fund (2006) *Briefing: Access to Health Care and Minority Ethnic Groups.* London: King's Fund.

Knudsen, K. and Wærness, K. (2008) 'National context and spouses' housework in 34 countries', *European Sociological Review* 24/1.

Labov, W. (1973) 'The logic of nonstandard English', in N. Keddie (ed.) *Tinker, Tailor . . . the Myth of Cultural Deprivation.* Harmondsworth: Penguin.

Lacey, C. (1970) *Hightown Grammar, the School as a Social System.* Manchester: Manchester University Press.

Laing, R. D. (2010 [1960]) *The Divided Self.* London: Penguin [Tavistock Publications, 1960].

Laing, R. D. and Esterson, A. (1970) *Sanity, Madness and the Family.* Harmondsworth: Penguin.

Lash, S. and Urry, J. (1987) *The End of Organized Capitalism.* Cambridge: Polity Press.

Latif, S. (2010) *Better Health Briefing Paper 18: Effective Methods of Engaging Black and Minority Ethnic Communities within Health Care Settings.* London: Race Equality Foundation.

Laurie, H. and Gershuny, J. (2000) 'Couples, work and money', in R. Berthoud and J. Gershuny (eds.) *Seven Years in the Lives of British Families.* Bristol: Policy Press.

Lawler, S. (2005) 'Disgusted subjects: the making of middle-class identities', *Sociological Review* 53/3.

Le Grand, J. (1982) *The Strategy of Equality.* London: Allen & Unwin.

Leach, E. R. (1967) *A Runaway World?* London: BBC Publications.

Lewis, J. (2001) *The End of Marriage? Individualism and Intimate Relations.* Cheltenham: Edwin Elgar Publishing.

Lewis, O. (1961) *The Children of Sanchez.* New York: Random House.

Licht, B. G. and Dweck, C. S. (1987) 'Some differences in achievement orientations', in M. Arnot and G. Weiner (eds.) *Gender under Scrutiny.* London: Hutchinson.

Lincoln, S. (2004) 'Teenage girls' bedroom culture: codes versus zones', in A. Bennett and K. Kahn-Harris (eds.) *After Subculture: Critical Studies in Contemporary Youth Culture.* Basingstoke: Palgrave Macmillan.

Lister, S., Reynolds, L. and Webb, K. (2011) *The Impact of Welfare Reform Bill Measures on Affordability for Low Income Private Renting Families.* London: Shelter.

Livingstone, S. M. (1988) 'Why people watch soap operas: an analysis of the explanations of British viewers', *European Journal of Communication* 3/1.

Lobban, G. (1974) *Data Report on British Reading Schemes.* London: Times Educational Supplement.

Lupton, R. (2004) *Schools in Disadvantaged Areas: Recognising Context and Raising Quality.* CASE Paper 76. London: Centre for Analysis of Social Exclusion, London School of Economics.

Lyotard, J.-F. (1984) *The Postmodern Condition: A Report on Knowledge.* Manchester: Manchester University Press.

Mac an Ghaill, M. (1992) *Young, Gifted and Black: Student–Teacher Relations in the Schooling of Black Youth.* Buckingham: Open University Press.

Mac an Ghaill, M. (1994) *The Making of Men: Masculinities, Sexualities and Schooling.* Buckingham: Open University Press.

MacDonald, D. (1965) 'A theory of mass culture', in B. Rosenberg, and D.M. White (eds.) *Mass Culture.* Glencoe: Free Press.

Machin, S. and Vernoit, J. (2010). 'Academy schools: who benefits?' *CentrePiece* 15/2 Autumn, available at http://cep.lse.ac.uk/pubs/download/cp325.pdf.

Mack, J. and Lansley, S. (1985) *Poor Britain.* London: Allen & Unwin.

Mack, J., Lansley, S. and Frayman, H. (1992) *Breadline Britain 1990s: The Findings of the Television Series.* London: London Weekend Television.

Mackenzie, C. S., Gekoski, W. L. and Knox V. J. (2006) 'Age, gender and the underutilization of mental health services: the influence of help-seeking attitudes', *Aging and Mental Health* 10/6.

Marcuse, H. (2002[1964]) *One-Dimensional Man.* London: Routledge.

Margo, J., Dixon, M., Pearce, N. and Reed, H. (2006) *Freedom's Orphans: Raising Youth in a Changing World.* London: Institute of Public Policy Research.

Marmot, M. (2004) *Status Syndrome: How Your Social Standing Directly Affects Your Health and Life Expectancy.* London: Bloomsbury.

Marmot, M. (Chair) (2010) *Fair Society, Healthy Lives: The Marmot Review, Strategic Review of Health Inequalities in England post-2010,* www.marmotreview.org/.

Marsland, D. (1989) 'Universal welfare provision creates a dependent population: the case for', *Social Studies Review* 5/2.

Matheson, J. (2010) 'The UK population: how does it compare?' in *Population Trends 142.* London: Office for National Statistics.

McIntosh, S. (1988) 'A feminist critique of Stanley Parker's theory of work and leisure', in M. O'Donnell (ed.) *New Introductory Reader in Sociology* (2nd edn). Walton-on-Thames: Nelson.

McKeown, T. (1976) *The Modern Rise of Population.* London: Edward Arnold.

McKeown, T. (1979) *The Role of Medicine.* Oxford: Blackwell.

McKinlay, J. B. (1977) 'The business of good doctoring or doctoring as good business: reflections on Friedson's view of the medical game', *International Journal of Health Services* 7/3.

McRobbie, A. (1994) *Postmodernism and Popular Culture.* London: Routledge.

McRobbie, A. (2000 [1991]) *Feminism and Youth Cultures.* Basingstoke: Macmillan.

McRobbie, A. (2008) 'Postfeminist passions'. *Guardian* 25 March.

McRobbie, A. and Garber, J. (1976) 'Girls and subcultures' in S. Hall and T. Jefferson (eds.) *Resistance through Rituals: Youth Subcultures in Post-War Britain.* London: Hutchinson.

Mead, M. (2001) *Sex and Temperament: In Three Primitive Societies.* London: Harper-Collins.

Middleton, S., Ashworth, K. and Braithwaite, I. (1997) *Small Fortunes: Spending on Children, Childhood Poverty and Parental Sacrifice.* York: Joseph Rowntree Foundation.

Miliband, R. (1974) 'Politics and poverty', in D. Wedderburn (ed.) *Poverty, Inequality and Class Structure.* Cambridge: Cambridge University Press.

Miller, D., Jackson, P. Thrift, N., Holbrook, B. and Rowlands, M. (1998*) Shopping, Place and Identity.* London: Routledge.

Mills, C. W. (1970) *The Sociological Imagination.* Harmondsworth: Penguin.

Mirza, M., Senthilkumaran, A., and Ja'far, Z. (2007) *Living Apart Together: British Muslims and the Paradox of Multiculturalism.* London: Policy Exchange.

Mitsos, E. (1995–6) 'Boys and English – classroom voices', *English and Media Magazine* 33 & 34.

Mitsos, E. and Browne, K. (1998) 'Gender differences in education – the underachievement of boys', *Sociology Review* 8/1.

Modood, T. (2006) 'Ethnicity, Muslims and higher education entry in Britain', *Teaching in Higher Education* 11/2.

Modood, T., Beishon, S. and Virdee, S. (1994) *Changing Ethnic Identities.* London: Policy Studies Institute.

Moon, N. and Ivins, C. (2004) *Survey of Parental Involvement 2003/04.* London: Department for Education and Skills.

Moriarty, J. (2008) *The Health and Social Care Experiences of Black and Minority Ethnic Older People*. Better Health Briefing Paper 9. London: Race Equality Foundation.

Mulvey, L. (1975) 'Visual pleasure and narrative cinema', *Screen* 16/3, included in L. Mulvey (2009) *Visual and Other Pleasures (Language, Discourse, Society)*. Basingstoke: Palgrave Macmillan.

Murdock, G. P. (1949) *Social Structure*. New York: Macmillan.

Murphy, P. and Whitelegg, E. (2006) *Girls in the Physics Classroom: A Review of the Research on the Participation of Girls in Physics*. London: Institute of Physics.

Murray, C. (1989) 'Underclass', *Sunday Times Magazine*, 26 November.

Murray, C. (1990) *The Emerging British Underclass*. London: Institute of Economic Affairs.

National Equality Panel (2010) *An Anatomy of Economic Inequality in the UK: Report of the National Equality Panel*. London: Government Equalities Office.

Navarro, V. (1976) *Medicine under Capitalism*. New York: Prodist.

Navarro, V. (1986) *Crisis, Health, and Medicine: A Social Critique*. London: Tavistock Publications.

Nazroo, J. (1997a) *Ethnicity and Mental Health*. London: Policy Studies Institute.

Nazroo, J. (1997b) *The Health of Britain's Ethnic Minorities: Fourth National Survey of Ethnic Minorities*. London: Policy Studies Institute.

Nettleton, S. (2006) *The Sociology of Health and Illness* (2nd edn). Cambridge: Polity Press.

Nichols, T. and Beynon, R. (1977) *Living with Capitalism*. London: Routledge & Kegan Paul.

Oakhill, J. and Petrides, A. (2007). 'Sex differences in the effects of interest on boys' and girls' reading comprehension', *British Journal of Psychology* 98.

Oakley, A. (1974) *The Sociology of Housework*. Oxford: Martin Robertson.

Oakley, A. (1981) *From Here to Maternity*. Harmondsworth: Penguin.

Oakley, A. (1984) *The Captured Womb: A History of the Medical Care of Pregnant Women*. Oxford: Blackwell.

Oakley, A. (1985) *Subject Women*. London: Fontana.

Oakley, A. (1989) *Women Confined*. Oxford: Martin Robertson.

Oakley, A. (1992) *Social Support and Motherhood: The Natural History of a Research Project*. Oxford: Blackwell.

Orr, D. (2011) 'The new enthusiasm for raging at anyone seen to be different' *Guardian* 10 March.

Paechter, C. F. (1998) *Educating the Other: Gender, Power and Schooling*. Abingdon: RoutledgeFalmer.

Pahl, J. (2005) 'Individualisation in couple finances: who pays for the children?' *Social Policy and Society* 4/4.

Pahl, J. (2008) 'Family finances, individualisation, spending patterns and access to credit', *Journal of Socio-Economics* 37/2.

Pakulski, J. and Waters, M. (1996) *The Death of Class*. London: Sage Publications.

Palfreyman, D. (2003) 'Independent schools and charitable status: legal meaning, taxation advantages, and potential removal', in G. Walford (ed.) *British Private Schools: Research on Policy and Practice*. London: Woburn Press.

Palmer, C. (1999) 'Tourism and the symbols of identity', *Tourism Management* 20.

Palmer, G. (2006) 'Disabled people, poverty and the labour market', in G. Preston (ed.) *A Route out of Poverty? Disabled people, work and welfare reform*. London: Child Poverty Action Group.

Palmer, S. (2007) *Toxic Childhood: How The Modern World Is Damaging Our Children and What We Can Do About It*. London: Orion.

Parker, H., Aldridge, J. and Measham, F. (1998) *Illegal Leisure: The Normalisation of Adolescent Drug Use*. London: Routledge.

Parker, S. (1971) *The Future of Work and Leisure*. London: MacGibbon & Kee.

Parker, S. (1976) 'Work and leisure', in E. Butterworth and D. Weir (eds.) *The Sociology of Work and Leisure*. London: Allen & Unwin.

Parry, G., Van Cleemput, P., Peters, J., et al. (2004) *The Health Status of Gypsies & Travellers in England: Summary of a Report to the Department of Health*. Sheffield: University of Sheffield, School of Health and Related Research.

Parsons, T. (1951) *The Social System*. London: Routledge & Kegan Paul.

Parsons, T. and Bales, R. F. (1956) *Family, Socialization and Interaction Process*. London: Routledge.

Patrick, J. (1973) *A Glasgow Gang Observed*. London: Eyre Methuen.

Payne, S. (2006) *The Health of Men and Women*. Cambridge: Polity Press.

Perry, E. and Francis, B. (2010) *The Social Class Gap for Educational Achievement: A Review of the Literature*. London: RSA.

Phillips, T. (2007) Interview in the *Guardian* newspaper, 31 January.

Philo, G. (ed.) (1999) *Message Received: Glasgow Media Group Research, 1993–1998*. London: Longman.

Philo, G., Henderson, L. and McCracken, K. (2010) *Shifting Attitudes to Mental Illness – Making a Drama out of a Crisis: Authentic Portrayals of Mental Illness in TV Drama?* Glasgow Media Group and Shift. Available at www.glasgowmediagroup.org.

Pilkington, A. (1997) 'Ethnicity and education', in M. Haralambos (ed.) *Developments in Sociology*, vol. XIII. Ormskirk: Causeway Press.

Postman, N. (1994) *The Disappearance of Childhood*. New York: Vintage Books.

Power, S. and Whitty, G. (2008). 'A Bernsteinian analysis of compensatory education'. Paper presented at the 5th Basil Bernstein Symposium, Cardiff University, 9–12 July.

Rapoport, R. and Rapoport, R. N. (1971) *Dual Career Families*. Harmondsworth: Penguin.

Rapoport, R. and Rapoport, R. N. (1976) *Dual Career Families Re-examined*. Oxford: Martin Robertson.

Rapoport, R. N., Fogarty, M. P. and Rapoport, R. (eds.) (1982) *Families in Britain*. London: Routledge & Kegan Paul.

Reay, D. (2009) 'Making sense of white working class educational underachievement', in K. Sveinsson (ed.) *Who Cares about the White Working Class?* London: Runnymede Trust.

Renold, E. and Allan, A. (2006) 'Bright and beautiful: high-achieving girls, ambivalent femininities and the feminisation of success', *Discourse: Studies in the Cultural Politics of Education* 27/4.

Rist, R. C. (1970) 'Student social class and teacher expectations: the self-fulfilling prophecy in ghetto education', *Harvard Educational Review* 40.

Ritzer, G. (2004) *The McDonaldization of Society.* London: Sage Publications.

Roberts, K. (1978) *Contemporary Society and the Growth of Leisure.* London: Longman.

Roberts, K. (1983) *Youth and Leisure.* London: George Allen & Unwin.

Roberts, K. (1986) 'Leisure', in M. Haralambos (ed.), *Developments in Sociology*, vol. II. Ormskirk: Causeway Press.

Roberts, K. (2001) *Class in Modern Britain.* Basingstoke: Palgrave MacMillan.

Robson, K (2003) *Teenage Time Use as Investment in Cultural Capital.* ISER Working Paper 2003–12. Colchester: University of Essex.

Rojek, C. (1995) *Decentring Leisure: Rethinking Leisure Theory.* London: Sage.

Rosenhan, D. L. (1973) 'On being sane in insane places', *Science* 179/470.

Rosenthal, R. and Jacobson, L. (1968) *Pygmalion in the Classroom.* London: Holt, Rinehart & Winston.

Rutter, M. and Madge, N. (1976) *Cycles of Disadvantage: A Review of Research.* London: Heinemann.

Rutter, M., Manghan, B., Martimore, P., Oustra, J. and Smith, A. (1979) *Fifteen Thousand Hours: Secondary Schools and their Effects on Children.* Shepton Mallet: Open Books.

Savage, M. (1995) 'The middle classes in modern Britain', *Sociology Review* 5/2.

Scambler, A (2008). 'Women and health', in G. Scambler (ed.) *Sociology as Applied to Medicine.* Oxford: Saunders Elsevier.

Scheff, T. J. (1966) *Being Mentally Ill.* Chicago: Aldine.

Schor, J. B. (1992) *The Overworked American: The Unexpected Decline of Leisure.* New York: BasicBooks.

Schultz, T. W. (1971) *Investment in Human Capital.* New York: The Free Press.

Scott, J. (1990) *A Matter of Record: Documentary Sources in Social Research.* Cambridge: Polity Press.

Scott, J. (1991) *Who Rules Britain?* Cambridge: Polity Press.

Scraton, S. and Bramham, P. (1995) 'Leisure and postmodernity', in M. Haralambos (ed.) *Developments in Sociology*, vol. XI. Ormskirk: Causeway Press.

Sewell, T. (1996) *Black Masculinities and Schooling: How Black Boys Survive Modern Schooling.* Stoke-on-Trent: Trentham Books.

Sewell, T. (1998) 'Loose canons: exploding the myth of the "black macho" lad', in D. Epstein, J. Elwood, V. Hey and J. Maw (eds.) *Failing Boys? Issues in Gender and Achievement.* Buckingham: Open University Press.

Shakespeare, T. (1998) *The Disability Reader: Social Science Perspectives.* London: Cassell.

Sharpe, S. (1976) *Just Like a Girl.* Harmondsworth: Penguin.

Sharpe, S. (1994) *Just Like a Girl* (2nd edn). Harmondsworth: Penguin.

Silva, E. B. (ed.) (1996) *Good Enough Mothering? Feminist Perspectives on Lone Motherhood.* London: Routledge.

Silver, H. (1987) 'Only so many hours in a day: time constraints, labour pools and demand for consumer services', *The Service Industries Journal* 7/4.

Skelton, C., Francis, B. and Valkanova, Y. (2007) *Breaking Down the Stereotypes: Gender and Achievement in Schools.* Manchester: Equal Opportunities Commission.

Smith, L. K., Pope, C. and Botha, J. L. (2005) 'Patients' help-seeking experiences and delay in cancer presentation: a qualitative synthesis', *The Lancet* 366/9488.

Smyth, E., Dunne, A., McCoy, S. and Darmody, M. (2006) *Pathways through the Junior Cycle: The Experiences of Second Year Students.* Dublin: Liffey Press.

Sodha, S. and Margo, J. (2010) *A Generation of Disengaged Children is Waiting in the Wings. . .* London: Demos.

Spender, D. (1982) *Invisible Women: The Schooling Scandal.* London: Writers and Readers.

Sproston, K. and Mindell, J. (eds.) (2006) *Health Survey for England 2004.* London: The Information Centre.

Stanworth, M. (1983) *Gender and Schooling.* London: Hutchinson.

Storey, J. (2003) *Inventing Popular Culture: From Folklore to Globalization.* Oxford: Blackwell.

Strand, S. (2012) 'The White British – Black Caribbean achievement gap: tests, tiers and teacher expectations', *British Educational Research Journal* 38/1.

Strinati, D. (1995) *An Introduction to Theories of Popular Culture.* London: Routledge.

Sugarman, B. (1970) 'Social class, values and behaviour in schools', in M. Craft (ed.) *Family, Class and Education.* London: Longman.

Sutton Trust (2011) *Degree of Success – University Chances by Individual School.* London: The Sutton Trust, available at: www.suttontrust.com/research/degree-of-success-university-chances-by-individual-school/.

Sutton Trust / Ipsos MORI (2010) *Young People Omnibus 2010 (Wave 16): A Research Study among 11–16 Year Olds on Behalf of the Sutton Trust.* London: The Sutton Trust, available at www.suttontrust.com/research/young-people-omnibus-2010-wave-16/.

Swann Committee (1985) *Education for All: Report of the Committee of Inquiry into the Education of Children from Ethnic Minority Groups.* London: HMSO.

Swayne, J. (2009) 'Commentary', at end of E. Ernst (2009) 'Complementary/alternative medicine: engulfed by postmodernism, anti-science and regressive thinking', *British Journal of General Practice* 59/561.

Szasz, T. (1972) *The Myth of Mental Illness*. London: Paladin.
Szreter, S. (2003) 'Szreter responds' letter, *American Journal of Public Health* 93/7.

Taylor, L. (1984) *In the Underworld*. London: Unwin.
Taylor, S. (1999) 'Postmodernism: a challenge to sociology', *'S' Magazine*.
Taylor-Gooby, P. (2005) *Attitudes to Social Justice*. London: Institute for Public Policy Research.
Thornton, S. (1995) *Club Cultures: Music, Media and Subcultural Capital*. Cambridge: Polity Press.
Tough, S. and Brooks, R. (2007) *School Admissions: Fair Choice for Parents and Pupils*. London: Institute for Public Policy Research.
Townsend, P. (1979) *Poverty in the United Kingdom*. Harmondsworth: Penguin.
Townsend, P., Davidson, N. and Whitehead, M. (1990) *Inequalities in Health: The Black Report and The Health Divide*. Harmondsworth: Penguin.
Toynbee, P. (2004) 'Charles is more keeper of the kitsch than heir to the throne', *Guardian* 30 June.
Toynbee, P. (2011) 'Faith schools: now even the church admits they're unfair', *Guardian* 23 April.
Troyna, B. and Williams, J. (1986) *Racism, Education and the State*. Beckenham: Croom Helm.
Tudor-Hart, J. (1971) 'The inverse care law', *The Lancet* 1.
Tudor-Hart, J. (2009) submission (para 222) in *House of Commons Health Committee, Third Report: Health Inequalities*. London: The Stationery Office. Available at www.publications.parliament.uk/pa/cm200809/cmselect/cmhealth/286/28602.htm.
Turner, B. S. (1996) *The Body and Society: Explorations in Social Theory* (2nd edn). London: Sage.

Urry, J. (1995) *Consuming Places*. London: Routledge.
Urry, J. (2002) *The Tourist Gaze*. London: Sage.

Venkatesh, S. (2009) *Gang Leader for a Day: A Rogue Sociologist Crosses the Line*. London: Penguin.
Vincent, C., Rollock, N., Ball, S. and Gillborn, D. (2011) *The Educational Strategies of the Black Middle Classes*. London: Institute of Education / ESRC.

Waldfogel, J. and Washbrook, E. (2010) *Low Income and Early Cognitive Development in the U.K.* London: The Sutton Trust.
Walford, G. (ed.) (2003) *British Private Schools: Research on Policy and Practice*. London: Woburn Press.
Walker, R., Howard, M., Maguire, S. and Youngs, R. (2000) *The Making of a Welfare Class?* Bristol: Policy Press.
Westergaard, J. and Resler, H. (1976) *Class in a Capitalist Society*. Harmondsworth: Penguin.
White, P. (ed.) (2005) *Biopsychosocial Medicine: An Integrated Approach to Understanding Illness*. Oxford: Oxford University Press.
Whitty, G., Power, S. and Halpin, D. (1998) *Devolution and Choice in Education: The School, the State and the Market*. Buckingham: Open University Press.
Whyte, W. F. (1955) *Street Corner Society* (2nd edn). Chicago: University of Chicago Press.
Wilkins, D., Payne, S., Granville, G. and Branney, P. (2008) *The Gender and Access to Health Services Study Final Report*. London: Men's Health Forum / Department of Health.
Wilkinson, R. and Pickett, K. (2010) *The Spirit Level: Why Equality is Better for Everyone*. London: Penguin.
Wilkinson, R. G. (1996) *Unhealthy Societies*. London: Routledge.
Wilkinson, R. G. (2005) *The Impact of Inequality: How to Make Sick Societies Healthier*. London: Routledge.
Willis, P. (1977) *Learning to Labour: How Working Class Kids Get Working Class Jobs*. Farnborough: Saxon House.
Witz, A (1992) *Professions and Patriarchy*. London: Routledge.
Womack, S. (2011) 'The best days of our lives?' in *Britain in 2011*. Swindon: Economic and Social Research Council.
Woods, P. (1979) *The Divided School*. London: Routledge.
Woodward, K. (2000) 'Questions of identity', in K. Woodward (ed.) *Questioning Identity: Gender, Class, Nation*. London: Routledge.
Wright, C. (1992) *Race Relations in the Primary School*. London: David Fulton.

Young, M. and Willmott, P. (1973) *The Symmetrical Family*. Harmondsworth: Penguin.

Zaretsky, E. (1976) *Capitalism, the Family and Personal Life*. London: Pluto Press.

Illustration credits

Chapter 1 © andipantz/iStock; © andipantz/iStock; © Bob Ingelhart/iStock; © Ken Pyne; © Franziska Richter/iStock; © Ken Pyne; © Ken Pyne; © Ken Pyne; © Bob Ingelhart/iStock; © Ken Pyne; © Crown Copyright 2012.

Chapter 2 © Aman Khan/iStock; © Aman Khan/iStock; © tunart/iStock; © Paula Connelly/iStock; © Slobo Mitic/iStock; Musée du Louvre, Wikimedia Commons; © megamonalisa.com; © megamonalisa.com; © megamonalisa.com; © Ken Browne; © Ken Browne; © Ken Browne; © Ken Browne; © Ken Browne; © Ken Browne; © Ken Pyne; © Amanda Rhode/iStock; © Alex Nikada/iStock; © ericsphotography/iStock; © Ken Pyne; © Ken Pyne; © Ken Pyne; © tunart/iStock; © luoman/iStock; © Steve Geer/iStock; © Serdar Yagci/iStock; © Angel Herrero de Frutos/iStock; © Tomas Bercic/iStock; © Pavel Losevsky/iStock; © Michael Blackburn/iStock; © Soubrette/iStock; © Ted Foy/iStock; © Franky De Meyer/iStock; © Suzanne Tucker/iStock; © Ken Browne; © Ken Browne; © Soubrette/iStock; © Ted Foy/iStock; © Steve Debenport/iStock; © Cliff Parnell/iStock; © Jakub Niezabitowski/iStock; © franckreporter/iStock; © Helle Bro Clemmensen/iStock; © RSVP Music, Blue Skies Photography Bristol; taken from the movie *3 Idiots* © Vinod Chopra Films Pvt Ltd; © Juanmonino/iStock; © Alanna Jurden/iStock; © poco_bw/iStock; © Steven Allan/iStock; © Lise Gagne/iStock; © Vasko Miokovic/iStock; © Duncan Walker/iStock; © Chris Meadows/iStock; © Rob Broek/iStock; © SeanPavonePhoto/iStock; © fotoVoyager/iStock; © Eirene Mitsos; © Alexandr Tkachuk/iStock; © Ufuk Zivana/iStock; © Ufuk Zivana/iStock; © Ufuk Zivana/iStock; © Ufuk Zivana/iStock; © Ufuk Zivana/iStock; © James O. Jenkins; © iStock; © franz pfluegl/iStock; © Andres Balcazar/iStock; © Oktay Ortakcioglu/iStock; © Max Blain/iStock; © craftvision/iStock; © Ken Browne; © Joseph Jean Rolland Dubé/iStock; © gremlin/iStock; © Karina Tischlinger/iStock; © bobbieo/iStock; © mountainberryphoto/iStock; © Phil Berry/iStock; © www.warwick-castle.com; © Ken Pyne; © Gautier Willaume/iStock; © Tomaz Levstek/iStock; © Sean Locke/iStock; Linux inside2/Wikimedia Commons; matt buchanan/Wikimedia Commons; © Apple Inc. Courtesy of Apple Inc.

Chapter 3 © Marzanna Syncerz/iStock; © Marzanna Syncerz/iStock; © Anouchka/iStock; © iStock; © iStock; © Slobo Mitic/iStock; © Ken Pyne; © Skip O'Donnell/iStock; © Nuno Silva/iStock; © Reproduced by kind permission of PRIVATE EYE/Ken Pyne; © Justin Horrocks/iStock; © Anthony Rosenberg/iStock; © Ken Pyne; © diego cervo/iStock; © Slawomir Fajer/iStock; © Heiko Bennewitz/iStock; © Jelani Memory/iStock; © Maartje van Caspe/iStock; © Marcel Pelletier/iStock; © Ken Browne; © GYI NSEA/iStock; © Giacomo Pirozi/panos; © Compton Verney, *A Boy aged Two* by Marcus Gheeraerts the Younger, 1608; © Anouchka/iStock; © Sean Locke/iStock; © Ken Pyne; © binagel/iStock; © www.netdoctor.co.uk; © Mary Evans/iStock; © garysludden/iStock; © Hermann Danzmayr/iStock; © Amanda Rohde/iStock; © Gregory Lang/iStock

Chapter 4 © Alexander Raths/iStock; © Alexander Raths/iStock; © Mark Skinner/iStock; © Gordon Browne; © Gordon Browne; © Vasiliki Varvaki/iStock; © Mark Skinner/iStock; © David Freund/iStock; © Ken Pyne; © Andrew Gentry/iStock; © Crown Copyright (DWP); © Crown Copyright (DWP); © Crown Copyright (DWP); © Crown Copyright (DWP); © Crown Copyright (DWP); © Crown Copyright (DWP)

Chapter 5 © Elena Elisseeva/iStock; © Elena Elisseeva/iStock; © Stefan Klein/iStock; © Ugur Evirgen/iStock; ©Nicholas Sutcliffe/iStock; © Angel Herrero de Frutos/iStock; © Mikael Damkier/iStock; © Laurence Gough/iStock; © Ken Pyne; © Ken Pyne; © Richard Hobson/iStock; © Mark Evans/iStock; © Stefan Klein/iStock; © Ken Pyne; © Ken

Index

Using the index

If you can't find an item in this index, think of other headings it might be given under: the same references are often included several times under different headings. This index includes only the largest or most significant references found in this book, rather than every single occurrence of the theme. It is sensible always to check the largest references first, such as pages 239–44, before 125, 283 and 332. The chances are that what you're looking for will be in the largest entry, and this will save you time wading through a lot of smaller references. Numbers in blue refer to entries in the glossary. Between drawing up an index and the final printing of a book, there is often some textual movement, as printers' errors are corrected or the latest updates made. This means page references may occasionally not be as precise as is desirable. It is, therefore, always worth checking the pages on either side of the page references given if what you're looking for isn't there.